The Politician

by

ROBERT WELCH

Two dollars per copy

First printing, March 1963	10,000 copies
Second printing, May 1963	15,000 copies
Third printing, July 1963	25,000 copies
Fourth printing, November 1963	50,000 copies
Fifth printing (Library Edition), October 1964	10,000 copies
Sixth printing, December 1964	100,000 copies
Seventh printing, September 1970	25,000 copies
Eighth printing, March 1972	25,000 copies
Ninth printing, May 1975	25,000 copies

Library of Congress Catalog Card Number 64-8456
Manufactured in the United States of America

BELMONT PUBLISHING COMPANY
Belmont, Massachusetts 02178

There is nothing so powerful as
truth, and often nothing so strange.
Daniel Webster

CONTENTS

Truth will ultimately prevail where there is pains taken to bring it to light.

George Washington

Patriotism means to stand by the country.

It does not mean to stand by the President or any other public official save exactly to the degree in which he himself stands by the country.

It is patriotic to support him insofar as he efficiently serves the country. It is unpatriotic not to oppose him to the exact extent that by inefficiency or otherwise he fails in his duty to stand by the country.

In either event, it is unpatriotic not to tell the truth—whether about the President or anyone else—save in the rare cases where this would make known to the enemy information of military value which would otherwise be unknown to him.

Theodore Roosevelt

Please Note

Explanations are like government. Nobody loves them, but a minimum amount of both is a necessary evil.

The original manuscript of The Politician *has been reproduced herein, with typographical errors corrected and a few other minor changes as noted.*

The "documentation" for footnote purposes is not complete. Digging out the source materials five years later, for what was originally written as a private letter with no thought of publication, has not been easy for either myself or those who have helped me. More such footnotes will be added in later printings.

In the Epilogue *and elsewhere, especially in the footnotes written by others, there are occasional references to, and passages paraphrased from, earlier books, articles, and speeches of my own. But in this fight I sacrificed the comfort of modesty long ago. And it has seemed important to get within these covers as much contribution as I can make, within practicable limits, to a basic understanding of the Communist conspiracy—no matter where some of these thoughts have appeared before.*

Especially in the Prologue *and* Epilogue, *also, I have not dared make normal use of the editorial "we." For it might be misunderstood, and appear to some extent to involve others in a responsibility they do not share. So an abnormal use of the pronoun "I" has been unavoidable.*

From a professional viewpoint, there are too many different type faces and sizes in this book. It is because, trying to crowd in so much material, I have wanted to give each segment a readability in proportion to its importance.

Finally, some of the writing in this letter, especially in the informality of the language, and as to the order and arrangement of materials, is not up to the standard I would have set for myself in anything planned for publication. But it seems far better, for many reasons, not to attempt a face-lifting job on the manuscript at this time.

And so, with this much explanation but without apology, I now send The Politician *out into the world.   RW*

PROLOGUE

"And with forced fingers rude . . . before the mellowing year."

Thus John Milton complained of having to put pen to paper when the season was not yet ripe. And while this writer is certainly no Milton, we can sympathize with his feelings.

For never was this author under more compulsion, from more different sources and of a more varied hue, than to consent to premature publication of *The Politician*. By an increasing stream of letters from individuals, by resolutions passed at meetings of patriotic organizations, by personal pleas from many friends, he has been urged—and by the utterly unfair taunts of some Liberal publications has been dared—to make this "book" available to the public.

The situation has been difficult simply because this document was never written, nor intended, for publication at all. It was an adventure in one-man research which led to quantities of evidence and possible conclusions that surprised even the author. And it was sent personally and in confidence to various friends (too many, I'm afraid), in an effort to shake them out of their complacency and awaken them to both the dangers of the Communist conspiracy and the extent of its influence. Under these conditions a brief account of how the project came into existence would seem to be in order. For without such explanation both the character of the "book," and its purpose, would be badly misunderstood.

II

In December, 1954 I was riding back to New York from a visit up the Hudson, with three friends, in a car provided by one of those friends. They were well informed, we were able to talk freely, and the conversation became quite serious.

In the course of that conversation I expressed my concern over what appeared to me to have been the double-crossing by Mr. Eisenhower, in the Congressional elections just finished, of a number of conservative Republican candidates for both the

Senate and the House. He had promised to go into the states or districts of these candidates to help in their campaigns. With his immense popularity at that time such help was of great importance. These candidates had been led to count on that promised help, and to build their campaigns around it, more than was wise.

As these respective campaigns got under way, Mr. Eisenhower had found one excuse and reason after another for delaying and postponing his appearance in different areas, but always with the assurance that he would still be there. When these campaigns were all over, with no help from Mr. Eisenhower, our whole Congress had been moved a few notches further left by the defeat of several Conservatives. Just how much Mr. Eisenhower's smooth procrastination had contributed to those defeats it was hard to guess. But I expressed the opinion that this effect was probably intentional.

This surprised one of my listeners so much that, when I began to bring out parts of Mr. Eisenhower's earlier record which made such a view possible, this friend asked me if I would be willing to put my comments in the form of a memorandum which he could study. I agreed. And on my return to Boston I wrote him a letter of some nine thousand words, recapitulating the points I had made during our conversation.

This was the beginning of *The Politician*. I sent carbon copies of this letter to each of the other friends. And one or two of them immediately wanted additional copies sent to other friends. It was quite a while before I could have a new typing of the letter made, and in the meantime I had added a considerable amount to it.

The demand and this process continued until, some three years later, the letter had evolved into over two hundred pages reproduced by offset and collated with a plastic link binding. I still considered it a private unfinished manuscript for limited confidential distribution, but a study which might sometime be further expanded, modified, and probably moderated for formal publication.

Sometime before this I had given up my business responsibilities, and was devoting all of my time to the anti-Communist cause. I did not want what had been started simply as a private confidential letter at the request of a friend to get any further out of hand, even to please other friends; nor did I want the more studiously considered efforts I could now make, in this anti-Communist cause, to be twisted into a polemic path which I had never intended to follow. It was my purpose thereafter to lend out additional copies of *The Politician* to other friends only in quite rare instances. That purpose has been maintained.

Nor was it as naive as might appear for me to expect this "unfinished manuscript" to fade out of the picture and into oblivion. For this is exactly what was happening during the next two years. We had convincing indications that the lions of the Left, including Mr. Eisenhower himself, knew all about this manuscript when we began to push it into the past in 1958. *They* did not want it published, or brought out into the open, because there was too much devastating evidence in it concerning matters which they preferred to have forgotten. *We* did not want to publish it because the presentation of that evidence had never been prepared or put in shape for publication. Everybody was quite content to let the manuscript, and all copies of it, simply gather dust until it was pretty well forgotten; and until, so far as I was concerned, in some future years I might have the time to write a sound and complete volume of history dealing with events of the 1950's, into which the material in this manuscript could be incorporated.

But by the fall of 1960 the Left was beginning to learn of the existence, growth, and potential danger to themselves, of a new national organization known as The John Birch Society. They started looking for ways to damage and, they hoped, to destroy the Society. This organization had been building very solidly, and means of getting at it were not easy to find. In distress if not despair they seized upon this manuscript, written by the Society's founder long before the Society was formed, as a weapon for their attack. Despite the fact that the manuscript was no part of the materials or the beliefs of The

John Birch Society, and had been specifically disavowed at the founding meeting of the Society, the leaders of the Left made it the core of their first huge smear campaign against the Society as well as myself.

The opening assault, timed to coincide with the Republican National Convention in Chicago the first week of August, 1960, was in the *Chicago Daily News,* by a double-talking columnist named Jack Mabley (who also double-acts as a small-time politician). It was immediately picked up by that avidly "progressive" paper, *The Milwaukee Journal,* and two or three scattered lesser journalistic lights of the same tinge. Then, although some temporary damage had been done to the Society in the Chicago and Milwaukee areas, the subject was pretty much ignored by the rest of the nation's press, and the few reverberations began to die out. Whether this salvo had been fired by some eager beavers entirely on their own, or was inspired by strategists of the Left as—to mix our metaphors a bit—a trial balloon, we have no idea. But it was not until later, and in compliance with specific orders from Moscow, that the real barrage began.

The directive, making the destruction of anti-Communist groups a major assignment for Communists in 1961, was issued from the Kremlin early in December, 1960. And, as the 75-page report of the Senate Internal Security Subcommittee was later to make clear, the major brunt of that directive was borne in America by The John Birch Society. In late February, 1961 the implementation of this directive really got under way, through an article in the Communist *People's World* of San Francisco. This paper was ably assisted by a practically simultaneous and equally vicious attack in the *Santa Barbara News-Press,* which is published by Earl Warren's bosom pal, Tom Storke. *Time* magazine hastened to fall in step, even publishing in its article some errors of fact from the *People's World* (or from the same source), which had been specifically called to the attention of the *Time* reporter who interviewed me for the article. Then the whole Liberal-slanted press of America (and that means a very substantial proportion of the total press), immediately taking its cue from the *People's World*, or *Time*, or both, went all out in a continuous and extensive smear campaign against the Society which created a furore for many weeks. And the reverberations have lasted until today.

III

These attacks, in which the pundits of radio and television promptly joined the press, utilized falsehoods and distortions of many kinds. But the sensational, interest-compelling paragraphs of almost every smear consisted of sentences quoted out of context from *The Politician*. The Left had decided to accept the danger of having doubts about Eisenhower's policies and intentions considerably increased among reasonably well-informed people, for the sake of discrediting The John Birch Society in the eyes of the vast majority of Americans who were now completely deluded by years of propaganda.

The campaign was viciously unfair, especially in this feature, for many reasons. Not only, as I have said, was this manuscript no part of the beliefs or materials of the Society, but most of the members had never even heard of it before being blamed for what it said. They were being accused of something for which they had taken no responsibility whatsoever. Although I myself was perfectly willing to take the responsibility for whatever I had written, there was simply no way that I could defend myself or my statements without publishing the whole document of which these statements were a part. This the Leftists gambled, correctly, I would be unwilling to do; not because of any possible further damage to myself, but because of probable damage to the whole Conservative cause, through trying to lead people too rapidly into a realization of truths that they were unwilling to accept.

Also, I had never insisted that those who did read this manuscript had to arrive at my conclusions, or agree with the personal opinions expressed therein. In fact—and this is something which none of the smears in the press or over the air even mentioned—I had specifically stated in the document itself that I had no quarrel with those who attributed the

Communist-aiding actions of Eisenhower simply to political opportunism. There were some readers, indeed, who insisted and still insist that Eisenhower was simply too naive to know what he was doing; and that the whole incredible course of the history in which he had played so vital a part had been due to stupidity. And while many of those who read *The Politician* did come reluctantly to the same conclusion as my own, this personal opinion was still a minor part of the letter.

The damaging effect of the smears came, of course, from the charge that I was given to making "wild statements." Practically all that the press gave the public was these bare statements that were supposed to be so wild. Actually, as already indicated, the manuscript from which these few sentences were so roughly snatched consisted of over two hundred typed pages. Those pages contained a fairly compact and always accurate presentation of events, and an analysis of the motives, causes, and personalities involved in those events, which made up one important part of the horrible record of the Communist advance since the beginning of World War II. Despite the unusual and piecemeal manner in which the contents of these 287 pages had been put together, a lot of hard work and careful research had gone into their preparation. And very few indeed of those who ever read all of the pages in which these opinions were enmeshed, even those who still disagreed entirely with the bare statements so often quoted, ever came out with any feeling that there was anything wild about them. You yourself, my gentle but possibly hostile reader, quite likely will not share the personal opinions that I expressed, even after you have read this material which seemed to me to support those opinions. But I believe you will feel that there is a lot of disturbing and too little known (or remembered) history here, of however informal a nature, which deserves the attention of patriotic Americans.

For a number of reasons, therefore, some of which have already been suggested, I have at last decided to give to friends of mine, and to anybody else—friend or enemy—who really cares, an opportunity to read this manuscript *now, as is,* so that they can judge it for themselves. In doing so they may gain a better understanding of much that is happening today, through seeing current developments as merely an extension or completion of actions taken and trends initiated during the last Administration. And if the Liberals do not like this result of their unceasing and utterly unfair attacks, they have only themselves to blame. Any man, hounded long enough and mercilessly enough, for merely saying what he believes and doing what he thinks is right, is entitled at long last to defend himself.

Nobody has to tell us that, in its present shape, this document is neither a book of history nor a scholarly essay of any kind. Except for a few additions like this *Prologue* it remains what it has always been—basically a letter, originally written as an expression of personal and confidential views.

Finally, let me emphasize again that nobody has any slightest degree of responsibility for this manuscript, or for its past or present printing and distribution, except myself. It is worth repeating that neither The John Birch Society nor its members have ever had any connection with *The Politician* in any way, except to be the victims of smears aimed at them because of it. The founders of the Society having disavowed the document, the COUNCIL of the Society long ago officially made it clear that this was a purely personal property and problem of my own, with which they wanted nothing whatsoever to do in any way. Whatever present blame (or even possibly future praise) may accrue for the distribution of *The Politician* is mine alone—except for the moral encouragement given me by hundreds of friends to bring it out of seclusion and let it speak for itself. They feel that then, instead of being a skeleton in the closet, this manuscript may become a full-bodied and very effective instrument on the Americanist side of the fight which now engages us all. And I am following this advice.

THE POLITICIAN

AGAIN, PLEASE NOTE

In reading what follows it should be kept in mind that this final unpublished version was finished in June, 1958. Some of the references and statements are more readily understood if the date when they were made is remembered.

All footnotes, identified by page numbers and by index numbers within the page, are given in sequence in the back of the book. These footnotes, whether of explanation or documentation, have all been added during the fall of 1962, and the first two months of 1963, for this first published edition. There were none in any earlier copies of the manuscript.

Dear Reader:

This is not a book. It has not been published. It has not been offered for publication, nor intended for private publication by the writer.

This is an unfinished manuscript. A first and far shorter draft was completed in December, 1954, and shown to about thirty of my best-informed friends. A much longer version was finished in August, 1956, and has been read by perhaps sixty friends. This is a third, but by no means final, form of the composition. Its typewritten pages have been reproduced by a photo-offset process, and put together in this looseleaf binder, solely for the convenience of those who are asked to read it.

Such friends, of whom you are one, have been very carefully selected -- for reasons which will become obvious. Each copy of the manuscript is numbered, and this is No. _____. I am asking you to consider it as on loan to you, for your own eyes only, until it is returned. I hope you will consider the contents as strictly confidential, and will use precaution to keep the manuscript safeguarded while it is in your possession. But I shall not ask for it back in a hurry, because if anything happens to me I should like to have a goodly number of copies safely out in other hands.

Fully aware of the pressures on your time, I am nevertheless pleading with you to take enough of that time to read all of these pages carefully and without undue haste. Not only I, but other men of far more influence and achievement (whose names are known to you but should not be mentioned here), believe that you will consider this to be the most important manuscript or book you have ever read. This is not at all because of any skill or special knowledge or authority on my part. It is because of the importance -- to you, to your family, and to your country -- of the facts themselves which have been assembled here for your consideration.

Except in Chapter I (the accuracy of which I am willing to guarantee),[1] there is no information in these pages which has not already been widely published elsewhere. My undertaking has been merely to put together the various pieces, as they fit into one clear pattern, in order to make more obvious the frightening significance of the total picture.

Besides my main purpose, of calling to your attention the real import of this picture as I see it, there is one other reason for sending you the manuscript. The possibility cannot be ignored that ever-worsening circumstances may, at some future time, make advisable the publication of a book based on this material. Against that possibility I welcome, and shall greatly appreciate, any corrections of error, additions of significantly relevant fact, or criticisms or suggestions of any kind, you may be able and willing to give me.[2]

Sincerely,[3]

Robert Welch

INTRODUCTION

It is difficult for many of us to remember just what the score was, in the Cold War, only five years ago. So a brief review of the situation at that time may be helpful.

Joseph Stalin died on March 5, 1953. During the spring and summer of 1953 his death was a recent and most important event. Lavrenti Beria was still alive, to contest with Georgi Malenkov for dictatorial power. Affairs in the Kremlin were more unsettled than they had been since the purges of 1937. And throughout the world a fermenting doubt was at work as to whether Malenkov or anybody else would be able to establish the firm and efficient control over International Communism that had been exercised by Stalin.

The preponderant weight of evidence, on the authority of those best informed about the subject, was that the Russians had not yet produced even one atom bomb for themselves.[1] The few they had obtained for demonstration and prestige purposes had been assembled by them out of parts stolen from our plants. Even Harry Truman had subscribed to this view, in January, 1953, on the basis of all the knowledge that had been available to him as President. The Russians, while proceeding with their usual bluff and bluster, simply did not yet have any nuclear weapons.

General Van Fleet was in position to inflict a devastating defeat on the Chinese Communists in Korea. He himself has stated that, as late as April, 1953, he and the South Koreans could have won an overwhelming victory, and should have been allowed to do so.[2] Chiang Kai-shek had half a million soldiers on Formosa, straining at the leash to go back to the mainland -- either independently, or as our allies in

Korea.[1]

Japan had not yet been infiltrated by Communist influences as it has today. Ramon Magsaysay was in the very process of completely routing the Communists in the Philippines.[2] Ho Chi Minh was still having plenty of troubles with his civil war in Vietnam. Sukarno had not yet dared show his completely Communist hand in Indonesia. In Ceylon, extremely important as a base for any small wars around the perimeter of Asia, the United National Party was still in control; its dominant figure, Sir John Kotelawala (to become Premier in October, 1953) was vigorously pro-Western and anti-Communist.[3]

There were no strategically serious Communist advances yet in Africa. (Gamal Abdel Nasser was still a lieutenant-colonel; he became Vice-Premier of Egypt, under President Neguib, on June 18, 1953.)[4] The Middle East, except for little Israel, was still firmly anti-Communist. Turkey had shown her willingness actually to fight the Communists, by the troops she had sent to Korea. Greece was at that time solidly in the anti-Communist camp. So was Italy, with the Christian Democrats still in control.[5] England had thrown out the left-wing socialists and had a Tory government which, except for Anthony Eden, was at least a little bit awake to the Communist threat. West Germany had staged a remarkable recovery, and was taking the lead in trying to establish the anti-Communist European Defense Community. The enslaved people in Poland, in the Balkans, in all of the satellites, were as resentful and smoldering as they have ever been. The East Germans arose in the most determined and dangerous uprising the Kremlin ever had to face. The suicidal rebellion at the huge Vorkuta slave labor camps showed the inflammable conditions inside Russia itself.[6] There were a dozen fuses waiting to be lighted, and some already lighted which had to be stamped out in a hurry, all leading to charges of dynamite within the foundations of Soviet power.

The American government had saved the Soviet regime from financial collapse in 1933, and given its prestige and credit the vital hypodermic injection, by recognition. The American government had saved the Soviet regime from destruction by Hitler's armies, in 1942 and 1943, through intervention with both supplies and military force. The American government had made possible all of the postwar expansion of the Soviet empire, by acquiescence and frequently by collaboration in the Soviet subjugation of other nations. But in the spring of 1953 the American people were no longer in a mood to condone such a partnership. The American people had begun to wake up to the extent of Communist infiltration into our government and into every segment of our public life. They were, at long last, realizing the crime of "containment" and the folly of appeasement. And without the American government to hold over the Kremlin the umbrella of its protection, against storms rising on every side, the Kremlin faced a very precarious future. Not since the siege of Stalingrad had the whole Communist tyranny been in so much danger of being wiped off the face of the earth.

The sad truth is that this tyranny was actually saved, in this period of great vulnerability, by just one thing; by the inauguration, on January 20, 1953, of Dwight David Eisenhower as President of the United States. The circumstances of his election made it politically necessary for him to bring many good men into his government. The rationale of his election, and the temper of the American people, made it imperative for a while that he talk a good brand of anti-Communism. But the Communist influences which completely controlled him kept the reins of that control tight and effective. Subtly, cleverly, always proclaiming otherwise and finding specious excuses for what were really pro-Communist actions, these Communist influences made him put the whole diplomatic power, economic power, and recognized leadership of this country to work, on the side of Russia and the Communists, in connection with every problem and trouble spot in their empire. You only have to look at where we stand today, five years later, at exactly these same spots on the scoreboard reviewed above, to realize the truth of this assertion and the extent of this Communist success. It simply was not possible to lose so much ground, so rapidly, to an enemy so inferior, by chance or by stupidity. The explanation calls for a very sinister and hated word, but one which is by no means new in the history of governments or of nations. The word is treason. It is the province of this treatise to show the part played in these treasonous developments, however unwittingly or unwillingly, by Dwight Eisenhower; and how, as the most completely opportunistic and unprincipled politician America has ever raised to high office, he was so supremely fitted for the part.'

CHAPTER ONE

The Lieutenant Colonel . . . . .

The Olympic Hotel in Seattle is a massive stone building, with a huge oldfashioned main dining room that has been a treat to this weary traveler, and to thousands like him, on many occasions over many years. Nevertheless, in 1940 the Olympic Hotel badly needed business. Early that fall the manager hit upon a gesture of hospitality which he thought might serve as bait to bring in more customers. He was after, specifically, more patronage from the younger officers of the rapidly increasing U.S. Army forces at nearby Ft. Lewis. And he believed that if the colonels made The Olympic their social headquarters, the lieutenants surely would follow.

So the hotel manager telephoned a colonel with whom he had recently been on a fishing trip. He invited this gentleman to bring three or four other officers besides himself to dinner, in the manager's four-room apartment in the hotel. The colonel accepted. One of the officers he took along for the evening was a lieutenant colonel, by the name of Dwight D. Eisenhower. The only other guests were John Boettiger and his wife, the former Anna Roosevelt Dall, daughter of President Franklin D. Roosevelt.

Anna's place in her father's affections, and influence over him, were well known at that time. As soon as Lt. Colonel Eisenhower saw Mrs. Boettiger, and realized who she was, he asked to be seated next to her at dinner. Before dinner, during dinner, and after dinner, he monopolized her attention. They conversed together throughout the evening, to the visible

7

exclusion of the others present. But much of their conversation, naturally and necessarily, was overheard. And the burden of Ike's song for hour on hour was the greatness of Franklin D. Roosevelt. In telling the daughter how wonderful her father was, the lieutenant colonel managed to cover with fulsome praise practically all the words and works of the President.

Early the next morning Anna was on the telephone to her father in Washington. "I've found the man," she said. And she proceeded to tell the abnormally vain FDR what a hero-worshipper of his, and what a genius, she had discovered in an army uniform. Within a few days -- although the incident is completely and understandably ignored in Ike's own account of this period, in his ghost-written autobiography, Crusade In Europe -- Lt. Colonel Eisenhower was ordered to Washington for an interview in the White House.

A few weeks later Eisenhower, back at Ft. Lewis, was made Chief of Staff of the 3rd Infantry Division. Four months later, in March of 1941, he became Colonel Eisenhower, and was made Chief of Staff of the whole Ninth Army Corps. In June he was made Chief of Staff of the United States Third Army, with headquarters at San Antonio. There, in his own language, he "was brought closer to the problems of the Army of the United States as a whole." At the end of September, of that same year of 1941, he became a brigadier general. Five days after Pearl Harbor, or on December 12, 1941, he was called to Washington by telephone, in advance of written orders, by Walter Bedell Smith, who was conveying instructions from General George C. Marshall.

Brigadier General Eisenhower met General Marshall in Washington on December 14, and was immediately brought into war planning at the highest

level. On February 16, 1942 he was made Assistant
Chief of Staff of the War Plans Division. On March 9,
as the War Plans Division was replaced by the OPD
-- Operations Division of the War Department General Staff -- Eisenhower became its first head, with
the rank of Major General. On June 11 he was given
command of our "European Theatre of Operations";
and soon "fell into the habit" of having luncheon with
Winston Churchill at 10 Downing Street every Tues-
day, and dinner with Churchill at the latter's home
every Thursday. In July, 1942 he was given the three
stars of a lieutenant general. On February 11, 1943
less than two years from the time when he had still
been a lieutenant colonel, Eisenhower became a full
general. And ten months later, although he had never
been in combat command of even a battalion, and had
never seen a battle, General Eisenhower was made
Commander in Chief of all the Allied forces in Western Europe.[2]

We do not wish to imply, however, that this
meteoric rise was due entirely to the exercise of
Eisenhower's flattering charm on Anna Roosevelt
Boettiger, nor even to the personal favoritism of
her father which he thereby obtained. There were
more comprehensive forces at work. The first of
these was the overall and continuous brilliance of
Dwight D. Eisenhower as a politician. This aptitude
(which included some unsavory tricks for self-promo-
tion at the expense of his associates and superiors)
had already been well utilized, to give him the nebulous but profitable reputation of being "an outstanding officer. " For Eisenhower is not only all politician, so far as his ability is concerned. He is the
living embodiment of practically all of the skills and
attitudes that every ambitious politician would like
to possess.

His most obvious asset in political maneuvers

is the personal charm to which we have already referred. Few men have ever exemplified more conclusively Shakespeare's wise observation that "one
may smile, and smile, and be a villain." Woodrow
Wilson, for all the subtlety of his skill as a politician,
lacked this characteristic of disarming self-ingratia-
tion, which Franklin Roosevelt found so useful and
which Eisenhower has made even more so.

But Eisenhower is more like Wilson, and goes
far beyond him, in the second asset of his inventory
-- which is the successful pretense of not being a
politician at all. Here is, in plain and completely
provable fact, the "big lie"; the lie so big, and so
exactly the opposite of the truth, that it simply does
not occur to most people to examine it, as possibly
a lie, at all. La Rochefoucauld said: "It is a great
cleverness to know how to conceal one's cleverness."
With regard to his political cleverness Eisenhower
has performed this feat in the style of a master.

The General's contribution towards winning
World War II, for instance, was important; but it
was entirely that of a political "fixer." Whether
working with (or on) Darlan and de Gaulle, or
smoothing out frictions and disagreements between
the British and American chiefs of staff, his skill
was so great that even Alanbrooke said that "we, as
allies, were extremely fortunate to have such a
charming individual. As Supreme Commander what
he may have lacked in military ability he greatly
made up for by the charm of his personality."[1] Actually,
Eisenhower was so poor at strategy, tactics, and the
necessary qualifications for military command that
even his unceasing sponsor, George Marshall, once
cabled him in disgust that he was entirely too weak for
the position which he held.[2] He was, in fact, so indifferent a soldier that it became necessary for the top
authorities to shunt him aside and upstairs, in such

an exalted position that he had only political considerations to which to devote his energy and time, in order
that the real soldiers under him could get on with their
campaigns and the business of winning the war.' And
yet he came out of the war, and took a place in the
American public mind, as a great soldier; a man who
had won the war by his superb military generalship;
and a man so completely naive in politics that he
didn't even know what was happening, in the gigantic
build up of himself for the presidency. So firmly and
cleverly was this reputation established that not even
after five years of Eisenhower as President, during
which time he has continuously engaged in far more
dirty, more deceptive, and more ruthless behind-the-
scenes political manipulations than even Roosevelt
ever undertook, have the American people begun to
see the politician in the uniform of a soldier or under
the silk hat of the statesman.

So, returning to the discussion of Eisenhower's
rise in four years from being an unknown lieutenant
colonel to becoming the Supreme Commander of the
largest military force ever organized, with dozens of
the very ablest generals of Europe and America under
him, there are those -- even among his most severe
critics -- who attribute this fantastic ascent entirely
to his charm and political genius; to the same consciously employed smoothness that hypnotized Anna
Roosevelt and her father, and started Ike on his way.
And of course they could be right. But we think these
critics are entirely too optimistic, too generous, and
too blind to other influences which were sweeping him
along.

We believe that some very sinister but powerful
forces had already put their mark on Eisenhower as
a pliable tool of the future; that they recognized in
him a politician who, for personal promotion and
prestige and glory, would always be willing to sail

before the winds they created and to keep his compass pointed in the direction they desired. And we
believe not only that these forces were already helping the advancement of his career, at every turn,
but that this conclusion can be convincingly substan-
tiated by a careful enough study of the record.

We agree that the dinner in Seattle was extremely fortunate for Eisenhower and his promoters; and
that this opportunity to reveal himself to one of the
Roosevelt clan as so kindred a spirit was important.
But we also think that if this propitious opening had
not occurred, he or his behind-the-scenes manipula-
tors would have invented one which served almost as
well. While it is probable that Roosevelt's sheer
favoritism, once gained and held by the Eisenhower
flattery and charm, might alone have put Eisenhower
in a major-general's uniform before the war was
over, we think it took those sinister forces, of which
Roosevelt himself was a half willing but never quite
conscious captive, to parlay the Eisenhower winnings
into so grand -- and useful -- a final prize. And we
think this fact is the key to much of the tragic history
of the last fifteen years.

CHAPTER TWO

"Lucky Ike" . . . . .

For, let's go back to December 12, 1941. It was only the preceding Sunday that General George C. Marshall had woefully failed to use the telephone, or any other prompt means, to give General Short and Admiral Kimmel in Hawaii his own advance information as to the coming Japanese attack. Half of the American fleet had been deliberately decoyed as sitting ducks in Pearl Harbor, with Marshall's full knowledge and connivance, to induce the Japanese to strike. So afraid were he and Roosevelt that the Hawaiian commanders might somehow get some warning of Japanese intentions that they had even denied these commanders the possession of a "Purple" decoding machine, through which Kimmel and Short might themselves have learned at first hand what was afoot.[1] And while Roosevelt was equally guilty with Marshall of this particular piece of deliberate treason, I believe that the history of the two men and of the period will show a huge difference in motives. Roosevelt, being swept along and used by Communist forces which he thought he was using, avid for the glory and the power of being a wartime president and of tossing around millions of men and billions of dollars with a nod of his head, dreaming of accomplishing what Wilson had tried but failed to do, seeing himself sometime in the future as the world-worshipped hero who had saved it for democracy and perhaps even united it under his own leadership; Roosevelt thus saw the coming loss at Pearl Harbor as a worthwhile gambit for the sake of getting us into the war through a blow struck first

13

by an enemy.[1]

It was criminal. In fact, it was treason. But getting the enemy to strike first, in a war that seems inevitable, is nothing new in the history of nations. Those who would condone it can point to precedents in the past. And there are plenty of intelligent and otherwise patriotic Americans today who, recognizing and admitting everything we have stated above, still claim that Roosevelt was justified in making this calculated sacrifice in order to unite the country at once in wartime effort against enemies who sought to destroy it.[2] We vigorously disagree, but they have at least an understandable argument.

George Marshall's purpose, however, in our opinion, was not to save his country, but to carry forward Communist plans which would ultimately deliver it to Communism. His immediate goal was to get America into the war, at any cost, in order to relieve Stalin from the terrible pressure of the German armies. It was Japan who attacked us, but Marshall headed the necessary strength and influence which caused us to throw all of our gathering war might against Germany -- or in the form of supplies and armament directly to the aid of the Russians.[3] It was Marshall who insisted on our launching an immediate landing and second front in France, even in 1942, at whatever cost; and who kept on so insisting, even after the British had shown everybody else enough of the facts of life about crossing the Channel at that time to make the idea obviously absurd. Alanbrooke even charges that Marshall didn't have the slightest plan as to what Allied troops would do, if and after any of them actually landed in France, or even as to which way they should try to go.[4] This may be inaccurate or exaggerated. But it was prompted by Marshall's clamorous demand for a second front at once. The British, and even most of the American generals

14   The Politician

as soon as they got their bearings, merely thought that Marshall was horribly mistaken in this particular persistent view. But if they had realized that he didn't care what the fiasco -- and its continued repetition -- would have cost in American lives, provided it diverted German troops and attention from the Eastern front, they could more easily have reconciled this folly with the reasonable ability Marshall exhibited otherwise in carrying on the war.

For while this is certainly not the place to go into a hundred pages, to show that George Marshall always conducted the American side of the war for the benefit of the Kremlin, to the very best of his ability, or into a thousand pages of other details and circumstances to show all he accomplished for the Kremlin in the years following the war, it is necessary to enter the conclusion to which those pages would lead. I defy anybody, who is not actually a Communist himself, to read all of the known facts about his career and not decide that since at least sometime in the 1930's George Catlett Marshall has been a conscious, deliberate, dedicated agent of the Soviet conspiracy. There is, in my opinion, simply no escape from such overwhelming evidence.[1] But if the reader doubts this conclusion, as he has every right to do, and since I cannot stop to bolster it with the needed facts and arguments here, I ask him to accept it merely as a possibility for the present, and let us go on with our story.

At any rate, Marshall is justly famous for his memory of, and attention to, details.[2] It is true that he later was to testify under oath that he couldn't even remember where he had been or what he had been doing, during those fatal final hours on December 7, 1941, when he already knew that the Japanese bombers were nearing the Hawaiian coast. (It has now been reported, on good authority, that he spent most of the day at the Russian Embassy, conferring with Litvinov, who had arrived that morning. So his reluctance to remember is easy to understand.) But this same George Catlett Marshall had the memory and the motive, on December 12, to reach out by telephone for this one officer, Dwight D. Eisenhower, among hundreds of equal rank and superior experience. And the fact that Eisenhower was already known to be a favorite of the President undoubtedly made it seem much easier and more natural for Marshall to mark him as a protege of his own.

It must be remembered that these were the days when Roosevelt was completely dominated by Communist influences; when Lauchlin Currie and Harry Dexter White and dozens of their kind were flitting in and out of the White House and Washington with the vicarious authority of the President in their voices or at the ends of their fountain pens; when Roosevelt himself stated openly that Communists were among his personal friends, and turned the presidential spleen on anybody who didn't like them as well as he did.[1] It should be remembered that Roosevelt's court-packing scheme, to put over Communist-inspired New Deal measures despite the Constitution, was planned by the Communists and first announced by Earl Browder in a speech in Providence, Rhode Island. That in 1941 it was only three years since Roosevelt's attempted purge, of the Senators who had voted against this scheme, had been conducted by America's leading Communist, Earl Browder, from inside the White House.[2] And that it was to be only three years more before Alger Hiss would be playing his part at Roosevelt's right hand, despite everything both Martin Dies and the FBI had already done to indicate that Hiss was a Communist traitor.[3]

Please remember, too, that in all the countless conferences of the early war years, in Washington and London and everywhere else, it was usually George Marshall, speaking for the military, and Harry Hopkins, speaking for the President, who represented the United States or carried the real weight among our representatives.[1] It was Marshall and Hopkins who had by far the most to say about which generals should be moved or promoted into which commands, in the rapidly coalescing and increasing Allied forces. This was true at the very time that Harry Hopkins was specifically and almost solely responsible for the transmission to Moscow, through Great Falls, Montana, of secrets and documents concerning American power, fifty black suitcases full at that time; and of materials for the construction of an atom bomb, to help the Russians get started, years before we had produced one ourselves and while that production was still supposed to be the greatest secret in our history.[2]

It is to me inconceivable that under all the circumstances which prevailed, and with so many able and experienced generals available, Lt. Colonel Eisenhower could have been shot up all the way to Supreme Commander Eisenhower in so short a time, and with so obviously little military ability, without the Communist push behind him every step of the way. (Lord Alanbrooke, watching Ike's ascent to greatness while sadly conscious, from close observation, of his manifest unfitness for such responsibilities, and without any inkling of the real reasons for this ascent, could and did ascribe it only to Eisenhower luck.[3] But that luck, we believe, was provided directly from the Kremlin, with a hammer and sickle woven into every gorgeous piece.)

There are other possible explanations, of course.[4] And this one measure of tentative evidence does not prove that his unceasing promotion was due to Communist support. But please note that such support would explain this particular development very neatly and completely. And it is the total of so many developments and events, which the same premise would explain equally well, that makes the mathematical probability in favor of this explanation a practical certainty -- as I hope to show.

CHAPTER THREE

The Supreme Commander . . . . .

This is not a biography. I shall not try to give
any narrative coverage of Eisenhower's life, nor
even of any particular period of his life. So I see no
need for too strict attention to chronology, in connection with matters which seem relevant to my argument. But the first strong evidence of where Eisenhower's sympathies lay -- of where he thought it was
smart personal politics to have them lie -- as he began his wartime career, was his insistence on an immediate second front in France.[1] The plan for an
early Anglo-American invasion of Northern France,
which George Marshall and Harry Hopkins took to
London, in April, 1942, to persuade the British to
adopt, had been prepared by Eisenhower as the new
head of the Operations Division of our War Department.[2] It contemplated the beginning of the main
permanent invasion -- Operation Roundup -- with
eighteen British Divisions, in the spring of 1943.
American troops were to be poured over, through
Britain, as fast as they could be trained and trans-
ported, to increase this force rapidly to a million
men. But, in order to relieve Russia earlier, a
smaller preliminary landing -- Operation Sledgehammer -- was to be undertaken that very summer.
This was recognized as "probably sacrificial."[3] The
cost in British and American lives, however, did not
disturb Marshall, Hopkins, and Eisenhower, if they
could help out Stalin.
    I certainly do not claim to be any military strat-
egist. But the British wartime Chief of Staff has

written that "in the light of the existing situation his plans (meaning Marshall's plans, prepared by Eisenhower) for September of 1942 were just fantastic."[1] Many years later Eisenhower himself, with a reputation for military knowledge which now needed protection, wrote that "later developments have convinced me that those who held the Sledgehammer operation to be unwise at the moment were correct in their evaluation of the problem."[2] All of which could mean, of course, only that the utterly inexperienced "American Chief of War Plans," Eisenhower, had made a bad mistake in judgment. But it should be noted that this mistake in judgment was vigorously in favor of what Stalin wanted. (For instance the so-called Hollywood Democratic Committee,[3] consisting of a hard core of Communists and sympathizers, who had lost none of their enthusiasm through the Stalin-Hitler brotherhood period, were now screaming and kept on screaming for a second front -- in France and not through the Balkans. So did every other Communist front in America.) And it would be very difficult to find any "mistakes in judgment" which Eisenhower made later in the war -- of which there were plenty -- that were not in Stalin's favor. It is not too far-fetched to guess that so green a man had been put in so strategically important a position because the unfailing direction, which his "mistakes in judgment" would take, could be surmised with confidence.

Fantastic or not, the "Sledgehammer" plan was unceasingly urged by Marshall and Eisenhower throughout the fall of 1942. Then, in the spring of 1943, Eisenhower supported Marshall in his efforts to carry out Stalin's desires and get a cross-channel invasion started at once, despite the still utterly inadequate supply of troops, war materiel, and shipping for such a move. Eventually, in 1944, Stalin, George Marshall, and Eisenhower together were able to overrule Churchill and the British, stop the Allied forces which had invaded Italy from crossing the Po Valley into the Balkans, and open up their second front in France. This not only increased the relief for Stalin on the Eastern front, which was being provided by the Allied campaigns anyway, but from Stalin's point of view it accomplished what was now a far more important purpose. It left the Balkans wide open for the Soviet agents and Soviet armies to take them over, in the chaos that accompanied the German collapse.

Eisenhower's part in these decisions was increasingly important. Far more serious and revealing, however, than the lines of strategy which he supported as he moved into the councils of the mighty, were those "mistakes in judgment" which he perpetrated on his authority as Supreme Commander -- or on his own initiative, without proper authority, towards the close of the war and in the months following its end. Most notorious of these "mistakes" was his stopping of our troops from entering Prague and Berlin, in order to give the Russians time to reach and take those capitals, when both cities were begging to be allowed to surrender to the Americans.' The action was on a par with the transfer of troops out of Italy to France for a new front, instead of continuing the successful campaign through Italy. It served the same purpose of helping Stalin's postwar plans. But this decision was entirely, or primarily, Eisenhower's.

These orders to halt our troops were emphatically confirmed by Eisenhower -- he had already wired Stalin his generous "you go first" concession -- over the vigorous protest of Churchill, who could foresee the tremendous cost to the anti-Communist world in the ultimate political and economic effects of these pro-Communist "blunders." The best that can now be claimed, in support of this decision on Eisenhower's part, is that it was forced on him by George Marshall back in Washington, and that Marshall himself was bound by an agreement entered into at Teheran by Stalin, Roosevelt, and Churchill. The second half of this excuse is absurd, and is shown to be so by Churchill's own actions at the time Eisenhower halted his troops on the Elbe. As to the first part, it makes very little difference whether George Marshall told Eisenhower to do this, and Eisenhower obeyed, or Eisenhower told Marshall he was doing it, and Marshall approved. In either event, by the hypothesis of this letter, the Communists were telling both of them what to do. And no other explanation even makes sense.[1]

Just to complete the argument, however, it should be noted that the only agreement which could have been supposed to tie Eisenhower's hands in this way was the one already made for the postwar division of Germany into occupational zones. The eastward line of the zones allotted to the British and Americans ran about two hundred miles west of Berlin. But Eisenhower himself says: "This future division of Germany did not influence our military plans for the final conquest of the country."[2] He admits, or even boasts, that the troop-halting decision was his own, in this paragraph in Crusade in Europe: "A natural objective beyond the Ruhr was Berlin. It was politically and psychologically important as the symbol of remaining German power. I decided, however, that it was not the logical or the most desirable objective for the forces of the Western Allies." And he then gives several pages of specious reasoning to explain what he obviously realized would appear to have been his inexplicable -- and highhanded -- change in the plans to take Berlin which the British thought had already been settled.[3] It should be remembered that his book was written in time for publication in 1948; and that, in view of the true significance which has since been revealed of this and many other "blunders" by Eisenhower, he would undoubtedly attempt to put an entirely different light on this action if "writing" the same book today.

Of course, while Eisenhower was offered immediate peaceful surrender, it took the Russians three weeks of hard fighting, at an utterly unnecessary cost of thousands of lives, to reach Berlin. What took place then will show why the Germans had been so pitifully anxious to surrender the city to American occupying troops. When General Frank Howley entered Berlin on June 17, he found this incident typical: "A former secretary of mine, a girl of seventeen, had to be wheeled in a baby carriage several blocks down her street to a hospital, after seven Russian soldiers had taken turns raping her and her mother in their apartment.... Two hundred and thirty German girls were treated at the same hospital in a single day."[1] Actually, what the barbarian Russian soldiers did in Berlin, while Eisenhower kept our troops obligingly waiting in the outskirts, has been described, probably without exaggeration, as "the most ghastly and enormous raping and looting orgy which Christian Europe had ever had to suffer."[2] Soon thereafter, however, Eisenhower was in Russia, receiving from these "pals-in-arms" of his every honor and reward they could find to offer him, including an autographed photo of Premier Joseph Stalin.[3] There is not the least doubt that he fully deserved these marks of great appreciation from Stalin, or that he was going to deserve them even more.

One item in the list of reasons for such gratitude was what Eisenhower had done, in another and entirely different maneuver, to the future of the city of Berlin. By 1944 the U.S. War Department, under

George Marshall's domination, had already rejected Cordell Hull's 1943 proposal that the post-war occupation zones in Germany "be so drawn as to bring each into contact with Berlin. " It had already been accepted and agreed, among the Western allies, that Berlin would be entirely within the Russian occupation zone. So the question of a corridor into Berlin, from the other zones, became important. In February, 1944, the British suggested that such a post-war corridor be definitely planned by the European Advisory Commission. Again Marshall's War Department objected, saying that this matter of a corridor should be settled at the proper time by military representatives. In May, 1944, the European Advisory Commission closed up shop and turned its affairs over to Supreme Headquarters, Allied Expeditionary Force, of which Eisenhower was the head. From that time on, and through the clever preceding steps of Marshall which have been indicated above, the provision for an inviolable corridor into Berlin was solely the responsibility of Eisenhower as Supreme Commander.[1]

No such corridor was provided. The actual negotiations for the route between Berlin and the West were conducted by General Lucius Clay, under Eisenhower's command.[2] Then Eisenhower, sitting down with his friend, Marshal Zhukov, arrived at an understanding as to how the Russians would graciously permit passage in and out of Berlin along this route. But Zhukov was such a grand fellow and good friend that naturally no written agreement was needed; and this verbal "agreement" between Eisenhower and Zhukov is all the Western Allies, the Germans, and especially the people of Berlin, have had to depend on for their corridor to civilization. Of course Eisenhower "believed" that you could trust the Russians. It is a delusion under which he repeatedly claims to be laboring today.

The incredibly expensive Berlin airlift was just one of the costs of this "blunder." The other economic costs and the psychological and political costs, to the anti-Communist cause, have been beyond appraisal. Nor was the lack of a corridor the only pro-Russian monstrosity which Eisenhower arranged and allowed for Berlin. Just for one illustration of many less-noticed concessions, Hitler's old radio station, and the office building containing it, were turned over to the Russians, despite the fact that the building was in the British zone. One minor but sad consequence of this peculiar favor to the Communists was that, for years after the war, many anti-Communist refugees escaping from East Germany, and coming to this building first after crossing the line, would enter it for information. Nobody ever saw or heard of them again. Not only was it of great value for the Russians to have the use of this powerful radio station, but the building served as a beautiful trap for their most determined enemies.[1]

Our High Commissioner in Germany, John J. McCloy, said in 1951: "It's impossible for me to conceive how any group of sane men could have permitted the creation of a situation such as exists in the Russian zone of Germany today."[2] But if Mr. McCloy had been willing to accept the simple hypothesis that this situation was created by men, primarily George Marshall and Dwight D. Eisenhower, who were deliberately and consciously serving the interests of Russia rather than their own country, the puzzle would have disappeared like an exploded soap bubble. And it made no difference that some of these men were not traitors for the sake of treason, but only opportunistic politicians who knew where the real control of future events lay and by which side their bread was buttered.[3]

Let's look next at another tremendous boost given the Russian Communist plans by Eisenhower, for which he justifiably took some of the credit in 1948, but which he undoubtedly would prefer to disclaim today. This was the instigation and early implementation of the so-called Morgenthau Plan for the conversion of Germany into a goat pasture -- so that it could never stand as a bulwark against the eventual Russian march across Europe. But for the foresight, patriotism, and determination of just one man, James Forrestal (whom the Communists later, either directly or indirectly, murdered), Eisenhower and his Communist pushers would have succeeded in carrying out the complete and final devastation which they planned.

The egg of the Morgenthau Plan was laid during a discussion of Germany's future, which took place at Eisenhower's English headquarters, in August, 1944. In Crusade in Europe Eisenhower (or his Communist ghost writer, Joseph Barnes) says that the discussion arose because of the visit of Secretary Morgenthau.' But even in 1948 Mr. Barnes was careful not to have Eisenhower mention that Harry Dexter White and John G. Winant were also present at the meeting. As to primary responsibility for the plan, however, we can save a lot of rambling to assemble evidence by simply quoting Fred Smith, former Assistant to Secretary of the Treasury, Henry Morgenthau, who has stated categorically in print: "On August 7, 1944, in a tent in southern England, the Morgenthau Plan was born. Actually it was General Dwight D. Eisenhower who launched the project."[2] The same on-the-spot authority has also said of the plan that Eisenhower sparked it, Morgenthau organized it, and Harry Dexter White "built it." What the Morgenthau Plan set out to do was so barbarous, and its execution, if not arrested half way by the common sense which Forrestal was able to make prevail, would have been so disastrous to our own clear interests and to everybody except the Russian Communists, that no further emphasis on the significance of this plan, and of its origin, is needed here.[/]

Instead we should move on to another pro-Communist policy-crime, in which Eisenhower played a considerable part -- and of which, strangely enough, the egg seems also to have been laid at this same meeting on August 7, 1944. This was the egg which hatched into the Nuremberg trials.[2] Eisenhower quotes himself as having said on that inglorious occasion: "Prominent Nazis, along with certain industrialists, must be tried and punished. Membership in the Gestapo and in the SS should be taken as prima facie evidence of guilt. The General Staff must be broken up, all its archives confiscated, and members suspected of complicity in starting the war or in any war crimes should be tried."[3]

Considering the complicity of Franklin D. Roosevelt and George Marshall in starting the war with Japan, of which Eisenhower was certainly aware by 1944, the sanctimonious savagery of that part of the statement reached a new high in hypocrisy. And we can well imagine the burst of applause from Harry Dexter White. The intentional violation of some of the best established principles of international law, in order to promote the effectiveness of Russian terror, prestige, and control in Central Europe, was already clearly evident in this statement, without any regard to the facts involved or the utterly unfair way in which these new principles of ex post facto law were to be applied. But many of the circumstances which were really to make the Nuremberg trials such a heinous crime were still largely in the future. Not only did the raping and looting by Russian soldiers, in all of Germany which they occupied, exceed in barbarity anything of which their enemies were even accused at Nuremberg; but Eisenhower himself, as overall commander of the Western Allies, was just as responsible for the Stuttgart atrocity as were any of the German generals, tried at Nuremberg, for the actions of soldiers under their command. In that affair, long since fully proved despite everything the Eisenhower headquarters could do to keep it out of print, French Negro soldiers from Senegal (wearing American lend-lease uniforms) rounded up approximately four thousand German women of all ages in the Stuttgart subway and engaged in a raping orgy for three days.[1]

Senator Robert A. Taft said on October 5, 1946, that "the hanging of the eleven men convicted at Nuremberg will be a blot on the American record which we shall long regret."[2] But Randolph Churchill stated the case even more emphatically, and accurately. "Cold-blooded murder," was what he called the executions. The Germans were not hanged, he said, "for starting the war, but for losing it. If we tried the starters, why not put Stalin in the dock?"[3] As a matter of fact, the worst single atrocity of the whole war, the Katyn Forest Massacre, committed by Stalin's orders, did almost become a subject of the trials. The Russians were actually going to have the Germans tried for this crime. When the Polish Government-in-Exile presented to Supreme Commander Eisenhower incontrovertible proof that it was the Russians who had so brutally murdered these thousands of Polish officers, the accusation against the Germans was dropped. But Eisenhower then helped to suppress the evidence, to avoid any trouble it might cause the Russians. Back in this country the Pentagon made sure that Major General Clayton Bissell stamped top secret on the report of Lt. Col. John H. Van Vliet, Jr., clearly showing the Russian guilt for this mass murder, and buried it until long after the Nuremberg trials were over.[4]

Eisenhower was neither an official prosecutor nor judge at the Nuremberg trials. But he had helped actively to inspire them, in the planning that brought them about, and in the gathering of the completely one-sided evidence on which they were based. He fully approved of them, and the way they were conducted. He thereby helped, as much as any one man, to convince the Europeans of the horrible fate that would be in store for generals or statesmen who opposed the Russians, and that the Russian idea of justice would now prevail instead of the kind which Western Europe had hitherto accepted, at least in principle, since the days of the Romans.

You can, of course, find specious and perhaps plausible reasons, other than a plain desire to help the Russian Communists, for Eisenhower's actions in this connection, as elsewhere. But to do so requires considerable seeking and a lot of sophistry. While the explanation, as plain as day before the face of anybody who does not willingly close his eyes to it, that Eisenhower was making himself the trusted darling of the Extreme Left, leaves no loose ends around whatsoever. Also, this explanation is supported by an entirely different body of actions more or less simultaneous; by a course of action, for which Eisenhower was directly and almost solely responsible, so infamous, so extensive, and so innately pro-Communist in every aspect, that it should be given a separate chapter.

CHAPTER FOUR

"Operation Keelhaul"[1]. . . . .

On November 23, 1954, Lt. General Edward M.
Almond of the U.S. Army was testifying before a
Congressional committee in Washington. He was
asked if he had been familiar, during World War II,
with a man named Tinio. This was his reply:

"Yes, Sir. Tinio was a nomad from a Turkistanian area. I could not even locate it myself, if
I tried. He had a partisan band and to look at them
you would immediately decide they were cutthroat
pirates. This band was a band of his own. He was
a nomad. He came to Italy and joined with one of my
regiments. He became a very reliable patrol leader.
He many times and on more than one occasion occupied a sector of the front in the Apennines, virtually
unoccupied by regular military personnel, between my
right flank and the left flank of the Brazilian Division
which was just beyond me or east of me, in the winter
of 1945. He did such good work that he was known
throughout my division. I think we gave him a cer-
tificate of accomplishment or something, just to be
grateful about it.

"But one day soon after the war ended in Italy,
in 1945, I was queried from General McNarney's
headquarters, which he very properly did, because
he had the request from a Soviet mission that had
come to Italy. Apparently, they heard about this
Tinio. The specific enquiry to me was: 'Was there
a Turkistanian by the name of Tinio with a band or
a group operating in my sector?' I said: 'Yes, there
was one, but where he is now, I don't know.' They

said: 'Is he in your area now?'

"On investigation, I found he was still over there with the 370th Infantry, his friends. I got in touch with the colonel of that regiment. He said that he would and did talk to Tinio. He immediately discovered that he, Tinio, was very much alarmed, that the Soviets had queried about him. What he had done in his own country, I didn't inquire of him. I have no knowledge. He was a good fighter and on our side. But he was disturbed that the Russians wanted to know where he and his men were.

"I also attribute it to the fact that he was not a convert of the Communists or Soviets and that they were after him. I was ordered eventually to turn Tinio over to the Russians for transportation back to Russia. I did that with the complete conviction, based on the things I had gotten from Tinio and from those with whom he associated, that it meant his certain destruction, and that of his band...."[1]

The italics above are ours. This valiant refugee from Communism must have been very proud when he thought he had not only found, but had earned, sure political asylum for himself and his band, among friends -- among the great freedom-loving Americans whom he had aided. His mistake was tragic, and fatal. And the source of the orders referred to will be clear in due course.

At the end of the war the Russian army pushed into Hungary, plundering, torturing, and raping as they went.[2] Several thousand patriotic Hungarians put up a last ditch fight against this advance. When they could hold out no longer, they retreated far enough to surrender to American troops. The Russians set up a red regime, and this provisional government demanded the return of these prisoners by the Americans. There were no Hungarians on the compiled list of war criminals, so the American legal department in Germany refused to allow the extradition.

But a Mrs. Laszlo Endre, wife of one of these prisoners, had an uncomfortable premonition. On August 15, 1945 she managed to see Cardinal Rohracher, and asked him to intervene, to prevent these prisoners being delivered to the Communist government in Budapest. The Cardinal told her he had already spoken to General Mark Clark about this matter, and that General Clark was quite sure the prisoners would not be handed over to the Reds. But Mrs. Endre's well founded premonition was still working. Unsatisfied even by the Cardinal's confidence, she hunted up Countess Lili Alberti, an old school friend who was now working for the Allies. Mrs. Endre explained that she was seeking information as to the future safety of her husband and his colleagues. And there she got the true information, of which obviously neither the Cardinal nor even General Clark had been aware. The Countess told Mrs. Endre there was no hope. She said that all of these Hungarians, as well as all members of anti-Communist governments everywhere, would be delivered to the countries of their origin -- which meant for these Hungarians, of course, to the red so-called government now in their native Budapest. When Mrs. Endre then protested that General Clark had said this would not happen, the Countess simply answered: "I have seen the order. It is signed by Dwight Eisenhower."[1] The Countess' information and prediction were quite correct. All of these Hungarian patriots were extradited, even though the U.S. Legal Department in Germany never did sanction the extraditions, and many of them were publicly executed.

These two incidents, however, are simply tiny illustrations of a heartrending program, carried out on a massive scale, over a long period of time. Stalin had made up his mind to use the chaos of the war's end, the reach of his armies into countries which had harbored refugees from Communism, and the help of Dwight Eisenhower, to drag back to Russia for liquidation or slave labor everybody who had escaped his country since 1939, and who was still in Central Europe, regardless of what they had been doing since. This exercise of memory and vengeance, as a warning to others who might wish to run out from under the Communist tyranny, was to apply to men, women, and children; to civilians, and soldiers; to those who had fought in German uniform against the Allies, and alike to those who had fought against the Germans, as volunteers with the Americans and other allies, on many fronts. There were somewhere from two to five million victims involved. And Eisenhower saw to it that every one of them who could be found was returned, despite whatever cruelty and force were needed -- and despite the fact that to do so he had to violate not only international law, and the laws of humanity, but the actual laws of his own country as well.

Nor is any of this a matter of either guessing or interpretation. The clear proofs of responsibility are all in the records, if anybody wishes to dig deep enough to find them and work hard enough to put them together. The best defense that Eisenhower and his inner circle of supporters have had, against accusations concerning this whole monstrous crime, was for a long time simply a conspiracy of silence. This typically Communist treatment of opposing truth was so successful that the comprehensive brief of indictment against Eisenhower, prepared by Dr. Bela Hubbard prior to the 1952 elections, did not even mention forced repatriation. But as parts of the record were gradually brought out here and there by anti-Communist researchers and historians, until the horrible truth began reaching the floor of Congress -- as in the Bosch Resolution of February 8, 1955[1] -- the Eisenhower apologists have tried to brush off any personal guilt on his part by blaming an agreement at Yalta for both the policy and its execution.

This is deliberate distortion and falsification, of the worst order. It's true that there was an agreement at Yalta, signed on behalf of the United States by General John R. Deane on February 11, 1945, which provided for the exchange of prisoners of war and "liberated" civilians, regardless of their desires. They were to be returned to their "countries of origin."[2] Apparently under the influence of Alger Hiss, Secretary of State Stettinius and our delegation entered into this agreement despite everything Ambassador Joseph Grew, then Acting Secretary of State in Washington, could do to prevent it. Grew pointed out to Stettinius the agreement's illegality, its inhumanity, and its violation of the long established American principle of offering ready asylum to those persecuted for political views. Grew had already correctly stated our position with regard to Soviet nationals taken prisoner in German uniforms, in an official State Department note of February 1, 1945, to Nikolai V. Novikov, Soviet representative in Washington. He said that we could never forcibly repatriate Soviet nationals taken prisoner in German uniform, for the simple reason that international law required that they be treated as German prisoners of war. He quoted the Geneva Convention, which does not permit the retaining state "to look behind the uniform." This was an excellent doctrine, long shared by civilized nations. Grew sent Stettinius a copy of this note, along with many telegrams, to Yalta. But it was all to no avail. Stalin was determined to have his vengeance, and Messrs. Stettinius, Hiss, et al., had Deane sign on the dotted line.

(Of course Grew was forced out of the State Department shortly thereafter by Dean Acheson, who took his place. And a decade later this particular note was considered so damaging to the Roosevelt-Stettinius reputations and to the pro-Communist arguments about Yalta, that the cover-up boys who managed and "released" the Yalta papers omitted it altogether. A copy of the note was made available to Julius Epstein by John Foster Dulles, on Mr. Epstein's discovering and presenting clear proof that the note did exist.)[1]

It was on the strength of the Deane agreement at Yalta, therefore, that Dwight Eisenhower could claim to have signed the order, which Countess Alberti saw, for the return of the Hungarian patriots to "the country of their origin." The fact that this was no longer actually their country, but had been taken over by the Communists, the very people against whom they had been fighting, was a mere trifle which Eisenhower chose to ignore.

But his part in the whole brutal program is far more important and ignominious than this mere resort to sophistry to have a few thousand Hungarian anti-Communists surrendered to their torturers. Among the Yalta papers there is a letter from Anthony Eden to the U.S. Secretary of State, informing him of repatriations of Soviet nationals, from both England and Mediterranean areas, which had already been made, before Yalta; and stating that Allied Supreme Commander, Dwight D. Eisenhower, had already decided to extradite Russians as quickly as possible.[2] And it was not just Russian nationals concerning whom he had made this decision. Those readers with good enough memories will recall the wave of suicides of Polish officers, who had served gallantly as volunteers with our troops in Italy, when these men found that they were being forcibly returned by our army to their certain death in

a Poland which was now ruled by Stalin's Lublin Gang.
For some brief mention of this affair did get into the
American newspapers. But we were all too busy
celebrating the universal and eternal peace, which
had now been achieved, to pay any attention. And
these Polish officers, who could not by any stretch
of the imagination be considered prisoners of war,
were not covered by the Yalta agreement at all. The
responsibility for the merciless cruelty to these allies
rests squarely on the shoulders of the Supreme Commander, Dwight D. Eisenhower.

The most important single implementation of the
foul "Deane Agreement" was the destruction of General Vlasov's army. A Soviet Army Commander,
Andrei A. Vlasov, who was at heart a bitter anti-
Communist but an equally dedicated Russian patriot,
surrendered to the Germans in 1942. His intention
was to get their help in organizing a Russian army
to free Russia from the Bolshevik tyranny. But he
made it all too clear that he and his troops, even in
German uniform, would never fight against the Western allies; that he didn't think the Germans themselves,
or anybody but Russians, could ever conquer Russia;
and that he was not at all interested in a German victory, but only in freeing Russia from the Soviet tyranny. Even though this, if successful, would have established peace on the Eastern front, the Germans at that
time were riding high, and were so sure of being able
to conquer and rule Russia, that they wouldn't listen
to Vlasov's plans. Himmler tried only, and unsuccess-
fully, to use him for propaganda purposes. It was General Vlasov -- or one of his subordinate generals --
who gave the journalist, Erich Kern, the remarkable
definition of Bolshevism as "that terrible synthesis of
madness and crime, which holds my poor, unhappy
people in its grip." But he would have no part in helping to replace a Bolshevik tyranny with a Nazi tyranny,

and so for a long time the Germans would have no
part of him.

By 1944, however, the whole picture had changed.
The Germans were desperately looking for help from
any source. So it was Himmler himself who, at the
very end of 1944, supported Vlasov in the organization and equipment of three divisions of Russians --
refugees and prisoners of war -- in German uniforms
and as a part of the overall German army, to act as
a "Russian Army of Liberation." (They became
known as the ROA, from the Russian initials for
these words.) The divisions were formed, and were
in action, by early in 1945. But of course it was too
late. Their major effect was to anger Stalin by the
number of his troops, at some points on the Eastern
front, who immediately surrendered to ROA forces
as soon as they learned the identity of these people in
German uniforms against whom they were fighting.

As the coming German collapse became obvious,
General Vlasov ordered all of his units to march to a
pre-arranged spot in southern Austria. He and they
were prepared, if necessary, to fight to the last man
rather than be returned to Soviet Russia. But, quite
properly, he did not believe this would be necessary.
The situation of his forces might best be understood
by considering that of the Japanese on Hawaii at this
same time. Many of these Japanese, feeling that it
would be far better for Japan and the world in the
long run, to be rid of the imperialistic military
clique which controlled that country, had fought willingly and ably, however sad their hearts, in American
uniform as American soldiers against the Japanese
armies. But for Japan to have treated any of these
Japanese, who were captured in American uniform,
as anything but regular prisoners of war, would have
been unthinkable under international law. For us to
have entered into some agreement with Japan when

the war was over to turn over to that country, for torture and death, any of these Japanese who had served in our uniform in our armies, would have been incredible. So Vlasov certainly had reason to hope and believe that he and his men would be accorded the civilized treatment of uniformed prisoners of war; especially since everything that had happened at Yalta was then still as secret as the grave.

On the way to the redoubt in Austria the First ROA Division, under General Bunichenko, side-stepped enough to march to Prague. At that time Patton's forces, which had reached Pilsen, fifty miles away, had been pulled <u>back</u> about fifty miles by Eisenhower's orders (on the excuse later given that he couldn't spare the gasoline for them to march fifty miles <u>forward</u>), in order to allow the Russians under Marshall Koniev to take the city. The inhabitants had revolted against the Germans, the departing Nazis had set fire to the city, and sheer horror prevailed. Bunichenko's division arrived, restored order on May 6, 7, and 8, and slipped away as Koniev's troops came in. Having learned in Prague that Eisenhower intended to let Russian troops occupy all of Czechoslovakia, General Bunichenko marched his ROA First Division westward until they reached the nearest American forces, and surrendered his twenty-five thousand men to the United States 3rd Army on May 10, 1945. <u>The division was then forcibly disarmed, and compelled by United States tanks to march into the hands of the Red Army which was waiting for them.</u> And the mass suicides which took place had no effect on these orders or arrangements.

In the meantime General Vlasov himself had been received as a guest at United States 3rd Army Headquarters. Not knowing exactly what was happening to his men, but deeply disturbed, he wrote letters to Eisenhower as Supreme Commander, and to the various Western governments, pleading that his forces not be returned to the Soviets, and asking that he and his leading officers be allowed to stand trial before an International Tribunal. But the last thing Stalin wanted was to give Vlasov any chance to justify and explain his course. Vlasov's men, of all units, were already being turned over by force to the Russians. But even the Supreme Commander did not quite dare use force, or have the 3rd Army use force, to surrender General Vlasov himself to the Soviets -- especially since General Patton had tried to intercede on behalf of both Vlasov and his men. So, on May 12, 1945, Vlasov and his small staff were told that they had to go to the U.S. 4th Army Headquarters for a conference. The convoy, "protected" by four tanks, set off for the conference site. A few miles out it was intercepted by Red soldiers, who arrested Vlasov, and all of his staff, and took them away, while their "protective" escort calmly looked on. And the Red Army car, which had blocked the road and which contained the Red officers who carried out this "arrest," was one that had waited patiently at 3rd Army Headquarters all that morning, until the convoy got under way.' What finally happened to Vlasov and all of his men we do not know, and we certainly hate to think.[2]

The key to that last episode, however, which is also the key to Eisenhower's guilt in the whole repatriation crime, is the question that was already revolving around the use of force in these repatriations. It must be remembered that the examples we have given are merely that; simply illustrations of what was happening everywhere, over half of Europe, not only to volunteers with our armies, and prisoners of war in German uniforms, but to vast numbers of civilians, including women and children, hundreds of thousands of whom had been settled in their new lives in new countries for years. And the herding and

forcing of these people at bayonet point into box cars
to be shipped back to Russia, by our soldiers under
Eisenhower's overall command, was so brutal and
heartrending that even the Pentagon officially desig-
nated the program as "Operation Keelhaul" -- keelhaul being the most cruel form of punishment known
to the older navies. It was also brutal enough that
our own officers and men got so they couldn't take it,
but that is a point we are coming to presently.

Now some apologists for Eisenhower -- let us
repeat -- say that he was merely carrying out orders,
however infamous, as determined over his head at
Yalta. One answer to this is that the War Trials at
Nuremberg were conducted, right while much of
this program was going on, under the aegis and influence of Supreme Commander Eisenhower; and
that German generals were there being condemned
to death for nothing more than carrying out orders,
involving brutality, handed them by their superiors.
Eisenhower not only carried out the same kind of
orders, but never once even voiced a protest.

But that answer is really not necessary. The
truth is that Eisenhower tremendously exceeded any
official authority he had for the brutality of this program, even the authority of the Deane Agreement.
For in that agreement not one word was said about
using force to bring about these repatriations, and
even that weakkneed bunch of Stalin-worshippers
who perpetrated the Deane Agreement would not
have dared put themselves on record so far, in
violation of recognized international law, as to have
agreed to the use of force to implement Stalin's proposal.

Colonel Harold E. Potter, the army's own official historian, has stated that even the Yalta agreement could not justify forced repatriation. It did not
contain any reference to the use of force. According

to Colonel Potter's careful study and report, it was
the arbitrary interpretation of the Yalta agreement
by our Joint Chiefs of Staff which caused the use of
force and the tragedies of 1945-47. This would bring
us right back to George Marshall again, with Eisenhower delightedly carrying out Marshall's policies,
at least for most of 1945. And there is no doubt as
to where George Marshall stood, or that Eisenhower
could count on his support, as to every screaming,
struggling victim he shipped back into Stalin's hands.
But Colonel Potter's statement is not quite accurate,
for one thing; and does not indicate Eisenhower's
direct responsibility for the period when it became
accurate, for another.

In the first place, as we have noted, Eisenhower
decided on forcible repatriations, and began them,
before the Yalta agreement was reached, and while
the course was strictly contrary to such policy in the
matter as we did have. In the second place, Eisenhower just as vigorously used force to repatriate
Russian, Polish, and other nationals, who were
volunteers in our armies, and to whom the Yalta
agreement could not possibly apply, as he did with
regard to Russian nationals in German uniform.
And in the third place, for the first and most horrible ten months of this program, it was only Eisenhower's personal interpretation of the Yalta agreement that force might be used, and not that of our
Joint Chiefs of Staff -- although there is no doubt he
had George Marshall's tacit approval of what he was
doing.

Fortunately for our present purposes, the history of the period is quite clear as to this point. For
by August, 1945, both the American officers and en-
listed men in Europe were too sick at heart, over
what they were doing, to go on without some protest
being registered. They were not blaming Eisenhower

for the program, because they were allowed to assume that the source of these inhuman orders was somewhere beyond and above him, and that he was merely carrying out such orders, the same as they were. But they had had enough. So General Patch, Commander of the U.S. 7th Army, wrote to Supreme Headquarters on August 25, 1945, asking for specific written clarification as to whether he must use U.S. military units to <u>enforce</u> the involuntary repatriation of Soviet citizens. This laid it on the line. Up to that time the U.S. Joint Chiefs of Staff had not issued any such instructions, or made any such interpretation of the Deane Agreement, and Eisenhower had been proceeding strictly on his own. He didn't dare answer categorically this question, raised in this way. So he <u>now</u> referred the query to the Joint Chiefs of Staff in Washington. No answer came. George Marshall was soon to leave on his mission to China, where, in just fourteen months, he was to accomplish miracles towards turning that country over to Mao Tse-tung.[1] He was undoubtedly leery of committing himself so boldly to this European atrocity, under all of the prevailing circumstances. And for a few months it looked as though the remaining prospective victims might be saved. But on November 19, 1945, Dwight Eisenhower was brought back to Washington, to become Chief of Staff, U.S. Army, and hence <u>ex officio</u> a member of the Joint Chiefs of Staff. And thirty days <u>after</u> he assumed that <u>position</u>, or on December 20, 1945, at long last the Joint Chiefs of Staff answered General Patch's inquiry and announced their formal decision. It was that <u>all</u> Soviet citizens, who on September 1, 1939 had been resident inside the U.S.S.R., must be repatriated, disregarding their personal wishes and if necessary by means of force. And "Operation Keelhaul" was immediately resumed.[2]

While it may seem to the reader that we have gone into this matter of repatriation at considerable length, the truth is that we have condensed the whole sordid story to the best of our ability. We have omitted all description of the repatriation centers for Soviet nationals, who were separated from all other prisoners of war and displaced persons, and "segregated in centers of their own," where Soviet Repatriation Representatives had "the right to appoint the internal administration and set up the internal discipline and management of centers in accordance with U.S.S.R. military procedure and U.S.S.R. law. . . ."' (This quotation is from one of the official orders from Eisenhower's headquarters.) We have omitted all reference to some very revealing documents in the Pentagon archives, because it would take too long to bring their revelations into proper focus. And despite the regretted omission of any discussion of certain other aspects of the whole crime, we are going to move on to another subject after just one final point.

In Crusade in Europe there is tremendous falsification of history throughout the whole book, by omission, emphasis, slant, arrangement, and every trick an extremely cunning writer could devise. But Eisenhower and his Communist ghost-writer, Joseph Fels Barnes, were ordinarily too clever to put down anything which was categorically false. It was too dangerous. The story of the repatriation crime was too damaging, however, and the likelihood of the true story ever coming out apparently appeared too small, to justify the usual treatment. And so, although at least two million victims were involved, and the whole operation was of tremendous importance to postwar Europe, the book tries to gloss the story over in less than three pages of humanitarian generalities. (They are Pages 484-486 in the 1952 paperbound Permabooks edition.) And these two and one-half pages are a tissue of deliberate and direct lies. Just for one illustration, Eisenhower says on Page 485: "These policies and agreements (he is trying to blame Yalta, but is actually admitting he made the decisions) we first tried to apply without deviation, but we quickly saw that their rigid application would often violate the fundamental humanitarian principles we espoused. Thereafter we gave any individual who objected to return the benefit of the doubt."

I have in front of me, as I now write, a photostatic copy of Part II of an order issued from "Supreme Headquarters, Allied Expeditionary Force," dated "Revised May 1945," and entitled "Guide To The Care of Displaced Persons in Germany." Part II, Section 3, Heading 1, Paragraph 3 of that order says: "After identification by Soviet Repatriation Representatives, Soviet displaced persons will be repatriated regardless of their individual wishes." Another paragraph of that same order reads: "Enemy and ex-enemy displaced persons, except those assimilated to United Nations status, will be returned to their countries of nationality or former residence without regard to their personal wishes." These orders continued in effect, without any interruption until August, when General Patch raised his question; and then were confirmed by our Joint Chiefs of Staff, even as to the specific use of force, as soon as Eisenhower became a member and could put his influence to work. And both he and Joseph Barnes were well aware of these facts, when they wrote the falsehoods indicated above for publication in 1948.

"But why," the reader is asking, "if these facts are true, aren't they known?" The answer is that they are known today, just as the true facts about the Pearl Harbor betrayal finally became known, years later, through the books of Morgenstern, Admiral Kimmel, Admiral Theobald, and others.' As stated

in the foreword, there is nothing in this whole present
paper, except what is clearly shown to be only the
writer's personal interpretation or opinion, which
has not already been published with careful documentation. But if you ask why these facts were not known
earlier, and are not widely known, then that is quite
a different question. The answer, part of which will
be given in the next chapter, is probably the strongest
single part of the proof of my thesis. But in the meantime let's finally nail the evidence of this present chapter down in place.

There have been few crimes in history more
brutal and more extensive than this forced repatriation of anti-Communists, to which Dwight Eisenhower
committed the honor of the United States. Dragging
the honor and reputation of our country through such
pools of bloody betrayal, and thus convincing anti-
Communists of either the stupidity or the pro-Communism of the United States, was of course one of the
objectives. And while he had the "moral support,"
when needed, of plenty of other pro-Stalinists in our
government at that time, it was Eisenhower who gave
Stalin's monstrous plan of vengeance and warning all
of its teeth and its total effectiveness. You can find
excuses and reasons for Eisenhower's conduct, or for
various separate parts of it, by the dozen, if your
credulity can stand the burden. But there is one
simple, plain, straightforward reason which completely solves the whole problem, without leaving a
single loophole. And we do not need to spell it out
any more.

CHAPTER FIVE

The Hero . . . . .

Following Lenin's death in January, 1924, there took place in Moscow a long and merciless struggle for various levels of personal power. Both the large and little battles in this struggle were disguised as disputes over socialist doctrine, and over the correct policies for Leninist communism to pursue. During that unsettled period Joseph Stalin committed almost every conceivable mistake, of false prophecy, of self contradiction, of fumbling error and clumsy reversal, that any leader could possibly score. (Just for one quick illustration, it was Stalin's ill-advised telegram to M. N. Roy in Hankow, in 1927, which Roy was stupid enough to show to Wang Ching-wei, that destroyed at one blow most of the results of Borodin's years of work in China for the Communist cause.)[1] Nevertheless, by January, 1928, when Trotsky and thirty of his leading supporters were exiled to Siberia, Stalin had emerged as the victorious and vengeful tyrant in supreme command. How?

The answer, or by far the most important part of the several answers, is very simple. Stalin early obtained and steadily strengthened his "complete monopoly of all the means of information and comment, both in print and on the platform."[2] Boris Souvarine has written a long and minutely detailed history of those years, out of close personal knowledge of the actors and events. Souvarine points out that "the entire press belonged to him (Stalin) and praised his foresight unblushingly.... No despot in any age or in any country has ever enjoyed such powers of deceiving public opinion or, if that failed, of suppressing it. "[1]

Control over the media of information was clearly proved, during these four years of conflict, to be a vital element of strength in political conspiracy. The effort to obtain and exercise such control was henceforth established by Stalin as the most important factor in the practical mechanics of Communist attack, in every country and on every front. And this insidious suppression or smothering of the truth, with a parallel outpouring of clever distortions and falsehoods, has been the most powerful weapon which the Communists have employed in the thirty-years march towards their goal of world conquest.

In the United States, unlike Russia in 1924, there have been radio and television and movies and many other media to consider, besides an enormous number of publications. So the Communists, realizing both the size and the importance of their problem, went to work on it early and with proportionate energy. Naturally their very success has been used to hide that success from the vast majority of the American people. But the record, or enough of it to scare the daylights out of those who do study it, is all there for anybody who will take the trouble to put together the pieces.

In front of me, for instance, is a published list of two hundred top actors, writers, and directors in the movies who are either Communists or active Communist sympathizers. Most of them have been diligently slipping their poison into American minds for a generation. John T. Flynn's While You Slept [2] will show you the absolute Communist control for years of the powerful book-review sections of the New York Times and New York Herald Tribune, and the devastating ultimate effect of that control on public opinion. Harry Elmer Barnes' Struggle Against The

Historical Blackout[1] will show you how thoroughly
and successfully the true documentary history of
American foreign affairs for the past twenty years
has been kept from public knowledge. Frank Hughes'
monumental Prejudice And The Press[2] will show you
how cleverly but almost completely the Communist
pressures are exerted all along the journalistic line
to bring out the bias that the Communists want. And
there are plenty of other sources for finding the
clearly proved truth. The only trouble is that practically nobody reads them. The Communists have seen
to that, through the very controls that these sources
would expose.

It is worth while pausing here for just one illustration out of many, of just one way out of many, that
the whole scheme works. Early in 1957 there was
published Tito, Moscow's Trojan Horse, by Dr.
Slobodan M. Draskovich.[3] Writing with detailed knowledge of the country, the events, and the people involved, in 330 pages Draskovich made out a very convincing case that there never had been any real break
between the Kremlin and Tito; that Tito remained,
and always had been, one of the most loyal agents of
the Kremlin; that so-called Titoism or "nationalist
communism," instead of being a form of revolt a-
gainst Moscow, had actually been planned and directed
from Moscow at all times; and that Tito and Titoism
were the most useful weapons Moscow had for enabling
its Communist agents and sympathizers throughout the
free world to steer their respective countries down the
exact paths Moscow wanted them to follow. All of this,
incidentally, is something the writer of this letter has
been saying repeatedly and emphatically in print since
1951.[4] But Draskovich had both the authoritative knowledge and the standing as a scholar to make his book an
eye-opener to anybody who read it. It had the potential
effect of a blockbuster on the whole Titoist "independent

communism" myth.

But that myth has been built up to practically a
religious belief in this country, by the Edward Mur-
rows, Elmer Davises, Walter Lippmanns, Drew
Pearsons, Marquis Childs', Tom Stokes', and all of
the other pundits of the airwaves and the editorial
pages, who have told us exactly what we should do to
take advantage of so fortunate a falling out between
thieves. (Giving Tito himself over a billion dollars
was just one small and materialistic result of this
propaganda.) So what happened when Draskovich's
volume appeared? Did these opinion-molders and the
more academic experts behind them start calling
Draskovich names, or pointing out mistakes in either
his facts or his arguments, or supporting their declared positions against this devastating attack? Not
on your life. All of the academic experts went right
on turning out their articles and brochures, full of
solemn dissertations and even vigorous arguments
among themselves, as to how we and the other Western nations should take advantage of the Kremlin-Tito
rift. All of the popularizers, such as we mentioned
above, of these dishonest premises and dialectic conclusions, went right on filling our ears and eyes with
the exciting news and significance of the rising movement of communist nationalism. They just ignored
Draskovich and the truth he had set forth as if such
a man and his book didn't exist.

The result was very effective. When Draskovich's
book first came out, any number of the comparatively
few honest scholars and writers who did read it said to
themselves: "Well! How on earth are the supporters of
Tito, and of Titoism as an opportunity for the West, going to answer this?" So each one waited expectantly, to
appraise the various defenses when offered. But no defenses appeared. The expected defenders did not deign
even to notice such nonsense, nor to be interrupted in

their solving for us of the problem of how we were to lick Communism. And pretty soon each of the honest scholars and writers was unconsciously saying to himself: "Well, I guess this fellow Draskovich didn't know what he was talking about. Certainly his charges and arguments didn't amount to much, for they haven't disturbed the real scholars and analysts in the field enough for such experts even to pay any attention to them." So in a little while the temporarily puzzled honest scholars and writers were themselves again back on the same old bandwagon, merrily taking part in, and contributing their bit to, determining and building up plans as to how we were to make the best use of "communist nationalism." They had been swept by sheer noise, rather than the real prestige of the noisemakers, into forgetting the question in their minds as to whether the thing they were arguing about even existed. And if any one of them was persistent enough to pursue the thought which briefly held him, he soon found himself and his writings or speeches being accorded exactly the same completely effective and frustrating treatment -- of being simply ignored, while the dialectic wave passed on by and left him -- which rendered Draskovich's book a mere exercise in futility.

One important later incident shows both the brazenness with which this technique was carried out, and the extreme subservience to the Communist cause on the part of one of America's greatest media of information. Edward R. Murrow put the television facilities of the Columbia Broadcasting Company at the disposal of Tito for a slick propaganda job on the American people.[1] In order to give the affair some semblance of an objective television interview, certain "experts" on Yugoslavia had been allowed to send written questions to Tito in advance. His submission to this direct examination was supposed to prove

broadmindedness, or fairness, or something, on the
part of the promoters of the program.

Some honest-to-goodness experts on Tito and
Yugoslavia got wind of this plan, and tried to have
Slobodan Draskovich allowed to prepare some of the
questions. Dr. Draskovich was born and raised in
Yugoslavia, and until 1941 was a professor at the
University of Belgrade. His book, for all the silent
treatment given it by the reviewers, is scholarly,
penetrating, and unimpeachably authoritative. He is
almost certainly the best-informed expert on Yugoslavia in this country today. He would certainly seem
to have been the most logical man for an American television system to have asked to question Tito in an interview telecast to the American people. But of course
there wasn't a chance in the world of having anything
so logical or "objective" take place. Murrow and
CBS would have called off the whole interview and
program before they would have allowed Tito to be
asked the honest and revealing questions Draskovich
would have handed him -- or before they would have
called public attention to Draskovich and his book
through the prestige of even vicarious appearance on
this program.' Murrow was not only selling Tito to
the American public, but was also building up the "experts" in this country who are clearly in step in the
Left Wing parade.

One other illustration of this conspiracy of silence toward critics and embarrassing questions is
worth brief mention. In the spring of 1955 Congressman Bosch, a Republican of New York State, filed the
bill to which we have already referred, demanding an
investigation of the forced repatriation of displaced
persons after the war. The bill was based on very
serious charges, against very important people, in
connection with a tremendously important matter directly involving several million victims of cruelty

chargeable to our country. Not only was the bill quietly and permanently buried, but not one of the great press wire services ever carried a single word of news that such a bill had ever been filed.'

There are a dozen other equally skillful techniques which the Communists, their sympathizers, their dupes, and the plain opportunists in the public-information world (who know on which side of the ideological fence the greenest grass for their fodder is found), concertedly use to promote the Communist line. As a consequence of the operation of these techniques over a long period of time, the Communists now have almost as effective a veto as to what the American public shall not hear and see, and influence over the slant of what it does hear and see, as Stalin exercised in Russia in 1924. It takes only one smart Communist here, another one there, each one guiding the thinking and actions of ten fellow travelers, each fellow traveler influencing the thoughts and actions of ten egghead liberals, and so on through spreading circles, to carry on this domination without an impossible drain on Communist manpower and intellectual resources. And it is only with a knowledge of this domination of our media of mass information in mind that the point of this chapter stands out in its real significance. With that domination perennially observed and fully understood, however, the circumstance described in the next several pages becomes the most important single foundation for the hypothesis of this manuscript.

For President Eisenhower benefits from an incredibly good press, and has so benefitted for many years. Even the Left Wing, even when hitting hardest at Eisenhower policies, fights those policies and their other backers, but almost never attacks Eisenhower himself. I subscribe to, and regularly read, The Worker; its slightly more pretentious sister publication, the National Guardian; their very highbrow cousin, Max Ascoli's The Reporter; and other periodicals of varying shades of vermilion between bright pink and reddest crimson. I read The Daily Worker for years, until its suspension.' In none of those periodicals can I remember ever seeing a direct attack on Eisenhower himself.

In fact, the pattern of the Reds' publicized attitude towards Eisenhower was well exemplified in a speech on September 12, 1956, to an audience of Communists in New York City, by Blake Charney, Acting Chairman of the Communist Party. He said: "... Eisenhower in San Francisco, when he accepted his Party's nomination, made quite a speech. He spoke on peace and improving our relations with the U.S.S.R. It was evident to anyone who watched and heard him that he was a man of profound sincerity. "[2]

On the same front page of a copy of the National Guardian now in front of me, picked almost at random far down in the pile, I find these two contrasting paragraphs as to the treatment given Eisenhower, and that given anybody else in Washington -- who is supposed to be anti-Communist -- either Democrat or Republican.[3] "The logical man to head the probe, " reads one paragraph, in an article about the "Oil lobby whitewash, " "was Senator Albert Gore (D-Tenn), but the top brass was afraid he would be too tough. Johnson and Knowland, masters at in-fighting and specialists in the low blow that even the referee doesn't see, set up a special handpicked eight-man 'bi-partisan' committee to contain Gore. " I have italicized the lines that contain the knife, to set it off against the pat on the back in the next exhibit. "The President, " says a paragraph in another article, "was answering a letter which Premier Bulganin had written last September urging a new look at disarmament and the

ban on the bomb. It was a cordial exchange and the
world took heart. But the President did more than
smile. He made several important concessions. "
And even in the "capitalistic" press, such as the New
York Times and the Washington Post (God save the
United States!), you will find that whenever Mr. Khrushchev has been making his most malicious and sarcastic
cracks -- such as those about the stupidities Eisenhower
had been sold concerning "clean" bombs -- he has usually gone out of his way to add some such solemn declaration as that of course Eisenhower himself was "a
man of principle and integrity. "

Very early in 1956 Joe Glazer, "Educational
Director" of the United Rubber Workers Union, put
out a ten-inch long-playing record, containing four
songs by Glazer and collaborators. It was probably
the dirtiest piece of campaign material issued during
the year. It was so malicious that Paul Butler, Chairman of the Democratic National Committee, immediately made it clear that he had nothing to do with production or distribution of the record.' This was smearing by the Left Wing, strictly on its own initiative. The
smears were concentrated on Nixon, Humphrey, McKay,
Mrs. Hobby, Wilson, and Benson. But there was no
song nor even section of a song devoted to Eisenhower.
His name was mentioned only once, and then in the comparatively mild lines of the parody on Dixie, as follows:
"To Dixon-Yates you'll pay high rates
For Eisenhower and Nixon. "

It was Thomas L. Stokes, however, who really
summed up the point of this chapter, by gloating over
it. Stokes, during the last years of his life, was one
of the most unwavering and nauseating purveyors of
the Communist line among the supposedly reputable
columnists. And in March of 1956 he used one of his
daily columns to rhapsodize over the success of the
very tactics we are talking about. After some "ain't

it wonderful" introductory sentences, he got up to his main point: "an asset" of Eisenhower's "of which Democrats have been constantly conscious." "This," Stokes went on, "is the President's amazing personal popularity. In its extreme manifestations it becomes a sort of idolatry, beyond hero worship, that Democrats find themselves unable to explain in any precise fashion." We add, "and well they might." For we do not think there is any even plausible explanation except the one we are trying to set forth in this chapter.

Further along Stokes says that for all the idolatry of President Roosevelt, he was also bitterly hated. Which is true; for while he played with the Communists, they had to run him by persuasion and flattery, rather than by orders. So they were not willing, even if they had been able, to give Roosevelt the full benefit of such control over public opinion as they have today. Then Stokes smirks: "Our present President provokes nothing of that kind. Nobody seems to dislike him or,to put it the other way, virtually everybody seems to like him. ... The end result is to set him above the confusion of political conflict, above his party, above partisanship. The political effect of this aloofness is what plagues Democrats as they try to figure ways to reach him as a target. For he never seems to be blamed for acts of his administration, or even policies of his administration."

The italics are mine, but the rejoicing was that of Mr. Stokes. It continued: "Just now, for example, it is Secretary of Agriculture Ezra Taft Benson who is taking the heat as chief scapegoat. It is against him that discontented farmers spill their ire. It is his name that they repeat bitterly -- not 'Ike.'

"Similarly, the President's popularity is at an even higher level in the South, according to polls, than in 1952. ... He seems to get no reflected blame in the public school integration turmoil. This even

though well before the Supreme Court's decision
his administration had espoused a broad policy against
segregation which it had implemented in numerous
areas. . . . Southern anger strikes directly at the
Supreme Court, not at him, according to Southern
members of Congress.

"He appears, in short, to possess a peculiar
magic. "[1]

We agree. He certainly does. Even after Eisenhower sent troops to Little Rock, the attempts to
blame him were watered down into laments that poor
advisors had talked him into such a "blunder. " And
we are sure Pinky Stokes knew even better than we
do just how that "magic" had been achieved. A very
important part of the method begins with the fact that
the criticism of Eisenhower by the Communists, and
by their recognized agents and sympathizers, is always gentle, and just sufficient to give him the necessary protective coloration.

The pattern thus set by the leftists has been followed by both middle-of-the-road and -- till fairly
recently -- by even extreme right-wing critics; the
latter, in my opinion, having been unconsciously and
indirectly guided by this example consciously and
carefully established by the Left. Nobody wishes to
attack a man whom everybody seems to honor. As
to the "middle-of-the-road" commentators and edi-
torializers, we have simply been trying to make
more obvious and understandable what we believe any
informed man can daily see; namely, how heavily all
of our media of mass information are controlled or
influenced by the Communists and their socialist
buddies or gullible dupes. Consider now, not the
positive propaganda of these mouthpieces, but how insidious and ubiquitous have been the hatchet operations
of Drew Pearson, Edward R. Murrow, Elmer Davis
(when alive), and dozens like them. Or remember

the foul slanders about Taft and his family that were spread so industriously in Ohio during the 1950 Senatorial campaign by the pals of Walter Reuther, or the equally foul lies about McCarthy that were circulated all of the time by the pals of Eleanor Roosevelt. Why no lies, nor even innuendoes, about Eisenhower, ever? Stop to think that no man, though his ideological slant may range all the way from John Bricker's to that of Norman Thomas, escapes the organized invective campaigns of the Communists if or whenever he is known to oppose their plans. Then consider how natural it would seem under the supposed present circumstances for the Communists to set in motion their smear techniques against Eisenhower, and how many things there are in his record to lend themselves to ready use in such a campaign. When you consider these and other pertinent aspects of the situation during the last five years, the willingness of the Left Wing to permit and even augment the personal popularity of Eisenhower makes his relationship to the Left justly subject to deep suspicion.

This suspicion is increased by the fact that so much of his reputation is demonstrably phony, and his whole career so full of tempting morsels for the character assassin to seize upon. Just suppose that some real anti-Communist general, like Albert Wedemeyer, had had the smelly liaison with his female chauffeur that Eisenhower enjoyed with Kay Summersby.' Do you suppose that half the press of the country would be constantly playing up Wedemeyer (even if he were president), by pictures and by articles, as a wonderful family man? Or suppose MacArthur, as Supreme Commander in Europe, had been drunk and unavailable the night the Battle of the Bulge began. Can you imagine how many times that story would have been retold by the Communist-inspired columnists? Or suppose Taft, at the 1952 Republican Convention, had

made the dirty undercover deal with a candidate for
the Vice-Presidency that Eisenhower made. Then
think how such papers as the New York Post, the
Washington Post, the Toledo Blade, the Raleigh News
and Observer, the Atlanta Constitution, the St. Louis
Post, the Minneapolis Tribune, or the Des Moines
Register would have screamed their moral indignation
to the high heavens. But the very few objective reporters and columnists who have dared even tell this
story have gambled their careers in doing so.

Then it must be remembered that the Communists
do not need truth for their smear campaigns at all.
They will manufacture rumors out of whole cloth, if
necessary. If there are little fires from which to
start their lot of smoke, so much the better. What
couldn't they do, if they had the slightest wish to
hurt Eisenhower, with the report of his career at the
War College; or with his friendship for Anna Roosevelt Boettiger; or with his tax deal over a book he
didn't even write; or over the time he spends on golf,
and his obvious ignorance of what he is talking about
half the time at press conferences?

But from all the press and radio and television
sets of the nation, or almost all, the public gets the
unquestioned impression that Eisenhower is a great
general who won the war practically singlehanded, a
great President who is loyal to the finest American
traditions, a good man who may have some bad advisors but who is the acme of sincerity, personal
integrity, and intuitive wisdom. The fact, which is
easy enough to prove beyond a shadow of a doubt, is
that he is none of these things. As we have already
indicated, he was such a lousy soldier that practically
all authority except of a political nature had to be
taken out of his hands in order to win the war. He
is visibly trying to destroy by attrition the American
form of government. He follows orders of the White

House clique so willingly that he is frequently embar-
rassed because they haven't yet told him what his
opinion is, on some matter about which he is being
questioned; and he is demonstrably one of the most
insincere, vindictive, and hypocritical human beings
that ever lived.

This being true -- and I think even this treatise
will definitely prove that much, if you have the patience to bear with me to the end -- then why should
I, a conservative, Republican, anti-Communist, be
the one to point out these things? Why aren't the
Communists and their front men doing it, with their
organized means to reach a million times my audience? If Eisenhower really was the one man behind
whom the country could effectively unite in 1952 to
defend itself from Communism, and still is the one
best defender of the United States of America and the
free world from Communism, as the "liberal" hue
and cry has so loudly proclaimed, then why haven't
the Communists themselves torn his halo to shreds?
Why in heaven's name don't the Communists get to
work to tear him down instead of letting him remain
on a pedestal? The tearing down, to a devastating
degree, would be very simple for them to do. And
the one and only easy answer, or satisfactory answer,
to these questions practically jumps at you as soon as
they are asked.

CHAPTER SIX

The Candidate . . . . .

The imaginary setting, in which we ask you to join us at the beginning of this chapter, is not in the least necessary in order to establish the facts we present. Our purpose is solely to orient your thinking to the time and the circumstances involved, so that you can more easily follow our conclusions, or form your own, as to the meaning of what was taking place. Please go back with us, therefore, seven years.

It is 1951. Suppose you are a member of the secret top strategy board of the Communists in the United States; one of a group of perhaps three people, all completely above suspicion, whose whole purpose of existence is to plan and order the steps by which the Communists eventually take over this country. You or your predecessors have been unbelievably successful for twenty years. But there is a psychological pendulum in the attitudes of a people, which has a certain degree of inevitability of which you are well aware. So you recognize that there has begun to run, and to grow, a strong tide of feeling against the socialistic mood in which Communism thrives; against entanglement in international socialist plans; and against both the crimes and the theories of Communism itself.

This revulsion of feeling on the part of the American people, if properly led, unified, and given a chance to make its real underlying strength felt, is likely to wipe out many of your gains for the past several years, and to put a stop to your further progress for years to come. By destroying both your progress

in America and the tremendous value of that progress
to your plans over the rest of the globe, it may endanger the whole vast Communist conspiracy. And
this revulsion, because it is psychologically inevitable,
cannot be stopped. Under these circumstances obviously you must ride it, guide it, twist its direction,
frustrate it all you can, and roll with the punch.
You must be smart enough, brilliantly cunning enough,
to give ground to whatever extent, and in whatever
way, giving ground will still leave you in ultimate
control of the most powerful forces at work. Cunning,
deception, and bluff are practically all you and your
fellow top Communists have had to do with during
most of your conquest and enslavement of a third of
the world. Now is the time, with the imperative
need, for more of the same brilliant and realistic
strategy.

So. You and your fellow conspirators have this
politician, anxious to carry out Communist orders for
the sake of Communist support, in the very top rank
of the American army; a politician who owes his
whole career to you; one whom you have been building
up for years -- from the day when you managed to get
him jumped over several hundred superior officers to
be put in high command. It is becoming increasingly
known now, in 1951, that in 1941 and '42 the Communists were in direct or indirect control of almost
everything President Roosevelt did. You are aware,
therefore, that the very fact that this particular officer was selected and pulled up out of far lower ranks,
for so great a post, at that time, might be -- and certainly should be -- a warning note of suspicion to somebody. But you are too successful in your handling of
the media of mass information, and in your use of
means to silence anybody who might even breathe
such a suspicion, to worry about that. The scorn and
smear of your dupes and gullible echo-artists could

make what happened to Dr. Wirt[1] look tame, in comparison to what would happen to anybody who might be clearheaded enough to point a finger at this man or at this possible significance of his being chosen as he was.

And you have now cleverly and carefully, merely by encouraging and feeding the enthusiasm of others, surrounded this man with an incredible aura of ability and personal popularity.[2] You have been farsighted enough never to let him declare himself as either a Democrat or a Republican, or take any steps which would be too much of a handicap to your present plans. Although he made the mistake in 1942 of telling somebody that he expected to be President of the United States some day, and although so many things in his career since then have been part of a careful build-up towards making him President, you have succeeded in having him established in the public mind as above politics. He can pose as an unwilling candidate who would have to be persuaded to sully his naive soul with politics for the sake of his country's needs.

It's true that you have been saving this man, and blowing up his stature, in the hope that he might win the Presidency as the nominee of an increasingly and ever more openly socialistic-Communistic Democratic Party. For that party, in two more terms under such a man, could carry you through to complete final victory. You have even hoped that it might become possible to make him the nominee of both parties. That would greatly hasten the destruction of constitutional government in America, and make your establishment of a Communist dictatorship here that much easier and earlier.

But this is 1951, and realities have to be faced. In 1950 you turned every hidden weapon in the Communist arsenal on Taft.[3] He not only came through that battle stronger than ever, but in doing so he

showed just how terribly dangerous was that under-
current of revulsion against everything you planned.
And if Taft got the Republican nomination in 1952,
and was then elected -- as you knew better than anybody else he surely would be -- the game was up for
a long time to come. The weeding out of your planned
agents alone would be so drastic and such a blow that
you would practically have to start all over again,
painfully and slowly, at the next turning of the tide.

So, reluctantly but cleverly, you trot out this
"hero" you have been saving and have it suddenly
discovered that he is a Republican after all. By incredibly dirty steamroller tactics -- always accusing
the opposition of the exact crimes which you yourself
are committing, according to time-tried Communist
strategy -- you get him nominated.' And now, riding
that very revulsion which has endangered you, guiding
it as planned, you get him elected.

It still being imperative that you not give your
hand away, and that you make the necessary sacrifices
where they will hurt the least, you have him surround
himself, in the top official echelons of his administration, with men who look all right, and most of whom
are all right, except in the one vital spot of foreign
affairs. Letting these happy and gullible and highly
gratified Republicans achieve a few laborious and
comparatively petty victories concerned with our
domestic economy, such as eventual removal of the
excess profits tax, and playing up these turns away
from socialism as far more important and weighty
than they are, is a small price to pay as against what
might have happened.

In all the lower administrative ranks you still
have and maintain the holdovers from the New Deal
Administration, who will find ways to nullify any progress back towards a really free economy. Among your
man's semi-official and personal assistants you can

have him appoint just as many crypto-Communists and Communist sympathizers as you dare. And in the all-important field of foreign affairs you can still save the day entirely, with a New Deal favorite as Secretary of State who exactly fits your needs. For although he -- fortunately, from your point of view -- wears a Republican label, here is a man, a longtime protege and assistant of Dean Acheson, who has already proved that he knows how to play on your team. Here is just the Secretary of State to help your man Eisenhower, succeeding Truman, to go right on handing both military and diplomatic victories to the Communists all over the world on a silver platter, while always shouting loudly that he is doing, or is going to do, the opposite. What's more, by Eisenhower's very association with, and apparent working with, this coterie of "good" Republicans, in other matters, you will enable him to have his way in those all important <u>domestic</u> matters which really count -- stopping the exposure of your agents, and the whittling away of American sovereignty by international treaties and by the growing power of the United Nations.

You like this strategy, as it finally jells in the minds of yourself and your associates, and as it begins to work out according to plan, both because of its defensive necessity and because of some offensive advantages which it also offers. For one thing, as you let your man gradually show his hand more and more, especially in fighting exposure of Communists despite the contrary expectations of so many leaders and voters who supported him, you will definitely wreck the Republican Party for good -- or metamorphose it into another political agency of the Left. By forcing through the anti-segregation decision of the Supreme Court, which you certainly planned as far back as when you had Gunnar Myrdal brought over here to write his mammoth book,[1] you will also make it practically impossible for the coalition of conservative southern Democrats and conservative Republicans ever to be reestablished with the same strength again. In the very bitterness that you will stir up in the course of these developments, and in the split of the parties which you will thus engineer and enlarge, you may make an eventual nomination of your man by the controlling left-wing core of both parties possible after all. And if not, at the very least you will promote a steady breakdown of constitutional government within the United States, and will be moving the whole country ever nearer towards that civil war which may eventually become necessary to your plans.

There is one apparent problem. Although the support of Eisenhower for the Democratic nomination, which temporarily boomed in 1948 until you stopped it for very sound reasons from your point of view, came from such extreme left-wingers that Eisenhower's affiliations should have been obvious, there is no assurance in 1951 that your following will not now be thrown off the track by Eisenhower's announcement that he is a Republican. For this man is completely a "sleeper" in the Communist cause, a crypto-Communist whom you have built up, from the outside, as a great patriot. To make him the nominee of the Republican Party, which by the very spirit of the times will be committed to an anti-Communist crusade, you have the problem on your hands of letting your followers know, as far down into the rank and file as necessary, that he is your man. Enough Communists in the middle levels must be made aware of this so that their influence will cause even the rank-and-file Communists to lay off, to desist from the smear tactics against this man which would otherwise be so plainly called for by their whole past training. This is all the more necessary because you have kept him free of fully recognized Communist contacts and of publicized pro-Communist activities, in this country, which cannot be discounted as "misguided idealism" at the very worst.

But this problem is not difficult to solve. For instance, there is one maneuver in sponsorship, evidently for that purpose, which is quite interesting. You have your man show great and continuing reluctance to being a candidate until the proper time. Then you manage to have his "availability" discovered and officially proclaimed -- before any of the top-flight politicians like Sherman Adams or Henry Cabot Lodge are pulled into the act -- by a man whose name means nothing to a vast majority of the American people, even those fairly well informed about pro-Communist activities. But his name, for all of its apparent relative unimportance, is adequately significant to your friends "in the know." So a leftwinger named Leonard Finder becomes the official and widely publicized discoverer and promoter of Eisenhower for the <u>Republican</u> nomination. And the whole American press, gladly even if in large part unconsciously, does your job for you, of spreading the information to every corner of America, and to every Communist far enough up in the ranks to recognize its significance, that Leonard Finder wants Eisenhower to be the Republican nominee. This huge help to the solution of your problem is as simple as that, and as natural and easy in the regular pattern of Communist procedures. And there are plenty of other ways of passing the word down the line.

In the meantime, the leading pseudo-liberals in your following, or under the influence of your followers, have been cleverly and secretly lining up many ranking Republican politicians behind Eisenhower's candidacy. It is fairly easy to get men like Henry Cabot Lodge and Sherman Adams and Thomas Dewey, either because of their hatred of Taft, or their extreme internationalist views,' or both. After a certain amount of gathering strength has been shown, and your brilliant slogan, "Taft can't win," has been started rolling, it becomes easy and then easier to bring on the bandwagon even gullible "conservatives" like Sinclair Weeks and Eugene Pulliam. On the theory that half a loaf of conservatism is better for their country than no crumbs at all, these patriotic Americans are willing to close their eyes to the loss of much of what they stand for, in order to have the Republican Party win. The "I like Ike" stampede is on its way. And a slippery way it is.[2]

CHAPTER SEVEN

The Campaign . . . . .

Before looking at the quality of the Eisenhower
support in that campaign it is worth taking a paragraph or two to consider the character of a man and
a candidate who would allow on his own behalf such
dirty tactics as were so widely practiced. And any
thought that Eisenhower was not fully aware of these
tactics, or that he did not even encourage them, is
absurd. I have in my files a copy of a letter written
during the campaign to Eisenhower personally, by
one of his strongest supporters in the state of Kansas.
In this letter this supporter stated that it seemed to
him incredible Eisenhower could actually know the
foulness of the tactics being used on his side in
Kansas, and still condone them; and that this friend,
whom Eisenhower knew to be with him all the way,
was taking it on himself to tell Eisenhower just how
rotten the situation was. But certainly nothing happened, and no steps were taken, to clean up those
tactics. And what happened in Kansas was pure and
clean when compared to what happened later in
Georgia, in Louisiana, and in Texas.'
On a platform in Greater Boston, before a
large audience consisting of both Republican factions
-- of Republicans who were going to have to vote
later for either Taft or Eisenhower to get one of them
elected -- Sherman Adams spent an hour tearing Taft
to pieces, without the slightest regard for either truth
or decency. Taft supporters were kept quiet throughout this vicious harangue by the expectation of asking
questions at the end. But Adams quickly slipped away

without allowing any such opportunity. This was a typical performance. Yet it was Sherman Adams whom Eisenhower later, knowing all of that, made one of his chief advisers.' The use of any means to achieve an end is one of the fundamental planks of Communist strategy. And Eisenhower has never had the slightest hesitation about walking any such plank which they laid out for him.

Taft was noted for his good sportsmanship. Practically everybody, whether for him or against him, conceded that he was always a generous and tolerant opponent. It took blows far below the belt and far more vicious than even a political campaign justified before he ever complained about their unfairness. The only man who engaged in blows so incredibly foul in the 1952 campaign that Taft said he could never forgive them nor their perpetrator -- Taft himself said this was the only man he could never forgive -- was Clifford Case of New Jersey.[2] Yet Case is practically the only Republican or so-called Republican, running for the Senate since that time, whom Eisenhower as President has actively helped in his campaign. But he threw all the weight and prestige of his Presidential office into the battle to make Case a Senator.[3] The fact that even in that campaign, even with all of Eisenhower's help, Case had great difficulty keeping the charges as to his own Communist affiliations adequately squelched and ignored, has implications that are much to the point.

Any objective argument is usually weakened by the speaker's going into the "I happen to know personally approach." Yet there is one incident within my own experience which needs to be related here. In the spring of 1952, when I was running as a Taft-pledged candidate for the National Republican Convention, in the Fifth Congressional District of Massachusetts, I challenged the Eisenhower State Head-

quarters to supply a pro-Eisenhower speaker for a
debate or debates in my district, on the issues involved. Despite the fact that this challenge was
issued very early in the campaign, was constantly
reaffirmed, was made on the friendliest basis and
with the clear offer that our side would meet them
half way with regard to costs, choice of moderator,
time and place of meetings, and all other details, I
never did get an acceptance for even one full debate.
The nearest I came to it was the consent of the
Eisenhower headquarters, under the prodding of one
of the local women's Republican clubs, to send out a
speaker to debate with me, at the end of this club's
regular meeting for other purposes, and with each
of us to be allowed ten minutes.

It turned out, on the evening in question, that
the club had plenty of additional time available. I
argued that both speakers should take either twenty
or even thirty minutes. But my opponent insisted
that we stick to the ten minutes originally indicated.
After this had finally and quite positively been agreed
on, when he got up he spoke seventeen minutes, and
used every word and minute of that time to excoriate
Taft. This was despite the fact that the burden of the
most insistent appeals emanating from pro-Eisenhower speakers and writers everywhere was to the
effect that no Taft supporter, and no Republican,
should criticize Eisenhower because he might be our
candidate. In fact, as we look back now, we can see
how desperately -- and why -- the inner core of planners of the Eisenhower campaign were pushing this
argument, so as to keep conservative Republicans
from ever looking too far or too closely into the real
Eisenhower record. But of course, since one of their
major objects was to discredit Taft, they did not a-
bide by any such sportsmanlike arrangements themselves, anywhere or at any time. And those Repub-

licans who actually believed this speaker, at the end
of his seventeen minutes, although they had heard
nothing either good or bad about Eisenhower, would
not have been able to vote for Taft with good conscience
even if he had been nominated.

Now the real point is that this man, sent out by
Eisenhower's Massachusetts Headquarters without,
I am sure, either knowledge or investigation as to
who he really was, and who was on their speaker's
bureau undoubtedly because he himself had initiated
the action which put him there -- this man was Raymond V. Dennett. The name meant nothing to our
audience, and apparently meant nothing to the Eisenhower State Headquarters, except that he was head of
some local outfit known as the World Peace Foundation. (Alger Hiss had been a member of the board
of this foundation, but I'm sure they didn't know that
either.) And there seemed to be nothing to be gained
by my attempting to disillusion either that audience
or the State Headquarters at that time, by getting into
a fight over personalities. But I had in my possession
right then a photostatic copy of a document showing
that Raymond V. Dennett had been Secretary of the
Board of Directors, chairman of one of the most important committees, and an active participant in the
innermost councils of the Institute of Pacific Relations, at the very time during the war years and immediate postwar years when this institute was putting
in its cleverest and most telling blows to further the
Communist cause.'

Nor was this an isolated or unique instance of
the crypto-Communist rushing to Eisenhower's support. There is plenty of evidence that this type of
support rallied to Eisenhower in the primary campaign,
everywhere in the country that it was available and
could be effective.[2] And the roster of left-wingers
and super-liberals -- not necessarily Communists nor

even properly suspected of being Communists -- as
well as of known and open Communist sympathizers,
who were raucously rooting for Eisenhower, reads
like the invitation list for a national ADA convention.

First, however, let's go back four years. The
movement to "draft" Eisenhower for the Republican
nomination in 1948 had not been allowed by the Communist bosses to get far enough to demonstrate the
kind of birds-of-a-feather that he attracted. Eisenhower's letter to Leonard Finder, announcing that he
was not a candidate, was mailed on January 22, 1948.
It should be noted, nevertheless, that the man who
spearheaded the move, Stuart Scheftel, later was the
campaign coordinator for the "Democrat," Rudolph
Halley, when Halley won the Council Presidency of
New York City, as the candidate of the Socialist
"Liberal" ticket. And the only so-called Republican
of any prominence to get on this short-trip bandwagon was the notorious Charles Tobey of New
Hampshire, who had practically a perfect New Deal
voting record.

But when you turn to the list of those who --
knowing well what Eisenhower stood for and where
he belonged in the political spectrum -- tried to make
him the Democratic candidate in 1948, the flock is
something to behold. Among its leaders were Adlai
Stevenson, Millard Tydings, James Roosevelt, Frank
Hague, Jake Arvey, Franklin D. Roosevelt, Jr., (a
vice-president of Americans For Democratic Action),
A.A. Berle, Jr., Helen Gahagan Douglas (who had
won high political office through Communist support
and later lost it through supporting the Communists),
William O'Dwyer, David Dubinsky (who had raised A-
merican money to help the Communist forces in the
Spanish civil war), Claude Pepper (of whom the less
said the better), Chester Bowles (of whom we may
have more to say later), Walter Winchell, Drew

Pearson, Eleanor Roosevelt, most of the leaders of the Americans For Democratic Action -- and Sidney Hillman.

Now most of these people were not Communists at all. They were crooks like William O'Dwyer, political opportunists like Claude Pepper,' extreme left-wing intellectuals like Adlai Stevenson, and busybodies like Eleanor Roosevelt, who thought that either the world, or their political careers, or their standing with other intellectuals, or their safety from prosecution, would be improved by anything they could do to help the whole left-wing cause; and they recognized Eisenhower as a leading kindred spirit. Of those who probably were Communists, Hillman died before the issue came to a showdown; Dubinsky was still classified as a Trotskyite, or at least as a Dubinsky-Lovestone deviationist; and there was some reason in each case why the Communist strategy board, or the really top command, had not tipped off this particular individual that he was driving down the wrong fairway, at the wrong time. Or maybe the top command was anxious to see what might happen, and just had not yet made up its mind. At any rate, the real Communist power never got behind this drive, and just before the Democratic Convention Eisenhower made it clear that he was not a candidate for that nomination either. The Communist top command had decided that the chances of their reelecting Truman were good enough, and their danger if Dewey was elected was small enough, to justify saving Eisenhower for a greater need.

But when 1952 came around, and the prospect they then faced was either electing Eisenhower or having Taft as President, they pulled out all of the stops. And they didn't dare run Eisenhower as the Democratic nominee against Taft as the Republican nominee. For in the election campaign, as distin-

guished from the primary campaign, there would
have been no possible self-interest involved, on the
part of the Republicans, to keep them from exposing
Eisenhower's pro-Communist record. Not only,
considering the mood the country was in at that time,
would Taft have won in a walk by the time that exposure was completed, but their most useful "hero"
would have lost his usefulness for all future occasions. So they had to get rid of Taft, and put across
Eisenhower, in the primaries. In doing so, and in
getting the Republican Party and then the American
people to accept Eisenhower not only as a Republican,
but as a reasonably conservative Republican, they
put thousands of leading Republicans under a spell
so incredible that the word hallucination does not begin to describe it. Just the plain facts that were then
known as to Eisenhower's beliefs and actions, and the
nature of the following which was visibly supporting
him, was enough to make any high school student,
who looked at the situation honestly and objectively,
decide that the whole Republican Party had gone
crazy. We'll skip the "beliefs and actions" here,
because of an overlapping otherwise with other sections of this letter. But the character and quality of
the left-wingers who vociferously supported his campaign -- and with whom people like Sinclair Weeks
and George Humphrey and Charles Wilson willingly
and knowingly got in the same political bed -- should
have been sufficient to make the whole situation as
clear as a raid on a Sunday School picnic by neighbor-
hood ruffians.

In order to finish dealing with this topic without
seeming to belabor it unduly, however, let's lump
into one catalogue those strange specimens on whom
we turn our spotlight as having supported Eisenhower
in 1952, whether in the primary campaign, or after
he was nominated, or in both stretches. We might

begin the roll call with Norman Thomas, Stanley M.
Isaacs, Jacob Javits, Adam Clayton Powell, and
Arthur J. Goldsmith -- although it is hardly fair to
put Norman Thomas in such company. Thomas is
only a bleeding-heart exhibitionist, and professional
windmill, who is not a Communist, and whose support
of Eisenhower -- at that time -- was only lukewarm.
But the viciously pro-Communist records of the other
four are too well known to need any delineation here;
and they all put their whole weight into the Eisenhower
campaign. There is a considerable body of evidence
that Arthur Goldsmith even helped to "mastermind"
as well as finance it. What's more, the support of
all these men was well known -- and in the cases of
Isaacs, Javits, and Powell, highly publicized -- during the campaign itself.

Of the 1948 supporters listed several paragraphs
above, most were estopped from pushing the "Repub-
lican" Eisenhower in 1952 by the radiance of their
Democratic labels. But, as Emerson says, when
the half-gods go, the gods arrive. Among these gods
of the entertainment and literary world, who shouted
their heads off for Eisenhower in 1952, were Russell
Crouse, Oscar Hammerstein, Moss Hart, Quentin
Reynolds, Richard Rodgers, Arthur Schwartz, Howard
Lindsay, Arthur Loew, William Zeckendorf, Max
Kriendler, Faye Emerson, Humphrey Bogart, Lauren
Bacall, and Michael Straight.

It would be comforting to feel that our readers
would stay with us while we interpolated here another
whole book, equal in size to this one, just to point out
the Communist activities and affiliations of some
members of the above group; and to outline the ardent and longtime support of the Roosevelt-Truman-
Henry Wallace brands of "democracy" by the others.
We do not feel it, so we'll have to reconcile ourselves
to a small sampling job instead.

Quentin Reynolds, already cited by the House Committee on Un-American Activities for his Communist front activities, had even been a sponsor of one Communist organization which had the Soviet agent, Gerhardt Eisler, on its payroll; and had just taken the place, as editor of the notorious United Nations World, of Louis Dolivet, when that alien Communist was denied readmission to the United States in 1950 as "a dangerous Stalinite agent." The United Nations World had been so completely and consistently pro-Communist that even the United Nations had disavowed it in 1948. Among Reynolds' close associates on that magazine were Robert E. Sherwood, the New Deal liar who admitted that he had been consciously and deliberately lying when he wrote Roosevelt's "again and again and again" speech; and Thomas Mann, with thirteen Communist front citations, and a medal given him by Stalin's emissaries in East Germany as late as 1949.

Crouse, Hammerstein, Hart, Reynolds, Rodgers, and Schwartz had been original sponsors of the Independent Citizens Committee of the Arts, Sciences, and Professions, organized by the Communists in 1944. When this front got too well recognized for what it was, it changed its name to the National Council of the Arts, Sciences, and Professions, and put on the Soviet-directed Scientific and Cultural Conference for World Peace at the Waldorf Astoria in 1949.' Humphrey Bogart, one of the yellowest as well as reddest of Stalin's little helpers in Hollywood, and Lauren Bacall, had led the delegation of movieland Reds to Washington to tell the government and the American people just where they got off in trying to do anything to the ten Hollywood Communists who had been arrested. Michael Straight, a protege of Felix Frankfurter, and who had boasted that Harold Laski was the instructor who had influenced him the most, was the owner of the pro-Communist magazine, the New Republic. William Zeckendorf had contributed four thousand dollars to the Democratic Party for the 1950 election alone. Max Kriendler was a contributor to the National Committee For An Effective Congress, a letterhead organization through which to channel money and help to defeat anti-Communist Senators. Of the Committee which put on the Madison Square Garden spectacle to ballyhoo Eisenhower's campaign, which included many of the names in the list above, at least one-third of the members already had Communist-front citations to their credit. And it was this whole medley of left-wingers, and worse, who were actually giving the most vociferous support to the man whom the American people were electing for the very purpose of exposing and cleaning up such left-wing influences.'

Or maybe we should mention that Jacob Potofsky, successor to Sidney Hillman as president of the CIO Amalgamated Clothing Workers, had been a longtime and outspoken booster of Eisenhower for the Presidency, and still was. (He had once grouped Eisenhower with Henry Wallace and Claude Pepper, as among the leaders he really counted on to save the country by "progressive reform. ") Or Charles Marciotti, the Pennsylvania lawyer still registered as a Democrat, whose penchant for representing underworld characters had made him famous or infamous, as you prefer. Or Alvin Johnson, President-Emeritus of the Communist-slanted "New School" in New York -- of which Gerhardt Eisler's brother Hans was a member of the faculty. Or Sanford Griffith, a former broker now barred from Wall Street, but a big shot in the Anti-Defamation League. Or Joseph E. Davies, of Mission To Moscow fame,[2] the most blatantly and brazenly pro-Communist of all the ambassadors appointed by Roosevelt or Truman.[3]

These men were all snorting and tearing to get Eisenhower elected.

Or let's turn to the field of journalism, and its most scintillating stars. Drew Pearson, of course, not at all deterred by his past interest in whom the Democrats nominated, was now all out for Eisenhower, for the Republican nomination, and then for his election. So was John Franklin Carter, better known as Jay Franklin, a former avowed Fascist and then a ghost writer for both Roosevelt and Truman. So, of course, was Elmer Davis, who had headed the OWI during the war years, when that agency was more completely loaded with actual Communists and close fellow travelers than any other government department. (I gave page after page of the Communist make-up of Elmer Davis' OWI in The Life of John Birch, published in 1954.' But I'll not stop to repeat that documentation here.) Or Ted O. Thackrey, editor of the Daily Compass, successor to PM, and generally known as "the uptown edition of the Daily Worker." Among the staff writers for the Compass under Thackrey's management were Jennings Perry, Johannes Steel, I. F. Stone, and William S. Gailmor. In that paper, on August 19, 1951, Thackrey wrote: "As of today, there is but one man outstanding in the public view who meets one and all of these qualification requirements [for a Presidential candidate] .... This man, of course, is General of the Army Dwight David Eisenhower." And there isn't any doubt that Thackrey and his fellow Communists knew what they were talking about, so far as the qualifications they wanted were concerned.

When it comes to the publications themselves which were all out for Eisenhower, besides the United Nations World and the Daily Compass which we have already mentioned, we find also Marshall Field's Chicago Sun-Times; that completely pro-Communist

magazine, The Churchman, edited by Guy Emery Shipler, with eighty-five(!) Communist-front citations;
Max Ascoli's The Reporter; the Saturday Review,
whose Communist leanings John T. Flynn exposed so
well in While You Slept; and, moving into slightly more
respectable circles, such sharply left-wing papers as
the New York Post, the Washington Post, and literally
dozens more like them. To anybody at all familiar
with the two papers, the fact that the New York Post
and the Washington Post could support a man for the
Presidency should have made him utterly impossible
even for consideration as a Republican candidate --
and would have but for the willful blindness and opportunism of so many Republican leaders.

Finally, let's take one brief look at the strangest
corner of all in this red-tinted panorama. Way up in
Vermont, in and near the small town of Bethel, were
the "retreats" of such well-known Communists as Lee
Pressman, Nathan Witt, Marion Bachrach, and John
Abt. There was a whole huge nest of them. And in
1952 a patriotic but not too cautious Vermont woman,
Lucille Miller, began to point out, and to do her best
to get other people to pay attention to the fact, that
every one of these Communists was actively supporting Eisenhower's campaign. She didn't make any
headway, because it seemed preposterous -- except
to the Communists and their sympathizers. But
three years later, in actions based on other charges,
before a federal judge who had himself been one of
the objects of her criticism, and in which Mrs. Miller
was denied her constitutional rights, she was railroaded
to St. Elizabeth's hospital for the insane in Washington.

Eventually powerful enough public-spirited citizens,
interested in the case, forced the hospital to allow an
examination of Mrs. Miller by outside doctors -- who
stated that she was just as sane as they were -- and
she had to be turned loose. The smear and incarcera-

tion of Mrs. Miller, engineered ostensibly because
she later advised soldiers being drafted in peace time
to test the constitutionality of the draft act, served
to make the original facts which really got her into
trouble be glossed over and forgotten. Forgotten, that
is, by all but a few of us, who were likewise disturbed
in 1952 by the tremendous support of Eisenhower which
we knew to be of Communist origin or Communist sympathies. And we have recognized what happened to
Lucille Miller, however much it was dressed up and
disguised and made to look plausible, for the warning
it was intended to be; a warning to any and all anti-
Communists, whether it be General Kirke Lawton,
or Joe McCarthy -- or this writer --, not to get too
close to Eisenhower with the truth about his Communist backing and pro-Communist activities.' For the
truth is the one weapon he and the top conspirators
behind him could not withstand. And the full truth,
just about the Communist support and Communist-
inspired support which he received in the 1952 campaigns -- if there were any way to get this truth to
the American people through their shell of complacency, after crossing the smear barricade which the
Communists have erected -- would be enough to break
the whole Communist conspiracy in this country in
six months. But, alas, there is no possible way to
do it.

CHAPTER EIGHT

The Anti-anti-Communist'. . . . .

Eisenhower as President has initiated and
sparked a continuing, unhesitating, and highly successful effort to prevent any real exposure of Communists high up in government, and to minimize the
exposure of Communists in the lower echelons -- of
either the Truman Administration or his own. Of
course in both the strategy and the tactics of this operation he has been guided by, and taken orders from,
the Communist bosses who count on him merely for
the execution of their planning. But as the actual
"Chief Executive" he has carried out that planning
well, and willingly. He cannot put the blame on anybody else. For instance, even the usually pro-
Eisenhower U.S. News and World Report, although it
was also pro-McCarthy, admitted on December 11,
1953: "Mr. Eisenhower did not consult members of
his cabinet, members of Congress, or the Republican
National Committee before deciding to make an attack
on the ideas of Senator McCarthy. "[2]
    That this crusade in suppression had nothing
really to do with the personality, the methods, or the
shortcomings of McCarthy is clearly shown by the
fact that Eisenhower was just as emphatic and heavy-
handed in stopping the exposures by his own Attorney
General, Herbert Brownell, of Communist activities
under Truman. The chief difference was that, in
1953, in one week after Brownell began his intended
campaign of public information, with his exposition of
the Harry Dexter White case, Eisenhower was able to
silence Brownell by direct orders.[3] In doing so, he

made clear to all other members of his administration and of the Republican Party, whom he could control, that the surest way to the presidential doghouse was to expose Communists, past or present.

Eisenhower was not able, of course, to silence McCarthy at that time. But by devious means and slippery maneuvers dreamed up for him by the geniuses in the background, he was able to stymie McCarthy's investigation, at a crucial period, for nine months. This was long enough to prevent any revelation of where the trail of treason actually led in either the Army and its Loyalty Board or in the CIA; and long enough to ensure that McCarthy's investigations could finally be stopped altogether by a Democratic Congress -- which Eisenhower helped mightily to make certain would be elected, as we shall point out in the next chapter.

One of the straws which Eisenhower desperately grabbed, in the earlier days of his administration, as a means of discrediting and slowing down McCarthy, was the article by J. B. Matthews in the American Mercury.[1] In that conscientiously documented article Matthews carefully stated that perhaps ninety-seven percent of the Protestant clergy in America were above criticism in their attitude towards Communism. (He was too generous and too restrained, but that is another story.)[2] But he pointed out the damage that was being done by at least some of the other three percent who were following the Communist line. And it was Eisenhower personally who set the stage and made the arrangements for the terrific blast against Matthews which not only destroyed the effectiveness of the article, but made it a political necessity that Matthews be dropped from his new staff position with the McCarthy Committee.[3] In fact Joseph Alsop openly boasted, in the New York Herald Tribune, that Eisenhower had taken steps to stimulate the telegrams from clergymen of the Protestant, Catholic, and Jewish faiths, which prepared the way for his outburst. "The White House actively sought the opportunity," Alsop said, "indeed created the opportunity."[1] It surely did. One of the clergymen had not even read the telegram to which his name was signed until it appeared in the newspapers!

Many of us supposed, at the time, that the damage to Matthews and to McCarthy was the whole purpose of this maneuver. Since then I have followed the work of Myers Lowman, in Cincinnati, and of Edgar Bundy, in Wheaton, Illinois, who have been concentrating their studies on Communist infiltration into the Protestant ministry. It has now become evident that the Communists long ago decided to use this medium of influence on public opinion as one of the most important channels of their propaganda. Their tremendous success in doing so has not, I believe, been so much through Protestant ministers becoming Communists as through Communists becoming Protestant ministers. They have converted some, who were already ministers, to Communism, of course. And some young men with leftish leanings, going through the already infiltrated theological schools, have been made into full fledged Communists on the way. But probably more important than either group have been the young men who were already dedicated Communists, and hence believed that the end justified any means, who have gone through these pink theological schools and then become ministers and bishops, suspected of nothing worse than eggheaded liberalism. Lowman published, not long ago, a list of 2109 ministers, of the Methodist denomination alone, who are either Communists or fellow travelers.[2] He says his forthcoming lists for several other denominations are much larger -- the Unitarian list, somewhat naturally, being relatively the worst of all. Bundy, who was with the

Army Air Force Intelligence for seven years,[1] states categorically that, as bad as the Communist infiltration in the field of education has been, the percentage of Communists and Communist sympathizers among the Protestant clergy is twice as large as it is among educators.[2] So it may well be that turning the eyes of the American public away from any good look at this quietly dangerous development was as important, in the minds of Eisenhower and his bosses, as the more specific immediate purpose.

As to the Army-McCarthy hearings probably little needs to be said here. That the whole factitious proceeding was cooked up inside the White House was revealed in the hearings themselves.[3] That Secretary Stevens had originally intended to cooperate with Mc Carthy, gladly and diligently, in weeding traitors out of the Army, was obvious. It was equally obvious that he gradually changed, under pressure from the White House, until in the hearings themselves he reversed himself openly and brazenly with full White House approval. A very able and patriotic U.S. Army General, Kirke Lawton, found that he had sacrificed his career by merely doing his patriotic duty in trying to help to expose the Communists under his command at Fort Monmouth. Lawton was relieved of command and retired, not just to satisfy the vengeance of George Marshall and Dwight Eisenhower, but as another warning to those Army officers who might want to emulate his brand of patriotism. All of the artificial storm and fury, from which you might have thought -- and were supposed to think -- that McCarthy had committed every crime in the book from arson to treason, eventually boiled down to the question of a censure motion against McCarthy for language and methods supposedly unbecoming a Senator.[4] The censure motion was itself written, down to the last word and comma, by agents of the Communist-loaded National Com-

mittee For An Effective Congress,[1] and was introduced by a former supporter of the Morgenthau Plan
and the Nuremberg trials, a badly confused Senator
named Ralph Flanders, whose language and methods
have frequently been worse than anything of which
McCarthy was even accused. Then the White House
crew went to work, by subtle means and some not so
subtle, to influence the attitude and vote of a sufficient
number of Senators.[2] How many were driven by this
White House pressure, against their own wishes and
their own better judgments, to vote for the censure
of McCarthy, it is impossible to determine. But even
Flanders has since expressed his repentance and re-
morse for doing so.[3]

From these and many other items of evidence
incidental to the occasion it was clear that Eisenhower
was frantically determined, in whatever way and at
whatever cost, not only to liquidate McCarthy's investigations and McCarthy's influence, but to humiliate McCarthy personally in such vicious fashion as utterly to discourage any other patriot who might be
tempted to take up the same torch. The later black-
listing of McCarthy and his wife from the White House
social functions was not, in my opinion, just the result of a vengeful desire on Eisenhower's part to
humiliate still further a defeated enemy. It was a
coldly calculated way of impressing on would-be-
crusaders just what would happen to anybody who
dared become serious about exposing Communists.

It was not enough, however, just to scare off the
investigators. It was important that any who didn't
scare be ridiculed, frustrated, and blocked at every
turn. One blocking method which the Communists
had devised was the Truman security order of 1947,
which prohibited Congress from access to government
files on the loyalty of personnel. Another was the
1948 directive by President Truman, forbidding gov-

ernment officials to give information to Congressional committees without White House permission.'
It was under the authority of this second order, for
instance, that Major General Miles Reber, in September, 1953, refused to tell McCarthy's committee
who gave security clearance to certain army employees the Senator believed to be Communists.[2] Eisenhower had allowed Truman's directive to stand, as
he also had the earlier order concerning access to
government files. Both orders were clearly designed by Communists, for the protection of Communists. But worse was to come.

On Monday, May 17, 1954, the U. S. Supreme
Court handed down its decision requiring desegrega-
tion in all public schools.[3] The attention of press and
public were excitedly focused on that event for the
next many weeks, as was easily foreseen that it would
be. So on that same day, with the brilliant timing
which the Communists always make a part of their
strategy, Eisenhower quietly clamped a dictatorial
embargo on the supply of any information by government departments to investigating committees, which
made the Truman gag rule look almost cooperative,
and which has been in effect ever since.[4]

One illustration will easily show the significance
and effect of that directive. In 1956 the known strength
of Communist influence in the National Labor Relations
Board was a matter of concern to several congressiona
committees. The House Committee On Un-American
Activities, under Congressman Francis Walter, decided to investigate. It subpoenaed eight present employees of that agency. But none of them would testify,
about anything. And they didn't have to plead any first
or fifth amendments. Each one of them simply presented a letter, directed to him by the head of the
NLRB. Each one said that the letter to him had been
written after consultation by the head of the NLRB

with President Eisenhower. Each letter cited the Executive Order of May 17, 1954, to which we referred above. And that was that. The committee was helpless. Chairman Walter called the Eisenhower executive order "incredibly stupid";[1] but that was, in our opinion, both an erroneous and an entirely too generous description.

It will be remembered that of the three commissioners, who first ran what is now the NLRB when it was established by Roosevelt in the 1930's, one later proved to be an out-and-out crook, one later proved to be an out-and-out Communist, and nobody had to wait to know where the third member, Frank Graham, stood on the questions with which the board dealt. He was accurately described by an eminent lawyer who had many cases before him. "Frank Graham is not a Communist," this lawyer said. "He is entirely sincere. He is simply the most gullible jackass in America."

It was this precious trio who had set the pace and the pattern for the NLRB. As Senator McCarthy pointed out, "no federal agency during the last twenty years has had more influence upon the economic and social structure of the nation than the National Labor Relations Board." The continued subversion of that board has, naturally, been a prime goal for the Communists at all times. And they have been decidedly successful. The Communists have been placing their agents in top-level jobs in that agency from the beginning.[2] In 1940 a House Committee, headed by Representative Smith of Virginia, reported that the NLRB was heavily infiltrated. McCarthy knew well how heavily infiltrated it was in his day, but never reached the chance to do anything about it. Congressman Walter's committee tried and failed.[3] Other committees are well aware of the situation today, but know they can't get anywhere with an investigation, because of Eisenhower's protection of the Communists with his gag rule.

"The National Labor Relations Board," as Dan Smoot says, "has the power to make -- and does make -- arbitrary decisions which affect the lives of every person in the United States." We know that this agency in the past has been infested with, and at times dominated by, Communists. There is plenty of disturbing knowledge about its pro-Communist slant right now. But we are not permitted to find out just how badly infiltrated it is, or how many actual Communists are inside the Board guiding its activities, because Eisenhower says it's none of our business -- or of the business of Congress.'

This attitude and this executive order now stop cold, at every turn, any investigation of Communists in government. The order is also stretched to prevent the revealing of other information which the Communists do not want revealed, as in the hearing of the (old) McClellan Committee early in 1956 on the 1954 executive agreement, made by Eisenhower's Administration, to relax controls on free-world trade with Soviet nations. McClellan was able to get one or two small bits of general testimony from a couple of courageous technicians. They ventured that much, at the risk of their jobs, before refusing to answer more specific questions. The first testified that he believed one of the items taken off the embargo list was "the heart of our military communications system." The second, that beyond question the easing of curbs on the sales of electronic devices to the Reds had given them a "war advantage." And Mc Clellan more or less verified, by indirection, what everybody concerned already knew, that the agreement had cleared the way for the British to sell Soviet Russia seventy-four million pounds of copper wire which Russia so badly needed for its war machine.

But as to any and all details which would have enabled the committee to make any report or take any action, the witnesses clammed up, on the authority of this order.[1] For the order, as we have said, was not limited to personnel security matters, but prohibited government departments from giving Congressional committees any information. This Presidential directive works as a complete shield, behind which the Communists can do anything they wish, in any department, with impunity and without fear of exposure.

However, we have considerably more ground to cover in this chapter. We are trying to show the intention and result of some of Eisenhower's maneuvers to help the Soviet cause right here in America. After this much consideration of his success in preventing the exposure of Communists, the next place to look is at his actions in connection with the Bricker Amendment. And for that look we need a small bit of preparation again.

There are three paths of procedure by which the Communists might eventually take over the United States. One is a sufficient degree of infiltration to seize power by a peaceful coup d'etat, as they did in Czechoslovakia.[2] A second is through civil war, with the infiltrated Communists and their dupes aided, when the time comes, by all of the military might of the Soviet. This would be analagous to the method they used in taking over China; and it seems clear from all of their past history that they would not attempt the conquest of so powerful a nation as the United States, from the outside, without a sufficiently strong fifth column inside our country to convert the attack into a civil war.

The third path, however, and the one which seems likely to be relied on most heavily in their present plans, is more in accordance with Lenin's long-range strategy. This would follow the course of inducing gradual surrender of American sovereignty, piece by piece and step by step, to some international organization like the United Nations. These small separate bits of surrender of sovereignty can be made to subsidiary and affiliated organizations of course, such as ILO and UNESCO and WHO, as well as directly to the parent organization itself. Simultaneously with this course, and equally gradually, the Communists would be getting complete working control of this international complex of organizations. Both sets of steps, short and insidious at first, would be steadily increased in both length and brazenness. Until, eventually, a world-wide police state, absolutely and brutally governed from the Kremlin, would become a visible and accomplished fact. The rapidly growing purge of the Kremlin's enemies and tightening of its controls would then soon make the autocratic tyranny of a Communist dictator as complete as was that of Ghenghis Khan.

In this connection, therefore, Eisenhower's violent opposition to the Bricker Amendment, in the face of his willingness to compromise and negotiate with the Republican leadership about almost every other piece of legislation up to that time, must be added to the items which support my thesis. For the whole first two years of his administration the only matters concerning which he showed any dynamic leadership whatsoever, or concerning which he gave any appearance of even really caring what happened, were the exposure of Communists, the Immigration Act (which we'll discuss much later), and the Bricker Amendment.' On the last issue, as on the first, he went all out. He used every ounce of the power and prestige of his office and every measure of personal cajolery by himself as President, to persuade Senators -- even those who had originally sponsored the Amendment -- to change their previously announced positions and vote against it.

One Senator, who has read an earlier and shorter version of this letter, which contained twenty numbered items of argument, told me that the one item most convincing to him of the truth of my hypothesis was Eisenhower's course with regard to the Bricker Amendment. And this conviction arose from his own personal experience and observation. This man who, as Congressman, or Governor, or Senator, has been in high public office for more than twenty years, said that in all that time he had never seen as urgent, unreasonable, and unceasing pressure exerted on the members of either body of Congress by any President for any purpose, as Eisenhower put on him and the other Senators to defeat the original Bricker Amendment. And he was entirely willing to accept my explanation that, it having been absolutely imperative for the Communists to stop the building of this roadblock across the flow of American sovereignty into the United Nations, Eisenhower was carrying out Communist orders to stop it -- at any price.[1]

One cost of this course, among many, was such rampant hypocrisy on Eisenhower's part as alone to have raised a lot of eyebrows, had the eyebrows not been spattered and stuck with so much Communist mud already thrown into the eyes of the American people. For, as Merwin Hart has emphasized, the Constitution gives a President no part whatever in the amending process.[2] Eisenhower was not only well aware of this, but had fallen back on that principle to save himself embarrassment in connection with a proposed constitutional amendment limiting individual and corporate income taxes, which had been introduced into the Congress in January, 1953. He didn't want to show his hand, as actually being for the Marxist principle of ever higher taxes, and bitterly opposed to any such amendment, so early in the game. And he knew his opposition would not be necessary. So, on February 18, 1953, he wrote a letter to a member of Congress, in which he sanctimoniously sidestepped the question of his support of this H. J. Res. 103, as follows: "...I feel that it would be inappropriate for me to express my views on a proposed constitutional amendment, since a joint resolution proposing an amendment to the Constitution is not presented to the President for his approval."[1] This was a clear and sound statement of a well recognized principle. But the principle meant nothing, not too many months later, when all the influence he could possibly muster was needed to defeat another proposed amendment, which was more dangerous to Communist plans.

Another place where Eisenhower has played extremely well on the Communist team has been on the phony "bookburning" front. An outstanding example was offered by his widely publicized speech at Dartmouth College.[2] There he brought his best brand of disingenuous subtlety to the defense of the pro-Communist policy of USIA and our information centers abroad. These information centers in various foreign countries are not "public" libraries. They are supposedly supported by American taxes for the specific purpose -- however idiotic -- of presenting information favorable to the American way of life. These information centers had been shown, despite every obstacle placed by Eisenhower's State Department in the way of Cohn, Schine, and other investigators, to be loaded with books by Communist authors presenting the Communist viewpoint.[3] (They still are today.) But in his Dartmouth speech Eisenhower made it clear that anybody who would even suggest removing these books belonged to the book-burning, knowledge-destroying, persecution fraternity throughout history -- of which Hitler has been the most spotlighted contemporary example. This speech, which tremendously

supported Communist attitudes everywhere, a-
mounted to a clever but exact following of the Communist line, a deliberate confusion of the American
people.

By 1955 at least some of the conservative and
middle-of-the-road Republicans who had so mistaken-
ly supported Eisenhower for the Republican nomination began to be disillusioned and disturbed by what
"their man" was doing. They were actually surprised. They should not have been in the least. While
posing as an anti-Communist, Eisenhower has at all
times been one of the most vigorous and vicious anti-
anti-Communists in American public life. His whole
course, right here in this country, had always cleverly followed the sinuous Communist paths, and there
were plenty of visible markers of the course he was
traveling, for anybody who would take the trouble to
look. To point out a comparative few of these markers we need a flashback -- and a separate chapter.

CHAPTER NINE

The Pro-Communist . . . . .

Perhaps the first of the strong indicators of
Eisenhower's pro-Soviet stand in America is really
found in Europe. In the fall of 1945, when the Russians were starting to show their postwar hand,
many newspapers in the United States began to call
the obviously imperialistic Russian plans to the attention of their readers, in both editorials and news
columns. So Eisenhower, with his exalted position
guaranteeing wide publicity, let out a vicious blast
against the "crackpots" who were critical of Russian
diplomacy and actions.[1]

Also, while he was still in Europe in 1945,
Eisenhower accepted the invitation of Anna Rosenberg, on behalf of Sidney Hillman, to be the featured
speaker at the annual CIO Convention in 1946. Anna
Rosenberg was then running around Europe as the
"personal representative" of President Truman.
Hillman was already planning to promote Eisenhower
for the presidency, with the full force of the CIO and
its Political Action Committee behind him.[2] Eisenhower accepted Anna Rosenberg's invitation despite
the vigorous protest of many high-ranking American
Army officers. These officers were bitter at the
strikes, stoppages, and slow-downs in American
production, engineered by Communists in the CIO
after the second front in France had been opened and
Stalin was safe. Such actions had seriously impeded
the last years of the war effort, when Stalin wanted
to keep the war on the Western front going just as
long as possible. At that time, also, the CIO was

97

affiliated with the World Federation of Trade Unions, which even the AF of L was denouncing as Communist dominated. But in due course Eisenhower stood before the CIO Delegates in convention assembled, identified the CIO with "American labor," and praised their patriotism even to the extent of saying that they rightly shared in the laurels won by American troops on the battlefield.[1]

At about this same time (1946) Eisenhower accepted the annual Churchman award. (He had already received the so-called Page One Award of the Communist-controlled New York Newspaper Guild.)[2] The Churchman, which we have already mentioned before because of its later support of Eisenhower for the presidency,[3] was edited by the "Reverend" Guy Emery Shipler. Even at that time Shipler already had forty-eight citations in government files for his affiliations with Communist or Communist-front groups. The part the magazine and its editor were playing as adjuncts to the Communist propaganda apparatus was so obvious, to anybody who would take a look, that even Harold Ickes -- after first accepting an invitation to the dinner, before he took that look -- withdrew his name from the dinner committee and publicly blasted the sponsors.[4] But Eisenhower went all right, as the guest of honor, and received the award; and his attendance at the dinner was used to start a campaign for $250,000 to increase the activities of this pro-Communist magazine.[5]

And before we leave the matter of awards, we should undoubtedly give him credit for the one he received in 1945 from Freedom House. Probably the less said about Freedom House the better. You either know about that motley blot on American decency, or it would take entirely too many pages to put the "Reverend" Leon M. Birkhead and some of the other managers of its nefarious activities in their proper setting.

(We can't resist this much, however. Birkhead was
the man who, with Rex Stout as his partner in running
the "Friends of Democracy," hired the notorious'
scoundrel Avedis Boghos Derounian, alias John Roy
Carlson, to pass out anti-Semitic literature for three
months to good Americans, so that he could bring
charges of anti-Semitism against any who accepted
it and seemed interested.' -- And I once found myself
in a position where I had to introduce Derounian, to a
large audience, as the speaker of the evening. --
Birkhead was also the boss or guiding spirit of a man
named Buchanan, three times convicted as an auto-
mobile thief, who still got to Congress, became chairman of the Buchanan (Investigating) Committee, and
was probably the foulest individual who ever used his
Congressional authority to persecute patriotic and up-
right Americans. But that is too long a story, also.
And there have been plenty of other activities of
Freedom House just as bad.)

At any rate, the presiding officer at the Eisenhower award presentation was Rex Stout, former
editor and part owner of New Masses, an official
Communist Party weekly.[2] And to show you the kind
of man Birkhead and Stout felt sure they were honoring, let me point out that among others who have been
recipients of the same award are Roger Baldwin (who
once publicly stated "Communism is the Goal"), with
forty-two Communist-front citations in government
files; and Norman Corwin, radio director for the
United Nations, who has been officially cited sixty-
eight times for his Communist-front affiliations.

In 1949 Eisenhower became a member of the
board of the Carnegie Endowment for International
Peace. This board had, very reluctantly, and because they could no longer flout public opinion so
openly, accepted the resignation of Alger Hiss as
president. They had elected as his successor Joseph

Johnson, who had for years been the right-hand man of Hiss in our government. Then on December 12, 1949, this board, with Eisenhower now a member, passed a resolution deploring the "political pressure" being exerted on Dean Acheson for his defense of his friend Hiss. Eisenhower did not follow the leads of his good friends Acheson and Frankfurter, in serving as a character witness for Hiss, probably because his presence in Europe during the period of Hiss' most important activities would have kept the testimony from being of sufficient value. But in November, 1949, he did go out of his way personally to vouch for the loyalty of Philip Jessup, in a telegram to the McCarran Committee, when that committee was investigating the smelly activities of Jessup in the Institute of Pacific Relations.

It was as president of Columbia University, however, that Eisenhower got in some of his most effective blows for the cause. Best known of these was his acceptance of the grant, from the Communist puppet government of Poland, of thirty thousand dollars as an endowment for a "Chair of Polish Studies." He was warned by Columbia faculty members, as well as patriotic Polish citizens in this country, that the endowment was solely for the purpose of setting up a Communist propaganda center at Columbia. Dr. Arthur P. Coleman, an assistant professor in Columbia's Slavic Languages Department for twenty years, resigned in protest. But Eisenhower was not to be deterred. He accepted the grant, established the Adam Mickiewicz Chair, and appointed Dr. Manfred Kridl to fill it. Kridl was known to be a "noted Marxist." How satisfactory the whole transaction and the appointment of Kridl were, to the Communist government in Poland, was revealed on August 21, 1949, in a gloating report of the official Communist Polish literary weekly, <u>Odrozenia</u>, which said: "Our government entrusted the Chair to the excellent scholar, Dr. Manfred Kridl. "'

On June 8, 1949, Eisenhower, as a member of the Educational Policies Committee of the National Education Association, had signed a report issued by that committee stating that Communists should not be allowed to teach in American schools. Right at that very time he was arranging to accept the Polish Communist grant for Columbia, and it was just a month later that Dr. Coleman resigned and Dr. Kridl was appointed to the Columbia faculty. But this was hardly more than a straw in the wind. Somewhat less substantive but equally revealing was the well-publicized visit and homage Eisenhower paid to Professor John Dewey, the founder of "progressive education" in this country, and the idol of every Communist and pink in the educational world. What really mattered, however, was the comprehensive protection and coddling by Eisenhower, during the years of his active presidency of Columbia, of the whole giant Communist complex in that institution.

The truth, I believe, is that, had Columbia not already been such a haven for Communist professors and center of Communist influence, Eisenhower would neither have wanted, nor been offered, the job of being its president. Certainly he left it more Communist-slanted than he found it. At one time he was given a list of eighty-seven people on his faculty who had records of affiliation with Communist or Communist-front activities. Some of them undoubtedly were just dupes. But among them were such notorious, persistent, and industrious workers in the Communist cause as Walter Rautenstrauch, Dorothy Brewster, Bernhard J. Stern, Mark Van Doren, Gene Weltfish, Robert S. Lynd, Corliss Lamont, Leslie C. Dunn, Abraham Edel, Paul F. Brissenden, Phillip Klein, Harry Grundfest, Ernest J. Simmons, Boris M. Stanfield, Donald G. Tewkesbury, Edith F. Claflin, and Goodwin Watson.[2]

For any organization to be officially classified
by government agencies as a Communist front, then
as now, the evidence had to be conclusive -- and
practically blinding. Yet at that time the first five
names on this list already had citations in government files for participation in 62, 38, 31, 19, and 33
Communist fronts, respectively. Stern, under an
assumed name, had written a Marxist book put out
by the official publishing subsidiary of the Communist
Party. Miss Weltfish had been president of one organization classified by the U.S. Department of
Justice as Communist. And so it went, not only with
these five but with others named. Just for one more
illustration, the pro-Communist activities of Goodwin
Watson, the last name on the list above, filled sixty-
four pages in the exhibits from Congressional hearings. All of these facts and full information concerning all of those listed were supplied to General
Eisenhower.

It was not easy to do. At all times he angrily
denied and aggressively resisted any implication that
there was any taint of Communism in the Columbia
faculty at all. On August 18, 1948, the New York
Star carried on its front page a feature story, authorized by Eisenhower himself. Its opening sentence was:
"Dwight D. Eisenhower, president of Columbia University, last night vehemently denied that the University,
its staff and its textbooks bore any taint of Communism. "
(It is an interesting coincidence, pointed out by J. B.
Matthews, that, in another feature story on the same
front page of the same paper, Alger Hiss vehemently
denied that he was or ever had been a Communist.)
Further along in the same article Eisenhower was
directly quoted as follows: "I found no traces of
Communism among the deans, professors, and the
rest of the staff at Columbia, and I met them all. "
You can explain this any way you want to, but certainly

the easiest explanation is that it was simply a brazen
lie to protect the Communists.[1]

A few months later, in February, 1949, the American Legion officially appointed a delegation to call on
President Eisenhower of Columbia University and give
him the facts about Communists on his faculty. Eisenhower refused even to receive the delegation.[2] His attitude remained the same during his whole administration. Despite this resistance, the full information
concerning the eighty-seven faculty members was
given to Eisenhower, and did reach him. He ignored
it. Every one of the eighty-seven, plus Dr. Kridl and
a few others, were still teaching at Columbia when he
left. So far as I know, except for Rautenstrauch and
any others who may have died natural deaths in the
meantime, they are still there today.

Eisenhower himself claims, however, that his
greatest accomplishment while at Columbia was the
organization of Arden House and its program, The
American Assembly.[3] If he had said his "greatest accomplishment for the Communist cause," as he undoubtedly intended some of his readers to understand
his meaning, he would probably be right. The facilities
of this abnormally luxurious brainwashing emporium
were donated to Columbia by Averell Harriman. But
its organization of six-weeks courses of extremely
clever indoctrination for carefully selected American
business executives, and of its American Assembly
technique, was worked out under the direction and
with the approval of Eisenhower. These business executives are kept incommunicado, mixing and talking
only with each other and the staff, for the whole six
weeks. The combination of swank surroundings, intellectual flattery, "inner circle" atmosphere, "profoundly authoritative" lectures, and subtle thought
guidance, is so skillfully contrived that most of the
"graduates" come out as enthusiastic alumni, believ-

ing exactly what it was intended for them to believe, willing to put their names and lend their prestige to the "reports" they have been steered into preparing, and anxious to sell other business executives the idea of seeking the same wonderful experience. The fact that these "reports," which are collectively published in book form and widely distributed as objective studies, somehow end up following the exact Communist line on the subject covered, escapes them entirely. And by this time they are so beautifully brainwashed and smugly superior that they only get angry if you point it out. The net result is an increasingly powerful lobby, of supposedly hard-headed business men, for such Communist aims as strengthening the power of the United Nations (it is a United Nations flag, not an American flag, that hangs over the main entrance to Arden House); for recognizing the value of more trade by the United States with Russia, Red China, and the satellite nations; for understanding the inevitability and desirability of Red China's admission to the United Nations; for increasing American foreign aid; and for other long-range programs dear to the Communist heart.

The American Assembly is given plenty of buffer activities and protective coloring. There are other sessions at Arden House, such as those dealing with production or business management, which do an excellent and even (usually) an objective job in their respective areas. But for the last word in clever and "authoritative" propaganda, permeated by "scholarship" and bearing insignia which make it above suspicion -- especially suspicion by those innocents who helped to produce it -- Arden House is the elite studio among propaganda factories.

Eisenhower is entirely right. It is quite an accomplishment. Anybody who, through long study, knows the true essential facts of developments in the

Far East over the past twenty years, can see just how clever an accomplishment, by reading the book turned out by The American Assembly, called The United States And The Far East, which was published in January, 1957. Not since Lawrence Rosinger "And Associates" put together their The State Of Asia, for the Institute of Pacific Relations, has there been anything equal to it. The conclusions, brilliantly arrived at after so many pages of ostentatious scholarship and logic, could all have been set down in advance, in ten minutes, by anybody who knew the Kremlin's propaganda line in that area at that time. And on April 2, 1957, I, as a director of the National Association of Manufacturers, received from The American Assembly a letter quoting, and endorsed by, the Director of the Education Department of the NAM, offering to send me free The United States And The Far East, and other publications of The American Assembly, on request.

Then, in March, 1958, I received from The American Assembly, Columbia University, New York 27, N. Y., notice that I could have the "Final Report of the Twelfth American Assembly," also free on request. This is described as a 200-page book, prepared under the "editorial supervision" of Philip C. Jessup (concerning whose pro-Communism see Page 219 of this treatise). Its title is ATOMS FOR POWER: UNITED STATES POLICY IN ATOMIC ENERGY DEVELOPMENT; and of the seven authors listed in the contents, the place of honor is given to J. Robert Oppenheimer!'

Arden House is indeed an accomplishment, in the field of propaganda, which would call for my admiration if it did not intend my destruction. In my opinion Mr. Eisenhower and the Communist bosses can well be proud of what they have achieved, from their point of view, at Arden House. It was his greatest pro-

Communist achievement as <u>president</u> of Columbia --
though exceeded by far, in ultimate value to the Kremlin, by another enterprise he initiated during the same
period.'

CHAPTER TEN

The Republican' . . . . .

We need a change of pace. The continued exposition and analysis of Eisenhower's pro-Communist activities can wear out both reader and writer with their monotony. So, while we have skipped any reference to his greatest single contribution to the Soviet cause during his "civilian" years, let's leave that item for a later chapter. In this one we ask you to look with us merely at the political and ideological record of the man whom the Republican Party accepted as its candidate, and sold to the American people -- in the first campaign anyway -- as a reasonably conservative Republican.

The story begins on November 9, 1909, in Abilene, Kansas. Dwight Eisenhower, then nineteen years old, made a political speech at a rally of "The Young Men's Democratic Club." He declared himself a Democrat, waxed oratorical in showing why any "intelligent young man" would become a Democrat, and accused the Republican Party of "legalized robbery."[2] He has been a Democrat, of the left-wing New Deal variety, ever since. During his years at West Point and as an army officer, naturally he was inactive politically. Or reasonably so. But whenever his political coloration did come out through his uniform, it showed him to be a Roosevelt-worshipping Democrat. In 1944, on his own statement (according to Washington correspondent Arthur Sylvester, who heard him make it), he voted for Roosevelt against Dewey.[3] He also persuaded others to vote for Roosevelt, among them Dr. Daniel Poling. Dr. Poling has said: "I've

107

voted the Republican ticket at every single election except 1944, when General Eisenhower personally prevailed upon me to cast my vote against Governor Dewey of New York and vote for Roosevelt and the New Deal. "

There is plenty of proof that, in thus plugging Roosevelt and the New Deal, Eisenhower was not doing any violence to his own beliefs, even with regard to our domestic economy. At a private dinner at the "F" Street Club in Washington, in 1947, at which several Republican Senators were present, the question of inflation was discussed. Eisenhower offered his solution to the problem. Inflation could easily be licked at any time, he said, by a simple action on the part of the industrialists and other business leaders of the nation. They merely needed, by joint and voluntary agreement, to forego all profits for a year -- or for two years if necessary.' Eisenhower's ignorance of the functioning of the American business system could have been as colossal as this would indicate, but his ignorance of human nature could not. Here was bitter and deeprooted hostility to the American business system, advanced under the umbrella of ignorance. That a man either holding such a belief, or pretending to do so, could ever have been given the Republican nomination, for the Presidency of the United States, is a sad revelation of the venality and opportunism of a lot of Republican politicians. It also proves conclusively that Eisenhower's proper political classification was in the red fringes of the Democratic Party.

In 1948 Eisenhower was entirely willing, up to the last stretch, to be nominated by that party. William Ritchie, former Democratic Chairman of Nebraska, said Eisenhower told him personally on the Monday before the Republican Convention that he was ready to accept the Democratic nomination. He then withdrew

-- on the orders and for the reasons, we believe, that we have stated in earlier parts of this treatise. But Harry Truman, with whom he had been and still was in very close contact, thought of him unquestionably as a Democrat right up to the fall of 1951.[1]

Now it is perfectly all right for a man to be a Democrat, even an A. D. A. Democrat, if that school of political philosophy expresses his own honest beliefs. It is also true that the terms "Republican" and "Democrat" are not precise, and that their ideological boundaries were overlapping, even in 1952. But they had not overlapped sufficiently for men of the political affiliations and known beliefs of Milton and Dwight Eisenhower to call themselves Republicans. Both words still conveyed certain clear significances to the American people. Even the seeds of confusion planted by Earl Warren and Wayne Morse on the West Coast, for the purpose of making the principles and positions of the two parties indistinguishable, had not yet borne sufficient fruit to be of much moment anywhere except in their respective states. Throughout the rest of the country people generally recognized Republicans as Republicans and Democrats as Democrats, almost as clearly as they recognized men as men and women as women, despite a certain number of neuters and indefinables in both sets of classifications.

But in 1952 Dwight Eisenhower suddenly announced that he was a Republican. And his campaign manager, Henry Cabot Lodge, rounded out the pretense by declaring that "Ike" had been a lifelong Republican.[2] In plain language, both statements appear to have been calculated and deliberate falsehoods, made for the purpose of stealing the Republican nomination from Robert Taft. Lodge was at the best a sleazy politician -- as the people of Massachusetts had already fully discovered -- looking for a political victory. But Eisenhower and his more intimate

backers had much more farreaching purposes in mind.
One of them was to destroy the Republican Party as
an organizational crystallizer of the anti-socialist and
anti-Communist strength in the United States. And
their progress in that direction, since Eisenhower
usurped control of the party, has been steady, determined, and increasingly successful.[1]

During the 1952 campaign Eisenhower lied constantly and unblushingly about his beliefs and intentions. The record is all there for anybody who wants
to go back and read his speeches.[2] About the only
place he told the truth was when he assured the people of Tennessee that TVA would have his hearty blessing as President. He had even warned his "liberal"
associates at his NATO headquarters in Paris not to
be disturbed by anything he said during the campaign;
that after he was elected they would find he was just
the same Eisenhower they had known in the past.[3]
During the first year or two of his administration it
was expedient for him to tread lightly in matters of
domestic legislation. Finding specious reasons to delay the removal of the excess profits tax, making sure
that the corporate tax remained at fifty-two percent,
otherwise putting on the brakes against any real return to American principles of taxation and of government in general, and simply holding the New Deal-So-
cialist fort against the expected current attacks, was
about all he dared to do for a while.

The record will show that he did hold onto most
of the so-called New Deal gains, giving up very little
ground, even temporarily, until he and his fellow-
socialists could start marching forward again. And
he allayed suspicion as to what he really was about,
by paying constant and flag-waving lip service to
American economic and political principles. But, to
anybody who would stand off and look at developments
objectively, this lip service was proved by every turn

of events to be rankest hypocrisy. Eisenhower invariably came out with some bombastic phrase, to the effect that we must all work like dogs to stop creeping socialism, at the very time when he was most ardently supporting those men and those measures, of his own administration, which were actively helping socialism to creep upon us more insidiously and further than ever before.

By the end of 1954 his increase in <u>domestic</u> governmental spending had already started. It was half a billion dollars more than for 1953. His first extension of Social Security coverage had already been accomplished. The mouthings of his Secretary of Labor, the attempt to scuttle the Taft-Hartley Act, and the obvious behind-the-scenes support by Eisenhower himself of the top labor leaders and of some of their most ambitiously radical plans, were already so revealing that one high-ranking official of the Department of Commerce resigned in disgust. He then told an audience, of which this writer was a member, that the incredible support of the labor bosses, at the expense of management and of the American people, stemmed straight from the White House.

By 1954 Eisenhower and his advisers were constantly probing for points of weak resistance, at which they could put over some new advance of statism. During that summer they tried hard to get the Federal Government into the health insurance business, through a "reinsurance fund."[1] They had already established the Department of Health, Education and Welfare, which the Republicans and conservative Democrats had successfully kept the A.D.A. crowd from doing under either Roosevelt or Truman. They had set up that coddler of the inefficient and truster of the untrustworthy, a paternalistic monstrosity known as the Small Business Administration. In the President's economic report at the beginning of 1955 he urged that the country accept a Keynesian doctrine now known as the "compensatory budget theory." By this plan, budgets would have little or no relation to the money actually needed to run the government, but their size would be determined by the need -- in the minds of the central planners -- for either expanding or contracting the nation's economy at a given time.

Within the first two years of his administration Eisenhower accumulated a deficit of over eight billion dollars, against a deficit accumulated by Truman, in seven budgets, of only about five and one-half billion dollars, with the Korean War going full blast under Truman. (Even the thinly balanced budgets for a year or two thereafter, achieved by George Humphrey and Harry Byrd and others despite Eisenhower, used all the additional tax revenue of a growing economy, without leaving so much as a measly billion dollars for reduction of the dangerous national debt.)[1] He had already given his encouragement to a projected program of spending for public works that is making anything Roosevelt initiated look like peanuts. Within one more year, or by the end of 1955, the government investment in surplus farm products was almost six times what it had been at the end of 1952, when the Eisenhower Administration took over.[2] A similar expansion of bureaucratic reach and power, although done as quietly as possible, was taking place in every area of our national life. The continuous efforts to emasculate the legislative branches of our government, to subordinate the judiciary to political purposes, and to concentrate more power in the executive branch, had already begun. All of these developments were directly opposite to the principles of American government which Eisenhower had been elected to maintain and restore. What's more, they were exactly what he was still

claiming, in pious generalities, to be trying to prevent. And this was just the slow starting glide, the
innocent-seeming getting-under-way, of the toboggan
ride to come. We shall have just a little more to
say, about that toboggan ride we are now on, in a
later chapter.

Simultaneously with this massive ideological
movement to the left there had been a much sharper
political drive in the same direction. The ruthless
weeding out of the followers of Taft, and of conservatives in general, from positions of influence within
the Republican organization, had started the minute
Eisenhower was elected.' At the same time Eisenhower did an effective job of dragging his feet, a
very clever job but one so extensive as to provoke
widespread comment and criticism, in not giving
jobs to Republicans at all; not even jobs which, despite Civil Service regulations, were open and supposed to be available to a new administration as
favors to the party faithful. The magazine, Human
Events, charged on September 15, 1954, that no
federal administration in history had so strikingly
disregarded party loyalty in this respect.

It was not until the mid-term elections of 1954,
however, that the clear intent to sabotage the whole
Republican Party became evident to anybody who
wasn't blinded by wishful thinking. The violent opposition of the administration to McCarthy and to the
Bricker Amendment brought on, first, a lethargy in
what were normally the hardest working units of the
party machinery. This showed up especially in a
failure to raise money. And they brought on, second, a stay-at-home tendency on the part of millions
of conservatives on election day, which visibly decided many of the important outcomes. (Consider
Joseph Meek's candidacy for the U.S. Senate, in
Illinois, for one clear-cut illustration of both factors

at work.)' These results, nevertheless, could have been considered incidental and even unintentional. The striking failure of the Eisenhower Administration to "take care of the party," in patronage, could at that time have been put down to stupidity or ingenuousness. But not so the plan, directed from the White House, to purge conservative Senators and Congressmen in the forth-coming elections, which plan was well-known within high ranks of the party as early as March of 1954.[2] By September it was known that the White House had been making overtures to "liberal" GOP Senators to work for the ousting of Knowland as Republican leader in the next session. And also by September, Leonard Hall, National Chairman of the GOP, who was doing his utmost to hold the party together despite these disruptive maneuvers, was being given the brush-off by White House assistants, and having an extremely difficult time in ever seeing Eisenhower at all.[3]

Nor can there be any slightest question about the disruption of, and damage to, the party being intentional. Eisenhower not only refused to do any campaigning for, or to give any White House moral support to, the Republican Senatorial and Congressional candidates -- with the single exception of the Communist-supported Clifford Case of New Jersey. He left their campaigns permanently disorganized through his deliberate delaying tactics with regard to his expected support, which support was never forthcoming. Then, at the very last minute, he went through face-saving motions, of which a high-school politician would have been ashamed, with his fantastically childish scheme of chain telephone calls.

The notorious James Michael Curley of Boston boasts that at the end of his first mayoralty campaign he and his henchmen spent the night, after the last rally was over, waking people up at their homes all

over the city. On finally getting somebody to come
to the door at two o'clock in the morning, the Curley
henchman would identify himself as a friend of Mr.
Kenny, Curley's opponent, and then ask the newly
awakened man or woman to be sure to vote for Kenny
the next day. Naturally, every one of these people
was so angry that he actually went to the polls next
day, whether he had intended to do so or not, in order
to vote against Kenny; and he got all of the friends he
could to do likewise. Whether somebody in the Eisenhower entourage knew of this political trick, and the
chain telephone campaign was started in part because
of the reverse effect it might have on the fortune of
those candidates thus "supported," we don't know.
It seems unlikely, because Eisenhower and his advisers well knew that the "you call ten people and ask
each of them to call ten people and so on" technique
would actually peter out before it had any measurable
effect at all, except to provoke ridicule. But this was
the contribution -- the sole contribution -- which a
President of the United States offered in support of
the party which had elected him as its standard
bearer only two years before.

To anybody who observed Eisenhower's conduct
in the 1954 Congressional campaign, objectively and
without any preconceived confidence that he was a
loyal Republican, his treason to the party was unmistakable. The defeated Republican candidates, stunned
and disappointed, generally attributed his action to
political naivete. But that is a commodity in which
Eisenhower and his advisers are singularly lacking.
And if these defeated candidates, or anybody else,
had looked at what transpired against the supposition
of this paper, they would have found much to disturb
them.

It is true that a conclusion that Eisenhower was
a willing tool of the Communists, based on that cam-

paign alone, would have been utterly unjustified. It is true, of course, that there is nothing in this whole chapter which proves any such conclusion, and which cannot be explained in other ways. But it is also true that if his being a politician owned by the Communists is accepted as a working hypothesis, then <u>everything</u> in the whole chapter is completely covered, and made immediately intelligible, by that one explanation. The Communists wanted Eisenhower as President, standing out in single glory above a repudiated Republican Party. They wanted, to work with him, a Democratic Congress -- the more "leftwing" the better. And the final blocking of Joe McCarthy by that Democratic Congress was just one of the many objectives they had in mind, to be achieved by the combination.

Owen Lattimore once advised our State Department to let China fall to the Communists without having it appear that we pushed it. [1] We believe that the record reveals a similar intent on the part of Eisenhower, with regard to the Republican Party.[2] The purpose of himself and his bosses was to get the Republican Party destroyed without their appearing to have had any hand in its destruction. We shall return briefly to the story of that attempted murder, which was cleverly planned to look like suicide -- and to the "resurrection" of a substitute corpse -- in the next chapter.

CHAPTER ELEVEN

<u>The Modern Republican</u> . . . . .

One of Eisenhower's admirers has pointed out
that, from the summer of 1945 until the end of 1948,
his greatest preoccupation was with demobilization,
as rapidly as possible, of the American armed
forces. We are sure this was true. For as long as
the United States had such tremendous armed might,
ready at hand to be used, Stalin could not breathe altogether easily about his brutal conquests in eastern
Europe. He had sufficiently controlling influence
over the Truman government to be able to count not
only on its acquiescence in these barbarous betrayals
of Poland, Yugoslavia, Czechoslovakia, and other
nations, but on Washington's active help. Stalin
could not be entirely sure, however, as to what
might develop in the 1948 American elections. If a
man like Taft should become President, with any
considerable military power in Europe still at his
disposal as Commander in Chief, then some of
Stalin's plans, especially with regard to East Germany, might become impossible to carry out.
    With every American division broken up, there-
fore, with every trained pilot sent home without re-
placement, with every million dollars worth of
American war materiel deliberately blown up or
sunk, Stalin felt that much more secure against any
reversal of the fortune which was favoring him at
every step. And Dwight Eisenhower, probably more
than any other one man, brought successful efforts
to bear to make Stalin thus feel secure from a military point of view -- with respect to those conquests

which Dean Acheson, more than any other one man, was helping him to complete.

Then, once the American machine which won World War II had been destroyed, once we had gone through a period of comparative helplessness so far as ground forces and conventional weapons were concerned (roughly 1948-1952), then everything was ready for the next step. This was the rebuilding and redeployment of the armed forces of the United States in such ways as actually to help the Communists in their future plans. The whole NATO scheme was a major part of that step. We have now spent on NATO more than three hundred billion dollars, for which we have absolutely nothing to show except the ill will of our NATO allies.[1] The energy and the billions devoted to this most gigantic hoax in all history would easily have been sufficient to make the United States invulnerable against any conceivable enemy. Instead, more money than our total admitted national debt has been cunningly poured down the NATO drain. One purpose was simply to create that debt. Another was to put confusion twice confounded throughout the whole community of Western nations, in the place of any real opposition to the Communist military potential.[2]

This whole development is chiefly interesting here, however, because it has been so closely paralleled by what has happened to the American Republican Party. The first objective of Eisenhower and the Communist bosses, as we have tried to make clear in the preceding chapter, was to destroy its actual and potential strength as a bulwark against the advance of Communism. This had really been completed by the time of the 1954 Congressional elections. Once the Republican Party had been made an innocuous wreck, and Joseph McCarthy had been smeared and hounded to his death, the way was cleared for the next step. This was to rebuild a so-called Republican Party, after the image of the Harry Truman Democratic Party; so that, even though deprived of political offices and strength, it would actually and positively help the Communists in their plans to take over the United States. This Eisenhower has already gone far towards accomplishing, under the influence of the pro-Communists around him.

The story really begins in 1950, more than two years before he was elected President. In that year there was formed a tenuous organization known as Republican Advance. Among its official founders and unofficial but enthusiastic sponsors were John Davis Lodge (of Connecticut, brother of Henry Cabot Lodge), James Duff, Clifford Case, Christian A. Herter, Clifford R. Hope, John Heselton, Jacob Javits, Walter Judd, John Foster Dulles, Russell Davenport, Walter Williams -- and Richard M. Nixon. This organization was given both financial and moral support by the Americans For Democratic Action! Russell Davenport was a leader in both; and Francis Biddle, one of the most new-dealish of Roosevelt's cabinet members, publicly stated that he would like to see Republican Advance and Americans For Democratic Action become formally affiliated, since "both are working towards the same end." Biddle was quite right, too; and that end, despite the ignorance of this fact on the part of some members of both groups, was the gradual communization of the United States to make easier its absorption into a world-wide Communist empire ruled from the Kremlin.

Then, in 1952, the "Citizens For Eisenhower" group was organized. Among its founders and leading spirits were Stanley M. Rumbough, Jr. (son-in-law of Mrs. Joseph E. Davies), and Walter Williams.

It issued a policy statement much along the lines of that previously issued by Republican Advance, but somewhat less brazenly worded as to its socialist objectives. Gradually these two organizations worked together and pulled together until they became one and the same thing; and until the combination, with Eisenhower as both a front and a tool, had a grip on the metamorphosed Republican Party even stronger than the control of the ADA over the Democratic Party.[1]

In the 1956 elections the planned nationwide campaign to elect Eisenhower by a huge majority, while at the same time to defeat or weaken Republican candidates for the Senate and House, was pointedly successful. Of the four Republican Senators specifically marked for purging, only Welker of Idaho was up for re-election.[2] He was defeated, and an extreme left-wing Democrat elected in his place[3] -- mainly through the efforts of the Eisenhower following -- right at the time that Eisenhower himself was carrying Idaho by a comfortable margin. Also, since Eisenhower had announced in advance -- through Paul Hoffman's article in the October 26, 1956 issue of Collier's,[4] through Robert J. Donovan's book, Eisenhower, The Inside Story,[5] and even more by his own actions -- that he and his views were far more important than the Republican Party as a whole,[6] the very setback to orthodox Republicans, which his own left-wing gang engineered, was hailed by him as a mandate from the people to get on with the revolution.

It was from the results of this deliberate treason to the Republican Party that Eisenhower's bosses acquired the brazen nerve to have him begin openly preaching and putting into practice the more extreme and undisguised tenets of state socialism. What the Wall Street Journal[7] and other diehards of the faith complained of, as a "change in direction" on the part

of Eisenhower, stemmed from the assurance given
the Communist planners and their collaborators by
the 1956 election. The success of Republican Advance, Citizens For Eisenhower, Committee For An
Effective Congress, Americans For Democratic Action, CIO-PAC, and other organized supporters of
the revolution, in glorifying Eisenhower himself while
making monkeys out of all those who dared oppose him
and his machine of "modern" Republicans, was the
climax to four years of more widespread, intensive,
continuous, and unbelievably dirty behind-the-scenes
political activity than had ever before been dreamed
of in America. Nor is any slightest cessation of this
knifing of the conservatives, or of kicking and stamp-
ing on those already down, in sight or intended. As
of September, 1957, the Citizens For Eisenhower
treasury had a war chest of seven hundred thousand
dollars.' Although $160,000 of this money belonged
to the GOP National Committee, the Citizens For
Eisenhower boldly refused all demands that it pay
this debt. Here was the nest egg for a much greater
campaign fund for the same subversive activities in
the 1958 and 1960 elections.

Actually, there was no change-in-direction whatsoever after 1956. There was merely a quickening
of the pace, and a new boldness in revealing the direction in which Eisenhower had been moving, as fast as
he dared, all of the time. For now he and his bosses
were not having to buck a Republican Party. They
had destroyed it, and reconstructed it, so that the
new Party was one of the instruments for building
their socialist state.

We are not going to make any attempt here to
measure the extent of the socialization of our country
by the forces working through Eisenhower, either
during the four years when he had to keep a wary eye
on the conservative political support he was double-

crossing, or since he has been able to thumb his nose at the utterly routed real Republicans and move "forward" with greater ease. To do so would require a great deal of laborious research. And the degree of socialization is increasing so rapidly that the results would be out of date before the research was completed. But the reading of a few different gauges here and there, as of different dates, just as those readings happen to come to hand, is both interesting and revealing.

As of the summer of 1957 the federal government owned three million more acres of land in the continental United States than it had when Eisenhower was inaugurated. It had already owned the equivalent of the total areas of Maine, New Hampshire, Vermont, Massachusetts, Connecticut, Rhode Island, New York, New Jersey, Pennsylvania, Delaware, Maryland, Virginia, South Carolina, Florida, Alabama, Tennessee, Kentucky, West Virginia, Ohio, Indiana, Illinois, and Mississippi. (If this seems incredible, check it for yourself. Our authority is Tyre Taylor, General Counsel Of The Southern States Industrial Council.)[1] Three million acres is comparatively a very small increase in this total of slightly more than four hundred million acres, but the direction should be sharply the other way.[2]

In 1952 Eisenhower, as a candidate, told the people of Tennessee how much he favored TVA.[3] In 1953, paying lip service to conservatism as a part of his act for the whole nation when he first went in as President, he called the TVA a good example of creeping socialism. In his 1957-58 budget, he asked for 14.7 million dollars of new funds for TVA, against 5.3 million dollars the previous year. And the drive both to expand TVA (especially in its steam plants) and to create new TVA's really got under way.[4]

Despite the futile and frustrating effort of Ezra

122   The   Politician

Taft Benson to bring some common sense and honesty into the farm program of the Eisenhower Administration, the forces controlling that administration have pushed the government ever further into socialistic follies which cannot even be accounted for, except with tongue in cheek, by stupidity. Typical of the criminal contradictions and coercions engaged in by the Agriculture Department have been its actions in the field of poultry raising. During the three years ending in June, 1957, six different government agencies poured out more than thirty-five million dollars to encourage increased poultry production. But during that very same time a seventh agency spent thirty-six million dollars buying up surplus eggs, to remove them from an oversupplied market; and the Department of Agriculture was constantly warning chicken-and-egg farmers to curtail production.[1]

It is the Soil Bank scheme, however, enacted into law in 1956 and now in full operation, which makes the paternalistic controls of American farming planned by newdealers Henry Wallace or Charles Brannan look like the "reactionary" policies of McKinley -- both as to the substance of the present law and in the absurdities of its administration. A House inquiry has revealed farmers receiving government payments for crop failures on land where they were paid not to grow any crops at all; and cases where government-owned land was leased to private operators, who were given more under the Soil Bank provisions for letting it lie idle than they were paying rent to the government.[2] Such details are themselves important, because of the deliberate intention they show to bury all common sense under the inefficiencies and controls of a mushrooming bureaucracy. But they are far overshadowed by the total effect of the Soil Bank plan and other modern-

Republican policies, as best illustrated by Eisenhower's own boast -- that federal subsidies, of one kind or another, now account for one-half of our total farm income![1]

Coupled with a shouting for ever larger appropriations "for defense" have gone such treasonous inefficiency and exorbitant waste in the spending of military billions as to make a deliberate "intention to squander" beyond question. In fairness it should be stated that this trend was already strongly in evidence, as the "rebuilding" of our armed strength got under way in the latter years of the Truman Administration. But it has gone so far now that the Navy's having on hand a 72-year supply of canned chicken and a 60-year supply of ketchup doesn't even surprise anybody. When a 60-year supply of hamburgers for the whole American Army was located in one depot in New Orleans, and reported to an Assistant Secretary of Defense, it turned out that the Army had lost all track of even having such a depot, and didn't know it existed. In 1955 it was disclosed that the Defense Department was paying thirty-three million dollars per year in interest and storage charges on three billion dollars' worth of excess clothing it could never use.[2] There is no question but that the colossal wastefulness, of which these are but isolated examples, is far greater and more widespread, today. Nor is there any question in this writer's mind that it was cleverly planned that way by some of the sinister forces behind our "great military President" -- the same forces which were at work in this field before he ever became President.[3]

As the Wall Street Journal said on March 29, 1957, "the federal government has aided education since pioneer days, when certain sections of land were set aside to support schools. But only in the past two years has there been serious consideration of using federal funds for general aid to public schools." (Italics mine. RW) But the pressure for such federal aid, under Eisenhower, has been continuous, dirty, frequently based on statistics proved to have been utterly false, and is steadily increasing. [1]

A fifteen-man Study-Committee of the President's own Commission on Intergovernmental Relations submitted a 154-page report on Federal Aid To Education, which said: "We have been unable to find a single state that cannot afford to make more money available to its schools or that is economically unable to support an adequate school system." [2] Yet in the face of that report Eisenhower presented to the Eighty-fourth Congress a Federal School Aid program that would have cost two billion dollars -- for an entering wedge. [3] And Eisenhower has pushed relentlessly since then, at the back door, front door, and all side doors, to get the federal government really embarked on the subsidization, and consequent control, of public education. If ever there has been a stacked deck, it was the so-called White House Conference on Education. At that Conference its head, Neil McElroy (now Secretary of Defense) used, or condoned and permitted the use of, the strictly Communist tactic known as "group dynamics," for the purpose of extracting the desired recommendations. [4] The actual case for "Federal Aid" is so demonstrably poor that even this well-staged maneuver was not decisively successful. But no amount of facts, arguments, or opposition has kept Eisenhower from leading the socialist pack in yelping ever louder for increasing federal subsidies of every kind. And the pack is steadily gaining on its goal.

On June 30, 1954, the Federal Housing Administration was holding the bag on eighteen billion dollars' worth of mortgages on private homes, with only about a two percent reserve to protect the Amer-

ican taxpayer from having to bail it out of its liability
(something for which any banker would go to jail). I
don't know the total today, for it is about as hard to
get up-to-date figures out of our government as it is
to get hold of the internal telephone book of the United
Nations (which indirectly reveals the structure of its
administration and the character of its personnel).
But I do know that the amount has increased materially
since 1954, and was upped by more than two billion
dollars in the summer of 1957 alone. (All of this
outlay, incidentally, is entirely outside of appropriation controls, or the budget, and hence outside of the
admitted national debt.)

The expansion of Social Security under Eisenhower, both in the number of people covered and in
the amount of benefits paid, has been as rapid as
Norman Thomas or even Earl Browder could possibly have asked. By December, 1957, the monthly
payments under OASI alone were ten times what they
had been in 1947; and the modern Republicans were
boasting that they had added ten million persons to
the Social Security rolls.'

While this mushrooming process continues un-
abated, Eisenhower has now taken a vigorous personal
lead in expanding unemployment compensation to cover thirty-nine weeks of idleness instead of the usual
twenty-six, and to land the federal government with
both feet in the middle of responsibility for such payments. On May 23, 1958 the NAM News properly
asked how the federal government could lend unemployment compensation money it did not have to
states not needing it; and pointed out that Eisenhower's proposal would alone add about one and one-
half billion dollars to the federal deficit for next
year. Even the Boston Herald, about as namby-
pamby a defender of our once free-enterprise economy as Leverett Saltonstall or Irving Ives, stated

editorially on March 27, 1958:

"The proposal of the President for an extension of unemployment compensation looks an awful lot like a wave of the future. It seems to forebode the time when every person on reaching an employable age will automatically become eligible for pay for the rest of his life whether working or not." Actually this whole move is just one more tremendous step towards establishing in the United States the Marxian principle of "from every man according to his ability, to every man according to his need" -- a principle which the Communists found utterly unworkable for themselves in Russia, but are doing their utmost to impose on us as one means of breaking down our morale and sabotaging our productive strength.

In 1950 the federal government had 1,863 agencies, with 1,961,029 civilian employees. By the end of 1955 it had 2,135 agencies, with 2,362,142 civilian employees. Most of this increase, of approximately eighty thousand civilian employees per year, had taken place under Eisenhower. (It included the addition of one whole new department, Health, Education and Welfare, which the Republicans had successfully prevented time after time when it had been advanced by Oscar Ewing and Harry Truman, but which Eisenhower put over for his ILO pals in this country.) We cannot tell you what the total is today; and we would trust no statistics given us until we knew how much of the total had been by-passed and omitted, as outside of some official classification. But just in the 1957-58 budget alone there was provision for the open addition of 31,500 new federal employees, and the advertised additions are not the ones we have most to fear. For every time you hear the Hoover Commission (sincerely but gullibly) praise Eisenhower because his administration has followed

one of its suggestions and dropped five thousand
federal employees, just look around carefully. You
will find that, simultaneously, it has quietly added
ten thousand bureaucrats somewhere else. (The
State Department, just for one illustration, has been
carefully giving everybody the impression that it had
about thirteen thousand employees -- and will probably keep on doing so. But early in June of this year,
1958, Bryton Barron stated under oath that the State
Department had more than thirty-four thousand employees, and nobody dared refute him.)[1]

By the spring and summer of 1957 Eisenhower's
bosses, the 1956 elections behind them, began letting
him really play his hand. His proposed budget for
1957-58 called for <u>domestic</u> spending of 30.9 billion
dollars, against the highest figure under Truman (for
1952-53) of 19.7 billion dollars.[2] Almost all of this
increase was involved in federal "welfarism" of one
kind or another, despite the high level of prosperity
at the time, and the fact that there were seventy-two
million jobs available. As to the proposed 1958-59
budget, little needs to be said here after all of the
hubbub (almost entirely futile) which it has caused.
The important point about the present outlook and
trend is not a budget for the next fiscal year of something approaching eighty billion dollars -- plus tremendous sums authorized in ways to by-pass the budget -- but the fact that even with appropriations of
such magnitude it is almost certain that Eisenhower
and his busy helpers will <u>achieve</u> a deficit in this next
fiscal year of at least ten <u>billion</u> dollars.[3] And we say
"achieve" advisedly because we believe the largest
deficit they can manage to pile up is their definite
goal and purpose.

The hypocrisy Eisenhower has shown, with regard to every action we have outlined, has been beyond belief were it not for the complete documentation

available; and has been exceeded only by his hypocrisy in the conduct of foreign affairs, which is not our concern at this point. There is not a single step, on this road to complete socialism we have so inadequately described, at which he has not studiously proclaimed one thing while doing exactly the opposite. We have refrained from showing this monumental hypocrisy at every step by quoting his own words directly out of his own mouth, solely to keep the length of this chapter from getting out of hand. (Such quotations fill one whole folder in our files.)

But we'll at least illustrate how daring and how brazen this hypocrisy can be, by referring to it in connection with a final item which more or less epitomizes the theme of this particular chapter. On June 4, 1957, to the Conference of Governors at Williamsburg, Virginia, Eisenhower picked up and expounded the years-old slogan of the NAM, "bring government back home" -- without, of course, giving the NAM any credit. He asked the governors of the forty-eight states to join with his administration in creating a task force to start transferring, or recommending the transfer of, various functions now performed by the federal government back to the states. He almost drooled at the mouth in advocating that the flow of money to Washington and then back to the states (with the inevitable leakage and "freight charges") be stopped or greatly reduced. This was to be in order "that Government remains responsive to the pressing needs of the American people"; "that, in meeting those needs, each level of Government performs its proper function -- no more, no less"; and that "thus we will pass on to those who come after us an America free, strong, and durable."

The real purpose of this nauseating bombast was to distract attention from the fact that in the very budget, right then before Congress, Eisenhower was rec-

ommending and urging the longest steps ever taken
towards reducing the states to mere handout and administrative tools of the federal government. The
sugar-coated poison by which this atrophying of
states' responsibilities is mainly accomplished is
called "grants-in-aid." In 1930 there had been one
federal aid or handout program involving the states,
and that had to do with highways. But by June, 1957
there were already sixty-seven such programs
operating, under which the state governments, after
turning over their own proper food to Washington,
then looked to Washington to be fed. And in the one
budget about which Eisenhower was concerned when
he made his Williamsburg speech, there was provision for fourteen entirely new grants-in-aid programs, bringing the total of such elaborate participa-
tions by the federal government in strictly state affairs to eighty-one. What Eisenhower was saying,
in a speech obviously planned carefully for him, as
to both timing and content, by his Communist bosses,
was exactly the opposite of what he was using all the
prestige of his Presidential office to accomplish at
that very minute.

The total of federal grants-in-aid to the states
during the last three fiscal years under Truman
ranged between two billion two hundred million and
two billion four hundred million dollars. By the fiscal
year of 1956 under Eisenhower they had climbed to
three billion six hundred million. For fiscal '57
they were estimated at well over four billion dollars,
and for fiscal '58 they are estimated at more than
five billion.[/] That shows just how much Eisenhower
wishes to turn functions of government and corresponding taxing powers back to the states.

Contrary to some popular conceptions, in all of
this increasingly rapid movement towards an all-
powerful completely socialistic central government,

Eisenhower has led the way, fought for the legislation he wanted with every political trick at the disposal of a President, and has been successful largely through the support, not of Republicans, but of the left-wing Democrats in Congress -- and outside. Holmes Alexander pointed out, on May 13, 1957, that on every one of the fourteen roll calls on the 2.8 billion dollars for Health, Education and Welfare in the then proposed budget, the Democrats in the House voted to sustain this spending and the Republicans voted to cut it. The whole Eisenhower budget that year was emphatically supported by Harry Truman, Adlai Stevenson, and G. Mennen Williams! Leaning on the support of the leftists in the Democratic Party, in connection with the 1958-59 budget, and everything else Eisenhower proposes, has now gone ever further. Eisenhower now even believes, obviously, that before too much longer, with the full support of his modern Republicans and the Walter Reuther Democrats (almost indistinguishable) he will be able to impose price and wage controls on the American economy. For while we have been at war with Russia for thirteen years, it is only now when that fact can be used to speed up the rigid socialization of this country that Eisenhower has decided this is war, and that we are not enjoying a glorious peace for which he himself has been chiefly responsible.

In April, 1957, Norman Thomas, six-time candidate for President of the United States on the Socialist ticket, stated that "the United States is making greater strides toward socialism under Eisenhower than even under Roosevelt."[1] His gloating was well justified.[2] To Roosevelt's mind, his steering of this country toward socialism was only a piece of clever political chicanery. To Eisenhower and his bosses it is a deliberate and all-encompassing purpose. And in some expressive vernacular we can assure Mr.

The Modern Republican   131

Thomas that "he ain't seen nothing yet, " as we shall
further emphasize in a later chapter.

CHAPTER TWELVE

The President Of The United States . . . . .

    We return to the record of betrayal of America's
interests, and of help to the Communist cause, on
the international scene. It cannot be called incredible,
because the acts and events which constitute that
record have actually occurred. But there is no word,
short of incredible, that is strong enough to describe
it.
    On January 20, 1953, Dwight Eisenhower was
inaugurated as the thirty-fourth President of the
United States. He thus became, automatically and
immediately, captain and quarterback of the free-
world team, in the fight against Communism. In our
firm opinion he had been planted in that position, by
Communists, for the purpose of throwing the game.
    We are all familiar with this technique in the
sports world, despite its fortunate rarity. Contrary
to all sporting instincts and moral principles, and at
the expense of disloyalty to teammates with whom the
traitor may have worked for years, ball games have
been "thrown" for no greater incentive than a money
reward. It is extremely shortsighted to assume that
the most cunning, deceptive, and ambitious gangsters
the human race has ever known would not, with world
rulership as their goal, contrive to have their opposition double-crossed at some stage by the leader of the
opposition.
    There is nothing new about this kind of calculated
betrayal, even in statecraft. It was only eighty gen-
erations ago that fascist Sparta set out to conquer all
of the Greek world, including of necessity democratic

Athens. Sparta was a slave state, with only a very small percentage of its total population in the citizen class, and with those citizens rigidly ruled as to their every act and thought by an oligarchy at the top. In the long struggle Sparta made full use of satellite city-states, beginning with its neighbors; of pro-Spartan groups and infiltration in other city-states, including Athens itself; and of an ideological appeal which made as powerful and tricky a weapon as communism is today. The comparison of the long continued struggle between Sparta and Athens with the present one between Russia and the United States probably affords the most exhaustive and complete parallel in all human history. And when that earlier struggle culminated in the Peloponnesian War, it was the treason of Athen's own great politician-general, Alcibiades, which brought about her defeat and capture by Sparta. Alcibiades, rich, famous, honored, and powerful, was the one man most Athenians would have found it most difficult to think of as a traitor. But the final sentence in the otherwise very poor biography of Alcibiades in the Fourteenth Brittanica is well worth keeping in mind: "Superficial and opportunist to the last, he owed the successes of his meteoric career purely to personal magnetism and an almost incredible capacity for deception."

Here was famous historical precedent, though not the only one, for the Kremlin's use of Eisenhower to deceive America. But to assume that this double-crossing would not be subtle, hard to spot, even harder to prove, and disguised as a valiant fight against the Communists themselves, is sheer stupidity. Not only would they want a clever actor, possessed of great personal magnetism, in the role -- and they have one -- but they know that the convincingness of any actor in any drama depends to a large extent on the "stage props" and the supporting perform-

ance of other actors. That part of the deception
their propaganda machine and infiltrated organization were all set to supply, through long preparation,
before they ever undertook such a strategem.

So, to return to the football analogy, Eisenhower did not, in January, 1953, pick up the ball and
immediately start running down the field in the wrong
direction. This was too long a field, with the game
extending over years instead of minutes. Long before he reached his own goal posts he would have
been tackled by loyal members of his own team, and
then kicked out of the game. Instead, he has managed
repeatedly to have his team thrown for huge losses,
while always pretending to be planning the plays, giving the signals, and offering the leadership which
should result in ground gained for our side. Many of
his most showy end plays have resulted in disastrous
setbacks for our side, and many of his forward passes
have been intercepted by the enemy, with resulting
large gains for their side. His routine line-bucking
day-by-day plays merely reach the same results more
slowly. These results have been ascribed to tough
luck, or poor support, or superior enemy strength,
or anything else but the true explanation. Which is
not only that Quarterback Eisenhower has always
made sure the signals called, for any play, were
thoroughly caught and understood by the enemy before
the play was started. The truth is that, as a usual
rule, it has been the enemy who has told him which
play to call. So naturally they were prepared to meet
it. The advantage for the enemy has been added to
the further one that Eisenhower himself, and a varying number of other players on our varsity squad at
different times, have actually been trying to lose
ground, so far as they could do so without letting that
intention become apparent. It is not surprising,
therefore, that our team has been steadily pushed

back, crippled, and demoralized until, without a decisive change for the better in both line-up and management, ultimate total defeat is now just a matter of time.

To give the full story of all those plays of the past five years, to explain the extent and method of the treachery involved in each case, and to appraise the loss of ground, of players, and of morale resulting from each play, would take many books the size of this document. A proper and reasonable presentation of just this single section of the Eisenhower story would, we believe, leave no slightest doubt that he has been under the control of the Soviet management since he first got into the game. But we have to be practical, in every move undertaken to defeat this conspiracy; even in the effort to convince an inner circle of patriots of its existence and frightening progress.

So, except for an occasional flashback, we'll abandon the football metaphor as no longer useful. We'll simply string together, in this chapter and the next, a compilation of some of those acts and events, to which we have made generalized reference, with a minimum of the background and explanations which should also be given. And we believe it will make for both conciseness and clarity if we number the items.

1. It has been a well-nourished impression that the deliberate failure of our forces to fight the Korean War to win it, or even to seize victory when it was ours for the taking, is solely chargeable to the Truman Administration. This is simply not true. On March 26, 1955 General James A. Van Fleet, who had been Commander of the United States Eighth Army in Korea in the spring of 1953, all but charged treason in the White House in a speech which was given very little attention in the American newspapers. "Victory was denied us back in April and

May of 1953, when we had the enemy on the run, "
Van Fleet said. "We could have won here and we
should have won. "[1]

The period referred to, it should be noted,
was three to four months after Eisenhower had
been inaugurated. It was also just two months after the death of Stalin, on March 5, 1953. So the
disingenuous excuse of our fearing to pursue or
even to accept victory, lest it provoke the Russians
to start a third World War, was even more transparent than it had been. The United Nations resolution of October, 1950 had stated that the unification
of Korea was the object of our fighting.[2] The one
thing which, after the Inchon Landing, had kept us
from driving the Communists out of all Korea, and
achieving that unification, was the Communist influence in Washington. After Eisenhower's election
that Communist influence was even more decisive.[3]

2. After the death of Stalin, and because of
various other factors which we shall touch upon in
due course, the Communists were extremely anxious for peace in Korea. They were delighted to
have the American President make a trip to Korea,
and suggest by his actions that he was practically
suing for peace -- which Eisenhower obligingly did
-- both for appearances in Asia, and because this
made it more plausible for them to force on us the
ignominious terms and arrangements which we later
accepted.[4] But in the United States Eisenhower
claimed credit for bringing about the peace. The
truth is that the Communists were calling the turn,
and Eisenhower was merely going through the appropriate motions from this end.[5] If the Communists
had not wanted peace, for their own reasons, they
would still be fighting.[6]

3. Eisenhower's chief of our negotiation team
at Panmunjom was John Foster Dulles' law partner,

Arthur Dean. By the most favorable possible interpretation of his previous career, Dean was both a
hopeless fathead and an unconscionable liar. We'll
comment briefly on that characterization in another
connection. But even if he be given the benefit of
every doubt concerning his loyalty -- which takes a
bit of doing -- putting Arthur Dean in this spot was
like sending Little Red Riding Hood to make a deal
with the wolf. This is something nobody would do
unless he was on the side of the wolf.

One illustration of Dean's perspicacity was his
acceptance of the so-called Neutral Nations Super-
visory Commission for enforcing the terms of the
truce, supposedly in both North and South Korea. Although the Communists had insisted on the appointment of this Commission, they never did allow it to
do any inspecting in North Korea at all. But for two
years after the truce, and although Syngman Rhee
had refused to recognize its authority from the beginning, members of this Commission went all over
South Korea, and sent reports to the Communists
on everything that was taking place. For two of the
nations which Arthur Dean had accepted as neutrals
between the Communists and non-Communists, for
this Commission, were Poland and Czechoslovakia.
Eisenhower not only gave every sign of approving
this idiocy; but two years later, and fifteen months
after Dulles had promised Rhee faithfully to get this
monstrosity out of his country, Eisenhower as Commander-in-Chief allowed orders to be issued to A-
merican soldiers to shoot Koreans, if necessary, in
order to protect these Communist spies from being
bodily put out of South Korea.'

4. Our treatment of the so-called prisoners of
war was exactly on a par with Eisenhower's repatriation cruelties in Europe in 1945. These men were
not regular prisoners of war at all. They were anti-

Communists who, at the risk of their lives, had deserted from the Communist troops into which they had been impressed, and come over to us on the strength of our specific promises to let them go where they would be safe when the war was over. We had dropped leaflets to this effect month after month behind the Communist lines, and most of these prisoners had shown up clutching these leaflets in their hands, to demonstrate their faith in its promises. But we had put them in stockades. And at the time of Mr. Eisenhower's truce we physically forced them to submit to interrogations and so-called "explanations" of Communist agents, of so brutal a nature that an official American observer, writing in the Saturday Evening Post, quoted a Swiss lieutenant with the UN Repatriation Commission as saying that he had rather have seen all of these prisoners shot outright than subjected to the ordeal we made them suffer.[1]

Everything about the Panmunjom negotiations was designed to weaken our prestige, and the confidence in either our strength or our honor, in Asia, while it enhanced the prestige of the Communists, and increased the Asiatic's fear of opposing them. And nothing about the whole proceedings served this dual purpose better than our cruel breach of faith with these prisoners. But for the courage and honor of Syngman Rhee, in unilaterally releasing all he could at one swoop -- despite the castigation he knew this would bring down on his head from Washington -- Mr. Eisenhower and his pal Nehru would have had their way. Every one of these prisoners would have been turned back over to their Communist masters. And this would have been especially true of those fifteen thousand Chinese prisoners who signed a petition in blood to be sent to Formosa instead.[2]

5. From a strictly American point of view, the action with regard to our own men who had been taken

prisoner by the Reds was even worse. The final official cease-fire in Korea occurred on July 27, 1953.
But five months later, at the end of 1953, the official
figure for Allied prisoners, still unaccounted for,
was 3,421. At least ninety percent of these were A-
mericans. This said nothing of the 20,000 South Korean soldiers and 80,000 kidnapped South Korean civilians,
held in North Korea -- and still held there today --
about whom we have never even voiced a mild protest. This figure did not include any of our boys who,
according to irrefutable evidence gathered by Mark
Clark and confirmed by other American generals, had
been deliberately murdered in cold blood while defense-
less prisoners of war, and dumped into trenches dug
for that purpose.' The Defense Department, on the
basis of a report from General Ridgway, had already
given the total of captured United States military personnel who were thus murdered by the Communists as
eight thousand.²

The figure of 3,421 referred to Allied prisoners,
assumed to have been alive on July 27, 1953, who had
not been returned in accordance even with the shameful truce which we did sign, and for which Eisenhower
claimed credit as a great accomplishment. But not
only did Eisenhower do absolutely nothing about having
these boys returned, he visibly was a party to the attempt to have most of the American people forget they
existed, until the Chinese Communists themselves
later brought the issue into the limelight for blackmail purposes. Then Eisenhower further gave his
at least passive blessing to the release, at different
times and by various agents and agencies of our government, of the most confusing sets of figures, as to
how many prisoners were involved, that most of us
have ever tried to cope with in historical research.³

In the meantime these prisoners had been used,
and were still being used, by the Chinese Commu-

nists, as tremendously valuable pawns in their propaganda war, for showing the people of Asia how little the supposedly great American government was either able or willing to look out for even its own uniformed soldiers. And this was done, in our opinion, not over Eisenhower's objection, but by his willing connivance and help. There are three specific actions, as well as his conspicuous lethargy in the matter, to justify this harsh conclusion.

First, one of the most important objectives of the Chinese Communists in this blackmail procedure was accomplished in the long series of meetings, over seventy in number, between their Wang Ping-nan and our Ambassador U. Alexis Johnson. For such formal and well publicized meetings between one of our top diplomats and one of their diplomats, with us in the position of suppliant, served excellently to take the curse off our official non-recognition of Red China, so far as their prestige in Asia was concerned. All they had to do, month after month, was to run pictures or news reports of Ambassadors Johnson and Wang at their latest meeting. The Chinese Communists thus established the appearance, for those with whom they were most concerned, that as a practical matter we must and do recognize Red China as an equal, even as an equal from whom we have to beg. And these futile meetings, which served absolutely no other purpose, could have been discontinued by Eisenhower at any time, and could never even have been started without his approval.[1]

Second, the Chinese Communists promoted these prisoners from pawns in the game to major pieces, when they brought the United Nations into the act. For the United Nations has never officially admitted that there is any legitimate government at Peiping either. But its pro-Communist Secretary-General, Dag Hammarskjöld,[2] went to Peiping hat in hand, beg-

ging on behalf of the United Nations -- as superior
to the United States -- for some small crumbs of
mercy in the way of giving America back its soldiers.
And a pro-American President with any guts would
not only never have approved and encouraged such
an abject pilgrimage, glorifying Red China and accomplishing nothing else; he would never have permitted it.'

Third, Eisenhower made it perfectly clear to
the Chinese Communists that they could keep these
prisoners, and treat them any way they wished, with
impunity. For in November, 1954, when the Peiping
regime was going through its cruel farce of spy
charges against thirteen of our men whom it had
selected for that honor, Eisenhower announced that
the United States Government would take every step
"within peaceful means" to obtain their release.²
Eisenhower knew, just as well as the Communists
themselves, how little attention they would pay to
anything except force; and this was simply a method
of opening the door to all of the diplomatic maneuvers, always implying recognition on our part, in
which they wished to engage.

It is difficult for the American public to grasp
the almost incredible value of growing prestige, and
of the appearance of success, to Communist plans
and progress. You have only to read the Communist
press for a while, to see how they picture every little
flame of concession by us on a huge fire of victory
for themselves, to realize the place of prestige in
their thinking. The Communists proceed everywhere
on the theory that if you seem to be winning, if you
can make enough people think you are winning, then
you are winning. In today's propaganda-enmeshed
world, that theory has a lot of soundness, especially
in Asia. Nowhere is sheer prestige so important as
on that continent. And there are few things we have

done that have helped the Chinese Communists more to increase their prestige, with their own enslaved subjects and with all of the other people in Asia, than this: We have let them keep, mistreat, display, and make bargaining tools out of, our men in uniform, after a truce had been signed in which they specifically agreed to return those men. Eisenhower has not only been a willing party to that play at every stage, but he even found a way to let the Chinese Communists reap an additional benefit from their actions, as we shall see.

6. At the end of 1953 we consented to a meeting of the foreign ministers of the so-called Big Four, to be held in Berlin in February, 1954. That meeting could serve no possible purpose except to build up Malenkov's stature and the Kremlin's influence. It was designed to prove, on both sides of the Curtain, that Moscow had lost nothing in forcefulness or diplomatic skill by the transfer of power from Stalin to Malenkov. And Eisenhower, largely through his Secretary of State, helped in that achievement in every way he could. Mr. Dulles even set up a silly argument as to the proportion of these meetings to be held in the Russian Zone of Berlin. He said "one-fourth," with the obvious implication that the Russians were just one-fourth of the Big Four. The Communists insisted that one-half of the meetings be held in the Eastern Zone. This would of course suggest to a watching world that the Russian power and point of view were to be given equal weight in these conferences with those of the other three members combined. As soon as Mr. Dulles had insisted firmly enough and loudly enough on the "one-fourth" position, so that the whole world really was watching, he then backed down and agreed to meet one-half of the time in the Eastern Zone, exactly as the Russians had demanded.

Not only have we handed the Communists one diplo-

matic victory after another, on silver platters in a
steady parade, since Eisenhower became President.
We have constantly gone out of our way, as in the a-
bove case, to make those victories more shining,
and appear even more important than their actual
substance would have indicated. It bears repeating
that the Communists thrive on prestige and the aura
of success, far more than on what they win by tanks
or bullets. And we believe that a detailed history of
international diplomacy during the past five years
will show a clearly recognizable plan at work, on
the part of Eisenhower and our State Department, to
increase the Kremlin's prestige in every practicable
way at every feasible opportunity; and a parallel
plan at work to wear down America's own prestige
by attrition and erosion. This has been accomplished
despite the fact that a vast majority of the employees
of the State Department, who are entirely loyal citizens, have not consciously been a party to this treason
nor aware of its occurrence. In a game that is being
"thrown" by two or three players, the other players
merely have to be hoodwinked as to what is happening.

7. Accomplishing nothing else at this Berlin
Conference, we said over and over that we would
not even dream of having the so-called Big Four admit Communist China to such a conference, as the
Russians were insisting. Washington, of course,
had not officially admitted that this bunch of cutthroat
rebels, which called itself the Chinese People's Republic, even was a government. On January 27, 1954
Secretary Dulles proclaimed to the whole world that
letting them into such a meeting would be an attempt
to secure for Communist China "a position in the
councils of the world which it had not earned."[1] He
could have put the objection on far stronger grounds,
but that hardly matters. For only three weeks later,
or on February 18, Dulles again backed down com-

pletely, and the announcement was made that the meeting was to be held in Geneva.' And Eisenhower used the fact that the Chinese Communists were still holding our men as prisoners, not as a reason for forbidding the conference, but as an excuse for encouraging it, on the pretext that we might thus be able to do something about their release!

8. So, in the late spring of 1954, we accorded the Chinese Communists the de facto recognition which was so important to them, by admitting them to a Big Five conference at Geneva. And we met with these murderers, who were still brazenly mistreating our soldiers, not as belligerents to discuss their violations of the truce, but as equals in a round-table discussion of the problems of the world. It is easy to imagine what that alone did to lift the Communist standing in Asia. But far worse was yet to come. For while we gave the appearance of not knowing what the Berlin Conference was leading up to, nor what the Geneva Conference was all about, the Communists were aiming at a very definite and important goal.[2] This was, to hand their agent, Ho Chi Minh, the better half of Vietnam. Their success was unalloyed. Time Magazine summarized it very well. "At Geneva," Time said, "the Communists got precisely what they sought; a vast slice of Indochina, and a stance from which to take the rest, plus formal recognition of their military conquests and time to do their further will."[3] And even Kiplinger, the myopic purveyor of truths that come up and bite him, put much of the responsibility on Eisenhower, blaming Eisenhower for lack of either action or decisiveness at crucial stages in the negotiations.[4] In other words, Eisenhower put on a good act, in the role of being an easy mark instead of a traitor.

But he did more. Just how completely we, the United States, were a party to, and identified with, this further surrender to Communist aggression, was carefully dramatized by some Dulles-type statements, this time of Eisenhower himself. During that same spring of 1954, for instance, while Ho Chi Minh was carefully synchronizing his military action with the negotiations in Geneva, and while Eisenhower was doing absolutely nothing towards relieving the fortress of Dienbienphu, he nevertheless went out of his way to explain gravely that Indochina must not be allowed to fall to the Communists, because, if it did, neighboring nations would also topple as surely as pushed dominoes.[1] And on June 30, he proclaimed emphatically, and bombastically: "I will not be a party to any agreement that makes anybody a slave."[2] Then, only three weeks later, with his full blessing, a top official of our government sat in, without protest, at the establishment of another ignominious truce, this one making very unwilling slaves out of thirteen million Vietnamese.

CHAPTER THIRTEEN

<u>Leader Of The Free World</u>[1] . . . . .

In the spring of 1953, for reasons which we have
already summarized, the fortunes of the Kremlin
were at a low ebb. Its straining bluff was having to
be stretched much thinner than usual. And when the
East Germans rose against their Communist Masters,
on June 17, 1953, their courage could easily have
started a rollback of the Iron Curtain that would
have continued until the whole world was free. Certainly they had every reason to believe, from our own
loud professions of purpose, that they would receive
help and encouragement from the West. But this
writer has received reports, which he believes, as
follows: That in anticipation of help from us, leaders
of the revolt tipped off secret agents of our government in advance; that these agents promptly and hopefully forwarded the information to Washington; that as
a result the Russians were informed by Washington of
what was brewing twenty-four hours before the revolt
started; and that this twenty-four hours advance notice
was of extreme importance in enabling the Kremlin to
crush the uprising, before it made sufficient headway
to become a real civil war.[2] And we stood by as passively, while these anti-Communists were slaughtered
by the thousands, as we later did when the Russian
tanks with Mongolian crews rolled through the streets
of Budapest.

From that time on the outlook of the Communists
once again took a long trend of steady improvement.
By the end of 1954 the Kremlin in Moscow, and all of
the little branch kremlins elsewhere in Europe and

Asia, were busily consolidating their gains to date and implementing Moscow's new schemes of aggression and expansion. We continue for one more chapter our listing of some of the ways in which Eisenhower gave major support to those Soviet aims.

9. The biggest consolidation job the Communists have faced, since the early 1920's in Russia itself, has been in China since 1949. The psychological problem was enormous. And the core of that problem was to get the millions on the mainland to think of the Peiping regime as a permanent government, however unpopular, rather than as a gang of rebels, however temporarily successful. Eisenhower began the year 1955 by a mighty contribution to the success of that undertaking. In one of the most skillful, as well as most costly and disastrous, intentional "fumbles" of his playing career, he had our government announce, with his visibly enthusiastic approval, that what we wanted was a "cease-fire" in the Formosa Strait.[1]

To the mass of the American people, utterly unfamiliar with the situation in the Far East or the background of this statement, it suggested another lump of peace, and sounded wonderful. To the Red Chinese it was so marvelous a propaganda weapon that their radio stations could not refrain from gloating as they constantly rebroadcast and made references to this new American policy. To all of the anti-Communists on that side of the Pacific, the statement was a morale-shattering repudiation of Chiang Kai-shek's official position, and of everything our alliance with him was supposed to mean. It would take too much room here to paint in the catastrophic effects of that world-publicized repudiation, so we'll simply paraphrase one small part of the long and flaming cable which Life Magazine's correspondent, John Osborne, sent from Hong Kong. He said -- in

effect, and quite correctly -- that if the United States
had deliberately dropped a hostile bomb on Chiang Kai-
shek's government buildings in Taipei, we could not
have done more damage to the whole anti-Communist
cause throughout southeast Asia.[1]

Then, just to supply substance to back up words,
in suggesting an attitude which Peiping was gleefully
proclaiming as our gradual "abandonment" of Formosa,
our government compelled Chiang to give up the Tachen
Islands. The evacuation by the Nationalist Chinese,
of both their troops and the civilian inhabitants of the
Tachens, and the surrender to the Communists of these
islands -- right off against Chiang's original birthplace
and home -- was a bitter blow to the pride and prestige
of the Nationalist government. It was forced on the
Nationalists against their will and, despite some specious excuses given, for no sound reason except to help
the Red Chinese boasts that they would eventually take
over Formosa as well. The boasts were then further
abetted by the purposely equivocal position we adopted
with regard to the defense of Quemoy and Matsu. These
islands were actually saved by Chiang, making it clear
that his troops would fight for them to the last man, regardless of what America did. The Communist bosses
in Moscow and Washington were not willing to bring the
issue to a head, and endanger all of their steady progress through diplomacy, by a military invasion. But
Eisenhower had engineered a very serious gain for
Mao and Moscow, and loss of ground by Chiang and
ourselves, through one of the most disingenuous yet
most effective pro-Communist acts he has ever perpetrated.[2]

10. The Country now defined as Austria is about
four-fifths the size of our state of Ohio, in both area
and population. Its industrial output and total income
are, of course, much smaller fractions of their par-
allels in Ohio. But from 1945 to 1955 this little

country was looted by Russia of half a billion dollars
worth of oil and industrial equipment, plus untold
amounts of personal property and goods seized by the
Red Army. During this time, offsetting the Russian
looting so as to keep the people from starving, we
poured into Austria one billion dollars of foreign aid.
Then, on May 15, 1955, John Foster Dulles signed
the Austrian Peace Treaty.

This treaty not only accepted and validated all of
the prior Russian robbery. It decreed that Austria
must further pay Russia over the next ten years 320
million dollars worth of oil and manufactured goods.
It turned over to Russia all property in Austria belonging to Germans even though most of it had been
acquired prior to the anschluss of 1938 -- estimated
to be worth one and one-half billion dollars. For
certain of these properties to which title was thus
handed to Russia, but which physically were left in
Austria, Austria was obligated to pay 150 million
dollars. The treaty required that the United States
withdraw all troops from Austria, thus severing the
connection over the Brenner Pass between NATO
forces in Germany and those in Italy. It left Austria
ringed by the Red Armies in Czechoslovakia, Hungary,
and Yugoslavia. It specified the kind of organizations
which should be allowed to exist in Austria, requiring
that all "Fascist-type" associations -- which of course
meant any organization that was remotely anti-Communist or even honestly neutral -- had to be dissolved.
The treaty, in its wording alone, was pure Communist
drool and propaganda all the way through, which meant
that the United States became officially a party to these
expressions of the Communist viewpoint. It gave the
Russians practically a first mortgage on all of Austria,
and put the country under Russian shackles to make
sure that the Austrians worked for the next ten years,'
under Russian slave drivers with their armies right

behind them, for the benefit of the Russian economy. It opened the door almost exclusively to Communist infiltration, indoctrination, and the usual political coercion of the Austrian people during the next ten years. It put four hundred thousand refugees at the mercy of the Communists for "repatriation." And it did all of this under the guise and pretense of giving Austria its sovereignty and freedom.

This is the treaty which Eisenhower helped the Russians to ram down the throat of a helpless small country, and which he glorified to the American people as a great victory for the West -- a victory due to the generosity of the Russians and their new spirit of goodwill. In his message to the United States Senate, when he submitted this treaty, Eisenhower wrote that "the reversal in policy by the Soviet Government. . . has now permitted the conclusion of an Austrian Treaty and has won for freedom another important triumph."[1] He railroaded it through the Senate under such a demand for haste that even O'Mahoney of Wyoming spent half an hour objecting, and emphasizing the Senate's reluctance to act so hurriedly.[2] During the total debate of two and one-half hours, one Senator interviewed twenty of his colleagues. "They had either not read the Treaty or had only a glimmer of its contents."[3] Nobody had had a chance to read even the Senate Committee's report on the treaty, for the report did not come out until the next morning.[4] But Eisenhower insisted on immediate ratification, and got it, by White House pressure and by assurances from both Dulles and himself that this treaty was in the best interests of the American government.

If this incident had stood alone, it could be charged to stupidity. But it did not. The Austrian Treaty was just one part of a steadily repeated pattern of aid to the Soviet cause. If the treaty had been forced on us, Eisenhower's handling of it could be put down as the normal chicanery of a politician in self defense. This was not the case. Our government had taken the lead in bringing about this treaty, or had been a very willing party to it. We do not like epithets or harsh language in this letter, because we are aware that ordinarily they weaken our case. But there are occasions when only plain language, whether harsh or not, will adequately or accurately describe a situation or an act. The plain simple fact is that Eisenhower's assurances about the Austrian Peace Treaty, to both the Senate and the people of the United States, were brazen lies, as anybody who will take the trouble to study the background and read the treaty can see for himself. And that fact is important.[1]

11. No matter how the Kremlin line has shifted, nor what the line has been for any particular period, Eisenhower has adjusted his policies, and the policies of our government so far as he could control them, to tie in with that line. Make due allowances for the Kremlin's long and brilliant adherence to "gradualism" in its plans for world conquest; for its firmly maintained principle of never going too far too fast. Then look objectively at the whole panorama of Eisenhower's actions and his (frequently contradictory) words. You will find that in the role of Judas goat assigned him by the Kremlin, he has pranced just as nimbly and faithfully to any current theme from Moscow as have Earl Browder or Eugene Dennis.

The most striking illustration of this enthusiastic adjustment to the Moscow mood was during the build-up of sweetness and light leading to the Summit Conference, and then that conference itself.[2] Eisenhower's characterization of the Austrian Treaty as a great concession by the Soviet served the extra purpose of helping to brew the so-called "Spirit of Geneva."

The Treaty was ratified on June 17, 1955; the Summit Conference opened in Geneva on July 18, 1955. But this was only one small light turned on to show the beauty of peaceful coexistence. Another was the order issued to the F.B.I., in July, 1955, to make no arrest of Communists during the Summit Conference. Much worse was the action taken with regard to the shooting down of our Navy plane, on June 23, 1955, off the coast of Alaska. The Navy had absolute proof that this plane was deliberately attacked, well out over international waters -- which meant that our fliers were brutally murdered. The Russians not only did not deny it, but admitted it by conceding that they "might have been wrong." The truth was that they wanted the whole world to know of the incident; to see what they could do to the United States with impunity and still have the U.S. President come smilingly to meet them at Geneva. This was apparently the actual purpose of the attack. And it was entirely successful. The U.S. Navy was asked by the White House, which of course amounted to an order, to suppress the news, until after the Geneva Conference, lest it sour the "warm accord" expected there.

But the really huge light of this same kind was Eisenhower's radio-television talk to the nation on the evening of July 15, 1955. This was, as he said, "within a matter of minutes" before he was to leave on a trip "unprecedented for a President of the United States." He called it a trip "to engage in a conference with heads of other governments in order to prevent a war." Further along he stated that his purpose was "to attempt, with my colleagues, to change the spirit that has characterized the inter-governmental relationships of the world during the past ten years."[2] Here was a plug for the "peaceful coexistence" line which was then the chief burden of Moscow's ballyhoo, that could not have been surpassed by Khrushchev himself.

Later the speech moved into its tone of glowing
optimism as to what might be expected from this
conference,[1] when, as Eisenhower put it, so many
others had accomplished nothing but propaganda for
the participants. Not propaganda for the Communists, note, but with blame clearly and equally placed
on us, as trifling with men's hopes in order to engage
in propaganda. For Eisenhower well knew that his
speech would be carried in newspapers all over the
world. But this conference was to be different, he
said, because from all earlier conferences one in-
gredient had been missing. That was "an honest
intent to conciliate, to understand, to be tolerant,
to try to see the other fellow's viewpoint as well as
we see our own." Then came the real sales pitch,
expressed as one of the causes of optimism, as follows: "Another item. Did you note this morning the
speech made by Premier Bulganin in Moscow? Every
word he said was along the line that I am now speaking.
He talked of conciliation and tolerance and understanding."[2] We think it unlikely that Malenkov, or whoever
was the real boss and planner at the Kremlin, had both
of these speeches, the one by Bulganin and the one by
Eisenhower, written by the same person. For it would
be hard for one person to get exactly the right slant of
the appeal to two such different audiences. But we
haven't the least doubt that each speech was written
according to specific instructions from the Communist dictator, and that the context, timing, and beautiful meshing together of the two speeches was all
planned in the Kremlin.

As to any reality in this promise of a world
freed from the Cold War, or even as to Eisenhower's
belief in any such possibility, that is an incredible
absurdity. He knew what had just happened to our
Navy plane. At that exact time, as he and Dulles

both well knew, Moscow was giving a hundred million
dollars to Ho Chi Minh for the specific purpose of stirring up more trouble in Indochina.   At that very time,
as he also knew, the Kremlin had <u>already</u> laid the trap,
which the Summit Conference was to enable it to spring
on Adenauer.   And one of the very reasons he was proclaiming for believing in the new conciliatory attitude
of Moscow, the Austrian Peace Treaty, he knew to be
a complete fraud in that respect.   But Eisenhower
went right on playing this same Russian game when he
arrived at the conference itself; and again, with all
of America and the world listening,when he returned
home.   At Geneva he told the assembled prime ministers, and hence the world, that he was "profoundly
convinced" that the Russians desired peace, just as
he did.   He dwelt at length on the need for friendship
and "a new spirit"; and he talked so much and often
about building a "bridge" between East and West that
one cynical reporter said he sounded like a general
in the Corps of Engineers.[1] He refused to get down
to business in any negotiations at all, stuck to gen-
eralizations about making progress wherever possible, and exuded exhortations for everybody to get
together.

And get together, of course, they did.   It is doubtful if there has ever been another conference of heads
of state and top-level diplomats at which there was so
much horseplay, drinking, exuberant good fellowship
-- and photography.[2] All of which, of course, was
exactly what the Russians wanted most!   Plus, to be
sure, an agreement for the meetings immediately to
follow "at the ambassadorial level," including those
between Chou En-lai's assistant, Wang Ping-nan and
our U. Alexis Johnson, to which we have already referred.   Plus such minor dividends as a deal to stop
the launching into Soviet territory of bible-carrying
balloons, by Billy James Hargis, "in order to carry

out the Eisenhower-Bulganin plan of peaceful coexistence." But it was the hail-fellow well-met acts in front of the cameras that made the Summit Conference the most valuable single propaganda event for the Russians in which they had ever engaged.

Neither Eisenhower nor anybody else in our delegation showed any clear idea of anything that we had in mind or wanted to accomplish. So far as they were concerned the purpose of this conference was to hold a conference. It does not take hindsight to see, and even in the spring of 1955 it was perfectly clear to plenty of people besides McCarthy, that there was absolutely nothing America could gain or even hope to gain from Eisenhower's attendance at the Summit Conference. And without his attendance and blessing, obviously there would have been no conference. In our football analogy, this was a forward pass thrown directly into the arms of a waiting enemy player with a clear field in front of him. As a consequence, the Communist gains were tremendous.[1] With minor exceptions they stemmed entirely from the boisterous spirit of camaraderie which prevailed, and the indisputable evidence of that good fellowship in the thousands of pictures, that made the whole conference a field day for the camera men.[2] We'll list briefly just a few of the major benefits of the Communists.

A. Most important was the firm foundation laid at Geneva for Communist claims that the West welcomed peaceful coexistence, and gladly accepted it at face value.[3] For fear of revolt among their subjects is an ever present and stern reality in the minds and plans of the lords of the Kremlin. Here was clear proof that even Eisenhower himself, the head of the one Western nation in which the enslaved peoples put most hope of help, had abandoned any thought of "liberation," and was in fact a bosom pal of the very tyrants they wanted to overthrow. [1]

A year later one of the best intelligence services, for information from behind the Iron Curtain, printed this paragraph:

"Our correspondents in Moscow and satellite capitals report that every possible boast is being made that Britain and America have accepted the 'new Soviet regime'; therefore 'Russians' should support their own government and satellite peoples should back their Communist regimes; also, it is useless for refugees to hope for the support and sympathy of Western governments since these capitalist powers 'have made peace with communism' and therefore the refugees would do better to return home. "[2]

This campaign was designed not only to break the spirit of resistance and revolt in both Russia and the satellites, but to discourage any attempt even to escape; and to help to persuade everybody behind the Curtain that they might as well accept the inevitable, make the best of a bad situation, and fall in line as hopefully as possible with Communist planning and the Communists' claims that they can produce a better life.[3] It has been so successful that, in their resulting assurance of greater safety, the Communists have been able to allow considerably more freedom across the Iron Curtain boundaries in both directions. And by far the greatest single factor in producing that success were the pictures of Eisenhower practically with his arms around Khrushchev and Bulganin at the Summit Conference.

The campaign which was started so effectively by the great show at Geneva has produced such defeatism among Soviet bloc anti-Communists almost everywhere that there is now, according to all reliable reports, only one practicable way it could be overcome. This would be by the United States breaking off diplomatic relations with Soviet Russia and with all of the Soviet-dominated satellites. Such action, and only such action, the anti-Communists say, "will convince us that Bulganin's and Khrushchev's claims of American support are false."[1] And our readers can easily imagine just how much chance there is of that taking place so long as Eisenhower is President.

B. There has been an equal and parallel effect of the Summit Conference, and of the "spirit of Geneva" which it inaugurated, in discouraging anti-Communism among both the peoples and the governments outside of the Iron Curtain.[2] In fact, the evidence of a "rapprochement" between the United States and Russia had become so convincing by one year later that leading publications all over Western Europe were speaking openly of "the United States-Soviet Alliance." On May 16, 1956, for instance, Der Spiegel, a paper in Hamburg, ran a story about diplomatic European developments. Its headline for that story was the startling phrase: "The American-Soviet Alliance." And this was no rare exception.[3] Perhaps it should be pointed out, too, that the Eisenhower government had not allowed any grass to grow under its feet in encouraging that feeling in Europe, by various other acts since the Summit Conference. We could list several, but space and time forbid.

C. The real significance and effect of the Summit Conference was less understood in the United States than anywhere else in the world. This was because of the falsely favorable light by which this performance, like so many of Eisenhower's steps of conscienceless cooperation with the Soviet, were shaded to look like adventures in idealism. And not even McCarthy often dared to point out the true import of the acts of the President himself, because it was too difficult to make that import clear, through the fog of pseudo-idealism with which the Communists and their dupes had surrounded him. But even in America the Summit Conference did make it unmistakable that the plank in the 1952 Republican platform, calling for efforts toward liberation of the enslaved peoples,[1] had been formally and completely discarded. Eisenhower had already been referring to any attempt of Chiang Kai-shek to liberate his fellow countrymen on the mainland as "aggressive war," in which he would have no part.[2] "Aggressive war" was, of course, the exact term by which Moscow wished to have described any attempt at liberation,[3] by anybody, anywhere. The Summit Conference went further and made a much weaker form of the Truman-Acheson policy of "containment,"[4] now called "peaceful coexistence," our visibly official policy. The Republican Party and the American people meekly accepted this callous betrayal of one of the very principles that had helped most to get Eisenhower elected. So the rest of the world, duly observing, henceforth proceeded on the justified assumption that the American people, as well as the American government, had simply washed their hands of any concern about the whole tragic problem.

D.   The Summit Conference was completely responsible for forcing on Konrad Adenauer a tragic reversal of his policy and of his whole previous course. Among the many disastrous results of our folly in participating in that hypocritical carnival show, none was more harmful to the anti-Communist world than the effects in Germany.

For there Adenauer had personified the whole anti-Communist position. That position was one of solid refusal to consider the tyrants in the Kremlin as within the pale of civilized human beings, or to deal with them on any such basis. He had done a

superb job of standing firm against all of Moscow's
blandishments and pressures. Then the leaders of
our government, and of England and France, engaged in their boisterous display of friendship with
these same tyrants -- with the spotlight of world
publicity turned on the exhibition. This cut the
ground of public opinion right out from under Adenauer. "Why, " the Germans now began to ask themselves and each other, "if the American President
and other highest officials are willing to treat the
lords of the Kremlin as boon companions, and find
it advantageous to fraternize with them, does our
Chancellor persist in such obstinate, unrealistic,
and harmful aloofness?"

The Kremlin, always masterful at timing, had
invited Adenauer to Moscow just before the Summit
Conference began. When the conference was over
the invitation still stood, and was pressed anew.
Adenauer found his position more and more untenable. Finally he decided it was best to go. But only
after he and the rest of his delegation were in Moscow did the Russians put their cards on the table and
reveal the clever trap which they had prepared. Without an iota of shame they announced that, ten years
after the war was over, they still held 9,626 German
soldiers and officers as prisoners. They would send
these prisoners home if Adenauer would agree to the
exchange of ambassadors, and to the establishment
of regular diplomatic relations between the Federal
Republic and the Soviet Union.

It was a tough spot in which to place any man.
The Kremlin had been willing to go to great lengths,
and undertake long and careful planning, in order to
obtain this diplomatic recognition by West Germany.
But it was a bad mistake on the part of Adenauer to
have gone to Moscow. He had been tricked into a
nasty hole, and had to face the consequences. He did

not feel that he could go back home emptyhanded, and leave these prisoners exiled any longer at the mercy of their barbarian captors. He agreed to the Russian terms.

It was a far more important concession than might at first appear. The deal not only seriously weakened Adenauer's prestige and position, in his relations with the Kremlin. It practically forced him into a situation which has made his former un-yielding stand against "negotiations" and appease-ment far more difficult to maintain. And it put the Kremlin, which thus became the only government to have ambassadors in both West Germany and East Germany, in the center of the stage for its constant juggling with the most explosive issue in all Europe -- the unification of Germany.[1]

The renewal of publicity about the great personal friendship between Eisenhower and Zhukov, the dis-couragement by Eisenhower of any hope on the part of Eden and Faure of getting any concessions whatso-ever out of the Russians, and many other aspects of the Summit Conference deserve comment, but there is much other ground still to cover. So let's leave the Geneva carnival with one final remark concerning its bearing on our main theme. It simply was not possible for Eisenhower to agree to, and then attend, the Summit Conference, and put on the exhibition which he did of fraternizing with the Kremlin tyrants -- for them to publicize all over the world -- without being fully aware of the harm it would do the anti-Communist cause everywhere, and of the tremendous help it would be to the Kremlin in all of the ways we have mentioned. And he did everything he possibly could, in the execution of his assignment, to increase that harm on one side and help on the other.[2]

Any adequate effort, however, to continue this enumeration of Eisenhower's actions undermining the anti-Communist cause since the 1955 Summit Conference, would be almost endless. So at this point we'll stop separating such items by giving them numbers, and simply summarize the developments in this area as briefly as we can.

The real key to both the purpose and the results of American foreign policy, as conducted by Eisenhower and his State Department over the past few years, is the extent to which they have contrived to make the United States hated, laughed at, and held in contempt -- in Europe, in the Middle East, in the Far East, in Africa, in South America, everywhere. The evidence of this feeling arises unmistakable on every hand; from the statement of Prime Minister Karamanlis of Greece just before the elections in that country in 1956, that no Greek politician could say a good word for America without the risk of being hurt politically,[1] to the treatment accorded Vice-President Nixon and his wife on their tour of South America in the spring of 1958.

Ventriloquist Edgar Bergen once asked his created character, Mortimer Snerd, a very frank question. "Mortimer," Edgar said, "how can you be so dumb?" "Well," drawled Mortimer, "I'll tell you. It ain't easy!" And we are sure that John Foster Dulles, who seems to have been assigned the Mortimer Snerd role in our international puppet show, feels the same way.[2] To stage-manage an unending series of betrayals of America's allies and of our country's best interests, and to have those betrayals accepted one after another as mere stupidities, obviously has not been easy. So much explanation and background would be required, to put each of these dozens of "blunders" of the Eisenhower-Dulles act in its true light, that we shall attempt nothing more here than an indication of a few spots where the light might profitably be focused.[3]

Since the claim has been so loudly and adventitiously shouted by the liberals, that the resentment of the United States and its Vice-President in South America was due to our parsimoniousness in handouts to South American countries, the reader might consider the following exhibit. Greece is, both in area and population, about twenty-five percent larger than the island of Cuba. Into this non-industrialized, poverty-stricken small country we had poured approximately one billion four hundred million dollars in foreign aid up to June 30, 1957.' And Greece, at the time James Forrestal died in 1949, had become a solidly dependable member of the anti-Communist bloc. Yet in the last six years Eisenhower and Dulles have succeeded, by dozens of barely perceptible steps, in finally and almost completely reversing the orientation of Greece, until today that last non-Communist country of the Balkans is ripe for the Communist plucking whenever the Kremlin thinks the proper time has come. It wasn't easy, even with so much money to spend in the wrong ways and to put in the hands of the wrong people, to alienate so many good friends of America, and to weaken the anti-Communist leaders among the Greeks themselves, to so disastrous an extent. But the results are plainly visible; and even the cunning steps by which these results were accomplished can be discerned and analyzed too, by anybody who has the time for the study required.

Much of the clever "fumbling" by which the United States has helped Communist aims with regard to other countries, however, has been easier to identify. In general it follows the same formula which we have tried to make readily recognizable to our readers. This consists of loudly proclaiming a United States policy or position, in "unalterable" support of some anti-Communist stand favorable to one of our allies, until the whole world, including the ally in question,

knows that this is the official and announced policy
of the American government; and of then sharply
backing down from and abandoning that policy, so as
to give disastrous and even decisive importance to
our reversal. And recent history is simply loaded
with illustrations of this formula at work.

During the winter of 1957-58, for instance, the
Eisenhower Administration loudly and emphatically
insisted -- especially to the chancelleries of Europe
-- that no new summit conference or other United
States talks with the Soviet Union were admissible
without an advance understanding of some kind concerning progress towards German reunification. This
was the sine qua non of any conference at all. Yet on
March 12, 1958, in Manila (so that the statement
would get tremendous play in the world press and
practically none in the American papers), Dulles announced that the United States would no longer insist
on the reunification of Germany even being put on the
agenda of the expected summit conference.' This
statement cut the ground right out from under Adenauer, who didn't even try to hide that he felt he had
been betrayed. It stimulated a tremendous resurgence
of the spirit of "neutralism" towards Russia, in Germany; and was one of the clear markers of the beginning of the fall of all Western Europe, into a
state of "neutralist" dependence on the "good will"
of Russia for such autonomous existence as its nations will still enjoy.

The same kind of doublecrossing of France and
England, throughout the whole Suez episode, had already prepared the way for our repudiation of Adenauer to be even more impressive to all of Europe.
Dulles, with an overbearing arrogance towards allies
which was itself calculated to weaken anti-Communist
unity, had insisted that France and England leave the
whole trouble with Nasser in his hands, for him to

have settled through full American support of a Canal
Users' Association.   When it finally became plain
that he had no slightest intention of living up to his
promises, England and France embarked on their ill-
fated invasion.   It is almost certain that this step was
encouraged, and sold to the British and French governments, by Communist influences within those governments, because the Communists knew they could
use Dulles and Eisenhower and the power of the American government to convert the invasion into a tragic
fiasco.[1] The net results were: (1) to make England
and France look like silly third-rate powers, in the
whole Middle East, where their influence had been
so strong for so long;[2] (2) to glorify Nasser, in the
eyes of the whole Arab world, as the native hero who
had reduced the lions to slinking cats;[3] (3) to create in
both England and France a hatred and distrust of the
American government, especially among the real anti-
Communists in those countries, which later actions
would make even more fatal to any defense of Western Europe.[4]

Not only, as is now well known, were all of these
steps and results planned in advance, at least as far
back as the Twentieth Congress of the Communist
Party in Moscow, in February of 1956; not only were
the results successfully achieved; but Dulles and
Eisenhower carried out their part in the Kremlin-
conducted drama with consummate skill.   Eisenhower
even added to the bitterness of the most patriotic
British through many personal touches.   He ordered
the British and French to pull their armed forces
back out of the Suez territory, as if they had been
tributary powers;[5] and he rubbed salt in the wound by
using "cavalry barracks language" in confirming these
orders personally to Anthony Eden over the transatlan-
tic telephone.[6] When Eden pleaded to be allowed to
come to Washington to state the British case, Eisen-

hower at first agreed; and then publicly humiliated
Eden further by cancelling the consent before the
British Prime Minister could catch a plane.' As to
Dulles, anybody who thinks we are hard on this
Kremlin-serving hypocrite ought to read the British
newspapers of November and December, 1956. They
were not excoriating him because of disagreements
in points of view, but because of deliberate lies he
had told members of the British government, on
which they had depended as truth.[2] The London magazine, Punch, later summed up their whole attitude in
a long and bitter article which ended with the "discov-
ery" that Mr. Dulles was a schizophrenic. "There
exists within him," it said, "a vigorous majority in
favor of guaranteeing to tell the approximate truth
between 11 A. M. and 3 P. M. on Sundays, Washington
time. By other bits of him it is still felt that . . .
such a concession would undermine the entire basis
of Mr. Dulles' position. "[3]

It is with regard to our hand in the French troubles
in North Africa, however, that we find both the clear-
est and the most recent example of our government's
most skillful, determined, and brazen service to the
Soviet. (1) We have given all kinds of encouragement
and support to the Communist-controlled F. L. N.
(Front de la Liberation Nationale), which is committing the atrocities and stirring up all the trouble in
Algeria. (2) We have pretended to be trying to help
the French settle these troubles, even to having Mr.
Dulles' right-hand man, Mr. Murphy, insist on telling the French just what to do[4]-- and what they must
do, to retain American "support" -- in Tunisia and
Algeria. (3) Eisenhower personally caused the fall
of the Gaillard government, by personally demanding
its acceptance of policies of appeasement (which of
course only made matters worse, as they were intended to do), and by making our intervention so bla-

tant as to precipitate a crisis in the French parliament.' (4) And the net results are that Mr. Murphy in particular and the American government in general are associated with miserable failures, hated by the most patriotic and anti-Communist Frenchmen for having really caused those failures, and have so messed up the whole situation that there is little chance even de Gaulle can keep it from getting worse. The cards in all of North Africa are completely stacked on behalf of the Communists, and an objective study of the developments there over the past three years will show conclusively that Eisenhower (and Dulles) have played a leading part in stacking those cards. The brutal pro-Communist pressure exerted on Gaillard's government, and the current double-crossing obstructions to any prospect de Gaulle might otherwise have of working out a sound anti-Communist solution to the Algerian affair, merely climax a long and successful series of Eisenhower's interferences in North Africa on behalf of Soviet aims.[2]

And let us repeat, in final conclusion to this chapter, that the three or four "shows" to which we have turned our dial are simply illustrations of what is going on all over the world. On the other side of the planet from Paris our government, after turning a very cold shoulder to the rebels in Sumatra against the Communist dictator, Sukarno -- whose power in Indonesia we largely created by driving the Dutch out for him -- our government has been openly selling arms to Sukarno. These he can add to those being received from Russia and Red China, to put down the anti-Communist revolt. And just to make our pro-Communist position clear, our ambassador recently gave a dinner for Sukarno. All Southeast Asia, horrified, views this discouragement of opposition to a Communist dictator now consolidating his position, and this deliberate demonstration of high regard for the dictator himself, as a further huge step of betrayal to the anti-Communist cause. Even the Nationalist Chinese press in Formosa has stated caustically that there is no misunderstanding after these incidents as to where the sympathies of the American government really lie.

They are right. There should no longer be any misunderstanding of where Eisenhower's sympathies lie, by anybody -- even by good Americans who were foolish enough to support him for the Republican nomination in 1952.'

CHAPTER FOURTEEN

The One-Worlder[1] . . . . .

It was at least forty years ago when this writer first thrilled to Tennyson's lines:

> "Till the war-drum throbbed no longer,
> and the battle flags were furled
> In the Parliament of man, the Federa-
> tion of the world.
>
> "There the common sense of most
> shall hold a fretful realm in awe,
> And the kindly earth shall slumber
> lapped in universal law. "

The poet paints a picture which every human being of good will and good conscience would like to see become a reality. The desire for permanent and world-wide peace, maintained by a just and honorable world-wide government, has become increasingly stronger during the recent centuries while the world itself was growing increasingly smaller. A federation of all nations, strong enough to make warfare between different nations as infrequent and unlikely as warfare between the American states, has become a great ideal.[2] And the Communists have been just as quick to prostitute this ardent longing to the service of their conspiratorial purposes as they have every other humanitarian sentiment or noble dream of modern man.

The Communists want a world government, all right. And they are willing to work towards it through every form of "federation" (like the United Nations)[3] and "parliament" (like the International Labor Organization) that can be devised. But the "one world" government they want is a monolithic tyranny, ruled from Moscow through administrative satrapies -- as they have made overwhelmingly clear, by both words and actions, for over thirty years. The "federations" and "parliaments" which they have been so instrumental in setting up, or go to such lengths to control, are regarded by the Communists as ultimately nothing more than additional agencies and forces, manipulated by them to hasten the surrender of national sovereignties to the Kremlin's international police state. And among the silliest of all the self-deceptions of the Western nations is that they can play along with this game, hoping against cold reality that these organizations will somehow prove to be, or can be converted into, something other than Soviet pawns.

If a group of honest men were to play poker, at which their lives were the stakes, with a group of known crooks determined to snuff out those lives, and were to concede to the crooks the privilege of cheating at every turn, while the honest men bound themselves by ethical standards and the rules of the game, the stupidity of the action would be beyond all understanding And that, of course, is what appears to be happening in the United Nations, UNESCO, ILO, WHO, and in all the rest of the international monstrosities. It is what appears to be happening in the countless moves by the United States, unilaterally, to gamble our substance and sovereignty against unsigned checks on a nonexistent bank account of future good will. But if a sufficient percentage of those supposedly "honest men," and the most influential among them at that, are really stooges of the crooks, using their influence and leadership to make participation in the game by themselves and their friends seem plausible, then the mystery disappears and only the foul odor of

treachery remains. And it is only when that interpretation is placed on the efforts of the Eisenhower
Administration to promote one-worldism that such
efforts make any sense at all.

This is not the time or place to point out the continuing flavor given the United Nations by Alger Hiss,[1]
ILO by Albert Thomas,[2] WHO by Brock Chisholm,[3] or
to document the effective domination of all such organizations by the Communists and their sympathizers
today. But we must take a few pages to highlight a
fraction of Eisenhower's most important contributions
towards the creation of a united socialist world -- in
the exact sense and for the exact purpose desired by
Moscow. And among the greatest of these contributions has been his determined drive for vastly expanded, permanent, American "foreign aid," to be
slanted more and more directly in favor of Soviet
satellites and dependencies.

Just to analyze our foreign-aid program adequately would take many volumes.[4] One of its intrin-
sic and vital long-range purposes, a socialist egalitarianism between nations, has seldom even been discussed in the American press. We are all aware that
socialism intends and implies a leveling process, as
to both property and income, between the individuals
within any national boundaries -- except for the special and tremendous prerogatives of the police-state
bureaucrats who run the show. Most of us realize
that the progressive and confiscatory income tax,
for instance, is one of the many Marxian tools designed to see that ultimately no man, no matter how
much more industrious and ambitious than his neighbors, has more of anything than do those neighbors.[5]
But we are inclined to forget that what the Communists demand is <u>international</u> socialism, under which
no nation (or area, or province of Moscow, which had
once been a nation) would have more of anything than

any other nation.

As the Communists get ever nearer to their goal of total world conquest, they are visibly putting more drive behind the subsidiary goal of egalitarianism between nations.' For just as a socialist economy within national boundaries, that denies individuals the privilege of bettering their own lots except through government rewards, makes it much easier to rule any people by a bureaucratic tyranny, so will a socialized equality between nations and races make control by the gangsters at the top far easier to maintain. In theory, this means bringing the poorer and less industrialized nations up to a certain level of property, production, and prosperity. In fact, of course, and as all human experience has shown, it means bringing the richer nations down to one level of poverty for all. But the Kremlin gangsters are not especially concerned about that. It is the leveling of the differences which is vital to their plans. The constant pouring of American billions into the poorer countries, if the stream can be made large enough, is intended as a psychological even more than a substantive step, of huge import in the direction of ultimate equalization.

But there are many intermediate purposes which American foreign aid is intended to accomplish for the Soviets in the meantime. The key to the shorter-range purport of the whole program lies in the supposedly subtle, arrogantly esoteric, arguments by which it is supported. Americans by the millions say to each other such things as: "I can't follow the reasoning in giving planes to Tito"; or, "How on earth our paying a Negro jazz artist like Dizzy Gillespie more salary than we pay the President of the United States, to take his band to Syria and Yugoslavia, does any good in the fight against Communism, is beyond me"; or "With as much wastefulness in the program as has been exposed, it is hard to see whether the gains are worth the cost." And the summarization of all these comments would be: "Of course I'm not on the inside of all the diplomatic bargaining and purposes involved, but from where I sit most of this foreign-aid business doesn't make sense to me." If these Americans could ever simply turn their minds around, however, and look clearly, plainly, objectively, at American foreign-aid as a program deliberately designed, continued, and constantly expanded, for the specific and conscious purpose of helping the world-wide Communist conspiracy, the whole program and everything about it would immediately make very solid sense indeed.

The fact that the very conception of American post-war foreign aid was inspired during the war by Earl Browder and other Communists would not be too difficult to prove. Some of the most important seeds are to be found in Browder's book, Teheran, published in 1944.[1] The part that Communists like Alger Hiss, Harry Dexter White, and Frank Coe played, in getting us embarked on this program, is already fairly well known.[2] The way in which, from the very beginning with UNRRA, so much of our foreign-aid money was brazenly steered, to direct help of the Communists,[3] by men like Dean Acheson and Herbert Lehman, is all a part of the record.[4] The fact that the middle part of this program was identified with the name of George Marshall is significant; it was a tip-off to the top-flight Communists everywhere in the world as to what was afoot.[5] And today, although a great number of both visionaries and practical politicians have been beguiled into supporting foreign aid, the strongest, most vociferous, and most persistent pressure for its continuance and increase is coming from the extreme Left -- with Eisenhower leading the pack. I have never seen one word against our foreign aid program in either The Daily Worker or the National

Guardian; nor, for that matter, in the two great news-papers whose editorial points of view follow those of The Daily Worker most closely, the New York Times and the Washington Post.

The truth is that, as the Communists well realize, even though the American people do not, there are five major forms of harm to ourselves in this scatter-ing of our billions. First is the sheer expense.[1] On top of all the other wild extravagancies of our govern-ment, this program is doing its part towards taking us, with increasing rapidity, into that cruel and crush-ing form of bankruptcy which results from wiping out the value of our currency.

Second is the effect of our incredible wasteful-ness, in making us the laughing stock of the world, subject to the ridicule of the very people whose friend-ship we are supposed to be winning.[2] When just one out of our ten foreign-aid offices in the small country of Iran, with fifty-five employees including stenographers, has fifty-three official automobiles and forty-one native chauffeurs, we are not making friends out of the Irani-ans but overbearing fools out of ourselves. Yet this case is a sample par for the course.[3]

Third is the tremendous help we give to socialist governments. They use our millions to cover up the results of their economic folly, to keep themselves in power, to increase the socialization of their respective countries, to fasten their bureaucratic grip more tightly over the daily lives of their citizens, and to create a climate ever more favorable for the poisonous vines of Communism.[4]

Fourth is the extent, already mentioned, to which our foreign-aid money is channelled into direct subsidization of the Communists.[5] The stock illustra-tion is the more than a billion dollars we have given Tito.[6] But from the UNRRA funds which we handed Madame Sun Yat-sen and the Lublin Gang a dozen years ago, to the ninety million dollars we gave Gomulka in 1957, to Eisenhower's present demands for enormous regular gifts to all Communist satellite governments, the record of this idiocy is continuous. Only this year for the first time, however, have the supporters of foreign aid conceded that one of its purposes is to bribe the satellite governments not to revolt against the Kremlin.[1] In other words, the Eisenhower Administration is now shamelessly -- if not yet quite openly -- using American taxpayers' millions as one of the effective weapons of the Kremlin for keeping its puppets happily rewarded and under easier control. And the American people have been so brainwashed and befuddled, by the pro-Communist propaganda issued right by our government, that they do not recognize this course as either idiocy or treason.

The fifth harmful effect of our checkbook invasions, however, is even more important and much more fundamental. With our dollars, and our locust swarms of agents to spend those dollars, we act exactly like foreign conquerors everywhere today. Tens of thousands of our "occupying" forces, both civilian and military, lord it over the natives of the countries where they are stationed; and, as the very reason for their existence, go about telling the poor benighted natives what to do and how to lead their lives. (In 1955, for instance, we spent nine hundred thousand dollars in Turkey, organizing and setting up labor unions, so that the Turks would have better industrial relations!)[2]

The Kremlin-controlled Communist conspiracy is actually the most ambitiously imperialistic force that has ever come into existence on our planet. But a key maxim of Soviet policy is: Always accuse your opponent, first and loudly, of those very crimes which you yourself are committing. And since they realized they could never make us appear to anybody, for very long, as imperialists by the sword, they have steered us into becoming imperialists by the dollar. It is very easy for Russian agents and Russian propaganda to point to us as imperialists; to convince the natives everywhere that we are imperialists; and to get us hated and feared accordingly. For we have actually become imperialists, meddling in the lives, the economics, the politics, and the foreign policies, of almost every remaining country in the free world; and doing so as extensively, as obnoxiously, and almost as damagingly, as ever did a Caesar who had taken over such countries by the sword.

We even help the Communists' propaganda by giving them names on which to hang their charges. By adding a "Truman Doctrine" for Greece and Turkey and then an "Eisenhower Doctrine" for the Middle East to a once highly respected but now easily distorted Monroe Doctrine, we have appeared to intend ultimately to promulgate American "doctrines" which would definitely establish us as imperialist "protectors" of countries all over the world. Nothing could serve the Russian propaganda and psychological needs today better than the announcement, some eighteen months ago, of the so-called Eisenhower Doctrine.[1] It led immediately to newspaper headlines all over the world such as: AMERICA SEEKS TO DOMINATE THE MIDDLE EAST. In our opinion, it was deliberately planned and intended for that purpose. The Eisenhower Doctrine epitomizes not only the folly of our course, but the clever treason which determines it.[2]

Whereas Harry Truman was usually too dumb to realize the specific purposes for which his name and his authority were being used, however, Eisenhower has personally played too clever a hand in the Communist game, too long, in too many different sets of circumstances, for any such assumption even to be reasonable. Especially has he had his hand, consciously, continuously, and emphatically in the promotion of foreign-aid spending. In 1957 he threatened to call a special session of Congress if the foreign-aid appropriation he had currently demanded was cut by just the 13% which was indicated.[1] Although a very suspicious secrecy about what was to be done with the money made it difficult for even Congress to learn any of the details, it was possible to find out that this proposed new appropriation included fifteen million dollars of economic aid for Tito plus "some" military assistance, and many other grants of equally doubtful character.[2] Yet Eisenhower insisted that reducing this foreign-aid appropriation would put the interests of the United States in real jeopardy, and strongly implied that the reduction by even a few millions would be a life-and-death matter for our national security.[3] As the Wall Street Journal said on August 16, 1957, it was almost impossible to find the President's statements about foreign-aid even credible. We insist that they were quite credible and quite understandable, once you realized on which side of the fence he was working.

The repetition of that same drive for huge foreign-aid appropriations in 1958, with the drive again spearheaded by Eisenhower himself, is raging right while these pages are being revised. Its character can be judged from the fact that on May 22 the chairman of a House Appropriations Subcommittee angrily called a halt to the subcommittee hearings on foreign aid because of the "unprecedented pressure campaign" being exerted on members of Congress by the White House.[4]

The U. S. News and World Report can hardly be called biased in this connection, for every page of every issue breathes its childishly unquestioning admiration for Eisenhower. But on August 23, 1957 that magazine said: "President Eisenhower's unusual interest in foreign aid, leading to White House pressure of a kind not exerted for any other legislation, is reported by some Republican leaders in Congress to be a mystery to them." In view of the provable tremendous harm which our foreign-aid program is doing to the United States and the whole anti-Communist cause, such members of Congress (in both the 1957 and 1958 sessions) might well have regarded Eisenhower's eternal pressure for its expansion, and for its frozen projection into future years, as a mystery indeed. But once you accept the perfectly simple fact of Eisenhower's real intentions, that mystery also completely evaporates.

Next to American foreign aid, in promoting one-worldism, Communist style, has now emerged that manifestation of peaceful coexistence known as the "cultural exchanges." And it was Eisenhower's participation in, and actions during, the first Summit Conference, which made this program even possible. For not until escape to America, or defection to the West of any kind, had been made to appear hopeless, through the ostentatious friendship of the American President with the Kremlin brass, did the Soviet Union dare start letting its citizens out of the prison of its borders, to come to the United States in huge and unending delegations of every kind. Then, when the flood got under way, these delegations received the smiling blessing and studied encouragement of Eisenhower at every turn.

The real purposes of these visits are too obvious, and the real composition of the delegations is now too well known, for us to belabor either point here. Instead, we'll let one illustration simply project the whole argument. After the Russian crew of "housing authorities" had visited many other cities, it came to Boston. A refugee friend of ours got an article into a local newspaper,[1] revealing that one member of this gang, named Manikov, really was quite an authority on housing: He was second in command of all the slave labor camps in Russia. Mr. Manikov, learning of this article and of the warm welcome awaiting him here from the Polish and Lithuanian refugees, dropped out of his delegation before arrival, to join it somewhere later, and never did show in Boston. Actually he was typical of the kind of trusted hard-core Communist agents which the Kremlin has been sending on these excursions, even though most of them have escaped the similar embarrassment of being specifically recognized and identified.

One little-noticed effect, out of the many harmful results of letting all these delegations of Communist agents and spies roam the whole country, has been the terrific dampening of the anti-Communist ardor of various refugee groups and racial minorities from the satellite nations. For on seeing how cordially such visiting Communists were treated by our government and -- following government example and urging -- by our chambers of commerce and other business organizations, the Americans of Polish or Latvian or Lithuanian origin, and from many other ancestral sources, have begun simply to drop their active anti-Communism in despair. With the United States itself so visibly pulled into the one-world orbit of Communist spying, influence, and governmental reach, they have decided it is folly for themselves -- and even greater folly for their relatives in their respective homelands -- to fight against this spreading monstrous tyranny any longer.[2]

But all of that is, in a way, only a plus on the real returns. A royal welcome is given to the "Christian ministers" from Soviet Russia, at the

Council of Churches meeting in Evanston.[1] The
Moiseyev Russian folk dancers put on their show
in Washington's Capitol Theatre (and many others
throughout the country). "Everybody" attends,
including of course John Foster Dulles and his
brother Allen. During the intermission our Secretary of State visits backstage and chitchats with the
troupe on how much happiness they are spreading
among the American people.[2] As Fulton Lewis says,
it was all very chummy, and not made any less so
by the fact that it was the very same evening when
the Kremlin announced it had executed Nagy.[3] Nor
by the fact that the American guest conductor of this
dance group pleaded the Fifth Amendment rather than
tell whether he was a Communist.[4]

A half-starving pianist from Texas, named Van
Cliburn, is invited to play in Moscow, is awarded a
prize, and returns to be given a ticker tape parade
and welcome down Broadway -- to be sure the Russian generosity, appreciation of talent, sense of
fair play, and ability to make any American artist
famous, are all given the widest possible publicity.
Then Tovarish Van Cliburn gives a concert, in
Washington's Constitution Hall of course, during
which the "distinguished" audience stands at rapt
attention while the Communist Internationale is
played.[5] (And how many members of Mr. Eisenhower's
administration thrilled to this foreshadowing of the
coming dawn when -- in the words of that anthem --
the Communist Internationale shall be the human
race -- nobody will ever know.)

Mr. Cyrus Eaton lavishly entertains Soviet
scientists at his Pugwash estate, and Soviet diplomats at his home in Cleveland.[6] And Eisenhower himself is so anxious to show his high regard for every
loyal Communist that he makes strenuous efforts to
have representatives of the Kadar puppet government

of Hungary attend his second inauguration, almost
before the dead bodies of the Hungarian fighters for
freedom, killed by these Kadar Communists, have
been picked up from the streets of Budapest.

From literally ten thousand such evidences that
Communists are just the same as everybody else,
only more so, most of the native anti-Communist
American patriots are learning -- or we are supposed
to be learning -- the hopelessness of our cause. The
spreading "good will" of one-worldism, which not
only includes the Communist murderers but which
they visibly dominate, gains momentum from these
acts of "neighborliness" and "togetherness" every
day. And the support of Eisenhower personally,
through both words and example, for a steady increase in such visits and "cultural exchanges" and
"international courtesies" of every sort -- that also
is exerted almost daily, with all the power of the
Presidency behind his maneuvers.

The question of GATT and American tariffs is
too long, complicated, and bitterly controversial,
for us to go into it here. But there is one specific
angle of this question which is directly pertinent and
important to our present discussion. It is being more
and more admitted, and will probably soon be boasted,
by the tariff-destroyers led by Eisenhower, that one
of their goals is the complete wiping out of national
boundaries in all matters of economics. Now if we
really could have completely free trade, which was
not a one-way street, between all the peoples of the
world, there are few Americans who would object.
But of course what the Eisenhower pack is seeking is
something entirely different. They want the tariff
barriers removed, so that any and every country in
the world can dump their products in the United States;
while the currency licenses and controls of foreign
governments, and numberless other restrictions in-

cluding outright prohibition, make American exports to those same countries -- even of goods or in areas where our technological advantages would enable us to compete with the immensely cheaper foreign labor -- utterly impossible.' And don't let any sophomoric or dishonest "liberal" economist tell you foreign interests cannot sell goods in America for American dollars without also eventually buying the equivalent in some form of American goods, for otherwise they would have nothing to do with the money. There are at least two things to do with it, which the Communist governments in particular, now dumping shoes or crockery in America, or acquiring American dollars through other "exchanges" throughout the world, find extremely attractive. One is to convert it into gold (which they are allowed to do, though American citizens are not), and withdraw that gold to spend anywhere in the world. The other is to invest those American dollars in acquiring control or voice in American industrial enterprises. They have already followed both procedures to the tune of billions of dollars.[2]

Here again we see the great "leveling" principle at work. But we see something else at work, too, which is of even more interest at the minute. That is the psychological conditioning of the American people to the idea of weakening, and eventually eliminating, national boundaries. When the United States becomes, in economics, just an area, not a nation, it will have been taken a long way towards becoming politically just an administrative area in a Communist-socialist one-world. And Eisenhower is taking us in that direction, through that means, just as fast as he can possibly contrive the proper steps -- or his Communist bosses can contrive them for him.

We have already touched on NATO, so far as it affects, and defeats, any honest American defense against Communist military power. But again there is another and different point which needs to be spotlighted here. Briefly, the three chief features of the North Atlantic Treaty Organization are: (1) its incredible cost; (2) its acceptance by the American people as a substitute for a real defense program;[1] and (3) its subordination of American armed forces and American decisions to the control of an international organization.[2] No. 3 only is our present concern.

Comparatively few Americans have even yet waked up to the fact that the statute binding us into NATO -- which Senator Taft fought so vigorously and so vainly -- was in several respects a direct repeal of our Declaration of Independence.[3] Our military secrets, our defense plans, and the disposition of our forces, have been put into the hands of a "Standing Group, " composed of officers of three countries, France, Britain, and the United States, with equal representation. And Walter Lippmann -- who does know what goes on and is very happy about it -- has gloated that "the deciding reason for limiting the war to the Korean peninsula, for not expanding it into China, was that American strategic air power is not only committed to the defense of the Atlantic Community but that <u>it cannot as a matter of technical procedure be employed except with the full and willing collaboration of Great Britain and France.</u>" We have italicized the important part of this boast. The United Nations can only argue, recommend, and bring public and private pressures to bear, as to what we do with our planes, ships, and troops. The "Standing Group" of NATO can <u>command.</u>

Most Americans have forgotten that NATO was dreamed up and initiated by Dean Acheson, and fathered by Harry Truman under Acheson's guidance. They recall only its "implementation" and leadership by Dwight Eisenhower, without realizing that the sig-

nificance of this fact is even more sinister than that
of the other two. Nor do they realize that the surrender of any part of American sovereignty to an organization of fifteen nations -- even though that organization was supposedly formed for the purpose of opposing
the Soviet Union -- is a huge step, psychologically and
substantively, in the direction of eventual surrender
of more and more of that sovereignty to one-world
organizations increasingly controlled by the Communists.

The truth is that the Communists do not care
whether the dilution of American sovereignty, and
the breaking down of the Americans' belief in and
reverence for the independence of their action, is
accomplished by our participation in the United Nations, by our contracted submission to NATO, by the
activities of the United World Federalists, by each of
a dozen other instrumentalities, or by all of them
working together. But the ultimate Communist Internationale is not to be a federation of nations, and
contemplates an elimination of national boundaries
and national patriotisms. Every weakening of such
boundaries and such patriotism -- and especially of
the United States boundaries and the formerly fierce
and proud American patriotism, is a corresponding
gain for Communist purposes. And the further truth
is that you cannot find one single important way or
means of weakening our national sovereignty and our
sentiment for that sovereignty which Eisenhower has
not been using or promoting for years, to the very
best of his remarkable ability and the full extent of
his power.

On October 25, 1957, President Eisenhower and
Prime Minister Macmillan of England issued a joint
statement in which they said: "The concept of national
self-sufficiency is now out of date. "' We do not know
just what the British law covering such a situation

may be. We do know that for a President of the
United States such a statement, and even more his
countless efforts to support it by his actions, constitute a deliberate violation of his solemn oath of
office, justifying his immediate impeachment; and
that the lack of any move for such impeachment itself shows the almost unbelievable extent to which
he and his Communist bosses have been able to
make the American people lose their conscience,
their courage, and their sense.

CHAPTER FIFTEEN

The Propagandist . . . . .

In 1949 Herbert Lehman and a group of associates formed an outfit known as the National Committee
For A Free Europe, Inc. Just how much Lehman
knew or wanted to know about fighting Communism
is revealed by his actions while head of UNRRA, when
he channeled its rehabilitation millions out through
such Communists as Madame Sun Yat-sen in China
and the Lublin Gang in Poland.

By what precise steps has never been quite clear,
but with the personal blessing of Dean Acheson and
the financial aid of his State Department, in 1950 this
embryonic organization grew into the Free Europe
Committee, Inc. This was a semi-public, semi-
governmental agency (the government's participation
and control have purposely been kept confused and
undefinable to this day). The Free Europe Committee then fathered two offsprings: The Crusade For
Freedom, which would raise money; and Radio Free
Europe, which would spend most of it. In that same
year the Crusade For Freedom, under the presidency
of General Lucius Clay, launched the first of its annual gigantic fund-raising campaigns. (Clay had done
as much as any other one man to help Eisenhower to
mess up the Berlin situation so favorably for the Russians.) As most Americans have now forgotten, and
most commentators and reporters giving the early
history of Radio Free Europe seem to prefer to omit,
that first campaign was built largely around the prestige and the synthetically created popularity of General Dwight D. Eisenhower. It got under way with a

nationwide radio speech by Eisenhower, appealing to the American public to support so noble a cause as enthusiastically as he endorsed it.' And it was Eisenhower's part in the establishment of Radio Free Europe which, as indicated at the end of Chapter IX above, we consider his greatest achievement on behalf of the Kremlin during his years as president of Columbia.

In 1951 one of Eisenhower's closest personal friends and political associates, C. D. Jackson -- later to be a member of his White House "Palace Guard" -- moved in as president of the Free Europe Committee. For the next few years, in that capacity, Jackson controlled the planning and dominated the policies of Radio Free Europe.[2] To anybody really familiar with C. D. Jackson's past history and actions, what then began to happen would have been no surprise -- even if the American people had taken any slightest interest, after putting up their money, in what was being done with it.

At any rate, the first country chosen to be restored by the magic of C. D. Jackson and his Radio Free Europe to the ranks of the free world was Czechoslovakia. Since May 1, 1951 the powerful Czechoslovak station of Radio Free Europe, near Munich, has been broadcasting to that country, in its native languages, for twenty hours a day. To do the job correctly, Eisenhower's pal, Jackson, set up a so-called Council of Free Czechoslovakia to conduct this psychological warfare. And the composition of that committee was something to behold.

For in 1945 a group of Czech renegades had got together in Moscow, formed a "national front" Czech government with Stalin's blessing, and then had followed the Red Army into Czechoslovakia, much as the Lublin Gang had done in Poland. It was this group which, through the positions its members were able to take and the front organizations they formed, paved the way for the Communists to take over the country in the coup d'etat of February, 1948. Yet, of the twenty-five men on Jackson's Council of Free Czechoslovakia, twenty had been members of this "national front" aggregation.[1]

The president of Jackson's Council was Dr. Peter Zenkl, who had been deputy prime minister under the Communist Prime Minister Gottwald. The foreign-secretary of Jackson's Council, Dr. Hubert Ripka, had written in a book published just the year before: "We are not naive enough to believe that our country can be governed without the Communists."[2] In an earlier book he had written: "We Czechoslovaks make no secret of our genuine satisfaction that Soviet Russia is beginning to participate in European and world politics as a strong world power."[3] An important member of Jackson's Council was Vaclav Majer, who had been minister for food under Prime Minister Gottwald. And the rest were all of the same stamp.

The actual broadcasting at Munich under Jackson's direction was in charge of Pavel Tigrid-Schoenfeld, a self-styled "former" Communist, who surrounded himself with Reds, and excluded every Czech patriot who had ever shown the slightest hostility to Communism. While back in the New York office, in charge of what might be called the "Czech desk," Jackson installed Ferdinand Peroutka, who had been a leading socialist advocate of Czech collaboration with the Communists before the Communists took over his country.[4] Much of Peroutka's "fighting" of Communism from New York consisted of nasty remarks about Senator McCarthy, General MacArthur, and Senator Taft, to be broadcast in Europe. In his commentary broadcast from Munich on August 3, 1952, reporting with obvious jubilation

the defeat of Senator Taft at the Republican Convention, Peroutka proclaimed: "For Europe it is decisive that the last remainders of isolationism have
been removed, and that a sound policy has been carried to victory."' And that, my friends, was nothing
compared to the usual stuff you were paying for with
your money, to be broadcast over Radio Free Europe
as a means of pushing back the Iron Curtain.

Perhaps we should give you a really fair sample,
to confirm the above statement. The second country
on C. D. Jackson's list for salvation was Hungary.
His selection of collaborators, agents, and committee members for that operation was even worse than
for Czechoslovakia, so we'll skip the details here.
And this bunch of Communists and Communist-sym-
pathizers really went to town. In fact the pro-Communism of their broadcasts was so blatant that in
1954 the West German government, catching several
of the leaders out of the country simultaneously, refused to give them visas to get back in, and threatened
to throw the whole station right off German soil. For
months these Communists were waiting around all
over Europe, drawing pay from Radio Free Europe
for doing nothing, until the pressure from the Eisenhower Administration on the German government was
sufficient to get everything restored to its status quo.
But that's getting ahead of our illustration, which occurred on December 11, 1951. On that evening, a
few months after this station of Radio Free Europe
had started its crusade to encourage the Hungarians
in their opposition to Communism, a Communist
named Imre Mikes, using the pseudonym of Gallicus
as he did for all of his regular broadcasts, under the
sponsorship and at the expense of the American people,
announced:

"In our 'The Living Hungarian Culture' column
Hungarian poets will speak to the nation.... We shall

now read the poem of Laszlo Szabo, poet of the People's Democracy. It's title is: The Age Of Stalin. " Then, with his approval and admiration obvious, he read it. And just to show you we are not fooling about what went on, we'll take the space to give that poem in full, in a literal translation. Here it is.

The Age Of Stalin

To the future generation taking our place and
    from which the heroes of Tomorrow emerge
I dedicate my poem, to fix the rhythm and com-
    memorate the timeless creations of the Age
    of Stalin.
Never forget it: that which we start building
    today, every stone of it is a cornerstone
    on steel base, and on it our new age is
    built, an age where work is a necessity and
    the new Communist order reigns supreme.

I should start with him, who is always with
    us, whose smile beautifies all the young ...
It was he who, for all times to come, de-
    feated the exploiters, and achieved final
    triumph for the sacred cause -- Lenin.
But where Lenin is the branch, Stalin will be
    the flower, when Lenin is the spark, Stalin
    will be the flame;
And true to his solemn vow to the master, he
    now faithfully carries out Iljich's testament,
    and with strong and sure hands leads hu-
    manity toward the final goal -- classless
    society...

My country, I am speaking to you now --
    Soviet blood was shed in glorious battles

so you can become a country... now at
last the dreams of Doza, Kossuth and
Petofi came true and Rakosi is leading
you toward great glorious goals!
In our country work has become glory and
honor, and new heroes emerge from the
work-contests; every carload of steel is
a month or a year in our favor: time that
takes us ahead on our way to socialism.

Now eight hundred arms defend your peace,
my country -- and you are guarding the
peace of eight hundred million ...

In the fire of class-struggle thus ripens and
boils Tomorrow, and the lame will walk
and the blind will see, man will turn his
back on poverty and disease, and his
machines will topple the walls of class
differences.
This is the true empire of Truth, the one
Marx was writing about -- Marx the
great prophet.
And over all of our days, like a torch on the
mountaintop, or a statue of granite, rises
the great guardian of our peace, Stalin,
opening his arms wide -- to embrace the
peoples of the world!

This is the kind of propaganda for Americanism
that was going out over Radio Free Europe in 1951,
under Eisenhower's close friend, C. D. Jackson. It
is the kind that kept right on going out after Eisenhower became President. For instance, at 12:15
P. M. , on May 3, 1953, over the Czechoslovak station, in the "Sunday Comments of Ferdinand Peroutka":
"Eisenhower's program, on the other hand, even

though America's factories have not been national-
ized, stands for the concept of world socialism.
There is no better way to describe it. This is socialism. ... The aim of the program outlined by the
President of the United States is to socialize life. " [1]

That was certainly encouraging to the anti-
Communists of Europe. As was this, on May 1,
1954, at 2:50 P. M. : "Today, on May 1st, we convey
our greetings to all those who are dedicated to the
faith in democratic socialism. "[2] To Communists, of
course, May 1 corresponds to our July 4; "democratic socialism" is their own phony term for the
Communist ideology; and such broadcasts frequently
end with the playing of the Communist Internationale.

It is propaganda of exactly the same purport --
though slightly more subtle -- which is going out over
Radio Free Europe today, under the direction of
another of Eisenhower's close friends, Willis D.
Crittenberger. Fulton Lewis has been making that
fact incontrovertibly clear with example after example, for months -- to those who were not too wil-
fully blind, or too indifferent, to see the truth staring
them in the face. And anybody who tries to cut down
on the money handed Radio Free Europe by the government (even though it is supposedly a private agency),
or to reduce the public's contributions to Radio Free
Europe, or to change its policies, or to inaugurate
a Congressional investigation of the monstrosity, has
run into and will run into the determined and vicious
opposition of Eisenhower, personally and as President, every step of the way.

Of course a lot of milk-toast anti-Communism
has been put out over Radio Free Europe. Of course
a little real anti-Communism has been interspersed
at rare intervals -- when, where, and how it would
do the least harm -- for the record. Of course the
Russians have gone through the motions of "jamming"

The Propagandist   193

Radio Free Europe stations at times,' and of having such jamming widely publicized in the American press. After all, the Communists, engaged in winning the whole world with a careful and gradual deception as their major weapon, do not engage in such deception casually, or as a sideshow; nor do they often make the stupid mistake of overplaying their hand. They give each piece of deception the full professional touch. They know it would be ridiculous, or at least entirely too risky and foolhardy, to expect the American people to permit and maintain the activities of Radio Free Europe, unless when the crises arrive Radio Free Europe could pull some samples of acceptable anti-Communism out of its records, and could give semi-plausible explanations for its general course. But the exhibits are not convincing, and the specious explanations are not plausible, to anybody who looks far enough into the whole record.

The story of the United States Information Agency (first made a separate bureau by Eisenhower after he became President)[2] and of Voice of America[3] is just as revealing. But every chapter of this book has to be selective rather than comprehensive. And there are two other entirely different categories of Eisenhower's brilliant public-relations accomplishments for the Kremlin that we wish to cover in this one.

First is the use of official Washington, and especially of the White House itself, as a means of publicizing and glorifying foreign Communists and collaborators with Communists -- to the immense advantage of themselves and discouragement of the anti-Communists in their respective countries. The beginning of the breakdown of the political control of Italy by the Christian Democrats, for instance, and of the development of the present dangerous power

there of Nenni's Communist-controlled Left-Wing
Socialists and of Enrico Mattei, really came with the
death of De Gasperi on August 19, 1954; but it was
given a tremendous boost by the election on April 29,
1955, of Giovanni Gronchi as President of the Republic. Gronchi, although a Christian Democrat (in the
same way that Eisenhower is a Republican), was
elected with the strong and known help of Communist
support and votes;' and from the very hour of his inauguration speech he began pressing for the extreme
left-wing parties to be admitted to the government --
to an extent in this speech which, according to the
New York Times, "went beyond the wildest hopes of
the Communists and fellow travelers."[2]

Signor Gronchi immediately started encroaching
on the powers of his prime minister, stealing the
limelight, advocating "neutralism" for Italy, and
boasting: "I was the first to advocate a so-called
opening to the left and I am still in favor of it." This,
of course, was just the kind of man Eisenhower was
looking for, to honor in Washington. In short order
Gronchi was invited on a "visit of state" to this
country, was royally entertained at the White House,
and was shown every mark of Eisenhower's approval
and esteem. To the American people this meant
nothing. Even if they had ever heard of Gronchi,
they attached no significance to his being entertained
in Washington.[3] But in Italy our treatment of President Gronchi was of great importance in building up
his prestige. (To add real body to the insubstantial
pageant of our hospitality and favor, the World Bank
extended to Gronchi's government seventy million
dollars -- the largest development loan it has ever
made in Europe.) And to the politicians of Western
Europe, watching all of this with some lingering
amazement, it was made elaborately clear that the
way to gain the blessing and the help of the White

House was to collaborate with the Communists.

Nor was it necessary to be in any way pro-American to attract the rain of Presidential favors from Washington. In fact, just the opposite, as the next exhibit in this preposterous parade of Eisenhower favorites was to demonstrate beyond all doubt. For Achmed Sukarno of Indonesia first came to the world's serious attention by leading a mob which burned the President of the United States in effigy, as an imperialist, in the streets of Batavia.[1] And although our government was the one decisive factor in driving the Dutch out of Indonesia for him, in establishing him as the "president" and now the virtual dictator of the so-called Republic of Indonesia, and is right now supplying him the arms to put down the Sumatran rebels against his Communist dictatorship,[2] Sukarno has never ceased being an outspokenly bitter enemy of the United States. Before, _during_, and since he was accorded the honor -- and tremendous help to his personal position in Indonesia -- of the longest state visit in the history of our country,[3] Sukarno has excoriated the United States at every turn.[4]

When you think what an invitation to Chiang Kai-shek for an official visit to America, and his being feted in Washington, would mean to the whole anti-Communist cause in Eastern Asia, and how easy it would be to arrange; and when you then think how damaging to the anti-Communists and helpful to the Communists was our lavish hospitality to, and fawning over, Sukarno;[5] then, just from that consideration alone you can realize how definitely and deliberately the White House and our State Department are giving every aid and encouragement to our Communist enemies that they dare.[6] And increasingly they dare a great deal. For it was not enough to have Sukarno spend nineteen days roaming this country and being royally entertained as the guest of our government, or to have him address a joint meeting of both houses of Congress convened in his honor, or to give him all the publicity about his glorious reception in America. (This was publicity which he immediately used to great advantage for the Communists in Red China, during his visit to his friend Mao that directly followed his visit to his friend Eisenhower.) On top of these "routine" arrows for his propaganda bow, Eisenhower arranged to give him a few silver-tipped ones as well -- such as sending Eisenhower's personal plane half way across the Pacific, to pick up Sukarno and bring him to our shores; and such as the high praise which Eisenhower went out of his way to give Sukarno's remarks.[1] Nothing was too good, nor even good enough, for the man whose troops, at that very time, were murdering wholesale the Christians of the Moluccan islands who had been our most unswerving friends in all Oceania for twenty years.[2]

Then came Mr. Nehru. His aggressive activities on behalf of the Communists throughout all of the foul negotiations at Panmunjom should alone have been enough to get him recognized forever as the mortal enemy of the United States.[3] If any reader will just brush aside the smoke of "neutralist" nonsense about Nehru, blown so blindingly by his "liberal" friends in this country, however, and start looking at the actual facts of his work with and for the Kremlin for more than thirty years, they cannot escape the conclusion that he is a loyal viceroy of the Kremlin in India today. In the No. 6 issue of ONE MAN'S OPINION[4] we gave many pages of evidence to support our belief that Nehru was, and long had been, a conscious wholehearted agent of the Communists. We cannot repeat that evidence here. But since at least 1927, when Nehru became vice-president of the first important world-wide Communist front, the League Against Imperialism formed in Brussels; through

the late 1930's, when he was sending shiploads of
food to the Communist butchers who were trying to
take over Spain; through 1949, when the whole plane-
load of American correspondents, returning to tell
the truth about what was happening in Indonesia, was
destroyed in Bombay by an "accident" so convenient
for Nehru's good friend, Sukarno; until the present
time, when he is brazenly using hundreds of millions
of American dollars to make India socialist in her
domestic economy and Communist in her international
alignment; during all of this period Nehru's status can
be most easily clarified by a very old illustration.'

Thirty years ago here was an animal that considered itself a tiger, associated regularly and actively with other tigers, and was accepted by them
as a leader among tigers. Since then this animal
has never ceased to look like a tiger, act like a tiger,
spring like a tiger, roar like a tiger, smell like a
tiger, or side with the tigers in all of their raids on
the lambs. What possible basis is there for Washington's straining and pretended assumption that this
animal might be a lamb today, acting the way it does
merely because it is afraid of the other tigers?

What's more, Nehru has continuously directed
his pro-Communist energies against the United States
as the chief target of his enmity -- as any good Communist would. But he was invited to pay us a state
visit, was given an immeasurable amount of free publicity in our press and over the air, and was treated
-- for the world to observe -- with all the respect
and cordiality due to a great friend and ally. In fact,
Eisenhower personally went much further than even
the most cordial formalities would have required.

For obvious political reasons there had been a
break, in the parade of the captains and kings of Communism to our shores, from June, 1956 until after
the election that fall. But not long after; Mr. J.

Nehru arrived in December, white riding breeches and·all. There are millions of Asiatics whom Nehru wishes to reach, with the kind of propaganda provided him by his glamorous reception in America, to whom a picture is literally worth ten thousand words, because of their illiteracy. So he has skillfully made of the sloppy white pants (called <u>churidar</u> in their Kashmir habitat) a trademark by which he can readily be recognized in any photograph. And the cleverly contrived, brilliantly posed, picture of Nehru, wreathed in smiles, rushing up the White House steps and practically into the arms of an equally friendly and smiling Eisenhower, who was coming out the White House door to greet him (so that the well known and clearly recognizable <u>outside</u> of the White House would be the setting of the photograph) -- that picture alone was worth as much to the worldwide Communist parties as if America had started dropping bombs on Bangkok and Baghdad.[1]

Mr. Eisenhower's gushing remarks about the "privilege and honor" thus given himself, of receiving Nehru like a long-lost brother, were merely additional dividends on the performance, for the sake of Asiatics sufficiently informed to be aware that Nehru was stabbing America in the back at every opportunity.[2] But, as usual, substance was added to the glory accorded our exalted guest. Shortly before his arrival our government gave him -- pardon us, sold him -- six hundred and fifty-two million dollars' worth of wheat, cotton, rice, and other farm products. At least, that is the price our government had paid for the merchandise. We sold it to Nehru for 360 million dollars, on paper. Out of that 360 million we gave him back 54 million as an undisguised gift. We allowed him a "long-term credit" for 234 million dollars of it. The remaining 72 million dollars, all Nehru was actually paying for the 652 million dollars' worth, we were to take from India in goods we were then to give away in other parts of the world.' And this was all entirely aside from the "negotiations" then being conducted, for some long-term "loans" in real money, towards paying the ten billion dollars estimated cost of India's new five-year plan. If you will concede our claim that we are not here discussing this matter as one of the follies of foreign aid, but solely from the point of view of propaganda, we believe you will then admit that just as the makings of pro-Communist propaganda alone our treatment of Nehru was pretty powerful stuff. And it was primarily Eisenhower's words, actions, and influence which made that treatment something for the Kremlin boys really to write home about.

The magazine Human Events,[2] and other dependable sources of Washington information, convincingly stated it to have been the original intention of Eisenhower and his State Department to have Nehru followed in this parade of Communist visitors by Tito, and then Tito by Khrushchev and Bulganin themselves. And Kiplinger, who can see neither the past nor the future except through the eyes of the Eisenhower Administration, bravely announced on December 29, 1956: "Tito probably will visit sometime in early spring... Washington and Gettysburg. Both are easy to control against riots and demonstrations." It was discovered, however, that the brainwashing of the American people was not yet far enough advanced for quite such daring gestures of camaraderie with the top Communist tyrants to be feasible. So those "spectaculars" in Eisenhower's pro-Communist propaganda displays were postponed until the market was in a more responsive mood.

There is a third kind of pro-Communist propaganda activity, which Eisenhower has been carrying on, which has largely escaped seriously critical attention. For the separate, apparently spontaneous pieces have been too little recognized as parts of a long-range deliberate, cumulative program. This program has two sections. One might be identified as "The Spirit of Geneva Extension Course by Correspondence," although it began long before the Summit Conference which was supposed to have given birth to the "Spirit of Geneva." The other could be called: "Pot Shots for the Pravda Line by the President of the U.S.A."

To illustrate the second section first, we ask you to take a look with us at a fraud known as The Little Red Schoolhouse of New York City. It is a private "progressive" school, of which Randolph B. Smith is director. At least Randolph B. Smith is one of the names he uses -- the one for this purpose. Even under that name he has a Communist-front record a mile long. His record of helping Communists and Communist causes goes back at least as far as 1940, and continues without break right up to this morning. In 1952 he took the Fifth Amendment rather than answer under oath as to whether he was a member of the Communist Party.[1] Mrs. Randolph B. Smith also used the Fifth Amendment, to avoid telling whether she was a member of the Communist Party, whether she had tried to recruit teachers for the Communist Party when she supervised the N.Y. State WPA nursery school project, and a lot of other things.[2]

Associated with the Smiths in running the Little Red Schoolhouse, either as teachers or as trustees, have been Hubert T. Delany, Norman Studer, Basil Bass, Dr. Barbara Biber, Adele Lithauer, and other birds of the same feather, all well known to bird watchers who turn their glasses on the nesting grounds of the Communists. To put it bluntly, the Little Red

Schoolhouse is a notorious show place of Communist sympathies. Yet on February 28, 1958, at a dinner in New York celebrating the twenty-fifth anniversary of Mr. Smith's pro-Communist educational enterprise, the highlight of the affair was a personal message from President Eisenhower commending the school for "searching out new paths for the training of free citizens."

As the VFW's Guardpost pointed out, a congratulatory message from the President of the United States is a prize eagerly sought after by many institutions.' But, to the best of our knowledge, no other private school in the country has ever received this kind of blessing from Eisenhower. He singled out one which carries the word "red," as a brazenly revealing part of its name, on which to bestow such a prize.

Of course the usual claims are made, even by those who condemn this action on the part of Eisenhower, that he was not aware of what he was doing, and was merely guilty of letting himself be imposed on by some bad advisors. This is, in our opinion, as absurd as the thought that he didn't know what he was doing in 1946 when he accepted the Churchman award, or in 1949 when he installed the Communist-endowed chair of Polish history at Columbia. And -- to look at a far more important illustration of his potshot propaganda -- he was equally aware of the significance and the ultimate purpose of what he was saying when, in October, 1956, he defied the American Congress with regard to aid to Tito. "My finding," he announced, "that Yugoslavia is not participating in any policy or program for the Communist conquest of the world is based upon the fact that the ideology and doctrine of the Yugoslav Communist Party appear to adhere to the concept that each nation should determine for itself which kind of a society it wishes and that there should be no interference by one nation in the internal affairs of another."[1]

In that involved sentence there are three entirely separate statements of "fact." Every one of the three was utterly false, and being daily proved false by Tito's words and actions at that very time, as Eisenhower well knew. But more relevant to our present discussion than his specious excuse for renewing military aid to Tito (which he was determined to supply anyway) was his use of the occasion to give a tremendous boost to the current Communist propaganda line. The Kremlin was extremely desirous of promoting the belief in the Western nations that the people in the satellite countries were glad to accept Communism, provided only that it was "nationalist" Communism, "independent" of Moscow. It was partly to strengthen this belief that Moscow had planned and provoked the Hungarian revolt. The concept of "nationalist" Communism as a means of weakening the U.S.S.R. is a vital part of the Kremlin's recent and present strategy of deception, and -- under Moscow's direction -- has been played up by every important Communist or Communist stooge in the world for the last few years. Eisenhower simply followed his orders and did his part. And he had hardly sat down, after thus praising Tito's principle of non-interference by one nation in the internal affairs of another, when Tito himself made a speech (November 15, 1956) praising the Soviet Union for having interfered in the affairs of Hungary, and saying: "...we must defend the present government of Kadar, we must support it."[2]

Eisenhower's playing of the Kremlin's propaganda pipes for the Communists naturally turns out many different tunes. One of the most effective, which he has played several times, has been his repeated and "generous" defense of "neutralism," as corresponding to the neutral attitude taken towards foreign entanglements by the United States during the first 150 years

of its existence. Nothing could be less like the "neutralist" subservience of Nehru's India to the purposes
of the Kremlin than America's rugged independence
from 1783 to the beginning of Wilson's second term in
1917. But Eisenhower has not only helped the Kremlin mightily with this tune. He has gone much further;
and, by pointing out, in support of such wise "neutralism, " the dangers facing a weaker nation in a military
alliance with a stronger one, has frightened some of
our own allies, especially West Germany, into added
doubts about its pro-Western position.

Parallel to this has been Eisenhower's support
of the "anti-colonialism" slogan, which the Communists have used so maliciously to stir up trouble in
Asia and Africa. He has enthusiastically compared the
efforts of Communist-led gangs in Indonesia or Algeria,
to establish Communist-controlled satrapies of Moscow
in those areas, with our own aims in 1776. For instance, in his "State of the Union" message in January, 1957, Eisenhower said that "today's expressions
of nationalism are, in spirit, echoes of our forefathers'
struggle for independence. "[1] Nothing could have been
farther from the truth, or better calculated to make
the Communists' propaganda line more useful against
our allies and ourselves.

As Louis Budenz long since pointed out, the long-
range Communist battle cry is "Peace" -- peace always, of course, on Communist terms.[2] A contemporary offshoot of that hardy Communist strategy is the
drive for disarmament. In fact, as this is written, and
almost entirely unknown to the American people, Mr.
Dulles has already consented (at Manila, on March 14,
1958) to a new summit conference at which disarmament will be the only topic on the agenda.[3] In the noble
cause of getting us disarmed Mr. Eisenhower is doing
all he can to help the Kremlin -- in propaganda as otherwise. On May 22, 1957, he "served notice that he now

favors a supreme effort to reach a disarmament agreement with the Soviet Union. " He said that something "just has to be done in the interest of the United States " to end the arms race.' Admiral Radford, chairman of the Joint Chiefs of Staff, having summed up this nonsense the preceding Sunday with the one sentence, "We cannot trust the Russians on this or anything, "[2] Eisenhower issued what amounted to a sharp rebuke to Radford. He made it clear that he preferred the point of view of his special disarmament adviser, Harold Stassen. He said he was prepared to meet the Russians halfway and -- here is the crux of the pro-Communist propaganda -- that his chief concern was to make sure that "we are not ourselves being recalcitrant " or "picayunish. "

Standing on any principles whatsoever, in our dealings with Moscow, is in Eisenhower's language being picayunish. And we are sure that is correct; for moral principles of any kind are, with him, most picayunish considerations indeed. One of his most revealing propaganda forays for the Communists has been his high praise of, and bold attempt to give wider readership to, Eric Hoffer's book, The True Believer. The whole thesis of this book is that any man who has any real faith, or beliefs, or principles, to which he is willing to pay anything more than lip service, belongs to the lunatic fringe. It cleverly holds up to ridicule those thousands of Americans, of whom this writer hopes he is one, who not only believe there are certain eternal truths which should guide the human race, but are willing to fight for that belief and to die for it if necessary. The book is visibly a part of the subtle but long-continuing and increasingly successful Communist efforts to break down Americans' traditions, sense of values, and confidence in the righteousness of their opposition to anything -- including Communism. And Mr. Eisenhower highly recommends it, as one of his favorite volumes.[1]

Along the same line was Eisenhower's at least left-handed boost for The Investigator.[2] This long-playing record, selling for $5.95, which held up to vicious scorn not only Joseph McCarthy, but any and all Congressional committees investigating Communists, and the whole United States Senate as well, was written and peddled by one Reuben Ship. Ship was an identified member of the Communist Party who took the Fifth Amendment four times before being ordered deported to Canada as a proved alien Communist.[3] When this record came in from Canada, the Communist Daily Worker plugged it with huge delight. (So, of course, did the New York Times.)[4] But a large part of its sale of around a hundred thousand copies -- at $5.95 per record -- was due to the fact that Eisenhower was reported, and did not deny, to have enjoyed it immensely. (The New York Times: "A spokesman for the Little White House in Augusta, Georgia, declined to comment on reports that President Eisenhower had heard and enjoyed the recorded version of the program.")[5]

But both the number and the range of Eisenhower's efforts to give a lift to Communist propaganda, at home and abroad, are almost unending. On the only occasion when I have ever known him to speak with approval of American scientists and their achievements (now supposedly so outclassed by their Russian counterparts), he carefully went far out of his way to hold up as examples -- Einstein and Steinmetz! The first of these, as most Americans do not know, had been run out of Germany and had come to America, not because he was Jewish, but because of his pro-Communist activities. He continued those activities in this more complacent country, with increasing boldness, to the day of his death. The second, Steinmetz, had been chiefly famous for his pro-Communist sympa-

thies even in those distant days when most Americans
thought Communism was some kind of a foreign joke.
And it is a standard, undeviating -- and cumulatively
effective -- practice of Communists always to glorify
other Communists when you have a chance.

At the other end of the range, it is interesting
to note that when "President" Nasser of the United
Arab Republic arrived in Moscow this spring for his
lengthy visit, and greeted his hosts with "Our people
know the Soviet Union stands for peace," the whole
sentence somehow sounded familiar to many Americans. It should have. Those were almost the exact
words Eisenhower had used in greeting Zhukov, on
arrival at Geneva in 1955.' With illustrations in between those two we could fill a book, if we were writing one on that subject. In fact, we could almost fill
a book with Eisenhower's disingenuous confessions
and implications that the prolongation of the Cold War
was due just as much to our unreasonableness and
selfish purposes as to any fault of the Russians.

But this chapter is already getting far too long.
So let's turn only briefly, in conclusion, to the "felicitations" department. Since as soon as he dared
after he became President, and with greatly increased
frequency and cordiality after the Summit Conference,
Eisenhower has poured out these countless expressions
of his personal good will towards the Communist tyrants in Moscow and the satellite states. And of course
their wide publication behind the Iron Curtain has been
of inestimable value to the Kremlin, in discouraging
their restless slaves from dreaming of American aid
for any revolt they might start.

Not all of this visible favoritism to Communist
potentates and diplomats has even been through written
or spoken words. There are other ways. It is unshakable protocol, for instance, that when a new ambassa-

dor from any country arrives in Washington, he can
do absolutely nothing until he has been received by the
President. And when the extremely able Dr. Holling-
ton Tong replaced Dr. Wellington Koo (who was actually dean of the Washington diplomatic corps), as Ambassador from Nationalist China, Dr. Tong was pointedly and insultingly kept cooling his heels for three weeks
before being admitted to the White House. But then
came Mikhail Menshikov, who had advanced his career
by using our UNRRA money, in 1946, to feed only the
pro-Communist Poles, while allowing the Polish patriots to starve. When Menshikov arrived as the new
ambassador from the Soviet Union, Eisenhower all but
met his plane. Not only was he received at the White
House immediately, but Eisenhower even arranged for
a picture to be taken of himself and Menshikov together (deliberately and admittedly breaking all precedent
in such cases), for the propaganda use of the new ambassador.' Out of an infinite total of such "little things "
have the Communists built up their prestige which now
blankets the world.

Also, the felicitous concern can be in the other
direction, with equal gain for the Kremlin. At Geneva
in 1955 Bulganin told Eisenhower: "We hope you decide
to run again. " To be sure that statement was given
sufficient publicity, world-wide, as being unmistakably
authentic, Eisenhower himself repeated it to a meeting
of Congressional leaders when he returned to Washington, and Drew Pearson sent it on its way.² More recently, another slippery left-winger, John Gunther, who
happens to be a biographer, admirer, and friend of the
President, has given wide circulation to the observation: "So far as I could tell, the Kremlin bosses were
strongly pro-Eisenhower, although cool to Nixon. " ³
Again there was much useful grist for the Communist
propaganda mills in having it widely known, in the right
places, that the Kremlin tyrants were entirely satisfied

with the friendly and helpful stooge whom their supporters had contrived to put in the White House.

But Eisenhower has given them plenty of more
clean-cut grist for the same mills. On November 7,
1955, for instance, he sent a personal message to
Kliment Voroshilov, "President" of the Soviet Union:
"On this national anniversary of the Soviet Union, I
am happy to convey to Your Excellency and to the peoples of the Soviet Union the best wishes of the people
of the United States for progress toward a permanent
and just peace."[1]

Voroshilov, it should be remembered, is really
famous for just one thing. When the city of Kiev surrendered to the Bolshevik troops, it was on the specific promise of Voroshilov, advanced to induce the surrender, that the thousands of loyal Czarist army officers in that city, with their wives and children,
would be allowed peacefully to leave for their homes
or wherever they wanted to go. Instead, the minute
the surrender was complete, Voroshilov had all of the
men shot forthwith, and put their wives and daughters
in brothels "for the health of his army." When he
actually boasted of this foul treachery fifteen years
later to William Bullitt, and Bullitt could not refrain
from commenting on the treatment of the women,
Voroshilov explained it didn't make any real difference
that they too had not been shot at once, for they were
all dead within three months anyway.[2]

Eisenhower well knew all of this, of course.
He also knew that November 7, 1955, was not the thirty-
eighth anniversary of the founding of the Soviet Union
as pretended, but of the bloody Bolshevik revolution;
for the Soviet Union was not even founded until 1922.
But James Hagerty, Presidential secretary, when
asked why Eisenhower had gone so far out of his way
to set a precedent of this kind, replied it was simply
"because the President wanted to send a personal mes-

sage to Voroshilov and the Russian people."[1]

He set a precedent, all right. On January 1, 1958, the President received direct, by commercial cable, greetings from " the Russian leaders, " extending to him "best wishes " from the Russian peoples and " from us personally." It went on to declare Russian dedication to the "noble goal " of friendship and cooperation between the American and Russian peoples. It stated the conviction of these leaders that by uniting their strength, the United States and the Soviet Union could bring about the "great, ardent dream of humanity" -- "peace on earth " and "freedom from fear." Eisenhower immediately sent a reply, reciprocating the greetings, and expressing the earnest hope that the New Year would bring "a firmer and better understanding " between citizens of the two countries. He forwarded it by Western Union Telegraph. There was no going through stiff or formal diplomatic channels, you will note, when such palsy-walsy friends wanted to wish each other "happy New Year," and to have all the world see just how palsy-walsy they were.[2]

Anniversaries, of course, of any kind, real or phony, have served as the most useful excuse for such messages, coldly calculated to give the Communist murderers an aura of the highest respectability, and to make resistance to their power appear hopeless. And the Eisenhower testimonials have by no means been confined to the murderers in the Kremlin itself. For example, on July 22, 1957, he sent the following message to Aleksander Zawadski, "President of the Polish Council of State, " whose real boss, Gomulka, had only recently finished putting down the Poznan and Warsaw riots: "On the occasion of the official holiday of Poland, I am happy to convey my personal greetings to Your Excellency and to extend to the people of Poland the very good wishes of the people of the United States."[3] And it should be noted that the Polish holiday which

Eisenhower thus glorified is in celebration of the day in 1948 when the last anti-Communist members of the Polish government were ousted, and Stalin's Lublin Gang took over complete and formal control of Poland, making it officially a Communist dictatorship and a Soviet satellite.

Or, for another example. On November 29, 1957, Eisenhower sent this message to Tito: "I am happy to convey to Your Excellency my greetings and felicitations and to the people of Yugoslavia those of the people of the United States on this anniversary of the Federal Peoples' Republic of Yugoslavia."[1] Since the most important step in the establishment of the so-called Republic of Yugoslavia had been the public murder of Mihailovich, the best friend America ever had in the Balkans and the staunchest anti-Communist, there is an especially nauseating odor about this bouquet to the butcher of Belgrade.[2]

We'll skip all other examples, however, except one. That is Eisenhower's long-continued, tremendously publicized attitude of esteem and affection for his "buddy," Marshal Georgi K. Zhukov. That flirtation has been used to serve many purposes, all of them for the benefit of the Kremlin.[3]

An INS despatch of June 5, 1954 read as follows: "Eisenhower Marks Tenth Anniversary of Normandy Landings. The President cited the wartime cooperation among the Allies as an example of what can be accomplished when nations work together toward a common goal, and recalled 'his pleasant association with the outstanding Soviet Marshal Zhukov.' " In May, 1955, Eisenhower let it be known that he and his friend Zhukov had been exchanging private letters. And Eisenhower continued to keep the press and the world informed of the unbroken romance, at every feasible opportunity.

One of the results of this highly advertised com-

radeship was to promote a feeling with the general
public that not all of the Soviet leaders are bad, that
there could be good Communists and honorable Communists, and that Zhukov was one of those exceptions.
Until finally there came the time when Eisenhower's
bosses dared to have him use his touted comradeship
with Zhukov, whom he called "an honest man" even
though "a confirmed Communist," as the launching
platform for a rocket of Communist propaganda that
startled even the complacent American people.

Having failed, temporarily anyway, in the plan
to have Tito and then Khrushchev and Bulganin visit
Washington, Eisenhower began plugging for the next
best thing to serve Communist propaganda purposes.
On July 17, 1957, he told his news conference it might
be helpful if his wartime friend, Marshal Zhukov --
then Soviet Defense Minister -- would exchange visits
with our Defense Secretary Wilson. (That he has not
given up at all on the idea of bringing Khrushchev over
to be feted as our guest is shown by his statement in
March of this year, 1958: "By no means do I fear the
results on America of a visit by Mr. Khrushchev." [1]
Naturally he didn't say anything about the "result on"
the rest of the world, which would be the chief purpose
of the visit.)

At any rate, in the course of this July 17, 1957
news conference, Eisenhower -- naturally saying nothing about Zhukov's 1956 performance as "the butcher
of Budapest" -- delivered the following almost incredible "confession":

"I must say that during the years that I knew him
(Zhukov) I had a most satisfactory acquaintance and
friendship with him .... We had many long discussions
about our respective doctrines .... We tried each to explain to the other just what our systems meant, to the
individual, and I was very hard put to it when he insisted that their system appealed to the idealistic .... And

I had a very tough time trying to defend our position ...."

Eisenhower then went on to explain Zhukov's point of view: That our system of government was materialistic, because it allowed each individual to do whatever he wanted, and to look out for himself; while the Communist system was idealistic, because it insisted that the individual give himself to the state and sacrifice for the state. "I am merely saying, " he ended up in answer to a question, "that against that kind of a belief you run against arguments that almost leave you breathless, you don't know how to meet them. "'

There is the completely phony ideological line of the Communists, put in its most favorable possible light; brilliantly condensed into a few sentences of easy words, and reduced to an ad personam type of argument that the man in the street can understand; given a human-interest touch that magnified its attention-getting quality a hundredfold; and spouted for the Kremlin, with the "profound sincerity" the Communists so gleefully eulogize, under the most skillfully arranged circumstances for enormous publicity, by the President of the United States. It would have been interesting to sit in on the briefing sessions at which his Communist bosses prepared him to mouth their supreme argument with what was (for Eisenhower) such unusual coherence and conciseness.

CHAPTER SIXTEEN

Associates And Appointments.[1] . . . . .

In other places in this treatise we have already
touched on Eisenhower's association with, praise of,
and praise by, high-ranking Communists. Of course
we have omitted many illustrations -- such as his
going so far out of his way to invite Khrishna Menon
to the White House, and to treat Menon as an honored
friend.[2]

Perhaps the most important and revealing of the
instances omitted takes us back some thirteen years.
For Eisenhower is the only man, Russian or American or of any other nation, who was ever allowed to
have his picture taken with Stalin (just the two of
them together) at the tomb of Lenin. We think it is
highly significant that an American would be willing
to pay that kind of homage to Lenin, or to let himself be thus "honored" by the Communists as one of
their half-gods and heroes. But in this way and others
Eisenhower and Stalin were presented as comrades,
in both the casual and the technical senses of that
term, to all of the Russians, and to all of the eastern
European peoples whom Stalin's agents were right
then in the process of bludgeoning into slavery.

Let's leave the we-belong-to-the-same-fraternity
displays, however, and turn to another kind of association of Eisenhower with Communists -- in this case
of a less exalted level than his military and diplomatic
comrades. It is equally revealing. For if you will
look closely enough you will find that there has always been one (or more) very clever Communist
right at his elbow, to guide him, to give him his or-

ders, or to receive his reports, ever since he reached a position of any importance. During the war, for instance, Supreme Commander Eisenhower had as press control officer of his headquarters a man named Cedric Belfrage.[1] And very little comment about this character is needed for those familiar with the more active Communist agents over the past twenty years. Sworn and uncontradicted testimony exists that he was a member of the Soviet espionage group headed by Jacob Golos, and that he was a secret party member with a party alias.[2] After the war he wound up in America as editor of the pro-Communist weekly, the National Guardian.[3] About three years ago he was deported as a Communist alien. And the fact that he was not able to find some loophole, to stall or prevent this deportation as so many others have done, was probably due to the wish of Eisenhower's bosses to see Belfrage out of any possible range of the renewed interest of a Congressional committee.

Another illustration is that during these same war years Colonel Hans Habe, of Eisenhower's Psychological Warfare Staff, was his right-hand man in that nebulous activity. Habe, with half a dozen aliases used in the Communist service, wound up in the chaos of postwar Germany, with a fistful of American money, establishing, running, and subsidizing pro-Communist newspapers. We have lost track of him since.

Even for his book, Crusade In Europe, Eisenhower's chief ghost writer was Joseph Fels Barnes. Not only have Barnes' activities shown him to be a Communist, but he has been independently identified as a Communist agent, on their own personal knowledge, by Whittaker Chambers, Louis Budenz, General Alexander Barmine, Dr. Karl A. Wittfogel, and Hede Massing.[4] Among those who also helped Eisenhower in connection with his book in one way or another were

Gabriel Hauge, Clifford Case, and Joseph E. Davies.[1]
Hauge is a member of the Bilderberg Group,[2] but we'll
skip further mention of his suspicious activities here,
because it would require too much time. We have already touched on the Communist support and connections of Clifford Case.[3] As to Joseph E. Davies, his
unceasing pro-Communist sympathies and actions
are typified by this statement, which he made to an
audience in Chicago in February, 1942: "By the
testimony of performance and in my opinion, the word
of honor of the Soviet Government is as safe as the
Bible."[4] As it had been only two years since the Soviet Union had seized Latvia, Estonia, and Lithuania,
in deliberate violation of their most solemn agreements with these small nations, and as Mr. Davies
was well aware of this "testimony of performance,"
he left no possible doubt as to his own character or
purposes. Nor have his actions in all the years since
left room for any reasonable doubt that Eisenhower's
good friend, Joseph Davies, was working for the
Kremlin at every turn.

To continue this chapter in this style, however,
when there is so much material like the above available, would make it as long as this whole paper was
intended to be. So we'll skip all of the documentation
and most of the comment in listing just a few more of
the Communists, Communist sympathizers, or extreme leftwingers with whom Eisenhower has personally been on very friendly terms. Such a list
would include: John G. Winant, Harry Dexter White,
Henry Morgenthau, Jr., Anna M. Rosenberg, Sidney
Hillman, Pearl Mesta, Jacob Javits, W. Averell
Harriman, Milton Katz, and Harry Hopkins.

The American people have not yet waked up to
the clear evidence that Harry Hopkins, instead of being the fumbling half-mystical dogooder for which
they took him, was one of the most successful Com-

munist agents the Kremlin has ever found already planted in the American government, and then developed to supreme top-level usefulness.[1] By the time they do, if ever, one piece of that evidence, strange to say, may well be that Dwight Eisenhower called Hopkins one of the greatest and <u>most loyal</u> Americans he had ever known.[2]

Eisenhower's praise of Harry Hopkins is not nearly so revealing, however, as his almost incredible eulogy of Ralph Bunche. As far back as 1936 Bunche was writing glowingly of "the principles of equality and humanitarianism advocated by the Soviet Union," and was working in close association with James W. Ford. Archibald Roosevelt has produced and distributed a 44-page detailed study of Ralph Bunche, showing beyond doubt that Bunche has been consciously and energetically working for the Communist cause for more than twenty years.[3] And yet, on September 25, 1949, Eisenhower stated in a speech, made as president of Columbia University, that Ralph Bunche was "the greatest statesman this country has ever produced."[4]

Another exhibit of Eisenhower's close personal involvement with the Communists and near-Communists is to be found in the story of the National Committee For An Effective Congress. This organization, considerably left of the Americans For Democratic Action, was formed in 1952. Of its thirty-nine officers and letterhead sponsors, more than thirty were either known Communists, Fifth Amendment Communists, or fellow travelers who invariably follow the Communist path.[5] This Committee (which later, incidentally, actually wrote every word of the Censure Motion against McCarthy that Senator Flanders introduced)[6] raised money during the 1954 campaign for the support of Senators Humphrey and Taylor and other extreme leftwingers of the Dem-

ocratic Party.[1] The only Republican Senator whom
they supported was Margaret Chase Smith of Maine,
which merely confirms what some of us think of her.
It is the clear purpose of the Committee For An Effective Congress to wreck the Republican Party,[2]
to put extreme radicals in control of the Democratic
Party, and to promote the rapid movement of this
country into the orbit of Communism by any means.

Now set this fact and development alongside the
fact that Paul Hoffman has been one of Eisenhower's
strongest supporters, best personal friends, and
most dependable agents for implementing Eisenhower's ideas concerning world affairs. Then note
that Paul Hoffman contributed one thousand dollars
to the Committee For An Effective Congress; and
having done so, did everything he could to cover up
and hide this contribution, until Fulton Lewis stated
and proved that it had been made. And it is Paul
Hoffman, financial supporter of this Communist-
dominated Committee For An Effective Congress,
who contends that his close friend Eisenhower has
been the savior of the Republican Party.

Finally, let's look briefly at one more exhibit in
this category, namely Philip Jessup.[3] Dr. Jessup had
been one of the most important men in the Institute of
Pacific Relations during all the years of its most important treasonous activities. Working hand in glove
with his close friend, Frederick Vanderbilt Field, he
had done everything he could to turn China over to the
Communists and, after the mainland was lost, to see
that both Korea and Formosa were abandoned to the
Communists as well.

Jessup had been officially listed as the sponsor
of several Communist fronts.[4] He was a protégé of
Dean Acheson. He was a great friend of Alger Hiss,
and had appeared as a character witness for Hiss at
both Hiss trials.[5] He was a vigorous supporter of

Owen Lattimore. In hearings before a Senate Committee, in October 1951, he was caught deliberately lying under oath about his previous attitude towards our recognition of Red China.' The evidence of his pro-Communist sympathies, and of his unceasing and energetic efforts on behalf of the Communist cause, was -- and is -- overwhelming. Equally important for this discussion, those sympathies and actions were fully known to Eisenhower. But Jessup has been a close friend, adviser, and teammate of Eisenhower's for many years; and still is at this writing, in 1958.

They have been associated together, along with John Foster Dulles, Alger Hiss, Joseph Johnson, and some other famous characters, at the Carnegie Endowment For International Peace -- of which Dulles, Hiss, and Johnson were successive Presidents. We described Jessup's major achievement for Eisenhower's great pride, Arden House, on Page 105 of this manuscript. Nor has the relationship been one-sided. For on March 18, 1950 Dwight Eisenhower went far out of his way to vouch personally for the loyalty of Philip Jessup, in a letter to the Subcommittee of the Senate Committee on Foreign Relations, which was holding hearings on Jessup's nomination as Ambassador-at-Large. And this Subcommittee recommended against the appointment, because of Jessup's pro-Communist associations and leanings, despite Mr. Eisenhower's gratuitous whitewashing of his friend.² But both men have been well aware that the American people are extremely short as to memory and long as to complacency.³

It is the chief purpose of this chapter, however, to turn the spotlight on the general run of appointments which Eisenhower has made since he became President, and to adumbrate their significance. We have already discussed the necessity which he could not dodge, and the advantages he was able to utilize, of appointing some good Republicans and sound Americans to his first cabinet. But his concession to political realities practically ended at that point. Since that time his appointments have almost invariably been characterized by one or more of these three purposes: (1) To split the Republican Party, and weaken the conservative faction, by giving jobs to leftwing Republicans, whenever anybody calling himself a Republican was appointed at all; (2) to frustrate and break down the whole Republican Party, as well as to gather strength and implementation for socialistic measures, by giving important jobs to leftwing Democrats; and (3) to put actual Communists or Communist sympathizers into influential positions, to whatever extent the political climate made it feasible. Eisenhower's catering to this third purpose has steadily increased during the last two or three years.

The political affiliations of some of Eisenhower's appointees, however, are as vague and as mysterious as were his own. Also, the categories above do sometimes overlap with regard to a particular individual; that is, he may appear to be a leftwing Democrat, for instance, and actually be a Communist. So we are going to list below some forty appointments made by Eisenhower, or which could not have been made by department heads under him if he disapproved, without trying to separate them into three classifications. But we shall try, in most cases, to make clear the place of the appointment in this whole story, by at least a brief word of comment.

1. Milton Eisenhower[1]

Presidential Adviser. At least in appearance. Had always been an ardent New Dealer, to put it mildly, and still is. Proof of at least pro-Communist leanings is implicit in his support of Owen Lattimore, and of others like him, at Johns Hopkins.[2] In

my opinion the chances are very strong that Milton
Eisenhower is actually Dwight Eisenhower's superior
and boss within the whole Leftwing Establishment.
For one thing he is obviously a great deal smarter.

2.   Maxwell E. Rabb

Presidential Adviser, and assistant for relations
with minority groups. First official title, "Associate
Counsel" for the President; then "Secretary To The
Cabinet." Now in private law practice. Drew a salary all during 1952, while helping to run the Eisenhower campaign, for a post he never filled with the
Democratic-controlled Senate Judiciary Committee.
The staff director of this committee did not even know
him.[1]

Max Rabb is a very clever and cagey man. Proof
that he is a Communist sympathizer would not be
easy, except as a logical deduction from his overall
actions and visible purposes. In masterminding the
steal of the Republican nomination at Chicago in 1952,
however, he followed so faithfully and cleverly the
exact Communist technique, of always accusing your
enemy, first and loudly, of the very crime which you
yourself are committing, that the long arm of coincidence would be strained in reaching so far.

3.   John Foster Dulles[2]

Secretary of State. America's Case Against
Secretary Dulles & Company was presented by Senator William E. Jenner in an article in the April, 1956
issue of the American Mercury. We covered a certain amount of additional ground on Pages 23 to 28
of the June, 1958 issue of American Opinion.[3] We'll
try to summarize these and other appraisals here as
briefly as we can.

John Foster Dulles is the man who chiefly persuaded Thomas E. Dewey and the Republican "opposition, " in 1944 and 1948, to go along with, instead of
fighting, the pro-Communist foreign policies of the

Roosevelt and Truman Administrations. Dulles has at all times been a close friend, admirer, associate, consultant, and political protégé of Dean Acheson.[1] Senator Jenner says that "Mr. Dulles is Mr. Acheson's identical twin." Dulles became officially a right-hand man of Acheson, in 1950; and was so completely a part of the Communist-dominated Truman foreign-policy menagerie that he no longer gave Who's Who In America his address as 48 Wall Street, New York, which was his law office, but as "Office: Department of State, Washington."[2]

Certainly his appointment was a strange and disillusioning one to be made by the kind of Republican which President Eisenhower was pretending to be in 1952.[3] Among other visible parts of his record, Dulles had been a prominent and much publicized member of the first meeting of the World Council of Churches, at Amsterdam in 1948, when that body officially declared capitalism to be just as bad as Communism.[4] Dulles neither protested nor disavowed the statement, which was fully in accord with his own expressed convictions, and which was given so much publicity in this country that I actually heard it, being loudly bleated over a radio from the club house, while I was playing golf.

For many reasons and after a lot of study, I personally believe Dulles to be a Communist agent who has had one clearly defined role to play; namely, always to say the right things and always to do the wrong ones. The Japanese peace treaty, the Austrian peace treaty, and his very definite doublecrossing of the British government in the Suez affair are all cases in point. In speeches and public statements Dulles is always the proponent of the real American position, the man who announces the policies and intentions which the American people want to hear, and which they recognize as right.[5] He thus serves to convince the American Congress and people that the administration is <u>trying</u> to do the right thing. Then Dulles backs down, or is overruled, or appears to be forced by circumstances and pressures he can't control to reverse himself; the government does exactly the opposite of what he has said it would do; and the defeat of our side is worse than if he had never spoken at all. But the American people simply do not grasp that it was all planned that way in the first place.

Although it certainly will not strengthen my argument any, it may perhaps be worth while, just to give the reader a break from so much monotonously respectable language, to quote somebody else's summation of Dulles' character. Once, in a small group, I asked a good friend of mine and prominent American, whose name at least is well known to every reader of this document but who has never held any political office, what he thought of Dulles. After a moment of hesitation he replied, so that everybody could hear: "I think John Foster Dulles is a sanctimonious, psalm-singing hypocritical son of a bitch, and I know him very well." If Syngman Rhee, Chiang Kai-shek, Nuri es-Said, and other real anti-Communists in the governments of our allies throughout the world, could be persuaded to voice their real thoughts, I am sure they would agree with that sentiment, if not with its phrasing. For it is certain beyond dispute that Dulles (or our State Department as run by Dulles), has been selling them and their countries down the river into Communist hands, as cleverly as he knew how and as rapidly as he dared.

4. Martin Durkin

First Secretary of Labor. Robert Taft said his appointment was incredible. It <u>was</u> -- so incredible and so revealing that even Eisenhower couldn't make that one stick. But his aims are shown by the fact that he made it at all.'

5. Theodore C. Streibert[1]

First head of the newly independent United States Information Agency. Announced at the beginning of his term that under him the Voice of America would avoid "going violently anti-Soviet." It certainly has. He also stated that "where there are two sides to a question here we shall be sure to give both sides."[2] Taking American taxpayers' money to present, to the people of the satellite nations, the Soviet side of the phony issues they stir up, would be bad enough. Streibert's choice of agents to present the American side, over Voice of America, has been even worse. Eisenhower could get away with so brazen an appointment even then, simply because it seemed to the American people too minor for them to give any of their attention.[3]

6. (In preparing this manuscript for publication it has seemed more logical to deal with the name originally listed here under "Associates." And this has been done.)

7. Chester Bowles

Ambassador To India. Actually a holdover from the Truman Administration, who was replaced by Eisenhower on May 15, 1953. But this "foot-dragging" was inexcusable, and quite revealing as to Eisenhower's purposes, to anybody who really looked behind the scenes. For while Bowles' sympathies had not yet been too well exposed to the public, they were well known to the insiders. And fortunately we can put Bowles in his proper niche here with just one simple fact: He was one of the principal owners of the pro-Communist publication, PM.[4]

8. Charles E. Bohlen

Ambassador To Russia.[5] This appointment, also made so early in the Eisenhower Administration, was declared even then by a discerning few to be a portent of things to come.[6] Senator McCarthy claimed that there were sixteen pages of derogatory material about Bohlen in the FBI security file on him. Senator Wayne Morse, ardently pro-Bohlen, referred at first to "two or three," then to "six or seven," and finally admitted fifteen such derogatory reports.[1]

Bohlen was a protégé of Acheson, and another close friend of Alger Hiss.[2] Even at the hearings on his confirmation he still brazenly supported the Teheran, Yalta, and Potsdam conferences and agreements, in each of which he had participated in a minor capacity. He was vigorously endorsed by Senators Humphrey and Lehman. He was confirmed, despite his record, because most of the Republican Senators put peace in the Republican Party at this stage above an honest foreign-affairs policy, and shared the feeling expressed by Senator Taft that the appointment of Bohlen was a relatively minor question, not worth fighting over. They were wrong. For Eisenhower was edging Communist sympathizers, right out of the old Acheson-Hiss coterie, into every position of importance that he dared. The total impact of this program was very important indeed. And the total of these "relatively minor matters not worth fighting over" added up to a very clear revelation of the game Eisenhower was playing. But nobody, or very few indeed, even wanted to look.[3]

9. Arthur H. Dean

Chief American Negotiator in the truce with the Communists at Panmunjom. Already mentioned far earlier in these pages, so we'll add little more about him here. His sympathies can readily be seen from the fact that early in 1954 he stated publicly, with the prestige of an American "Ambassador," that we should take a "new look" at Red China and "be prepared to admit them to the family of nations."[4] Had already given Red China at Panmunjom everything they could think of to ask for except the White House dome. Long-time law partner of John Foster Dulles.

Arthur Dean was the one man who, more than any other, had blocked every effort to clean up the Institute of Pacific Relations from the inside, and had kept it firmly and aggressively on its pro-Communist course. In addition to all of which he is, right on the plain written record, one of the most brazen and incorrigible liars that ever competed in that category with Alger Hiss.[1]

10. Allen W. Dulles[2]

Head of the CIA. Brother of John Foster Dulles. (They have a sister in the State Department whose pro-Communist slant is less disguised).[3] Law partner of Arthur Dean.[4] Allen Dulles is the most protected and untouchable supporter of Communism, next to Eisenhower himself, in Washington.

How many millions of dollars of American taxpayers' money Allen Dulles has turned over to Walter Reuther's stooge, Irving Brown, to promote Communism in fact while pretending to fight it (through building up the left-wing labor unions of Europe), nobody will ever know. How many millions he has turned over to David Dubinsky and Jay Lovestone, both admitted Communists but claiming to be anti-Stalinist Communists, on the specious excuse that it is best to fight the Kremlin through such opponents, nobody will ever know. How many millions he has supplied to the NTS, the phony Russian refugee anti-Communist organization, to enable its world-wide branches to wreck real anti-Communist organizations, none of us will ever know. Nobody is allowed by the Eisenhower Administration to get close enough even to ask. When a man as highly regarded and highly placed as Major General Trudeau, Director of Military Intelligence, even began to suggest that the CIA under Allen Dulles was of no help in safeguarding America against Communism, Trudeau found himself quickly removed from office as head of Military Intel-

ligence and sent to routine duty in the Far East.
When Senator McCarthy, at the very height of his popularity with the American people, began casting even
random glances at the CIA, his days were immediately numbered.

When a patriotic young American goes into intelligence work, especially against as ruthless an enemy
as the Communists, he knows that he is risking his
life. He knows that he must count on his own courage,
skill, and resourcefulness. But he has every right to
expect loyalty to America on the part of those above
him in his own agency. One month before that shuttle-
cock defector, Otto John, went over to the East German Communists, however, he spent a whole day in
Allen Dulles' headquarters in Washington. Then, immediately after John's defection, our agents in Central
Europe began losing their lives. The inside report is
that more than 160 were exposed and killed within the
next several weeks. The inference that Otto John took
with him from Washington the information that made
this possible is clear. Of course there is no way to
prove it. McCarthy, if he had been given the full power of the United States Senate behind his investigation,
might have been able to uncover the whole rotten story,
and to show that the CIA is the most Communist-infested of all the agencies of our government. But Eisenhower was able instead to turn the power of the U.S.
Senate onto the destruction of McCarthy. And Allen
Dulles still goes his slippery way.[1]

11. Arthur F. Burns

Off-and-on Economic Adviser and Super-adviser
to the President. Typical of the kind of economic advice Burns hands out were his statements in 1955 that
"our system of free and competitive enterprise is on
trial" and that government "must be ready to take
vigorous steps to help maintain a stable prosperity."[2]
It is quite probable that the job of "economic adviser"

has been merely a coverup for Burns' liaison work between Eisenhower and some of his bosses in the Establishment.

12.   John J. Corson

Appointed to head a panel of advisers to the President on higher education, especially as to recommendations to the President, for him in turn to make to Congress, on Federal Aid To Education.   This appointment was not subject to approval by Congress, because the "briefing panel" was set up and paid under the President's "emergency funds," for which he does not have to account.   Mr. Corson's general point of view can be shown by this paragraph from a paper which he wrote for "The Social Welfare Forum":

"As things stand today, government alone can provide the security that families, churches, and charitable agencies did in the past.   The pension programs provided by employers and labor will constitute nothing more than the frosting on the cake.   Government must provide basic security, and this means a frank guarantee of a minimum of well-being for every individual, not alone for a fifth of the people at the bottom of the scale."[1]

You can certainly tell in advance just the kind of advice concerning federal aid to education that Mr. Eisenhower will get, knows he will get, and wants, from any panel headed by Mr. Corson.   And we have listed this relatively quite minor appointment here because it is so completely typical of the kind of appointments Eisenhower is consistently making on the lower as well as the higher levels.

13.   James E. Mitchell

Secretary of Labor.   Mitchell has not been one whit less devoted to the aims of the most leftwing labor bosses, or less active on their behalf, than Durkin would have been.   He has just been quieter and more subtle about it.   From rebuking the American employ-

er-delegate to the ILO for opposing seating of the
Russian Communist so-called employer-delegates,
to repeatedly declaring himself against state right-
to-work laws, Mitchell has shown himself to be the
answer to Walter Reuther's prayer. And this writer
has heard a man, formerly highly placed in the Department of Commerce, publicly make the statement,
based on his own knowledge and experience, that behind the scenes the White House fully supports
Mitchell's most biased activities on behalf of the
most ambitiously tyrannical labor leaders.

14.   Arthur Larson

At first, Undersecretary of Labor. Now, Director of U.S.I.A.   As Undersecretary of Labor,
Mr. Larson publicly favored a union shop. When
asked whether he thought that an individual ought to
be forced to join a union if he didn't want to do so,
Larson replied: " That's a case of the individual, as
so often happens in our lives, having to conform to
the will of the majority. "[1] Mr. Larson proclaims
himself as a great believer in the " American center, "
to which he says that he himself, Adlai Stevenson,
Dean Acheson, and President Eisenhower all belong.[2]
He also says positively that in all of these expressions he is stating Eisenhower's beliefs as well as his
own.[3] We have no doubt that he is right.[4]

15.   G. Bernard Noble

Head of the Historical Division of the State Department. Actually is a holdover from the Truman
Administration, but despite the extensive use of the
civil service alibi by the Eisenhower Administration,
it would be easy enough to get Noble out of this spot
if they wished to do so. Under Noble's management
of the Division, the suppression, distortion, and falsification of the documents and records concerning
our foreign policy have been so continuous and so
shameless that two career men in the Division, Bryton

Barron and Donald Dozer, gave up their jobs rather than be a party to such machinations.[1]

16.   Simon E. Sobeloff

At first Solicitor General of the United States, in which position he selected and controlled thousands of lawyers working for the federal government. Was then appointed by Eisenhower as Judge of the Court of Appeals for the Fourth Judicial Circuit.

In 1955 the administration began its drive -- later implemented by a Supreme Court decision -- to allow bureaucrats accused of subversive activities to "confront their accusers."   This plausible sounding piece of legalistic hocus-pocus was a clever scheme for forcing exposure of FBI agents and informers working within the Communist party. It was another disastrous blow to whatever internal security system we still have left. The Department of Justice prepared a brief against the proposal. Sobeloff as Solicitor General refused to sign the brief!

We do not think there is any doubt that Sobeloff's known sympathies can fairly be described as un-American. We can see no possible excuse for his appointment to either of his jobs by a Republican president. But we can see plenty of reason for it, just the same.

17.   James Hagerty

Presidential Secretary. We know nothing about his background. But his actions speak for him -- and even more for President Eisenhower. Among the accomplishments of which Hagerty is openly most proud is his part in planning and carrying out the scheme to destroy McCarthy.[2]

18.   James B. Conant

High Commissioner To Germany. We do not contend that Conant is a Communist, any more than we do about Hagerty or some of the others above. We do contend that the appointment of Conant to that specific job was made by a pro-Communist President for the spe-

cific purpose of damaging the Republican Party and
the anti-Communist cause.' Conant had been a zeal-
ous New Dealer, and an ardent advocate of the Morgenthau Plan. What a man for a Republican President to send to Germany, to help to tie them to us
as allies against the Communists!

19.   David K. E. Bruce

Ambassador To West Germany.² The chief significance of this appointment by Eisenhower was the deliberate nose-thumbing affront to the Republican Party.
Bruce has been an active and partisan Maryland Democrat all of his life. He was Ambassador to France
and Undersecretary of State under Truman, and a
close supporter of the Truman Administration. In
1956 he supported Adlai Stevenson and contributed
one thousand dollars to the Democratic Party. One important Republican Senator said that his colleagues were
incensed at this appointment of "another Democratic
campaign contributor to an important diplomatic post."³
Making the Republicans incensed and frustrated, of
course, was exactly what Eisenhower wanted.

20. Amory Houghton

Ambassador To France, to succeed Clarence
Dillon, whose appointment we did not bother to discuss. Amory Houghton was chairman of the board of
the Corning Glass Works. The fact that Corning Glass
had been involved in one criminal and five civil anti-
trust actions brought by the Department of Justice
over the past several years, or that its board chairman resigned from the War Production Board in 1942
under eyebrow-raising circumstances, did not bother
Eisenhower any in appointing this board chairman to
an important ambassadorship. We have a strong suspicion that these possible objections were overweighed
on the favorable side by considerations of which only
one tiny facet stands revealed. In 1951, when a Communist sympathizer and bad security risk, Dr. E. U.

Condon, gave up his post as head of the U. S. Bureau
of Standards because of actions of the House Committee on Un-American Activities,' he was immediately
given the job of Director of Research of the Corning
Glass Works.

This does not mean to say that Amory Houghton
or his firm had done anything wrong, to get the persistent attention of the Department of Justice. The
anti-trust suits may have been typical examples of New
Deal government harassment, for all we know. But
it does show how very little the "clean-as-a-hound's-
tooth" Administration, which couldn't sign the natural gas bill because somebody had merely attempted
to bribe somebody else in connection with it, really
cares about such considerations except when they
make a grand excuse for actions it desires to take.

On the other hand the argument that Houghton's
firm employs twenty thousand people and that therefore he could not be expected to be responsible for individuals employed will not hold when the nature of
Dr. Condon's job is remembered. The position of
Director of Research of the whole enterprise simply
could not be given to anybody in the Corning Glass
Works without the approval of the Chairman of the
Board. This does not imply that Amory Houghton is
a Communist. It does indicate a "softness" towards
them, a willingness to discount Communist sympathies and employ and work with people having such
sympathies -- which would serve Eisenhower's purposes almost as well.

21. (The name listed here, in the confidential
letter, has been omitted in preparing this manuscript
for publication, as being no longer of any importance
in the context.)

22. Fred Seaton

Secretary of the Interior, to succeed Donald
McKay. This was a part of the move, which began

immediately after the 1956 elections, to replace even
those reasonably sound men whom Eisenhower had put
in his first cabinet, with the kind of men he wants. In
fact, we believe Eisenhower's urging of McKay to run
for the United States Senate, in Oregon, may have been
primarily to make room for Seaton as his successor
in the cabinet.

There was a topflight career man in the Department of Interior, available to succeed McKay. He was
so logical a choice, and so urgently recommended by
leading Republicans, that many assumed he would be
given the job. But Eisenhower thumbed his nose at
them again, and appointed Seaton. To give all of
Seaton's qualifications that appealed so to Eisenhower
would take many pages. But we can summarize them
in just one sentence. During his brief term as a so-
called Republican Senator from Nebraska, Fred Seaton
was ranked higher than any other Republican in the
whole United States Senate, by the Americans For
Democratic Action, for voting exactly the way the ADA
wanted him to vote.'

23.   Maxwell S. Stewart

Writer for the Department of Health, Education
and Welfare. Stewart puts out the official "Public
Affairs" pamphlets for that department. They are
intended to have, and probably do have, considerable
influence in forming American public opinion on many
subjects. Stewart is typical of hundreds of such writers, public relations experts, and other propagandists
throughout the various departments who, while not actually appointed by Eisenhower, could not be where
they are without his approval. They could not be there
unless these department heads sensed that they are
pleasing Eisenhower by having such "liberals" on
their staffs. As for this man's type of "liberalism,"
there is at least nothing equivocal about it. He was a
former recruiting agent for American students to at-

tend Moscow Institute, a leading participant in the affairs of the Institute of Pacific Relations during the peak years of its pro-Communist accomplishments, and his name has appeared as a member of more than fifty organizations which have been cited by government agencies as subversive.[1]

24.   Joseph E. Johnson

Appointed as chairman of a committee to investigate United States participation in the conferences and activities of the ILO. This committee, of the executive department of the government, was all that the NAM and the U.S. Chamber of Commerce got for their request that the ILO be investigated by a Congressional committee, as a prerequisite to continued nomination by the NAM and U.S. Chamber of an employer-delegate.

How smoothly, subtly, and irresistibly the Communists bowl over or push aside all opposition, to their patient but sure progress along the roads they have chosen, was never more clearly revealed than in the NAM board meeting when it was decided to nominate an employer-delegate for 1957. Will McGrath and this writer led the fight for dropping out, and not lending our prestige any longer to a group in which we were completely powerless, and which was using our participation and prestige simply to help them in their plans to enslave us.[2] The vote was very close. About five votes either way would have made the difference, And at least five or six of those who voted for continued participation either stated on the floor, or told me afterwards, that they did so solely on the strength of the Johnson Committee report. This report, supposedly based on a careful and objective investigation made by a committee appointed by the President, and headed by a man of the caliber of the President of the Carnegie Endowment For International Peace, carried tremendous weight in their minds. And it recommended that we not only stay in the ILO, but greatly increase our interest and participation in its affairs. Not a one of these NAM directors knew, or would have paid any attention even if told, without at least a hundred pages of convincing background material to open his eyes, these plain and important facts: Joseph E. Johnson was a protégé of Alger Hiss, who had worked in various government agencies as a subordinate and right-hand man of Hiss for years; and when the trustees of the Carnegie Endowment simply had to drop Hiss, as a concession to public opinion, they did all they could to repair damage to the Communist cause by appointing his disciple, Joseph E. Johnson, to succeed him as president of the Endowment. And Eisenhower had become a member of this board of trustees at the time. The report and recommendations of Joseph Johnson and his committee, with regard to the ILO, could have been foretold in advance almost to the last comma, and certainly were foreseen by Eisenhower when he made the appointment.

25. Earl Warren

Chief Justice of the United States Supreme Court. Warren is probably not a Communist, although the ardent advocacy of him for the Presidency by Eleanor Roosevelt, Joseph Rauh, Jr., and many of their ilk, makes one wonder. As does the sharp turn taken by the Court, in support of rabidly pro-Communist measures, since Warren became Chief Justice.' But that he is actually and at least an extreme leftwing socialist, as well as a consummate hypocrite, was clearly shown by some articles that he wrote for the Saturday Evening Post many years ago. As by almost everything else in his whole career.

26. Robert McKinney

United States Delegate to the new International Atomic Energy Agency. Robert McKinney was the publisher of a Santa Fe newspaper, an ardent Democrat who vigorously supported Adlai Stevenson and viciously attacked Eisenhower in the 1956 campaign. He even resorted to the typically Communist tactics of lying about Eisenhower's health and promoting a whispering campaign against Mrs. Eisenhower. All but the last of these facts were told to Eisenhower personally by General Pat Hurley.[1] Yet three months later, under pressure from his associates -- or direct orders from his Communist bosses -- Eisenhower appointed this man to the group which is to share our atomic know-how and atomic wealth with the rest of the world.

We think that one explanation of this strange episode is quite simple. We think that Robert McKinney is a Communist sympathizer or fellow traveler who had never grasped the full significance of the support of Eisenhower by Leonard Finder, or been told -- until quite recently -- where Eisenhower really stood. And that Eisenhower had never heard of McKinney until a few months ago, because McKinney's rising importance in the Communist scheme of things is of recent vintage. But a little matter like McKinney's slander campaign against Eisenhower was quickly forgotten, when their Communist bosses decided to have Eisenhower put McKinney in a very strategic position to work for the cause.[2]

27.   Harry P. Cain

Head of one of the loyalty boards.

Cain, former U.S. Senator from Washington, once was an outstanding conservative. He was deprived of his Senate seat by "liberals" with a lot of Communist help. He is one of the most conspicuous examples of an increasing number of men who have decided that anti-Communism was a losing cause, that a Communist victory was merely a matter of time, and that if you can't lick 'em -- join 'em! His change of heart obviously was convincingly shown, or made known,

to Eisenhower or the Communist bosses, before Cain
was appointed to head a loyalty board. In that position
he, like any neophyte who must prove himself to his
new associates, has out-Tydingsed Tydings in clear-
ing and whitewashing men who were visibly Communist agents.[1] If possible, he has been even more dili-
gent in that respect than Pierce Gerety, another Com-
munist-favoring loyalty board chairman on whom we'll
not bother to bestow autonomy in this discussion.

28. William J. Brennan, Jr.
Member, U. S. Supreme Court.

One of the most telling blows the Communists and
their liberal dupes were able to strike against Mc-
Carthy was the accusation that he called everybody a
Communist. It wasn't so at all. But naturally, since
he had taken on the job of running down and exposing
Communists, he found plenty of occasion and need to
use the term.

In this treatise, especially in this chapter, we are
somewhat in the same position. For naturally we are
seeking to list and discuss primarily those people
whose appointments have a direct bearing on the thesis
of this paper. So we appear to be calling almost everybody a Communist, a Communist sympathizer, or Communist helper of one kind or another, merely because
we have no reason to be mentioning the good men in
Washington, in all branches of the government, who
have no Communist sympathies whatever. Actually a
vast majority of the Senators and Congressmen, in
particular, are completely loyal Americans. For, as
Fulton Lewis has pointed out, "The liberal-left within
the Republican Party has little representation in the
Congress; it is concentrated among Presidential
appointees."[2]

But it is Presidential appointees, specifically,
whom we are discussing. That brings us back to Mr.
William J. Brennan, Jr. And the plain truth is that

Brennan's pro-Communist leanings were so clearly established in his record that we do not believe he could possibly have been confirmed for the Supreme Court only three or four years ago, before the smooth Eisenhower-Communist machine had worn down, browbeaten, and completely demoralized so much of the anti-Communist strength. Anybody sufficiently interested should look up the October 6, 1956 issue of <u>Human Events</u>, for as much of Brennan's history as Frank Hanighen dared to publish. One of McCarthy's very last efforts was to try to get the Senate to pay some attention to the plain facts about Brennan.[1] The Senators were too cowed by past experience to do so. Now McCarthy is dead, Brennan sits on the Supreme Court bench, and the Communist flood slowly engulfs all of the opposition.[2]

29. John S. Graham

Member, Atomic Energy Commission

Graham, a Democrat, served as Assistant Secretary of the Treasury under Truman. That's all we know about him. It is also all we need to know, to make evident Eisenhower's unceasing purpose of scuttling the Republican Party, and to show the continuity of the same influences through all recent Administrations.

30. (The name listed here, in the confidential letter, has been omitted in preparing this manuscript for publication, as being no longer of any importance in the context.)

31. Neil McElroy

Secretary of Defense.

This is another step in the left-grading of the original cabinet. McElroy's only publicized contribution to the leftwing drive up to the time of his appointment -- that we know about -- was his chairmanship and handling of the White House Conference On Education. The performance known as "group dynamics" is completely a Communist technique, invented and developed by them as a clever means of manipulating the opinions within supposedly free-discussion democratic assemblages, so as to distill out of these gatherings exactly the opinions that the Communist planners wanted arrived at in the first place. McElroy made assured and brilliant use of this technique, in order to come up with a report from this conference favoring the federal government's getting both feet into public education, despite the clear record that the report did not represent the views of a majority of even the carefully selected pawns on this chessboard. So, as other better informed writers have already pointed out, there was reason to regard Mr. McElroy with considerable skepticism.[1] And we can report, out of our own knowledge, that he was already so regarded by many of the outstanding conservative citizens of his home town of Cincinnati.

Since McElroy was made Secretary of Defense, he has shown his true colors much more emphatically. He has been an outspoken advocate of "changing our way of life" because of the Russian threat; that is, of regimenting our whole social organization under bureaucratic economic and political controls.[2] This would impose on us exactly that form and degree of state socialism under an all-powerful central government, which the Communists are so anxious to bring about as a major step towards pulling a communized America into a worldwide Communist regime.

In his own proper area of activity, McElroy has gone all out in support of Eisenhower's tricky and dangerous "reorganization plan!" for our armed services,[3] which would come nearer to establishing by legislation the foundations for a military dictatorship than any measure the Communists and their dupes have yet proposed.[4] And in supporting this scheme with all of the immense power at his command, McElroy has shown himself just as well versed or well tutored in other Communist techniques as he was in the one called group dynamics. He has made it crystal clear to every high officer of all of the services that the way for any such officer to wreck his career is to express any doubts about this reorganization plan.'

We have no idea whether Neil McElroy is an actual Communist sympathizer, or just an opportunistic left-wing politician "on the make." But he has certainly been doing the Communists' work for them with assurance and determination -- which it was obviously known he would do when he was appointed to so high a job.

Charles Wilson was, in our opinion, an able and honorable but very gullible businessman when outside his own bailiwick, completely befuddled by the snares of Washington. (Almost as befuddled as that earnest and sincere but now pathetic patriot, Sinclair Weeks, whose gullibility and helpfulness in the Eisenhower schemes have made him, simultaneously, a favorite and a laughingstock of the whole Left Wing.) But we think that Wilson was a far safer man to have in the spot of Secretary of Defense than his more brilliant and sophisticated successor.

32. Ellsworth Bunker
Ambassador To India.

And now we are back in the striped-pants and tinsel world of diplomacy. Mr. Bunker we happen to know and to have worked with personally. And we can assure you there is nothing in his smooth and charming front to suggest any smelly skeletons in his rear. But there seldom is.

At any rate, Bunker is a life-long Democrat, who served as both Ambassador to Argentina, and then Ambassador to India, under Truman. Which may establish the only point really involved in his appointment. But being of a mean and suspicious nature, we cannot help mentioning at least one bag of bones which somebody found in his immaculate-looking closets. Mr. Bunker is, and for sometime has been, a member of the board of trustees of the Institute of International Education,

Inc. A well-informed friend of mine says that describing the Institute as an actual branch of the Communist International, on the basis of the listing on
Page 6 of The Communist Conspiracy, issued on May
29, 1956 by the House Committee on Un-American
Activities, is to make a too "dogmatic interpretation
of a complicated relationship." Nor is there any
question but that plain eggheaded liberals have found
their starry-eyed way onto the Institute's board, as
in the case of all other associations promoting one-
worldism. But we confess to a strong prejudice
against any organization of which Stephen Duggan and
Ed Murrow have been the driving forces, and against
any man who would accept their leadership.[1]

    33. Lawrence G. Derthick

U.S. Commissioner of Education.

    Derthick is a "liberal" Tennessee Democrat,
and a close friend and protégé of Senator Estes Kefauver. So we see no reason to gild the lily. But
what an appointment to be made by a Republican President!

    34. Gordon Gray

Defense Mobilization Director.

    Gray is a "liberal" North Carolina Democrat,
who was considered "liberal" enough to have been
acceptable as a successor to Frank Graham as president of the University of North Carolina. Actually we
think that Gray, for all of his currently fashionable
"liberalism," is a reasonably able and entirely patriotic American. But his appointment was another
nail in the coffin of the Republican Party.

    35. John K. Emmerson

Counselor to the American Embassy in Lebanon.
Also brought back to Washington temporarily, at the
height of the Suez Affair, to assist Henry Cabot Lodge
in the United Nations.

    Emmerson is one of the men who helped to sell

out China to the Communists. He was a favorite
visitor to the Chinese Communists in Yenan in the
early 1940's, and reported favorably to our government on the Japanese Peoples Emancipation League,
which was strictly and completely a Communist organization. And he was one of four State Department
advisers in China, assigned to the staff of General
A. C. Wedemeyer at the close of the war, whose reports Wedemeyer said "were strongly slanted in favor
of Communist aims, contrary to fundamental American
policy and harmful to our fighting ally, the Nationalist
Government." Emmerson has now been in a position
for two years to help in the sellout of Iraq, Turkey,
and our friends in the Middle East, exactly as he did
in China a decade ago. And yet the American people
are surprised -- and the Eisenhower Administration
pretends to be surprised -- at the developments in
Lebanon and Iraq which are taking place right while
these pages are being written.'

36. Robert C. Strong

Counselor to the American Embassy in Syria.

On October 7, 1957, Attorney George S. Montgomery, Jr., of New York,sent the following telegram
to Secretary of State John Foster Dulles:

HAVE RECEIVED CONFIRMATION FROM
SENATOR WILLIAM JENNER THAT ROB-
ERT C. STRONG ON SEPTEMBER 30 AND
PRESUMABLY TODAY IS CHARGE D'AF-
FAIRES IN THE ABSENCE OF THE UNITED
STATES AMBASSADOR AT THE EMBASSY
IN DAMASCUS SYRIA STOP PARTIAL RECORD
OF THIS MAN ESTABLISHES THROUGH SEN-
ATE INVESTIGATION THAT DURING THE
YEARS 1949 AND 1950 ACTING AS CONSUL GEN-
ERAL WITH THE POSITION OF CHARGE D'AF-
FAIRES ON THE ISLAND OF FORMOSA FIRST
HE EXERTED EVERY EFFORT TO ASSIST THE

RED COMMUNIST CHINESE TO OVER-
THROW THE CHINESE NATIONALIST
GOVERNMENT AND CHIANG KAI-SHEK IN-
CLUDING THE SURRENDER OF FORMOSA
SECOND HE SENT DELIBERATELY FALSI-
FIED REPORTS AS TO THE STRENGTH OF
THE COMMUNIST CHINESE AND THE WEAK-
NESS OF THE NATIONALIST CHINESE PRE-
DICTING IMMEDIATE FALL OF CHIANG
KAI-SHEK IN ORDER TO ACHIEVE THIS VERY
OBJECTIVE THIRD HE EXCLUDED MEMBERS
OF THE INTELLIGENCE STAFF OF GENERAL
DOUGLAS MACARTHUR FROM THE ISLAND
OF FORMOSA FOURTH THAT HE SUMMARILY
DISMISSED A MILITARY ATTACHE WHO IN
DESPERATION HAD MADE A DIRECT ACCU-
RATE REPORT TO THE WAR DEPARTMENT
STOP DO YOU THINK YOU ARE PROPERLY
PROTECTING THE INTERESTS OF YOUR
COUNTRY BY PERMITTING SUCH A MAN TO
REPRESENT THE UNITED STATES AT A TIME
AND PLACE AS CRITICAL AS ANY IN THE
WORLD ACCORDING TO YOUR OWN STATE-
MENTS STOP DO YOU EXPECT AMERICANS
ANXIOUSLY WATCHING PROGRESS OF EVENTS
IN THE NEAR EAST TO REMAIN TRANQUIL IN
THE FACE OF SUCH INCREDIBLE ENTRUST-
MENT OF POWER.

That seems to take care of Mr. Strong's background and purposes. But the clear answer to Mr.
Montgomery's question was that Mr. Dulles -- and
Mr. Eisenhower and their Communist bosses -- did
expect the American people to remain ignorant, complacent, and passive, while the betrayal of our remaining friends in the Middle East was completed,
and that Mr. Dulles was right.

37. Raymond Ludden

In Office of Personnel, State Department, with especial responsibility for the Middle East.

In the fall of 1945 Raymond Ludden was summarily fired from his job in the American Embassy in Chungking, by General Pat Hurley, and sent home by Hurley, as too pro-Communist to be allowed to represent the United States in China in any capacity. So strongly were the Communists entrenched in our State Department, however, that almost immediately Ludden was sent back to China -- Hurley having resigned in the meantime -- and soon was assigned by the State Department as an adviser to General Wedemeyer. He was one of the four advisers referred to by Wedemeyer in the quotation two sections above, whose reports were so strongly slanted in favor of Communist aims. And this is the man who is now sitting in Washington and determining, more than anybody else, which employees of the State Department shall be sent or kept in the Middle East, "to save that area from the Communists."

The fact that a number of exactly the same so-called diplomats, who were directly responsible for the treasonous betrayal of our friends in China, are now in positions of equal influence with regard to developments in the Middle East, can have only one realistic explanation.

38. Llewellyn E. Thompson, Jr.

Ambassador To Russia.

Between 1946 and 1949 the Free World lost practically all of Eastern Europe to the Communists. The Kremlin did not have the military power to take over these nations by force of arms, and it certainly did not have the moral influence and popularity for its agents to be welcomed by the peoples of these nations as their new rulers. The enslavement of Roumania, Bulgaria, Hungary, Yugoslavia, Poland, and Czechoslovakia was accomplished by diplomatic betrayals, always aided and abetted by our State Department, followed by police-state suppressions of all opposition, always with the acquiescence of our State Department and frequently with actual help supplied by it. In some cases, as in Poland, this active aid by our State Department in the betrayal of the country, and in its subjugation to the Kremlin's agents, was carried out right under the eyes of an honest and horrified American Ambassador who did everything he possibly could to make his protests heard.[1] The slipperiness, cunning, and determination of our State Department during those few years, in helping Stalin to make satellite slaves out of the people of Eastern Europe, is utterly unbelievable to anybody who has not studied the gruesome details at considerable length. But by 1949 the job was practically finished. There remained only the formalization of the Kremlin's rule over East Germany, in 1950, to make Communist sway over all of Eastern Europe complete.[2]

The chief of the State Department's Eastern European Affairs Division, from 1946 to 1949, was Llewellyn E. Thompson, Jr.!!

We'll skip all of Mr. Thompson's other accomplishments for the cause but one. He was responsible for the negotiations concerning, and for the details and wording of, the Austrian Peace Treaty. President Eisenhower sent him a "Distinguished Service" citation for that achievement. Whenever the Kremlin bestows a medal on some butcher of a million peaceful people, for his "dedication to peace," thus using an exact reversal of the language and principles once understood and honored by the civilized world, we can no longer look virtuously askance at such mockery of man's history and customs. Eisenhower's honoring of Thompson for "the successful conclusion ... of the Austrian State Treaty" was of exactly the same Communist pattern. The American people, deceived, unaware, complacent, and morally indifferent, are being eased into the world of George Orwell without even knowing what is happening to them. When we learned that Charles E. Bohlen was being transferred from Moscow to Manila, our first thought was: "God help the Philippines."[1] On learning that his successor in Moscow was to be Llewellyn E. Thompson, Jr., we revised that prayerful thought to "God help the United States of America."[2]

39. (The name listed here, in the confidential letter, has been omitted in preparing this manuscript for publication, as being no longer of any importance in the context.)

40. James D. Zellerbach[3]
Ambassador To Italy.

We believe our readers are sufficiently familiar with the Institute of Pacific Relations for us not to need to fill in any more details about that instrument of Communist achievement. And Mr. Zellerbach was not only a member of its board of trustees during its busy season, and one of its financial angels, but he joined with Arthur Dean in preventing any cleanup of the organization from the inside.

We think that the purpose and activities of the Fund For The Republic are familiar enough to our readers for no further comment about that Communist-aiding agency to be needed.[4] And Mr. Zellerbach has been a director of the Fund For The Republic for years.

We are sure we have talked enough about the National Committee For An Effective Congress, not to need to add anything here. And Mr. Zellerbach is one of its thirty-nine members.

In our book all of these things are very bad and very revealing. But we do not think all three of them together tell as much about where Mr. Zellerbach's sympathies really lie as the fact that he is a close friend of, and strongly supported by, Paul Hoffman. But the sensitivity of the U.S. Senate to subversive tendencies has become so calloused, and most of its members so supine, under the unceasing Eisenhower pressures to have leftwing appointments confirmed, that it not only ratified the appointment of James D. Zellerbach in the face of his record; it refused even to hear witnesses who asked to testify in opposition to that appointment. [1]

With the forty names we have listed here, and similar appointees we have discussed elsewhere in this paper in other connections, we have hardly scratched the surface. Our most glaring -- but entirely conscious -- omission has been that of C. D. Jackson, filling the apparent position of Gadabout-at-Large.[2] My wife is the specialist in our family on Mr. Jackson, and has assembled some thirty or forty pages showing his pro-Communist leanings and almost incredible record. But the material is simply too long and too involved to put in proper order here.

We have said nothing about the appointment to the Atomic Energy Commission of one Isidor Isaac Rabi,[3] born and raised in Austria, a former roommate of the traitor Klaus Fuchs at Los Alamos, and more recently a member of the faculty of Columbia University. We have said nothing about the record of the ubiquitous George V. Allen, who succeeded Arthur Larson as head of USIA. We have omitted any previous reference to Robert Murphy, No. 2 man in the State Department. Murphy has shown such an amazing capacity for making America hated, and for getting it blamed by the natives for their troubles, in the Belgian Congo, in Algeria, in France, in the Middle East, and everywhere he has turned his meddling hands,[4] that the consistency of the results makes "poor luck" utterly absurd as an explanation. We have given no attention to Mr. John A. McCone, nominated by Eisenhower to replace Admiral Strauss on the AEC, although McCone was a favorite office-holder under Truman, and is a trustee of the Communist-infested California Institute of Technology,[1] where Linus Pauling is such a shining light. And please give us credit for restraint. We have not said one word in this chapter about Sherman Adams. We do wish to repeat, however, that if Adams sheds many more crocodile tears over the "unfairness" of the Oren Harris Committee, he is going to ruin his vicuna coat.[2]

There are dozens of other high-ranking appointments, and literally hundreds at lower levels, which would merely add their weight to the purport of this chapter. For Eisenhower and his Communist bosses and their pro-Communist appointees are gradually taking over our whole government, right under the noses of the American people. Even in our armed forces the same treasonous controls are gradually being established. Kirke Lawton, who tried to live up to his oath of office as an American army officer, by cooperating in the exposure of Communist agents under his command at Ft. Monmouth, found his career ruined, and has been traveling about the country as a lost soul for three years. But Zwicker, who visibly lied under oath to protect the Communists above him, who were in turn protecting the Communists at Ft. Monmouth,[3] has been promoted.[4] And the White House and Eisenhower personally engaged in an extraordinary lobbying campaign to make sure that Zwicker's promotion was confirmed.[5]

In similar vein we could go on for many pages. But this is enough, we hope, to make the pattern and the purpose clear. We think that an objective survey of Eisenhower's associates and appointments shows clever Communist brains, aided by willing Communist hands, always at work to give the Communists more power, and to weaken the anti-Communist resistance. We also think that, while this detail from history does not strictly involve the case of an appointment, there is one very fitting and revealing item with which to end this chapter. In the 1956 campaign for the Presidency, Eisenhower had the open and enthusiastic support of Harry Bridges. And we believe Bridges knew what he was doing, even though the American people did not.

CHAPTER SEVENTEEN

The Word Is Treason . . . . .

So certain and so rapid has now become the succession of world-shaking events, of crisis on top of
crisis, that the memory of the American people concerning earlier crises has become even shorter than
it was before. There is one important result, of this
obliteration of impressions by ever new and heavier
impressions, on which Eisenhower's Communist
bosses have counted with assurance. As each new
development on the Cold War front takes place, the
American people are stuffed to the gills with arguments, in infinite detail, as to why the President
did this or did not do that, and are set to debating
with each other as to the soundness or wisdom of
every piecemeal action or statement of the administration -- with all such arguments and grounds for
debate carefully pitched on the foundation that the
administration is seeking the best possible course
for bringing about the ultimate defeat of Communism.
Only as any one major development begins to recede
enough in perspective, so that the American people
could look at it whole, is there any real chance of
widespread suspicion arising that the whole premise,
on which the battle of opinions has been fought, was
fraudulent in the first place. But by that time a new
development has turned the attention of the public
once again on the tweedledum-against-tweedledee con-
troversies connected with the new crisis. Yet it is
only by getting outside, away from the individual
trees and the underbrush, that there is any chance
of seeing a woods correctly; and the only way we

have of quickly grasping the nature and important
features of any new woods we may find ourselves in
at a particular time is by recalling what we have
learned from similar experiences in the past. So
let's look back, very briefly, at just a few of these
"woods" we have recently been through.

Who, for instance, is paying any attention today
to the International Atomic Energy Agency, about
which there was so much shouting only two years
ago? Yet the sell-out of this country's interests and
safety to the Communists, which Eisenhower engineered through that scheme, is far more obvious today than it was then. The Agency grew out of a
proposal which Eisenhower personally made to the
United Nations in 1953.[1] The Charter creating the
Agency was approved by the General Assembly of
the United Nations in October, 1956. In due course
that Charter, in the form of a treaty, was then presented to the United States Senate.

As some concern and indignation did arise over
this monstrous betrayal, Eisenhower began making
his customary claims of astonishment on discovering
some of the features of the treaty[2] -- exactly as he
did with regard to provisions of his own "civil rights"
bill. In this case, however, the hypocrisy was carried even further. For at the very time Eisenhower
was expressing pious surprise at some of the terms
of the Charter, his associates were shouting that the
Senate must accept it for the explicit reason that this
whole plan was President Eisenhower's own idea.
(Of course nobody brought forth the fact that helping
Russia to get its hands on more nuclear fuels has been
an obsession with Eisenhower ever since he took such
pains in 1945 to see that Soviet troops got possession
of the Czechoslovakian Uranium mines.)[3] In July,
1957, the treaty was ratified -- and promptly forgotten.

It shouldn't have been. Any member of the United Nations is automatically eligible to join the International Atomic Energy Agency. Any country, such as Red China, although not a member of the United Nations, may be taken into the Agency by a two-thirds vote of those nations that are already members. Russia almost burned out a bearing in its haste to set the example of ratification. Some eighty other nations had already joined or signified their intention of joining before we did. But the Agency meant nothing until the United States joined, since sharing our atomic materials and knowledge was the reason for its existence. We now pay one-third of the cost of running the outfit (besides supplying all of the nuclear fuel for it to manage), but have only one vote in eighty concerning its management. The head of the Agency today is a Czechoslovakian Communist.[1]

Eisenhower had already committed us in advance to membership, as far as he dared, by his statement of November 18, 1956 (immediately after the elections) as follows: "It will be our policy... to seek to conduct our operations in support of nuclear power development abroad in consonance with the policy of the International Atomic Energy Agency, in whose endeavors we shall take our full part."[2] On October 23, 1956 he had sent a telegram to the conference which was drafting the Agency's statute, as follows: "The United States will make available to the International Agency, on terms to be agreed with the Agency, 5000 kilograms of the nuclear fuel, Uranium-235, from the 20,000 kilograms allocated last February by the United States for peaceful uses by friendly nations."[3] And even before we had joined, the Atomic Energy Commission was using the Agency as an excuse for sharing our knowledge, by declassifying information of considerable value in the production of fissionable material.

The Word Is Treason

253

Practically all of the nuclear scientists have stated that there is no clear line between the production of such materials for power development and its production for bombs.[1] The Agency has no control over what its member nations do with the nuclear fuel allotted to them out of the pool we provide. According to the charter of the Agency we could be obligated by the Agency to deliver our fissionable material directly to such nations as Yugoslavia, Russia, or even Red China.[2] And responsible authorities say that the 20,000 kilograms of U-235, which we were committed from the beginning to put into the pool, would make enough atomic bombs to wipe out every major city in America.

By the original terms of this commitment, our contribution of the remaining fifteen thousand kilograms of that twenty thousand was contingent on the same amount being contributed by all of the other nations of the world combined. But the President could modify that condition at any time. (He may already have. Once the Senate ratified the Charter, this Agency did a clever disappearing act from the pages of American newspapers.) Or he could cause delivery to be made by ourselves on the mere <u>promise</u> of delivery by other nations. Or Russia could actually put fifteen thousand kilograms into the pool, to match ours, and the Agency could then simply -- and perfectly legally -- turn the whole thirty thousand kilograms over to Russia. The only single safeguard against that whole lot, or any amount allocated by the Agency to any nation at any time, being used to produce bombs, is the "treaty" with those nations which constituted the Agency's charter.

There is not one treaty of any substance with any non-Communist nation which Russia has lived up to since the Communists came to power in that country. But Eisenhower urgently insisted that we put our necks

into this noose, in reliance on the Russian promise
not to monkey with the rope. The whole insidious
scheme, to wipe out the one military advantage over
Russia which we still had,' and to put the power to
destroy us right into Communist hands, was variously
described -- even by those who opposed it -- as an
exercise in starry-eyed idealism; or as a premature
and incautious play in world politics; or as simply un-
surpassable folly. Frankly, we do not believe it was
any of those things. We think it was camouflaged but
deliberate treason; and that the camouflage consisted
primarily of our unwillingness to use the senses God
gave us and look squarely at plain facts.

Despite the small amount of space we gave to so
large a subject as foreign aid, we are not going to
plunge again into that wild blue yonder. But we do
want to take a quick squint, from the point of view
of this chapter, at one or two little clouds in that sky
which have now floated off in the distance.

Incredible enough was Eisenhower's early and
ardent championing of a loan by us to Gomulka's government of Poland.² This insistence could not be
justified by any naive belief in Gomulka's "nationalism" and independence of Moscow, because Eisenhower had been equally insistent on establishing the
"Chair of Polish Studies" at Columbia, when no such
excuse was even suggested. But nobody, at all informed on the situation, could possibly believe the
"independence" myth anyway, for many reasons.
We'll cite just two.

It was stated right in the arrangements for the
forty-five million dollar "loan" that five million dollars of this money was to be used for equipment to
increase Poland's deliveries of coal to Soviet Russia
-- on which tributary deliveries Poland had fallen
behind. It was perfectly clear that the Kremlin was

not only helping Gomulka to get this money, in every way that it could, but was telling Gomulka exactly what to do with it, to help Soviet Russia the most, when he got it.

Also, at the very time of the successful negotiations for this loan, Gomulka's government was itself extending loans and credit to Ho Chi Minh, to strengthen the Communist grip of that Moscow agent in Indochina.' In other words, Big Soviet Brother Russia was giving Little Soviet Brother Poland the pride and prestige of itself being big brother to a still smaller child of the Soviet family -- namely Ho Chi Minh's government in North Vietnam. There is no other possible reason why a financially hard pressed Poland should be giving handouts to a small Communist regime on the other side of the world, with which it had no historic affiliation whatsoever, except that the whole maneuver was ordered by Moscow to promote solidarity within the Communist family and for other propaganda purposes. And to carry out these purposes required only a small slice of the money which we ourselves were providing Communist Poland. Once again Eisenhower's action did not even make sense, except as a means of helping the Communists in their world-wide plans.[2]

Equally incredible was Eisenhower's enthusiasm for handing out additional hundreds of millions of dollars to Nehru in support of India's Second Five-Year Plan, when the very plan he was boosting had been drawn up by P. C. Mahlanobis and Oscar Lange. Mr. Lange had left the faculty of the University of Chicago in 1945, renounced his American citizenship, and become a high official of the Communist government of Poland -- which he still is. Professor Mahlanobis' loyalty to the Kremlin is equally clear. Yet Eisenhower was eager to have these men decide how huge sums of American money were to be spent -- supposedly to make India less vulnerable to Communism![1]

But we would be willing to rest our case, as to what the whole mountain of foreign-aid evidence proves about Eisenhower's real purposes, before any honest jury which had not been completely hypnotized, on just one thin string of that evidence. And that is his continued and unshakable determination, supported by all of the power of the Presidency, to keep right on sending military supplies to Tito. We have already reminded our readers of the way Eisenhower not only defied Congress, in the fall of 1956, with regard to aid to Yugoslavia, but converted that defiance into a marvelous piece of propaganda for the Communists. What we wish to emphasize here is that military aid to Tito has been one of Eisenhower's personal pet projects for years; a project which, but for Eisenhower's unceasing and aggressive backing, would have been dropped long ago.

The best that could <u>ever</u> be said of aid to Tito, the murderous Communist tyrant of an enslaved people, was that it was supreme folly. But even that "admission against interest" became idiotic by the summer of 1956. For in June of that year Tito spent three weeks in Moscow as a guest of the Kremlin. At the end of that visit he and Zhukov signed joint communiques announcing that their governments stood shoulder to shoulder for various causes dearest to the Kremlin's heart, including the unification of Germany by "negotiations" rather than by free elections, and the handing of Formosa over to Red China. Tito awarded Zhukov Yugoslavia's highest decoration, <u>The Order Of Freedom</u> (no fooling, that's what they call it); and Zhukov stated, with Tito's full approval, that in any future war their two countries would fight shoulder to shoulder "for the well-being of mankind."[2]

Since that time, while Tito has of course gone through some of his usual off-again on-again mouthings about his independence of Moscow, in reality he has openly and continuously acted as the Kremlin's ally and agent, guiding Nasser, Nehru, and others according to Communist instructions. He is not only irrevocably our enemy, as he always has been; but any pretense that he is not a part of the top Moscow Communist hierarchy has become ridiculous. Yet in May, 1957, after a short interlude caused by Congressional awareness of these obvious facts, the State Department announced plans to resume shipments of military aid, including jet planes, to Tito; and further announced that this was with the specific approval of President Eisenhower.[1] Shortly thereafter Eisenhower emphatically reaffirmed that such shipments would be continued. They were, to the tune of some fifty-five million dollars' worth of military equipment during the fall of 1957, with special attention to jet planes. The shipments are still being continued today.[2]

During Eisenhower's tenure of office the United States has "invested" nearly three-quarters of a billion dollars (on top of all other aid to Tito) to arm the Yugoslav Communists. The Yugoslav army now has twenty-eight divisions, eight of which have been wholly equipped by the United States -- to help overrun Western Europe on the ground whenever the Kremlin is ready. But the proportion of United States equipment in the Yugoslav Air Force is immensely higher. Almost all of Tito's combat-worthy planes have been given him, by us -- which really means by Eisenhower. This arming of a known enemy with our military equipment could not be any more clearly of treasonous intent if the planes were being delivered direct to Moscow. It is sheer hallucination to regard it in any other light.

Professor Slobodan Draskovich says, and proves, in his book, Tito, Moscow's Trojan Horse: "To pro-

mote Titoism ... for the sake of communist world conquest, makes sense. To promote Titoism for the sake
of freedom, does not."[1] Frankly, we believe that
Eisenhower fully agrees with Draskovich. We believe
that he insists on sending military aid, especially jet
planes, to Tito, specifically because it does help the
Communists in their plans for world conquest. And
we believe that the reader, if he will be honest with
himself, cannot even find any other plausible explanation.

Eisenhower has waged an unrelenting campaign
to break down our immigration laws, and nullify our
immigration restrictions, in order to increase the
flood of aliens now pouring across our borders. And
the criminal and subversive part of this flood, just
from what is actually known, is enough to make any
American's hair stand on end.

Eisenhower's program -- like so many of his
other activities -- is a continuation and expansion of
one begun under the Communist-dominated Truman
Administration. Since 1948 we have legally received
into this country, under three special laws pushed
through for that purpose, four hundred thousand "displaced persons" and two hundred thousand "refugees,"
in addition to our normal quota of immigrants. How
many of them have been Communists there is no way
of guessing with any reasonable accuracy. Any man
who tried to do a conscientious and proper screening
job, in admitting these immigrants, has been either
discharged or transferred. (As Almanzo Tripp,
Robert C. Alexander, and others will gladly testify.)[2]
Eisenhower's urgent recommendations, if followed,
would now be adding at least 378, 000 -- Congressman Francis E. Walter estimates 500, 000[3] -- immigrants annually to the influx provided by the Walter-
McCarran Act. How many of these would be Commu-

nists can be surmised only from the pressure by Communist fronts to get Eisenhower's proposals adopted.[1]

As the July 15, 1957 <u>Bulletin of the Southern States Industrial Council</u> pointed out, the study and preparation that went into the Walter-McCarran Act were the most extensive, and over the longest period of time, ever devoted to a single piece of legislation by the American Congress. The Act became law, over the Communist-dictated veto of President Truman, on June 26, 1952, by a vote of 278 to 113 in the House and 57 to 26 in the Senate.

Prior to that time, our immigration laws and naturalization policy were not coordinated, and our whole program for admitting immigrants was a snarl of separately enacted and conflicting statutes. The Walter-McCarran Act straightened out the conflicts, cleared away many injustices, carefully made humanitarian provision for emergencies, and put our whole procedure on a generous but sensible basis.[2] It is an excellent law -- to everybody except those who wish to admit enough Communists to form a fifth column large enough to help mightily in our destruction.

But the Communists don't like it. They call it "fascist," "racist," and all the other smear names they can devise. The House Committee on Un-American Activities disclosed in the spring of 1957 that the Communists had created more than 180 fronts for the specific purpose of bringing about "grass roots" pressure on Congress to destroy the Walter-McCarran Act. Today they have more than 200 organizations on this assignment. And <u>leading the pack</u> of these would-be destroyers, with his idealistic-sounding subterfuges and his unceasing "emergency" proposals, is Dwight D. Eisenhower. Congressman Walter himself said, specifically of these attempts to punch fatal holes in the Walter-McCarran Act, that "the pressure from the White House is stronger than any I have seen in my twenty-one years in Congress and by far the most effective."[1]

(Let us call attention, in passing, to the recurrence of this same description of White House pressure, by different Congressmen and Senators in connection with entirely different pieces of legislation. Eisenhower has a diligently earned reputation for being gentle, lackadaisical, even indifferent about much that goes on around him, and ready to compromise tolerantly and generously with views that differ from his own. But let any matter come up in which the Communists are vitally concerned! Then the legislators involved, separately and repeatedly, report that the "White House pressure" on them, always to go along in the direction desired by the Communists, is the greatest they have ever known. This is just as true whether the issue be the Bricker Amendment, Foreign Aid, or Immigration.)

Another quotation from Congressman Walter, our country's greatest authority on the immigration problem and on legislation connected with it, is also well worth noting. On Monday, February 11, 1957, the United Press reported a statement made by Walter, the day before, in a radio debate with Senator Jacob K. Javits. The Congressman had said that, of the Hungarian refugees admitted to the United States, the first 6200 had all been Communists, including some secret police agents; and that the United States Refugee Relief Administration had taken 6200 visa numbers, belonging to "real refugees" from Europe, assigned those numbers to these Hungarian Communists, and thus provided for their permanent lawful residence in this country.[2] Some of us, including this writer, had been saying in print that this was happening, weeks before Congressman Walter gave such official confirmation. Nor is there the least doubt that thousands of the other Hungarian "refugees" admitted, with so

much fanfare made over them, were also Communists.[1]
And it will be easily remembered that it was Eisenhower who made more and louder "humanitarian"
noises, about rushing all of these "refugees" to our
shores, than any other man in America.

If Madame Roland were living today, she could
amend her famous lament to "Humanitarianism --
what treason is committed in thy name!" For on
top of the speciously legalized flood of immigrants
of suspicious character, the influx of illegal entrants
is even worse. The Communists went diligently to
work, with their usual organized fronts, on both
methods of massive infiltration, in the early 1930's.
We have now reached the point that, on the solidest
authority, from three to five million unnaturalized
aliens are illegally within our borders.[2] Nothing is
being done about them, and the Eisenhower Administration, largely through Max Rabb, made it clear
that it will "get" anybody who tries to do anything
about them.[3] In New York City alone, in just one recent year, the files on between fifty and seventy-five
thousand illegal aliens were stamped "Closed" and
simply stored away.[4] Today the streams of such
aliens, known to contain a large proportion of subversives, are pouring in on us in ever greater volume, from Canada, from Cuba, from Mexico, and
from other sources. And not even an honest and
patriotic member of the Immigration Service could do
anything to stop even the most notorious subversive
from entering.

We'll pause for one quick illustration, just to substantiate that last point. There are known to be at
least fifty thousand Communists in Havana alone. And
in the district office of the Immigration Service in
Miami you will find, on any visit, dozens of files on
Communist agents whom that office knows to be en-
route to America, from or through Cuba, at that very

time -- in order to enter the United States illegally and remain here. But the Immigration Service cannot intercept a single one. Why? Because Eisenhower's State Department has waived -- for more than two years now -- all documentation for all persons coming to this country from Cuba, if they claim they are coming for less than twenty-nine days. On being asked about this ruling, the State Department explained: "The law says we may waive documentation in certain emergency cases so we gave a blanket order." "But," the State Department was then asked, "what is the emergency to justify the waiver?" They replied: "The emergency is the terrific pressure we are under to get people into the United States."[1] And that pressure stemmed right back to Max Rabb, using all of Eisenhower's power and prestige, with Eisenhower's full knowledge and consent.

Actually, the breakdown of our whole immigration barrier and screening service, for the visible purpose of letting Communists and those who can be controlled by Communists pour in, is so brazen and so nearly incredible that we cannot begin to present the matter properly in the space available here. Again, a whole book is needed. But for anybody who wishes to get at least some inkling of the treason involved in this area, right through the Truman Administration and then increasingly under Eisenhower, we recommend a speech made by Mr. Richard C. Arens, Staff Director of the Committee on Un-American Activities, on April 18, 1957.[2] Its sheer recital of facts will, or should, chill your spine. It will also go far to explain how the Communists now control enough numerical voting strength in this country, as a marginal body which they can influence to go in either direction (or both directions at once, as in 1956), to bring off the miraculous stunts that have been puzzling the analysts out of their sleep ever since Truman was reelected. (For a shocking confirmation of the growing Communist influence in our elections, please note that in the California primaries a couple of months ago 425,000 votes were cast for a known Communist as a candidate for an important state office!)[1] Any conservative or anti-Communist politician in America today is having to face not only the honestly Democratic or "liberal" voters in his constituency, but a sizable bloc -- depending on the area -- of controlled votes that are not amenable to reason or arguments of any kind. That the Eisenhower State Department and its Immigration Service are deliberately and constantly increasing this bloc is common and public knowledge to everybody who has studied the plain facts. That Eisenhower personally is fully aware of this program, and is its chief supporter, is the plain fact that we wish to make clear here.

For six years Eisenhower and his associates have carried on a persistent and energetic campaign to break down the independent sovereignty of the United States, and to submerge that sovereignty under international agreements and the control of international agencies. The open boasts of the United Nations crowd -- as in the book, Revolution On East River, by James Avery Joyce[2] -- that there is a day-by-day de facto surrender of American sovereignty to the UN, are well justified. And Eisenhower's support of this transfer of sovereignty by installments is continuous. He has emphasized over and over, for instance, that our troops are to be used, in implementation of the Eisenhower Doctrine, under the control of the United Nations Security Council.[3]

In that Council we have one vote in eleven; Russia has a veto power over everything it doesn't like; and the United Nations Secretary for Security Council Affairs, who would have the most direct control of any such troops, has been either a Russian Communist or a Yugoslav Communist ever since the United Nations was founded.[1] Also today, since a smooth, clever, and quiet "reorganization" of the inner workings of the UN was put through about four years ago, it is administratively almost completely under the thumbs of a triumvirate consisting of Dag Hammarskjöld, Ralph Bunche, and a Soviet "diplomat," Ilya S. Tchernychev.[2] The whole Secretariat and administrative staff below them consists almost entirely of people of the same stripe. Yet, right while this is being written, Eisenhower is doing his utmost to put into the hands of this group our prestige, our interests, and the command of our armed forces, in the Middle East. We are supposed to be fighting Communist aggression there, but Eisenhower will see that we turn over to these same Communists the control of everything we do in the fight.

In this connection the drive to put our money also, as well as our troops, under the command of this same body is worth noting. Two of Eisenhower's favorite lieutenants, Harold Stassen and Christian A. Herter,[3] have spent much time in building up the arguments and working on public opinion to have us spread our foreign aid to all of the world under a new dispensation. Either we must enter into a partnership with Russia, whereby benevolent Russia and rich America together help to "develop the underdeveloped nations" -- which is the exact plan Earl Browder set forth for the future, in 1944[4] -- or we must contribute the money first to a United Nations pool, and let the United Nations then allocate our aid to the have-not nations, according to its superior wisdom and more impartial approach. Herter began plugging this Browder line months before he was taken into the Department of State.[5] And while, fortunately for the United States, Childe Harold seems at present to be a lost cause,

Eisenhower will find plenty of other helpers in his steady whittling away of America's substance and sovereignty, for this purpose and many others.

As one means to that end Eisenhower has entered into more than four hundred so-called "Executive Agreements," all of them completely by-passing Congress, and many of them committing this country to obligations and aims of which even a supine Congress would never have approved. And most of these agreements Eisenhower was able to put into effect, unhindered and uncriticized, simply because not enough members of either the Congress or the public ever heard of them at all.

There are many other ways in which Eisenhower has gradually been putting his <u>official</u> weight more openly on the side of International Communism. But we'll make one illustration of these other ways suffice here. This instance came a few months after the Summit Conference. He forced on our National Security Council a formal policy of encouraging satellite governments to "maintain military alliances" with the Soviet. We'll let the intensely pro-Eisenhower <u>Christian Science Monitor</u> tell the story:

"It was recognized that if the 'spirit of Geneva' was to lead to a safer and easier relationship between Washington and Moscow, Washington would have to renounce any encouragement to movements in Eastern Europe which in any way could appear in Moscow's eyes as a threat to its security.

"On the basis of these assumptions the National Security Council, under the leadership of the President himself, decided to take a truly extraordinary step. It framed a policy under which the United States actually would encourage the governments of Eastern Europe to remain the military allies of the Soviet Union."'

"Extraordinary" was the right word. This policy,

stripped of all the specious dialectics used to disguise it, and looked at through glasses not clouded by the mists of Communist doubletalk, has just one objective: To make the whole Soviet System more closely knit, less vulnerable to revolt, and more powerful as an enemy of ourselves. And please note that this huge victory for the Kremlin was obtained "under the leadership of the President himself."

Of course the material for this chapter is endless, but the patience of our readers is not. While we believe, therefore, that a thorough investigation of such crises and affairs as those identified by "Little Rock," "Sputnik," "NATO Paris Conference," and many others, would reveal Eisenhower's hand at work in every case, skillfully aiding Communist aims, we are simply going to indicate the direction a very few of those investigations might take, as briefly as we can.

A most interesting subject for detailed study would be Eisenhower's role in connection with the segregation storm in the South; his part in bringing about that storm, in subtly promoting its increasing violence, and in steering it towards the ultimate objective of his Communist bosses who planned the whole thing far in advance. This writer, in a six-thousand word article published two years ago, pointed out that the whole "civil rights" program and slogan in America today were just as phony as were the "agrarian reform" program and slogan of the Communists in China twenty years ago; and that they were being used by the same people, in the same way, for exactly the same purpose -- of creating little flames of civil disorder which could be fanned and coalesced into the huge conflagration of civil war.'

The real "activists" and inciters on both sides of the issue don't care any more about actual Negro "rights" than they do about growing mushrooms on the moon. What they want is the bitterness, strife, and the results of that strife -- such as the acceptance of the use of federal troops to put down local "rebellion" -- which can be brought about by urging both sides to resistance and violence. The whole program in America, from its strong but deceptive appeal to the idealistic, to the ruthless utilization of conflicting human emotions to create a maximum of trouble, is remarkably similar to the one carried out in China. This program is of too typical a Communist pattern, in every thread, for it not to have been woven by Communist hands from the beginning. And Eisenhower's central responsibility for inaugurating and carrying forward this program is too clear for argument. But for any more detailed analysis of the strategy and tactics employed by Eisenhower and his Communist bosses in this scheme, we shall have to refer any interested reader to the article mentioned above. [1]

It is now well-established that several of the largest foundations in the United States are operating under directives "so to change the economic and political structure of this country that it can be comfortably merged with the Soviet Union, " or to that effect. From the time when the Institute of Pacific Relations, using $2,600,000 of the money of these foundations, was so important a factor in the betrayal of China to the Communists, right up to the support by these foundations of trouble-making agencies in the South today, they have been extremely powerful influences, at work, in a hundred different ways, on behalf of International Communism.

When the Reece Committee set out, however, to expose the tremendous support of Communist activities by the foundations, it was Representative Hays[2] who, by such antics and obstructionism as have never

been witnessed in any other hearings of a Congressional committee, made it literally impossible for
the Reece Committee to do its job at all. And Hays
boasted that he was acting on behalf of the White
House, with Eisenhower's personal blessing.[1]

As to Sputnik, we would begin with a hundred
pages to substantiate Igor Gouzenko's flat assertion
that the combination of spying and treason was more
responsible than all other factors combined for the
Soviet exploit in the earth satellites race.[2] We think
that, even from what is known, we could convince
any open-minded American that the Soviets were kept
well informed of everything we had; and that our own
launching of an earth satellite was deliberately held
back for years to enable Russia to launch one first.

With that established, we would then begin the
look at Eisenhower's part in the whole deal, with the
following transcript from a Congressional committee
hearing as a starting point.[3]

Senator Symington: "Mr. Lamphier, I think...
the so-called ballistic missile was started in 1946 and
canceled in 1947 when the Army Air Corps was part of
the Army.... Is that correct?"

Mr. Lamphier: "Yes, sir. We checked the records before we came and it was July of 1947."

Senator Symington: "At which time, I think the
record should show that the Chief of Staff of the Army
was General Eisenhower."

At a later point I would certainly bring in the fact,
publicized by David Lawrence, that it was President
Eisenhower's decision to separate work being done by
the Services on intercontinental missiles from work
on satellites, and to put emphasis on the former.
Short of the actual use of missiles in a shooting war,
the public cannot tell how much feet-dragging has been
contrived in work on the ICBM, or how far Russia
may have stolen and utilized our own developments to

be ahead of us in that field too. But her achievement in putting the first earth satellite into orbit was to be visible to the whole world as a propaganda stunt of immeasurable value. And we think that the overwhelming importance of Eisenhower's scheming and authority, in providing the Communists with this great "victory," could be proved beyond question.

Leaving other large affairs and long-term developments untouched at all, we still wish to crowd in here a few miscellaneous items which demonstrate which way, and how strong, the Eisenhower wind has been blowing. President Remón of Panama, for instance, was a real anti-Communist. Before he was assassinated he had been very strict on Communist agitation; so strict, in fact, that his unpopularity with the Eisenhower Administration was obvious.[1] And we have read reports which we believe that our government was holding up Panama's rental on the Panama Canal, as a part of pressures amounting to a blackmail effort, to get Remón to ease up on arrests of Communist spies.[2]

During the Hungarian revolt, and after the anti-Communists despaired of getting the help which they had been led, by Radio Free Europe, to believe we would provide, Franco offered to send arms, provided only that Adenauer would allow Franco's planes to land on West German soil for refueling. Adenauer agreed. With unwonted haste, our State Department went to work immediately to prevent this arrangement from being carried out. And "it took Eisenhower's prestige as President to bring enough pressure to bear on Franco and Adenauer," in order to keep the Hungarian patriots from getting arms through this plan Franco had devised.[3]

With regard to the present mess in the Middle East, we'd like to remind our readers that during the Indochina crisis, while Dienbienphu was still holding

out, Eisenhower emphatically and constantly overruled the Pentagon, as to any thoughts of our stepping
in on the side of the anti-Communists. And at the
time of the Suez affair, let <u>Intelligence Digest</u> state
the case: [1]

"Whereas American pressure on Mr. Ben Gurion
to withdraw from the Sinai Peninsula was so tremendous (even that word is hardly adequate) and of such
a nature as to be virtually irresistible, the Pentagon
was not in agreement with the White House. The
Pentagon approved of both Israel and Anglo-French
military action. The Pentagon well understands the
Middle East strategic situation and wants Nasser out.
It not only approved but was envious of the recent military moves.

"What the State Department did was President
Eisenhower's personal policy. He entirely disregarded the Pentagon's advice. He insists that placa-
tion of Nasser is the way to win over the whole Afro-
Asian bloc against Russia, and brushes aside any advice to the contrary." (And the article then went on to
show how Nasser was working directly for the Soviet
all over the Middle East.)

BUT -- in the present crisis, Eisenhower has
used the advice of his Joint Chiefs of Staff as his excuse for sending American troops into Lebanon. On
July 14 he went through all the motions of listening to
a whole afternoon's debate, at a meeting attended by
both Dulles brothers, many other officials of the executive branch, and twenty-two Congressional leaders.
Two hours later, he ruled for armed intervention, supposedly on the strength of what the Pentagon representatives had advised, against much opposition. [2]

Anybody who thinks this decision really depended
on this advice, or was not cut-and-dried before the
meeting, or that the meeting itself was anything but
sheer window dressing, is showing a naivete that ap-

parently no amount of past experience can dispel.
Columnist Bill Cunningham, commenting on the
"swiftness and smoothness" with which our troops
moved into Lebanon, points out that "we were completely alerted and ready. The plans obviously were
already drawn."[1] There is no doubt about that. Eisenhower's Communist bosses had already planned
all of the early steps in this new crisis, <u>and their
timing,</u> and the bases for all of the usual rash of arguments as to the wisdom of the course -- far in advance.

We have stayed clear of predictions in this document, and we have a healthy respect for James Russell Lowell's advice: "Don't never prophesy onless ye
know." But we think the easiest way to show just why
Eisenhower's bosses arranged for our present intervention in Lebanon is to look at the inevitable result.
It is perfectly obvious that, when "the dust has settled" in the Middle East, four things will have happened:

(1) Our remaining prestige and influence in the
Middle East will have been destroyed as completely
as was that of France and England, through the "backing down" which we forced on them at the time of the
Suez affair.

(2) The prestige of the United Nations, our subservience to the United Nations, and the Kremlin's
domination over the United Nations, will all have been
immeasurably increased.[2]

(3) Nasser, as a viceroy of the Kremlin, will be
in complete and dictatorial power over the whole
Arab World.[3]

(4) Western Europe will be supplied the oil, on
which its whole economy so heavily depends, on the
sufferance and "good will" of Nasser and the Kremlin; and the Kremlin will use this all-decisive weapon as a means of forcing ever more appeasement and

"neutralism" on the governments of Western Europe.

It was to bring about these things -- while of course pretending just the opposite -- that Eisenhower landed our marines on the soil of Lebanon.

Winding up this list of maneuvers for which "the word is treason," we ask the reader's forbearance for one more rotten apple out of the foreign-aid barrel. Right now Eisenhower is vehemently proclaiming that restoration of the 872 million dollars, tentatively cut from what is known as "the President's foreign-aid program," is vital for "fighting Communism." But the little Southeastern nation of Laos has been receiving one of the largest per capita handouts of our foreign-aid money anywhere in the world -- forty million dollars per year for its two million inhabitants. According to Eisenhower it would be disastrous to our fight against Communism to slash any part of that sum for Laos scheduled for the coming year. But the man who controls the spending of this American money -- the Minister of Planning and Rehabilitation in Laos -- is the open leader of the Communist movement in that country!

It is simply impossible any longer to classify the gift of jet planes to Yugoslavia, or of forty million dollars per year to Laos, as stupidity. This is plain unadulterated treason -- and everybody knows it. But the game has gone so far that nobody knows how to do anything about it. For, as Sir John Harington said long ago, if treason prospers sufficiently, then none dare call it treason. And this certainly applies to those patriots in our government who are well aware of what is happening.

Finally, we'll end this parade with a rather strange exhibit, whose significance is lost on most Americans but well understood by those Europeans it is most intended to impress. This is a booklet, put out by NATO for distribution in Europe, with an excellent picture of Eisenhower on the cover. In the caption under this picture, and also inside the booklet, the title of its hero is given as: Citizen General Eisenhower. This description, going back to the days of the French Revolution for the background of its meaning, very clearly implies to any informed European that the man assuming or accepting such a title is definitely on the revolutionary side, the Jacobin side, in any struggle between the surging proletariat and the forces of traditionalism. And clearly this booklet, with this caption under the picture on the cover, could not or would not have been put out by NATO without Eisenhower's approval. Standing alone, the episode would mean little. But when added to all of Eisenhower's other actions in Europe, to show his sympathies with the Communist cause and friendship for the Kremlin tyrants, it becomes just one more convincing and discouraging symbol of hopelessness to the Kremlin's enemies.

Standing alone -- as I said in the beginning -- Eisenhower's maneuverings on behalf of the Kremlin, in connection with atomic fuel, with immigration, through NATO, or through any other activity touched on so inadequately in this chapter, could each somehow be explained on the basis of gullibility or idealism or ignorance. But when put together they add up entirely too plainly to another answer.

In September, 1956, Mr. Stanislaw Maskievicz, a former Premier of the Polish Government-in-Exile, announced sadly that he was returning to Poland. He made it clear that this was not due to any "return home" propaganda of the Moscow line, and that he would remain an ardent anti-Communist as long as he might live. He said simply: "I consider it my duty to return to my native country because America and Britain have betrayed us."'

Maskievicz, though voicing the sentiment of all satellite Europe, was not quite right. The <u>peoples</u> of America and Britain have not betrayed the enslaved peoples of Europe, consciously or intentionally or in any way except through their complacency and ignorance. But Eisenhower, and many men of lesser standing like him in both governments, have deliberately betrayed not only Mr. Maskievicz's Poland, and the patriots of Hungary, and the subjugated people of all Eastern Europe, including Russia itself;[1] they have equally betrayed, with equal deliberateness and intent, the people of England and America as well. Eisenhower's betrayal to the Communists of his own country, and of the free world it was supposed to be leading, has been so determined, so steady, and so effective, that his purpose seems to me unmistakable.[2]

Several questions will naturally arise in the mind of any normal reader.

The first is, if so many situations within our government are as bad as I have described them, why do not a few good patriotic Americans here and there simply resign, tell the true story, and blow the whole mess wide open? The answer is that they do, constantly.

That is, they resign and tell the story, with complete documentation out of their personal knowledge. And the results are the most discouraging single feature of the whole life-and-death struggle in which we are now engaged. They butt out their brains against a wall of complacency, reinforced by Communist propaganda, and die of broken hearts. From Dr. Wirt in 1934,[3] through Arthur Bliss Lane in 1948,[4] to Bryton Barron in 1956,[5] the roll is long and pathetic. The truth, in pieces -- even as large a piece as Arthur Bliss Lane was able to reveal -- gives no terror to the Communists. They smother it with ease, and ruin the man who tells it.

Arthur Bliss Lane, for just one illustration, was an able career man in our diplomatic service, with an impeccable reputation, for thirty years. As our Ambassador to postwar Poland, he saw with his own eyes, lived through, and fully understood, the acts of perfidy by which Dean Acheson, Donald Hiss, and others turned over Poland to the Communists. He gave up his career, as a conscious sacrifice, for the specific purpose of telling the truth to the American people. He put that truth in his book, I Saw Poland Betrayed. And neither his sacrifice nor the book created even a ripple.

During the following years Arthur Bliss Lane became a good friend of mine, and has visited in my home. I know what happened to him, and how pathetic was his death. I also know that Dean Acheson and Donald Hiss are both still members of a highly respected law firm in Washington. Their help to Communist causes has been so glossed over by the opinion-molding rollers of the Communist propaganda machine, and is regarded with such indifference, that the Chairman of the Tax Committee of the United States Chamber of Commerce does not have the least scruple about being a partner in the same law firm.

The Communist influence over the total information reaching us through all media, and over the resulting attitudes of the American people, is simply overwhelming; so overwhelming today that a frontal attack against the Communists is like walking head-on into a mowing machine, and has become one of the more unpleasant forms of suicide.

A second question is: Could Eisenhower really be simply a smart politician, entirely without principles and hungry for glory, who is only the tool of the Communists? The answer is yes. With the benefit of comments from friends who have read earlier versions of this document, I have made this revision of the manuscript from that point of view. And the whole letter had already come to be known as <u>The Politician.</u>

For it is obvious that the Communist thinking and planning for Eisenhower's actions, and for the tenor of his public statements, are all done by others. He is only the shell through which the Communist mix of action and propaganda is extruded. He is kept playing golf, or "on vacation," or otherwise out of the way all that the exigencies of the Presidential office will possibly permit. This is for the very purpose of keeping the road clear for actions to be taken and decisions made, in his name, to suit Communist needs -- and without him having to know both the real reason and the specious reason for every detail of what he "does." McCarthy pointed out, what could readily be observed, that frequently "they" had not had a chance to tell Eisenhower what his opinion was on some matter until after his decision had already been announced.

It is at least conceivable, of course, that he is simply too dumb to understand what he is doing. This would mean that over a period of twenty years he had somehow been led to fit all of his actions into policies and plans which helped the Communist cause, and had been constantly pushed up by the Communists into positions where he could help them more, without ever realizing what the Communists were doing with him, or for him. This would require a naive belief in his own brilliance or his own innocent good fortune, however, paralleled by actual operations of the long arm of coincidence, which most observers not born yesterday might find difficult to accept. While any reader is welcome to look at Eisenhower's whole life in that light, therefore, if he wishes to do so, we'll give the viewpoint only passing consideration here.

Which means that the only serious alternative to the theme of The Politician is even more disturbing. It is the suggestion, which cannot be ignored, that Eisenhower's motivation has been more ideologically honest than shallowly opportunistic. Or, to put the matter bluntly, that he has been sympathetic to ultimate Communist aims, realistically and even mercilessly willing to help them achieve their goals, knowingly receiving and abiding by Communist orders, and consciously serving the Communist conspiracy, for all of his adult life.

The role he has played, as described in all the pages above, would fit just as well into one theory as the other; that he is a mere stooge, or that he is a Communist assigned the specific job of being a political front man. In either case the Communists are so powerfully entrenched by now that, even if Eisenhower disappeared from the scene, all the momentum and strength of the forces we have seen at work would still have to be overcome before we would be reasonably out of danger. The firm grip on our government, of the forces that have worked through Eisenhower, is more important than Eisenhower himself. And so long as I can make clear the power and pervasiveness of the conspiracy, as it reaches right inside the White House, I have no wish to quarrel with any reader who finds it easier to believe that Eisenhower is a more personable Harry Truman than that he is a more highly placed Alger Hiss.[1] For such an interpretation of his conduct brings us out at almost exactly the same point, so far as the disastrous effects on the present and future of our country are concerned.[2]

For the Communists can now use all the power and prestige of the Presidency of the United States to implement their plans, just as fully and even openly as they dare. They have arrived at this point by three stages. In the first stage, Roosevelt thought he was using the Communists, to promote his personal ambitions and grandiose schemes. Of course, instead, the Communists were using him; but without his knowledge or understanding of his place in their game. In the second stage, Truman was passively used by the Communists, with his knowledge and acquiescence, as the price he consciously paid for their making him President.' In the third stage the Communists have installed in the Presidency a man who, for whatever reasons, appears intentionally to be carrying forward Communist aims. And who, in situations where his personal effort and participation are needed, brings to the support of those aims all of the political skill, deceptive cunning, and tremendous ability as an actor, which are his outstanding characteristics.

With regard to this third man, Eisenhower, it is difficult to avoid raising the question of deliberate treason. For his known actions and apparent purposes certainly suggest the possibility of treason to the United States, no matter how he may rationalize it to himself as loyalty to an international dream.

CHAPTER EIGHTEEN

The Present Danger . . . . .

This paper is much longer than I wanted it to be. But the subject is big, and broad, and important. Even with the ninety thousand words used, I have barely scratched the surface of all the mud that might be revealed underneath. The Communist design for taking over the planet involves trickery and schemes and organized implementation of almost infinite diversity and ramifications. The best we have been able to do was simply to give an inkling of what is going on, in just one channel of activities, in the workings of the largest, most complex, most solidly organized, most realistically flexible, and most ambitious conspiracy the world has ever known.

According to an official NATO statement, the Communists now have over six million men under arms, with sufficient war materiel and equipment of every kind for at least twice that many.[1] They have over twenty thousand planes, a large proportion of which are modern jets. They are building more planes rapidly, and have more than trebled the airfields in eastern Europe, which will handle jets, within the past few years. They have more submarines than all the other navies of the world put together; 450 against about 65 with which the Germans all but destroyed Allied shipping.[2]

While we do not think that NATO is the most trustworthy source of information about anything, there are independent advices which indicate that this is a factual military report. The number of submarines, for instance, is confirmed by Jane's Fighting Ships, which has long been the final authority on that subject.[1] Jane's also says that since World War II the Russians have built more naval destroyers and cruisers than all the rest of the world combined. It cannot be doubted that the Russian total war potential is tremendous, modern, and constantly increasing.

We have 1,500,000 men under arms, scattered all over the world, in comparatively small and isolated detachments where they could be mowed down like match sticks in a surprise attack. The truth is, we planned it that way. And in the obvious opinion of Ridgway[2] and other patriotic generals, the strength and morale and fighting potential of our armed forces, instead of improving over the past few years, has steadily deteriorated.[3] In my opinion, this was "planned that way" also.

I do not pretend to know the comparative total fighting strength of the United States against that of Russia. Our Strategic Air Command is supposed to be extremely powerful, and let's hope that it is. But I do know that the American people have been beguiled into putting their confidence, as to their own safety, in allies who will be more of a burden than a help in any showdown; and in that glittering and expensive soap bubble called NATO, largely blown up by Eisenhower, to which we have already referred.

We have spent the money for defense all right, because spending American money was a prime objective of Eisenhower and his Communist bosses. But what we have got for it is another and doubtful matter. Even Kiplinger says that the waste in connection with our military establishment is bigger than anybody knows.[4] We strongly suspect it is far bigger than even Kiplinger knows. Everybody knows that the three divisions, Army, Navy, and Air Force, have long been fighting disastrously among themselves. I believe it is possible to prove that the fighting was subtly encouraged and partly caused by Eisenhower, for many purposes -- including ultimate support of the dictatorially dangerous reorganization plan he is now promoting.

We are not supposed to worry too much, however, about our ability to withstand the Communists in an aggressive conventional war. For they will be deterred from using their potential, so the theory goes, by our superiority in the field of atomic weapons. But nowhere has treason been more rampant than in connection with our building and handling of our atom bombs.

The security regulations in our atomic energy plants have been lax, and rotten, beyond all credibility. Five years ago the chief of security training and administration for our Atomic Energy Commission resigned, after finding how bad conditions were and how little he could accomplish to improve them. He gave a year of his life to writing a book, to tell the American people his belief, based on his own knowledge and observation, that the Communists had simply walked off from our plants with enough parts for Russia to assemble at least twenty atom bombs of their own before they ever built one.

Nobody paid any attention, and beyond question the situation is even worse today. We do not know what is happening to the bombs we are building; where they are being stored or under whose control. We cannot be sure that many of them are not being shipped -- like jet planes to Tito -- where they will immediately be at the disposition of the Kremlin.

We have reason to believe that, at long last, for the past two or three years Russia has actually been building atom bombs of its own. Its stockpile of such bombs, whether manufactured, stolen, or both, does not have to match ours, nor even to be large. It is taken for granted that we will not use such a bomb first, while Russia will not hesitate to do so. In the case of so destructive a weapon the element of surprise would more than offset an inferiority in numbers. So it does not seem that our "deterrent" should be counted on too heavily or too long.

Except that these millions of men and hundreds of submarines and dozens of hydrogen bombs and earth-circling missiles are held up by the Russians for us and other nations of the world to worry about, however, I don't think we should worry about them. In other words, it is their existence, and the mere threat of their use, which gives them far more value in the propaganda war than they are likely to have in a shooting one. For we think the Kremlin plans to take us and the rest of the world over without any big war, if possible. Then, having established enough control so that there can be no large clear-cut war between Communist and non-Communist nations, but only civil wars, separate little wars on which they can concentrate all of their force that may be necessary against single enemies, one at a time -- then the Kremlin gangsters will use their armies and ships and planes all right, and even atom bombs if necessary, to suppress "insurrections" and to consolidate their organizational tyranny. We think that today the chance of their success in these endeavors is terrifying.

It is, as it has been, the cunning of the Communists and not their martial might that we have to fear -- until after they have taken us over. But in the meantime this martial might has become one of their increasingly important weapons in the psychological war which they wage so eternally and so successfully. And their cunning has the benefit of long experience and many victories to support it.

The Communists now have six thousand schools and colleges teaching political warfare, propaganda, agitation, and subversion.[1] The most important objective of all that tremendous effort is to encircle, infiltrate, and take over the United States. Towards that end they are making remarkable progress.

The legislative branch of our government has been brought so far in line that it will ratify an Austrian Peace Treaty without debate, approve the appointment of a Zellerbach without a question, and listen to the speech of a Sukarno with applause.

Our Supreme Court is now so strongly and almost completely under Communist influence that it shatters its own precedents and rips gaping holes in our Constitution, in order to favor Communist purposes. Its "Red Monday" decisions in 1957 were described by a notorious Communist in California as "the greatest victory the Communist Party ever had."[2] This gloating comment may have been entirely correct. Just one result of those decisions was that more than three hundred known Communists or Communist sympathizers were actually <u>restored</u> to their positions within our federal government. Other results were equally disastrous to the anti-Communist cause; and other decisions by the Supreme Court since then have been equally bad.[3]

As to the Executive Department of our government, it has become, to a large extent, an active agency for the promotion of Communist aims -- as the preceding more than two hundred pages of this book have tried to show. It is certain that the situation must grow worse, under present circumstances, even if and when Eisenhower ceases to be President, unless we can understand and undo so much that he has accomplished. There is one important reason for this which most Americans have not stopped to notice. We still see and read about hearings of the House Committee on Un-American Activities and the Senate Internal Security Subcommittee, although so much of the steam has now been let out of their boilers. And we take for granted that these patriotic legislators are looking for flagrantly dangerous Communists wherever they can find them. But this is not the case. They are looking for such Communists everywhere <u>except in government.</u>

You may discover either committee investigating, or seeking to expose, Communists in labor, or in education, or in the entertainment world -- though their efforts are pathetically small and brutally handicapped in proportion to the size and power of the enemy. But no longer do you ever see such a committee even questioning a suspected Communist in government. For Eisenhower's gag rules have made the field of government out of bounds to such committees, and have made utterly useless their even attempting to investigate Communists in government agencies.' In fact, these committees cannot even get answers from anybody <u>inside</u> government to any questions they might ask concerning suspected Communists <u>outside</u> of government. For those same gag rules, issued and enforced by Eisenhower, prohibit agencies of the executive branch from giving these Congressional committees any information whatsoever, about anything. So both Communists and their activities, in departments like State and Treasury and Commerce, are as free to multiply as rabbits on a farm grown to weeds.

But the recent progress of the Communists in non-governmental areas of our public life has been almost as great as within the government itself. Since Eisenhower became President, practically all of the <u>known</u> termites have come out of their holes and begun going boldly about their business again. Communist sympathies and even actual pro-Communist subversive activities are daily made more respectable, not only by our government, but by our labor unions, our great universities, the councils of our religious denominations, much of our press, and the complacency of our people. Owen Lattimore more safely ensconced at Johns Hopkins,[1] Dirk Struik restored to the good graces of M. I. T., Alger Hiss expounding at Princeton,[2] Robert Oppenheimer lecturing at Harvard, Telford Taylor speaking at West Point, Communist "clergymen" from Russia welcomed as members of religious councils in this country, openly Communist labor union leaders thumbing their noses at laws designed to weed them out; all of these are but symptoms of a spreading, deepening Communist influence throughout our national life.

The primary objective of these brazen exhibitions of Communist leanings is to metamorphose Communist conspirators into just members of another political party; to make treason not treason at all, but merely a difference of opinion. And we have been heading rapidly, under Eisenhower's leadership, toward the acceptance of that Communist point of view

In the meantime, the official Communist party in this country has become almost negligible in strength and influence, in comparison with the legions of crypto-Communists and undercover agents of the conspiracy. It will remain so for a while, even if and after the status of a recognized political party is attained. For the unknown and especially the unsuspected Communists can accomplish so much more for the cause. Only the small fry, as a general rule, are and will be allowed to sacrifice their effectiveness for the sake of Party size and activities.

In Czechoslovakia in 1947 the Communist Party was accorded the same standing as any other political organization. A great many open Communists had been duly elected to various government positions, including the second highest office in the nation. Yet, when the coup d'etat came in February, 1948, the most surprising part of the whole affair was the number of important people -- in business, in the professions, in education, in government -- who turned out to be Communist agents, whom nobody had ever suspected of Communist sympathies at all. It is childish for us to assume that the same thing is not much more true in the United States today, where the Communists do not yet have the advantage of a legalized status and complete respectability, where the job to be done is immensely greater, and where the goal is so much more important.

There are known to be at least thirty huge espionage rings operating in this country, against the two or three that have been only partly exposed.[1] Beyond any question the secret Communists are many times as numerous and immeasurably more potent and dangerous than the known or suspected ones. On June 14, 1956, Bella Dodd testified to her certainty that the secret strength of the Communists in this country was greatly and rapidly increasing all of the time.[2] Fulton Lewis published, in the summer of 1957: "Your editor is informed by U. S. intelligence experts that Soviet agents continue to receive secret cooperation from highly placed Americans. In one known case a Soviet agent, under twenty-four hour surveillance, was observed visiting the homes of nationally-known political personalities, a respected jurist, and a leading industrialist."[3] And of course not only is the FBI helpless to do anything about this situation, but all really effective exposure of Communist agents has now been completely stopped.

The bosses of the International Communist Conspiracy are playing the United States exactly like a huge fish on the end of a line. They never reel in too fast. They let out a little line when necessary. They show patience and skill and determination. Little by little they have been wearing down the fish's fight and resistance, and hauling him gradually closer, until their assurance of pulling in their catch becomes ever greater and the hour nearer at hand. They are doing the same thing with other and lesser fish throughout the world, and have been for a long time, netting them one by one.

In playing these fish the Communist bosses know and use every trick of the art. Brilliant timing is one. It was no accident, for instance, that the treatment of Nixon in South America occurred during a lull between Soviet-precipitated international crises, so that there would be no competition for headlines in the newspapers, nor interference with the fullest worldwide publicity for this heaping of indignities on the Vice-President of the United States.

Another trick is the prostitution of existing political machinery to their uses. With the aid of their socialist allies and gullible dupes, the Communist bosses have now manipulated our "primaries" system so that anti-Communists no longer have any way to make their voices heard or their votes count, in national elections, or now even in many state elections. There are dozens of other wiles, artifices, and maneuvers on the grand scale; some of them for the main purpose of simply creating so much and such widespread confusion of thought that few people know whom to believe or what to believe about anything. And just as a fish is allowed to exhaust himself in his seeming escape, by running a taut line, we are being taken into the Communist camp more and more under the guise of fighting Communism.

Only the honest anti-Communist refugees, who have lived through the same conditions in other countries seem to understand what is happening. A Chinese friend of mine, a well-known educator, says: "All of the same signs are now visible here as in

China in the 1930's, when nobody would believe them."
A Polish refugee says: "Now I realize we are living
through what we witnessed in Poland more than twenty
years ago." There are others by the score who make
the same observations and issue the same warnings.
But nobody here will listen, or believe them, either.
As Dr. Schwarz of Australia truly says: "Our ignorance, our complacency in the face of an <u>observable</u>
<u>impending</u> catastrophe is so profound that it verges
on insanity itself."[1]

But as the fish is pulled nearer, the net is all
prepared. The blueprint has already been drawn,
and actually published, for the declaration of complete martial law by Eisenhower or any President at
the first touch of emergency. J. Edgar Hoover himself has said that beyond any doubt thousands of Communist agents have worked themselves into the most
strategic possible positions, ready to emerge when
the time comes and carry out their parts for Mother
Russia.[2] The seizure of radio and television stations,
the broadcasting of false information, the appearance
of false leaders, the incredible planned confusion and
terror, if the Communists should decide to strike suddenly as they did in Czechoslovakia, is a nightmare to
consider.

The fundamentally decent American mind just
will not grasp the kind of enemy with which it has to
deal. One disastrous manifestation of this innocence
is that the American people refuse to suspect Eisenhower of complicity in the Communist plot, despite
all of the clear evidence right in front of their faces.[3]
Even those to whom I entrust this manuscript, unless
already well informed as to a lot of the background,
will be reluctant to believe the indictment. For here
we have another case of the Communists' most disarming technique -- the use of the Big Lie; the lie <u>so</u>
<u>big</u> that nobody will believe it is a lie.

Yet what has happened in so many countries in the thirteen years since 1945 -- and which would have been even more incredible thirteen years ago -- must be believed. What has happened in this country during the past five years must also be believed. And some-body has caused it. To shut our eyes to the most ob-vious and probable causes, simply because we don't like them, is to be as silly as the Communists want us to be.

To paraphrase Elizabeth Churchill Brown, "the only enemies the American people have to fear are the enemies in their midst."[1] The most conspicuous and injurious of these enemies today, I believe, is named Dwight David Eisenhower. He is either a will-ing agent, or an integral and important part, of a con-spiracy of gangsters determined to rule the world at any cost. And it is probably an appropriate way to end this treatise by simply summarizing how far this conspiratorial group has already gone toward total victory.

From 1924, when Lenin died, until 1929, Stalin was occupied with winning dictatorial power in Russia. From 1929 to 1933 he was busy saving this regime, of which he had become dictator, from utter collapse. Our recognition in 1933, giving his credit and pres-tige throughout the world a tremendous boost, was the turning point in that struggle. From 1933 to 1936, by indescribable mass cruelties and murders, Stalin whipped the Russian economy into enough compliance with socialist planning to make it at least a going con-cern. From 1936 to 1938 Stalin's energy and cunning were taken up with the great purge and the mock trials, whereby he cut down all of the tall corn around him, and made his own eminence and power absolute. But all of this time, by infiltration into other coun-tries, he had been looking ahead to the day when he could really get started on Lenin's strategy for the Communist conquest of the world.

When the second World War -- which the scheming of his agents in other capitals so largely helped to bring on -- began in 1939, Stalin was ready to make use of the opportunities which he knew it would bring. Keeping, through the influence of his agents, the eyes and anger of other nations focused on the crimes and conquests of Hitler, he himself embarked on a series of far more brutal crimes and more extensive conquests -- which he and his successors have continued right up till today. Here is the chronological history of Communist conquests up to the point where both chronology and conquests cease to be discrete, and were made intentionally vague by the Kremlin itself.

1. Russia taken, 1917. Boundaries determined by Treaty of Brest-Litovsk, 1918.

2. Union of Soviet Socialist Republics organized, 1922. Besides the reduced Russia listed above, there were taken into the U.S.S.R.:

> Russian Armenia, Azerbaidzhan, Georgia, Ukraine, Byelorussia.

3. Estonia, Latvia, Lithuania, Eastern Poland, Karelian Isthmus of Finland. Seized 1939-40. Temporarily lost to Germany during World War II. Reverted to U.S.S.R. in 1944.

4. Mongolia, 1945.

5. Albania, Yugoslavia, Hungary, Roumania, Bulgaria, 1946.

6. Poland, 1947.

7. Czechoslovakia, North Korea, Manchuria, 1948.

8. Mainland of China, East Germany, 1950.

9. Tibet, 1951.

10. North Vietnam, 1954.

Since 1954 the Kremlin, partly to keep from mak-

ing its rapid progress toward world rule too obvious,
has been establishing or solidifying "neutralist" dependencies, instead of satellites; and has preferred
an increasing permeation of Communist influence
throughout all the remaining countries of the world, instead of the more revealing step of formally taking any
of them over. And before offering any readings of the
levels of this influence, we should take a quick look at
one or two gauges which definitely record Communist
progress from various points of view.

At the last congress of International Communism,
just before World War II, delegates from all the Communist Parties of the world represented a total of
slightly more than four million members. But in
November, 1957, at the triumphant meeting in Moscow
to celebrate the fortieth anniversary of the Bolshevik
Revolution, delegates came from seventy-five Communist Parties, with thirty-three million members.
This is approximately an <u>eight hundred percent ex-
pansion</u> in the twenty years. And that is just about
the rate of growth of Communist power throughout the
world during that time, no matter from what angle
you measure it, or with what unit of comparison.

Since the Communist masters do not have -- nor
want -- but from one to five percent of any subject
population as members of the actual party, we can assume three to four percent as a rough average. These
thirty-three million party members, therefore, constitute the hard core of tyranny over almost a billion
subjugated people. This figure is confirmed by our information from many other sources. But twenty years
ago the total Communist-ruled population was only
around a hundred and twenty-five million. And practically all of the huge difference has been added since
the end of the war.

From the summer of 1945 to the summer of 1958
the Communists have <u>averaged</u> adding to their empire

seven thousand newly enslaved subjects every hour.
And let us remind you that these people —— of Czechoslovakia or of China or wherever they may be —— have
the same love for their families, think of concentra-
tion camps with the same despairing horror, and feel
exactly the same pain under torture, as do you and I.
Seven thousand more human beings, just like ourselves have been brought under the incredibly brutal
rule of a Communist police state, on the average,
every hour, twenty-four hours of every day, 365 days
of every year, for the past thirteen years. And today
this rate of conquest and enslavement is being rapidly
accelerated.

A far-flung and insidious tide may not even
seem to be rising, at any specific spot briefly
watched. But the rate of its rise can be determined, by measurements made at long enough
intervals -- as we have done above. And how
much it has already climbed up the sides, and
seeped into the eddies, of areas once firm and
dry, can also be noted. We have undertaken to
assess how far the Communist tide has gone,
percentage-wise, towards swallowing up such
areas entirely. Our observations for that purpose have been as conscientious and objective as
I could make them. We present the results, on
the next two pages, exactly as they appeared in
The American Opinion Scoreboard for 1958, and
as published in the July-August, 1958 issue of
the magazine. '

The American Opinion Scoreboard

In the following tabulation we have undertaken to estimate the present degree of Communist influence or control over the economic and political affairs of almost all of the "nations" of the world. (The omissions have been due to lack of size, importance, or autonomy.) The chief source of such control or influence may be Communist-run labor unions (as in Uruguay), or Communist sympathizers in government (as in India), or powerful Communist political parties (as in Italy), or highly successful Communist agitation and propaganda (as in Mexico). The total extent of Communist control or influence over any country, however, is due to the impact of all Communist pressures, direct and indirect, visible and undercover, working together. In most cases, of course, that total cannot be measured with any exactness. But we believe the appraisals given below to be conservative, as of June 1, 1958.

It is only when this scoreboard is compared with any similar one, which might have been compiled as recently as 1952, that its significance becomes so shockingly apparent. The progress of the International Communist Conspiracy has now become so great and so rapid that the Kremlin's biggest concern is no longer guns or butter. It is how to keep the remainder of the free world, and especially the people of the United States, from realizing the speed and certainty with which the Communists are completing their conquest of the planet. We intend to publish a revised scoreboard once a year until the conspiracy is entirely successful or has been entirely destroyed.

COMMUNIST INFLUENCE
As A Percentage Of Total Control

1.	Aden	20 - 40	19.	Chile	40 - 60
2.	Afghanistan	80 - 100	20.	Communist China	100
3.	Albania	100	21.	Nationalist China	0 - 20
4.	Argentina	40 - 60	22.	Colombia	20 - 40
5.	Australia	0 - 20	23.	Costa Rica	20 - 40
6.	Austria	20 - 40	24.	Cuba	40 - 60
7.	Belgian Congo	0 - 20	25.	Czechoslovakia	100
8.	Belgium	20 - 40	26.	Denmark	20 - 40
9.	Bolivia	40 - 60	27.	Dominican Republic	0 - 20
10.	Brazil	40 - 60	28.	East Germany	100
11.	Britain	20 - 40	29.	Ecuador	0 - 20
12.	British Guiana	80 - 100	30.	Egypt	100
13.	Bulgaria	100	31.	El Salvador	20 - 40
14.	Burma	60 - 80	32.	Ethiopia	60 - 80
15.	Cambodia	80 - 100	33.	Finland	60 - 80
16.	Canada	20 - 40	34.	France	40 - 60
17.	Central African Federation		35.	French Equatorial Africa	20 - 40
		0 - 20	36.	French Togoland	40 - 60
18.	Ceylon	60 - 80	37.	French West Africa	40 - 60

The Scoreboard

38.	Ghana	80 - 100	72.	Outer Mongolia		100
39.	Greece	40 - 60	73.	Pakistan	20 - 40	
40.	Guatemala	60 - 80	74.	Panama	60 - 80	
41.	Haiti	20 - 40	75.	Paraguay	0 - 20	
42.	Honduras	40 - 60	76.	Peru	20 - 40	
43.	Hungary	100	77.	Philippines	20 - 40	
44.	Iceland	80 - 100	78.	Poland		100
45.	India	60 - 80	79.	Portugal	0 - 20	
46.	Indonesia	80 - 100	80.	Roumania		100
47.	Iran	20 - 40	81.	Saudi Arabia	60 - 80	
48.	Iraq	20 - 40	82.	Sierra Leone	20 - 40	
49.	Ireland	0 - 20	83.	Singapore	60 - 80	
50.	Israel	40 - 60	84.	Somalia	40 - 60	
51.	Italy	40 - 60	85.	South Korea	0 - 20	
52.	Japan	20 - 40	86.	South Vietnam	40 - 60	
53.	Jordan	20 - 40	87.	Soviet Union		100
54.	Kenya	20 - 40	88.	Spain	0 - 20	
55.	Laos	80 - 100	89.	Sudan	20 - 40	
56.	Lebanon	40 - 60	90.	Sweden	20 - 40	
57.	Liberia	20 - 40	91.	Switzerland	20 - 40	
58.	Libya	60 - 80	92.	Syria		100
59.	Luxembourg	20 - 40	93.	Tanganyika	20 - 40	
60.	Madagascar	20 - 40	94.	Thailand	40 - 60	
61.	Malaya	40 - 60	95.	Tibet	80 - 100	
62.	Mexico	40 - 60	96.	Tunisia	80 - 100	
63.	Morocco	60 - 80	97.	Turkey	0 - 20	
64.	Nepal	60 - 80	98.	Uganda	20 - 40	
65.	Netherlands	0 - 20	99.	Union of South Africa	0 - 20	
66.	New Zealand	0 - 20	100.	United States	20 - 40	
67.	Nicaraugua	20 - 40	101.	Uruguay	40 - 60	
68.	Nigeria	20 - 40	102.	Venezuela	20 - 40	
69.	North Korea	100	103.	West Germany	0 - 20	
70.	North Vietnam	100	104.	Yemen	80 - 100	
71.	Norway	40 - 60	105.	Yugoslavia		100

THE OVER-ALL RECKONING

Basic Communist strategy for conquest of the world, as laid out thirty-five years ago and relentlessly followed ever since, consisted of three steps: (1) Take eastern Europe; (2) next take the masses of Asia; (3) then take the rest of the world, including the United States. The Communists completed their first step in 1950; the second step is now about three-fourths accomplished; and they have gone at least one-fourth of the way towards carrying out their third step. Which means that the Communists have now covered about two-thirds of the total distance to their final goal of world-wide dominion. And the momentum and the speed of their progress are steadily increasing.

In support of our score for No. 100, the United
States, we wish to add just one specific item. It
derives from, and illustrates, the Communist domination of the unions which control many strategic
parts of our economy and our defense. It is factual
rather than interpretive, and it is easy to understand.

Seventy-five vital links in the most secret communications of our government, including those of the
Pentagon to Air Force bases in New York, Maine,
England, Canada, and Newfoundland, are all available
to the members of one union, the American Communications Association. But this union was kicked out
of the CIO in 1950, as being too Communist even for
that outfit.[1] In May, 1957, the president of this union
and five other officials and members invoked the
Fifth Amendment when questioned about Communist
membership.[2] Yet the members of this union are --
and for years have been -- in position to put their
hands on any and all messages over these top-secret
channels of our government's own communications
system.[3]

The significant point of the above paragraph,
however, is that this door to betrayal is known to be
wide open; and nobody -- in Congress, in the executive branch, in the Pentagon itself -- nobody even
dares to try to close it. Those who want it kept open
are too completely in charge. And this is just one
more indication of how powerful the Communist influence has now become in almost all of our federal
agencies.

But actually a large part of this treatise has
served, we hope, to support the bracket of Communist influence within which we have listed our own
country. We believe that the Communists have already gone more than twenty percent of the way
towards taking us over. We do not believe that
their influence has yet reached forty percent of

total control of our whole social, economic, and political organizations. And we believe that the score which we have assigned to the United States is correct.'

Because the level of Communist influence in certain Middle Eastern countries has markedly moved upward, since this scoreboard was prepared as of June 1, we also wish to call attention here to the increasingly precarious position of Western Europe. By looking at a map you can readily see how, for the Communists, the road to Paris has led through Peking -- and then back through Calcutta, Cairo, and Damascus -- exactly as Lenin and his associates predicted and planned thirty-five years ago. Note the present encirclement of Western Europe. There is Russia itself (and its firmest satellites) to the north and east. Then you follow clockwise around the Mediterranean, with Syria, Egypt, Libya, Tunis, Algeria, and Morocco. Then jump across the British Isles, and on the northwest are Iceland and Norway. The Communists are now in position to close in on Western Europe and take it, at any time they think it is strategically wise to do so. And, incidentally, they would kill or capture our own men scattered over that continent like so many helpless boy scouts, if they found it desirable or necessary to use force at all.

Repeatedly over the past forty years, and increasingly during the past thirteen, we have been told about one mistake after another which the Communists were making. Time after time we have been told that some mistake they had made, or some supposed reverse they had suffered, was so important that the whole Communist system was about to go up in smoke. The only answer to such nonsense, and all we really need to show us how real and how imminent is our danger, is simply: Look At The Score.

As we said in The Scoreboard, the Communists now are at least two-thirds of the way towards carrying out Lenin's strategy, and ruling the whole world. They are gaining speed and momentum fast. We are now the only real obstacle left in their way. And we have a Communist, or a politician who serves their purposes every bit as well, sitting right in the chair of the President of the United States.

Mr. Khrushchev was being cute, cautious, and clever when he said that our grandchildren would be living under socialism. Even that remark was meant to disarm us, by making the danger seem remote.' If we do not wake up to the real facts fast, and wake up enough of our fellow citizens, it will be our children and ourselves living as enslaved subjects of the Kremlin -- possibly within five years, and certainly within ten to fifteen years at the very most. The danger is present, and it is very clear.

EPILOGUE

The manuscript you have just read, may we add this one more time, was begun in December, 1954 and, with repeated additions, finished in June, 1958. A great deal has happened since then which supports the thesis of that manuscript. We shall make no attempt here to mention even a major part of the most important items of this evidence. We shall confine our attention instead to just a few developments, of which a brief discussion will usually serve a double purpose. For not only do these episodes from contemporary history show further repeated and decisive aid, to the Communist march toward global conquest, by influences within our Government which fully utilized Eisenhower's authority as President; but they show the continuity of the same all-important aid to the same programs, by the same influences, under the next Administration. Although we are still too close to the picture to attempt to fix responsibility on individuals in the new Administration by cumulative evidence, as we can now do for the period from 1952-1960, it is clear that there has been no change in the course or purpose of our Government as a whole. It still remains, as it became under Eisenhower, the most powerful force promoting the world-wide Communist advance.

II

Most conspicuous of the illustrations, of course, has been Cuba. The delivery of Cuba into Communist hands, and eventual conversion of Cuba into the Communist spearhead for subjugating all of the Americas, really began with an order of the Eisenhower Government on March 14, 1958, which suspended all deliveries of arms to the legitimate government of Cuba. At the same time Castro was allowed, by transparent subterfuge, to get all the arms from this country that he needed. The undermining of the Batista government, and support of Castro, continued to parallel in many other ways — although on a telescoped scale as to both time and area — the undermining of Chiang Kai-shek and help to Mao Tse-tung which had delivered China into Communist hands a dozen years before.

There was no slightest justification for our Government, or any responsible agency or official within that Government, to claim ignorance of Castro's true nature and purposes. Our Ambassador to Cuba, Earl E. T. Smith, an earlier Ambassador, Arthur Gardner, and our Ambassador to Mexico, Robert C. Hill, all tried to tell our State Department that Castro was a Communist. The record was clear and conclusive.[1] By or before the time when Castro seized Havana, and while he probably could not have survived a month without the recognition and help of our Government, several objective students of the Latin American scene—especially Dr. J. B. Matthews, Fulton Lewis, Bob Siegrist, and this writer—were publicizing the fact that he was an agent of the Kremlin and had never been anything else.

But obviously Castro knew what to expect from the Eisenhower Administration. For in November, 1958, when Castro was still an outlaw in the Oriente hills, there was an exchange of messages between Dr. Milton Eisenhower and himself. Just what plans, procedures, and timing were discussed in these messages, it would undoubtedly be hard to discover. But a few weeks later, on January 1, 1959, Castro seized Havana and established his tenuous hold over the whole island. Just one week later, on January 7, 1959, Eisenhower recognized this group of known Communist murderers—Fidel Castro, Raoul Castro, Che Guevara, and their associates—as the legal government of Cuba. And he did so on the very day that *Hoy,* the Communist newspaper, appeared in Havana for the first time in six years.

From then on Castro was entertained in Washington by Eisenhower's Undersecretary of State, Christian Herter; was glorified at Harvard by Archibald MacLeish and McGeorge Bundy; was assured by Assistant Secretary of State Roy Rubottom, that the United States wanted to help "the Cubans" with whatever they needed; and was repeatedly told (with full publicity, of course), by Eisenhower's new Ambassador to

Cuba, Philip Bonsal, that the United States was in general sympathy with Mr. Castro's glorious revolution. Mr. Bonsal emphasized that Washington was willing to overlook and forget all of the mistreatment of American citizens and insults to the American Government being constantly and brazenly perpetrated by Castro's regime.

The program was obvious, and by no means new. It called for using American support, American prestige, American money, and American good will to build up Castro, and get him solidly established. While at the same time, and as rapidly as he could put each new solidification of his power under his belt, Castro was increasingly making clear his subservience to Moscow and actual enmity for the United States, so as to lay the groundwork for the next stage in this Communist advance. That stage began when, on January 3, 1961—as one of the last official acts of the Eisenhower Administration—Washington severed diplomatic relations with Cuba. This was beautiful timing, from the point of view of the Communists. It enabled the Kennedy Administration to inherit Castro as a clear-cut enemy. There would be no confusion left in the public mind, as a result of its ever having had Castro as a protégé, to confuse the image of firm hostility which was to be the theme of the next act in the same play.

For Castro was now strongly enough entrenched to do without any visible backing from Washington. He could openly declare that he was and always had been a Communist, and take other steps to establish himself ostentatiously as an official Viceroy of the Kremlin, without running any risk or stirring up any resistance which he would not be prepared to handle. Through a few well planned insurrections and invasions, which were doomed to merciless defeat in that very planning by which they were provoked, stimulated, arranged, and betrayed, Castro expected to eliminate even the potential of effective opposition.

Having leaned on Washington to make himself strong enough to be a conspicuous Communist enemy, Castro's game now was to raise himself higher, to an entirely new level of prestige and power, by repeated defeats of the United States, diplomatically and even militarily. To that end he was able to count on the full cooperation of Washington at every turn. As was easy enough to predict, by anybody who stood off and looked objectively at the Communist formulas and policies at work.

In fact at a public meeting in Los Angeles, just two or three days before the actual "invasion" at the Bay of Pigs took place in April 1961, but when it was an open secret that such an invasion was "in the works," this writer had no hesitation in prophesying what would be the actual results of that "invasion." This was in answer to a question from the floor. And having been "on the road" with a crowded schedule of speeches and meetings for the preceding week, and thus having seen nothing more than headlines, I replied that I could venture no opinion as to details. But that, when all of the smoke had cleared away, I was sure the audience would find three things to have happened.

First, Castro would have been made tremendously stronger and safer within Cuba itself, because of the anti-Castro patriots who would have been killed or captured. The latent resistance to Castro would have been so discouraged and broken, by the defeat and the reprisals, that Castro would not have to do any serious worrying again about insurrection for a long time to come. This was the same formula used in Poland and in Hungary in the fall of 1956.

Second, the United States would have lost immeasurably in prestige, and in damage to any position of moral, political, or military leadership it still had left. For we would not only be publicized and criticized everywhere for having tried to "meddle in the internal affairs of a small nation," but even more because we had completely and pitifully failed in the attempt—so far as our *supposed* purpose of helping the anti-Communists was concerned. This was the same formula used in Vietnam in 1954, in Lebanon in 1958, and more recently in Laos.

Third, Castro's prestige would have been greatly enhanced

everywhere throughout Latin America, because he would be glorified as the wonderful little Cuban David, who had stood up to, and defeated, that great gringo Goliath, the United States. This was the same formula used in the Suez Affair on behalf of Nasser, to build up his prestige tremendously at the expense of the British and the French. And the worst of it, of course, was that all of these things, in connection with the Cuban fiasco, would have been *planned to happen*, in just this way, from the very inception of the whole scheme.

There was no question about these developments, even in advance, nor has there been any question about what took place. They were all a part of the total Communist strategy, which was that the United States would first *create* this enemy, Castro, and then lose to him at every turn. Nor is there any question but that the same controlling influences, in both the Eisenhower and Kennedy Administrations, have been diligently carrying out this strategy and are still doing so today. The only difference, as already indicated, is that we can now look at the Eisenhower Administration whole, while it is still too early in the Kennedy Administration for any effort to establish individual responsibilities of new participants with equal assurance. Let me simply emphasize instead, in support of the "continuity" theme, that among those prominently connected with the humiliating and disastrous Cuban fiascos under Kennedy have been Allen Dulles, William Wieland, Richard Bissell, Philip Bonsal, and Roy Rubottom, all of whom were equally prominent and active under the Eisenhower régime.[1]

III

There has been the same continuous drive at work, towards the goals desired by the Kremlin, in another area, where a whole bundle of separate but closely related activities are tied together in one sinister bundle which might be labelled: *Disarm and Surrender.*

The real drive to condition the minds of the American people for a gradual acceptance of this fantastic program began with the launching of Sputnik, in the fall of 1957; and with the reports of the Gaither Committee and the Rockefeller Brothers Fund Study Group, which were timed so professionally to augment the impact of Sputnik as a propaganda weapon. We were supposed to see for ourselves, simply from the fact that Sputnik was running around overhead, that we should start thinking about "peace" on any terms. But just in case some of us were too dumb or too patriotic to get the point, it was spelled out for us by the two Foundation-sponsored "advisory" groups.

Both reports preached defeatism with unblushing shamelessness. The *London Economist*, on January 4, 1958, said of the Gaither group: "Broadening its task almost beyond recognition, it concluded that the Soviet Union stands a good chance of gaining such a military lead by 1961 that it could then destroy or neutralize the United States." Its basic theme was that we should forget about any shooting war, and look to other solutions to our desperate situation, because the United States would probably lose any such war anyway. While the Rockefeller report itself said: "It appears that the United States is rapidly losing its lead over the U.S.S.R. in the military race . . . . Unless present trends are reversed, the world balance of power will shift in favor of the Soviet bloc . . . . . . However, it is not too late if we are prepared to make the big effort required now and in the years ahead."

Both reports, and Sputnik itself, were intended to lay the groundwork for more foreign aid, for wilder Government spending of every kind, for increased bureaucracy, for more regimentation of our economy, curtailment of our freedoms, and changes in our whole American system to make us more like Soviet Russia. Every one of these purposes fitted into the grand design: So to change the economic and political structure of the United States that it can be comfortably merged with Soviet Russia. But the most important specific purpose with which we are concerned here was scaring the American people into a mood where they would be increasingly willing to resign themselves, however reluctantly, to considering the surrender of our nation into such a "merger" on "peaceful" terms. And the fact that this whole scarehead alarm was based on a Soviet show-off stunt, which was almost certainly made possible by thievery of both plans and production from ourselves (whose military forces had already been able to put a Sputnik in orbit more than a year before, and had been held back from doing so simply on orders from Washington)[1]—this was not allowed to reduce the effect of the propaganda drive on the mass American mind. This mind had already been too thoroughly brainwashed during five full years under Eisenhower.

A next important piece of construction on this foundation base, therefore, was the see-saw but unceasing drive for a cessation of atomic bomb testing by ourselves (far more sinister in its psychological suggestion than in its relation to our actual military strength), along with various other widespread pushes for "unilateral" disarmament. While still more important was the carefully "leaked" disclosure that various individuals and agencies, within or closely tied to our Government, *were studying the advisability and the methods of "strategic surrender" by our country.*

Of course the "leaking" was phony, as it had been in connection with the Gaither Report, simply to obtain more attention and more appearance that this was really "high-level inside stuff." For on August 5, 1958, Brig. General Thomas B. Phillips (U.S.A. Retired) wrote an article which was published in the *St. Louis Post Dispatch,* with the following headline and leading sentence: "Question Of When United States Should Surrender In All-Out Nuclear Attack Studied For Pentagon—scientists are proceeding on assumption Russia has achieved, or is rapidly gaining, intercontinental military superiority with missiles." And some extracts from the article are:

> Three non-profit scientific agencies working for the Defense Department or the services are making studies as to whether the United States can survive and continue to fight after an all-out nuclear attack. One is studying the conditions when surrender would be advisable, rather than to try to continue a war that is already lost . . . .
>
> A straw in the wind, showing the direction of some thinking,

> is the publication of a book, *Strategic Surrender,* by Paul Kecs-
> kemeti; Stanford University Press, 1958. The book is a Rand
> Corporation Research study. The Rand Corporation is a non-
> profit scientific agency operated for the Air Force by a group of
> universities . . . .

> 'What present weapons portend,' Kecskemeti writes, 'is an
> extreme disruptive effect, which . . . points to the possibility of
> surrender of a different sort: surrender without fighting.'

Naturally Eisenhower denied the story by General Phillips,
or that we were contemplating anything but victory over Communism. But Milton Eisenhower was one of those who had
recommended that such a plan of gradual surrender be prepared. And at the very time of this denial there was a "World
Brotherhood" meeting going on in Bern, Switzerland, in which
Eisenhower's close friend, Paul Hoffman, was one of the leading
participants. Others present included Arthur H. Compton and
John J. McCloy. The conclusions arrived at by this assemblage
—and you can be sure "group dynamics" did not have to be
used to produce these conclusions—have been summarized by
Dan Smoot as follows: [1]

> We must recognize that the communist countries are here to
> stay and cannot be wished away by propaganda. All is not bad in
> communist countries. Western nations could learn from com-
> munist experiments. We should study ways to make changes
> in both systems—communist and ours—in order to bring them
> nearer together. We should try to eliminate the stereo-type atti-
> tudes about, and suspicion of, communism. We must assume
> that the communist side is not worse than, but merely different
> from, our side.

Now note how smoothly but firmly Eisenhower was going
along with this whole movement, and how little his denials
meant about this—or about anything else. In October 1956,
he had said that for us to stop H-bomb tests would be a "declaration of a moratorium on common sense."[2] On December 17,
1957, he had stated that "to stop these tests . . . could increase
rather than diminish the threat of aggressions and war."[3] But
during the fall months of 1958, and within a few weeks after
the above statement was issued by the World Brotherhood
group, Eisenhower suspended all nuclear testing, and there were

no more such tests throughout the rest of his Administration.[1]

But the clincher to all of this defeatist drive came from Joseph E. Johnson, close friend, longtime associate, and protégé of Alger Hiss. Joseph Johnson had also been a good friend and associate of Eisenhower, in the Carnegie Endowment for International Peace, and in many other activities, including the whitewash job on the ILO which he had done as an official appointee by Eisenhower. And on February 2, 1959, Mr. Johnson stated:

> From now on, every decision facing the United States in this (foreign policy) field must be taken in the light of the fact that a good part of this country could be destroyed . . . . We must be prepared to fight limited wars, limited as to weapons and as to goals, to stabilize a situation temporarily, tide things over. But victory is no longer possible.

So naturally the next step was up to Khrushchev. And since all of this was exactly in tune with what he had been demanding for three or four years, the form of that step was clearly indicated. On September 15, 1959, Khrushchev gave a speech before the United Nations in which he outlined the Communist program for world peace and security. The title of the speech was "General and Complete Disarmament and International Control." He carefully avoided any reference to the armed forces of the Soviet Union, of course. But otherwise, and for everybody else, he proposed a *three-stage program* for world disarmament. And within a few months various groups and organizations began to spring up, advocating "peaceful coexistence and unilateral disarmament" for the United States.

Which brings us at last, and again, to the theme of continuity between the two Administrations. For under Kennedy our government is not only following the recommendations of Khrushchev's speech, but is carrying out those recommendations aggressively and precisely. In the fall of 1961 President Kennedy proposed a *three-stage program* for world disarmament under United Nations control. Each member nation was to begin immediately placing segments of its military forces under UN command, and thus contributing to the creation of a UN "peace force."[1] And Adlai Stevenson, United States Ambassador to the United Nations, nailed the intent down by stating: "In fact, the United States program calls for the total elimination of national capacity to make international war." Secretary of Defense McNamara began actual implementation of the program by gradually "phasing out" our first strike weapons systems. And at the beginning of the brutal United Nations attack on Katanga the United States Government supplied several planes and other military equipment to this "peace force" of the United Nations.

In September, 1961, Congress, strongly pressured by the Executive Departments in general and the State Department in particular, enacted legislation which established the "U. S. Arms Control and Disarmament Agency." At approximately the same time our State Department issued its Document No. 7277, entitled *Freedom From War,* which set forth a United States program for world disarmament, but specifically for United States disarmament, to be carried out in three stages. Nor did the State Department even bother to hide the startling extent to which its program is taken directly from the blueprint supplied by Khrushchev in his speech of September 15, 1959. Then in April, 1962, Mr. Arthur Dean, as President Kennedy's special envoy on disarmament matters, replacing Dean Rusk, offered the United States disarmament program as a treaty to be accepted and made binding by the United Nations. Again, this proposed treaty suggested the same three-stage disarmament plan recommended by Khrushchev in 1959. And the understanding—which our State Department will neither confirm nor deny—is strong in Washington that the Department is definitely planning total transfer of our military forces to the United Nations within three years.[2]

As to the continuity between Administrations, please note that at the World Brotherhood meeting in Switzerland in 1958, which played so timely and revealing a part in this whole movement, and of which we listed above the participants who were a part of Eisenhower and Company, the other leading Americans in attendance included Herbert H. Lehman, Eleanor Roosevelt, and Adlai Stevenson. And that John J. McCloy, properly counted above as a part of the Eisenhower inner circle in connection with that conference, is now, under Kennedy, chairman of the General Advisory Committee for the U. S. Arms Control and Disarmament Agency. Note also that Arthur Dean, who conducted—in fact so ignominiously mis-conducted—the Panmunjom truce negotiations for Eisenhower, was Kennedy's official representative who proposed the United States disarmament plan to the United Nations. There is some consolation for American patriots in the fact that this whole left-wing team, despite all of their audacity and brazen exercise of power, does not yet have enough top-flight players to go around. So they have to use many of the same players on both the mislabelled "Democratic" and "Republican" squads. But the fact remains that these total influences, making of bipartisanship an asset instead of a liability, have been driving the United States down the road to *Disarm and Surrender,* in a planned stampede which began with Eisenhower's blessing, and which did not even miss a stride when Kennedy took over as their Commander-in-Chief.

IV

Probably the one single event which was most damaging to the anti-Communist cause throughout the world, however, of all such events during the last two and one-half years of the Eisenhower Administration, was the visit of Khrushchev to this country. For while the strong and widespread protests within the United States kept it from being turned, in fact, into the tumultuous triumph which had visibly been planned by our State Department and expected by Khrushchev himself, the Communist publicity team was able to make it look enough like such a triumph to serve their purposes. The mere presence of Khrushchev in the United States as a "state" guest of our country, plus what various officials of our Government *were* able to arrange in the way of honors, dinners, demonstrations, and top-level hospitality, supplied all the grist needed for the Communist propaganda machine. Especially when the usual Communist lies were fed into the same hopper with factual reports, in whatever proportions seemed best for a particular batch in view of the use to be made of the finished product.

The Belgrade radio was constantly blatting away, for instance, with such absurdities as this: "Mr. Peace, as Premier Khrushchev is now generally known to the American people, arrived in San Francisco today." Or: "The American people are now generally agreed that the landing of Premier Khrushchev on their shores is the most important since that of Columbus." While the two official books glorifying Khrushchev's tour indulged in no such self-defeating nonsense. In the editions for English-speaking readers they are hardbound, beautifully printed, full of pictures showing Khrushchev being made welcome all over America and in some places royally treated. Conversations and incidents are recorded in a casual and convincing style.

There are editions of these books in Spanish, for Latin American consumption, which sell for about the equivalent of three dollars each in the various countries. I have been told that one Japanese edition sells for about sixty cents, regardless of its cost, in order to reach a wide enough audience in that country. All over the world, through books, broadcasts, newspaper reports, and all media of communication, both the fact and the significance of the visit were hammered into the consciousness of the whole literate population. And you can readily imagine what this evidence of the friendship for Khrushchev on the part of the United States Government, including its very highest officials, and of the willingness of the American people to accept and support this friendship—what this did to strengthen the hands of the pro-Communist politicians, and to weaken and demoralize those still trying to save their own countries from being taken over, in every area of the remaining "free world." It was even more of a blow to any dreams of resistance, among the enslaved peoples of the satellite nations and of Russia itself, when most of those dreams were still somehow based on the persistent and pathetic hope that the United States would yet help them, if and when they ever undertook to throw off their Communist chains. And even in our own country the

Khrushchev reception and tour was one more huge step towards two Communist goals. One was to make more millions of Americans come to feel that the Lords of the Kremlin were not so different from other prime ministers, presidents, and politicians; and that maybe we should follow the wisdom of our own political leaders and work for closer and more friendly relationships. The other goal was to make informed and realistic anti-Communists throw up their hands in despair or become hopelessly demoralized.

How much Eisenhower was personally responsible for this visit we do not know. But he certainly played his part, as host to his imperial visitor, with all necessary enthusiasm and visible cordiality, to make that visit as effective for the purposes behind it as he could. And he had already had plenty of practice. For the Khrushchev visit was merely a temporary culmination of what I have repeatedly called elsewhere "the preposterous parade." A huge and highly publicized welcome in America— that is, highly publicized in the native press and other media—to build up the prestige at home of the Kremlin's favorites, and to disintegrate their opposition or warn their rivals to fall in line, had already been used on behalf of Gronchi, Sukarno, Nehru, Nkrumah, Castro, and many more, before the Kremlin utilized the formula for its own full benefit through the Khrushchev expedition.

But the same parade then continued, for the same less epic but still important purposes, after Khrushchev's tour as before. During the last two and one-half years of the Eisenhower Administration the tremendous benefit of this treatment was given to such Communists, pro-Communists, and politicians who were *personae gratae* with the Communists as Sékou Touré of Guinea, Fanfani of Italy, Segni of Italy, Mateos of Mexico, Ibrahim of Morocco, and—for a second helping—Sukarno of Indonesia.

Which once again brings us to the matter of continuity. For we have seen exactly the same program carried out, for the same purpose, under Kennedy. In fact one aspect of that purpose—or one use of the formula—has become even more clearcut. Both Ben Bella and Juan Bosch supply excellent illustrations.

During the early stages of the FLN's guerilla atrocities in Algeria, Ben Bella had been arrested, sent to France, and imprisoned for his crimes. So he had spent the last six years of the conflict in jail—or what was described to the general public as "in jail." For up until the time when the French Army and its patriotic influence had been almost destroyed by de Gaulle, none of even the pro-Communist governments with which France was repeatedly cursed had dared release Ben Bella altogether. So they merely allowed him to play a leading role, in this FLN "insurrection" against France, from his jail headquarters, by remote control. And only the insiders or the very well-informed knew that, for the last three years of that struggle, Ben Bella's "jail" was supplying him "country-club" comforts and facilities; or that even from this setting inside France he was the dominant leader of the FLN, and the favorite of Moscow. In fact some of the other FLN Communist leaders, actually in the fight in Algeria, didn't even know. Or maybe they just tried to convince themselves that it wasn't true.

So when de Gaulle, having finally completed his patiently cunning and gradual betrayal of Algeria into Communist hands, began withdrawing the shattered French Army from Algeria and turning that unhappy country over to the FLN, there was for a while considerable confusion and even some fighting among the FLN leaders actually in the field as to who was going to become the boss. And the Kremlin could not, or at least preferred not to, come right out and announce that Ben Bella was their chosen and anointed viceroy to run Algeria on their behalf. The first step, therefore, was to arrange for a United States Government plane to go to France, pick up Ben Bella from his "jail," and transport him, with respectful recognition of his importance, to Algiers. Then Moscow and its unconfused agents in Algeria enabled Ben Bella to win the internecine struggle in short order. But neither the masses of the Algerians being enslaved, nor even the ordinary newspaper readers elsewhere in the world, had an adequate way of learning promptly enough, to suit Moscow's and Ben Bella's purposes, that he really was the Kremlin's "white haired boy," and not just another ambitious native criminal and traitor gambling his life for the chance of coming out on top.

So this problem was quickly and easily solved, by the time-tested method. Just as soon as it was at all practicable after Ben Bella had been set up as the top man among the Communists in Algeria, he was sent on a typical visit to Washington—of exactly the kind which had been so similarly helpful to Sukarno and Castro before him. And not only was this vicious Communist criminal royally entertained by President Kennedy and glorified by our State Department. But to make the significance of the visit unmistakable, and to have it given the greatest possible publicity by a dramatic touch, Ben Bella was accorded the 21-gun salute, reserved for visiting heads of state, right on the White House lawn. He had thus received the figurative "tap on the shoulder" which made him henceforth a member of the same viceroyal club with Tito, Gomulka, Mao Tse-tung, Sukarno, Castro, Kwame Nkrumah, and some dozen more of the Kremlin's regional butcher boys—about half of whom had themselves had their status recognized by the same formality. Nobody from then on could possibly doubt who was the boss in Algeria; and Ben Bella could get on with those massacres and tortures of tens of thousands of his fellow Moslems, who had been faithful to France, which are now going on throughout Algeria with almost no notice whatsoever in the American press.

We do not need to belabor the point to the same extent with regard to Juan Bosch. But while every reasonably well informed student of the Conspiracy sensed that this longtime criminal, Communist, and close friend and protégé of both Betancourt and Castro, had been brought to power in the Dominican Republic by the same forces that arranged the assassination of Trujillo, the gradual maneuvering which the Communists have carried out in the Dominican Republic since that assassination, and before they could safely and solidly establish Juan Bosch in power, had been very confusing to the outside world. So confusing that, with Juan Bosch now going through one of those temporary periods — a la Castro — of claiming not to be a Communist, there was need for the usual step to wind up that confusion without delay. So you all saw pictures of Juan Bosch, as the newly elected "President" of the Dominican Republic, being entertained by our own President at the White House. Or if not, you can be sure that everybody in the Dominican Republic did, and everybody else in all of Latin America who is concerned about the now rapid Communist take-over of one country after another in that continent and a half. And in the near future you will find each or most of the new Communist viceroys in Latin America being given the same treatment, as rapidly as their victories and the Kremlin's blessing justify this accolade.

IV

To continue this chapter in this same manner, however, could make it an endless catalogue instead of the mere sampling that was promised. So let's skip the U-2 affair with the comment that *everything* about it appears to have been handled in the manner that would best serve Soviet interests, no matter what the intentions of some of those involved may have been. Let's skip the Khrushchev-Eisenhower "Summit" Conference in Paris in May of 1960 with the comment that the arrangement of the two names tells the story. In 1955 the Soviets had been very proud, and it had been a tremendous boost to their prestige, just for Khrushchev and Bulganin to be allowed to meet on equal terms in a Summit Conference with the President of the United States. By 1959 the lowering of America's standing throughout the world, and parallel increase in the showy pretenses of the Soviets, had gone so far—had been helped so much by the worldwide actions of the Eisenhower Administration itself—that top billing for Khrushchev in the second Summit Conference was implied by Soviet attitudes and undoubtedly accepted as reasonable by most of the international audience.

To make the point clearer, however, and to enable the Soviets to draw the last ounce of benefit from the opportunity, it was arranged that Eisenhower would meekly sit still for a tongue-lashing from Khrushchev over the U-2 matter. With the cameras grinding and the sound tracks rolling for reproduction of the show all over the planet, the President of the United States allowed himself to be bawled out by the Premier of the Soviet Union in language which, even in the phony English translation, was coarse and insulting; but which in the original Russian, for the benefit of all eventual audiences which spoke that language, was obscene and profane.[1] All of which was simply a part of the scenario.

Let's skip the betrayal and overthrow of that great anti-Communist, and heroic friend of our country, Syngman Rhee, without going into any of the details of the Eisenhower Administration's nefarious part in that disaster. Let's skip the acquiescence and collaboration constantly given by the Eisenhower State Department to Castro and Betancourt in their long continued and finally successful joint effort to destroy the ablest anti-Communist in Latin America, Rafael Trujillo. In fact, let's skip everything else about the final quarter of the eight-year game carried on under Eisenhower as the ostensible quarterback. While for those who would like to know more about some of the separate plays whereby we invariably and unceasingly lost so much ground, let me insert a "commercial" by adding that most of them — including all items mentioned above—have been covered at one time or another, to some extent and usually in fairly full detail, in the pages of the monthly magazine *American Opinion*. As will be future events of the same tragic substance and significance in future issues, as the program of betrayal of our friends and elevation of our enemies by our Government, now unbroken since 1944, rolls on through the present and successive Administrations.

In closing this added chapter it seems appropriate for me to call the reader's attention to certain fundamentals which underlie the whole cruel nightmare in which the world finds itself today. The first falsehood is the basic theme of all Communist strategy and tactics. By what I have called elsewhere "the principle of reversal," they present themselves, their purposes, their reasons, their actions, their philosophy, their history, and everything about themselves and their enemies, and about the sociological environment of both, as almost the exact opposite of what the truth would show. By "peace," for instance, they mean unceasing war—*their kind of war*—until there is no opposition left to the Communist tyranny. By the "liberation," of a country like Cuba, they mean the imposition on Cuba of a Communist dictatorship, and the use of cruel repression until all resistance is wiped out. By the struggle against "colonialism" they mean taking over, from the beneficent rule of civilized powers, those parts of the world where the standards of living, of education, and of individual freedom were gradually being lifted by those civilized powers, and converting such areas into colonies of the Soviet Empire—the most cruel and oppressive "colonial" tyranny the world has ever known. By a "dictator" they mean an anti-Communist like Chiang Kai-shek, who has spent his life trying to establish a republican form of government for all of China; and by a "democratic leader" they mean a Communist like Khrushchev, who has made himself an autocratic tyrant by being personally responsible for the torture and murder of millions of his fellow human beings.

But this principle of reversal goes far beyond the science of semantics, and involves every segment of human activity—morality, education, economics, politics, diplomacy, the arts, religion, *and even science*. In every aspect of man's relationship to God and to his fellow man, the Communists turn the truth, and even the search for truth, upside down. This is not from weakness, but from strength and determination. As a deliberate matter of policy, as the foundation stone of their conspiracy, they strive consciously for amorality instead of towards moral perfection; desire to achieve ruthlessness rather than compassion; seek to show the utter worthlessness of individual man and to degrade him to a status lower than that of the ants; worship Hate instead of Love; and encompass all of their plans within a Universal Lie, that is to be made reality by an infinite number of large and little lies which promote its purpose. And it is the very audacity of this diabolic program which has helped them mightily to go so far with their cruelties and cunning.

This brings us to the most important of their separate Big Lies. The first is that Communism is a movement of the down-trodden masses, against their oppressors. The truth is exactly the opposite. Communism is imposed on every country, from the top down, by a conspiratorial apparatus, headed and controlled by suave and utterly ruthless criminals, who are recruited from the richest families, most highly educated intellectuals, and most skillful politicians within that country. The rest of the show, including all of the noise made and work done by the poor "revolutionary" beatniks and dupes at the bottom, is mere pretense and deception. This is part of the reason why it is always tremendously easier for the Communists to take over a highly industrialized, prosperous, and highly educated country like Czechoslovakia—when it is reached in the time table of their grand strategy for global conquest—than a poor, non-industrialized, and uneducated country like China. It is also why the condition of the masses, even their economic condition, to say nothing of their spiritual condition, is always worse after Communism has been imposed on them than it was before. The accuracy of this analysis has been unmistakably clear, in the whole record of the Communist advance, ever since the modern Communist movement was founded, as a *gospel of hatred,* by a brilliant intellectual named Karl Marx and a prosperous manufacturer named Friedrich Engels. But until the opponents of Communism learn where to look for their enemies, and are courageous enough and realistic enough to look unflinchingly in the top echelons of their nation's political, educational, financial, industrial, and professional activities, these cunning and power-seeking criminals, who have been helped into their exalted positions through the very fact that they are Communists, will continue to take over one country after another with less than three percent of the total population at the time the take-over is accomplished. And we have seen no sign from God that the United States is to be any exception.

The second of these two biggest separate Lies is that Communism is "the wave of the future." The exact opposite is true

—and the top Communists themselves know it. The whole conspiratorial Communist movement and advance, which is bringing such incredible suffering to the world in our generation, is so completely contrary to the current of man's course that only once before in all recorded history have we had anything like it on any comparable scale. That was when fascist Sparta, with an internal structure very similar to that of Soviet Russia today, using the same conspiratorial methods behind a phony ideological front, gradually took over one Greek city-state after another and imposed its brutal system on the whole Greek world, including Athens. Then, while "all marveled but none grieved," the gigantic but tenuous bubble burst, man's common sense and desire for freedom reasserted themselves, Sparta receded into oblivion without contributing anything to our civilization, and Athens went on to its period of greatest splendor.

Except for a vastly speeded up re-enactment on a compressed scale, of the same scenario of collectivist thinking, tyranny, and terror, which took place in the French Revolution, there has not been anything else like the Spartan horror to plague mankind until the present Communist conspiracy. And it will just as surely go the same way in time. Communism, far from being "inevitable," or "the wave of the future," or a culminative stage in man's progress, would appear only as one of the huge jokes or hoaxes of history but for the cruelty and suffering involved. Actually, in the best illustration I can give (and which I have used many times before), Communism resembles nothing so much as a huge dirty boil on the body of mankind. Like any such boil, it is very painful; it is seeping poisons into the bloodstream; it could even become dangerous to the whole body; and it badly needs to be lanced and drained, so that the composite human system can be restored to at least normal comfort and health again.

Communism is about as much a "wave of the future" as was the Manichaean philosophy of the Third Century or the witchcraft terror of the Seventeenth. Its intellectual pretensions deserve only ridicule and contempt. But because of the size and power which the Conspiracy has now attained, the massive cruelties and suffering which it has imposed, and its destructiveness to everything worth while in our civilization, we have to take it very seriously indeed. Its rapidly increasing danger to ourselves arises primarily from the fact that the fundamentally decent American mind simply refuses to recognize the kind of enemy with which we now have to deal. The primary purpose of this book, and of its publication, has been to try to bring sufficient realism into all of our thinking about the Conspiracy to save ourselves from the same fate—however temporary in the long perspective of history—as the billion victims whom it has already enslaved.

Finally let me say that the publication of this book is not for me a happy occasion. We live today in a world which none of us—except the conspirators who have made it this way—wanted. Our consciences, and our sense of responsibility to those who come after us, bring up duties and drive us to actions which we do not welcome, and which are beyond all of the normal expectations of our lives. This book is an excellent example. For I doubt if anybody ever tried so hard to avoid publication of a volume which he knew to be true, and for which there was known to be so ready a sale. I do not relish the experience of condemning others, nor of living myself amid a torrent of protests and condemnations. But it takes a great deal to wake up even those perfectly good and patriotic citizens who have had so skillfully and patiently bestowed on them so large a vested interest in error. And I hope that this bit of history will ring and continue to ring like a disturbing alarm clock in the minds of many men.

For this is history in substance, although not in format or in literary quality. Who is afraid of history, and why should there be excited protests against it? This is not history written in the style and manner I would have preferred, nor that I used in *May God Forgive Us*. But that doesn't alter its validity one iota. And if this history contains facts that are unpleasant and disturbing to both the reader and myself, *that is the fault of those who made the history, not of him who wrote it.*

BIBLIOGRAPHY

I

Addresses, Articles, Interviews, News Conferences, Remarks, Speeches, And Statements By Dwight D. Eisenhower.

1943

"Appeal to the King and People of Italy," *Current History*, September; page 66.

"Foot-Slogging Soldier," *Life*, November 22; page 32.

"Message to the French People," *Current History*, August; page 396.

"Proclamation, September 8, 1943," *Current History*, November; page 248.

1944

"Message to the People of Europe," *Current History*, July; pages 36-37.

"Orders on Germany," *Current History*, November; pages 412-15.

1945

"Ike, War Correspondent: He Talks a Straight Story," *Newsweek*, June 25; page 44 *et seq.*

"National Strength Is a Necessity," *Vital Speeches of the Day*, December 1; pages 108-10.

"Our Great Team," *Vital Speeches of the Day*, July 1; pages 549-50.

"Peace: An Absolute Necessity," *Vital Speeches of the Day*, July 1; page 551.

"Quality of America's Fighting Men," *Vital Speeches of the Day*, July 1; page 546 *et seq.*

"Summation of Army's Arguments in Favor of Merger of War and Navy Departments," *Congressional Digest*, December; page 314 *et seq.*

"Two Statements on V-E Day," *Current History*, June; pages 491-92.

"V-E—Unconditional Surrender," *Vital Speeches of the Day*, May 15; page 452.

1946

"America's Army's Role," *Vital Speeches of the Day*, December 1; pages 127-28.

"Summary of Operations in Northwest Europe," *New York Times Magazine*, May 5; pages 8-9.

1947

"Over-All Security of the United States," *Vital Speeches of the Day*, September 15; pages 715-18.

1948

"Democratic Citizenship," *Vital Speeches of the Day*, November 1; page 34 *et seq.*

"For a Sick World," *Time*, May 17; page 55.

"Open Letter to America's Students," *Reader's Digest*, December; pages 1-5.

"Support for Western Europe," *Vital Speeches of the Day*, May 15; pages 461-63.

1949

"Age of the Individual," *Vital Speeches of the Day*, June 15; pages 518-19.

"Lincoln Had the Proper Attitude Toward Power," *Vital Speeches of the Day*, March 15; pages 335-36.

"Middle Way," *Vital Speeches of the Day*, September 15; pages 708-11.

"Open Letter to Parents," *Reader's Digest*, February; pages 11-14.

"What Kind of Government Ahead," *Vital Speeches of the Day*, November 15; pages 66-8.

1950

"Crusade for Freedom," *Vital Speeches of the Day*, October 1; pages 746-47.

"Freedom Is Everybody's Job," *Scholastic*, September 27; page 7 *et seq.*

"Give the Public the Facts," *Vital Speeches of the Day*, June 1; pages 484-86.

"Harmony in the Armed Services," *U.S. News & World Report*, February 3; pages 13-18.

"Lincoln," *Rotarian*, February; page 11.

"World Peace," *Vital Speeches of the Day*, April 15; pages 386-91.

1951

"Assurance of World Security Through American Leadership," *U.S. Department of State Bulletin*, February 19; pages 285-87.

"Defense of Western Europe," *Vital Speeches of the Day*, February 15; pages 258-62.

"Eisenhower Reveals Europe's Plight," *U.S. News & World Report*, September 7; pages 82-91.

"Eisenhower's Stand," *Time*, December 24; pages 14-15.

"Unity of Purpose Urged for Security of North Atlantic Area," *U.S. Department of State Bulletin*, February 12; pages 245-51.

"Unity of West Europe Essential for World Security," *U.S. Department of State Bulletin*, July 30; pages 163-65.

"Where Ike Stands," *Reader's Digest*, November; pages 15-18.

1952

"Address of General Eisenhower," *U.S. News & World Report*, August 29; pages 90-91.

"Address of General Eisenhower," *U.S. News & World Report*, September 5; pages 88-90.

"Address of General Eisenhower to the AFL," *U.S. News & World Report*, September 26; pages 97-100.

"Aims of the Republican Party," *Vital Speeches of the Day*, August 1; pages 610-11.

"Atlanta Address of General Eisenhower," *U.S. News & World Report*, September 12; pages 88-90.

"Basic Issues," *New York Times Magazine*, November 2; page 9.

"Candidates Take Their Stands on Issues That Decide Votes," *U.S. News & World Report*, October 31; pages 18-19.

"Cincinnati Address of General Eisenhower," *U.S. News & World Report*, October 3; pages 112-14.

"Cleveland Address of General Eisenhower," *U.S. News & World Report*, October 3; page 70 *et seq.*

"Dangers Europe Faces As Ike Sees Them," *U.S. News & World Report*, June 6; page 34 *et seq.*

"Defense Unity: Ike's View," *U.S. News & World Report*, December 12; pages 26-28.

"Eisenhower Tells What He Wants for Children," *Parents' Magazine*, October; page 37 *et seq.*

"First Anniversary of SHAPE As an Operational Headquarters," *U.S. Department of State Bulletin*, April 14; pages 572-79.

"Flint Address of General Eisenhower," *U.S. News & World Report*, October 10; pages 106-07.

"General Eisenhower Asks Release From SHAPE Assignment," *U.S. Department of State Bulletin*, April 21; pages 614-15.

"General Eisenhower's Latest Size-Up of the World Situation," *U.S. News & World Report*, February 1; pages 22-24.

"General Eisenhower's Views on Possible Cuts in Mutual Security Funds," *U.S. Department of State Bulletin*, May 26; pages 840-41.

"General Eisenhower's Visit to Korea," *U.S. Department of State Bulletin*, December 15; pages 948-49.

"Ike Speaks for Himself," *U.S. News & World Report*, June 13; pages 90-93.

"Ike Tells What He Saw in Korea," *U.S. News & World Report*, December 12; page 44.

"Indianapolis Address of General Eisenhower," *U.S. News & World Report*, September 19; pages 86-87.

"Interview With Eisenhower," *U.S. News & World Report*, March 28; pages 13-16.

"Milwaukee Address of General Eisenhower," *U.S. News & World Report*, October 17; page 100 *et seq.*

"New York Address of General Eisenhower," *U.S. News & World Report*, October 24; pages 96-100.

"Off the Cuff Answers by General Eisenhower," *U.S. News & World Report*, August 29; page 26 *et seq.*

"Philadelphia Address of General Eisenhower," *U.S. News & World Report*, September 12; pages 84-86.

"Remarks of General Eisenhower at Wheeling, W. Va.," *U.S. News & World Report*, October 3; page 72.

"Responsible Citizens," *Vital Speeches of the Day*, June 15; pages 514-17.

"San Francisco Address of General Eisen-

ment of State Bulletin, May 11; page 673.

"Military and Economic Policy," *Vital Speeches of the Day,*" May 15; pages 457-58.

"Mutual Security Program for 1954 Presented to Congress," *U.S. Department of State Bulletin,* May 25; pages 735-42.

"Our Sovereign Faith in Freedom and Dignity," *Vital Speeches of the Day,* October 15; pages 2-5.

"Pan American Union: A True Community of Equal Nations," *U.S. Department of State Bulletin,* April 20; pages 563-64.

"Peace in the World," *Vital Speeches of the Day,* May 1; pages 418-21.

"President and the Press," *U.S. News & World Report,* February 27; pages 113-15.

"President Defends Right to Meet Accusers Face to Face," *U.S. News & World Report,* December 4; page 113.

"President Favors Increased Aid to Migrants From Europe," *U.S. Department of State Bulletin,* May 4; pages 639-41.

"President Recommends Commission to Review Commercial Policy," *U.S. Department of State Bulletin,* May 25; pages 747-48.

"President Suggests Study of Immigration and Nationalities Act," *U.S. Department of State Bulletin,* May 18; pages 730-31.

"President to Young Republicans," *U.S. News & World Report,* June 19; pages 92-94.

"President Warns Against Cuts in Mutual Security Funds," *U.S. Department of State Bulletin,* August 3; pages 158-59.

"President's Letter to Syngman Rhee on Proposed Korean Armistice," *U.S. Department of State Bulletin,* June 15; pages 835-36.

"President's Message," *American Forests,* December; page 9 *et seq.*

"President's Views on Spies As an Issue in 1954," *U.S. News & World Report,* November 27; page 123.

"Recommendation for Increased Aid to Korea," *U.S. Department of State Bulletin,* August 10; page 193.

"Recommendations for Extension of Trade Agreements Act," *U.S. Department of*

State Bulletin, April 27; pages 634-35.

"Reorganization of Foreign Aid and Information Programs," *U.S. Department of State Bulletin,* June 15; pages 849-56.

"Representative Government: An Expression of Faith," *U.S. Department of State Bulletin,* October 26; page 541.

"Soviet Progress in Development of Atomic Weapons," *U.S. Department of State Bulletin,* October 19; page 508.

"State of the Union," *U.S. News & World Report,* February 13; pages 93-99.

"This Continent a Single Entity," *Vital Speeches of the Day,* December 1; pages 98-100.

"Tribute to Teachers," *School Life,* March; page 81.

"Use of Surplus Agricultural Commodities for Emergency Aid," *U.S. Department of State Bulletin,* July 13; pages 60-61.

"U.S. Aid to Bolivia," *U.S. Department of State Bulletin,* November 2; pages 584-86.

"U.S. Dependence on Foreign Trade," *U.S. Department of State Bulletin,* October 26; pages 539-41.

"U.S. Position on Iranian Oil Dispute," *U.S. Department of State Bulletin,* July 20; pages 74-76.

"U.S. Views on German Unity," *U.S. Department of State Bulletin,* August 3; pages 147-49.

"What Eisenhower Says About the Bomb," *U.S. News & World Report,* October 16; page 42.

1954

"Administration's Policy," *Vital Speeches of the Day,* October 15; pages 788-89.

"Agricultural Trade Act Signed," *U.S. Department of State Bulletin,* August 2; pages 165-66.

"Atomic Power for Peaceful Use," *U.S. Department of State Bulletin,* September 20; page 396.

"Atomic Stockpile for Peace," *Vital Speeches of the Day,* January 1; pages 162-65.

"Basic Prosperity to Be Sustained," *Vital Speeches of the Day,* January 15; pages 194-95.

"News Conference Statement by the President," *U.S. Department of State Bulletin*, August 2; page 163.

"9 Billions in Medical Bills—President's Answer: Reinsurance," *U.S. News & World Report*, January 29; pages 96-98.

"No Road Blocks to Co-operation—President's Promise to Nation," *U.S. News & World Report*, November 12; page 98 *et seq.*

"Our Legislative Program," *Vital Speeches of the Day*, July 1; pages 546-49.

"Pan American Day, 1954," *U.S. Department of State Bulletin*, April 12; page 564.

"Peace in Freedom," *U.S. Department of State Bulletin*, November 8; pages 675-79.

"Policy on Wool Imports," *U.S. Department of State Bulletin*, March 15; pages 393-94.

"Political Campaign Gets Up Steam," *U.S. News & World Report*, September 3; pages 98-102.

"President Asks Governors to Visit Korea," *U.S. Department of State Bulletin*, February 22; page 273.

"President Against Restricted Fish Imports," *U.S. Department of State Bulletin*, August 2; pages 166-67.

"President Eisenhower: Americans Will Defend Rights," *U.S. News & World Report*, August 6; page 58.

"President Eisenhower Speaks on Education at Defiance College," *School Life*, January; pages 49-50.

"President on Foreign Economic Policy," *U.S. Department of State Bulletin*, September 13; page 371.

"President Proclaims American Educational Week," *National Education Association Journal*, November; page 513.

"President Reports on Progress Toward Mutual Security," *U.S. Department of State Bulletin*, September 13; pages 381-85.

"President Requests Studies of Barley and Oats Imports," *U.S. Department of State Bulletin*, September 6; pages 340-41.

"President Speaks," *Newsweek*, June 7; pages 24-25.

"President's Forecast: Good Times Ahead," *U.S. News & World Report*, February 5; pages 44-49 *et seq.*

"President's Views," *U.S. News & World Report*, November 19; pages 92-94.

"President's Views on Treaty Making," *U.S. Department of State Bulletin*, February 8; page 195.

"Principles of U.S. Foreign Policy," *U.S. Department of State Bulletin*, September 13; pages 359-62.

"Programs for Building National and International Security," *U.S. Department of State Bulletin*, February 1; pages 143-48.

"Protocols on German Occupation and Accession to NATO Transmitted to Senate," *U.S. Department of State Bulletin*, December 6; pages 847-56.

"Pursuit of True Peace," *Vital Speeches of the Day*, September 15; pages 1474-76.

"Recommendation Concerning U.S. Foreign Economic Policy," *U.S. Department of State Bulletin*, April 19; pages 602-07.

"Recommendation Relating to Mutual Security Program," *U.S. Department of State Bulletin*, July 5; pages 35-37.

"Red China," *U.S. News & World Report*, July 16; page 29.

"Reduction of U.S. Forces in Korea," *U.S. Department of State Bulletin*, January 4; page 14.

"Reply to U.S.S.R. on Atoms for Peace Program," *U.S. Department of State Bulletin*, November 15; pages 733-34.

"Responsibility of the Newspaper," *Vital Speeches of the Day*, July 15; pages 593-95.

"Shining Evidence," *Time*, October 18; pages 17-18.

"Significance of Allied Landing in Normandy," *U.S. Department of State Bulletin*, June 21; page 959.

"Size Up by the President," *U.S. News & World Report*, January 22; pages 120-23.

"State of the Union: President's New Program," *U.S. News & World Report*, January 15; pages 65-70.

"Statesman and the State," *Vital Speeches of the Day*, September 1; pages 674-76.

"This Great Country of Ours," *Vital Speeches of the Day*, April 15; pages 413-16.

"Time of Great Decisions," *U.S. Department of State Bulletin*, May 10; pages 702-04.

"Tribute to Commander and Men of Dien-Bien-Phu Garrison," *U.S. Department of State Bulletin*, April 12; page 542.

"Turkish President Awarded Legion of Merit," *U.S. Department of State Bulletin*, February 15; pages 249-50.

"U.N. Human Rights Day, 1954," *U.S. Department of State Bulletin*, December 20; page 963.

"U.S. Aid for Home Builders: Low Payments, Loan Insurance," *U.S. News & World Report*, February 5; pages 72-74.

"U.S. Assurance to France," *U.S. Department of State Bulletin*, June 28; pages 990-91.

"U.S. Speaks From Strength," *U.S. News & World Report*, December 31; page 45.

"What Could Get U.S. Into War in Asia: Mr. Eisenhower Gives His View," *U.S. News & World Report*, May 21; pages 89-90.

"What Eisenhower Said About Indo-China in April," *U.S. News & World Report*, July 30; page 21.

"What Eisenhower Says About Indo-China Now," *U.S. News & World Report*, July 30; page 21.

"What Eisenhower Says About Russia and the U.N.," *U.S. News & World Report*, August 20; page 81.

"What the President Said About Indo-China," *U.S. News & World Report*, February 19; page 58.

"What the President Said About Prisoners of Reds," *U.S. News & World Report*, December 10; page 53 *et seq.*

"Where Business Stands in Second Republican Year," *U.S. News & World Report*, August 20; pages 85-86.

"World Trade Week, 1954," *U.S. Department of State Bulletin*, May 24; page 801.

1955

"Activities Under the Agricultural Trade Development and Assistance Act," *U.S.*

Department of State Bulletin, January 31; pages 200-06.

"Adapting U.S. Military Strength to Meet Changing World Conditions," *U.S. Department of State Bulletin*, January 17; pages 87-88.

"Amendment to Public Law 480," *U.S. Department of State Bulletin*, August 29; page 362.

"As a Crusader," *Newsweek*, June 6; page 82.

"Benefits to the United States of Participation in Proposed Organization for Trade Cooperation," *U.S. Department of State Bulletin*, April 25; pages 678-81.

"Big Four Conference: What Ike and Churchill Say," *U.S. News & World Report*, April 8; page 64.

"Business Ahead As Ike Sees It," *U.S. News & World Report*, January 28; pages 42-46 *et seq.*

"Commerce and World Peace," *U.S. Department of State Bulletin*, May 23; pages 842-43.

"Communist Treason in Our National Life," *U.S. News & World Report*, September 9; page 144 *et seq.*

"Developments in the Near East," *U.S. Department of State Bulletin*, November 21; page 844.

"Eisenhower Intelligence," *New Republic*, September 12; page 5.

"Eisenhower: Prospects for Peace Are Brighter," *U.S. News & World Report*, August 5; page 123.

"Eisenhower Talks About Peace," *U.S. News & World Report*, May 6; page 25.

"Eisenhower Urges Lowering of Iron Curtain," *U.S. News & World Report*, July 29; page 111.

"Eisenhower: You Are More Than Union Members," *U.S. News & World Report*, December 16; pages 130-31.

"Eisenhower's Reaction: Disappointment," *U.S. News & World Report*, January 21; page 93.

"Enactment of Trade Agreements Extension Act of 1955," *U.S. Department of State Bulletin*, July 4; pages 25-26.

"Exchangee Denied Permanent Residence Immigration Status," *U.S. Department* of *State Bulletin,* July 11; pages 83-84.

"Exploring the Avenues to Peace," *U.S. Department of State Bulletin,* June 20; pages 987-89.

"Faith in the Future of the American Republic," *U.S. Department of State Bulletin,* March 14; pages 439-40.

"From the President's State-of-Union Messages 1954 and 1955," *School Life,* February; page 65.

"Furthering Foreign Economic Policy of the United States," *U.S. Department of State Bulletin.* January 24; pages 119-22.

"Government Program for Low-Income Farmers," *Current History,* June; page 368.

"Guildhall Address, July 12, 1945," *The Nation,* July 9; pages 23-24.

"Health Message," *Congressional Digest,* March, page 69 *et seq.*

"How Ike Would Aid Schools," *U.S. News & World Report,* February 18; pages 78-79.

"Ike: I Do Not Like Politics, But—," *U.S. News & World Report,* June 10; page 32.

"Ike on Peace," *U.S. News & World Report,* August 12; pages 96-98.

"Ike on Salk Vaccine: It Will Eliminate Polio," *U.S. News & World Report,* May 20; page 32.

"Ike on Zhukov: We Were Friends," *U.S. News & World Report,* February 18; pages 88-91.

"Ike Outlines His Political Creed," *U.S. News & World Report,* September 23; pages 114-16.

"Ike Tells How U.S. Will Work for Peace," *U.S. News & World Report,* July 1; pages 96-98.

"Ike: U.S. in a Better Position Than Ever Before," *U.S. News & World Report,* May 27; page 106 *et seq.*

"Ike Versus Ike," *American Mercury,* October; page 146.

"Ike's Plan for Arms Inspection," *U.S. News & World Report,* July 29; page 82.

"Ike's Stern Warning, Chou's Bristling Reply," *U.S. News & World Report,* February 4; pages 66-68.

"Increased Duties on Imported Bicycles," *U.S. Department of State Bulletin,* September 5; pages 399-401.

"Meeting of Heads of Government at Geneva," *U.S. Department of State Bulletin,* August 1; pages 171-77.

"Meeting the Human Problems of the Nuclear Age," *U.S. Department of State Bulletin,* June 27; pages 1027-30.

"Message From the President to Ben Wright," *Field & Stream,* November; pages 80-81.

"Mission of Radio Free Europe," *U.S. Department of State Bulletin,* February 21; page 295.

"Mutual Defense Treaty With Republic of China Transmitted to Senate," *U.S. Department of State Bulletin,* January 24; pages 150-52.

"Need for Greater Public Understanding," *U.S. Department of State Bulletin,* April 11; pages 609-11.

"Need for Peaceful Settlement of Near East Problems," *U.S. Department of State Bulletin,* November 28; pages 894-95.

"New Spirit of Cooperation in the Search for Peace," *U.S. Department of State Bulletin,* August 8; pages 215-17.

"President and Chancellor Adenauer Exchange Views on Geneva Meeting," *U.S. Department of State Bulletin,* August 15; page 259.

"President and Soviet Premier Exchange Views on Inspection," *U.S. Department of State Bulletin,* October 24; pages 643-47.

"President Eisenhower's Statement at Press Conference," *Aviation Week,* May 30; page 14.

"President Eisenhower's Views on Potential Use of Atomic Energy," *U.S. Department of State Bulletin,* November 14; page 787.

"President's Views on Administration of Foreign Economic Program," *U.S. Department of State Bulletin,* March 7; page 388.

"Problems Are Not Inherently Insoluble," *U.S. News & World Report,* July 29; pages 99-101.

"Promoting the Security of the United

States and the Free World," *U.S. Department of State Bulletin*, January 31; pages 163-70.

"Ratification of Geneva Conventions for Protection of War Victims," *U.S. Department of State Bulletin*, September 19; pages 454-55.

"Recommendations for Amending Refugee Relief Act," *U.S. Department of State Bulletin*, June 13; pages 951-53.

"Recommendations for 1956 Mutual Security Program," *U.S. Department of State Bulletin*, May 2; pages 711-17.

"Sample of Ike's Technique," *U.S. News & World Report*, March 18; pages 34-35.

"Search for Peace," *Vital Speeches of the Day*, May 15; pages 1218-20.

"Second Progress Report on the Agricultural Trade Development and Assistance Act," *U.S. Department of State Bulletin*, August 1; pages 197-203.

"Special Assistant to the President for Developing Disarmament Policy," *U.S. Department of State Bulletin*, April 4; pages 556-57.

"State of the Union—Eisenhower Scans Future: The Outlook Is Good," *U.S. News & World Report*, January 14; pages 92-99.

"Statement by President Eisenhower," *U.S. Department of State Bulletin*, November 7; page 728.

"Testimony of a Devout President," *Life*, December 26; pages 12-13.

"Time for New Franklins," *Time*, June 20; pages 16-17.

"To Seek the Road to Peace," *U.S. Department of State Bulletin*, July 25; pages 131-33.

"Toward the Good of Us All," *U.S. Department of State Bulletin*, August 8; pages 217-18.

"U.N. Human Rights Day, 1955," *U.S. Department of State Bulletin*, December 26; pages 1048-49.

"U.S. Policy on Defense of Formosa," *U.S. Department of State Bulletin*, February 7; pages 211-14.

"U.S. to Continue Support for Free Viet-Nam," *U.S. Department of State Bulletin*, March 14; page 423.

"What Ike Says About Chance of War," *U.S. News & World Report*, February 11; page 31.

"What Ike Says About Khrushchev and Arms Cuts," *U.S. News & World Report*, July 15; pages 85-87.

"What Ike Says About Zhukov," *U.S. News & World Report*, March 4; page 57.

"Why President Favors a Big 4 Meeting," *U.S. News & World Report*, May 20; pages 38-39.

"World Cooperation on Peaceful Uses of Atomic Energy," *U.S. Department of State Bulletin*, August 22; pages 300-01.

1956

"Accelerating the Development of Nuclear Power Abroad," *U.S. Department of State Bulletin*, December 10; pages 926-27.

"Anniversary of Philippine Independence," *U.S. Department of State Bulletin*, July 16; page 93.

"As Ike Sees Farm Problem," *U.S. News & World Report*, April 13; page 58.

"As Ike Sees the Revolt in Soviet Satellites," *U.S. News & World Report*, November 2; page 46.

"Big Decision, His Health, Warren, the Coming Campaign," *U.S. News & World Report*, February 17; pages 81-82 *et seq.*

"Bill Amending and Extending Sugar Act Signed," *U.S. Department of State Bulletin*, June 18; pages 1016-17.

"Brighter Hopes for Peace," *U.S. Department of State Bulletin*, January 2; page 3.

"Carrying the Fire," *Time*, June 11; pages 29-30.

"Case for Security," *Time*, October 15; page 28.

"Communist Imperialism in the Satellite World," *U.S. Department of State Bulletin*, November 5; pages 702-03.

"Congress Must O.K. Before Marines Fight in Mideast," *U.S. News & World Report*, April 13; page 90 *et seq.*

"Correspondence Between President Eisenhower and Premier Bulganin Concerning

Nuclear Tests," *U.S. Department of State Bulletin*, October 29; pages 662-64.

"Correspondence of President Eisenhower and Premier Bulganin Concerning Control of Armaments and Reduction of Armed Forces," *U.S. Department of State Bulletin*, August 20; pages 299-305.

"Correspondence of President Eisenhower and Premier Bulganin on Disarmament and U.S.-Soviet Relations," *U.S. Department of State Bulletin*, March 26; pages 514-18.

"Crusade for Freedom," *U.S. Department of State Bulletin*, April 16; page 636.

"Death of President Samoza of Nicaragua," *U.S. Department of State Bulletin*, October 15; page 573.

"Departure of President Sukarno," *U.S. Department of State Bulletin*, June 18; pages 1005-06.

"Developing the Atlantic Community; President's Letter to Senator George," *U.S. Department of State Bulletin*, May 21; page 836.

"Developments in Eastern Europe and the Middle East," *U.S. Department of State Bulletin*, November 12; pages 743-45.

"Distribution of Additional Quantities of Uranium 235," *U.S. Department of State Bulletin*, March 19; pages 469-71.

"Exchange of Correspondence Between President Eisenhower and Soviet Premier Bulganin," *U.S. Department of State Bulletin*, February 6; pages 191-95.

"Farm Legislation, 1956," *Current History*, September; pages 168-69.

"How Eisenhower Sizes Up Feuding in the Armed Forces," *U.S. News & World Report*, June 1; pages 54-55.

"How Eisenhower Views the Suez Situation," *U.S. News & World Report*, August 17; page 52.

"How Ike Sizes Up Trouble in Mixed Schools," *U.S. News & World Report*, September 14; page 43.

"How Ike Views the Drive Against Nixon," *U.S. News & World Report*, August 10; pages 29-31.

"How Ike Would Spend More Billions Abroad," *U.S. News & World Report*, March 30; pages 88-90 *et seq.*

"How the President Answered the Big Question," *U.S. News & World Report*, March 9; pages 64-68 *et seq.*

"I Shall Accept the Nomination," *Vital Speeches of the Day*, March 15; pages 322-24.

"Ike Asks New Spirit in Russia," *U.S. News & World Report*, August 17; page 105.

"Ike Cites the Record: Peace at Home and Abroad," *U.S. News & World Report*, September 28; pages 141-43.

"Ike: Full Picture Will Show No Loss in Security," *U.S. News & World Report*, May 11; page 114.

"Ike Points to His Record—More Jobs, Inflation Checked, U.S. Spending Down, Labor Peace," *U.S. News & World Report*, October 19; pages 134-36.

"Ike Says H-Bomb Test Must Go On," *U.S. News & World Report*, October 12; page 56.

"Ike Spells Out Farm Program—Cut Crop Surplus, Keep Soil Bank, Extend Credit," *U.S. News & World Report*, October 5; pages 125-27.

"Ike Stands on His Record, Says Democrats Talk Bunk," *U.S. News & World Report*, October 12; pages 144-46.

"Ike Talks About His Health, Bulganin, Chance of War," *U.S. News & World Report*, March 16; pages 92-94 *et seq.*

"Ike Talks of Running Mate: I thought of a Whole Group," *U.S. News & World Report*, August 31; pages 32-35.

"Ike's Explanation: How U.S. Figures in School Disputes," *U.S. News & World Report*, September 21; page 50.

"Ike's Own Summary of the State of Union," *U.S. News & World Report*, January 13; pages 97-98.

"Ike's Own Words About Running," *U.S. News & World Report*, January 27; pages 26-29.

"Importance of Restoring Funds Cut From Mutual Security Program," *U.S. Department of State Bulletin*, July 23; page 144.

"Increased Tensions in Middle East," *U.S. Department of State Bulletin*, November 5; pages 699-700.

"International Atomic Energy Agency Es-

eign *Policy Bulletin*, November 15; page 36 *et seq.*

"Significance of London Conference on Suez Canal," *U.S. Department of State Bulletin*, September 10; page 405.

"Simplifying Customs Procedures," *U.S. Department of State Bulletin*, August 13; pages 273-74.

"Special Statement Prepared for *NEA Journal*," *National Education Association Journal*, October; page 410.

"State of the Union," *Vital Speeches of the Day*, February 1; pages 226-33.

"Strengthening the Defense of the United States and Its Allies," *U.S. Department of State Bulletin*, January 30; pages 147-54.

"Sure Safeguards Needed Before Bomb Tests Can End," *U.S. News & World Report*, November 2; pages 98-100.

"Third Progress Report on the Agricultural Trade Development and Assistance Act," *U.S. Department of State Bulletin*, January 23; pages 130-38.

"Three Guidelines to Peace," *Scholastic*, May 3; page 17.

"2-Billion-Dollar Program for Federal Aid to Schools," *U.S. News & World Report*, January 20; pages 102-04.

"U.N. Human Rights Day, 1956," *U.S. Department of State Bulletin*, December 17; pages 949-50.

"U.S. Concern for Hungarian People, Statement by the President," *U.S. Department of State Bulletin*, November 5; page 700.

"U.S.—Hungarian Friendship," *U.S. Department of State Bulletin*, December 10; page 913.

"U.S. Participation in the United Nations During 1955," *U.S. Department of State Bulletin*, September 3; pages 382-84.

"U.S. Policies and Actions in the Development and Testing of Nuclear Weapons," *U.S. Department of State Bulletin*, November 5; pages 704-15.

"U.S. Rejects Soviet Proposal to Use Force in Egypt; Urges U.S.S.R. to Withdraw Troops From Hungary," *U.S. Department of State Bulletin*, November 19; pages 795-97.

"U.S. Views on Polish Trials," *U.S. Department of State Bulletin*, October 8; page 552.

"War, Hungary, Inflation—How Eisenhower Sizes Them Up," *U.S. News & World Report*, November 23; pages 125-26 *et seq.*

"We Cannot Be Partisans—We Are All Americans," *U.S. News & World Report*, April 27; pages 122-24 *et seq.*

"We Must Be Patient, We Must Be Understanding," *U.S. News & World Report*, March 23; page 104.

"What Ike Says About Nixon Now," *U.S. News & World Report*, March 23; page 36.

"What Ike Says About Suez, Health, the Campaign Ahead," *U.S. News & World Report*, September 7; pages 78-81.

"What Ike Sees Ahead: '56 Better Than '55," *U.S. News & World Report*, February 3, pages 102-17.

"What Ike Tells Voters," *U.S. News & World Report*, October 26; pages 122-24.

"What Is the Job to Be Done," *Vital Speeches of the Day*, October 15; pages 2-4.

"What President Would Do to Help U.S. Farmers," *U.S. News & World Report*, January 20; pages 78-82 *et seq.*

"Why Ike Vetoed Farm Bill—And Democrats' Reply," *U.S. News & World Report*, April 27; pages 109-12 *et seq.*

"Why U.S. Must Test More H-Bombs," *U.S. News & World Report*, May 4; pages 122-23.

"Woodrow Wilson Centennial Year Proclamation," *U.S. Department of State Bulletin*, May 14; page 806.

"Working Together for International Understanding," *U.S. Department of State Bulletin*, June 4; pages 915-20.

1957

"Advantages to the United States of Membership in Proposed Organization for Trade Cooperation," *U.S. Department of State Bulletin*, April 22; pages 657-58.

"Anniversary of Fall of Bataan," *U.S. Department of State Bulletin*, April 29; pages 679-80.

"As Ike Sees It: Cost of Peace Comes

U.S. News & World Report, August 30; page 24.

"Ike Says This About a Clean Bomb," *U.S. News & World Report*, July 5; page 26.

"Ike Talks About His Health, Living Costs, Mideast Troubles," *U.S. News & World Report*, March 15; pages 132-36.

"Ike Talks of Foreign Visitors, Dulles, Sending Troops Abroad," *U.S. News & World Report*, February 8; pages 86-88.

"Ike Tells Why Top Men Are Hard to Hire," *U.S. News & World Report*, August 9; page 90.

"Ike's Plea to Israel; Ben-Gurion's Answer," *U.S. News & World Report*, March 1; pages 65-70.

"Ike's Views on Inflation, Cuts in Budget, What Congress Did," *U.S. News & World Report*, September 13; pages 102-04.

"Inflation a Threat to Sound Economy," *Vital Speeches of the Day*, October 15; pages 2-3.

"International Atomic Energy Agency Comes Into Being," *U.S. Department of State Bulletin*, August 19; page 307.

"International Economic Situation," *U.S. Department of State Bulletin*, February 11; pages 222-25.

"Let's Not Throw Away Engines of This Ship of State," *U.S. News & World Report*, May 10; pages 110-12.

"Letter From the President to Representative Durham," *U.S. Department of State Bulletin*, July 29; page 217.

"Letter of President to Be Included in U.S. Passports," *U.S. Department of State Bulletin*, August 12; pages 275-76.

"Little Rock Story, in the Words of Eisenhower, Faubus, Governors," *U.S. News & World Report*, October 11; pages 102-09.

"Meaning of Kremlin Purge—As Ike and Dulles See It," *U.S. News & World Report*, July 26; pages 85-86.

"Message From President Eisenhower to American Council on NATO," *U.S. Department of State Bulletin*, February 18; page 252.

"Middle East," *Vital Speeches of the Day*, January 15; pages 200-03.

"Mohammed V, Sultan of Morocco, to Visit to U.S.," *U.S. Department of State Bulletin*, July 1; pages 19-20.

"Mutual Security Program for 1958 Presented to Congress; Message of President Eisenhower," *U.S. Department of State Bulletin*, June 10; pages 920-26.

"No Cut-Rate Price for Security," *U.S. News & World Report*, May 24; pages 134-36 *et seq*.

"No Reason to Grow Hysterical—No Additional Threat to U.S.," *U.S. News & World Report*, October 18; pages 118-20 *et seq*.

"Opening of Islamic Center," *U.S. Department of State Bulletin*, July 15; pages 102-03.

"People-to-People Program," *U.S. Department of State Bulletin*, November 11; page 747.

"President and Prime Minister Kishi Exchange Views on Nuclear Tests," *U.S. Department of State Bulletin*, October 21; pages 635-36.

"President Asks for Authorization for U.S. Economic Program and for Resolution on Communist Aggression in Middle East," *U.S. Department of State Bulletin*, January 21; pages 83-88.

"President Commends Israel on Decision to Withdraw," *U.S. Department of State Bulletin*, March 18; page 433.

"President Comments on Trade With Red China," *U.S. News & World Report*, June 14; page 134.

"President Eisenhower's Views on House Joint Resolution 16," *U.S. Department of State Bulletin*, August 12; pages 296-97.

"President Exchanges Greeting With British Prime Minister," *U.S. Department of State Bulletin*, February 4; page 174.

"President on Arms Cuts—Our Offer Always Stands," *U.S. News & World Report*, July 12; pages 104-05.

"President on State and Federal Powers," *U.S. News & World Report*, October 4; page 59.

"President Requests Investigation of Imports of Dairy Products," *U.S. Department of State Bulletin*, July 1; pages 33-34.

Bibliography

"President Talks About Budget and Helicopters," *U.S. News & World Report,* April 5; pages 92-94 *et seq.*

"President Tells Why He Sent Combat Troops to Little Rock," *U.S. News & World Report,* October 4; pages 64-65.

"President Tells Why U.S. Spending Must Go Up," *U.S. News & World Report,* January 25; pages 146-50.

"President's First Hint of Compromise," *U.S. News & World Report,* July 26; pages 100-01.

"President Sets His Goal: Help to Heal Divided World," *U.S. News & World Report,* February 1; pages 118-19.

"Progress in International Financing," *U.S. Department of State Bulletin,* October 14; pages 595-99.

"Queen Elizabeth II Visits the United States," *U.S. Department of State Bulletin,* November 11; pages 742-46.

"Recommended Revision of Immigration and Nationality Act," *U.S. Department of State Bulletin,* February 18; pages 247-50.

"Resignation of Sir Anthony Eden As British Prime Minister," *U.S. Department of State Bulletin,* January 28, page 130.

"Sale of Long Staple Cotton From National Stockpile," *U.S. Department of State Bulletin,* July 29; page 209.

"Salute to Argentine Air Force," *U.S. Department of State Bulletin,* December 9; page 929.

"Science in National Security," *Vital Speeches of the Day,* November 15; pages 66-69.

"Should the President Get Tough With Congress? Should He Take Gifts?," *U.S. News & World Report,* August 16; pages 104-05.

"State of the Union," *Vital Speeches of the Day,* February 1; pages 226-29.

"Status of American Education," *School Life,* March; pages 5-6 *et seq.*

"Statute of International Atomic Energy Agency Transmitted to Senate," *U.S. Department of State Bulletin,* April 15; pages 615-16.

"Summary of Important Facts in Earth Satellite Program," *U.S. Department of State Bulletin,* October 28; page 673.

"Tenth Anniversary of Greek-Turkish Aid Program," *U.S. Department of State Bulletin,* April 1; page 539.

"Tenth Anniversary of Marshall Plan," *U.S. Department of State Bulletin,* June 24; page 1002.

"U.S. Issues Commemorative Stamp Honoring President Magsaysay," *U.S. Department of State Bulletin,* September 16; pages 472-73.

"U.S. Proposes Two-Year Ban on Testing Nuclear Weapons," *U.S. Department of State Bulletin,* September 9; pages 418-19.

"U.S. Will Not Sacrifice Security to Worship a Balanced Budget," *U.S. News & World Report,* November 22; pages 114-15.

"Voice of America," *Vital Speeches of the Day,* March 15; pages 322-23.

"Way Eisenhower Sees His Budget Fight With Congress," *U.S. News & World Report,* May 31; pages 113-16.

"What Eisenhower Said About Labor Rackets," *U.S. News & World Report,* May 3; page 104.

"What Eisenhower Says About Federal Versus State Power," *U.S. News & World Report,* November 1; pages 118-19.

"What Eisenhower Sees Ahead for U.S. Business," *U.S. News & World Report,* February 1; pages 106-10.

"What Ike Said About Secretary Wilson," *U.S. News & World Report,* February 8; page 89.

"Who Should Cut the Budget? President Gives His Views," *U.S. News & World Report,* March 22; pages 96-98.

"Why U.S. Ships Are Cautioned on Travel in Mideast Waters," *U.S. News & World Report,* April 26; page 100 *et seq.*

"Wider Education of Our People," *Vital Speeches of the Day,* May 1; pages 418-20.

1958

"Academic Training for the Foreign Service," *U.S. Department of State Bulletin,* November 3; pages 689-90.

"Action by Congress Urged by President,"

Congressional Digest, November; page 262 *et seq*.

"Arab Development Plan," *Vital Speeches of the Day*, September 1; pages 675-78.

"Before Any Tax Cut, We've Got to Make Sure We Are Right," *U.S. News & World Report*, April 11; pages 102-03.

"Budget Message of the President," *U.S. Department of State Bulletin*, February 3; pages 169-79.

"Business Outlook Now, As the President Sees It," *U.S. News & World Report*, January 24; pages 91-93.

"Brotherhood of Christmas," *U.S. Department of State Bulletin*, January 20; pages 91-92.

"Colombo Plan Nations Hold Tenth Annual Meeting; Welcoming Remarks by President Eisenhower, November 10," *U.S. Department of State Bulletin*, December 1; pages 853-57.

"Columbus Day, 1958," *U.S. Department of State Bulletin*, November 3; pages 688-89.

"Communist Threat to Peace in Taiwan Area," *U.S. Department of State Bulletin*, September 29; pages 481-84.

"Crisis in Lebanon," *Vital Speeches of the Day*, August 1; pages 612-13.

"East-West Size-Up of Peace Outlook— And the Cold War," *U.S. News & World Report*, January 3, pages 83 and 85.

"Eisenhower Letter That Jolted Khrushchev," *U.S. News & World Report*, August 1; pages 66-67.

"Eisenhower on Summit Talks: We Will Never Close Door," *U.S. News & World Report*, March 14; page 93.

"Eisenhower: The Decline Is Slowing Down," *U.S. News & World Report*, May 30; page 61.

"Eisenhower: Things Are Good and Getting Better," *U.S. News & World Report*, October 31; pages 98-101.

"Eisenhower to Khrushchev—Differences Between Us Are Basic," *U.S. News & World Report*, August 8; page 69.

"Eisenhower to Khrushchev: The Real Way to End H-Tests," *U.S. News & World Report*, April 18; page 78.

"Eisenhower's Ground Rules for U.N. Summit Talks," *U.S. News & World Report*, August 1; page 47.

"Eisenhower's Own Words on Inflation, Integration, Mideast," *U.S. News & World Report*, August 15; pages 91-92.

"First Anniversary of Ghana's Independence," *U.S. Department of State Bulletin*, March 31; page 517.

"47th Anniversary of Founding of Republic of China," *U.S. Department of State Bulletin*, November 3; pages 692-93.

"Freedom Under Law," *U.S. Department of State Bulletin*, May 19; page 831.

"Free-World Cooperation and America's Security," *U.S. Department of State Bulletin*, July 21; page 103.

"From the President: Terms for Halting Atom Tests," *U.S. News & World Report*, August 29; page 29.

"Government Will Act in a Sound and Timely Fashion," *Vital Speeches of the Day*, April 1; pages 359-61.

"How Eisenhower Sees the Business Future," *U.S. News & World Report*, January 31; pages 78-79.

"How Ike Answers Critics of Shake-Up in the Military," *U.S. News & World Report*, April 25; pages 120-23.

"Ike Answers Bulganin With Charter for Peace," *U.S. News & World Report*, January 24; pages 116-20.

"Ike on Anti-Semitism, Quemoy, Politics in Foreign Affairs," *U.S. News & World Report*, October 24; page 93.

"Issues: Defense, Prosperity—At Stake: Control of Congress," *U.S. News & World Report*, January 31; pages 88-89.

"Meaning of the Election, As the President Sees It," *U.S. News & World Report*, November 14; pages 128-29.

"Meeting of Heads of Government of NATO Countries," *U.S. Department of State Bulletin*, January 6; pages 3-16.

"National Aeronautics and Space Act Signed by the President," *U.S. Department of State Bulletin*, August 25; page 327.

"NATO Conference at Paris," *U.S. Department of State Bulletin*, January 13; pages 47-52.

"No Use of Going to Summit if Soviets

Essential to Welfare of U.S.," *U.S. News & World Report*, July 25; pages 74-76.

"President Urges U.S.S.R. to Support U.S. Proposal for an International Inspection System in Arctic," *U.S. Department of State Bulletin*, September 8; pages 395-96.

"President Vetoes Bill Increasing Duty on Treated Seed Wheat," *U.S. Department of State Bulletin*, September 8; pages 395-96.

"President's 1958 Farm Message," *Congressional Digest*, March; pages 75-77.

"President's View: Red Hands in Unrest Around the World," *U.S. News & World Report*, May 23; pages 96-98.

"Problems at Home and Abroad—How Eisenhower Sees Them Now," *U.S. News & World Report*, August 29; pages 60-61.

"Real Story of Berlin, Report on Civil Rights, Red Missiles," *U.S. News & World Report*, December 19; pages 64-65.

"Red China, Schools, Adams—Here Are Eisenhower's Views," *U.S. News & World Report*, October 10; pages 80-83.

"Religious and Civil Liberty," *The Christian Century*, October 22; page 1195.

"Security and Peace," *U.S. Department of State Bulletin*, March 17; pages 411-15.

"Special Message on Education," *School Life*, March; page 5 *et seq.*

"State of the Union," *U.S. Department of State Bulletin*, January 27; pages 115-22.

"Tax Cut? Recovery? U.S. Policy Abroad? —Here Are Ike's Views," *U.S. News & World Report*, June 6; pages 98-99.

"10th Anniversary of International Educational Exchange Program," *U.S. Department of State Bulletin*, February 17; pages 248-49.

"Time for Greatness," *Vital Speeches of the Day*, January 1; pages 162-65.

"U.S. and Argentina Reaffirm Support for Concept of Joint Consultations," *U.S. Department of State Bulletin*, August 4; pages 209-10.

"U.S. and Brazilian Presidents Reaffirm Inter-American Solidarity," *U.S. Department of State Bulletin*, June 30; pages 1090-91.

"U.S. and Brazilian Presidents Support Summit Meeting at U.N.," *U.S. Department of State Bulletin*, August 18; pages 281-82.

"United States Dispatches Troops to Lebanon," *U.S. Department of State Bulletin*, August 4; pages 181-86.

"U.S. Nuclear Tests to Demonstrate Reduction in Radioactive Fallout," *U.S. Department of State Bulletin*, April 14; page 601.

"U.S. Offers to Negotiate Nuclear Test Suspension," *U.S. Department of State Bulletin*, September 8; pages 378-79.

"U.S. Participation in the United Nations During 1956," *U.S. Department of State Bulletin*, February 10; pages 235-37.

"U.S. Participation in the United Nations During 1957," *U.S. Department of State Bulletin*, August 4; pages 218-21.

"U.S. Position on Soviet Continuance of Nuclear Weapons Testing," *U.S. Department of State Bulletin*, November 24; page 810.

"Vice President Nixon Returns From South American Tour," *U.S. Department of State Bulletin*, June 9; page 950 *et seq.*

"What Eisenhower Thinks of the Sherman Adams Case," *U.S. News & World Report*, June 27; pages 76-77.

"What Ike Says Now About Taxes, Recession, H-Bomb, Defense," *U.S. News & World Report*, April 18; pages 118-20.

"What It Means to Be President," *U.S. News & World Report*, May 9; pages 50-51.

"What the President Said About Little Rock—And Governor Faubus's Reply," *U.S. News & World Report*, August 29; page 26.

"When President Is Disabled: Here's Eisenhower's Views," *U.S. News & World Report*, March 14; page 78.

"Why the President Calls for 3.9 Billion More in Foreign Aid," *U.S. News & World Report*, February 28; pages 90-93.

"World Trade," *Vital Speeches of the Day*, April 15; pages 399-401.

"Address, February 11, 1959," *Congressional Digest*, April; page 106 *et seq.*

"Address, May 6, 1959," *Vital Speeches of the Day*, June 15; page 526.

"Aiding the Less Developed Nations, a Cooperative Venture; Remarks by President Eisenhower," *U.S. Department of State Bulletin*, October 19; pages 531-32.

"Chairman Nikita S. Khrushchev of the Soviet Union Arrives for U.S. Visit," *U.S. Department of State Bulletin*, October 5; pages 476-79.

"Confidence in the Continuing Growth and Strength of America," *U.S. Department of State Bulletin*, May 4; pages 620-21.

"Eisenhower on Mikoyan, Missiles, Taxes, Civil Rights," *U.S. News & World Report*, January 23; pages 90-92.

"Eisenhower: There Is Progress; Khrushchev: Good—And Bad," *U.S. News & World Report*, October 12; pages 103-04.

"Exchange Between President Eisenhower and Chancellor Adenauer," *U.S. Department of State Bulletin*, October 12; page 501.

"Exchange of Persons—A Gateway to Peace," *U.S. Department of State Bulletin*, February 23; pages 260-61.

"Federal Responsibility in Education," *School Life*, January; pages 5-6.

"Freedom and the Search for Peace," *U.S. Department of State Bulletin*, June 1; page 783.

"From Eisenhower: Aims of His Trip Abroad, Warning on Steel," *U.S. News & World Report*, December 14; pages 96-97.

"From the President: Answers on Future of Dulles, Berlin Crisis," *U.S. News & World Report*, February 27; page 71.

"F.S.I. Holds Graduation Ceremonies for First Senior Office Class, Remarks by President Eisenhower," *U.S. Department of State Bulletin*, July 6; pages 35-36.

"How Ike Sees the Big Issues—Summit, Steel Strike, Castro," *U.S. News & World Report*, November 9; page 100.

"How Ike Sizes Up Khrushchev," *U.S. News & World Report*, September 28; pages 88-89.

"How Tough a Labor Bill?; Views of Eisenhower and Meany," *U.S. News & World Report*, August 17; pages 109-12.

"Ike on Chances for a Summit Meeting: No Brighter," *U.S. News & World Report*, June 29; page 68.

"Ike on Inflation, Highways, Housing, Medical Cost," *U.S. News & World Report*, May 25; pages 114-15.

"Ike Views U.S. Budget, Bonds," *U.S. News & World Report*, February 27; page 100.

"Ike's Answer to Demand for More Arms Spending," *U.S. News & World Report*, March 23; pages 42-43.

"Ike's Views on Budget, Politics, Troubles in Latin America," *U.S. News & World Report*, July 13; page 92.

"Ike's Views on Steel-Wage Talks," *U.S. News & World Report*, June 29; page 99.

"Ike's Views on Summit, Steel Talks, Interest Rates," *U.S. News & World Report*, June 15; pages 90-93.

"Importance of Understanding," *U.S. Department of State Bulletin*, April 27; pages 579-83.

"Inflation and Its Cure—As the President Sees It," *U.S. News & World Report*, November 16; pages 99-101.

"International Commerce and the Paths to Peace," *U.S. Department of State Bulletin*, May 11; page 670.

"Maintaining World Peace and the Security of Free Nations," *U.S. Department of State Bulletin*, February 9; pages 198-205.

"McElroy and Ike Say This About a First Blow," *U.S. News & World Report*, March 16; pages 38-39.

"New Labor Laws Eisenhower Wants Passed," *U.S. News & World Report*, February 6; pages 97-98.

"No Ground War in Europe," *Time*, March 23; pages 13-14.

"Pledge to the Peoples of the World," *U.S. Department of State Bulletin*, January 12; pages 47-48.

"President: Americans Are Entitled to Expect Better," *U.S. News & World Report*, October 5; pages 111-12.

"President and Queen Elizabeth Open St. Lawrence Seaway," *U.S. Department of State Bulletin*, July 20; pages 75-76.

"President Approves Legislation Extending P.L. 480 Program," *U.S. Department of State Bulletin*, October 12; pages 515-16.

"President Approves Meeting on World Refugee Year," *U.S. Department of State Bulletin*, May 18; page 708.

"President Comments on D.L.F. Proposals by Senator Fulbright," *U.S. Department of State Bulletin*, June 22; pages 926-28.

"President Disapproves Increase in Tariff on Tartar Imports," *U.S. Department of State Bulletin*, April 13; pages 529-30.

"President Eisenhower Accepts Resignation of Secretary Dulles," *U.S. Department of State Bulletin*, May 4; pages 619-20.

"President Eisenhower Dedicates Library at Abilene," *U.S. Department of State Bulletin*, November 2; pages 620-23.

"President Eisenhower Makes Informal Visit to Mexico," *U.S. Department of State Bulletin*, March 9; pages 331-32.

"President Eisenhower Sends Greetings for Opening of American Nation Exhibition," *U.S. Department of State Bulletin*, August 17; page 229.

"President Eisenhower Visits Italy, Turkey, Pakistan, and Afghanistan," *U.S. Department of State Bulletin*. December 28; pages 931-34.

"President Lays Cornerstone of New CIA Building," *U.S. Department of State Bulletin*, November 23; page 743.

"President of El Salvador Concludes Talks With President Eisenhower," *U.S. Department of State Bulletin*, April 6; pages 478-79.

"President Offers Soviet Premier Alternative Approach to Test Ban," *U.S. Department of State Bulletin*, May 18; pages 704-06.

"President Recalls His War Days," *U.S. News & World Report*, January 23; page 23.

"President Recommends Membership in Inter-American Bank," *U.S. Department of State Bulletin*, June 8; pages 849-51.

"President Urges Congress to Act on Draper Committee's Recommendations on U.S. Military Assistance Program," *U.S. Department of State Bulletin*, July 13; pages 46-49.

"President Uges Soviet Premier to Accept Test Control Measures," *U.S. Department of State Bulletin*, June 8; pages 825-27.

"President's Business Forecast: An Era of Prosperity If—," *U.S. News & World Report*, January 30; pages 77-78.

"President's Grand Tour," *U.S. News & World Report*, November 16; pages 65-66.

"President's View on His Health, Loyalty Oath, Panama," *U.S. News & World Report*, December 14; page 95.

"Presidents of Mexico and United States Reaffirm Ties of Friendship," *U.S. Department of State Bulletin*, November 2; pages 624-27.

"Private Letters of the President," *Life*, March 16; pages 104-06 *et seq.*

"Role of the Teacher in Promoting Peace and Understanding," *U.S. Department of State Bulletin*, October 5; pages 479-81.

"Science and the State," *Time*, May 25; pages 12-13.

"Significance of Fourth of July," *U.S. Department of State Bulletin*, July 27; pages 116-17.

"Sound Dollar," *Vital Speeches of the Day*, July 15; pages 578-79.

"Sound Dollar, a Foundation Stone of American Leadership," *U.S. Department of State Bulletin*, May 18; pages 706-07.

"State of the Union," *U.S. News & World Report*, January 16; pages 60-64.

"Steel, Labor Laws, Summit—President's Latest Views," *U.S. News & World Report*, November 2; pages 78-79.

"Strengthening the Instruments of Freedom," *U.S. Department of State Bulletin*, May 18; pages 707-09.

"Tenth Anniversary of the North Atlantic

Treaty Organization; Remarks by President Eisenhower," *U.S. Department of State Bulletin*, April 20; pages 543-46.

"Tribute to John Foster Dulles," *U.S. Department of State Bulletin*, June 8; page 833.

"U.S. Accepts Statue of Bolivar From Government of Venezuela," *U.S. Department of State Bulletin*, March 16; page 378.

"United States and Soviet Union Exchange New Year Greetings," *U.S. Department of State Bulletin*, January 26; pages 131-32.

"United States Role in the World Refugee Year; Statement by President Eisenhower," *U.S. Department of State Bulletin*, June 15; page 872.

"United States Welcomes Agreement on Solution of Cyprus Problem," *U.S. Department of State Bulletin*, March 16; pages 367-68.

"Uniting the Free World Through Religion and Education," *U.S. Department of State Bulletin*, September 28; pages 447-48.

"Universality of Lincoln's Ideals," *U.S. Department of State Bulletin*, March 2; page 298.

"Western Berlin and Nation's Defense," *Vital Speeches of the Day*, April 1; pages 354-57.

"What Eisenhower Expects From Khrushchev's Visit," *U.S. News & World Report*, September 21; page 128 *et seq.*

"When Khrushchev Visits U.S.—The Things Ike Wants Him to See," *U.S. News & World Report*, August 24; pages 82-84.

"World Eisenhower Saw . . . The One He'd Like to Build," *U.S. News & World Report*, January 4, 1960; pages 85-86.

"World of Growth, a World of Law," *Time*, December 21; page 11.

1960

"Address to Uruguayan Congress, Montevidio, March 2," *U.S. Department of State Bulletin*, March 28; pages 483-86.

"America's Goal," *Vital Speeches of the Day*, August 15; pages 651-55.

"Bonds That Unite U.S. and Latin America," *U.S. Department of State Bulletin*, October 10; pages 557-58.

"Challenge to Khrushchev—Eisenhower's Blueprint for U.N.," *U.S. News & World Report*, October 3; pages 88-92.

"Eisenhower: Disregard Parochial Views," *U.S. News & World Report*, February 15; page 59.

"Eisenhower: No One Wants Another Pearl Harbor," *U.S. News & World Report*, May 23; page 56.

"Eisenhower's Philosophy About a U.S. That Is Second Best," *U.S. News & World Report*, February 15; page 89.

"Eisenhower's 7 Orders to Protect the Dollar," *U.S. News & World Report*, November 28; pages 52-53.

"Eisenhower's Views on Politics, Rockefeller, Recession," *U.S. News & World Report*, July 18; pages 108-09.

"Food, Family, Friendship, Freedom," *Vital Speeches of the Day*, January 15; pages 223-24.

"Forging a Comonwealth of Nations," *U.S. Department of State Bulletin*, November 14; pages 743-47.

"Four Powers Agree on May 16 As Date for Summit Meeting; Message of President Eisenhower to Mr. Khrushchev," *U.S. Department of State Bulletin*, January 18; page 77.

"From Eisenhower: The Nixon Role in Government," *U.S. News & World Report*, September 5, page 79.

"From the President of the United States to the White House Conference on Children and Youth," *School Life*, March; page 5 *et seq.*

"Hemisphere Cooperation for Better Municipal Government," *U.S. Department of State Bulletin*, November 21; pages 799-80.

"How Ike Views Segregation: Local Matter—Up to a Point," *U.S. News & World Report*, March 28; page 94.

"How's Business? This Is the President's Answer," *U.S. News & World Report*, August 22; page 46.

"I Have Difficulty in Restraining My Indignation," *Time*, August 8; page 12.

"Ike on Religion, U.N., Congress," *U.S.*

News & World Report, September 19; page 90.

"Ike on Rhee: A Great Man," *U.S. News & World Report*, May 9; page 41.

"Ike: Too Many Getting the Bomb," *U.S. News & World Report*, April 11; page 38.

"Ike's 4-Billion-Dollar Plan for More Aid Abroad," *U.S. News & World Report*, February 29; pages 107-11.

"Improving World Health and Nutrition," *U.S. Department of State Bulletin*, September 19; pages 441-43.

"International Balance of Payments," *Vital Speeches of the Day*, December 1; pages 98-100.

"Key to Common Progress," *Vital Speeches of the Day*, April 1; pages 354-55.

"King and Queen of Denmark Visit Washington," *U.S. Department of State Bulletin*, November 7; pages 717-19.

"Major Issues Facing Congress," *Vital Speeches of the Day*, September 1; pages 676-78.

"Most We Can Hope for Is Ease of Tension," *U.S. News & World Report*, May 9; page 73.

"Mutual Security, Its Principle and Program," *U.S. Department of State Bulletin*, May 23; pages 811-14.

"Mutual Security Program for Fiscal Year 1961; President's Message to Congress," *U.S. Department of State Bulletin*, March 7; pages 369-75.

"North Atlantic Council Holds Ministerial Meeting at Istanbul; Message From President Eisenhower," *U.S. Department of State Bulletin*, May 23; pages 839-40.

"Path of Common Sense Is Still Open to Khrushchev," *U.S. News & World Report*, June 6; pages 120-23.

"President Asks for Discretion in Purchase of Dominican Sugar," *U.S. Department of State Bulletin*, September 12; pages 412-13.

"President Comments on Financial Discussions With Germany," *U.S. Department of State Bulletin*, December 19; pages 925-26.

"President Congratulates Dr. Rhee on Well-Earned Retirement," *U.S. Department of State Bulletin*, May 30; page 859.

"President Directs Use of Mutual Security Funds for Office of I.G.C.," *U.S. Department of State Bulletin*, May 30; page 859.

"President Eisenhower Completes Visits to 11 Countries in Europe, Middle East, South Asia, and Africa," *U.S. Department of State Bulletin*, January 11; pages 46-57.

"President Eisenhower Departs for the Far East," *U.S. Department of State Bulletin*, July 4; pages 7-8.

"President Eisenhower Makes Official Visit to Portugal," *U.S. Department of State Bulletin*, June 6; pages 907-08.

"President Eisenhower Replies to Letter Regarding Meeting With Soviet Premier," *U.S. Department of State Bulletin*, October 17; pages 595-96.

"President Eisenhower Visits the Far East," *U.S. Department of State Bulletin*, July 25; pages 123-39.

"President Eisenhower Welcomes India—Pakistan Indus River Pact," *U.S. Department of State Bulletin*, October 10; pages 577-78.

"President Emphasizes U.S. Desire for Progress on Disarmament," *U.S. Department of State Bulletin*, April 4; page 514.

"President Expresses Views on World Court and Disarmament," *U.S. Department of State Bulletin*, January 25; pages 128-30.

"President Meets With Heads of U.N. Delegations of New Nations," *U.S. Department of State Bulletin*, November 7; pages 713-15.

"President: Our Defense Is Strong, Awesome," *U.S. News & World Report*, February 29; page 91.

"President Pledges U.S. Cooperation to Promote Social Progress and Economic Growth in the Americas," *U.S. Department of State Bulletin*, August 1; pages 166-70.

"President Reiterates U.S. Position on Guantanamo Naval Base," *U.S. Department of State Bulletin*, November 21; page 780.

"President Seeks Authority for U.S. Participation in I.D.A.," *U.S. Department*

"U.S. States Position on U-2 Incident; Statement by President Eisenhower," *U.S. Department of State Bulletin*, May 30; pages 851-52.

"U.S. Urges Soviet Union to Cease Unilateral Action in the Congo," *U.S. Department of State Bulletin*, September 26; page 473.

"U.S. Welcomes Security Council Discussion of RB-47 Plane Incident," *U.S. Department of State Bulletin*, August 8; pages 211-12.

"Western Powers to Continue Efforts for Peace Despite Disruption of Paris Meeting," *U.S. Department of State Bulletin*, June 6; pages 904-07.

"What Mr. Eisenhower Said Ten Years Ago," *U.S. News & World Report*, February 1; page 104 *et seq.*

"What President Eisenhower Says About Intelligence Estimates, the Space Race," *U.S. News & World Report*, February 8; pages 50-51.

"What the Good-Will Trips Did—A Report From Eisenhower," *U.S. News & World Report*, July 11; pages 91-92.

"When Ike Was Asked About Politics, Defense, Missiles," *U.S. News & World Report*, January 25; pages 90-91.

"World Court," *Vital Speeches of the Day*, October 1; pages 738-39.

1961

"Budget Message, Transmitted to Congress," *Congressional Digest*, March; pages 80-82 *et seq.*

"Certain Satisfaction," *Time*, October 20; page 27.

"Creed for Republicans," *U.S. News & World Report*, June 12; page 99.

"Eisenhower Recollects," *New Republic*, October 30; page 6.

"Farewell to the Nation," *U.S. Department of State Bulletin*, February 6; pages 179-82.

"How Eisenhower Sizes Up the World Today," *U.S. News & World Report*, August 21; pages 63-65.

"Liberty Is at Stake," *Vital Speeches of the Day*, February 1; pages 228-30.

"Message, December 16, 1960," *U.S. Department of State Bulletin*, January 9; pages 39-40.

"My Views on Berlin," *Saturday Evening Post*, December 9; pages 19-29.

"NASA to Promote Commercial Use of Communication Satellites," *U.S. Department of State Bulletin*, January 16; page 77.

"Now That I Am a Private Citizen," *Saturday Evening Post*, May 13; pages 19-21 *et seq.*

"Ranging the Field," *Time*, December 1; pages 13-14.

"Soviet-American Relations," *Saturday Review*, January 21; pages 44-45.

"Speech, a Pamphlet and It's Ike Versus Jack," *U.S. News & World Report*, October 2; page 98.

"State of the Union," *Vital Speeches of the Day*, February 1; pages 232-38.

1962

"Are We Headed in the Wrong Direction?," *Saturday Evening Post*, August 11; pages 19-25.

"How Much Freedom of Speech for the Military," *U.S. News & World Report*, February 5; pages 78-79.

"I have Great Respect for Kids," *Seventeen*, February; pages 64-65 *et seq.*

"Ike Asks: Is Morality Declining?," *U.S. News & World Report*, May 14; page 16.

"Ike Takes a Look at the GOP," *Saturday Evening Post*, April 21; pages 15-19.

"Real Threat to Liberty, As Ike Sees It," *U.S. News & World Report*, May 21; page 15.

II

Addresses, Excerpts From Books, Interviews, Remarks, Signed Magazine Articles, And Speeches About Eisenhower And Related Matters.

Ace, Goodman, "Fireside Chit Chat: Meet the Prez," *Saturday Review of Literature*, June 20, 1953, page 31.

Acheson, Dean, "Foreign Policy and Presidential Moralism," *The Reporter*, May 2, 1957, pages 10-14.

Adams, Sherman, "Bipartisan Government

Due Says Eisenhower's Political Chief of Staff," *Newsweek,* November 17, 1952, pages 26-27.

Adams, S. (cont.), "Critical Days of Ike's Three Illnesses," *Life,* May 26, 1961, pages 92-94 *et seq.*

———, 'Ike's Awkward Alliance With the Old Guard," *Life,* May 19, 1961, pages 134-36 *et seq.*

———, "What Goes On in White House When the President Is Sick," *U.S. News & World Report,* December 20, 1957, pages 88-89.

Adkins, Bertha Sheppard, "Vote Republican," *Independent Woman,* October, 1956, pages 3-4 *et seq.*

Agar, Herbert Sebastian, "Prayer for the New President," *Saturday Review of Literature,* January 17, 1953, pages 7-8 *et seq.*

Allen, George Edward, "My Friend the President," *Saturday Evening Post,* April 9, 1960, pages 23-25 *et seq.*

Alsop, Joseph Wright, "World Puts It Up to Ike," *Saturday Evening Post,* January 17, 1953, pages 26-27 *et seq.*

———, and Alsop, Stewart Johonnot, "Dreadful Dilemma of the Democrats," *Saturday Evening Post,"* July 23, 1955, pages 28-29 *et seq.*

———, "What the GOP Must Do to Win," *Saturday Evening Post,* September 13, 1952, pages 32-33 *et seq.*

Alsop, Stewart Johonnot, "Just What Is Modern Republicanism," *Saturday Evening Post,* July 27, 1957, pages 18-19 *et seq.*

Arnolt, Jessie Ash, "Little Ike's Hometown," *Christian Science Monitor Magazine,* May 19, 1945, page 4.

Ascoli, Max, "Curse of Indecision," *The Reporter,* October 17, 1957, pages 12-13.

———, "Kingdom of the Spirit," *The Reporter,* February 2, 1954, pages 10-11.

———, "Let's Pretend," *The Reporter,* December 10, 1959, pages 14-15.

———, "Miracle," *The Reporter,* August 11, 1955, pages 12-13.

———, "Preface," *The Reporter,* April 14, 1960, page 12.

———, "President and His Party," *The Reporter,* January 12, 1956, page 10.

———, "President and the Rabble," *The Reporter,* December 16, 1954, page 7.

———, "President Takes the Lead," *The Reporter,* January 5, 1954, page 6.

———, "President's Second Year," *The Reporter,* March 2, 1954, page 9.

———, "Second Act of God," *The Reporter,* June 28, 1956, page 7.

———, "This Spell of Langour," *The Reporter,* March 7, 1957, page 10.

———, "Time Has Come, Mr. President," *The Reporter,* July 21, 1953, pages 6-7.

———, "Turning Point," *The Reporter,* October 20, 1955, page 10.

———, "What Price Peace?," *The Reporter,* February 10, 1955, pages 12-13.

———, "Whose GOP?," *The Reporter,* August 9, 1956, page 10.

Baldwin, Hanson Weightman, "As Eisenhower Sees It Two Years After," *New York Times Magazine,* June 2, 1946, pages 7-9 *et seq.*

———, "Men of Destiny, Leaders in North Africa," *New York Times Magazine,* June 20, 1943, page 5.

———, "Two Generals: The Climax of the Drama," *New York Times Magazine,* July 6, 1952, page 3 *et seq.*

Barcella, Ernest L., "Ike's 70th Year: A Fitness Report," *Today's Health,* April 1960, pages 20-23 *et seq.*

———, "To See Ike, See Shanley," *Nation's Business,* August, 1956, pages 32-33.

Bartnett, Lincoln, "General Ike Eisenhower," *Life,* November 9, 1942, pages 112-14 *et seq.*

Bell, Elliott Vallance, "Election Results," *Vital Speeches of the Day,* January 1, 1953, pages 170-73.

Bendiner, Robert, "All Aboard for the Coattails Special," *The Reporter,* June 28, 1956, pages 24-27.

———, "Eisenhower and the Liberals," *The Nation,* April 10, 1948, pages 388-90.

Berger, Josef, "No Eisenhower Diary, History Is the Loser," *New York Times Magazine,* March 13, 1960, page 46 *et seq.*

Berger, Oscar, "Biography of General Ike,"

New York Times Magazine, October 13, 1946, page 20.

Berle, Adolf Augustus, Jr., "Folly of Demagogy; Brownell's Attack on President Truman Over White Case," The Reporter, December 22, 1953, pages 6-8.

Berman, Daniel M., "Cain and the President," New Republic, June 25, 1956, pages 10-15.

Bess, Demarie Caughey, "Are Generals in Politics a Menace," Saturday Evening Post, April 26, 1952, pages 28-29 et seq.

———, "Army's Favorite General," Saturday Evening Post, October 3, 1942, page 19 et seq.

———, "He United an Invasion Army," Saturday Evening Post, August 7, 1943, pages 18-19.

———, "How Eisenhower Produced a Foreign Policy," Saturday Evening Post, November 7, 1953, page 17 et seq.

———, "When He Talks, Ike Listens," Saturday Evening Post, November 17, 1955, page 24 et seq.

Bhatia, Prem, "When Ike and Nehru Meet," New Republic, December 10, 1956, page 9.

Binkley, Wilfred Ellsworth, "No Place to Hide," New Republic, November 15, 1954, pages 8-9.

———, "Will the Republicans Learn From Defeat?," New Republic, November 16, 1953, pages 13-15.

Binsse, Harry Lorin, "June Day in Washington," Commonweal, June 29, 1945, page 253.

Bishop, James Alonzo, "Day With Dwight D. Eisenhower," Cosmopolitan, July, 1956, pages 18-25.

Bolles, Blair, "Eisenhower's New Method," Foreign Policy Bulletin, July 15, 1953, page 3 et seq.

Boyle, Andrew, "Toward a United Europe," Commonweal, January 26, 1951, pages 391-92.

Bozell, L. Brent, "Dr. Javits and Mr. Hide," National Review, September 22, 1956, pages 8-11.

———, "Tiger in the White House," National Review, April 26, 1955, page 392.

Bracker, Milton, "Four Star Scotty; General Eisenhower's Pet," New York Times Magazine, October 17, 1943, page 2.

———, "Our Hard-Hitting Invasion Chief," New York Times Magazine, January 2, 1944, page 5 et seq.

Brant, Irving, "Tragedy of Eisenhower," New Republic, November, 3, 1952, pages 5-6.

Brinton, Crane, "Accounting to the American Public," Saturday Review of Literature, November 20, 1948, pages 9-18.

Brown, Charles, "Bucking for the East," Newsweek, October 27, 1952, page 26.

———, and Nicholson, Norman, "I Shall Go to Korea," Newsweek, November 3, 1952, pages 26-27.

Brown, John Mason, "General, the Governor, the Grassroots," Saturday Review of Literature, October 18, 1952, pages 10-13 et seq.

Brown, Lawrence R., "Eisenhower: The Bait and the Trap," The Freeman, September 24, 1951, pages 809-13.

Brown, Nona Baldwin, "When the President Goes on TV," New York Times Magazine, August 16, 1959, pages 14-15.

Brown, Stuart Gerry, "Civil Rights and National Leadership: Eisenhower and Stevenson in the 1950's," Ethics, January, 1960, pages 118-34.

———, "Eisenhower and Stevenson in the McCarthy Era: A Study in Leadership," Ethics, July, 1959, pages 233-54.

Bryson, Lyman, "Signs and Symbols in the Presidential Campaign," Commonweal, April 6, 1956, pages 14-16.

Bullitt, William Christian, "Please Don't Steal the President's Time," Reader's Digest, August, 1953, pages 38-40.

Bundy, McGeorge, "November, 1952: Imperatives of Foreign Policy," Foreign Affairs, October, 1952, pages 1-14.

Burnham, James, "How the I.P.R. Helped Stalin Seize China," The Freeman, June 30, 1952, pages 643-54.

———, and Schlamm, William S., "Should Conservatives Vote for Eisenhower-Nixon?," National Review, October 20, 1956, pages 12-15.

Butcher, Harry Cecil, "My Three Years With Eisenhower," Saturday Evening Post, December 15, pages 9-11 et seq.; December 22, pages 10-11 et seq.; De-

Bibliography

cember 29, 1945, pages 22-23 *et seq.;* January 5, pages 26-27 *et seq.;* January 12, pages 26-27 *et seq.;* January 19, pages 28-29 *et seq.;* January 26, pages 24-25 *et seq.;* February 2, pages 22-23 *et seq.;* February 9, pages 28-29 *et seq.;* and February 16, 1946, pages 28-29 *et seq.*

Butcher, H. (cont.), "Would Eisenhower Run," *Reader's Digest,* August, 1951, pages 7-9.

Byrnes, James Francis, "Statement of Governor Byrnes," *U.S. News & World Report,* September 26, 1952, pages 96-97.

Carlova, John E., "General Eisenhower's Narrow Escape," *Reader's Digest,* June, 1955, pages 51-54.

Carr, Christopher, "Eisenhower and the Future," *Commonweal,* January 9, 1953, pages 349-51.

Carr, Eugene, "How Ike Can Swing a Big Labor Vote," *Saturday Evening Post,* October 4, 1952, page 36 *et seq.*

Carroll, Wallace, "Eisenhower: An Indication of a Mood," *New York Times Magazine,* February 21, 1960, page 16.

Cassels, Louis, "White House: A Different President," *Nation's Business,* March, 1957, pages 34-35 *et seq.*

Cater, Douglass, "Folklore of an Electronic President," *The Reporter,* July 12, 1956, pages 15-18.

————, "Loneliest Job in a Crowded White House," *The Reporter,* June 25, 1959, pages 11-16.

————, "President and the Press," *The Reporter,* April 28, 1953, pages 26-28.

Catton, Bruce, "One Year Too Late; Time for Change Is Past," *The Nation,* January 9, 1954, pages 24-26.

————, "Wanted: A President; Mr. Get-Along Isn't One," *The Nation,* July 4, 1953, pages 8-9.

Cerny, Karl H., "Mr. Eisenhower: The Reluctant Critic," *America,* May 26, 1962, page 291.

Childs, Marquis William, "Eisenhower," *Look,* July 22, 1958, page 28 *et seq.*

————, "Why Ike Said No," *Collier's,* August 28, 1948, pages 14-15 *et seq.*

Christman, Henry, "Great Soldier and Good Citizen," *Saturday Review of Literature,* December 1, 1945, page 52 *et seq.*

Clark, Edward, "Ike's Mexican Holiday," *Saturday Evening Post,* April 21, 1962, pages 20-25.

————, "Visit to a Famous Farmer," *Life,* July 7, 1961, pages 61-68 *et seq.*

Clemens, Cyril, "Some Eisenhower Profiles," *Hobbies,* December, 1953, page 127 *et seq.*

Coffin, Tristram, "Drive to Stop Eisenhower," *New Republic,* October 1, 1951, page 9.

————, "Strange Romance: Ike and GOP," *New Republic,* November 19, 1951, page 14.

————, "Ten Men Ike Counts on Most," *Nation's Business,* April, 1954, pages 29-31 *et seq.*

Cogley, John, "Dwight Eisenhower, a Good Man," *Commonweal,* January 20, 1961, page 436.

————, "Legend and the Candidate," *Commonweal,* October 24, 1952, page 56.

————, "We Like Ike," *Commonweal,* September 14, 1951, page 542.

————, "Who's a Hypocrite?," *Commonweal,* April 15, 1955, pages 33 and 47.

Collins, Fredric William, "Erosion of the Presidency," *The Nation,* August 17, 1957, pages 63-64.

————, "Liberation: Evolution of a Policy," *The Nation,* March 30, 1957, pages 272-75.

————, "Our Om-Niscient President," *New Republic,* June 1, 1959, pages 11-15.

————, "Republican Congress Discovers the Trouble With Ike's Foreign Policy," *United Nations World,* August, 1953, pages 13-17.

————, "Sitzkrieg on the Budget Line," *The Nation,* June 15, 1957, pages 513-15.

————, "Who Makes the Decisions," *New Republic,* December 17, 1956, pages 8-10.

————, "Who Runs America?," *United Nations World,* June, 1953, pages 15-19.

Cook, Fred J., "Scoops by *Time* and

Newsweek," The Nation, May 17, 1958, pages 448-49.

Craig, Lillian, "Magic of the Personal Touch," *Reader's Digest,* July, 1953, pages 89-91.

Crawford, Kenneth Gale, "Eisenhower Can Be Drafted," *Saturday Evening Post,* November 15, 1947, pages 15-17 *et seq.*

————, "New Ike," *Newsweek,* August 17, 1959, pages 20-22.

————, "Our Man," *Newsweek,* July 25, 1955, pages 18-20.

————, "Visit to Gettysburg," *Newsweek,* July 3, 1961, page 27.

————, and Lavine, Harold, "After Four Years . . . Squaring Off Again," *Newsweek,* August 27, 1956.

Creel, George, "Study in Planned Futility," *The Freeman,* March 10, 1952, pages 365-68.

Cutler, Robert, "I Shall Vote for Eisenhower," *Atlantic Monthly,* October, 1956, pages 46-50.

Dangerfield, George, "Cult of Ike, Threat to the Presidency," *The Nation,* June 16, 1956, pages 504-05.

Daniel, Clifton, "With General Eisenhower at SHAEF," *New York Times Magazine,* March 4, 1945, page 5.

Daniel, E. C., "Supreme Test for the Allied Commander," *New York Times Magazine,* June 11, 1944, pages 5-7 *et seq.*

Daniell, Francis Raymond, "Churchill Seeks His Last Prize From Life," *New York Times Magazine,* January 4, 1953, pages 12-13.

————, "SHAEF: Eisenhower's Thinking Machine," *New York Times Magazine,* July 30, 1944, page 9 *et seq.*

————, "Ten Who Will Lead the Invasion," *New York Times Magazine,* January 23, 1944, page 6.

Davenport, Walter, "People, Politics, and '56," *Collier's,* March 2, 1956, pages 19-21.

Davis, Forrest, "Did Marshall Prolong the Pacific War?," *The Freeman,* November 5, 1951, pages 73-75.

Davis, Kenneth Sidney, "Abilene Factor in Eisenhower," *New York Times Magazine,* December 9, 1951, pages 12-13 *et seq.*

————, "Candidate From the Sticks," *Saturday Review of Literature,* June 7, 1952, pages 18-19.

————, "Eisenhower and Stevenson," *New Republic,* July 29, 1957, pages 13-15.

————, "Eisenhower and the Forty Farmers," *New Republic,* November 9, 1953, pages 9-12.

————, "Five-Star Finalist," *American Magazine,* July, 1945, page 17 *et seq.*

Davis, Maxine, "He's the President's Personal Physician," *Good Housekeeping,* August, 1954, pages 70-71 *et seq.*

Deakin, James, "Haggerty: Voice Behind the Throne," *New Republic,* August 27, 1956, pages 7-9.

Denson, John, "Eisenhowers at Home Abroad," *Collier's,* July 28, 1951, pages 13-15 *et seq.*

De Toledano, Ralph and Hadley, Arthur, "Last Speeches," *Newsweek,* November 10, 1952, pages 26-27.

De Voto, Bernard Augustine, "One-Way Partnership Derailed," *Harper's,* January, 1955, pages 12-15 *et seq.*

De Weerd, Harvey Arthur, "General Eisenhower," *American Mercury,* July, 1945, pages 16-25.

Dewey, Thomas Edmund, "Dewey Jumps to Ike's Defense: Hits Adlai for Name Calling," *U.S. News & World Report,* October 12, 1956, page 104 *et seq.*

————, "Eisenhower and the Next Congress," *Look,* October 19, 1954, pages 63-66.

————, "Elect Eisenhower," *Collier's,* October 25, 1952, page 20 *et seq.*

————, "Why I'm for Eisenhower," *Collier's,* May 17, 1952, page 15 *et seq.*

Downing, Francis, "After the Tumult and the Shouting," *Commonweal,* August 1, 1952, pages 409-10.

Draper, William Grafton, "I Fly the President," *Look,* August 20, 1957, pages 26-34.

Drummond, James Roscoe, "What Makes Ike Laugh?," *Collier's,* January 8, 1954, pages 15-19.

Drury, Allen, "Enigma of Gettysburg," *The Reporter,* December 29, 1955, pages 20-21.

Duff, James, "President Must Lead," *Newsweek*, August 24, 1953, page 23.

Dulles, John Foster, "Illness of President Eisenhower," *U.S. Department of State Bulletin*, October 10, 1955, page 566.

Earle, Edward Mead, "Man Who Might Have Been President," *Atlantic Monthy*, December, 1948, pages 85-86.

Edwards, Willard, "Mr. Eisenhower and the Socialized State," *American Mercury*, August, 1955, pages 7-12.

Elson, Robert T., "Eisenhower Boom Worries the Politicians," *Life*, August 25, 1947, pages 34-35.

———, "Question: What Is Ike Like?," *Life*, June 2, 1952, pages 75-76 *et seq.*

———, "Taft or Eisenhower," *Life*, August 6, 1951, pages 86-88 *et seq.*

———, "What Did Eisenhower Say?," *Life*, December 29, 1947, page 20.

Emrich, Duncan B. M., "Poet and General," *Saturday Review of Literature*, March, 1948, pages 9-11 *et seq.*

———, "War in 3 Pages," *New York Times Magazine*, May 5, 1946, page 8.

Evans, Medford, "Are Soviet A-Bombs Russian?," *The Freeman*, January 12, 1953, pages 266-68.

Feld, M. D., "Eisenhower: Constitutional Monarch?," *New Republic*, March 26, 1956, pages 8-9.

Fellers, Bonner, "How to Have the ICBM and a Better Defense and Still Cut the Budget $10 Billion," *Human Events*, October 12, 1957, page 4.

Finder, Leonard V., "Ike Will Not Run in '56," *Look*, October 18, 1955, page 11.

Fisher, John, "Editor's Easy Chair; Who's in Charge Here?," *Harper's*, February, 1958, page 10 *et seq.*

Fitch, Robert Elliot, "American President As Philosopher-King," *New Republic*, August 13, 1956, pages 11-13.

———, "Piety and Politics," *Antioch Review*, Summer, 1955, pages 148-58.

Fleming, Denna Frank, "Does Eisenhower Mean War?," *The Nation*, October 25, 1952, pages 374-77.

Flynn, John Thomas, "Our Phony War on Communism," *American Mercury*, February, 1954, pages 17-21.

Folliard, Edward Thomas, "Boredom of Convalescence Persuaded Ike to Run Again for the Presidency," *Nation's Business*, August, 1956, pages 19-20.

———, "Change in Public Attitude Helps President Guard Health," *Nation's Business*, September, 1957, pages 25-26.

———, "Changes Ease White House Routine," *Nation's Business*, June, 1956, pages 25-26.

———, "Democrats Disagree on Strategy and Tactics As GOP Rides High With Ike," *Nation's Business*, April, 1956, pages 25-26.

———, "Denver Mood," *Nation's Business*, October, 1954, pages 21-22.

———, "Eisenhower: A Tough Old Man at Sixty-Nine," *Nation's Business*, October, 1959, pages 23-24.

———, "High-Rank Stumping in New Jersey," *America*, October 7, 1961, page 6.

———, "Ike Could Name GOP Candidate," *Nation's Business*, November, 1955, pages 23-24.

———, "Ike Could Win Again, Politicians Agree," *Nation's Business*, October, 1960, pages 27-28.

———, "Little Things Can Snowball; Eisenhower-Truman Feud," *America*, January 3, 1959, page 390.

———, "Man Who Makes Music Wherever He Goes," *America*, November 21, 1959, page 229.

———, "New Spirit Enters the White House," *Nation's Business*, August, 1955, pages 17-18.

———, "Old Guy Joins a Private Club; Ex-Presidents," *America*, January 28, 1961, page 557.

———, "Our Very Popular President," *America*, October 31, 1959, page 119.

———, "Shooting War Over Berlin?," *America*, March 28, 1959, page 734.

———, "Washington Asks: Will Ike Use Whip or Patience?," *Nation's Business*, January, 1957, pages 21-22.

———, "Washington Front," *America*, August 8, 1959, page 585.

———, "Washington Mood," *Nation's Business*, January, pages 21-22; June, pages 21-22; July, pages 21-22; December, 1953, pages 21-22; March, pages 19-20; June, pages 21-22; July, pages 19-20; August, 1954, pages 19-20; February, 1955, pages 21-22; November, 1957, pages 25-26; October, 1958, pages 27-28.

———, "Why President Believes Russia Will Keep Her Word on Peace," *Nation's Business,* July, 1957, pages 21-22.

———, "With Ike in Europe," *America,* September 26, 1959, pages 770-72.

Freedman, Max, "Washington in Focus," *The Nation,* January 22, 1955, pages 64-65.

Freeman, Douglas Southall, "Ike Gets Vote of Southern Historian," *Life,* September 22, 1952, pages 53-54 *et seq.*

Freeman, Ira Henry, "Eisenhower of Columbia," *New York Times Magazine,* November 7, 1948, pages 12-13 *et seq.*

Gallicus, "Eisenhower Africanus," *New Republic,* November 1, 1943, pages 609-12.

Gayn, Mark J., "Europe Voted for Eisenhower," *The Nation,* June 21, 1952, pages 599-600.

———, and Tupling, Lloyd, "Ike at Home and Abroad," *The Nation,* November 1, 1952, pages 402-06.

Gehman, Richard B., "He Produces the President," *Good Housekeeping,* November, 1955, pages 64-67.

Genet [Janet Flanner], "Letter From Paris," *New Yorker,* March 3, 1951, pages 85-91; January 26, 1952, pages 76-80; July 26, 1952, page 40 *et seq.;* December 14, 1957, page 126 *et seq.*

Gerrity, John, "Making Crowds While the Sun Shines," *New Republic,* October 20, 1952, page 7.

Gervasi, Frank, "Say the Word, Ike!," *Collier's,* November 29, 1947, pages 16-17 *et seq.*

Graebner, Norman Arthur, "Eisenhower's Popular Leadership," *Current History,* October, 1960, pages 230-36 *et seq.*

Gafton, Samuel, "Does Ike Get Things Done?," *Collier's,* September 4, 1953, pages 60-65.

Gray, H. D., "Eisenhower for President," *New Republic,* July 30, 1951, page 2.

Grosvenor, Gilbert Melville, "When the President Goes Abroad," *National Geographic Magazine,* May, 1960, pages 588-649.

Gruenther, Alfred Maximilian, "Eisenhower at Seventy, an Intimate Album," *New York Times Magazine,* October 9, 1960, pages 23-25.

Gunther, John, "Eisenhower I Know," *Reader's Digest,* April, 1952, pages 15-17.

———, "With Eisenhower in Sicily," *Collier's,* September 25, 1943, page 11 *et seq.*

Hale, William Harlan, "Every Man an Ambassador," *The Reporter,* March 21, 1957, pages 18-19.

———, "Facts About Ileitis," *The Reporter,* June 28, 1956, pages 4-6.

———, "That War We Fought," *New Republic,* May 6, 1946, pages 664-65.

Hall, Leonard Wood, "Party Chairman's Views of President's Plans," *U.S. News & World Report,* December 9, 1955, pages 26-28.

Halle, Louis Joseph, "Eisenhower Approach: McCarthy and Nasser," *New Republic,* April 8, 1957, page 7.

Halsey, Margaret, "Revolution of Non-Expectation," *New Republic,* July 3, 1961, pages 15-17.

Hammond, Mary K., "1952 Election," *Current History,* January, 1953, pages 26-31.

Hansen, Harry, "Report of a Citizen," *Survey,* January, 1949, page 50.

Hard, William, "Run Against Ike!," *Reader's Digest,* January, 1956, pages 17-21.

Harger, Charles Moreau, "Abilene's," *New York Times Magazine,* November 22, 1942, page 39.

———, "At Abilene It Was Always Ike," *Rotarian,* September, 1945, pages 16-18.

———, "Eisenhower I Know," *Reader's Digest,* April, 1952, pages 17-18.

Harris, Louis, "How Voters Feel About Ike's Health," *Collier's,* July 20, 1956, pages 17-19 *et seq.*

Harris, Seymour Edwin, "Democratic Prosperity, Fiction or Fact," *New Republic,* November 3, 1952, pages 14-15.

Harrison, Gordon, "Can Eisenhower Save

the GOP?," *Harper's,* January, 1952, pages 21-26.

Harrison, G. (cont.), "New Conservatism; GOP Liberals Take Over," *The Nation,* June 2, 1956, pages 44-45.

Harsch, Joseph Close, "Eisenhower the Good," *New Republic,* December 12, 1960, pages 13-15.

————, "Eisenhower's First Hundred Days," *The Reporter,* May 12, 1953, pages 9-12.

————, "One View of Eisenhower," *The Nation,* June 7, 1952, pages 542-43.

Hatch, Alden, "Prexy Plan of General Ike," *Collier's,* September 13, 1947, page 11 *et seq.*

Hauser, Ernest O., "Inside Eisenhower Headquarters," *Saturday Evening Post,* November 17, 1951, pages 19-21 *et seq.*

Haushalter, Walter M., "Our Leftist Clergy," *The Freeman,* June 2, 1952, pages 573-75; June 16, 1952, pages 618-20.

Hazlitt, Henry, "Eisenhower So Far," *Newsweek,* August 24, 1953, page 65.

————, "Ike and the Economic Outlook," *Newsweek,* March 19, 1956, page 98.

————, "Ike's Semi-New Deal," *Newsweek,* February 15, 1954, page 80.

Heard, Alexander, "Eisenhower Challenges the Solid South," *The Nation,* July 26, 1952, pages 65-67 *et seq.*

Herald, George W., "Memo to Mr. Eisenhower," *United Nations World,* January, 1953, pages 16-19.

Herling, John, "World's Number One Quiz Program," *New York Times Magazine,* June 9, 1957, page 11 *et seq.*

Herter, Christian Archibald, "Secretary Herter's News Conference of March 9," *U.S. Department of State Bulletin,* March 28, 1960, pages 487-93.

————, "Secretary Replies to Senator Wiley on President's Missions Abroad," *U.S. Department of State Bulletin,* July 11, 1960, pages 47-48.

Hibbs, Ben, "We Need Eisenhower," *Saturday Evening Post,* May 3, 1952, page 17.

————, "Will the GOP Commit Suicide at Chicago?," *Saturday Evening Post,* July 5, 1952, page 10.

High, Stanley, "Man Closest to the President," *Reader's Digest,* June, 1953, pages 17-20.

————, "What the President Wants," *Reader's Digest,* April, 1953, pages 1-4.

Holmes, Julius Cecil, "Eisenhower's African Gamble," *Collier's,* January 12, pages 14-15 *et seq.;* January 19, 1946, pages 27-30.

Hoyt, Palmer, "I'll Vote for Eisenhower," *The Nation,* October 20, 1956, pages 319-21.

Huie, William Bradford, "But Who Does Ike Like?," *American Mercury,* March, 1952, pages 124-28.

————, "Memo to General Eisenhower," *American Mercury,* January, 1952, pages 124-28.

Hutchinson, Paul, "President's Religious Faith," *Life,* March 22, 1954, pages 150-52 *et seq.*

Hyman, Herbert Hiram, and Sheatsley, Paul B., "Political Appeal of President Eisenhower," *Public Opinion,* Q. 17, No. 4, 1953, pages 443-60.

Hyman, Sidney, "Absorbing Study of Popularity," *New York Times Magazine,* July 24, 1960, page 7 *et seq.*

————, "Eisenhower Glow Is Fading Away," *The Reporter,* September 19, 1957, pages 11-15.

————, "Eisenhower's Presidency: The Known and the Foreseeable," *The Reporter,* March 22, 1956, pages 13-17.

————, "Inner Circles of the White House," *New York Times Magazine,* January 5, 1958, page 10.

————, Portrait of the President As World Leader," *New York Times Magazine,* December 6, 1959, page 23 *et seq.*

————, "Problems of a Lame Duck President," *New York Times Magazine,* January 18, 1959, page 11 *et seq.*

————, "War of Presidential Succession," *The Reporter,* June 25, 1959, pages 9-11.

Ickes, Harold LeClaire, "Eisenhower Was Here," *New Republic,* November 19, 1951, page 21.

Inglis, David Rittenhouse, "Evasion of H-Bomb Issue," *New Republic,* November 5, 1956, pages 7-8.

Ingrim, Robert, "What Eisenhower Has

Learned in Europe," *American Mercury,* January, 1952, pages 7-13.

Javits, Jacob Koppel, "Republican's View," *Commonweal,* August 17, 1956, pages 483-86.

Johnson, Alvin Saunders, "Dr. Johnson Explains," *New Republic,* October 4, 1954, page 23.

———, "Eisenhower for President," *New Republic,* November 26, 1951, page 2.

Johnson, Gerald White, "As Any Didymus Can See," *New Republic,* February 4, 1957, page 8.

———, "Congress and Geneva," *New Republic,* August 1, 1955, page 12.

———, "Gentlemen's Agreement, Proposals Made at U.N.," *New Republic,* September 1, 1958, page 9.

———, "Health Issue, 1824," *New Republic,* July 23, 1956, page 9.

———, "Hold Your Breath; Closing of the Moratorium on Nuclear Bomb Explosions," *New Republic,* January 11, 1960, page 10.

———, "How Many Won't Vote?," *New Republic,* September 19, 1955, page 16.

———, "Invisible Man," *New Republic,* November 14, 1955, page 16.

———, "Is This Trip Necessary?," *New Republic,* January 25, 1960, page 10.

———, "Lamb Is Led," *New Republic,* October 15, 1956, page 12.

———, "Let Dag Do It," *New Republic,* April 8, 1957, page 10.

———, "Sing, for God's Sake," *New Republic,* November 30, 1959, page 9.

———, "Superficial Aspect," *New Republic,* December 7, page 13; December 21, 1953, page 16; January 4, page 15; June 21, 1954, page 17; January 17, page 16; February 28, page 15; March 14, page 6; March 28, 1955, page 16.

———, "Superficial Aspect: Senator Knowland's Warning," *New Republic,* January 31, 1955, page 17.

———, "Two Eisenhowers?," *New Republic,* March 26, 1956, page 16.

———, "What the People Said," *New Republic,* November 26, 1956, page 9.

———, "Whistling While We Work," *New Republic,* October 30, 1961, page 10.

———, "Why Did He Do It?," *New Republic,* March 12, 1956, page 23.

Kandel, Isaac Leon, "General Eisenhower on the Purposes of Higher Education," *School & Society,* October 30, 1948, page 292.

Kefauver, Estes, "Man, Not Principles," *New Republic,* November 17, 1952, pages 10-11.

Kemler, Edgar, "New Deals and Old," *The Nation,* January 21, 1956, pages 44-45.

Kissinger, Henry Alfred, "Khrushchev Visit, Danger and Hopes," *New York Times Magazine,* September 6, 1959, page 5 *et seq.*

Kittler, Glenn D., "Follow Ike," *Better Homes and Gardens,* October, 1955, pages 70-71 *et seq.*

Kleiman, Robert, "12 Bosses Mess Up Eisenhower's Job," *U.S. News & World Report,* July 27, 1951, pages 11-15.

Klein, A., "Inside Eisenhower," *New Republic,* July 16, 1956, page 3 *et seq.*

Kluckhohn, Frank Louis, "With Eisenhower at Headquarters," *New York Times Magazine,* January 10, 1943, page 5 *et seq.*

Knebel, Fletcher, "Crisis, Ike's Heart Attack," *Look,* December 27, 1955, pages 21-25.

———, "Did Ike Want Nixon?," *Look,* October 30, 1956, pages 25-27.

———, "How Ike Made Up His Mind," *Look,* May 1, 1956, pages 19-21.

———, "Ike's Cronies," *Look,* June 1, 1954, pages 57-61.

———, "Inside Story of the Ike-Truman Feud," *Look,* September 6, 1955, pages 21-25.

———, "On the Spot: The President's Doctor," *Look,* September 18, 1955, page 88 *et seq.*

———, "What Ike Doesn't Like," *Look,* May 15, 1956, pages 41-42 *et seq.*

Knowland, William Fife, "This Is the Way Ike Gave the Word," *U.S. News & World Report,* July 20, 1956, page 34.

———, "This Is What They Said," *American Mercury,* September, 1957, page 47.

Kornitzer, Bela, "Story of Ike and His 4 Brothers," *U.S. News & World Report,* July 1, 1955, pages 46-52 *et seq.*

Kramer, Dale, "Eisenhower: Issue of Power," *New Republic,* June 14, 1948, pages 12-14.

Krock, Arthur, "Impressions of the President and the Man," *New York Times Magazine,* June 23, 1957, page 5 *et seq.*

Laguerre, Andre, "Optimist in Arms," *Life,* July 16, 1951, pages 108-09 *et seq.*

Lahey, Edwin Aloysius, "Eisenhower Moves Right," *New Republic,* September 22, 1952, page 8.

———, "Ike, an Innocent at Home," *New Republic,* June 30, 1952, pages 15-16.

Lansing, Alfred M., "Ike's Fishing Secrets," *Collier's,* April 15, 1955, pages 30-33.

Lavine, Harold, "Eisenhower Will Run," *American Mercury,* September, 1951, pages 3-6.

———, "Ike Forging an Army on Faith," *Newsweek,* July 23, 1951, pages 26-29.

———, "In an Impressive Role," *Newsweek,* August 30, 1954, pages 15-17.

———, "In the Heat of Texas," *Newsweek,* June 30, 1952, pages 24-25.

———, "Taft on the Team," *Newsweek,* September 22, 1952, pages 23-25.

Lawrence, David, "After Six Months," *U.S. News & World Report,* July 17, 1953, page 108.

———, "Bleeding America," *U.S. News & World Report,* September 19, 1952, page 96.

———, "Eisenhower Compass," *U.S. News & World Report,* April 24, 1953, page 116.

———, "Farewell to the Faithful Servant," *U.S. News & World Report,* January 23, 1961, page 112.

———, "Heart That Faltered," *U.S. News & World Report,* October 21, 1955, page 164.

———, "Ike's Quandry—An Answer," *U.S. News & World Report,* February 17, 1956, page 176.

———, "Illegality Breeds Illegality," *U.S.*

News & World Report, October 4, 1957, page 144 *et seq.*

———, "Inaugurating Character," *U.S. News & World Report,* January 23, 1953, page 104.

———, "Inside the Republican Party," *U.S. News & World Report,* February 3, 1956, page 136.

———, "Man of the Era," *U.S. News & World Report,* January 6, 1956, page 120.

———, "Office Seeks the Man," *U.S. News & World Report,* August 1, 1952, page 100.

———, "Only Answer?," *U.S. News & World Report,* November 15, 1957, page 176.

———, "Purposeful Trip," *U.S. News & World Report,* November 16, 1959, page 124.

———, "Smearing a Peace Plan," *U.S. News & World Report,* September 12, 1952, page 92.

———, "There Is No Fourteenth Amendment," *U.S. News & World Report,* September 27, 1957, page 140 *et seq.*

———, "Treason's Biggest Victory," *U.S. News & World Report,* June 28, 1957, page 152 *et seq.*

———, "What's the Mandate?," *U.S. News & World Report,* November 28, 1952, page 116.

———, "Which Commander-in-Chief?," *U.S. News & World Report,* October 12, 1956, page 152.

———, "Which Constitution?," *U.S. News & World Report,* September 13, 1957, page 128.

———, "Who Is Forsaking the Republican Platform?," *U.S. News & World Report,* May 31, 1957, page 140.

———, "Year Is a Long Time," *U.S. News & World Report,* November 18, 1955, page 184.

Lawrence, William H., "Mr. President What Do You Think Of . . . ," *New York Times Magazine,* December 27, 1953, page 9 *et seq.*

———, "One-Candidate Show," *New York Times Magazine,* August 10, 1952, page 38.

Lear, John, "Ike and the Peaceful Atom," *The Reporter*, January 12, 1956, pages 11-21.

——, "White House Brain Map," *Saturday Review*, December 14, 1957, page 48 *et seq.*

Lefever, Ernest W., "Candidates' Religious Views," *The Christian Century*, September 19, 1956, pages 1072-75.

Lehman, Irving J., "Spirit of America," *Vital Speeches of the Day*, July 1, 1945, page 552.

Laviero, Anthony Harry, "Eisenhower: A Six Month Audit," *New York Times Magazine*, July 19, 1953, page 9 *et seq.*

Lindley, Ernest Kidder, "At a Time of Calm," *Newsweek*, October 10, 1955, page 49.

——, "Consequences of the Republican Convention," *Newsweek*, July 21, 1952, page 31.

——, "Eisenhower and Independents," *Newsweek*, January 21, 1952, page 29.

——, "Eisenhower and Truman," *Newsweek*, November 12, 1951, page 34.

——, "Eisenhower, Dulles and Korea," *Newsweek*, December 8, 1952, page 23.

——, "Eisenhower in '56," *Newsweek*, August 20, 1956, page 36.

——, "Eisenhower Message," *Newsweek*, February 9, 1953, page 21.

——, "Eisenhower on the Road," *Newsweek*, October 13, 1952, page 30.

——, "Eisenhower Significance: Ike Own Best Salesman," *Newsweek*, June 16, 1952, page 26.

——, "Eisenhower's Methods," *Newsweek*, March 2, 1953, page 23.

——, "Eisenhower's Ordeal," *Newsweek*, May 26, 1952, page 29.

——, "Eisenhower's Political Dilemma," *Newsweek*, November 19, 1951, page 27.

——, "Has Ike Cooked His Goose?," *Newsweek*, December 22, 1947, page 24.

——, "Health Issue," *Newsweek*, March 12, 1956, page 32.

——, "Historic Message," *Newsweek*, January 18, 1954, page 33.

——, "Ike—A Year Later," *Newsweek*, October 26, 1953, page 35.

——, "Ike and the Future," *Newsweek*, June 3, 1957, page 36.

——, "Ike's Decision," *Newsweek*, June 25, 1956, page 32.

——, "Ike's Republicanism," *Newsweek*, September 3, 1956, page 33.

——, "Mr. Eisenhower's Choice," *Newsweek*, December 13, 1954, page 30.

——, "Mr. Eisenhower's Congress," *Newsweek*, August 23, 1954, page 27.

——, "Mr. Eisenhower's Dilemma," *Newsweek*, November 2, 1953, page 26.

——, "Mr. Eisenhower's Strategy," *Newsweek*, September 13, 1954, page 36.

——, "National President," *Newsweek*, November 12, 1956, page 79.

——, "New Conservatism," *Newsweek*, February 8, 1954, page 32.

——, "New Regime Takes Over," *Newsweek*, January 26, 1953, page 29.

——, "Off to a Good Start," *Newsweek*, December 1, 1952, page 21.

——, "People's Decision," *Newsweek*, February 20, 1956, page 37.

——, "Pilot in a Storm," *Newsweek*, April 29, 1957, page 40.

——, "President and Congress," *Newsweek*, June 8, 1953, page 34.

——, "President Eisenhower's D-Day," *Newsweek*, December 7, 1953, page 30.

——, "President Shows His Hand," *Newsweek*, December 28, 1953, page 17.

——, "President's Diagnosis," *Newsweek*, November 16, 1953, page 33.

——, "President's Election Stake," *Newsweek*, October 11, 1954, page 37.

——, "President's Fight," *Newsweek*, January 25, 1954, page 27.

——, "President's Party Role," *Newsweek*, November 9, 1953, page 30.

——, "Salute to Ike," *Newsweek*, January 16, 1961, page 29.

——, "Step Towards Bipartisanship," *Newsweek*, January 11, 1954, page 29.

——, "Toward the Center," *Newsweek*, September 10, 1956, page 34.

——, "What Is Sound Politics?," *Newsweek*, February 22, 1954, page 30.

Lindley, E. (cont.), "Who Controls in Washington?," *Newsweek,* March 23, 1953, page 30.

———, "X-raying the Candidates," *Newsweek,* October 22, 1956, page 44.

Lodge, Henry Cabot, Jr., "Does the Republican Party Have a Future?," *Saturday Evening Post,* January 29, 1949, page 23 *et seq.*

———, "Eisenhower and the GOP," *Harper's,* May, 1952, pages 34-39.

———, "Why I Believe in Eisenhower," *Atlantic Monthly,* June, 1952, page 49.

Loftus, Joseph A., "Eisenhower's Formula for Relaxation," *New York Times Magazine,* September 5, 1954, page 10 *et seq.*

Lovett, Robert M., "Eisenhower and Korea," *The Nation,* January 24, 1953, page 88.

Lubell, Samuel, "Can Eisenhower Be Re-Elected?," *Saturday Evening Post,* February 12, 1955, pages 26-27 *et seq.*

Luce, Henry Robinson, "To Ike, the Wall Rises Between Opposing Ideas of Man," *Life,* September 8, 1961, pages 46-49.

Martin, Joseph William, Jr., "Case for the Republicans," *Saturday Evening Post,* October 13, 1956, pages 34-35 *et seq.*

Masse, Benjamin Louis, "Skipper Charts Progressive Course," *America,* January 21, 1956, page 443.

Mauldin, William H., "Eisenhower I'll Always Remember," *The Reporter,* September 23, 1954, page 45.

McCarten, John, "Letter From Washington," *New Yorker,* March 13, 1954, pages 114-25.

McCarthy, Joseph R., "McCarthy-Eisenhower Dispute: Senator McCarthy Gives His Rebuttal," *U.S. News & World Report,* December 11, 1953, page 40.

McConaughy, James Lukens, Jr., "While Eisenhower Proposes, the Old Guard Disposes," *Life,* June 21, 1954, pages 124-26 *et seq.*

McKenzie, Robert Trelford, "Ike: Stuck With Dick," *The Nation,* September 1, 1956, pages 170-72.

McMahon, Patrick, "Third Party?," *American Mercury,* August, 1953, pages 41-44.

McWilliams, Carey, "General Taft and Mr. Eisenhower," *The Nation,* July 12, 1952, pages 23-24.

———, "President's Illness," *The Nation,* October 8, 1955, pages 293-96.

Menken, Jules, "General Eisenhower's Report," *National Review* (of England), August, 1946, pages 127-34.

Michel, Ernest W., "My Long Journey to Eisenhower," *Reader's Digest,* December, 1960, pages 135-39.

Michie, Allan Andrew, "Great Decisions; Behind the Scenes With Eisenhower," *Reader's Digest,* August, 1944, pages 112-18.

Middleton, Drew, "Close-Up of Eisenhower As Negotiator," *New York Times Magazine,* May 29, 1955, page 7.

———, "Eisenhower Epic: Victory in the West," *New York Times Magazine,* May 6, 1945, pages 10-11 *et seq.*

———, "Eisenhower Faces East," *United Nations World,* February, 1951, pages 17-20.

Miller, William Lee, "Liking of Ike," *The Reporter,* October 16, 1958, pages 18-22.

———, "Politics Is So Confusing," *The Reporter,* November 27, 1958, page 14.

———, "Religion, Politics and the Great Crusade," *The Reporter,* July 7, 1953, pages 14-16.

———, "Unspecific Discussion, Not Dealing in Personalities," *The Reporter,* June 8, 1954, pages 29-30.

Millis, Walter, "Generals Take a Stroll," *Saturday Review,* June 1, 1957, page 20.

Mintener, James Bradshaw, "Why I Shall Vote for Eisenhower," *The Christian Century,* October 15, 1952, pages 1186-88.

Mitgang, Herbert, "Cordially His; Letter to the President-Elect," *New York Times Magazine,* January 18, 1953, page 18.

Moley, Raymond Charles, "After Minnesota," *Newsweek,* March 31, 1952, page 92.

———, "Candidates Alone Can't Win," *Newsweek,* September 8, 1952, page 104.

———, "Columbia's Commander-in-Chief," *Newsweek,* July 7, 1947, page 100.

———, "Eisenhower Situation," *Newsweek,* September 22, 1947, page 100.

———, "Eisenhower the Symbol," *Newsweek,* August 27, 1956, page 96.

———, "Excessive Abuse," *Newsweek,* November 30, 1953, page 112.

———, "Ike Learns His Trade," *Newsweek,* September 20, 1954, page 108.

———, "Man and the Candidate," *Newsweek,* August 25, 1952, page 92.

———, "Man and the Party," *Newsweek,* October 27, 1952, page 120.

———, "No Skirmish," *Newsweek,* November 16, 1953, page 112.

———, "No Time for Committees," *Newsweek,* December 9, 1957, page 108.

———, "Party Rule in Senate," *Newsweek,* July 2, 1956, page 76.

———, "Rediscovering Congress," *Newsweek,* August 24, 1953, page 80.

———, "Senator and the General," *Newsweek,* January 21, 1952, page 96.

———, "Shackles of Victory," *Newsweek,* May 18, 1953, page 120.

———, "You Can Elect Ike," *Newsweek,* November 3, 1952, page 112.

Moorehead, Alan, "Montgomery's Quarrel With Eisenhower," *Collier's,* October 5, 1946, pages 12-13 *et seq.*

Morgenthau, Hans Joachim, "What the President and Mr. Dulles Don't Know," *New Republic,* December 17, 1956, pages 14-18.

Moriarty, Rowland T. and McCord, Frederick A., "Ike, Mamie and the Neighbors," *Saturday Evening Post,* November 3, 1956, pages 32-33 *et seq.*

Morris, Joe Alex, "New Ike in the White House," *Saturday Evening Post,* October 16, 1954, pages 32-33 *et seq.*

———, "What Kind of President Will Ike Make?," *Saturday Evening Post,* January 3, 1953, pages 20-21 *et seq.*

Morrow, Hugh, "GOP Will Never Be the Same," *Saturday Evening Post,* April 2, 1955, page 25 *et seq.*

Mortimer, Lee, "Rudolph Halley's Comet," *American Mercury,* November, 1951, pages 87-95.

Morse, Wayne Lyman, "Portland Address of Senator Morse," *U.S. News & World Report,* October 31, 1952, page 96 *et seq.*

Mowery, William Byron, "Certain Young Captain," *American Magazine,* August, 1948, page 60.

Muller, Edwin, "How the Rhine Battle Was Planned," *Reader's Digest,* June, 1945, pages 27-31.

Murkland, Harvey Banta, "Great Journey," *Newsweek,* March 7, 1960, pages 25-27.

Murphy, Charles John Vincent, "Budget, and Eisenhower," *Fortune,* July, 1957, pages 96-99 *et seq.*

———, "Eisenhower Shift," *Fortune,* January, pages 82-87 *et seq.;* February, pages 110-13 *et seq.;* March, pages 110-12 *et seq.;* April, 1956, pages 112-16 *et seq.*

———, "Eisenhower's White House," *Fortune,* July, 1953, pages 74-77 *et seq.*

———, "What Ike Faces in Korea," *Life,* December 1, 1952, pages 51-52 *et seq.*

———, "White House Since Sputnik," *Fortune,* January, 1958, pages 98-101 *et seq.*

Neely, Matthew Mansfield, *et al.,* "President and His Church," *U.S. News & World Report,* April 8, 1955, pages 50-52.

Nehru, Jawaharlal, "Impact of Eisenhower Visit—As India's Leader Sees It," *U.S. News & World Report,* December 28, 1959, pages 50-53.

Neuberger, Richard Lewis, "Principles Over the Brink; Defeat of Hell's Canyon Dam Proposal," *New Republic,* August 13, 1956, pages 6-7.

———, "West, Eyes on Korea," *New Republic,* November 17, 1952, page 7.

Nevins, Allan, "Can the Clock Be Turned Back?," *New York Times Magazine,* November 23, 1952, page 9 *et seq.*

———, "Firm Basis of Anglo-American Unity," *New York Times Magazine,* March 17, 1957, page 9 *et seq.*

———, "Free World Gains Strength," *Nation's Business,* January, 1954, pages 22-23.

———, "Leadership: A Mysterious Qual-

Bibliography

the Negro," *Reader's Digest*, October, 1954, pages 61-64.

Priest, Ivy Baker, "Ladies Elected Ike," *American Mercury*, February, 1953, pages 23-28.

Puleston, W. D., "Blunders of World War II," U.S. *News & World Report*, February 4, 1955, pages 107-39.

Raskin, A. H., "How Eisenhower Plans to Deal With Depression," *Commentary*, May, 1954, pages 423-30.

Ratcliffe, Samuel Kerkham, "America at War: Three Careers," *Contemporary*, February, 1949, pages 81-86.

———, "General Eisenhower's Triumph," *Contemporary*, December, 1952, pages 321-26.

———, "Truman, Taft, and Eisenhower," *Contemporary*, March, 1952, pages 130-34.

Reese, Seward Phillips, "Dwight D. Eisenhower: Presidential Candidate," *Vital Speeches of the Day*, April 1, 1952, pages 354-59.

Reston, James Barrett, "Dilemma of the White House," *New York Times Magazine*, June 1, 1958, pages 7-9 *et seq.*

———, "Ike, Like Baseball, a National Institution," *Time*, September 19, 1955, page 42.

———, "Ike's Press Conference: Crisis Into Opportunity," *Time*, August 23, 1954, page 23.

———, "Inquiry Into Four Political Assumptions," *New York Times Magazine*, February 17, 1952, page 7 *et seq.*

———, "Memo on the Two Presidential Candidates," *New York Times Magazine*, August 24, 1952, page 7 *et seq.*

———, "President After a Year," *New York Times Magazine*, January 17, 1954, page 9 *et seq.*

———, "Wholesale Indiction; Summary of Newspaper Articles," *Time*, July 11, 1960, pages 54-55.

Reynolds, Quentin, "How They Work Together Under Eisenhower," *Reader's Digest*, December, 1951, pages 9-14.

———, "Mr. President Eisenhower," *Life*, April 17, 1950, pages 144-46 *et seq.*

———, "Winner: The People," *United Nations World*, October, 1952, pages 13-16 *et seq.*

Richberg, Donald Randall, "What of the Future?," *Vital Speeches of the Day*, January 1, 1953, pages 168-70.

Riesel, Victor, "Labor and Eisenhower," *American Mercury*, February, 1953, pages 59-66.

Riggs, Robert Langmuir, "Democrats Like Ike," *New Republic*, May 30, 1955, pages 14-16.

———, "Hungry Sheep Look Up and Are Not Fed," *New Republic*, January 30, 1956, pages 5-6.

———, "Press and the President," *New Republic*, May 24, 1954, pages 10-12.

Roberts, Chalmers M., "Battle on the Rim of Hell: President Versus War Hawk," *The Reporter*, December 16, 1954, pages 11-14.

Roberts, Charles, "At the Scene," *Newsweek*, June 18, 1956, pages 38-41.

———, "Bomb and a Barrage," *Newsweek*, October 29, 1956, pages 29-30.

———, "Ike—Warming Up," *Newsweek*, October 31, 1960, page 20.

Roberts, Edward V., "D-Day: As Seen by Eisenhower," *New York Times Magazine*, June 6, 1954, page 14 *et seq.*

Robinson, Donald B., "Future of Dwight Eisenhower," *American Mercury*, April, 1948, pages 391-99.

Rockwell, Norman, "Day I Painted Ike," *Saturday Evening Post*, October 11, 1952, pages 24-25 *et seq.*

Roper, Elmo Burns, "Public Opinion and the Election," *Saturday Review*, August 11, 1956, pages 9-10.

Roth, Philip, "Positive Thinking on Pennsylvania Avenue," *New Republic*, June 3, 1957, pages 10-11.

Roudakoff, Paul P., "Ike and Zhukov," *Collier's* July 22, 1955, pages 82-85.

Rovere, Richard Halworth, "Ascendancy Regained," *Spectator*, September 4, 1959, page 288.

———, "Eisenhower: A Trial Balance," *The Reporter*, April 21, 1955, pages 14-20.

———, "Eisenhower and the New President," *Harper's*, May, 1960, pages 31-35.

———, "Letter From Bermuda," *New*

Yorker, December 19, 1953, page 104 et seq.

Rovere, R. (cont.), "Letter From Denver," New Yorker, November 5, 1955, pages 137-43.

———, "Letter From Washington," New Yorker, January 19, page 56 et seq.; June 21, 1952, page 86 et seq.; April 4, pages 89-95; May 2, pages 99-109; July 25, 1953, page 44-49; August 28, 1954, page 68 et seq.; July 16, 1955, pages 69-75; January 21, pages 96-98 et seq.; March 10, page 74 et seq.; June 23, 1956, page 74 et seq.; January 26, pages 78-80 et seq.; November 2, pages 159-64; December 7, 1957, pages 141-44; June 13, pages 119-22 et seq.; December 19, 1959, pages 115-18.

———, "No Change," Spectator, June 15, 1956, pages 812-13.

———, "Reporter at Large," New Yorker, September 27, pages 96-105; October 4, 1952, pages 58-65.

———, "Republican Prospects," Harper's, June, 1953, pages 34-41.

———, "Second Eisenhower Boom," Harper's, May, 1950, pages 31-39.

———, "State of the Presidency," Spectator, January 10, 1958, page 33.

Rushmore, Howard, "Heard on the Party Line," American Mercury, April, 1955, page 128.

Rutstein, David Davis, "Doctors and Politics," Atlantic Monthly, August, 1956, pages 32-35.

Saltonstall, Leverett, "Ike Should Be Nominated," Collier's, July 5, 1952, page 23 et seq.

Sancton, Thomas, "They're After Eisenhower," The Nation, November 6, 1948, page 515.

Schlesinger, Arthur Meier, Jr., "What Eisenhower Was," The Nation, May 25, 1946, pages 629-30.

Schoenbrun, David F., "Ordeal of General Ike," Harper's October, 1952, pages 25-34.

Schorr, Daniel, "Traveling Salesmen for Two Ways of Life," New York Times Magazine, March 13, 1960, page 22 et seq.

Schuyler, George, "F.E.P.C. Is a Fraud,"

The Freeman, July 14, 1952, pages 697-700.

Scott, Hugh, "Republican's View," The Reporter, February 17, 1953, pages 31-33.

Seide, Ray, "How I Selected Westerns, Bought Socks and Prepared Paintings for President Eisenhower," Esquire, March, 1962, pages 47-49.

Sevareid, Eric, "Democrats' Tactics," The Reporter, May 5, 1955, page 30.

———, "Dynamic Conservatism," The Reporter, March 24, 1955, page 25.

———, "Is Any Man Indespensible?," The Reporter, October 20, 1955, page 20.

———, "President's Grand Tour," The Reporter, November 26, 1959, page 6.

———, "Two Inaugurals," The Reporter, February 7, 1957, page 4.

———, "Will the President Run Again?," The Reporter, March 10, 1955, page 30.

Shaffer, Samuel, "Ike's Dilemma," Newsweek, September 29, 1952, pages 23-25.

———, "Newsweek Polls Senate; It Will Be Ike; It Will Be Adlai," Newsweek, June 20, 1955, pages 25-26.

———, "Report on New Hampshire: Testing Ground for Ike," Newsweek, January 14, 1952, pages 27-29.

Shalett, Sidney M., "We Bring You Now the President," Saturday Evening Post, May 21, 1955, pages 32-33 et seq.

Shannon, William Vincent, "Eisenhower As President; Critical Appraisal of the Record," Commentary, November, 1958, pages 390-98.

———, "Eisenhower Paradox," Commonweal, March 23, 1956, pages 639-41.

Sharp, Samuel Leonard, "Ultimatum Verses Negotiation; Eisenhower's Foreign-Policy Speech," New Republic, April 27, 1953, pages 7-8.

Sheerin, John Basil, "New Cabinet and the Old Deal," Catholic World, January, 1953, pages 241-45.

———, "Scandal at Little Rock," Catholic World, October, 1958, pages 5-7.

Shelton, Willard, "Acheson Flounders; Eisenhower's Report to Congress," The Nation, February 10, 1951, pages 123-24.

———, "Pitfalls Ahead for Eisenhower," *The Nation*, July 19, 1952, pages 48-50.

Skillin, Edward Simon, *et al.*, "Our Choice for President," *Commonweal*, September 26, 1952, pages 595-98.

Slichter, Sumner Huber, "Why I Am for Eisenhower," *New Republic*, October 22, 1956, page 15.

Smith, Beverly Waugh, "Day in the Life of the President," *Saturday Evening Post*, January 30, 1954, pages 26-27 *et seq.*

———, "Here's What's Behind Ike's Grin," *Saturday Evening Post*, September 27, 1952, pages 32-33 *et seq.*

———, "I Watched Eisenhower Campaign," *Saturday Evening Post*, November 1, 1952, pages 26-27, *et seq.*

Smith, Margaret Chase, "Why Vote for Eisenhower?," *Woman's Home Companion*, November, 1952, pages 38-39.

Smith, Merriman, "Eisenhower I Know," *Look*, March 8, 1955, pages 23-29.

———, "Evolution of Eisenhower As Speaker," *New York Times Magazine*, August 7, 1955, page 18 *et seq.*

Smith, Walter Bedell, "Eisenhower's Six Great Decisions," *Saturday Evening Post*, June 8, pages 9-11 *et seq.*; June 15, pages 18-19 *et seq.*; June 22, pages 22-23 *et seq.*; June 29, pages 26-27 *et seq.*; July 6, pages 20-21 *et seq.*; July 13, 1946, pages 26-27 *et seq.*

Smoot, Dan, "Sacrificing for Communism," *Dan Smoot Report*, April 8, 1957, page 4.

Snyder, Howard McCrum, "Progress Report on a Famous Patient," *U.S. News & World Report*, December 23, 1955, pages 92-95.

———, and White, Paul Dudley, "What the Doctors Say About the President's Health," *U.S. News & World Report*, December 30, 1955, pages 22-24.

Spaatz, Carl, "Eisenhower and Air Power," *Newsweek*, June 16, 1952, page 30.

Sparkes, Boyden, "Eisenhower's Mission in America," *American Magazine*, December, 1948, pages 24-25 *et seq.*

Sparkman, John Jackson, "Full Measure of Health Is Vital," *U.S. News & World Report*, March 15, 1956, pages 126-28.

Stanford, Neal, "History Made Again at Gettysburg," *Foreign Policy Bulletin*, January 15, 1957, page 67.

———, "Is U.S. Slipping or Advancing?," *Foreign Policy Bulletin*, July 1, 1956, page 155.

———, "Real Eisenhower," *Foreign Policy Bulletin*, January 15, 1955, page 67.

———, "Status of the President's Leadership," *Foreign Policy Bulletin*, September 1, 1957, page 187.

———, "Was Latin American Tour a Success?," *Foreign Policy Bulletin*, April 1, 1960, page 107.

———, "Why Ike Will Run Again," *Foreign Policy Bulletin*, February 1, 1955, page 75.

Steinberg, Alfred, "Toughest Job in the World," *Reader's Digest*, May, 1954, pages 7-10.

Stevens, Francis B., "Ike's Aims on a New Trip Abroad," *U.S. News & World Report*, February 1, 1960, page 66.

———, "U.S. and the Vatican," *U.S. News & World Report*, December 14, 1959, page 75.

———, "Why Ike Is Going Halfway Round the World," *U.S. News & World Report*, November 23, 1959, page 55.

Stevenson, Adlai Ewing, "Summit and the Campaign—Democrats Chart Their Course," *U.S. News & World Report*, May 30, 1960, pages 81-82.

Stokes, Richard L., "U.S. Had No Secrets; The Great Falls-Washington Axis," *The Freeman*, January 12, 1953, pages 263-66.

Straight, Michael Whitney, "Dear Stub, Signed Dwight," *New Republic*, December 27, 1954, pages 13-15.

———, "How Ike Reached the Russians at Geneva," *New Republic*, August 1, 1955, pages 7-11.

Strout, Richard Lee, "President and the Press," *New Republic*, January 11, 1954, pages 15-16.

———, "Twenty-Second Amendment: A Second Look," *New York Times Magazine*, July 28, 1957, page 5 *et seq.*

Sullivan, Leonor Kretzer, "Lack of Leadership in Washington," *Vital Speeches of the Day*, June 1, 1957, pages 489-92.

Sulzberger, Cyrus Leo, "Intimate Portraits of the Four," *New York Times Magazine*, May 15, 1960, pages 15-17 *et seq.*

Sulzberger, C. (cont.), "Old Friends, Old Collaborators," *New York Times Magazine*, October 25, 1953, page 9.

Swomley, John M., Jr., "Eisenhower Portent," *The Christian Century*, January 30, 1952, pages 124-26.

Taft, Robert Alphonso, "Taft Press Conference After Meeting With Eisenhower," *U.S. News & World Report*, September 19, 1952, pages 90-93.

Taylor, Allan, "What Ike Believes," *Collier's*, March 1, 1952, pages 18-19.

Toth, Charles W., "Dwight D. Eisenhower: Presidential Candidate," *Vital Speeches of the Day*, April 1, 1952, pages 359-64.

Truman, Harry S. "Day Ike Snubbed Me," *Look*, May 24, 1960, pages 25-33.

Tully, Andrew F., "Ike's Bunkered Haven, Burning Tree Camp," *Collier's*, August 5, 1955, pages 52-55.

Udall, Stewart Lee, "Eisenhower and Congress," *New Republic*, June 3, 1957, page 3 *et seq.*

Uhler, John Earle, "Eisenhower-Darlon Understanding," *Catholic World*, February, 1943, pages 523-29.

Varney, Harold Lord, "Eisenhower Midway," *American Mercury*, March, 1955, pages 9-16.

Volkov, Leon, "Ike's Strategy," *Newsweek*, April 25, 1960, page 32.

Waithman, Robert, "Eisenhower and America," *Spectator*, February 23, 1951, page 234.

Weinman, Martha, "Mr. Eisenhower Builds His Dream Home," *Collier's*, September 17, 1954, pages 23-27.

Welles, Benjamin, "Ike, the Man," *Ladies Home Journal*, February, 1953, pages 11 *et seq.*

Welsh, Alexander, "Sir Walter Scott and Eisenhower," *New Republic*, January 23, 1961, pages 16-17.

Wertenbaker, Charles Christian, "Eisenhower in Victory," *Life*, June 25, 1945, pages 84-86.

Weyl, Nathaniel, "Red Star Over Cuba," *Human Events*, January 13, 1961, pages 21-24.

White, Theodore Harold, "Army at Bay," *The Reporter*, March 30, 1954, pages 11-13.

White, William Smith, "Eisenhower Opens the Last Act," *Harper's*, December, 1958, pages 80-83.

———, "Eisenhower's Dangerous Legacy of Good Will," *Harper's*, March, 1960, pages 100-05.

———, "Evolution of Eisenhower As Politician," *New York Times Magazine*, September 23, 1956, page 11 *et seq.*

———, "Has Eisenhower Changed the GOP?," *New York Times Magazine*, March 18, 1956, page 11 et seq.

Williams, Gerhard Mennen, "Plea to the President," *The Reporter*, February 18, 1960, pages 24-26.

Williamson, Samuel Thurston, "Four Star Fighting Men," *New York Times Magazine*, May 2, 1943, pages 14-15.

Wilson, Harper Hubert, "Crisis of Democracy; White Case," *The Nation*, November 21, 1953, pages 417-20.

Wilson, Richard Lawson, "Eisenhower in the U.S.S.R.," *Look*, September 15, 1959, pages 26-27.

———, "How Eisenhower Views His Presidency," *Look*, November 8, 1960, pages 73-76 *et seq.*

———, "Ike Has Decided There Will Be No War," *Look*, April 20, 1954, page 106 *et seq.*

———, "Ike Makes Himself Available As He Bids for Popular Support," *Look*, April 7, 1953, pages 71-72 *et seq.*

———, "Ike's Second Term Tragedy," *Look*, January 7, 1958, pages 9-11.

———, "Why Ike Doesn't Want a Second Term," *Look*, June 28, 1955, pages 21-23.

Winner, Percy, "Belated Bid for French Votes," *New Republic*, November 24, 1952, page 9.

———, "Demagogue and the Kremlin," *New Republic*, November 3, 1952, page 16.

———, "Europe Cools Toward Ike," *New Republic*, September 22, 1952, page 9.

———, "Europe Likes Ike," *New Republic*, April 14, 1952, page 9.

———, "Ike and the Old Guard," *New Republic*, July 28, 1952, page 7.

———, "Ike's Two Campaigns," *New Republic*, March 31, 1952, page 9.

———, "Who Likes Ike?," *New Republic*, October 27, 1952, page 9.

Wittmer, Felix, "Freedom's Case Against Dean Acheson," *American Mercury*, April, 1952, pages 3-17.

Wolfe, Henry Cutler, "Mr. Four Star," *Saturday Review of Literature*, December 2, 1944, page 62 *et seq.*

Wright, Gordon, "Thucydides and Eisenhower," *Virginia Quarterly Review*, Winter, 1955, pages 115-24.

Wyden, Peter, "Ike Comes to Town," *Newsweek*, July 11, 1955, pages 21-22 *et seq.*

———, "Take the President Out of the White House!," *Saturday Evening Post*, February 16, 1957, pages 24-25 *et seq.*

Yearly, Clifton Krebs, Jr., "Presidency Today," *Commonweal*, September 19, 1958, pages 607-10.

III

Unsigned Magazine Articles About
Eisenhower and Related Matters.

AMERICA

1953

"C. U.'s New Rector and New Alumnus," December 5; page 253.

"Eisenhower's Message of Hope," December 19; page 313.

"President Grows," July 25; page 413.

"President Scores," August 8; page 449.

"President to the People," May 30; page 238.

"Selling the Eisenhower Peace Plan," May 2; page 125.

1954

"President Attends Red Mass," February 13; page 493.

"President on Preventive War," August 28; pages 513-14.

"President Prays," October 9; page 29.

"President to the Press," May 8; pages 154-55.

"Profile of the President," January 23; page 414.

"White House Farm Plan," June 26; page 334.

1955

"John Marshall Confronts the Floods," September 10; page 549.

"President and Congress," January 15; page 393.

"President's Illness," October 8; page 30.

1956

"Decision Awaited," March 3; page 602.

"Immorality of Neutralism," June 23; page 298.

"Intellectual Point Four," June 9; page 255.

"Now Ike's the Boss," December 8; page 286.

1957

"Foreign Aid," June 1; page 278.

"President Speaks; Little Rock Crisis," October 5; page 2.

"Second Term Begins; Legislative Program," February 2; page 494.

1958

"President Passes Test; State-of-the-Union Address," January 18; page 442.

1959

"Eisenhower in Asia," November 21; page 225.

"President Visits the Vatican," November 21; page 230.

"Presidential Posture on Berlin," March 21; page 707.

"We Will Not Retreat One Inch," March 28; pages 735-36.

1960

"After the President's Visit," March 19; page 727.

"In the Wake of the Japanese Debacle," July 2; page 410.

"Neutralized Africa? President's Proposal," October 8; pages 35-36.

"No Ugly American; In India's Book," January 2; page 388.

1961

"Eisenhower's Farewell," February 4; page 587.

ATLANTIC MONTHLY

1952

"Atlantic Report on the World Today," October; page 12 *et seq.*
"Washington," November; page 12 *et seq.*

1953

"Atlantic Report on the World Today," May; page 10; July; page 9; August; page 4 *et seq.*

1955

"Atlantic Report on the World Today," March; page 4 *et seq.;* April; page 8 *et seq.*
"Watch on the Potomac," July; page 10.

1956

"President's Health," June; page 6 *et seq.*

1957

"Atlantic Report on the World Today," May; page 12 *et seq.;* July; page 4 *et seq.*

BUSINESS WEEK

1951

"What Europe Needs Is Arms," February 10; page 22.

1952

"Changing the Business Climate," November 8; pages 27-31.
"Eisenhower Submits a Report Card," April 12; page 196.
"Eisenhower's Problems Take Shape," July 26; page 144.
"End of an Era," November 15; page 184.
"Getting Ready to Take Over," November 15; pages 27-28.
"Ike Can Get a Share of the Labor Vote," July 19; page 114 *et seq.*
"Ike's Problem: To Swing Taft's Midwest," July 19; pages 30-32.
"Seat of Power Shifts; Government-in-Embryo," December 27; pages 25-26.

"What Eisenhower Stands For," January 19; page 98 *et seq.*
"Why Ike Talked to the AFL," September 20; page 31.

1953

"Appealing to the People," May 23; pages 27-28.
"Eisenhower: A Study in Contrasts," December 5; pages 32-33.
"Eisenhower Plan," December 19; page 188.
"Eisenhower Shapes a Businessman's Government," January 14; pages 30-32.
"Governing Less on Purpose," August 8; pages 25-26.
"Reshuffling White House Team," September 5; pages 23-24.

1954

"Eisenhower in Charlotte: Patriotism and Strategy," May 29; pages 98-100 *et seq.*
"Forward Look in Washington," February 13; page 196.
"Piled-Up Desk at White House," October 23; page 27.
"President's Program," February 6; page 140.
"Pushing Business Expansion," January 9; pages 27-28.
"State-of-the-Union Message," January 16; page 192.
"Who'll Make Foreign Policy? Bricker Amendment," January 30; page 121.

1955

"Economic Plan With Political Meaning," January 15; pages 30-32.
"Gettysburg Gets Set to Serve As Temporary Capital," November 5; pages 28-29.
"Making the Best of Misfortune," October 8; page 192.
"News That Shook the Nation," October 1; pages 27-30.
"Peace, Freedom and Expansion," January 15; page 172.
"Second Look at the Economy; Joint Committee on the Economic Report," February 5; pages 112-14.
"Washington: Business As Usual," October 8; page 25.

"Washington Outlook," October 8; pages 37-38; November 26; pages 37-38; December 24; page 35.

"White House Team Carries On," October 15; pages 158-160.

1956

"New Presidency," March 10; pages 25-27.

"No Strings Attached," November 17; page 200.

"President at a Crossroads," February 18; pages 25-27.

"President Gives His Answer," March 10; page 176.

"Race Against the Calendar," June 16; pages 23-24.

"Toward a Common Goal," September 1; page 152.

"Washington Outlook," January 7; pages 37-38; January 14; pages 35-36; june 23; page 39; October 6; pages 39-40.

"What the Decision Means," March 3; pages 27-39.

1957

"Business Goes On, but Not As Usual," December 7; pages 26-28.

"Crisis in the White House," November 30; pages 25-27.

"Defending His Budget," May 18; page 39.

1959

"Eisenhower Seeks New Order," December 5; pages 23-24.

"Europe Greets New Eisenhower, and U. S. Wins New Strength," September 5; pages 32-33.

"Moving Toward a Berlin Policy," March 21; page 174.

"New, Fighting Eisenhower," May 23; pages 25-28.

"Reasserting Leadership in Asia," December 19; pages 23-25.

"TV's Splurge on Eisenhower Trip," December 12; pages 29-31.

"Washington Outlook," April 25; pages 39-40.

1960

"Eisenhower Plays Good Neighbor," March 5; pages 25-27.

"Mending Fences in East Asia," June 18; pages 27-29.

THE CHRISTIAN CENTURY

1945

"Eisenhower on Conscription," July 25; pages 854-55.

1947

"Eisenhower for President?," October 15; pages 1230-31.

"Eisenhower Will Head Columbia," June 9; page 843.

1951

"Eisenhower and the Two-Party System," November 21; page 1332.

1952

"Are There Two Eisenhowers?," October 29; page 1243.

"As the Campaign Closes," October 29; pages 1246-48.

"Eisenhower a Candidate," January 23; page 91.

"Eisenhower Elected," November 12; page 1307.

"Unbridged Gulf," February 6; pages 150-51.

"Voice of the People," November 19; pages 1343-45.

1953

"Alien to America," July 22; pages 838-39.

"Eisenhower Blueprint," February 18; pages 182-84.

"New Hand at the Helm," January 14; pages 40-41.

"President at His Best," December 9; page 1411.

"President Offers a Christmas Gift; Plan for a Pooling of Nuclear Materials," December 23; pages 1493-95.

"President Stakes Down His Faith," February 11; page 155.

1954

"Eisenhower As President," February 10; pages 167-69.

"Eisenhower at Assembly of World Council," September 1; page 1048.

"President Makes a Great Speech," November 3; page 1325.

"Special Letter to a Special Assistant; President Eisenhower's Letter Appointing Nelson A. Rockefeller Special Assistant," December 29; page 1572.

1955

"President's Illness Overshadows U. S.," October 5; page 1131.

1956

"Election Results," November 14; page 1315.

"President to Run for Term Two," July 25; page 867.

"President's Illness Concerns the Nation," June 20; page 739.

1957

"President Balances His Judgement," June 19; page 747.

1959

"President of All the People?," December 16; page 1459.

COLLIER'S

1946

"Did Eisenhower Lose the War?," August 3; page 74.

1950

"It Ain't No Sin," April 1; page 74.

1952

"All Cards on the Table," August 30; page 74.

"Here's How We Vote," November 1; page 74.

"Ike Is My Boy," September 6; pages 64-66.

"Man for Leadership," August 9; page 74.

"Why They Like Ike," June 28; page 74.

1953

"Lay Off, Friends, Lay Off," April 18; page 78.

"Right Man for the Job," January 24; page 70.

"They Like to Think They Look Like Ike," May 30; pages 18-19.

1954

"Horse He Can't Ride," September 3; page 86.

"Ike Needs a Politician," March 19; page 118.

"Inseparable Twosome; Hobbies and Relaxations of Chief Executives," January 22; page 110.

"Look at the Record," February 5; page 110.

1956

"From Plebe to President; Ike As His Classmates Remember Him," June 10; pages 92-97.

"President's Health," April 13; page 106.

COMMONWEAL

1945

"Parade," July 6; page 275.

1951

"Eisenhower Mission," January 12; pages 340-41.

"Out of the Wilderness," November 21; page 155.

1952

"Campaign," October 31; page 83 *et seq.*

"Candidate Eisenhower," January 18; pages 364-65.

"Eisenhower As Eisenhower," September 5; page 525.

"Eisenhower As Taft," September 19; pages 572-73.

"Eisenhower Candidacy," May 9; page 109.

"Eisenhower Victory," November 14; pages 131-32.

"Final Stages; Campaign Speeches," October 24; pages 54-55.

"General and the Press," June 20; page 262.

"General's Crusade," July 25; page 379.

"General's Return," December 26; page 297.

"They'd Rather Be Right," June 27; page 286.

"Trouble With Crusades," August 29; page 499.

1953

"Conflicting Duties," August 28; page 506.
"Gauntlet Is Down; McCarthy's Declaration of War Upon the Administration," December 11; pages 247-48.
"Great Persuader," February 13; page 463.
"Hail and Farewell," January 23; page 391.
"On Again, Off Again; The President's Recent Speech in Boston," October 9; page 4.
"President and Politics," November 6; pages 108-09.
"President and the Bomb," October 23; pages 52-53.
"Purgers and the President," June 26; page 290.
"Shadows of the Past," December 4; page 213.
"Time for a Change," June 5; page 215.
"To Live in Peace," May 1; page 87.
"Where Was Mr. Hughes?," September 4; page 53.

1954

"Ambiguous Blessing," September 10; page 549.
"Bipartisanship and Responsibility," January 15; page 367.
"Drawn Battle," March 19; page 591.
"Fall Elections," July 16; pages 356-57.
"New Ike?," January 8; page 344.
"President's New Leadership," December 17; pages 299-300.

1955

"Disengagement," May 27; pages 195-96.
"Modest Achievement," May 13; page 139.
"Our Debt to President Eisenhower," October 7; page 3.
"Political Prospects," October 14; page 29.
"Sweetness and Light," August 5; pages 435-36.
"Wishing Won't Make It So; Contemporary Mood of the American Mind," August 26; pages 507-08.

1956

"Before the Election," November 2; page 115 *et seq.*

"Books and Politics," July 20; page 384.
"Candidate Eisenhower," March 16; pages 607-08.
"Eisenhower As Hobson," August 10; page 458.
"Executive Suite," June 8; page 242.
"Health Issue," July 6; pages 335-36.
"Mr. Eisenhower Again," September 7; pages 551-52.
"Primaries, Anyone?," February 3; page 448.
"President and Politics," May 4; page 111.
"President's Illness," June 22; page 228.
"President's Personal Victory," November 23; pages 195-96.
"President's Sense of Duty," January 20; page 393.
"Time of Decision," September 28; pages 623-24.
"Two Men," September 21; pages 599-600.

1957

"Eisenhower and the Old Guard," June 21; page 294.
"Little Rock and the Future," October 18; pages 59-60.
"Mr. Eisenhower and the GOP," February 22; pages 525-26.
"Mr. Eisenhower and the Right Wing," May 10; page 141.
"Mr. Eisenhower's Second Term; Inaugural Address," February 8; pages 475-76.
"Plea to the White House," February 8; page 477.
"President and the Governor," October 4; page 5.
"President's Health," March 22; pages 628-29.
"President's Press," May 3; page 116.
"Should Mr. Eisenhower Resign," December 20; page 27 *et seq.*

1959

"Eyes on the Presidency," September 4; pages 459-60.
"No Ground War?," April 3; page 5 *et seq.*
"Old Guard and the President," February 13; pages 509-10.

"Ike Sees the U. S. As Only Candidates Can," October 27; pages 38-39.

"Ike's Command Decision," October 6; page 32.

"Ike's Great Crusade," July 21; page 28.

"Ike's Roster Lengthens," April 7; pages 40-41.

"Liberation Issue," September 22; page 30.

"Man and His Mission," December 15; pages 23-29.

"Man on His Way Over, Man on His Way Back," June 2; pages 26-27.

"Minnesota Spells It Out," March 31; pages 31-33.

"New Chief Finds Men New to Government," December 1; pages 43-45.

"1912 Overture to 1952," June 23; pages 21-27.

"Nixon Fights, Wins and Weeps," June 23; pages 25-31.

"People, Gowns, Hope, All New," December 8; pages 38-39.

"Redeclaration of Independence," November 17; pages 33-41.

"This Ain't the Army, Mr. Ike," June 30; pages 26-28.

"Voters See Close-Up of Eisenhower," June 16; pages 15-21.

1953

"Bermuda Makes Modern History," December 14; pages 24-29.

"Books, Words and Deeds," June 29; page 32.

"Fateful Dinner in a Quonset Hut," May 25; page 44.

"Fresh Hope, but Hard Reality; President's Address to the United Nations," December 21; page 10.

"Ike Finds a Fairway," February 23; pages 26-27.

"*Life* Visits the President-Elect," January 12; pages 94-95.

"Look Folks, I'm Speaking French," November 23; page 42 *et seq.*

"Noble Inaugural," February 2; page 24.

"My Colorado Golf Cronies," August 24; page 26.

"President Has Some Fun and Relights Hope of Peace," April 27; pages 34-35.

"President's Appointments," February 16; pages 22-25.

"State of the Nation," July 6; page 16.

"United Nations Applaud, a Humble Man Listens," December 21; pages 6-9.

1954

"Agenda for the Alliances of the U.K. and the U.S.A.," June 28; pages 22-23.

"From *Erehwon* to Somewhere; Freedom to Take the Initiative," January 18; page 24.

"Past a Point of No Return; President's Break With McCarthy," May 31; page 37.

"Robert Montgomery Presents President As a Pro," April 19; pages 28-29.

1955

"Eisenhower and Geneva," August 1; page 29.

"Everyone Is Glad to See Ike Up and Around," November 21; pages 40-41.

"Flock of Visitors As Patient Gains," November 14; pages 70-74.

"Helicopter Cabinet," December 5; pages 56-57.

"New Eisenhower in Command," February 28; page 31.

"Nuclear 1955 for D.D.E. '15," June 20; pages 32-33.

"Presidential View of the Biggest Issue," January 17; page 35.

"World Watches a Window; President's Illness," October 10; pages 35-43.

1956

"All-Out Stevenson Go, Against the Ike Glow," October 15; pages 30-37.

"Biggest Town Meeting: Republicans' Salute to Eisenhower," January 30; pages 117-18.

"Campaign in the Homestretch," November 5; pages 56-63.

"Doctors Say He's Able; Is He Willing?," February 27; pages 38-39.

"Drama of President's Yes," March 12; pages 18-25.

"How to Be Right and Be President; Farm Bill Veto," April 30; page 52.

"Ike, Adlai, and American Ardor," September 3; page 41.

"Interlude on the Farm," October 8; page 63.

1955

"Cap'n Ike and Mr. Sam," January 25; pages 30-31.

1956

"Ike's Family Tree," November 13; pages 40-41.

1957

"President's Office," January 22; pages 42-43.

THE NATION

1947

"President Ike," July 5; page 3.

1951

"General Talks," November 10; page 389.

1952

"Bob Vs. Ike; Durkin Appointment," December 13; page 541.

"Eisenhower As Symbol," February 23; pages 168-69.

"Eisenhower: Silent Symbol," January 19; pages 51-52.

"Ike's Peace Program," August 23; page 141.

"Issue of Principle," October 4; pages 287-89.

"Platform Was the Payoff," July 19; pages 42-43.

"Question for Eisenhower; Trade Policy," October 11; pages 316-17.

"Shape of Things," January 26; page 69.

"Speak Up, General! McCarthy Vs. Lenard Schmitt," August 30; pages 162-63.

"Stake in Stevenson Victory," October 18; pages 341-43.

"Stevenson Narrows the Gap; Policies Altered to Fit; Battle of Columbia," October 25; pages 369-70.

"What You Lose if Ike Wins," October 18; pages 344-51.

"Who Likes Ike Now?," June 14; page 567.

1953

"Circus on the White House Lawn; McCarthyism," March 14; page 217.

"Foreign Policy: Ike's or Taft's?," June 6; page 465.

"Mr. Eisenhower's Proposal," December 19; pages 538-39.

"Present Danger, a Call for Leadership," December 12; pages 529-31.

"President Vanishes," September 19; page 221.

"President's Prayer," January 31; page 91.

1954

"McCarthy's Dilemma," March 13; pages 211-12.

1955

"From Guildhall to Geneva," July 9; pages 21-22.

"Is the President a New Dealer?," February 26; page 170.

"Politics and the Budget," January 29; page 89.

1956

"Dulles Edits Eisenhower," June 23; pages 521-22.

"Eisenhower Candidacy," July 21; page 49.

"Election Views From Abroad," October 27; pages 338-44.

"Great Decision," March 10; pages 189-90.

"Office and the Man," June 30; page 541.

"Pause That Refreshes," June 16; page 501.

1957

"Day of Speeches: November 13, 1957," November 23; page 377.

"Plus and Minus," November 16; page 333.

"President's Illness," December 7; page 417.

"Who's to Blame for Mr. Dulles?," February 9; page 109.

1958

"Bully for *Time*," March 8, pages 197-98.

"Mosquito Men," February 1; page 89.

"Speech That Won't Be Made," November 15; page 349.

1959

"Bon Voyage, Mr. President," December 12; page 429.

"General Remains Calm," March 14; page 217.

"Peace Juggernaut," September 12; page 121.

"Risks of Leadership," September 5; page 101.

"Stereotype and Reality," December 26; page 477.

1960

"Eisenhower and the Other Generals," February 13; page 129.

"Great Tranquilizer," July 9; pages 21-22.

"Nemesis," June 11; page 501.

1961

"Farewell and Hail," January 28; page 69.

1962

"Ike the Heretic," July 14; page 3.

NEW REPUBLIC

1947

"Like Ike?," October 27; page 5.

1948

"Democrats Boom Eisenhower," April 12; pages 10-13.

"Eisenhower Out?," February 2; pages 5-6.

"Rebellion, an Army, but No Chief," July 19; page 5.

1949

"Eisenhower on Education; Federal Aid," June 27; page 8.

1951

"Eisenhower's New Crusade," February 12; pages 5-6.

"Washington Wire," January 15; pages 3-4.

1952

"Dilemma of Candidate Eisenhower," July 21; pages 5-6.

"Eisenhower and 1952," January 14; page 5.

"Eisenhower or McCarthy," February 18; page 7.

"Eisenhower's Hard Choice in Korea," December 1; page 5.

"Has Eisenhower Delayed Peace in Korea?," November 10; pages 5-6.

"Knights and Knaves in Eisenhower's Great Crusade," July 28; pages 13-17.

"McIke," October 13; page 7.

"Mr. Eisenhower States His Views," June 16; pages 5-6.

"Stubbed Toes and Hardening Arteries," November 17; pages 5-6.

"Washington Wire," June 16; pages 3-4; October 20; page 3; November 3; pages 3-4.

"Why Voters Change Their Minds," October 27; pages 21-25.

1953

"Above and Beyond," May 4; page 7.

"Bermuda, No Golf for Eisenhower," June 1; pages 5-7.

"Eisenhower's Speech, the Greatness and the Weakness," April 27; pages 5-7.

"Has Eisenhower Joined McCarthy?," November 16; pages 7-8.

"President's Atomic Plan," December 21; pages 5-8.

"Umbrella Without Stays," November 9; page 7.

"Washington Wire," July 13; page 2; August 3; page 2; August 10; page 2; November 23; page 2; December 21; page 2.

1954

"Eisenhower at Abilene," November 22; pages 126-127.

"Eisenhower, the Decisive Test," December 6; pages 7-8.

"Ike and Joe," March 8; page 3.

"President's Sincere Vagueness," October 4; page 4.

"Two Years of Eisenhower," October 11; pages 1-19.

"Washington Wire," March 15; page 2; June 7; page 4; August 23; page 2; October 18; page 2; November 8; page 2; December 6; page 2; December 27; page 2.

1955

"Eisenhower's Cowardice: Ladejinsky Case," January 24; pages 6-7.

"Formosa: The Chance for Peace," February 7; pages 6-8.

"Not a Politician," July 4; pages 4-5.

"President From Today to January, 1957," October 3; pages 3-7.

"State of the Union," January 17; pages 5-15.

"To Run or Not to Run: Everybody Has an Answer," March 14; page 3.

"Washington Wire," March 7; page 2; May 9; page 2; October 3; page 2.

1956

"All's Well," June 25; page 2.

"Bunch of the Boys: Golfing Partners," September 10; page 2.

"Dispelling Doubt; Still Convalescent," July 23; page 2.

"Doctors and Mr. Eisenhower's Decision," January 2; page 3.

"Eden and Ike," February 13; page 5.

"Eisenhower's Contribution: What He Did Not Do," September 10; pages 3-4.

"Future With a Past," September 3; pages 3-5.

"H-Bomb Gesture," October 1; page 2.

"I Get Discouraged; Off to Georgia," April 16; page 2.

"Inside Story," July 9; page 2.

"Lack of Ideas," August 13; page 2.

"Leadership: Two Views," April 30; page 3.

"Ninth Hole," April 23; page 2.

"No Aid for Schools," July 16; page 2.

"Peace of Mind," October 1; pages 3-4.

"Persuading the President," June 18; page 2.

"Presidency," March 5; pages 3-4.

"President," June 18; page 3.

"President's Health," September 3; pages 9-16.

"Prospects of a Part-Time President," March 12; pages 3-5.

"Reversal by Dulles," June 18; pages 5-6.

"So Little Time," May 21; page 2.

"Solace From the White House," June 11; page 2.

"Washington Wire," February 27; page 2.

"What a Product! Republican Kick-Off Dinner," April 30; page 2.

"What I Believe; Upper Colorado Project," April 23; page 5.

"When the Wind Blows," October 22; page 2.

"While We Wait," July 2; page 5.

"Who Me? Departmental Difference," December 17; page 2.

"Work and Play," March 26; page 5.

1957

"Captain, My Captain," March 25; page 3.

"Day Congress Surrendered Unconditionally; From a Revised American History Published in 1987," April 29; page 7.

"Eisenhower, Faubus and the Court," September 30; page 5.

"I Do Want to Say This," June 17; page 7.

"Next Four Years," January 28; page 2.

"Responsible Rule and the President," December 16; page 5.

"Solace or Security?," November 4; pages 3-4.

"Wages of Sin," January 7; page 2.

1958

"Misleading the President," March 17; page 5.

"Without Eisenhower," September 8; page 3.

1959

"Is This What the President Means to Say?," March 23; page 9.

"T.R.B. From Washington," December 7; page 2.

1960

"Age of Damocles; Criticism of State-of-the-Union Message," January 18; pages 3-5.

"Dick and Ike," October 7; pages 7-8.

"President's Trip," March 14; page 5.

"Who Was in Charge? Recapitulation of the U-2 Incident," June 13; page 2.

1961

"Eisenhower Legacy," January 16, pages 3-5.

NEW YORK TIMES MAGAZINE

1945

"General Ike: The War Record of a Soldier," June 17; pages 6-7.

1949

"Ike in '52? Truman Thinks So," December 19; pages 13-14.

"Ike, the Atom, and '52," August 1; pages 15-17.

"Ike Wants to Make One From Three," March 7; page 20.

"Ike's Dangerous Choice," October 10; pages 25-26.

"Pal Ike, Pal Harry," December 26; pages 14-15.

"Truman and Ike the Real Winners," November 21; page 21.

1950

"American Assembly," October 30; page 81.

"Eisenhower Set to Shoulder the Burden of Bolstering Europe As Vital Frontier," December 18; pages 22-23.

"Farmer Eisenhower," December 4; page 18.

"Ike's Formula," April 10; page 22.

"What's Behind the Eisenhower News," November 6; pages 17-18.

1951

"Bigger and Better," August 27; page 38.

"Eisenhower Prods Lagging Notions," July 16; page 32 et seq.

"Eisenhower Rallies Fighting Spirit," February 12; page 15.

"General Ike Encounters Apathy on Tour," January 22; page 36.

"Green Light for General Ike in '52," August 13; page 15.

"H-T's Man," November 5; pages 60-61.

"Ike Returns to a Troubled Continent," January 15; page 36 et seq.

"Ike Shaping Up As Definite '52 Bet, Though Taft Drive Is Gaining Speed," July 2; pages 14-15.

"Ike's Command Post," October 8; page 25.

"Ike's Place," January 8; page 36.

"Ike's Political Plans? Later; What He Wants Now Is Guns," November 19; pages 23-24.

"Ike's Tour Stirs Russian Resentment," January 29; page 32 et seq.

"Ike's Week," February 12; pages 15-16.

"Setting Up Shop," March 5; page 38.

"What the President Told Ike; What Ike Told the President," November 12; pages 27-28.

1952

"Back to the U.S.A.," June 9; pages 23-25.

"Call to Higher Duty," March 31; pages 24 et seq.

"Campaign," September 15; pages 23-27.

"Candidates' Views on Business," October 13; page 84.

"Charting the Course," July 28; pages 25-26.

"Choosing His Cabinet Team, Ike Eases Orderly Transition," December 1; pages 17-18.

"Citizen Ike," June 16; pages 23-25.

"Debate on Aid-to-Europe Cuts Spotlights Ike and Taft Views," May 19; pages 27-28.

"Eisenhower and Stevenson: Where They Stand," August 4; page 29.

"Eisenhower Returning to Fight; Won't Let Taft Win by Default," March 10; pages 25-26.

"Europe Relieved and Pleased at Eisenhower's Nomination," July 21; pages 39-40.

"Fight in Committee," July 21; page 26.

"Foreign-Affairs Debate," July 7; pages 18-19.

"Foreign Policy Accent," August 18; pages 17-18.

"General Set a Killing Campaign Pace, Slams at H.S.T.," October 20; pages 30-31.

"Good-Bye Ike," June 2; page 33.

"Having Won Personal Victory, Ike Must Keep GOP United," November 17; page 25.

"Hello and Farewell," May 12; pages 43-44.

"Holding His Fire," September 8; page 25.

"How the Eisenhower Victory Was Achieved, Ike's Brain Trusters Made Shrewd Plans to Outsmart the 'Pros' Behind Senator Taft," July 21; pages 23-25.

"H.S.T. on Ike," January 21; page 24.

"Ike and H.S.T. Make History; Smooth

"Salute and Good Sense," November 23; page 57.

"Stalin Bid, Churchill Visit, Launch Ike Into New Year," January 5; page 13.

"Victory Won, a Greater Victory Hoped For," December 21; page 32 et seq.

"Washington Trends," July 27; page 15; August 31; page 15.

"What Kind of Change?," November 16; page 30.

1954

"Ambitious Eisenhower Program Is Up to a Splinter Congress," January 11; pages 17-19.

"As Ike Goes," May 3; page 24.

"Boomerang," August 30; page 20.

"Captain in the Potomac Storm," December 13; pages 23-24.

"Epitaph," August 23; pages 63-64.

"From Where Ike Sits: His Role in the Race, the Issues," October 25; pages 32-34.

"Home to the Prairie," November 22, pages 28-29.

"Ike and a Wave of Optimism," August 23; pages 15-16.

"Ike at 64; Confident," October 18; pages 25-26.

"Ike Is Their Patient," July 2; pages 16-17.

"Ike's Famous Stag Dinners, Who Gets Invited, Why, and What Happens," November 29; pages 26-28.

"Ike's Program: What He Will Get From Congress," January 18; page 23.

"Life of Looking Into Lenses," April 26; page 31.

"McCarthy Story; The Last Word," December 20; pages 18-19.

"Man Above Party?," November 29; pages 24-25.

"Man in Charge," January 25; page 82.

"Mr. Eisenhower Turns Pro—And the Politicians Perk Up," February 8; pages 19-20.

"Next the Great Debate," December 6; pages 23-24.

"Pressure on Ike," November 1; pages 18-19.

"Senator Knowland: He's a Man Hard to Stop," December 13; pages 26-28.

"State of Mr. Eisenhower," August 9; pages 15-17.

"These Are the Men Ike Listens To," June 14; pages 27-29.

"They Still Like Ike," September 13; page 30.

"Ties of Our Big Three: How They Got That Way," May 10; page 40.

"Visitor to the Desert," March 1; page 21.

"White House Assist," January 18; page 51.

"We Like Ike in '56," December 20; pages 19-20.

1955

"Appointment With Ike, Who Gets to See Him—Who Doesn't—And Why," April 18; pages 27-30.

"As the President Sees It," August 8; pages 17-18.

"At Gettysburg, the President Frets a Little, Wants to Do More," November 28; pages 32-34.

"Big Story," October 10; page 68.

"Calculated Risk," May 9; pages 25-26.

"Clinical and Monetary," March 21; pages 27-28.

"Congress: Filling a Vacuum," July 11; pages 17-18.

"52 Out of Ike's Two Hundred," August 15; page 18.

"GOP and the White House," October 24; pages 25-26.

"Grand New Party? Eisenhower Is Changing the GOP—Here's How," April 4; pages 27-30.

"Hour of the Pollster," October 31; pages 31-32.

"If You Do, or You Don't," May 23; pages 29-30.

"Ike at the Summit: He Gets Along," July 18; pages 17-18.

"Ike in '56, a Poll of GOP Chairmen," December 12; pages 33-34.

"Ike: Precautions Only," December 19; pages 19-20.

"Ike's Illness, Europe Was Stunned, Confused, Then Prayerful," October 10; pages 55-65.

"Ike's Thinking on War," February 14; pages 23-24.

"In Between," August 29; page 16.

"Man at Peace With Himself," March 5; pages 21-22.

"Nixon Political Pull," April 23; pages 27-28 *et seq.*

"Politics: This Is the Mid-October Mood," October 15; pages 41-42.

"President: A New Pressing Role," April 9; pages 29-30.

"President's Campaign," April 30; page 29.

"President's Case," February 27; page 82.

"Ten Simple Facts," November 5; page 70.

"Trouble With the President—Painful, but Mild," June 18; pages 36-37.

"Under the Sun," January 9; pages 17-19.

"Way Ike Is Acting," January 2; page 11.

"What the President Reads," April 30; page 32 *et seq.*

"White House Headlines . . . That Were Not Printed," July 2; pages 48-49.

"Why It Went the Way It Did," November 12; pages 61-66.

"Will Ike Run? The Balance Sheet," February 20; page 29.

1957

"As a New Term Begins," January 28; pages 23-27.

"Do the Best You Can," January 28; page 28.

"Ike's Course—Nixon's Niche," December 9; pages 27-34 *et seq.*

"Men Around Ike—The Inner Circle Shrinks," January 21; pages 31-32.

"Mr. Fixits," March 25; page 32 *et seq.*

"Paris, the President, Prestige," December 16; pages 31-32.

"President . . . The South," October 7; pages 27-34 *et seq.*

"State of Ike Today," May 27; pages 35-37.

"State of the President Today," April 15; pages 31-32.

1958

"Fit or Failing: Viewers Choice," January 27; page 25.

"How the U.S. Rates the President Now," October 6; pages 22-24.

"Ike's New Crisis—GOP Revolt," January 27; pages 23-24.

"Mad At Ike? No, But . . . ," March 10; pages 27-31.

"Old College Try," December 15; pages 28-29.

"Spot Ike's In," November 10; page 50 *et seq.*

"To Tell the People," January 6; pages 15-16.

"What Ike Likes," June 23; page 98.

"Why Ike's Temper Showed," May 5; page 29.

1959

"Astonishing Headliner," September 7; pages 58-59.

"Black-Tie Affair," August 3; pages 51-52.

"81 Men and a Girl," December 21; page 82.

"Ike—A Sober Appraisal," February 2; pages 17-18.

"Ike in France," September 14; pages 36-38.

"Ike's Course—Ike's Choice," March 16; pages 21-22.

"Ike's Triumph: The Substance" September 7; pages 17-22.

"Momentous Mission," August 31; pages 31-32 *et seq.*

"On Ike's Triumphal Trail," December 21; page 36 *et seq.*

"On the Sunyside," March 2; page 42 *et seq.*

"President Eisenhower and His Curtain Raiser, on Our Peace Mission in a Jet-Quick World," December 14; pages 58-60.

"President—Global Mission," December 7; pages 51-54.

"President in Person," November 16; pages 45-48.

"Splashing Ink on Ike," January 5; page 45.

"Summit's Troubled Prelude," December 28; pages 23-26.

"White House and the Court, Eisenhower and Warren Are Far, Far, Apart," February 8; pages 24-25.

1960

"Boiling East—The President," June 20; pages 45-46 *et seq.*

Bibliography

THE REPORTER

SATURDAY EVENING POST

1956

"Country Still Needs Eisenhower," September 29; page 10.
"How Much Press Quizzing Should the President Endure?," September 1; page 10.
"There's No Demand for a GOP New Deal," August 11; page 10.
"What Ike Needs Now Is a Reasonable Congress," December 8; page 10.

1961

"Great American Patriot Retires to Private Life," January 21; page 10.

SCHOLASTIC

1943

"Victory Vignettes," October 11; page 9.

1948

"Hats in the Ring," May 3; page 12.
"Not Available," February 9; page 6.

1949

"General Ike Calls on a Teacher," April 6; page 22T.
"Temporary Duty for Ike," February 23; page 8.

1951

"General Eisenhower Reports," February 14; page 14.
"Ike Sees President," November 14; page 16.

1952

"Eisenhower Plans Korean Trip," November 19; page 15.
"General Ike," April 2; page 17.
"Hail to the Chief," November 12; page 15.
"Ike Quits NATO," April 23; page 16.
"Ike Says He's Willing," January 16; page 16.
"New President and World Affairs," December 3; pages 12-14.
"Republican Presidential Candidate," October 1; page 6.

1953

"Mister President," January 14; pages 10-12.

"New President at Work," February 4; page 16.
"No, One Hat," April 29; page 13.
"President Meets Press," February 25; page 14.
"President Visits Canada," December 2; page 20.
"U.S. Peace Offensive," April 29; page 13.

1954

"Ike Paints Abe," February 10; page 29.
"President Dedicates Eisenhower Memorial Museum," December 1; page 16.

1955

"Gettysburg, Temporary Capitol of America," November 17; pages 14-15.
"President Has Heart Attack," October 6; page 17.

1956

"Battle Page," November 1; page 16.
"Dwight D. Eisenhower," September 27; page 18.
"Elections and the Next Four Years," November 29; pages 14-15.
"From President's Desk," September 13; page 21.
"Ike Says Yes," March 15; page 19.
"Ike: Will He? Won't He?," February 23; page 11.
"Ike Wins Smashing Victory," November 15; page 17.

SENIOR SCHOLASTIC

1957

"Diplomats Get Around," March 15; page 15.
"King Saud, Ike Confer," February 15; page 11.
"Mend Anglo-U.S. Relations," April 5; page 17.
"U.S. Troops Used in Dispute," October 11; pages 14-15.

1960

"Green Light on Good Neighbor Highway," March 16; pages 12-15 et seq.
"Ike in Far East," September 14; page 26.
"Ike's February Tour," February 10; page 28.

"Ike's Tour a Triumph," March 9; page 18.

"Summit Talks Set for Spring," January 6; pages 16-17.

1961

"Ike's Farewell," February 1; pages 14-15.

TIME

1942

"Eisenhower of Britain," October 19; page 74.

"Ike and Men," November 16; pages 25-26.

"Pershing's Mantle?," July 6; page 24.

"Two Stars on the Schedule," April 13; page 68.

1943

"Ike's Way; Battle of Italy," September 13; pages 27-29.

"Up Ike, Up Andy," February 15; page 62 *et seq.*

1944

"Bath and Suvorov," April 24; page 68 *et seq.*

"Supreme Commander," June 19; pages 25-28.

"Wielders of the Weapon," January 3; page 22.

1945

"Eisenhower on War," June 25; page 17.

"Fate of the World," January 1; pages 20-23.

"Home to Abilene," July 2; pages 18-19.

"Salute to General Ike," June 25; pages 16-17.

1946

"Better Than the Pros," October 28; page 25.

"Dangerous Bill," April 22; page 22.

"Good Old Ike," January 21; pages 41-42.

"Highland Fling," October 14; page 46.

"Ike and the Noose," February 4; page 25.

"Report From the Boss," July 1; page 25.

1947

"Artful Dodger," January 13; pages 25-26.

"Everything to Gain," October 6; page 26.

"General Proposes," December 15; page 26.

"Gown for a General," June 30; page 19.

"How's That?," September 22; page 25.

"Ike for Columbia," July 7; page 63.

"In the Balance," June 23; pages 20-23.

1948

"Back to Normal," February 2; page 9.

"Freshman," May 17; page 42.

"General Takes Command," October 25; pages 43-44.

"Ike Says Goodbye," February 16; page 28.

"Ike's Crusade," November 22; pages 27-28.

"No! No! No!," July 19; page 22.

"Slams Across the Sea," December 6; page 22.

"Spring Vacation," April 26; page 24.

"Wake and Awaking," July 12; pages 11-12.

1949

"Hard Words," December 12; page 22.

"Send for Ike," February 21; page 22.

1950

"American Assembly," October 30; pages 78-79.

"Cutting Edge," April 10; page 19.

"Dear Ike," May 1; page 20.

"Happy Birthday to Ike," October 23; page 22.

"Ike IV," April 3; page 23.

"Just Trying to Get Along," November 6; page 19.

"Who's in Charge?," December 18; page 24.

1951

"Again Ike," January 15; page 20.

"Case Against Ike," August 20; page 14.

"Clues," December 10; page 21.

"Harnessing a Wave," December 17; pages 21-24.

"Ike Sees His Army," April 23; page 34.

"Ike's Trip," January 22; page 21; January 29; page 24; February 5; page 18.
"Inside Story," November 19; page 22.
"Man With the Answer," February 12; pages 15-18.
"Operation Ike," July 30; pages 11-12.
"Question of Ike," November 12; page 19.
"Question of Timing," September 24; pages 25-26.
"Travels and Testimonials," November 5; page 24.

1952

"Bob the Bugler," September 22; page 24.
"Bogged Down or Warming Up?," September 8; page 21.
"Clear Call," March 31; page 19.
"Closer Than Ever," May 5; pages 22-23.
"Come Home, Ike," March 17; pages 19-20.
"Defeat of the Messrs.," March 24; page 19.
"Different This Year," October 13; pages 22-23.
"Eisenhower: A Factual Sketch," April 7; page 23.
"Faith of an American," October 27; page 24.
"Faith of the Candidates," September 22; pages 55-56.
"Glory of Making Sense," July 21; page 11.
"High Road Back," June 9; page 19.
"Home to the Wars," April 21; page 21.
"Homecoming," June 16; pages 19-23.
"I Shall Go to Korea," November 3; pages 22-23.
"Ike in the West," October 20; pages 27-29.
"Ike Takes Over," August 11; page 16.
"Ike, Where Are You?," February 25; page 23.
"Ike's Answer," January 14; page 15.
"Ike's Faith," August 18; pages 12-13.
"Ike's Fourth Week," July 7; pages 13-14.
"Ike's Second Week," June 23; pages 15-17.
"Ike's Third Week," June 30; pages 15-16.
"In Business," December 29; page 10.

"Just the Beginning," September 1; page 10.
"Korean Trip," December 15; pages 15-16.
"Man of Experience," November 3; pages 23-27.
"Mutual Appreciation," September 29; page 13.
"New Age for an Old Continent," February 4; page 16.
"Next President's Health," October 13; page 65.
"On to Washington," November 24; pages 19-20.
"Orderly Transfer," November 17; pages 21-22.
"Original Ike," December 1; page 54.
"Packed and Ready," December 8; pages 19-20.
"Really Rolling," January 21; pages 17-18.
"Republicans," June 30; pages 13-17.
"Setting the Course," December 1; pages 9-10.
"Still Uphill," June 16; page 19.
"Strain of Waiting," January 7; pages 12-13.
"Techniques and Tactics," March 24; pages 19-20.
"To Be Done: Homework," July 28; page 13.
"Trial By Press Conference," June 16; page 53.
"Wardrobe Problems," August 25; page 12.
"We've Got Him," November 26; page 24.
"Will of the People," November 10; pages 21-22.
"With Renewed Confidence," December 22; pages 9-10.
"Word From the Midwest," April 14; page 23.

1953

"At the Commodore," January 12; pages 16-17.
"Correspondent's View," November 30; page 52 et seq.
"Crackdown," December 14; page 26.
"First Month," March 2; pages 12-13.
"Hope and Hoppers," January 5; page 10.

"Man of the Hour," November 12; page 17.

"Meet Your Problems," June 18; page 23.

"Midwestward Ho," October 8; pages 19-21.

"Older Wisdom," March 12; page 19.

"Poll's Point," February 20; page 15.

"Precaution for Ike," March 12; page 46.

"President's Plans," May 28; page 17.

"President's Task," March 5; page 17.

"Press and the President," January 23; page 69.

"Renewal of Leadership," March 19; page 21.

"Rising Barometer," October 22; page 21.

"Rising Tide," October 29; page 15.

"Rustle in Bug Tussle," October 1; page 24.

"Who's the Genius?," May 21; pages 21-22.

"Zestful Leader," September 3; pages 9-10.

1957

"Common Cold and 'Copters," March 4; page 21.

"Dark Valley," October 7; page 70 *et seq.*

"Decision at Gettysburg," December 9; page 19 *et seq.*

"Fretfull Fall, President Eisenhower's Popularity Rating," November 11; page 24.

"Ike's Ebb?," July 29; page 11 *et seq.*

"Meaning of Little Rock," October 7; page 21.

"Occlusion," December 9; pages 20-21.

"Patient: The President," December 9; pages 51-52.

"Quick, Hard and Decisive," October 7; pages 21-25.

"Republican Split," May 20; pages 26-27.

"Second Inaugural," January 28; page 17.

"That Old Magic," December 30; pages 20-22.

"Up From the Bungle," December 9; pages 57-58.

"What Next? As the Press Sees It," December 9; page 22.

1958

"Leadership Issue," October 13; page 19.

"New Leadership," June 20; page 11.

"Vacation Time," September 8; page 13.

"Westward Bound," November 17; page 21.

1959

"American Image," December 21; pages 9-12.

"Battle Orders," December 14; page 44.

"Brouhaha in the Hagertorium," September 14; pages 53-54.

"Come Rain, Come Shine," December 14; pages 12-14.

"Friendly Ike: A Man of Few Friends," February 16; page 20.

"Journey's Beginning," December 7; pages 19-20.

"Mission Accomplished," September 14; pages 21-23.

"Pages of History," December 28; pages 9-10.

"Playing the Ace," November 16; pages 28-29.

"Same Ike," August 24; pages 11-12.

"Side Effects," September 14; pages 31-32.

"Success and Responsibility," September 14; page 21.

"Success for an Idea," December 28; page 9.

"Tearing Down to Build Up," May 4; page 32 *et seq.*

"This Is What I Want to Do," September 7; pages 6-10.

"Waiting for Ike," August 31; page 20.

1960

"Benvindo, Eekee!," March 7; pages 12-13.

"Circles on the New Calendar," January 4; page 11.

"Far Places and Close Principles," January 18; page 14.

"Great Joy," January 18; page 34.

"Home Again," July 4; pages 9-10.

"Man of the Year," January 4; pages 11-16.

"On to Tokyo," June 20; pages 9-10.

"On With the Trip," June 27; pages 9-10.

"Operation *Amigo,*" March 14; pages 22-23.

1961

"About the Battle," September 22; page 26.

"Back to the Hustings," November 3; page 16.

"Ike's Helpers," June 6; page 44 *et seq.*

"Ike's Line on Labor," November 14, page 100 *et seq.*

"Ike's New Battle," June 6; pages 11-13.

"Ike's Plan: Use Law Less, and Use Bargaining More," September 26; page 66 *et seq.*

"Is '52 Another 1940," February 29; pages 14-15.

"Men of Power and Politics in 1952; Truman and Vinson, Eisenhower and Taft, Churchill, Stalin and Mao Tse-Tung," January 4; page 38 *et seq.*

"Next President: A Rich Man," October 10; pages 14-16 *et seq.*

"Russia Will Do the Guessing Now," December 19; pages 11-14.

"Squeeze on Eisenhower," April 4; pages 18-20.

"Strings on Eisenhower: How He Can Campaign," February 22; page 16.

"Taft Makes It a Battle," April 11; pages 18-20.

"Truman to Ike—Troubles of Shift," November 21; pages 13-15.

"What Eisenhower Will Do," November 14; pages 13-16 *et seq.*

"What Ike Can Do About Korea," December 5; pages 11-15.

"What Ike Carried Away From Korea," December 12; pages 36-38.

"What Ike Would Be Like," January 18; pages 11-13.

"What Won for Ike," November 14; pages 18-22.

"While Ike Waits, Taft Claims Victory," May 23; pages 29-30 *et seq.*

"Who Will Be Elected—Meaning of the Polls," October 31; page 11-14.

"Who's on Ike's First Team," September 26; page 20 *et seq.*

"With Candidates: A Size-Up," October 17; pages 30-33.

1953

"Adam's Ike's Right Hand, Chief of a Growing Staff," July 17; page 67 *et seq.*

"Author's Taxes: Truman, 75%; Eisenhower, 25%," March 13; page 42.

"Can Eisenhower Handle Congress," December 25; pages 15-17.

"Did Women Elect Eisenhower?," May 8; pages 45-46.

"Eisenhower's Aid Plan: Big," June 19; page 32.

"Eisenhower's Answer to Taft," June 5; page 40.

"Eisenhower's First 90 Days," April 24; pages 15-17.

"Eisenhower's Ideas on Strikes," March 6; pages 84-89.

"Eisenhower's Plan for Korea," March 13; pages 23-24.

"First Whistle Stop for '54," May 15; pages 69-72.

"Great Conspiracy: Communism Inside U.S.," August 28; pages 11-15.

"How Eisenhower Looks at His Job," April 3; pages 22-23.

"How Eisenhower Will Woo Congress," November 20; pages 34-36.

"How Ike Fared With Congress," August 7; pages 22-23.

"How Ike Works—And How Much," October 9; pages 48-50.

"How the Vote Looks to Ike," November 13; page 32.

"Ike and Mamie in the White House," January 23; page 17 *et seq.*

"Ike and Winnie—Cordial but Tense," December 11; pages 73-76.

"Ike and Winston Take Over," May 29; pages 25-26.

"Ike's Anti-Slump Setup: Ready to Use, if Needed," June 12; pages 71-73.

"Ike's Dinners Have a Purpose," July 3; pages 26-27.

"Ike's First Six Months," July 17; pages 22-24.

"Ike's Plan: Food to Win Friends," July 10; page 19.

"Ike's Own Money Troubles," September 25; pages 28-29.

"Ike's Plan for Old People," November 20; pages 98-100.

"Is Ike to Be Underpaid?," January 16; page 29.

"Men Who Lead Congress," June 12; page 64 *et seq.*

"Politics—Hard to Live With and Hard to Live Without," November 6; page 68 *et seq.*

"Real Power," January 23, pages 58-60.

"Ike's Life As a Patient," October 14; page 32.

"Ike's Plan to Avoid a War," May 6; pages 21-23.

"Is U. S. Getting Ready to Bypass Chiang Kai-Shek?," May 6; pages 82-86.

"It's Christmas All the Time for U. S. Presidents," December 16; pages 39-41.

"Memo From Denver," October 7; page 104 *et seq.*

"Minor Ailment, but—Eisenhower Stays Healthy," March 18; page 36.

"More Men Who Came to Dinner," April 8; pages 26-28.

"President's Progress—Denver to Washington to Gettysburg," November 18; page 14.

"Rocking Chair Routine: It Will Be New, Strange," October 7; pages 64-65.

"Will Ike Be a Reluctant Candidate?," January 21; page 39.

"Way Ike Is Remaking His Party," September 16; pages 26-27.

"Way Ike Makes Friends," March 18; pages 34-35.

"Week End With Farmer Ike," April 8; pages 30-31.

"What Eisenhower Wants for Everybody in 1955," January 21; pages 28-29.

"What Eisenhower's Friends Say; He Will Think It His Duty to Accept," June 17; pages 22-23.

"What Goes On at Ike's Dinners," February 4; pages 34-41.

"What Trial Heats Show for '56," March 11; pages 30-32.

"When Ike and Zhukov Write," May 6; page 24.

"When Ike Must Decide," December 30; pages 19-21.

"When Ike's Heart Faltered; Hour by Hour With Newsmen," October 7; pages 66-68 *et seq.*

"When Washington Moves to Gettysburg," October 14; pages 22-24.

"White House Moves to Gettysburg," November 25; pages 58-61.

"Why Ike Went Campaigning," July 8; page 21.

"Why Ike Will Run Again," June 17; pages 19-21.

"Why Republicans Like Ike," November 25; pages 29-31.

"Why the Vice-Presidency Is in the Spotlight," September 9; page 48 *et seq.*

"Will Ike Choose Surgery? Doctors Differ on It," October 21; page 26.

"Will Ike's Brother Stop Nixon?," October 28; pages 21-24.

1956

"Adlai and Ike—What They're Really Like," August 31; pages 36-38.

"Can Ike Crack South Again?," September 7; pages 28-29.

"Dinner That May Go Down in History," March 16; page 76.

"Eisenhower, Nixon—Many New Problems," November 16; page 60.

"Eisenhower or Stevenson, Next President a Wealthy Man," October 26; page 50 *et seq.*

"Eisenhower Story," November 2; page 62 *et seq.*

"Has Eisenhower Changed?," June 1; pages 38-40 *et seq.*

"Here's How Ike Broke the News," March 9; pages 46-49.

"Here's the Latest From Ike and His Doctors," February 24; page 29.

"History Makers of '56," January 6; pages 57-59.

"How Eisenhower Plans to Win," July 20; pages 31-34.

"How Ike and His Aides Work Out a Speech," October 5; pages 84-87.

"How Ike Makes the Big Decisions," April 20; pages 30-32.

"How Ike's Illness Changes Things," June 15; pages 27-29.

"How Many Shifting to or From Ike?," October 12; pages 35-36.

"If Ike Doesn't Run—," February 24; pages 27-28.

"Ike—A Campaigner With His Dander Up," August 24; pages 28-30.

"Ike's Decision Depends on Word From Old Friend," January 20; pages 61-63.

"Ike's Future," June 22; pages 23-25.

"Ike's New Plan for a Healthier U.S.," February 3; page 49.

"It Looks Like Ike, Unless There's a

"President's Health," August 15; page 21.

"Showing Congress Who's Boss," April 25; pages 46-49.

"Sports Ike Likes," October 24; page 16.

"Story of a Decision," July 25; pages 68-70.

"Truman Vs. Eisenhower—Again," December 19; page 8.

1959

"After Europe, Ike Now Primed for Khrushchev," September 14; pages 33-34.

"Big Change at the White House," May 4; pages 46-47 et seq.

"Crowded Calendar for the President," August 24; page 6.

"Doctor's Report on Ike: He's Fit," November 16; page 27.

"Eisenhower-Khrushchev Visits: The Argument Heats Up," September 7; pages 64-72.

"Face to Face at Last: Eisenhower and Khrushchev," September 21; pages 78-80.

"Guide to Eisenhower's Tour," December 7; pages 54-56.

"Ike's Troubles With the Allies," September 7; pages 35-38.

"In Asia—It's Ike by a Landslide," December 21; pages 33-39.

"Real Story of a Famous Feud," January 2; pages 75-78.

"Trouble All Around: Congress, Party, Staff," February 27; pages 54-57.

"Washington Mysteries: A Resignation, a Rift Denied," February 6; pages 40-41.

"What Ike's Trip to Europe Means," August 31; pages 35-37.

"What's on the President's Mind," August 3; pages 33-35.

"Who's Who on Ike's Tour," November 30; page 58.

"With Ike on His 69th Birthday," October 26; pages 86-87.

"With Ike on Tour: New Era in Diplomacy," December 14; pages 39-40.

1960

"As Eisenhower Looks to 1961," July 18; pages 63-65.

"At President Eisenhower's Elbow in South America," March 7; page 23.

"Can Ike End the Cold War," January 4; pages 38-41.

"Defending the Americas—Ike's Warning to Reds," March 7; pages 35-39.

"Ike on Tour: Why 15,000 More Miles," February 29; page 37.

"Ike: Travelingest President—What the Record Shows," March 21; pages 98-100.

"Ike Vs. Nikita: Who's Winning," March 14; pages 47-51.

"Ike's Defeat in Asia," June 27; pages 37-41.

"Ike's Era—Big Moments in 8 Historic Years," November 14; pages 48-54.

"World Peace in Our Time?," January 4; pages 74-75.

1961

"Eisenhower's Reaction to Dillon Appointment—Two Versions," January 2; page 79.

"It's to Be Five Stars Again for Ike Soon," March 13; page 14.

"Kennedy's Job for Ike," November 20; pages 25-26.

"Staff Size-Up of Two Presidents: Eisenhower and Kennedy," January 30; pages 38-39.

1962

"Ike Calls for a Change; Hits at U.S. Economic Laws," February 12; pages 23-24.

MISCELLANEOUS

1951

"Allied Council Communique on Establishment in Europe of an Integrated Force Under Centralized Control and Command," Current History, February; page 109.

"As They Were," Coronet, July; page 109.

"Battle for Better Schools Must Be Won," Parents' Magazine, April; page 40 et seq.

"Open Letter to General Eisenhower," American Mercury, December; pages 3-8.

"Top Reporters' Forum; Should Eisenhower Run for President?," United Nations World, September; pages 10-11.

1952

"American Elections," *Fortnightly*, December; pages 361-62.

"Editorial," *Twentieth Century*, June; pages 462-65.

"Eisenhower Is the Man," *United Nations World*, February; pages 14-15.

"Eisenhower's Victory; Post-Election Prospects," *World Today*, December; pages 499-504.

"How to Think About Eisenhower," *American Mercury*, May; pages 3-9.

"President Chances," *Spectator*, July 18; page 88.

"Republicans' Choice," *World Today*, August; pages 91-92.

"Views on American Education," *School Life*, December; pages 33-34.

"We Are Not for Eisenhower on June 1st," *American Mercury*, July; pages 3-5.

1953

"Half a Year of Eisenhower," *Fortune*, August; pages 91-92.

"Eisenhower in the Cartoons of the World," *United Nations World*, August; pages 22-23.

"Two Republican Parties," *United Nations World*, July; pages 5-6.

1954

"Inspiration in a Few Kind Words," *American Magazine*, October; page 12.

"Recovery From the Plague," *Harper's*, July; pages 16-18.

1955

"But What Kind of Flag? Eisenhower's Philosophy," *Fortune*, November; pages 99-100.

"Eisenhower in Excelsis," *Round Table*, September; pages 363-68.

"Pacific America: A Coalitionist President," *Round Table*, June: pages 249-54.

"President," *Economist*, October 1; page 17.

1956

"As Citizens and Farmers," *Farm Journal*, November; page 166.

"Eisenhower Era; Four Years of New

Republicanism," *Round Table*, September; pages 62-63.

"Ike's Health and Farmers," *Farm Journal*, July; page 8.

1959

"Man Not Running for Anything," *Fortune*, March; pages 87-88.

"President and the Russians," *Saturday Review*, September 19; page 22.

1961

"Inauguration Week," *Science*, January 27; pages 263-64.

IV

Books About Eisenhower And Related Matters

Adams, Sherman, *Firsthand Report*, New York: Harper & Brothers, 1961.

Alexander, Edgar, *Adenauer and the New Germany*, New York: Farrar, Straus and Cudahy, 1957.

Alexander, Holmes, *The Famous Five*, New York: The Bookmailer, 1958.

Allen, Robert Sharon, *Lucky Forward: The History of Patton's Third U. S. Army*, New York: Vanguard Press, Inc., 1947.

Baldwin, Hanson Weightman, *Great Mistakes of the War*, New York: Harper & Brothers, 1950.

———, *Power and Politics*, Claremont, California: Claremont College, 1950.

Barron, Bryton, *Inside the State Department*, New York: Comet Press Books, 1956.

———, *The Untouchable State Department*, Springfield, Virginia: Crestwood Books, 1962.

Bouscaren, Anthony T., *The Security Aspects of Immigration Work*, Milwaukee: Marquette University, 1959.

Bryant, Arthur, *Triumph in the West*, Garden City, New York: Doubleday & Company, Inc., 1959.

Buckley, William F., and Bozell, L. Brent, *McCarthy and His Enemies*, Chicago: Henry Regnery Company, 1954.

Bundy, Edgar C., *Collectivism in the Churches*, Wheaton, Illinois: The Church League of America, 1958.

Burnham, James, *The Web of Subversion,* New York: The John Day Company, 1954.

Byrnes, James Francis, *Speaking Frankly,* New York: Harper & Brothers, 1947.

Carlson, John Roy [Avedis Boghos Derounian], *The Plotters,* New York: Dutton Co., 1946.

——, *Undercover,* New York: Dutton Co., 1943.

Chamberlin, William Henry, *America's Second Crusade,* Chicago: Henry Regnery Company, 1950.

Childs, Marquis William, *Eisenhower: Captive Hero,* New York: Harcourt, Brace and World, Inc., 1958.

Churchill, Winston, *Memoirs of the Second World War,* Boston: Houghton Mifflin Company, 1959.

——, *The Second World War,* six volumes, Boston: Houghton Mifflin Company, 1948-1953.

Ciechanowski, Jan, *Defeat in Victory,* Garden City, New York: Doubleday & Company, Inc., 1947.

Cooper, Kent, *The Right to Know,* New York: Farrar, Straus and Cudahy, Inc., 1956.

Davis, Kenneth Sydney, *Soldier of Democracy,* Garden City, New York: Doubleday & Company, Inc., 1945.

Deane, John R., *The Strange Alliance,* New York: Viking Press, 1947.

De Toledano, Ralph, *Spies, Dupes, and Diplomats,* New York: Duel, Sloan and Pearce, 1952.

Doenitz, Karl, *Ten Years and Twenty Days,* Cleveland: World Publishing Co., 1959.

Dies, Martin, *The Trojan Horse in America,* New York: Dodd, Mead & Company, 1940.

Ehrman, John, *Grand Strategy,* London: H. M. Stationery Office, 1956.

Eisenhower, Dwight David, *Eisenhower Speaks,* selected and edited by Rudolph L. Treuenfels, New York: Farrar, Straus & Company, 1948.

——, *Peace With Justice,* New York: Columbia University Press, 1961.

——, *What Eisenhower Thinks,* edited and interpreted by Allan Taylor, New York: Thomas Y. Crowell Company, 1952.

Flynn, John T., *The Roosevelt Myth,* revised edition, New York: The Devin-Adair Company, 1956.

Forrestal, James, *The Forrestal Diaries,* edited by Walter Millis, New York: Viking Press, 1951.

Glaser, Kurt, *Czecho-Slovakia: A Critical History,* Caldwell, Idaho: The Caxton Printers, Ltd., 1961.

Grenfell, Russell, *Unconditional Hatred,* New York: The Devin-Adair Company, 1958.

Hatch, Alden, *General Ike,* New York: Henry Holt & Company, 1944.

Heinsohn, A. G., Jr., *One Man's Fight for Freedom,* Caldwell, Idaho: The Caxton Printers, Ltd., 1957.

Hull, Cordell, *Memoirs of Cordell Hull,* New York: The Macmillan Company, 1948.

Hunt, Frazier, *The Untold Story of Douglas MacArthur,* New York: The Devin-Adair Company, 1954.

Larson, Arthur, *A Republican Looks at His Party,* New York: Harper & Brothers, 1956.

Lord, Walter, *The Day of Infamy,* New York: Henry Holt & Company, 1957.

Kornfeder, Joseph Z., *Brainwashing and Senator McCarthy,* New York: The Alliance, Inc., 1954.

Lokos, Lionel, *Who Promoted Peress?,* New York: The Bookmailer, Inc., 1961.

Manly, Chesly, *The Twenty Year Revolution,* Chicago: Henry Regnery Company, 1954.

——, *The UN Record,* Chicago: Henry Regnery Company, 1955.

Morris, Robert, *No Wonder We Are Losing,* New York: The Bookmailer, 1958.

Martin, David, *Ally Betrayed,* New York: Prentice-Hall, Inc., 1946.

McCann, Kevin, *Man From Abilene,* Garden City, New York: Doubleday & Company, 1952.

McKeogh, Michael J., and Lockridge, Richard, *Sergeant Mickey and General Ike,* New York: G. P. Putnam's Sons, 1946.

Miller, Francis Trevelyan, *Eisenhower:*

Man and Soldier, Philadelphia: John C. Winston Co., 1944.

Moorehead, Alan, Montgomery, New York: Coward-McCann, Inc., 1946.

Patton, George Smith, War As I Knew It, Boston: Houghton Mifflin Company, 1947.

Pridonoff, Eric L., Tito's Yugoslavia, Washington, D. C.: Public Affairs Press, 1955.

Roosevelt, Elliott, As He Saw It, New York: Duell, Sloan & Pearce, Inc., 1946.

Root, E. Merrill, Collectivism on the Campus, New York: The Devin-Adair Company, 1961.

Rosamond, Robert, Crusade for Peace, Philadelphia: Lexington Publishing Co., 1962.

Smith, Merriman, Meet Mister President, New York: Harper & Brothers, 1955.

————, President's Odyssey, New York: Harper & Brothers, 1961.

Stripling, Robert E., and Considine, Bob, The Red Plot Against America, Drexel Hill, Pennsylvania: Bell Publishing Company, 1949.

Togo, Shigenroi, The Cause of Japan, New York: Simon and Schuster, Inc., 1956.

Truman, Harry S., Memoirs of Harry S. Truman, Garden City, New York: Doubleday & Company, 1955.

Utley, Freda, The China Story, Chicago: Henry Regnery Company, 1951.

Veale, F. J. P., Advance to Barbarism, Appleton, Wisconsin: C. C. Nelson Publishing Company, 1953.

————, War Crimes Discreetly Veiled, New York: The Devin-Adair Company, 1959.

Watts, Vernon Orval, The United Nations, Los Angeles: The Foundation for Social Research, 1955.

Weyl, Nathaniel, Red Star Over Cuba, New York: The Devin-Adair Company, 1960.

Whitney, R. M., Reds in America, New York: The Beckwith Press, Inc., 1924.

Willoughby, Charles A., Shanghai Conspiracy, New York: E. P. Dutton & Company, Inc., 1952.

Wittmer, Felix, The Yalta Betrayal, Caldwell, Idaho: The Caxton Printers, Ltd., 1953.

Workman, William D., Jr., The Case for the South, New York: The Devin-Adair Company, 1960.

A Correction Corrected

This note has been added in the fourth printing. It refers to the passage at the top of Page 28, concerning the raping orgy in the Stuttgart subway.

In the July 3, 1963 issue of *Tocsin,* published by Charles Fox, this passage was quoted under the heading *Correction Please!* — which is the title of a regular monthly feature in the magazine, *American Opinion,* edited by myself. The "correction" which *Tocsin* then offered was: "Only trouble is, Stuttgart has no subway."

We are afraid that Mr. Fox's unfortunate malice towards this writer—which he has made visible in numerous other ways — greatly exceeded his knowledge. He seems to be utterly unaware that the meaning of "underground electric railway," which he obviously ascribes to the word "subway," and which he apparently considers to be the *only* meaning of the word, is a provincialism which has not yet even been accepted by dictionaries of English anywhere except in the United States.

In Stuttgart itself, or anywhere in Europe among English-speaking people who also know German, the word "subway" would immediately be recognized as meaning *Unterführung,* but if used as a translation of *Untergrundbahn,* would only cause puzzlement and confusion. And even in the United States, as recently as when the Webster's New Collegiate Dictionary which I am now using was published (in 1958), the word "subway," for the meaning that Mr. Fox has in mind, was still considered as an "Americanism," rather than as a fully acceptable term. That dictionary defines "subway" as follows: "An underground way or passage; esp.: (a) A passage under a street, for pedestrians, or for the running of water or gas mains, telephone wires, etc. (b) *U. S.* An underground electric railway."

Yes, Stuttgart does have a subway, Mr. Fox. And the tragic horror which we record did take place as described.

RW

FOOTNOTES

Page: Note

1:1 The original was undated.

1:2 Each of the original copies was numbered.

2:1 This information was given me in writing and in detail many years ago, by a responsible person, with the understanding that his name would not be used.

2:2 Only one error of fact was ever found in this manuscript by the considerable number of well informed people who wrote me after reading it. But several different correspondents called my attention to that error, which occurs on Page 86. Although insignificant, it has been noted and corrected in this edition.

2:3 Each of the original copies was individually signed.

Introduction

3:1 See Medford Evans, *The Secret War For The A-Bomb* (Chicago: Regnery, 1954); and, by the same author, "Are Soviet A-Bombs Russian?," *The Freeman*, January 12, 1953, pages 266-268.

3:2 *New York Times*, March 27, 1955.

4:1 For an up-to-date appraisal of this situation, see *The Dan Smoot Report*, January 14, 1963.

4:2 Magsaysay would be the victim of one of those remarkable "accidents" which seem to occur to so many staunch and effective anti-Communists: "Just before his death in a plane crash President Ramon Magsaysay of the Philippines said to Walker Stone of the Scripps-Howard newspapers: 'They're going to try to bump me off in this campaign. They know they can't win if I live.' Whether this adds to the probability that the Magsaysay plane was sabotaged is questionable; but it would be instructive to know who 'they' are." *National Review*, March 30, 1957, page 295.

4:3 Kotelawala was defeated in April 1956 by the People's United Front co-

Page: Note

alition and Communists were immediately placed in the cabinet — the beginning of the end for Ceylon.

4:4 "Since our Central Intelligence Agency clandestinely helped Gamal Abdel Nasser to power, he has acted as a front runner for Khrushchev in the Arab World and in Africa. Since Nasser's ascendancy to power, with our help, Khrushchev has become a power in the Middle East." Robert Morris in *The Wanderer*, December 6, 1962. Doctor Morris, in 1953, was Chief Counsel of the Senate Internal Security Subcommittee.

4:5 And at that time the Christian Democrat Party was still a bulwark rather than merely a shell of anti-Communist strength.

4:6 For a first-hand account of these conditions, see Joseph Scholmer, *Vorkuta* (New York: Holt, 1954); and, John Noble, *I Was A Slave In Russia* (New York: Devin-Adair, 1958).

6:1 It is largely from the theme of this sentence that the original manuscript came to be dubbed *The Politician*.

Chapter One

8:1 Dwight D. Eisenhower, *Crusade In Europe* (Garden City: Permabooks, 1952 [originally published by Doubleday in 1948]), page 24.

9:1 *Ibid.*, page 106.

9:2 *Ibid.*, pages 23, 24, 27, 28, 31-37, 47, 68, and 235-237. See, also, John Gunther, *Eisenhower: The Man And The Symbol* (New York: Harper, 1951), page 61, where Mr. Gunther observes: "There is no record quite like this [Eisenhower's rise in rank] in the American Army."

10:1 Alanbrooke, *Notes On My Life* (unpublished Ms.), Vol. VII, pages 572-573, as quoted by Arthur Bryant, *The Turn Of The Tide* (Garden City:

Doubleday, 1957), pages 430-431 n.

10:2 Richard L. Stokes, "Eisenhower As A Military Man," *Human Events*, June 22, 1957, page 3.

11:1 Bryant, *The Turn Of The Tide*, pages 454-455.

Chapter Two

13:1 The antecedents of Pearl Harbor have been thoroughly exposed by a long list of scholars beginning with John T. Flynn's pioneering effort, *The Final Secret Of Pearl Harbor* (a pamphlet published by the author in 1945). See, also, George Morgenstern, *Pearl Harbor* (New York: Devin-Adair, 1947); Russell Grenfell, *Main Fleet To Singapore* (New York: Macmillan, 1952); Charles C. Tansill, *Back Door To War* (Chicago: Regnery, 1951); Charles A. Beard, *President Roosevelt And The Coming Of The War, 1941* (New Haven: Yale, 1948); Frederic R. Sanborn, *Design For War: A Study Of Secret Power Politics, 1937-1941* (New York: Devin-Adair, 1951); Harry Elmer Barnes and others, *Perpetual War For Perpetual Peace* (Caldwell: Caxton, 1953); and, Anthony Kubek, *Communism At Pearl Harbor* (pamphlet, Dallas: Teacher, 1962).

For first-hand accounts by participants in the events at Pearl Harbor, see Husband E. Kimmel, *Admiral Kimmel's Story* (Chicago: Regnery, 1955); R. A. Theobald, *The Final Secret Of Pearl Harbor* (New York: Devin-Adair, 1954); and, Toshikazu Kase, *Journey To The "Missouri"* (New Haven: Yale, 1950).

14:1 One of the leading court historians explained Roosevelt's mendacity as follows: "Franklin Roosevelt repeatedly deceived the American people during the period before Pearl Harbor . . . . He was faced with a terrible dilemma. If he let the people slumber in a fog of isolation, they might well fall prey to Hitler. If he came out unequivocally for intervention, he would be defeated in 1940, or shelved for a candidate more willing to let the masses enjoy their fool's paradise. If he was going to induce the people to move at all, he would have to trick them into acting for their best interests, or what he conceived to be their best interests. He was like the physician who must tell the patient lies for the patient's own good. . . .

"The country was overwhelmingly noninterventionist to the day of Pearl Harbor, and an overt attempt to lead the people into war would have resulted in certain failure and an almost certain ousting of Roosevelt in 1940, with a consequent defeat for his ultimate aims." Thomas A. Bailey, *The Man In The Street* (New York: Macmillan, 1948), pages 11-12.

See, also, George N. Crocker, *Roosevelt's Road To Russia* (Chicago: Regnery, 1956), pages 1, 17-18, and 37; Beard, *President Roosevelt And The Coming Of The War*, pages 56 and 135; and, Theobald, *The Final Secret Of Pearl Harbor*, pages 2-8.

14:2 For example, see Forrest Davis and Ernest K. Lindley, *How War Came* (New York: Simon & Schuster, 1942).

14:3 Winston S. Churchill, *The Grand Alliance* (Boston: Houghton-Mifflin, 1950), page 705; and, Robert E. Sherwood, *Roosevelt And Hopkins* (New York: Harper, 1948), pages 445-446.

14:4 Alanbrooke, *Diaries, 1939-1943* (unpublished Ms.), as quoted in Bryant, *The Turn Of The Tide*, pages 288-289.

15:1 For the single most important presentation of this evidence, see Joseph R. McCarthy, *America's Retreat From Victory* (New York: Devin-Adair, 1952).

15:2 Frederick C. Painton, "Vignettes Of America's No. 1 Soldier," *Reader's Digest*, January 1944, page 71.

16:1 Martin Dies, "They Tried To Get Me, Too," *U.S. News & World Report*, August 20, 1954, page 56 *et seq.* See, also, Robert E. Stripling, *The Red Plot Against America* (Drexel Hill, Pa.: Bell, 1949), Chapter 3. Mr. Stripling was the chief investigator for the House Committee on Un-American Activities.

16:2 John J. O'Connor, former Chairman of the House Rules Committee, recalled: ". . . During the years 1933-39, when I often visited the White House, as a Member of Congress, and later as Chairman of the Rules Committee, I saw Browder there on several occasions. In fact, during the President's 'purge' of 1938, Browder directed purge operations from the White House, from which he telephoned instructions, from time to time." O'Connor further stated that Browder "could enter the White House, at anytime, and through any door and without any invitation." *Letter from O'Connor to Howard Rushmore,* September 19, 1949, as printed in Subcommittee on Immigration and Naturalization of the Senate Judiciary Committee, Hearings: "Communist Activities Among Aliens And National Groups," September 7-29, 1949, (Part 2), page 800.

The influence of Browder at the White House reached far beyond domestic affairs. In May 1942 Browder was serving a prison sentence after being convicted for fraudulent use of American passports. Roosevelt commuted the sentence and, according to a White House statement, the commutation was granted "to promote American unity." *New York Times,* May 17, 1942.

But a few months later Browder was *inside the White House* again: "On October 12, 1942, in the midst of Stalin's golden harvest of influencing American opinion, the Communist leader Earl Browder went on a visit to Washington. It was a momentous trip, for Browder went there, in effect, as the ambassador of the Chinese Communists. Later, when his mission had been successfully completed, he described what had occurred as equivalent to 'an agreement among nations.' He had won the first round in what was to lead to the victory of Red China.

"In Washington Browder, by personal and specific invitation, had a conference with Sumner Welles, then Under Secretary of State. He was accompanied by Robert Minor, Assistant Secretary of the Communist Party, and was introduced to Mr. Welles by Lauchlin Currie, Administrative Assistant to President Roosevelt. Currie has been mentioned prominently by Elizabeth Bentley as a friend and co-worker of the Soviet underground infiltration in Washington.

"At this conference Mr. Welles assured Browder that the government of the United States 'desires Chinese unity and deprecates civil strife in China.' He stated that the United States would not favor Chiang Kai-shek against the Chinese Communists in order to aid 'unity' in China. This decision, promptly communicated to the Chinese Communists, gave them a terrific boost." Louis F. Budenz, *The Cry Is Peace* (Chicago: Regnery, 1952), pages 26-27.

16:3 Dies, "They Tried To Get Me, Too," *U.S. News & World Report,* August 20, 1954, page 56 *et seq.*

17:1 Churchill, *The Grand Alliance,* page 602; Sherwood, *Roosevelt And Hopkins,* pages 1, 4-5, and 101; and, McCarthy, *America's Retreat From Victory,* Chapters 2-4.

17:2 See George Racey Jordan, *From Major Jordan's Diaries* (New York: Harcourt & Brace, 1952).

17:3 Alanbrooke, *Notes On My Life,* VII, pages 589-590, as quoted in Bryant, *The Turn Of The Tide,* pages 430-431.

17:4 Willmoore Kendall saw the rise to prominence of George Marshall and Eisenhower as part of a pattern engineered by the Liberal Establishment — a pattern which would include the appointments of Charles E. Whittaker and William J. Brennan to the Supreme Court, and Nathan Pusey and Robert F. Goheen to the presidencies, respectively, of Harvard and Princeton. "New Fashions In Supreme Court Justices And Ivy League Presidents," *National Review,* October 12, 1957, page 327.

Chapter Three

19:1 See George Johnson, *Eisenhower* (Derby, Conn.: Monarch, 1962), page 64.

19:2 See Bryant, *The Turn Of The Tide*, pages 277 and 280; and, Sherwood, *Roosevelt And Hopkins*, pages 445-446.

19:3 See Bryant, *Op. cit.*, page 278; and, Winston S. Churchill, *The Hinge Of Fate* (Boston: Houghton-Mifflin, 1950), pages 314-315.

20:1 Bryant, *Op. cit.*, page 285.

20:2 Eisenhower, *Crusade In Europe*, page 91.

20:3 The Hollywood Democratic Committee was merely a new version of the Motion Picture Democratic Committee which "was a proven Communist-controlled 'front.'" It was set up in the Spring of 1938 and went out of existence about one year after the signing of the Stalin-Hitler pact on August 23, 1939. During the lifetime of the organization it followed the Communist line faithfully . . . (and) when the Communist Party line changed from isolation to pro-war because of the attack on Soviet Russia by Hitler, the Motion Picture Democratic Committee was revived under a slightly different name. This time it was called the Hollywood Democratic Committee. This committee, like its predecessor the MPDC, followed the Communist Party line. . . .

"On May 24, 1945, there was advance notice that the Communist Party line in the United States would again undergo a change. This notice was in the form of a letter from a leading French Communist, Jacques Duclos. This letter was published everywhere in the official Communist press, and it constituted a criticism of the past 'line' and demanded a change back to the program of Marx and Lenin which had been abandoned during the war. On June 6, 1945, the Hollywood Democratic Committee became the Hollywood Independent Citizen's Committee of the Arts, Sciences and Professions." *Red Fascism* (Compiled from State and Federal records by Jack B. Tenney, and published in 1947 by the Federal Printing Company of Los Angeles), pages 290-291.

21:1 Although the Germans repeatedly tried to surrender to the Americans and British, Eisenhower always turned them down because he claimed they were trying to create a rift among the Allies. Here are Eisenhower's own words on the subject:

"Their sole desire was to avoid the necessity of surrendering to the Russians. . . . It was at once obvious that the Germans were merely playing for time so that meanwhile they could evacuate the largest possible number of soldiers and civilians from the Russian front to behind our lines. They persisted even now in attempting to surrender the Western Front separately, going so far as to say that, whatever my answer might be, they intended to order their armies to cease fire upon the Anglo-Americans. They asked for an adjournment for 48 hours before signing the final surrender, allegedly to enable them to get the necessary orders to their outlying units, but actually, it was clear, only to gain further respite for the purpose above mentioned. They were informed that unless they agreed to my terms forthwith I would break off all negotiations and *seal my front, preventing by force if necessary, any further westward movement of German soldiers and civilians.*" (Italics added.) Dwight D. Eisenhower, *Eisenhower's Own Story Of The War* (New York: Arco, 1946), page 119.

22:1 "In his book, *Das Ende an der Elbe*, Juergen Thornwald [a German historian] reports the following events: 'On May 4, 1945, General Eisenhower radioed to Moscow that the Third Army stood ready to advance to the Elbe and Moldau rivers and that American forces were preparing to occupy the entire western part of Czechoslovakia. On the very same day, General Antonov, Stalin's chief of staff, hurriedly requested the American mission in Moscow to instruct Eisenhower not to advance beyond the Karlsbad-Pilsen line, and to avoid a melee of American and Russian troops. The American units could have advanced more than 100 miles, and certainly to Prague and the Elbe River, without encountering large numbers of Russians. Yet Eisenhower at once complied with Antonov's request, whose true purpose he failed to comprehend [sic].'

"Thornwald's knowledge of the Russo-American messages apparently was based on radio intelligence which was available to the German Fuehrer at the moment, Admiral Karl Doenitz. It is thus established that (a) there was no Washington-Moscow governmental agreement concerning the seizure of Prague; (b) the American Army was able to seize the Czech capital; (c) the leading American Generals [with Patton's Third Army] wanted to take the city; and (d) the fateful decision to abandon Prague was made by General Eisenhower himself and by nobody else." Peter Lawrence, "Eisenhower Loses Prague," *The Freeman*, September 10, 1951, page 780.

See, also, Winston Churchill, *Triumph And Tragedy* (Boston: Houghton-Mifflin, 1953), pages 457-458 and 463; Bernard Law Montgomery, *The Memoirs Of Field Marshal Montgomery* (Cleveland: World, 1958), pages 296-297; George Sokolsky, *Boston Evening American*, June 28, 1952; and, Albert L. Warner, "Our Secret Deal Over Germany," *Saturday Evening Post*, August 2, 1952, page 30 *et seq*.

22:2 Eisenhower, *Crusade In Europe*, page 437.

22:3 *Ibid.*, pages 437-440.

23:1 Frank Howley, *Berlin Command* (New York: Putnam, 1950), pages 65-66.

23:2 Austin J. App in Elizabeth Lutz, *German Women In Russian Hands* (a pamphlet, published in Philadelphia by Boniface Press, 1950), page 46.

23:3 See Eisenhower, *Crusade In Europe*, page 510. When General Bor-Komorowski, the great Polish hero, called on Eisenhower after the war, he found that Eisenhower had one — and only one — autographed photo on his desk — Stalin's. *Human Events*, June 11, 1951, page 1.

Eisenhower had been rewarded by the

Soviets earlier. In Washington, on April 11, 1944, Secretary of State Cordell Hull, on behalf of Eisenhower, accepted from Soviet Ambassador Andrei Gromyko the Order of Suvorov of the First Degree — the highest honor which can be bestowed by the Soviet Government. *New York Times*, April 12, 1944.

But perhaps the most satisfying award Eisenhower was to receive from the Soviets was on June 10, 1945 in Frankfort when Marshal Zhukov presented Eisenhower with the Order of Victory, which has been appraised as being worth $100,000. See Harry C. Butcher, *My Three Years With Eisenhower* (New York: Simon & Schuster, 1946), page 860.

24:1 The Berlin story from 1943 to 1961 has been ably summarized in *The Dan Smoot Report*, August 7 and 14, 1961.

24:2 See Lucius D. Clay, *Decision In Germany* (New York: Doubleday, 1950), pages 25-26.

25:1 Bill Cunningham in his column, *Boston Herald*, October 4, 1951.

25:2 *Ibid.*, October 14, 1951. Mr. McCloy's incredulity is a little surprising since, seven years before this, when he learned of the post war plans for Germany, he recognized them as calling "for the conscious destruction of the economy in Germany and the encouragement of a state of impoverishment and disorder." *The Forrestal Diaries*, edited by Walter Millis, (New York: Viking, 1951), page 11.

25:3 McCloy could have profited by his own mistakes. As Assistant Secretary of War, he had personally played an important role in allowing Communists to infiltrate the Pentagon during World War II. See Major Hamilton Long's booklet, *America's Tragedy — Today* (Privately published, 1950). Also, see McCloy's testimony before the House Military Affairs Committee, February 27, 1945.

26:1 Eisenhower, *Crusade In Europe*, page 323.

26:2 Fred Smith, "The Rise And Fall Of The Morgenthau Plan," *United Nations World*, March 1947, pages 32-37.

27:1 The Germans, despite all that Forrestal could do, did not get off lightly by any means. The modified version of the Morgenthau plan was cruel to say the least. See Freda Utley, *The High Cost Of Vengeance* (Chicago: Regnery, 1949).

27:2 Effective and scholarly critiques of the Nuremberg trials are Montgomery Belgion, *Victor's Justice* (Chicago: Regnery, 1949); Lord Maurice Hankey, *Politics: Trials And Errors* (Chicago: Regnery, 1950); and, F. J. P. Veale, *Advance To Barbarism* (Appleton: C. C. Nelson, 1953).

27:3 Eisenhower, *Crusade In Europe*, page 323.

28:1 Karl H. Von Wiegand, *San Francisco Examiner*, July 17, 1949.

The appearance of French Negro soldiers in 1945 must certainly have awakened the memories of the German people. After World War I "France quartered a considerable number of her Negro colonial troops in private residences in parts of the Rhine territory. Their insulting and at times brutal conduct towards the German women was regarded as an indication that France would go to extreme lengths to humiliate Germany. In December 1921, General Henry T. Allen sent to Secretary Hughes a complaint that had been filed with the High Commission by a delegation of German working men: 'We fear to leave our homes and go to work leaving our wives and daughters in our houses with these men. This question troubles us more than houses and more food.'" Tansill, *Back Door To War*, page 22.

28:2 *New York Times*, October 6, 1946.

28:3 *Time Magazine*, September 22, 1947, page 42.

28:4 On the Katyn Forest story, see Select Committee To Conduct An Investigation Of The Facts, Evidence, and Circumstances Of The Katyn Forest Massacre, Hearings: Parts 1-7, October 11, 1951-November 14, 1952, and Report of December 22, 1952; Joseph Mackiewicz, *The Katyn Wood Murders* (London: Hollis & Carter, 1951); F. J. P. Veale, *War Crimes Discreetly Veiled* (New York: Devin-Adair, 1959), Chapter 2; J. K. Zawodny, *Death In The Forest* (South Bend: University of Notre Dame Press, 1963).

The importance to the Russians of concealing the truth was evident to the veteran journalist William L. White when he visited the Soviet Union in 1944: "Moscow correspondents say the most severe political censorship was imposed on their stories of the Katyn Forest Massacre. . . ." William L. White, *Report On The Russians* (New York: Harcourt, 1945), page 127.

Chapter Four

31:1 Julius Epstein uncovered the existence of a classified document in the Historical Records Section of the Army in Alexandria, Virginia. The document bears the file number 383.7-14.1 and is titled: *Forcible Repatriation of Displaced Soviet Citizens — Operation Keelhaul*. "How We Served As Partners In A Purge," *American Legion Magazine*, December 1954, pages 14-15; 43-45.

32:1 General Almond's testimony appears in Senate Internal Security Subcommittee (cited hereafter as S.I.S.S.), Hearings: "Interlocking Subversion In Government Departments," Part 25, November 23, 1954, pages 2053-2054.

32:2 See Hawthorne Daniel, *The Ordeal Of The Captive Nations* (Garden City: Doubleday, 1958), especially Chapter 11.

The United States Ambassador to Hungary, at this time, described the Russian behaviour as "a period of calculated destruction. The Russian method of occupation follows a certain pattern necessitated by the differences between the East and West in standards of living.

"After a spearhead of disciplined troops which destroys any remaining opposition, propaganda shock troops arrive. Their job is to destroy all evidence of higher than Russian standards of living in enemy territory, before the ordinary soldiers appear upon the scene. A man who eats at a table and sleeps on a bed is considered a bourgeois. Boxes had to be substituted for tables and straw for beds. In Hungary such a policy meant destruction of workers' and peasants' homes as well as those of the wealthy classes." John Flournoy Montgomery, *Hungary: The Unwilling Satellite* (New York: Devin-Adair, 1947), page 210.

Mr. Montgomery has also included in his book (pages 239-245) an account of the Russian occupation of Hungary as seen by members of the Swiss legation and consulate in Budapest. The Swiss report describes the wholesale rape of women from age ten to seventy; the widespread looting; and, the theft of funds from banks and legation safes, including those belonging to other nations than Hungary.

Ferenc Nagy, former Prime Minister of Hungary, provides further proof of the absolute depravity of the Russian soldiers, men *and women*, who were unleashed upon Hungary: "I was dumbfounded also by the thoroughness of the occupation. Mass units of the Red army were found not only in the cities and on the lines of communication, but even on the smallest farms and in the fields. The people were in constant dread. The women of the small cities and the villages lived in hiding to escape assault.

"The life of the peasants in the vineyard districts was sheer hell, where Red soldiers found stores of wine. One could not speak of humanity, honor, decency, or the sanctity of the family to drunken Soviet soldiers. They raped half-grown girls and screaming grandmothers; they robbed the peasants of their animals, they stole the linen and in many places even the furniture. Tens of thousands of women and children were carried off and inflicted with venereal diseases by ruthless Red soldiers. Lack of doctors and medicine, and the innate shyness of the country-folk, prevented treatment.

"The barbarism of the Soviet occupy-

ing forces can best be judged by the fact that many thousands of Hungarian men were raped or forced to unnatural excesses by Russian women soldiers. The Reds established a recreation camp near Kecskemét for more than thirty thousand sick and convalescent women members of the Soviet army and police forces. From this camp, for instance, the Russian women banded together at night and swooped down upon the surrounding hamlets, kidnaping the men and sometimes holding them captive for days. Often these abductions led to the peculiar situation of women and girls hiding, not themselves, but their men in the forests and in haystacks to keep them from the disease-ridden Soviet women troops." *The Struggle Behind The Iron Curtain* (New York: Macmillan, 1948), page 63.

33:1 *World Survey,* June-July, 1956, page 8.

35:1 See *Congressional Record,* 1955, page 1947. For the bill itself, see Julius Epstein, "Will Congress Repudiate Forced Repatriation," *Brooklyn Tablet,* March 12, 1955.

35:2 See "Agreement Between The United States And The Soviet Union Concerning Liberated Prisoners Of War And Civilians," Department of State, *Foreign Relations: The Conferences At Malta And Yalta, 1945,* pages 985-987.

36:1 Julius Epstein, "An American Crime," *National Review,* December 21, 1955, pages 19-21; and, by the same author, "House Resolution 137," *Brooklyn Tablet,* May 28, 1955.

36:2 *New York Times,* March 17, 1955.

40:1 For the Vlasov incident, see Peter J. Huxley-Blythe, *Betrayal* (Fleetwood, England: Friends of National Russia); Testimony of Igor Bogolepov in S.I.S.S., Hearings: "Institute Of Pacific Relations," Part 13, April 2-May 29, 1952, pages 4479-4520 and 4553-4593; and, two articles by Julius Epstein, "How We Served As Partners In A Purge," *American Legion Magazine,* December 1954, pages 14-15; 43-45; and, "An American Crime," *National Review,* December 21,

1955, pages 19-21.

40:2 Colonel Igor Bogolepov, former Counsellor to the Soviet Foreign Office and formerly a member of Vlasov's Army, could shed no light on the fate of the Army but said that "General Vlasov's body, skewered on a meat hook, was exhibited in Moscow's Red Square." Richard L. Stokes, "A Tragic Tale Of Lend-Lease," *Human Events*, April 1, 1953.

43:1 For an excellent analysis of the Marshall mission, see George E. Sokolsky, "Out Of Their Own Mouths: The Betrayal Of Free China," *The Freeman* (Section Two), September 24, 1951.

43:2 And Operation Keelhaul continued into 1947. "A small part of the tragedy unfolded even on American soil. Many liberated Soviet soldiers were brought to the United States, chiefly to camps in Idaho. Virtually without exception, after the war, they begged for political asylum. But they were forced to board Soviet ships in Seattle and Portland. Over a hundred who resisted successfully were brought to a New Jersey camp. In the end these, too, were surrendered to Stalin, though we had to use tear gas to dislodge them from the barracks." Julius Epstein, "How We Served As Partners In A Purge," *American Legion Magazine*, December 1954, pages 14-15; 43-45. An extensive survey of Operation Keelhaul is in Huxley-Blythe, *Betrayal*, pages 6 and 7.

44:1 "Guide to the Care of Displaced Persons in Germany," Supreme Headquarters, Allies Expeditionary Force, G5 Division, Displaced Persons Branch, Revised May 1945, Part III, Section 3.

45:1 See Note 1 on Page 13.

Chapter Five

47:1 See Chiang Kai-shek, *Soviet Russia In China* (New York: Farrar, 1957), pages 50-51.

47:2 Boris Souvarine, *Stalin: A Critical Survey Of Bolshevism* (New York: Longmans, 1939), page 444.

48:1 *Ibid.*, pages 444-445.

48:2 (New York: Devin-Adair, 1958). See, also, two articles by Irene Corbally Kuhn, "Why You Buy Books That Sell Communism," *American Legion Magazine*, January 1951, pages 18-19, 53-63; "Who Are The Censors?," *Op. Cit.*, July 1954, pages 14-15, 59-61; and, Rosalie M. Gordon, "Why You Can't Find Conservative Books In Public Libraries," *Human Events*, September 8, 1961.

49:1 A pamphlet published by the author. It was revised and incorporated into Harry Elmer Barnes and others, *Perpetual War For Perpetual Peace*, Chapter One.

49:2 (New York: Devin-Adair, 1950).

49:3 (Chicago: Regnery, 1957).

49:4 See Robert H. W. Welch Jr., *May God Forgive Us* (Chicago: Regnery, 1952), pages 79-83.

51:1 For an excellent early account of Murrow's methods, see Victor Lasky, "The Murrow Myth," *Human Events*, July 9, 1955; and, for a later appraisal, see E. Merrill Root, "Edward R. Murrow: Uprooted," *American Opinion*, December 1962, pages 1-9.

52:1 Senator John Marshall Butler of Maryland placed Dr. Draskovich's opinion of the Murrow program in the *Congressional Record*, July 16, 1957, pages 11810-11811.

53:1 See Julius Epstein, "An American Crime," *National Review*, December 21, 1955, page 19.

54:1 Publication of *The Worker* has been resumed on a twice-a-week basis.

54:2 J. R., "Special Report: Minutes Of A Communist Party Meeting," *National Review*, October 6, 1956, page 15.

54:3 March 19, 1956.

55:1 See the *Boston Traveler*, February 24, 1956.

57:1 *Boston Traveler*, March 13, 1956.

58:1 Miss Summersby's experiences in the Eisenhower entourage have been recounted in *Eisenhower Was My Boss* (New York: Prentice-Hall, 1948). When last we heard of Miss Summersby she was a fashion coordinator for the Columbia Broadcasting System in New York. *Newsweek,* September 19, 1960.

59:1 Profits on *Crusade In Europe* were $1,000,000, and under ordinary circumstances would have been taxed at a rate of 77 percent. But the Truman Administration interpreted the profits as capital gains, subject to a tax of only 25 percent — a difference of $520,000 in Eisenhower's favor. See the *New Yorker Magazine,* October 30, 1948, pages 15-16; and, *Editorial* in *Washington Times-Herald,* November 22, 1951.

Chapter Six

63:1 By 1933 Dr. William A. Wirt, Superintendent of Schools in Gary, Indiana, had gained national fame for his intelligent plan to counteract progressive education. Wirt was invited to join Roosevelt's brain-trust.

Soon after his arrival in Washington he realized that he was in the middle of a pro-Communist web. He was drawn into a dinner party held by Miss Alice P. Barrows, an educational 'expert' from the Department of the Interior. Other guests included minor government officials and the Washington representative of *Tass,* the Soviet news agency.

Wirt summarized the context of the after-dinner conversation of his companions: "We believe that we have Mr. Roosevelt in the middle of a swift stream, and that the current is so strong that he cannot turn back or escape from it. We believe that we can keep Mr. Roosevelt there until we are ready to supplant him with a Stalin. We all think that Mr. Roosevelt is only the Kerensky of this revolution."

All this — and more like it — shocked Wirt enough to cause him to circulate a memorandum, describing his experiences, to about one hundred individuals. One of these, James H. Rand Jr., then President of Remington Rand Inc., read the memorandum in a hearing of the House Interstate Commerce Committee. Rand created such a furore that a five-man congressional committee was summoned to investigate Wirt's allegations.

Wirt, Miss Barrows, and five of the dinner guests testified in what can honestly be described as a disgraceful spectacle. Wirt was ridiculed and harassed by the three New Deal Democrats who formed the committee's majority. And their report was a whitewash of Miss Barrows and her cohorts and a smear of Wirt. In later years John J. O'Connor, one of the Democrats on the Committee, made a public apology for his role in the affair.

Miss Barrows took the Fifth Amendment before the Senate Internal Security Subcommittee in 1953 when asked about her connections with the Communist Party. Wirt suffered a loss of reputation and his job. He died a broken man four years after the trumped-up hearings. See Select Committee To Investigate Charges Made By William A. Wirt, Hearings (April 10 & 17, 1934) and Report (May 2, 1934); for Miss Barrows' testimony, see S.I.S.S., Hearings: "Interlocking Subversion In Government Departments," (Part 12), June 23, 1953, pages 830-840; and, Robert G. Moore, "The Tragedy Of Dr. William A. Wirt," *National Republic,* May 1954, pages 21-22 *et seq.*

63:2 For an early and perceptive analysis of this strategy, see Lawrence R. Brown, "Eisenhower: The Bait And The Trap," *The Freeman,* September 24, 1951, pages 809-813.

63:3 See Senate Subcommittee on Privileges and Elections of the Committee on Rules and Administration, Hearings: "Investigation Into The Ohio Senatorial Campaign," November 26, 1951, pages 3-76.

64:1 Taft wrote a memorandum in late 1952 describing his personal reflections upon the campaign tactics used to defeat him: "How I Lost The Nomination," *Human Events,* December 2, 1959.

65:1 Gunnar Myrdal, *An American Dilemma: The Negro Problem In Modern Democracy* (New York: Harper, 1944). The book was financed with grants of $250,000 by The Carnegie Corporation of New York. See Report of the Special

Committee To Investigate Tax-Exempt Foundations And Comparable Organizations, 83rd Congress, 2nd Session, December 16, 1954, page 89.

". . . Not surprising is the Court's acknowledgement of the influence of a notorious Swedish Communist, Gunnar Myrdal, as an 'authority' in its May 17, 1954, segregation decision in *Brown* v. *Board of Education* (347 U.S. 348), which has triggered racial conflicts in the United States like those envisioned by Stalin in his 'American Black Belt' program of negro domination." S.I.S.S., Hearing: "Limitation of Appellate Jurisdiction of the United States Supreme Court," February 19-March 4, 1958, page 1079.

Myrdal used as advisers in his work a host of Communists and fellow-travelers. See Senator James O. Eastland, "The Supreme Court's 'Modern Scientific Authorities' In The Segregation Case," a speech delivered in the United States Senate on May 26, 1955 (reprinted in pamphlet form by *American Opinion*, 1962). See, especially, pages 9-11.

67:1 For example, Dewey was most candid in explaining his support for Eisenhower: "I am an internationalist. That's why I am for Eisenhower. Eisenhower is a Republican at heart — but more important than that is that he is an internationalist." *Look Magazine*, September 11, 1951, page 97.

"Governor Sherman Adams . . . has selected many individuals of a strongly internationalist trend for high Government positions. It is believed that this is the result of the influence of Mrs. Adams, who for long has been an ardent booster of 'one world' causes." *Human Events*, April 8, 1953, page 1.

68:1 The genesis of "Taft can't win" and similar slogans is described in "Through All The Days To Be," *American Opinion*, June 1961, pages 9-41. See, especially, pages 24-28.

68:2 One very distinguished journalist was obviously disturbed over the circumstances surrounding the candidacy of

Eisenhower: "There is, of course, no obvious connection between Eisenhower and the Soviet apparatus that has been probably at work in the White House, the Department of State and elsewhere in the Administration. Yet there is a nexus in the fact that the command decisions carried out by Eisenhower, the policies he has so faithfully served have arisen, in indeterminate part, from this Soviet apparatus.

"When we ask, with Cicero, 'who laid these snares?' the answer takes us to White, to Lauchlin Currie, who administered the Far Eastern policies of Roosevelt during World War II; to Lattimore and to Hiss. Thus if we have a Truman-Marshall-Acheson-Eisenhower world polity we have behind it a White-Currie-Lattimore-Hiss mechanism of persuasion in high layers of the government with others whose names have not yet been certified.

"It would be unfair and uncharitable to attribute to Eisenhower any knowing collaboration with the bureaucrats and publicists who have been subverting America's world position. One can and must say that Eisenhower has been an unprotesting agent of this whole foreign policy complex." Forrest Davis, "Bob Taft's Decision," *The Freeman*, May 19, 1952, pages 527-530.

Chapter Seven

69:1 Georgia and Louisiana were part of what was commonly called "the Southern Steal" but undoubtedly the most brazen work was done in Texas: "The real story [of the Texas GOP primary] among other things is one of the CIO goons, innocent of any voting in their lives save Democratic voting, offering violence to genuine Republicans with a long record of voting Republican, who wanted to get into primary precinct meetings to vote for Taft." *Human Events*, June 4, 1952, page 1.

But in New Hampshire, during the first part of the campaign, the pattern had been established: "Recently Tex McCrary was so candid as to admit to a journalist doing a profile of him that he had fought hard and dirty against Taft in the crucial primary in New Hampshire. 'I planted people in every Taft audience,' he said. 'I would have mothers get up to say, 'I have a son who is being drafted — and he wants to ask you why your voting record is the same as Marcantonio's.' ' Such gifts as these to the advancement of political understanding were made by the very high and the very mighty, including — the author of such a book would find — the prince of political probity, Dwight David Eisenhower." Editorial, *National Review*, October 5, 1957, page 295.

70:1 During the campaign the runner-up award for ignoring truth and decency, however, belonged to Mrs. Claire Booth Luce. She was quoted as saying Taft's nomination would be "good news to Stalin." *Human Events*, September 3, 1952, page 3. Mrs. Luce would later receive from Eisenhower an appointment as United States Ambassador to Italy.

70:2 *New York Daily News*, August 5, 1954.

70:3 The Eisenhower-Case team was to be responsible for a disgusting campaign against Robert Morris who tried to prevent Case's reelection in 1960. See *For Better Or Worse*, a pamphlet published by the New Jersey Council For Preservation Of Republican Principles, 1960.

72:1 Dennett's name was one of the most prominently mentioned in the Institute of Pacific Hearings held by the Senate Internal Security Subcommittee in 1951-1952.

72:2 For example: " . . . the Big Secret — as we learn from our sources in the Twin Cities — was the turn-out of left wingers for Ike. Within the Ike organization in Minnesota, we understand, discussion of this matter is strongly discouraged, with many a 'sh-sh.' Now, all politicians know well the traditional strength of the left-wing Farmer-Labor element in Minnesota. Therefore it is interesting to note that the pro-Eisenhower *Minneapolis Star* lifted the hem of the curtain on March 19 when it said: 'The slim 32,000 vote showing of the Minnesota Democratic-Farmer labor voters gave support to suspicion that they helped boost Ike's edge.' " *Human Events*, March 26, 1952, page 3.

74:1 Pepper had been exposed time and time again in various sources. See "Red Pepper," *Time Magazine*, April 1, 1946; "Pink Pepper," *Saturday Evening Post*, August 31, 1946; William S. White (Pepper is one of the "leaders of the far left wing."), *New York Times*, September 21, 1946; Ralph McGill, "Can He Purge Senator Pepper," *Saturday Evening Post*, April 22, 1950 (subheads read: "Pinko Senator Pepper" and "left wing, long-in-office Pepper"); "Red Mantle," (September 30, 1946) and "Red Pepper," (April 7, 1947), *Newsweek Magazine*. Pepper's pro-Communist record has been summarized recently in *Counterattack*, October 26, 1962, pages 173-176. And now the House of Representatives has a member in Pepper who "had risen so high in the ranks of Stalin's friends that the *Daily Worker* declared him to be 'the best man in the Senate.' " Budenz, *The Cry Is Peace*, page 3.

Mr. Pepper was successful as a Democratic candidate for the House of Representatives from Florida's Third District (Miami) in November, 1962. Pepper received a hearty endorsement from President Kennedy: "During your many years in Congress, the people of Florida and of the nation had an outstanding and valiant fighter on behalf of the public interest." *Letter from Mr. Kennedy to Pepper*, as quoted by Drew Pearson in his Bell Syndicate column, May 7, 1962.

Vice-President Lyndon B. Johnson was the feature speaker at a fund-raising dinner for Pepper's campaign on October 16, 1962. See "A Review Of The News," *American Opinion*, December 1962, page 73.

77:1 This gathering and its participants have been described in HCUA: "Review Of The Scientific And Cultural Conference For World Peace," a report released on April 19, 1949.

78:1 Very early in the 1952 campaign, when Taft was a victim of a double-cross by Republican leaders in New Jersey, George Sokolsky made a strong attack upon one group of Eisenhower's supporters: "The Wall Street Supporters of General Eisenhower were jubilant. Such moneymen as George Whitney, Clarence Dillon, Harold Talbott, John Hay Whitney, and Winthrop Aldrich — Big Bankers — who are supporting Eisenhower and masterminding his campaign, operate as businessmen do in ruthless competition. . . . "

Then Mr. Sokolsky compared the acceptance of such ruthless supporters by Eisenhower to how General Douglas MacArthur would behave under similar circumstances: "He supports Taft; he opposes Eisenhower; he does not preclude his own candidacy. . . . The international bankers can exercise no influence on General MacArthur. My estimate of his attitude toward them is that he despises the use of money to corrupt the electoral processes of a free people. . . . " Broadcast on the American Broadcasting Company's network on March 23, 1952, as quoted in *Human Events*, March 26, 1952, pages 1 and 2.

78:2 (New York: Simon & Shuster, 1941).

78:3 The manipulation of Davies by Soviet diplomats has been described by Colonel Igor Bogolepov in his testimony before the S.I.S.S. See Hearings: "Institute Of Pacific Relations," (Part 13), April 2-May 29, 1952, pages 4512-4516, and 4557-4560.

79:1 Robert H. W. Welch Jr., *The Life of John Birch* (Chicago: Regnery, 1954; reissued by Western Islands, Boston, 1960).

80:1 There was probably nothing stranger or more revealing in this matter of newspaper support for Eisenhower than that given by the publisher of the *New York Times*: "The *New York Times* is supporting General Eisenhower for the Republican presidential nomination because it is so very frightened at the thought of Mr. Taft, according to the *Times* president and publisher Arthur Hays Sulzberger. Sulzberger made the statement in reply to a question by a member of a journalism class he addressed at the University of Pennsylvania, Friday. The publisher indicated his newspaper was 'frightened' of Taft because of his 'consistently isolationist' stand on foreign affairs while the *Times* had long been internationalist in its viewpoint. Sulzberger said if Taft and Mr. Truman were the rival presidential candidates next November, he believed his newspaper would support Mr. Truman." *Camden* (N. J.) *Courier-Post*, April 19, 1952.

Sulzberger certainly knew an internationalist when he saw one. Eisenhower had made his "internationalism" quite clear during his command of NATO. The *U. S. News* on July 27, 1951, reported: "He takes seriously the promise to act only one-twelfth American and one-twelfth British, French, Belgian, etc. On a mantel piece in his office stands a constant reminder of this pledge — miniature flags of the 12 Allies lining up like soldiers in a row." As quoted in *Human Events*, March 26, 1952, page 3.

For more examples of this "one-twelfth American" posture, see *Editorial* in *Washington Times-Herald*, November 29, 1951, and Frank Kirkpatrick, *The American Way*, Vol. II, No. 1, 1956, page 6.

81:1 See William Johnson and Thaddeus Ashby, "The Lucille Miller Story," *Faith And Freedom*, September 1955, pages 3-19.

Chapter Eight

83:1 "The species anti-anti-communist may be recognized by these eight distinctive psychological traits:

"(1) A strong American guilt complex. (2) A conviction that, while communism is undesirable, the real enemy to be fought is militant anti-communism. (3) Extreme deference to the views of Prime Minister Nehru of India and other uncommitted neutralists in the world struggle. (4) An impulse to lean heavily, in difficult situations, on that weak reed, the United Nations. (5) A tendency to minimize the Soviet threat to American security and to amnesia about the Soviet international record of annexations and broken treaties. (6) Pathological fear of losing alleged friends in Europe and Asia by any strong clearcut action against Soviet or Red Chinese aggression. (7) Belief that the American taxpayer owes a living to the 'underprivileged' nations of the world. (8) Conviction that no arguments, apart from wayward prejudice, can be advanced against the admission of Red China to the United Nations." William H. Chamberlin, *Appeasement: Road To War* (New York: Rolton, 1962), pages 51-52.

83:2 December 11, 1953, page 12.

83:3 When Brownell was so arbitrarily and summarily stopped cold by Eisenhower, the lesson was obviously not lost upon Brownell. And after Brownell had been in office three years, Frank Kirkpatrick was alarmed at how far Brownell had moved from his early anti-Communist position. Commenting on a speech by Brownell in Dallas on April 17, 1956, Kirkpatrick said:

"The only communists with which Attorney-General Brownell concerned himself were what he called the 'Soviet Reds,' especially those in South American countries. Mr. Brownell should be asked about communism in the United States. Brownell is the political boss of the F.B.I. and determines what the F.B.I. does. Mr. Brownell determines what happens to the information obtained by the F.B.I. But Mr. Brownell goes to Dallas and talks about 'Soviet Reds,' saying nothing about U. S. communists under his regime.

"Under Herbert Brownell, the Communist Party, U.S.A., is so free from interference that it has come out of its underground hiding places where the members went when the striped pants conspirators were shown to be directed by those with baggy knees. Let Mr. Brownell tell us why he brought about the freeing of Harry Bridges, a man convicted of being in this country illegally,

and who was ordered deported. Let Mr. Brownell tell us why he dropped the case against Owen Lattimore after Lattimore had been indicted by a grand jury.

"Why does Mr. Brownell not tell the President that experts are needed in this country to meet the advance of communism? In Dallas, Brownell spoke of experts being needed in South America, but what about the U.S.A.?" *The American Way*, Volume II, No. 4, 1956, page 23.

84:1 "Reds And Our Churches," July 1953, pages 3-13.

Columnist George Sokolsky expressed surprise at the criticism directed against Doctor Matthews and said: "I have known Matthews for nearly 20 years. He is the greatest authority in the United States on the subject of Marxism and its infiltration into this country. . . . Matthews is respected by every person who works in this field." *New York Journal American*, July 9, 1953.

84:2 A view shared by Baptist Minister Reverend Daniel A. Poling and Episcopal Bishop James P. DeWolfe. See Daniel A. Poling, "Clergymen Are Citizens Too," *Saturday Evening Post*, April 24, 1954, pages 26-27 *et seq.* See, also, the testimony of Benjamin Gitlow before the House Committee On Un-American Activities ("Investigation Of Communist Activities In The New York Area — Part 6," July 7, 1953), pages 2069-2136.

84:3 Doctor Matthews was not the first to sound the alarm. More than four years earlier J. Edgar Hoover had written: "Many Communist fronts have been operated under the guise of some church commission or religious body. It is ghastly to see the monster atheism being nourished in the churches which it seeks to destroy. Church leaders can stop this nefarious infiltration by taking vigorous action in the boards and commissions under church supervision. Individual ministers and church members can avoid being hoodwinked if they will stay close to the *fundamentals* of their faith." "God Or Chaos," *Redbook Magazine*, February

1949, as quoted by Edgar Bundy in *News And Views*, August 1957, page 4.

Five years later Mr. Hoover obviously supported Doctor Matthews' thesis: "Never a day passes that I do not receive reliable reports on Communist activities in many different parts of the nation. Almost no field of our society is immune to them. In the ranks of the concealed Communists today are labor leaders, educators, publicists, doctors, lawyers, businessmen, and even clergymen . . . . Even the clergy, as I have said, are not without their undercover Reds. The Communists realize that religion is our strongest bulwark against the encroachment of Marxist doctrines, and in some instances are trying to attack Christian faith at its wellsprings by influencing or winning over ordained ministers as recruits to aid the Party." "The Communists Are After Our Minds," *The American Magazine*, October 1954, pages 19; 85-88.

Much of the damage done to Matthews and McCarthy might have been offset if the House Committee On Un-American Activities had invited Matthews to testify under oath on the matters he covered in his article.

Matthews did not request a hearing but he indicated his willingness to testify in a letter to Chairman Harold Velde: "Hundreds of citizens from all parts of the United States have suggested that I appear before the Committee On Un-American Activities to present exhaustive documentation on the Communist infiltration of the clergy. . . . It is my firm conviction now, as it has always been, that a great service can be rendered the vast majority of the Protestant churches by the fullest exposure of the diabolical scheme of the Communist Party to cloak its conspiracy against the United States by utilizing, among other ways, that small minority of clergymen who are careless or contemptuous of their sacred vows." *Letter from Matthews to Velde*, July 15, 1953, as quoted by Matthews in an address at Orchestra Hall in Chicago, August 9, 1954. The Address has been printed and distributed by Circuit Riders,

Inc. of Cincinnati.

85:1   July 13, 1953.

85:2   See *A Compilation of Public Records 2109 Methodist Ministers*, Two volumes, (Cincinnati: Circuit Riders, 1956). Circuit Riders have also published *A Compilation of Public Records of 658 Clergymen and Laymen Connected With The National Council of Churches; A Compilation of Public Records 20.5% Equals 1411 Protestant Episcopal Rectors; A Compilation of Public Records: 614 Presbyterian Church U.S.A., Clergymen; A Compilation of Public Records: 660 Baptist Clergymen; 30 of 95 Men Who Gave Us The Revised Standard Version of the Bible;* and, *A Compilation of Public Records: 42% of the Unitarian Clergymen and 450 Rabbis.*

86:1   In the original letter this read that Major Bundy had been with the FBI for seven years. It was the one error of fact reported by readers of the confidential manuscript.

86:2   Mr. Bundy has made the results of his studies known through his book, *Collectivism In The Churches* (Wheaton: Church League of America, 1959); his monthly newsletter, *News And Views*; and through the publishing by the Church League of America of such works as the League's staff study, *A Manual For Survival*, 1961; and, J. B. Matthews, *Certain Activities Of Certain Congregational Clergymen*, 1961.

86:3   Special Subcommittee on Investigation of the Committee on Government Operations, Hearings: "Special Senate Investigation on Charges and Countercharges Involving: Secretary of the Army Robert T. Stevens, John G. Adams, H. Struve Hensel and Senator Joe McCarthy, Roy Cohn, and Francis P. Carr," Parts 31-37, May 13-24, 1954.

86:4   See *Congressional Record*, December 1, 1954, pages 16268-16277, 16279-16341, and, 16344-16346.

87:1   *Congressional Record*, July 19, 1956, page 13521.

87:2   For a summary of Eisenhower's anti-McCarthy activities, see *New Bedford*

(Mass.) *Standard-Times*, Dec. 10, 1954.

87:3 See *Human Events*, July 18, 1956, page 2.

88:1 See Senate Document No. 126, August 31, 1960, *Internal Security Manual* (revised), page 319.

88:2 Committee on Government Operations, Hearings: "Communist Infiltration Among Army Civilian Workers," September 8 and 11, 1953, pages 9-23.

88:3 See Note 1 on Page 65.

88:4 See Note 1 on Page 90.

89:1 *The Dan Smoot Report*, July 13, 1956, pages 1-3.

89:2 See J. B. Matthews, "The Years Of Betrayal," *American Mercury*, February 1954, page 43; and, James Burnham, *The Web Of Subversion* (New York: Day, 1954), Chapter 8.

89:3 *The Dan Smoot Report*, July 13, 1956, page 2.

90:1 *Ibid.* Representative John E. Moss, Democrat of California and Chairman of the Special Government Information Subcommittee, said that the Eisenhower Administration invoked executive privilege forty-four times in withholding information. "Time after time executive branch employees far down the administrative line from the President fell back on his letter of May 17, 1954, as authority to withhold information from the Congress and the public." Associated Press Dispatch, *Quincy* (Mass.) *Patriot Ledger,* March 12, 1962.

91:1 See Senate Permanent Subcommittee on Investigations of the Committee on Government Operations, Hearings: "East-West Trade," February 15-June 29, 1956, pages 16-17, 81, and 317-319; "Final Report," July 18, 1956.

For the role of Harold Stassen in the use of the "gag order," see L. Brent Bozell, "Trading With The Enemy," *National Review*, March 28, 1956, pages 9-12; "National Trends," *Op. cit.*, April 4, 1956, pages 8 and 12; and, *The Dan Smoot Report*, June 17, 1957, pages 1-6.

91:2 See Kurt Glaser, *Czecho-Slovakia: A Critical History* (Caldwell: Caxton, 1961); and, Jan Kozak, *And Not A Shot*

Is Fired (New Canaan, Conn.: Long House, 1962).

92:1 See Subcommittee of the Senate Judiciary Committee, Hearings: "Treaties And Executive Agreements," February 18-April 11, 1953; Frank E. Holman, *Story Of The "Bricker Amendment"* (New York: Committee For Constitutional Government, 1954); and, Roger Lea MacBride, *Treaties Versus The Constitution* (Caldwell: Caxton, 1955).

93:1 Mr. Frank Chodorov made an excellent analysis of the ramifications involved with regard to opposition against the Bricker Amendment: "There appear to be three groups enrolled in the 'New School of Internationalists.'

"First, there are the doctrinaire socialists, with whom must be included the whole congeries of planners who are convinced that the millenium can be attained through Big Government. The American tradition of limited government, with delegated power, bulwarked by the Declaration of Independence and the Constitution, is the impediment that must be overcome. The chink in the armor of that tradition, they have found, is Article VI. If international law is the supreme law of the land, then the Conventions and Pacts of the UN could serve to override that tradition. The UN becomes an aid to socialists, for breaking through the barrier of the Constitution.

"Then there is that agglomeration of sentimentalists who see in international sovereignty the cure for all the ills of national sovereignty. Their reasoning, if it can be called reasoning, runs like this: a number of small governments is bad; therefore, one monster world government is good. Their psychological quirk prevents them from seeing this *non sequitur,* even as it prevents them from learning anything from history.

"The third group consists of those conscious Communists who would put this country under the domination of Moscow, and who find in the UN an instrument for their purpose. The U.S.S.R. joined this organization only when it became evident that its Charter was amenable to their plan for world conquest, and there is reason to believe that American stooges wrought the Charter with that end in view. At any rate, the Charter presents no threat to U.S.S.R. sovereignty, only to ours.

"But, whether opposition to the Bricker amendment comes from this last group and their equally sinister fellow-traveller dupes, or from the first two, who believe they are motivated by high ideals, the fact is that all of them aim to liquidate the sovereignty of the United States. In short, there is a bit of treason in their hearts." "Again The Issue Is Freedom," *Human Events*, May 13, 1953.

93:2 *Economic Council Letter*, September 15, 1955, page 3.

94:1 See "What The President Cannot Do," *Open Letter from Attorney Robert B. Dresser to Eisenhower*, dated March 16, 1957, and placed into the *Congressional Record*, April 4, 1957, by Representative Ralph W. Gwinn of New York, pages A2844-A2845.

94:2 Dwight D. Eisenhower, "Book Burning: Where U. S. Officials Stand," *U. S. News & World Report*, June 26, 1953, pages 37-46.

94:3 For further information on these information centers, see Permanent Subcommittee on Investigations of the Committee on Government Operations, Hearings: "State Department Information Centers," March 24-July 14, 1953; and, the Committee's Report for 1953, released January 25, 1954, pages 25-28.

Chapter Nine

97:1 Eisenhower "called the journals which were critical of Russia 'crackpots' and told the Russians: 'We must keep our sense of values and not be upset by a few crackpots.'" *Los Angeles Examiner*, July 23, 1948.

97:2 In 1944 Hillman, as Chairman of the National Citizens Political Action Committee, had participated in Roosevelt's successful campaign for reelection. The NCPAC was described by the Special House Committee on Un-American Ac-

tivities as the "Communist Party's supreme bid for power throughout its twenty-five years of existence in this country . . . [and] it is clear that the major objective of this Hillman-[Earl] Browder-C.I.O. axis is the gaining of a dominant position of influence in the councils of the Democratic Party." Hearings: Appendix IX (1944), page 261. See, also, Edna Lonigan, "Anatomy Of The PAC," *The Freeman*, November 27, 1950, pages 151-154.

98:1 Gunther, *Eisenhower: The Man And The Symbol*, page 128. The speech was given on November 20, 1946 in Atlantic City, New Jersey.

98:2 *New York Times*, December 7, 1945.

98:3 See Page 80.

98:4 See *New York World-Telegram*, December 2, 1946.

98:5 The dinner was held in New York City on December 3, 1946.

99:1 For more details on the Birkhead-Stout-Derounian alliance, see John T. Flynn, *The Smear Terror* (a pamphlet published by the author, 1947). The contents of Mr. Flynn's pamphlet ran serially in the *Chicago Tribune*, beginning January 12, 1947.

99:2 As late as June 1961, a letterhead of Freedom House carried Stout's name as Treasurer. And over the years the type of names associated with Freedom House has not changed: Ralph Bunche, Norman Cousins, Arthur J. Goldsmith, Paul Hoffman, Jacob Javits, Max Kriendler, Whitney North Seymour, and Bishop James A. Pike are carried on the 1961 letterhead as members of the Board of Trustees.

And, as of October 1960, the letterhead of Freedom House's Bookshelf Committee showed Archibald MacLeish as Chairman, while the Committee included Philip Jessup, the Arthur M. Schlesingers, Sr. and Jr., Max Lerner, Elmer Rice, Edward R. Murrow, Chester Bowles, Norman Cousins, Aaron Copland, and William O. Douglas.

101:1 For further information see the *Los Angeles Examiner,* July 23, 1948; *Seymour* (Conn.) *Evening Sentinel,* March 13, 1952; and, "How Much Satellite Money For American Colleges," (Editorial) *Saturday Evening Post,* November 6, 1948, page 184.

101:2 See *Red-ucators At Columbia University,* published by the National Council for American Education. This dossier was compiled from hearings and reports of State and Federal investigative committees and agencies.

103:1 "The Years Of Betrayal," *American Mercury,* February 1954, pages 34-35. This must rank as one of the all-time heights of irony in the history of journalism. Eisenhower's remarks were given in an interview with his Communist ghost-writer — Joseph Fels Barnes!

103:2 *Ibid.*

103:3 *New York Times* as quoted in *The Tablet* (Brooklyn), September 11, 1954.

105:1 Oppenheimer's rehabilitation in public opinion was due in great part to the work of Edward R. Murrow and his television program, *See It Now,* broadcast over the CBS network. See Finis Farr, "Edward R. Murrow; Poet Of Mankind," *National Review,* July 11, 1956, pages 8-10.

106:1 For later activities of American Assembly-Arden House, see Dan Smoot's *The Invisible Government* (Dallas: The Dan Smoot Report, 1962), pages 144-146.

Chapter Ten

107:1 The myth of Eisenhower's Republicanism was promoted by Harry Hopkins and Robert Sherwood, masters of deception: "I had several long talks with Eisenhower during the 24 hours Mrs. Hopkins and I spent at his country place about 15 miles outside of Frankfurt. Amongst other things, Eisenhower told me that he and his family had always been Republicans and had voted against Roosevelt every time up until 1944; but

that he did vote for Roosevelt this last time. He discussed his future at great length, repeatedly emphasizing that he did not want to go into politics. This seemed to be apropos of nothing in particular that I had said. He told me, however, that a good many people passing through raised the question of his running for President — obviously on the Republican Ticket." *Memorandum of Harry Hopkins* as quoted in Sherwood, *Roosevelt And Hopkins,* page 913.

Sherwood, however, believes that Hopkins is inaccurate, in part. Sherwood recalls that Eisenhower told him personally in London in March of 1944 "that his family had always been Kansas Republicans but that he himself had never voted in his life." *Ibid.,* page 915.

At any rate, when Eisenhower had finished his eight years as a "Republican" President, his labors for the GOP were succinctly summarized as: "Mr. Eisenhower had made the Republican Party unintelligible." Editorial, *National Review,* May 8, 1962, page 314.

107:2 *Washington Times-Herald,* January 27, 1952.

107:3 *Newark Evening News,* November 19, 1951, as quoted in the *Clover Business Letter,* July 1962, page 4.

108:1 Gunther, *Eisenhower: The Man And The Symbol,* pages 130-131.

109:1 Press conference of January 10, 1952, as quoted in *U. S. News & World Report,* January 18, 1952, page 1.

109:2 *New York Times,* January 7, 1952. Lodge's reward for his campaign work would be the Ambassadorship to the United Nations where he would sometimes "talk a good fight" against the Soviets but they certainly knew he had prejudged them favorably: "We want peace with them [Soviet Russia] and I am convinced that they want peace with us." *New York Herald-Tribune,* February 6, 1946.

For an excellent summary of Lodge's work, see Edward B. Simmons, "The Real Record Of Ambassador Lodge," *Human Events,* June 23, 1960. An earlier, but revealing, analysis of Lodge's work at the UN is in Chesly Manly, *The UN Record* (Chicago: Regnery, 1955), especially Chapters III and VII.

110:1 Harold Lavine, Senior Editor of *Newsweek* wrote: "Eisenhower has succeeded where Roosevelt and Truman failed. . . . The Republican Party is a thoroughly demoralized body. . . . Republican morale was able to sustain five successive defeats, but it has crumbled completely as the result of Eisenhower's two great victories." *Commentary*, October 1958, as quoted in *Human Events*, December 22, 1958.

In an Editorial of January 8, 1958, the *Chicago Daily Tribune* stated: "The fact is that the Republican Party, as it has developed, or, more properly, degenerated under Mr. Eisenhower and his palace guard, now stands for pretty nearly everything that can be found in unadulterated form under a Democratic wrapper. The great achievement of the occupant of the White House, if such it can be called, is to have destroyed the Republican Party as a repository for any recognizable body of orthodox doctrine."

110:2 See 1952 under Part I of the Bibliography.

110:3 *London Times*, October 16, 1952, as quoted by Freda Utley, "Was It Planned That Way?," *Human Events*, January 1, 1955.

111:1 See "9 Billion In Medical Bills — President's Answer: Reinsurance," *U. S. News & World Report*, January 29, 1954, pages 96-98.

112:1 During Eisenhower's eight fiscal years the average annual budget deficit was more than three billion dollars and the national debt was increased about *twenty-seven billion* dollars.

112:2 Adlai E. Stevenson, as quoted in *New York Times*, October 26, 1956.

113:1 A former Republican Congressman from Nebraska explained how cleverly this was done: "During Ike's first weeks in office, a list of Taft Republicans to be purged was prepared at the White House. In this strategy the Modern Republicans did not make Roosevelt's mistake of announcing their aims. Instead they laid their plans secretly and no public exposure of their tactics ever appeared. The frequent disappearance of conservative Republicans from public office and political influence in the following years was mute testimony to the effectiveness of this liquidation policy." Howard Buffett, "Taft's Legacy And The 1960 Elections," *Human Events*, April 29, 1959.

114:1 See *Human Events*, October 20, 1954, page 2.

114:2 *Op. cit.*, March 3, 1954, pages 1-2.

114:3 *Op. cit.*, September 22, 1954, pages 1-2.

116:1 Lattimore's boastful admission of this action appeared in the *New York Compass*, July 17, 1949, as quoted in Joseph R. McCarthy's *McCarthyism: The Fight For America* (New York: Devin-Adair, 1952), page 62. Later Lattimore had the gall to say: "Chiang's Government collapsed from inner rottenness, not from lack of foreign support." *Baltimore Sun*, March 26, 1951.

116:2 Gunther, *Eisenhower: The Man And The Symbol*, page 89.

Chapter Eleven

118:1 See Medford Evans, "The Nature Of NATO,"*One Man's Opinion* (now *American Opinion*), November 1957, pages 11-23. See, also, *Two-Faced NATO* (booklet compiled and published by the National Defense Committee of the Daughters of the American Revolution, 1961).

118:2 In 1957 Major General Charles A. Willoughby noted that NATO "had less than *one-fifth* of the number of ready divisions . . . [the Western powers] had maintained in an average prewar year (1928)." "Our Strategic Blind Alley," *National Review*, November 9, 1957, pages 417-419.

119:1 J. C. Phillips, *Borger* (Texas)

News-Herald, circa October 1954.

120:1 For further information on Republican Advance, see George F. Hobart, "Liberal Republicans Look To '64," *National Review,* September 25, 1962, pages 227-229; Remarks of Senator Pat McCarran, *Congressional Record,* Eighty-Third Congress, Second Session, page 14337; and, J. C. Phillips, *Borger* (Texas) *News-Herald, circa* October 1954.

120:2 The others on the purge list (Senators Joseph McCarthy of Wisconsin, William Jenner of Indiana, and George Malone of Nevada) did not come up for re-election until 1958.

120:3 Frank Church.

120:4 "How Eisenhower Saved The Republican Party." On February 16, 1957, *Human Events* (page 1) reported that Hoffman claimed that the White House suggested the idea of the article and that he "wrote a draft and submitted it to members of the Palace Guard. The latter returned it to him, saying it was not strong enough and urging him to name names. Hoffman acceded to this request and the *Collier's* piece appeared in print in a new and tougher version, with the names."

120:5 (New York: Harper, 1956).

120:6 For example, Hoffman quotes Eisenhower as saying in the first year of his administration: "I can tell you one thing, if I ever do run again, it'll be as an independent (and not as a Republican)." "How Eisenhower Saved The Republican Party," *Collier's,* October 26, 1956.

120:7 January 14, 1957.

121:1 Fulton Lewis Jr., *Exclusive,* September 4, 1957, and February 19, 1958.

122:1 "Report From Washington," *Southern States Industrial Bulletin,* August 15, 1957, page 3.

122:2 By the end of 1960, however, the total of land owned by the federal government was 771,512,000 acres or 33.9 percent of the entire national domain. U. S. Department of Commerce, *Statis-* *tical Abstract of The United States, 1962,* page 193.

122:3 A. G. Heinsohn Jr., *One Man's Fight For Freedom* (Caldwell: Caxton, 1957), page 92.

122:4 *American Taxpayers Association Bulletin,* January 30, 1957.

123:1 "Social Planners' Paradise," *Free Enterprise,* June 1957.

123:2 *First National Bank of Boston Monthly Letter,* June 1957.

124:1 "They Said It In 1957," published by the author, Don Raihle, page 4.

124:2 *Human Events,* June 11, 1955. page 3.

124:3 Since many of these crimes and absurdities were perpetrated *despite* whatever Ezra Taft Benson, as Secretary of Agriculture, could do to prevent them, it is hard to imagine what *would* have happened if he had yielded to the increasing left-wing pressures to get him out. Fortunately, Eisenhower and his Administration needed a certain amount of protective coloration from the Conservative brush right up to the very end. And the Department of Agriculture was one of the places where a true Conservative as Secretary could do the least damage to their most important plans.

125:1 For an honest appraisal of the physical state of public education at the time, see Roger A. Freeman, *School Needs In The Decade Ahead* (Washington: Institute For Social Science Research, 1958).

125:2 "A Study Committee Report On Federal Responsibility In The Field Of Education," submitted to the Commission on Intergovernmental Relations by the Study Committee on Federal Responsibility in the Field of Education, 1955. Also, see Dr. Adam S. Bennion, "A Case Against Federal Aid," *News From The NAM,* December 9, 1955, pages 1-7.

125:3 In a letter to Congressman Ralph W. Gwinn, dated June 7, 1949, Eisenhower himself stated: "I would flatly oppose any grant by the Federal Government to all states in the Union for educational purposes. Such policy would

. . . completely decry and defeat the watchful economy that comes about through local supervision over local expenditures of local revenues . . . . Very frankly I firmly believe that the army of persons who urge greater and greater centralization of authority and greater dependence upon the Federal Treasury are really more dangerous to our form of government than any external threats that can be arrayed against us." *Congressional Record*, 1949, Page A-3690.

125:4 See Fulton Lewis Jr., *Exclusive*, August 21, 1957, pages 2 and 3.

See Pages 239-240 for more on "group dynamics."

126:1 "Eisenhower-Republican Administration Achievements, 1953-1956," *Pocket Reminder*, Precinct Organization, Republican Central Committee, Los Angeles, page 3.

128:1 Senate Subcommittee of the Committee on Appropriations, May 28, 1958, Hearings: "Departments of State, Justice, and Judiciary, and Related Agencies Appropriations, 1959," pages 774-775; and, Bryton Barron, "The Blackout Extended," *National Review*, September 15, 1956, pages 13 and 14. In Eisenhower's last fiscal year, there were 38,999 employees in the State Department. The budget expenditures for that Department had risen from $156,000,000 in 1954 to an estimated $453,000,000 in 1962. See Department of Commerce, *Statistical Abstract of the United States*, 1960, page 367; and, *Op. cit.*, 1962, page 381.

128:2 *The Wall Street Journal*, March 8, 1957.

128:3 The final deficit was $12.4 billion. United States Department of Commerce, *Statistical Abstract of the United States*, 1962, page 380.

130:1 United States Department of Commerce, *Statistical Abstract of the United States* (1956), page 398, and (1958), page 406.

131:1 *Harvard Times-Republican*, April 18, 1957. The *Harvard Times-Republican* was a newspaper published by the Harvard College Republican Club.

131:2 This was amply demonstrated two years later by Ambassador Henry Cabot Lodge, who, at a dinner honoring Khrushchev in New York, "boasted that the U.S. is a 'welfare state' and remarked proudly 'that the Federal Government . . . pervades our lives — that one adult in every five gets regular checks from the Government and that countless others receive occasional payments . . . and that 2,000,000 persons live in Government-subsidized housing.' " *Human Events*, September 30, 1959, page 2.

Chapter Twelve

137:1 *New York Times*, March 27, 1955.

Conclusions of the Senate Internal Security Subcommittee are also pertinent: "The senior military commanders (Generals George E. Stratemeyer, James A. Van Fleet, Edward M. Almond, Mark Clark, and Admiral Charles Turner Joy) in the Korean war theater who appeared before the . . . Subcommittee . . . believe that victory in Korea was possible and desirable . . . that the action required to achieve victory would not have resulted in world war III . . . [and] that political considerations were permitted to overrule military necessities. [They] expressed grave concern over the conduct of this first U.N. 'police action,' and hoped we would never again hazard our troops under similar circumstances . . . believe that possible subversion, wishful thinking, European orientation and Allied pressure denied them victory . . . believe that failure to win in Korea has jeopardized our position in the Far East . . . supplied some clues to possible subversion in Government departments, but were unable to make specific charges . . . expressed the hope that the investigation would be continued and would encompass the source from which their orders were received—the Pentagon, State Department, our allies, certain Ambassadors . . . [and] hoped that the subject of direction of a U.N. war would be satisfactorily clarified before the United States again commits its forces, its prestige, and its vital interest in another U.N. military engagement." S.I.S.S., Report: "The Korean War And Related Matters," January 21, 1955.

For the complete testimony of the senior military commanders in Korea, see S.I.S.S., Hearings: "Interlocking Subversion In Government Departments," August 10-December 29, 1954, Part 21 (Clark); Part 22 (Stratemeyer); Part 24 (Van Fleet); Part 25 (Almond); Part 26 (Joy).

137:2 ". . . The General Assembly . . . recommends that . . . all constituent acts be taken, including the holding of elections, under the auspices of the United Nations, for the establishment of a unified, independent and democratic Government in the sovereign State of Korea. . . ." *United Nations Bulletin*, November 1, 1950, page 449.

On June 7, 1953 Eisenhower agreed that the United States was "committed" to the unification of Korea but said: ". . . We do not intend to employ war as an instrument to accomplish the worldwide political settlements to which we are dedicated." *U.S. News & World Report*, June 19, 1953, page 18.

On June 11, 1953, in a speech at Mt. Rushmore, South Dakota, Eisenhower said: ". . . In the field of foreign affairs: We have dedicated our party resolutely to a policy seeking to strengthen and secure friendship and co-operation among all nations loving freedom and resisting tyranny. We have recognized that the power to stay free demands spiritual strength, economic strength, and military strength; and the fostering of all these is essential to true collective security." *Op. cit.*, page 92.

137:3 "President Eisenhower went somewhat further than Mr. Acheson was prepared to go in order to get a deal with Communists in Korea." *Op. cit.*, page 12.

137:4 Quite a contrast to earlier appearances. "The North Koreans must be defeated 'soundly. . . . We must defeat

them physically and defeat their intentions.' " Eisenhower in a press conference at San Francisco, July 26, 1950, *New York Times*, as quoted in 1952 by the "New Hampshire Eisenhower For President Committee" (Co-chairmen Sherman Adams and Mary S. Brown) in its campaign literature.

137:5 The motions were by no means unpopular in all quarters: "Tremendous pressures have been exerted on the Administration from many sides to take the peace offered and let our credit go. The pressures are exerted by the financial interests who want to do business with Stalin's successors and the anti-anti-Communists who believe that the Soviets, although they have sinned, are basically virtuous or 'progressive.'

"Abetting these appeasement influences are the British, confident that 'there'll always be an England' so long as there are other nations to throw into the greedy jaws of the Communist Moloch. Last but not least, there are the good men of little faith who have persuaded themselves and the President that the Republican Party's only hope of survival is to give the people what they want at the moment, namely peace, at whatever cost to the future security of the United States." Freda Utley, "Appeasement A La Mode," *Human Events*, June 24, 1953.

"It was the United States and the United Nations that were put in the position of suing for a truce. Certainly it was not our own tactics that were chiefly responsible for dragging out the truce negotiations for more than two years and 158 meetings by the top truce teams. If the Chinese Communists had had a sincere desire for a truce, they could have got it in one day and in one meeting. It was we who, over these two years, allowed ourselves to be accused and insulted daily and kept yielding one point after another.

"On the battlefield itself, the best we won was a stalemate; and we turned even this into the appearance of defeat by accepting a screening of our prisoners by a 'neutral' commission of five nations including, in addition to India, the two Communist satellites, Poland and Czechoslovakia. That this shameful concession was not necessary was proved when the Communists accepted a truce notwithstanding the action of President Rhee in liberating 27,000 anti-Communist North Koreans." Editorial, *The Freeman*, August 10, 1953, page 797.

137:6 In June, 1953, in the waning days of negotiations for a truce, when Syngman Rhee made his dramatic release of North Korean anti-Communist prisoners [see Page 139], "the State Department showed great alarm and expressed fear that the Reds would cancel the negotiations. But, within 24 hours it was evident that the Reds had no such intention and word from their camp indicated they were prepared to conclude an armistice regardless of what Rhee had done or said. What was the lesson of this surprise? That the enemy very much wanted a truce on the terms indicated and is willing to yield on other points — such as the Rhee release of prisoners." *Human Events*, June 24, 1953, page 2.

"The President accepted a Korean truce on terms that [Adlai] Stevenson, had he been in the White House, would probably have been forced to reject in order to prove to the country that he was a loyal American." *Harvard* (College) *Crimson*, as quoted by *National Review*, November 10, 1956, page 5.

As for the Communists themselves, they made no secret of their feelings with regard to the "truce": "In a message broadcast by radio, the North Korean and Chinese Communist commanders proclaimed a 'glorious victory.' And Russian Premier Georgi M. Malenkov sent telegrams to the leaders of North Korea and Communist China in which he called the armistice 'a great victory (for the Communists) in the cause of defending peace in the Far East and throughout the world.'" William H. Vatcher Jr., *Panmunjom* (New York: Praeger, 1958), page 203.

138:1 *Time Magazine*, August 22, 1955,

pages 21-22.

139:1 Major Charles Fogg (U.S.A.), "I Saw The Struggle In The 'Explanation' Tents," January 30, 1954, pages 28 *et seq.*

139:2 See Geraldine Fitch, "Defeat At Panmunjom," *The Freeman* August 25, 1952, pages 803-805.

140:1 See Mark Clark, *From The Danube To The Yalu* (New York: Harper, 1954), Chapter 19.

140:2 November 23, 1951.

140:3 "In 1959 UN delegates to the Panmunjom meetings demanded that the Communists account for prisoners they failed to return in the exchange so many years before, prisoners known to have been in Communist hands because of radio broadcasts made naming them or transmitting their voices or by testimony of fellow prisoners who were exchanged. The UN Command listed 1,648 ROK soldiers, 452 Americans, 20 British, 9 Australians, 8 South Africans, and smaller numbers from Turkey, Greece, Colombia, Belgium, and Luxembourg as unreturned, as well as 17,500 Korean civilians forcibly taken north. The armistice agreement provided a complete release was to be made. The only reply received at Panmunjom was that all POWs were released long ago." O. H. P. King, *Tail Of The Paper Tiger*, (Caldwell: Caxton, 1961), pages 522-3.

"At the close of the Korean War, a list of captured personnel was submitted to the Reds, along with a demand that they be accounted for. Included were 944 Americans who were known, by various means, to be in Communist hands. When the Reds defiantly refused to yield up any information about these men, the Administration did nothing to force their return. Instead, trying to persuade the Communists to be more reasonable, the US 'unilaterally reduced' the number from 944 to 540 — thus arbitrarily consigning 400 American servicemen to the oblivion of Red captivity.

"Meanwhile, Administration inaction has also contributed to the work of erasing these men from official memory. As the years elapsed, the 'Missing Persons Act' came into effect. Under this law, once enough months have intervened, the bureaucrats are permitted to make a 'finding of death' for missing personnel; thus our soldiers are not only abandoned, but are systematically written off as dead and expunged from the lists of the missing." M. Stanton Evans and W. B. Hicks Jr., "Massive Humiliation," *Human Events,* February 18, 1959.

141:1 These meetings, as of September 20, 1962, total 114. *New York Times,* September 21, 1962. John Cabot, the present U.S. Ambassador to Poland, on June 23, 1962, assured Mr. Wang in effect — what informed Americans already knew — that our Seventh Fleet would continue to protect the Chinese Communists from any invasion by Chiang across the Formosa Strait. See *New York Times,* June 27, 1962.

141:2 Dr. Conor Cruise O'Brien, an Irish diplomat and colleague of Hammarskjoeld, presented an interesting sketch of Hammarskjoeld's character in *The Observer* (London) in 1961. See William S. Schlamm, "European Survey," *American Opinion,* January 1962, pages 23-27.

142:1 Chesly Manly recalled that John Foster Dulles described Hammarskjoeld's trip as a "mission of intercession." But, said Manly: "The Communists undoubtedly regarded it as a kowtowing mission, not only on behalf of the UN but also of the once proud United States . . . [and] the Eisenhower administration ignominiously entrusted the fate of American military personnel, held in violation of the Korean armistice agreement, to the intercession of a mincing UN Secretary General who labors furtively but tirelessly to bring Communist China into the organization." *The UN Record,* page 94.

142:2 "There was a time when Mr. Eisenhower was not so hesitant to give unqualified support to Americans in the Far East. During the presidential election campaign of 1952 the publisher of *The Standard-Times,* Basil Brewer, sent a telegram to Mr. Eisenhower questioning whether it would be wise for the United States to 'take the chance of withdrawing from Korea' and whether the Korean war would be brought to an end by Eisenhower 'with the American boys still in Communist prison camps.'

"In a letter of reply to Mr. Brewer, dated Oct. 24, 1952, Mr. Eisenhower said, 'We are not going to withdraw from Korea and leave our boys in Communist prison camps.' The facts of the matter are, we ARE withdrawing from Korea and we ARE leaving our boys in Communist prison camps. . . . Now that the Chinese Communists defiantly have broken the Korean truce terms by refusing to free American prisoners of war, the President has reverted to 'pathetic words of protest.' " *New Bedford Standard-Times,* December 1, 1954.

144:1 *New York Times,* January 28, 1954.

145:1 *New York Times,* February 19, 1954.

145:2 The Viet Namese knew what was developing: "During the closing stages of the Geneva conference the Viet Namese, Cambodians, and Laotians literally besieged [Undersecretary of State] Bedell Smith, requesting American protection and help against partition and against any solution based on French capitulation in the north." *Intelligence Digest,* August 1954, page 2.

145:3 August 2, 1954, page 9.

145:4 *The Kiplinger Washington Letter,* July 3, 1954, page 2.

146:1 Press conference on April 7, 1954. See *U.S. News & World Report,* April 16, 1954, page 21.

146:2 Press conference, as quoted in *New York Times,* July 1, 1954.

Chapter Thirteen

147:1 "The American conscience can never know peace until these people are restored again to being masters of their own fate." The people referred to by the speaker were the Latvians, Estonians,

Lithuanians, Poles, East Germans, East Austrians, Czechoslovakians, Albanians, Bulgars, and Rumanians. The speaker was Dwight Eisenhower before the American Legion Convention, August 25, 1952, as quoted in *U.S. News & World Report*, September 5, 1952, pages 88-91.

"I am sure that the President will run, first because Europe wants him, and secondly because the people of the United States want him." Senator Alexander Wiley, Republican of Wisconsin, in January 1956, as quoted in Frank Kirkpatrick, *The American Way*, Volume II, No. 1, 1956, page 21.

147:2 The reports were confirmed in an analysis by a private British intelligence service which said that the East German underground fought "because an unknown radio in Western Germany led them to believe that an East German revolt would receive the support of the Western powers. By openly revolting the hard core of anti-Communist resistance was destroyed by the waiting secret police and further uprisings of a similar nature were prevented through lack of capable leadership.

"The *Washington Evening Star* dated December 18, 1954, carried a statement by . . . Jay Lovestone: 'The A.F.L. (American Federation of Labor) was responsible for helping to develop and inspire those persons who later became the leaders of the famous June 17, 1953, revolt of the workers in Eastern Germany.' Jay Lovestone was paid by Allen Dulles' C.I.A. along with David Dubinsky to accomplish this act which protected the Soviet domination of Eastern Europe." *World Survey*, December 1956, page 2.

For more recent exploits of Lovestone, see Hilaire du Berrier, *Labor's International Network* (New Orleans: Conservative Society of America, 1962).

148:1 Said *Human Events* (January 22, 1955, page 1): "Now, Eisenhower comes out with a 'cease-fire' proposal. The record on 'cease-fire' pacts is very bad. Experience shows they only give the Reds

time for a bigger military build-up. Then the Reds violate 'cease-fire.'" Of course, even the *suggestion* of a 'cease fire' proposal was a psychological bomb against Chiang Kai-shek, in his position as *the only legitimate ruler of all China*, who was doing his best to put down a criminal insurrection.

149:1 *Editorial*, January 31, 1955, page 29.

"The original and basic intention of United States policy had been to help us, but in the long run since the Korean War, it has simply tied our hands. It has permitted the enemy to strengthen his military position, and it has weakened our own. It stops us from doing what we might do, what it is our duty to do, to help our people." President Chiang Kai-shek of Nationalist China, July 25, 1961, DeWitt Copp and Marshall Peck, *The Odd Day* (New York: Morrow, 1962), page 149. Of course, Chiang is being either polite, or gullible. This has been made to *appear* as the original and basic intention. But certainly some of the people promoting this appearance have designed and foreseen exactly what would happen and has happened, from the very beginning.

This writer has many times pointed out this effect, among the many nefarious effects of our foreign-aid program; namely, the gradual tying of the hands of the real anti-Communists like Chiang, against any realistic anti-Communist action, through his dependence which we insidiously develop on the continuance of American foreign-aid.

149:2 A really crushing blow was delivered to Nationalist China by Secretary of State Dulles in a press conference on September 28, 1958, when he described a return of the Nationalist regime to the Chinese mainland as "highly hypothetical" and that, in any event, the United States had "no commitment of any kind" to help the Nationalist regime return to the mainland. See *Deadline Data*, September 28, 1958.

150:1 Not a new situation by any

means. "According to the Austrian Institute for Economic Research, during the ten-year [1945-1955] occupation of Austria, 21% of Austria's exports were sent compulsorily but illegally to the Soviet bloc. During the same time the legal export of Austrian goods amounted to 0.40% of her total exports. Soviet administered oilfields and the 300 or more former German-owned industries which the Russians confiscated in eastern Austria, shipped $108 million worth of goods annually to the Soviet Union and $25 million worth to the East bloc satellites. This included two-thirds of Austria's 3,000,000-ton average annual production of petroleum and about one-third of her total export of machinery." *New York Times*, December 23, 1955.

151:1 See *Congressional Record*, June 1, 1955, pages 7344-7345; or, "The Austrian State Treaty," Department of State Publication 6437 (released April 1957) page 99.

151:2 *New York Times*, June 18, 1955.

151:3 At least twenty of the Senators were interviewed. *Human Events*, June 26, 1955, pages 1 and 2. The debates on the treaty are in the *Congressional Record*, June 17, 1955, pages 8591-8613.

151:4 "Senator Jenner (R., Ind.) tried hard to persuade the Senators to wait at least until the Committee report was out before voting, but the well-oiled machinery of the internationalists easily downed such a request." *Human Events*, June 25, 1955, page 1.

152:1 The full text of the treaty and related agreements and declarations is contained in "The Austrian State Treaty," Department of State Publication 6437 (released April 1957); pages 76-90; and in the *Congressional Record*, June 17, 1955, pages 8580-8591.

"Among those members of Congress who keep abreast of expert opinion on our foreign policy, many are showing doubts, now, about the Austrian treaty. Far from being a highly encouraging sign of Russian conciliation, as Dulles claimed, it looks like Moscow 'put one over' not only on the Austrians but on the United States. Foreigners, constantly in touch with sources in Central Europe, say that the treaty welds little Austria even more closely to the economic might of the Soviet Union than previously realized, without any perceptible advantage to the lesser partner to the deal. Furthermore, extravagant hopes built on the treaty tend to make hitherto cool-headed Austrians warm up to Russia and forget the Soviet duplicity in the recent past." *Human Events*, July 9, 1955, page 1.

152:2 It was at this time that William Loeb, Publisher of the *Manchester* (N.H.) *Union Leader* wrote: "This newspaper now solemnly charges that President Eisenhower has done more to destroy the respect, honor and power of the United States than any President in its history." Editorial, "Prince Of Appeasement," June 23, 1955.

153:1 Columnist Bill Cunningham, *Boston Herald*, July 24, 1955.

153:2 *U.S. News & World Report*, July 22, 1955, pages 47-48.

The Communists in the United States had been working for almost two years to bring about a 'summit' meeting. In the Fall of 1953 at a secret national conference the CPUSA received its instructions from Moscow: "Both the needs and the possibilities of the present moment call for the development of a veritable crusade for peaceful negotiations, for a top-level meeting of the Big Powers. . . . It is to this end that we must turn all our energies, our utmost skill, tenacity and resourcefulness. . . ." As quoted by Dean Clarence Manion, *Manion Forum Network*, May 4, 1958.

154:1 Pessimism was the tone two months earlier: "It can be revealed that the President, meeting with Senate leaders on May 9, told them he did not like the idea of a conference, that he fully realized the danger of dealing with the Russians," *Human Events*, May 14, 1955, page 1.

154:2 *U.S. News & World Report,* July 22, 1955, pages 47-48.

155:1 As quoted by James Reston in his *New York Times* dispatch as it appeared in the *Boston Herald,* July 21, 1955.

155:2 "Perhaps the most telling comment on the 'Spirit of Geneva' was made by Bulganin. Bulganin said that the spirit of Geneva was created by martinis, and he gave President Eisenhower full credit. The White House made an official denial of this tribute, however, saying that the President prefers scotch." *The Dan Smoot Report,* August 10, 1956, page 6. See, also, *Associated Press Dispatch* from Geneva as it appeared in the *Boston Herald,* July 21, 1955, under the headline: "Red Chiefs Joke, Drink With West Cameramen."

156:1 "The Russians scored a tremendous success at Geneva: They managed to create a mood of optimism without giving way an inch on the crucial question of Germany. . . . On matters of substance their line has, in fact, hardened." *The Economist* (London), July 30, 1955.

"Eisenhower says he made no pact at Geneva and proclaimed that no agreement was reached at the conference; but he offered to the Soviets the right to mount an air patrol over our country that is not only illegal but is tantamount to surrendering the independence of the United States by giving the Soviets the right and power of surveillance over our military actions.

"Of this offer, even the pro-Eisenhower *New York Times* was forced to say: 'In the first place, it was generally regarded as unrealistic. Second, it is illegal under U.S. laws. Third, it seemed to other Western delegates to be a proposal which has no chance of being accepted. Fourth, . . . the idea apparently was not explored in any detail, if at all, with Congressional leaders, who make the laws.' " Frank Kirkpatrick, *The American Way,* May-July, 1955.

Seven years later Frank J. Johnson wrote of Geneva's effects: "The United States was really maneuvered out of taking any advantage of its superior power until Soviet scientists could create a counterdeterrent to 'massive retaliation.' " *No Substitute For Victory* (Chicago: Regnery, 1962), pages 29-30. From 1954 to 1961 Mr. Johnson served in Naval Intelligence as a specialist on all aspects of Soviet political and military strategy.

156:2 "But the Soviet got what might be called peace at no price at Geneva. The pictures of the 'Big Four' chatting wreathed in smiles, of Eisenhower shaking hands with Bulganin, were of inestimable propaganda value for Soviet policy on both sides of the Iron Curtain. In Poland and other satellite countries these pictures were widely circulated to point a moral. If the President of the United States is on such good terms with the Soviet rulers, what is the use of hoping for liberation, of keeping up any kind of resistance? These Geneva photographs represented the biggest imaginable handicaps for the political and psychological warfare efforts of the Free Europe Committee and the American Committee for Liberation from Bolshevism." William H. Chamberlin, "The Great Geneva Fraud," *The Freeman,* December 1955, pages 770-772.

156:3 "What exactly then is 'peaceful co-existence'? What do the Communists mean by the term? One of the best definitions appeared in the newspaper, *Soviet Russia* [S. Titarenko, "Why Wars Are Not Fatalistically Inevitable," August 17, 1960]:

Peaceful co-existence is the general line of the foreign policy of both the U.S.S.R. and the other socialist countries. This does not mean, of course, peace in the class struggle between socialism and capitalism or reconciliation of the Communist with the bourgeois ideology. Peaceful co-existence means not only the existence of states with different social systems, but also a definite form of class struggle between socialism and capitalism on a worldwide scale. This form includes giving up military means for solution of controversial international questions and, at the same time, presupposes an ideological and political struggle and economic competition. Socialism need not resort to war for victory on a world-wide scale. Its ideas will inevitably win through peaceful competition.

Translated, this means that the struggle shall go on as before, but that it shall be conducted exclusively on Soviet terms, that is to say, that the greatest strength of the West—the superior military power of the United States—shall be neutralized and shall not be employed as a counterweight to the spread of Communism. If we attempt any forcible opposition to Communism anywhere, we are not peaceably co-existing." Johnson, *No Substitute For Victory*, page 61.

Eugene Lyons pointed out that the objectives of Soviet conduct in 1955 were: "(1) to obtain access to Western technology, its products and its specialized personnel, by opening wide the sluices of trade and 'exchange of persons.' (2) To beat down actual and potential resistance in the Soviet orbit by demonstrating to its people that they cannot hope for free-world support—on the valid theory that without such hope opposition sentiment must wither and die." "The Bear Smiles Again," *The Freeman*, November 1955, pages 735-737.

157:1 Eisenhower did take a step backward a few weeks after the Summit meeting, but Eugene Lyons was not deceived: "Only a few weeks after descending from the Summit, President Eisenhower tried to brake the runaway inflation of optimism. In his Philadelphia address on August 24 he warns: 'There can be no true peace which involves acceptance of a *status quo* in which we find injustice in many nations, repressions of human beings on a gigantic scale, and with constructive effort paralyzed in many areas by fear. The spirit of Geneva, if it is to provide a healthy atmosphere for the pursuit of peace, it is to be genuine and not spurious, must inspire all to a correction of injustice, an observance of human rights and an end to subversion on a world-wide scale.' "

Said Lyons: "To demand that a totalitarian police state observe human rights, that world communism cease to be subversive, is to demand the impossible. The President must know that such conditions cannot be met, short of a successful anticommunist revolution in the Soviet empire. In effect, he was repudiating the illusions he had himself helped generate." Lyons, *Loc. cit.*

As James Burnham saw the situation: "When we not merely have formal diplomatic relations with Moscow's representatives but smile and joke with them, exchange family gifts with them, go to their parties and invite them to ours, then we are saying to the Soviet peoples in a voice much louder than Radio Free Europe's: These rulers of yours are in our eyes not usurpers, tyrants, aggressors and assassins, but legitimate governors and decent human beings. When we offer Moscow and its satellites treaties, disarmament pacts, trade agreements, we imply that the Communist regimes are here to stay, that their word can be trusted." "The Third World War," *National Review*, January 18, 1956, page 13.

157:2 *Inform*, May 22, 1956, page 2.

A statement by John Foster Dulles confirms the appraisal from *Inform*: "It is very important that this satellite situation should develop in such a way that the Soviet Union is surrounded by friendly countries." *U.S. News & World Report*, December 28, 1956, page 73.

The liberal Spanish scholar and diplomat Salvador de Madariaga said of the Summit Meeting: "The Soviet leaders have every reason to be satisfied with the outcome of the Geneva conference. They have been able to demonstrate to their own peoples that even their opponents are convinced of the peaceful desires of the Soviet Union, so that, if no peace prevails, the reasons must lie elsewhere. They have been able to show to the peoples of eastern Europe that they have practically nothing to expect from the West for their liberation, that the West is practically ready to recognize the status quo of the Russian conquests by the indirect method of a security post, insofar as an acceptable solution for the German question can be found. To the Communists in France and Italy they have proved that Moscow will hence-forward support those communist parties with the help of which they have already engulfed half of Europe. It is difficult to see what the leaders of the West can show to *their* peoples as a success of the Geneva conference." As quoted in William H. Chamberlin, "The Great Geneva Fraud," *The Freeman*, December 1955, pages 770-772.

And Frederick D. Wilhelmsen made this observation on the Eisenhower version of "containment": "Perhaps our President, the most ungrammatical statesman in modern history, is the most apt symbol for the Gnostic mist with which we wrap our determination to do nothing that would risk our fortune or commit our word. He anounced to the world that it was American policy to keep alive the hope for freedom within the satellite countries *and* that it was American polity not to encourage rebellion in those countries." "The Bankruptcy Of American Optimism," *National Review*, May 11, 1957, pages 449-451.

157:3 "The American position is now clear—except, curiously, to the American people. It was made clear by the revelations about State Department connivance in Soviet-Yugoslav efforts, last September, to deflect revolutionary sentiments in Eastern Europe into 'national Communist' channels; by the Eisenhower-Dulles assurances to Moscow, in the first days of the revolt, that the U.S. did not favor 'new governments' in Eastern Europe that would be 'potential military allies' of the West; by the failure of the U.S. government to lift a finger in the rebels' behalf once the bloodletting had begun; and, finally by the U.S. Secretary of State's formal repudiation, last month, of the revolutionary method of libera-

tion." L. Brent Bozell, "The U.S. Pushes 'National Communism,'" *National Review*, June 1, 1957, pages 516-517 *et. seq.*

158:1 *Inform*, May 22, 1956, page 2.

158:2 "Balloons for a visit by Russian leaders to the United States, set afloat by American 'liberals,' were deflated on Capitol Hill in the past week, as a result of release of a bipartisan congressional committee report. This House report severely condemns President Eisenhower's 'summit conference' of last August, saying that it 'seriously weakened anti-Communist sentiment in the Middle East and Southern Asia' areas. The committee covered 24 countries on its trip and spoke authoritatively on sentiment in territories between Greece and Japan.

"The feeling in many lands, said the Members of Congress, is that it is 'senseless for them to resist Communists if the West is going to accept the Communists into respectable society at Geneva.' The report states that many in the countries they visited 'were shaken' by the American inclination to 'strive for friendly intercourse with the Communists.' The congressional committee also said that 'the sweetness and light campaign reflected in friendly pronouncements by Americans, in the exchanges of visitors between the United States and the Soviet Union, and in other ways, tended to weaken the anti-Communist resolve of the peoples of the Middle East, Southeast Asia and the Far East." *Human Events*, May 12, 1956, page 2.

158:3 See William S. Schlamm, "Foreign Trends," *National Review*, June 13, 1956, page 12.

159:1 The text of which read: "The Government of the United States, under Republican leadership, will repudiate all commitments contained in secret understandings such as those of Yalta which aid Communist enslavements. It will be made clear, on the highest authority of the President and the Congress, that United States policy, as one of its peaceful purposes, looks happily forward to the genuine independence of those captive peoples."

159:2 For what Eisenhower's attitude meant to the regime of Chiang Kai-shek, see Rodney Gilbert, "Bewilderment In Taipei," *National Review*, September 28, 1957, pages 276-277.

159:3 I was using the word "liberation," of course, in its correct and normal meaning; and not according to invariable Soviet usage, whereby the "liberation" of a country means the imposing on that country of a tyrannical Communist dictatorship.

159:4 "Containment" was the policy so carefully designed and propagated by George F. Kennan. See his two articles, "The Sources Of Soviet Conduct," *Foreign Affairs,* July 1947, pages 566-582, and, "America And The Russian Future," *Op. cit.,* April 1951, pages 351-370. Both articles were reprinted in Kennan's, *American Diplomacy 1900-1950* (Chicago: University of Chicago Press, 1951), which, as might be expected, won the "Freedom House Award" for 1951.

Kennan served in the State Department for twenty-seven years before retiring on July 29, 1953—his last position being Ambassador to the Soviet Union. And during the years of the Eisenhower Administration, Kennan was at the Institute for Advanced Study at Princeton, New Jersey, where his friend J. Robert Oppenheimer was Director.

Kennan's "containment" policy, however, was preserved by United States support of NATO (which was based on Kennan's ideas, according to the *Wall St. Journal* in its editorial of November 20, 1959).

On March 7, 1961 President Kennedy appointed Kennan as Ambassador to Yugoslavia, in which position he has labored mightily on behalf of Tito. See transcript of the NBC television program, "Today," for interview with Kennan, as contained under remarks of Senator William Proxmire in the *Congressional Record*, July 9, 1962, pages 12041-12044.

For an excellent critique of Kennan's

mental processes, see M. Stanton Evans, "The Liberal Against Himself," *National Review*, December 22, 1956, pages 11-13.

161:1 William H. Chamberlin summarized the effects on Germany: "The Soviet government has achieved two important objectives in Germany. It has obtained double German representation in Moscow, an ambassador from the Federal Republic along with a representative of its puppet regime. It has acquired an embassy in Bonn which, in all probability, will not only be a center for subversion and espionage but also a magnet of attraction for all the disgruntled and confused Germans who have a vague feeling that they might make a better deal for their country by loosening or breaking their ties with the West." "The Great Geneva Fraud," *The Freeman*, December 1955, pages 770-772.

161:2 Eugene Lyons was particularly disturbed at the acceptability of "neutralism" which resulted from the Summit Conference: ". . . The Geneva 'summit' conference, suggesting as it did that even the United States and its allies had been converted to neutralism, set up behind the Iron Curtain tides of despair that have not yet wholly receded. People there know that new respectability granted to neutralism amounts to a surrender, and thus dooms their hopes for liberation; and they understand why the Kremlin, in counting its forces, publicly lists neutralist countries and parties in the pro-Soviet columns. Only in the free world are there men who think of themselves as anti-Communist and yet manage to approve of neutralism." "The Anatomy Of Neutralism," *National Review*, July 18, 1956, pages 9-10 *et seq.*

162:1 *U.S. News & World Report*, March 2, 1956.

162:2 In a speech before the *Philadelphia Bulletin* Forum at Philadelphia on February 26, 1956, Dulles said that at "the Summit Conference at Geneva President Eisenhower did more than any other man could have done to open up to the Soviet rulers the vista of a new era of friendly relations between our countries."

Yet, only a few minutes later Dulles quoted Khrushchev's speech to the Supreme Soviet of December 29, 1955: "If certain people think that our confidence in the victory of socialism, the teaching of Marxism-Leninism, is a violation of the Geneva spirit, they obviously have an incorrect notion of the Geneva spirit. They ought to remember once and for all that we never renounced and we will never renounce our ideas, our struggle for the victory of communism."

And Dulles knew what *the teaching of Marxism-Leninism* was, since earlier in this same speech, he described it as the necessity "to hate all who differ from the Soviet Communist creed" and "that only by violence could international communism achieve its destined goals." See complete text of Dulles' speech in *Facts Forum News,* June 1956, pages 9-11.

162:3 L. Brent Bozell expressed his shock as he reviewed fifteen incidents which highlighted the first three years of the Eisenhower-Dulles foreign policy:

"....July 1953: The Administration agrees to an armistice in Korea, and thus relinquishes an opportunity to liberate North Korea. This decision is made although the Korean military commanders 'believed that victory in Korea was possible and desirable . . . [and] that political considerations were permitted to overrule military necessity.' (Report of Senate Subcommittee on Internal Security, January 21, 1955.)

"....April 1954: President Eisenhower proposes a *modus vivendi* in Indo-China, and the U.S. thereupon acquiesces in a deal with the Viet Minh and Red China whereby twelve million human beings and half the country are handed over to the Communists.

"....August 1954: Administration spokesmen begin to describe U.S. policy as one of 'peaceful coexistence,' borrowing a term originally attributed to Lenin.

"....January 1955: The Administration directs Free China to abandon its advance base on the Tachen Islands; Chiang is assured that if he complies, the U.S. will help defend Quemoy and the Matsus.

"....March 1955: The Yalta papers are released, but the Administration bars repudiation of the 'enslavements.' President Eisenhower observes that 'There is nothing to be gained by going back ten years and showing that in the light of after event, someone may have been right, and someone may have been wrong.'

"....March 1955: The President, when asked if the U.S. intends to support Free China's liberation aims, announces: 'The United States is not going to be a party to an aggressive war.'

"....May 1955: Secretary Dulles reveals that the U.S. will help defend Quemoy and the Matsus only if they are attacked as part of a full-scale assault on Formosa —an unlikely Communist strategy.

"....May 1955: The U.S. signs the Austrian State Treaty which commits Austria to bind her economy to Russia's, to permit Communist political activity in Austria, and to refrain from participating in the defense arrangements of the Western democracies.

"....June 1955: The President observes that the Austrian Treaty is evidence that Soviet peace talk may be 'sincere,' and decides to meet with the Kremlin leaders 'at the summit' to find out for sure.

"....June 1955: The Senate, under heavy Administration pressure, rejects the McCarthy resolution which recommends obtaining a prior Soviet commitment to discuss Communist satellites at the summit meeting. McCarthy argues that the Communist slave empire is the cause of world tensions; but the Senate resists 'tying the President's hands.'

"....July 1955: In his opening address at the Geneva conference, the President alludes to the satellites, but drops the subject when Bulganin denies the existence of a 'problem.' The President discovers, however, that the Soviet Union sincerely wants peace, and concludes that the Geneva meeting was a 'success.'

"....July 1955: Secretary Dulles reveals that the U.S. will view any attempts by

South Korea and South Vietnam to free the northern halves of their countries as 'aggression,' and will oppose them.

"....October 1955: The U.S. offers to guarantee the boundaries of the Communist empire.

"....November 1955: President Eisenhower conveys to the Soviet Union 'the best wishes of the people of the United States' on the anniversary of the day the Communists took over Russia.

"....December 1955: The U.S. promotes the 'package deal' for admission of Communist satellites to the UN, thus acquiesces in the UN's ratification of Communist rule in eastern Europe. In this connection, President Eisenhower sends three personal cables to Chiang Kai-shek, urging the Chinese Nationalist government not to veto the admission of a Soviet creature called 'Outer Mongolia.'" "National Trends," *National Review*, January 11, 1956, page 14.

163:1 By December 31, 1961 the aid total to Greece was $2.9 billion. Lawrence Sullivan, Coordinator of Information for the House of Representatives, as quoted in Fulton Lewis Jr., *The Top Of The News*, October 8-12, 1962, page 328.

164:1 *London Times*, March 13, 1958.

165:1 The critical events of the Suez crisis developed rapidly: On October 30, 1956 the United States proposed in the UN Security Council that all member states "refrain from the use or threat of force" in Egypt. The Soviet Union supported the resolution while Britain and France vetoed it. But, on November 5, British and French parachutists were dropped in the Port Said area. On the following day British Prime Minister Eden told the House of Commons that Britain and France were ordering a cease-fire by midnight.

Said the *New York Times* (November 8, 1956): "... We have just witnessed the sudden and complete collapse of the Western position under the impact of what amounts to a Russian ultimatum."

165:2 "... They (Britain and France) learned that, singly or collectively, they are no great powers any longer. In the face of a virtual Soviet ultimatum — acidly answered by Mr. Eisenhower — they had to buckle under Washington's orders; the only alternative was to buckle under Moscow's orders. For the time being, given the Unholy 'Alliance' between Washington and Moscow, the orders of the Big Two were parallel." Melchior Palyi, "Russia's Two-Fold Triumph," *National Review*, February 16, 1957, pages 153-4.

165:3 "... President Eisenhower and Secretary Dulles consistently missed their opportunities, consistently thwarted Britain and France, and consistently (though of course unknowingly [sic.]) let themselves be used as pawns in the game played by Nasser and the rulers of Russia." Henry Hazlitt, "Timetable To Disaster," *National Review*, February 9, 1957, pages 133-5.

165:4 Leading Democrats viewed the Suez incident as a decisive factor in the re-election of Eisenhower: "The sudden tensions overseas made retention of Eisenhower imperative in the minds of the voters. . . . But the defeated Stevenson and his jilted adjutants confirmed in post-mortem that 'the war issue beat us.' The Stevenson campaign manager, Jim Finnegan, said 'It was an even thing electorally until the Middle East Crisis.'" Columnist Bill Cunningham, *Boston Herald*, November 11, 1956.

165:5 Said Brent Bozell: "The tragedy is that the last realistic opportunity for preserving the Middle East as a Western sphere faded out when British and French troops withdrew from Port Said at Mr. Eisenhower's behest." "The Mideastern Policy," *National Review*, January 19, 1957, pages 56-57.

165:6 Viscount Hinchingbrooke, as quoted by *The Wall St. Journal*, February 15, 1957.

166:1 *London Sunday Times*, November 25, 1956.

166:2 *Ibid.*

John Gordon in the *London Express* (November 11, 1956) optimistically said that Eden had "put an end to Dullesism. For which not only Britain, but all Europe will be mighty thankful." Arthur Veyses of the *Chicago Tribune Press Service* reported that "Britons in unmatched numbers are writing to the American embassy here [in London] and warning President Eisenhower and Ambassador Winthrop W. Aldrich that anti-American feelings in Britain are stronger than ever and won't soon be erased." *Boston Herald*, January 29, 1957.

And in a separate dispatch, on the same day, the *Chicago Tribune Press Service* reported that British newspapers were describing Dulles as "a dedicated ass, a blunderer, tactless, the greatest obstacle to British-American unity."

166:3 Claud Cockburn, "Sanctions," March 6, 1957, pages 326-327.

166:4 "This appointment provided still another clue to American intentions. We have already encountered Mr. Murphy in these pages (page 20). It was he who, as President Roosevelt's personal envoy, had told the Algerian nationalists in 1942 that the end of colonialism figured among the American war aims. There was no reason to believe that his views had changed substantially in the interval." Michael J. Clark, *Algeria In Turmoil* (New York: Grossett & Dunlap, 1960), page 366. For more on Mr. Murphy see 233:1 and 248:4.

167:1 This was the famous "secret letter," which of course could not possibly be kept secret. It prompted Soustelle's brilliant epigrammatic speech which precipitated the fall of the Gaillard Government.

167:2 At the time these paragraphs were written, de Gaulle had just come to power, and was *talking* an extremely strong and convincing anti-Communist line. Despite his horrible pro-Communist record of the past, I was willing to *hope* with Soustelle, de Serigny and many patriotic Frenchmen, that he had changed. I maintained that hope as long as I possibly could and then, in the summer of 1961, began to point out, with increasing emphasis and documentation, how de Gaulle himself was betraying Algeria and France itself into Communist hands. See *American Opinion*, September 1961, "If You Want It Straight," pages 1-5; December 1961, "If You Want It Straight," pages 1-7; July-August 1962, "Algeria: An Appeal To American Opinion," page 68; and, September 1962, pages 1-62, reprinted as "The Tragedy Of France," in the *American Opinion* Reprint Series.

168:1 "President Eisenhower's betrayal of our allies on this side of the Iron Curtain at Suez, and of our allies on the other side of the Iron Curtain in Hungary, has made clearer than ever before the extent and depth of the bankruptcy of his policy. . . . The Hungarian slaughter, the apotheosis of Nasser, the humiliation of Britain and Eden, the surrender of the Mideast to the Soviet Union (the Eisenhower Doctrine is as effective as a sledgehammer against termites)—these are the realities of our foreign policy of 1957.

"Chiang Kai-shek and Syngman Rhee learned the same lesson a little earlier. It is a very simple lesson: the 'axiomatic structure' upon which American foreign policy is based is surrender, surrender, and again surrender. Nor is this surprising; it is the logical outcome of Mr. Eisenhower's first axiom: war is unthinkable." Frank S. Meyer, " 'New Ideas' Or Old Truth," *National Review*, February 2, 1957, pages 107-108.

Chapter Fourteen

169:1 Less than a year after the Eisenhower Administration came to power, Willis Ballinger wrote: "It is now clear that the internationalism which for more than fifty years has schemed to destroy our sovereignty and sap our wealth was not halted when the New Deal was turned out of office. It is closing in fast for complete victory and under the auspices of a Republican administration.

"These are the sad facts: ONE: President Eisenhower believes in a world government.

"TWO: His brother Dr. Milton Eisenhower, whose influence with the President is well-known, is also a firm believer in a world government.

"THREE: Secretary of State Dulles is a staunch world government advocate. Two days after he was selected last fall to be Secretary of State, Dulles sent a congratulatory telegram to the Atlantic Union Congress meeting in Buffalo, praising the idea of Atlantic Union but suggesting that NATO be used as the basis for fashioning the contemplated international State.

"FOUR: The Bricker amendment to the Constitution which would close the door on any treaty over-riding the Constitution, is strongly opposed by President Eisenhower. Though this amendment is actually a product of the American Bar Association, and has been approved by a two to one vote by the Senate Committee which held hearings on it last session of Congress, the Administration blocked it from coming to a vote in the Senate. It offered a substitute known as the 'Knowland amendment'—a substitute which our Bar Association voted down as inadequate.

"FIVE: Before the Louisville Bar Association, Mr. Dulles admitted that through a mere treaty the Constitution could be scrapped—that power could be taken away from the States and given to Congress, power taken away from Congress and given to the Executive, or power taken away from the Federal and State Governments and given to an international body. Conceding that our national sovereignty could be destroyed through a treaty, Dulles at the time thought an amendment to the Constitution desirable. But before the Senate Committee holding hearings on the Bricker amendment Mr. Dulles opposed it—told the Senators it was not necessary as the administration had no intention of doing anything about the Genocide Pact and the Declaration of Human Rights—both denounced by our Bar Association as subverting our Bill of Rights and supplying a blueprint for world socialism. The next morning President Eisenhower cabled a congratulatory message to the Human

Rights Convention in Geneva. Only a few weeks ago our representative in the UN—Mr. Lodge—voted for the Genocide Pact." "America—Europe's Happy Hunting Ground," *Human Events*, December 23, 1953.

169:2 But Eisenhower had decided the search was over for such a federation when the United States joined the UN: ". . . The President sounded off on the subject of the UN before the United States Committee for United Nations Day. The interview was not given much play by the press generally, but it did not escape those in the legislative arm who happened to be in town. They were surprised to learn from Ike's lips that the U.S. is 'committed irrevocably' to the support of UN. He also claimed that 'there is obviously one deep and abiding bond that joins us together . . . you have faith and belief in the United Nations and so do I.' Few members of Congress would agree with this.

"And the President declared that the UN 'still represents man's best organized hope to substitute the conference table for the battlefield . . . who knows what could have happened in these past years of strain and struggle if we hadn't had the United Nations . . . .' A number of legislators who knew much more about the diplomatic struggle of the past few years than Eisenhower will scarcely find such thoughts intelligible, in view of our war against the Reds with 'one hand tied behind our backs' by the UN.

"Finally, the President emphasized that the UN 'is far more than merely a desirable organization in these days . . . . I think the United Nations has become sheer necessity.' Later, according to the *Washington Daily News* (Sept. 24), White House sources said that the President opposes the U.S. getting out of the UN if Red China is admitted." *Human Events*, September 30, 1953, page 2.

169:3 "The entire Red scheme for the U.N. was revealed in a Communist pamphlet, 'The United Nations,' issued in September 1945 by the People's Publishing House, Bombay, India . . . . According to this Communist pamphlet, the Soviet Union has three main objectives in the United Nations: 1. Use of the veto 'automatically' to prevent any restrictive or harmful action being taken against the Soviet Union. 2. To create disaffection among the peoples of non-Communist nations 'particularly those of Great Britain and the U.S.A.' and thus to frustrate the foreign policy of those nations. 3. To use the U.N. Trusteeship Council and the Specialized Agencies for warping the program of national independence among the 'colonial' nations; to detach all dependent and semi-dependent areas from any foreign influence except that of the Soviet Union; and to bring about the amalgamation of all nations in a single Soviet system." Alice Widener, *Behind The U.N. Front* (New York: The Bookmailer, 1955), pages 57-58.

171:1 "Undoubtedly, many of the Red-sponsored applicants were turned away at the U.N. door. But it appears that the cleverest of the American group [sent by Hiss] not only got through, they eventually maneuvered themselves into secure positions at Lake Success, and later rode an escalator all the way to the top level positions in the U.N. Headquarters in New York City." *Ibid.*, page 25.

171:2 See William L. McGrath, "The Surprising Case Of The I.L.O.," *American Opinion,* December 1959, pages 9-17, and, Don Knowlton, "What Communists Say In The ILO," *Ibid.*, pages 18-19.

171:3 See J. B. Matthews, "The World Health Organization," *American Opinion,* May 1958, pages 7-12; 31-35.

171:4 Excellent material on foreign aid may be found in the numerous reports and releases issued periodically since 1959 by the Citizens Foreign Aid Committee (1001 Connecticut Avenue, N.W., Washington 6, D. C.). Walter Harnischfeger of Milwaukee is Chairman and Brigadier General Bonner Fellers is National Director of the Committee. Every member of the Committee has been connected in one way or another with the United States foreign aid program.

171:5 ". . . in the most advanced countries the following will be pretty generally applicable . . . . A heavy progressive or graduated income tax." *Communist Manifesto of 1848.*

172:1 Note the drive, greatly and rapidly increased during 1961 and 1962, to sell goods manufactured in Communist countries in American retail stores. Our Government has been supplying hundreds of millions of dollars worth of American farm products to Poland. Out of the hogs fed by these farm products the Communist bosses of Poland, using slave labor at every step in the process, put up canned hams which are shipped to the United States and sold to American consumers at prices which are not determined in any way by the laws of economics or competition. Both retail and wholesale channels in the United States are heavily pressured by our State Department to stock and sell these Polish hams. And this is all a deliberate part of the leveling process, between Communist Poland and ourselves, which I was discussing in these paragraphs.

173:1 (New York: International Publishers), pages 52-55. Browder was merely following the line laid down by Joseph Stalin, as early as 1921. See Joseph Stalin, *Marxism And The National And Colonial Question* (New York: International Publishers, 1944), pages 115-116.

173:2 In its eulogy of Harry Dexter White, the *Daily Worker* (November 20, 1953) said: "White fought for massive economic and trade relations with the Soviet Union—to the tune of a $10 billion postwar credit—so as to enable us to obtain the raw materials we need . . . . White called for 'real aid' to Latin America and China . . . ."

The Communists were lavishing praise where it belonged. In 1954 a Senate Subcommittee found "documents were introduced into evidence which stated that in 1944 the Government was advised to conserve its minerals and that it should purchase some critical materials from foreign countries, including Russia. It was testified that this advice played a part in the subsequent increase in United States dependence on foreign nations for critical materials which are available in this Nation and in the other areas of the Western Hemisphere." *Report*, Minerals, Materials, And Fuels Economic Subcommittee, 83rd Congress, 2nd Session, June 23, 1954, page 6.

The Chairman of the Subcommittee, Senator George W. Malone, said that the policy makers in this regard were "the Harry Dexter White and Alger Hiss group." Statement released from Senator Malone's office in August 1954. Also see, James Burnham's *The Web of Subversion*, pages 48-50; 130-133; especially for the White-Coe relationship.

173:3 At the Frunze Military Academy in Moscow the students were told that "the distribution of the goods shipped by UNRRA should be made through the People's Committees; and by distribution of the goods of UNRRA should be thus acquired members for the Communist Party among opportunistic people." Colonel Jan Bukar in his testimony before the House Committee On Un-American Activities, May 14, 1953, page 20. Colonel Bukar, a Slovakian-in-exile, also testified that: "In the distribution of the goods through UNRRA the people who got any portion of the goods had to be enrolled as members of the Communist Party for the goods . . . [and] I want again to state that through UNRRA the Communist Party gained many members." *Loc. cit.*, page 21.

". . . Communist guerillas [in China] quickly destroyed the Yellow River flood rehabilitation work of UNRRA engineers, constructed at a cost of millions of dollars. They similarly destroyed roads and railways repaired with UNRRA funds. While engaged in this deliberate destruction, they were receiving UNRRA relief supplies. For we insisted that a due proportion of UNRRA aid be furnished to Communist areas." Freda Utley, *The China Story*, (Chicago: Regnery, 1951),

cxlvi

page 49. See also, by the same author, *Last Chance In China* (Indianapolis: Bobbs-Merrill, 1947), pages 108-110.

The UNRRA crowd would also share responsibility for the despicable Operation Keelhaul (See Chapter Four). "Hundreds of thousands of Soviet fugitives who evaded repatriation by our military monitors ended up in DP camps under UNRRA control. Again force was used —not outright violence now but propaganda, threats, lies, pressures—to make them go home. Eugene Lyons writes: 'The role of UNRRA in riding herd on Stalin's enemies, both under Herbert Lehman and Fiorello La Guardia, was hardly one to make Americans proud of their statesmen. La Guardia in particular showed himself insensitive to the fears and grievances of the Kremlin's runaway subjects. Since UNRRA was widely infiltrated by communists and fellow travelers in any case, the plight of would-be non-returners was far from enviable.

"[And] . . . hordes of DP's in American hands were cajoled and frightened into going behind the Iron Curtain. Under Lehman's successor, La Guardia, came the notorious secret 'Order No. 199.' This, to quote Lyons again, 'Not only instructed DP camp officials to effect 'speedy return' of Soviet nationals to their homeland in accordance with the Yalta agreement, but outlined pressures and hinted at punishments toward that end.' " Julius Epstein, "How We Served As Partners In A Purge," *American Legion Magazine*, December 1954, pages 14-15; 43-45.

173:4 The United States Ambassador to Poland, Arthur Bliss Lane, wrote: "Over my personal protest, Director General Herbert H. Lehman had appointed as director of the first UNRRA mission to Poland the Soviet member of the UNRRA council, Mr. [Mikhail] Menshikov, whose first duty would be the negotiation of an agreement with the Polish Government for the reception and distribution of UNRRA supplies. It was no surprise to me when in August

[1944] the agreement concluded in Warsaw provided that the Polish Government, and not UNRRA, should have complete jurisdiction over the distribution of UNRRA supplies in Poland." What this arrangement led to in the following months is described by Lane: ". . . as the agreement with the Polish Government gave UNRRA no control over the distribution of goods imported by UNRRA, Drury could not prevent supplies being used for political purposes. Certain types of supplies, such as blankets, could be purchased only by those persons holding a specified type of ration card issued solely to government employees or to members of the Workers and Socialist parties. And, although over ninety percent of the Polish people were Catholic, Catholic schools, hospitals and orphanages had difficulty in obtaining UNRRA supplies. One municipal official, in fact, told the bishop of his community that UNRRA supplies were not intended for "reactionary" organizations, such as the Roman Catholic Church. UNRRA supplies, chiefly canned foods, appeared in many of the Warsaw shop windows at outrageously high prices, and some goods were even peddled on the sidewalk in front of the Hotel Polonia." *I Saw Poland Betrayed*, (Indianapolis: Bobbs-Merrill, 1948), pages 143; 214-215.

173:5 Eugene W. Castle reveals that in a letter he received (September 26, 1956) from Senator A. Willis Robertson of Virginia, Mr. Robertson wrote: "Tom Connally (former U.S. Senator from Texas) told me that he asked General Marshall, after the word got out about the Marshall Plan, what it was, and he said Marshall answered, 'I will be damned if I know.'" *The Great Giveaway* (Chicago: Regnery, 1957), page 28 fn2. "Secretary of War Robert P. Patterson, in a letter to Hiss which was read at the first Hiss trial, said: 'I know that it was you and Clark Eichelberger who set up the Committee for the Marshall Plan.'" *Ibid.*, page 16.

174:1 For example: "Our UNRRA

spendings totalled $2,671,000,000. After it was disbanded, we were induced to allocate nearly a third of a billion dollars more to wind up its operations. With a total disregard of our national interests, UNRRA money was unreservedly given to the Communist-ruled nations behind the Iron Curtain. It fed discontented peoples and strengthened the Red grip on their governments." Eugene W. Castle, *Billions, Blunders And Baloney* (New York: Devin-Adair, 1955), page 47.

"Of the many mistakes by which we have propelled Soviet Russia into its present position of power, the organization and administration of UNRRA has been the gravest. . . . Of the fifteen countries assisted by UNRRA all but six are now wholly or partly in Communist hands." Hubert Martin in *Human Events*, May 23, 1951, page 8.

"Total foreign aid disbursements by the U.S. Treasury since World War II now add up to $86.9 billion, through December 31, 1961." Lawrence Sullivan, Coordinator of Information for the House of Representatives, as quoted by Fulton Lewis Jr., *The Top Of The News*, October 8-12, 1962, page 328.

174:2 "In the latter part of July (1956), the foreign staff of the *Chicago Tribune* met in conference at London. The Paris Chief was asked: 'What about the American foreign aid program? Do you think it is necessary?' He replied: 'Emphatically, no. And it's not just my opinion, either. I have talked with scores of American officials employed here by the United States government in the various organs which handle foreign aid and virtually every one had admitted privately and confidentially, that it is rightly called *operation rat hole.* 'But don't quote me,' they say, 'or I would be out in the streets tomorrow.' Gen. Eisenhower lived in France for several years, State Secretary Dulles has made countless trips to Europe, the government has ambassadors, consuls, special agents, and missions all over the place, but none have chosen to see the uselessness of the give-away policy. Newspapers and magazines in Europe certainly give them the facts if they will read them, as in the recent article in the French weekly *Match* on, *Why Americans are Despised in Europe*. Governments, officially, welcome these billions of American gift dollars because the money helps their budgets without resorting to taxation. They are naturally willing that the American taxpayer shoulder this burden.'" *The Dan Smoot Report*, August 3, 1956, pages 4-5.

174:3 See, Bernard S. Van Rensselear, "How Not To Handle Foreign Aid," *Reader's Digest*, February 1957, pages 25-30.

174:4 Alberto Osteria Gutierrez, *The Tragedy Of Bolivia* (New York: Devin-Adair, 1958. See, also, Willmoore Kendall, "Bolivian Follies," *National Review*, October 6, 1956, pages 11-13.

As former Ambassador Spruille Braden explains it: "Utter confusion has existed with our foreign aid funds in Bolivia. It has been publicly stated, more than once, with no denials, that our aid there has been used to maintain service on Bolivia's loans with the Export-Import Bank. That is, we American taxpayers have had our money taken away from us to loan to a Marxist government; then, when there appeared to be danger of a default on the loan, more of our money was given to cover the service to the Export-Import Bank. As nearly as can be estimated, we are today giving grants to Bolivia to pay between 39 and 47.5 per cent of her budget." "The Decline And Fall Of 'Uncle Sam,'" *Human Events*, February 3, 1958.

174:5 "Despite the intentions of foreign economic aid, its major effect, insofar as it has any effect at all, will be to speed the communization of the underdeveloped world. . . ." Milton Friedman in *Yale Review*, Summer Issue 1958, as quoted in the *Indianapolis Star* (Editorial), June 16, 1960.

174:6 By December 31, 1961 the total given to the Tito regime was $2.2 billion.

Lawrence Sullivan, Coordinator of Information for the House of Representatives, as quoted by Fulton Lewis Jr., *The Top Of The News*, October 8-12, 1962, page 328.

175:1 Fulton Lewis Jr. brought the entire foreign-aid-to-satellites program of 1958 into proper focus: "The Administration push for an expanded foreign giveaway to the Soviet satellites arouses opposition on both sides of the aisle. The White House now pressures for economic aid to all communist countries except Russia, Red China and North Korea. Theoretical justification for such aid is furnished by Secretary Dulles who argues that slow evolution towards 'freedom' is inevitable among satellite nations. He sees Yugoslavia and Poland as pioneers in this development, ascribes their relative 'independence' in part to U.S. aid. Any future upheavals in the order of the Hungarian uprising are discounted in advance. Mr. Dulles anticipates evolution towards democracy, rejects (and would discourage) revolution.

"It is in this context that the Administration supports the thinking behind Senator Kennedy's amendment to the foreign aid bill that would 'liberalize' the interpretation of the Battle Act. At present, economic aid to communist countries is prohibited except when the President certifies that such aid is necessary for our national defense. The new amendment would permit economic assistance to the satellites if the President decides that such aid would assist them in becoming more 'democratic' and more 'independent' of Russia.

"Senators Knowland and Bridges lead the opposition within the GOP. They object to the abandonment of the former liberation policy, consider as utopian the belief in the gradual evolution of the satellites toward freedom. In their view Poland and Yugoslavia are full blown communist dictatorships firmly welded to the Soviet Union despite secondary differences. They are no more deserving of U.S. economic aid than Russia itself. Your editor concurs, considers any economic aid to the satellites an indirect subsidy to the Soviet Union. The satellite countries squabble and compete among themselves for Soviet economic aid, and Khrushchev would welcome our relieving him of part of his burden. No amount of U.S. economic aid could lead to detaching the satellites from Moscow. They depend for economic survival on trade with the Soviet Union—their largest customer and largest supplier of necessary commodities.

"Also, the communist leaders in the satellite countries know that any serious move toward independence would lead to armed Soviet intervention. The Administration's new aid policy is interpreted (correctly) as a U.S. warning against an anti-Kremlin revolution, advance notice of U.S. refusal to help future insurgents. United States economic aid to the satellites is a form of bribery to induce their good behavior vis-a-vis the Kremlin." *Exclusive*, June 4, 1958, pages 3 and 4.

175:2 *New York Times* dispatch, as quoted by James C. Ingebretsen in his syndicated column ("Pause For Reflection"), *circa* July 1955.

176:1 See *U.S. News & World Report*, January 18, 1957, pages 135-138.

176:2 "Mr. Dulles now assures the House Committee on Foreign Affairs that U.S. forces would be sent into action in the Middle East only against armed aggression, and never to topple a Red government set up by subversion. ("We won't walk in to overthrow any government that was installed in that area . . . however it gets there," he said.) If that is so, the Eisenhower Doctrine is strategically meaningless, for it is inconceivable that the Soviet Union should ever advance upon the Middle East by force of arms." Editorial in *National Review*, January 19, 1957, page 53.

How "meaningless" the Eisenhower Doctrine proved to be over the next eight months was described in the same publication's editorial ("The Eisenhower Doctrine, Short Course," September 28, 1957, pages 270-271): "1A. The U.S. appeases Nasser at the expense of its two closest allies. 1B. The U.S. infuriates Nasser by freezing all Egyptian credits. 2A. The U.S. funnels money and arms into Israel. 2B. The U.S. funnels money and arms into Jordan, which regards Israel as its prime enemy. 3A. The U.S. invents the idea of an anti-Soviet Baghdad Pact, and persuades Pakistan, Iran, Iraq, Turkey and Britain to join it. 3B. The U.S. refuses to join the Baghdad Pact.

"4A. The U.S. encourages the big oil companies to develop the oil resources of the Middle East. 4B. The U.S. remains passive when Arab rulers violate their contracts with the oil companies and sabotage pipelines, and promotes UN backing for the dictator who deliberately blocks the canal through which the oil tankers pass. 5A. The U.S. proclaims that it will protect the Middle East from Moscow. 5B. The U.S. doesn't lift a finger to hinder shipment of Soviet arms and personnel to Middle East nations.

"6A. The U.S. acts as the principal patron of Zionism. 6B. The U.S. accepts the anti-Semitic employment regulations of the Arab monarchs. 7A. The U.S. supports Britain's defense of its treaty rights in Oman and Muscat. 7B. The U.S. supports, finances and arms King Saud, who arms the tribesmen who attack the British in Oman and Muscat. 8A. The State Department representative describes the Syrian crisis as a major and immediate threat to our national security. 8B. The President goes fishing."

177:1 See *New York Times*, August 14, 1957.

177:2 Senator William Knowland of California objected strenuously to the delivery of sabrejet planes to Yugoslavia, and urged that military items be sent on a priority basis to anti-Communist allies of the United States. See Fulton Lewis Jr., *Exclusive*, June 12, 1957, page 4.

177:3 See Eisenhower's television and radio addresses of May 14 and 21, 1957 in *U.S. News & World Report*, May 24, 1957, pages 134-138; and May 31, 1957, pages 108-112.

177:4 The Chairman was Otto E. Passman, Democrat of Louisiana. *United Press Dispatch* in *Manchester* (N.H.) *Union Leader*, May 23, 1958.

178:1 For those interested in pursuing this topic, see HCUA, Hearings: "The Kremlin's Espionage And Terror Organizations: Testimony of Petr S. Deriabin," March 17, 1959. Deriabin is a former officer of the USSR's Committee of State Security (KGB). See, also, S.I.S.S.: "Beware! Tourists Reporting On Russia," an analysis prepared by Eugene Lyons, February 5, 1960; and, the same Committee's: "The United States Through The Eyes Of Soviet Tourists," a staff analysis, 1960. An earlier summary of "cultural exchanges" appeared in the 1958 "Report of the American Bar Association Special Committee On Communist Tactics, Strategy, And Objectives," reprinted in *American Opinion*, December 1958, pages 31-51. See especially pages 41-42.

179:1 Rev. Oswald Blumit in the *New Bedford* (Mass.) *Standard-Times*, November 18, 1955.

179:2 The callous attitude of the Eisenhower Administration towards efforts of the Polish people to liberate themselves was summarized in an editorial in *National Review* (July 25, 1956, page 5) as follows: "The total response of our government to the Posnan [Poland] uprising has been: 1) a mild comment by the press officer of the State Department to the effect that Polish workers do not appear to be altogether satisfied with their present situation; 2) an offer by Mr. Harold Stassen, the President's Commissioner of Peace and Disarmament, to send free food — for distribution by the Polish Government — that is, the Government that shot down the workers."

Also, in *National Review* (August 1, 1956, page 22), Frank S .Meyer ("Principles And Heresies") noted that: "As that gallant gesture [Posnan] faded into defeat, and the bloody, systematic repression of a police state began to grind its remorseless course, Secretary [of Defense, Charles E.] Wilson, testifying before a Senate Committee, expatiated on the 'liberalization' of the Soviet Empire, and amiably discussed the Soviet leaders as if they were the executives of some rival Ford or Chrysler corporation."

180:1 See Edgar Bundy, *Collectivism In The Churches* (Wheaton: Church League Of America, 1958), Chapter 15. Also, by the same author, "Red Trek To Evanston," *National Republic*, June 1954, pages 5-6; 31-32.

180:2 "The Russians' performance, he [Dulles] went on, was an example of one group of people giving happiness to another 'and we'd all do well to try it on a broader basis.' " *New York Times*, June 17, 1958.

Just a week before the Secretary of State was being so effusive in his praise of the ballerinas some interesting observations were presented in *Pravda* (June 9, 1958).

Under the title "Cultural Exchanges Should Serve The Matter Of Rapprochement Between The Peoples," G. Zhukov explained that the Soviet officials planned "cultural exchanges" with the United States after witnessing the success Hitler enjoyed in France and the Soviets, themselves, enjoyed in Poland and Czecho-Slovakia. Zhukov recalled that Secretary of State Dulles had referred to Americans' love of travel and the Russians decided to take advantage of his idea. Consequently front-line personnel would be sent to the United States in various groups including ballet groups. No "reactionaries" would be invited to the USSR. The expected and planned results of "cultural exchanges" would be pro-Soviet propaganda implanted in the American visitors to the USSR and the same propaganda disseminated in the United States by the Russian groups. Zhukov was President of the Government Committee for "Cultural Exchanges with Foreign Countries" in the Soviet of Ministers of the USSR.

Whether or not it was planned that way, the Soviets discovered an important result of "cultural exchanges": "The first buds of cultural exchange — guest performances in the United States of Igor Moiseyev's Folk Dance Company, the Beryozka Dance Company, and the Bolshoi Ballet — dissipated the myth current among Americans about 'forced' labour in the U.S.S.R. Even the most obtuse of businessmen had it brought home to him that such pearls of world art can be produced only by people inspired by supreme freedom." A. Ajubei and others, *Face To Face With America* (Moscow: Foreign Languages Publishing House, 1960), page 24.

180:3 "A final note on 'cultural exchanges' concerns the Soviet murder, disclosed last week, of Premier Imre Nagy and General Pal Maleter of Hungary. Secretary of State Dulles, informed of the double killing, murmured 'tragic, tragic.' He then returned to his seat in the Loew's Capitol Theater to catch the last half of the Moiseyev ballet's opening performance in the Capital." *Human Events*, June 23, 1958, page 4.

180:4 Arthur Lief was the conductor and his testimony appears in HCUA, Hearings: "Communism In The New York Area (Entertainment)," June 18, 1958, pages 2537-2542. In less than five pages of testimony Lief invoked the first and fifth amendments sixteen times. He refused to tell the Committee if he was a Communist, whether he discussed his Communist Party membership with S. Hurok, the impressario who hired him, whether Communists obtained the job for him, whether he attended meetings with the ballet members outside the professional sessions of the ballet, or if he knew of other Americans working with the ballet who were Communists.

180:5 See *Human Events*, June 23, 1958, pages 3 and 4; and, John T. Flynn, "Behind The Headlines," over the Mutual Broadcasting System, as quoted in the *Manchester* (N.H.) *Union Leader*, June 21, 1958.

180:6 See, Hilary Grey, "The Cyrus Eaton Story," *American Opinion*, March

1959, pages 13-24.

182:1 This problem has practically become academic since with the passage of the Trade Expansion Act of 1962 the Congress has virtually surrendered all of its authority to regulate tariffs. And now the President has almost total authority to abolish tariffs. See *The Dan Smoot Report*, August 6, 1962 for an excellent analysis of the implications of this recent law.

182:2 For a more detailed discussion of one part of, and danger from, this Communist activity, see "If You Want It Straight," *American Opinion*, October 1962, pages 1-5.

183:1 The folly of such acceptance was early recognized and described by Lawrence R. Brown in "Why Stalin Has Spared Europe," *The Freeman*, March 12, 1951, pages 361-363. Mr. Brown was particularly disturbed that the first major implementations of NATO policy were instigated by Acheson and Marshall whom he described as "two tried and true friends of Soviet expansion."

183:2 For a brief but excellent study of the background, history, and nature of NATO, see *Two-Faced NATO*, published by the National Defense Committee, Daughters Of The American Revolution, 1961.

183:3 Taft's foresightedness was never better displayed than in his opposition to NATO. Less than three months after Eisenhower's inauguration, April 8, 1953, Taft's analysis and fears were formally confirmed. William Moore, in a factual report from Washington to the *Chicago Tribune*, recorded that "State Department officials acknowledged today that they are bargaining away American sovereignty and the rights of individual States, in peacetime, in the North Atlantic Treaty Organization. Asked by Senator Hickenlooper (Republican, Iowa) what legal authority they had to transfer American sovereignty to other nations, they cited the President's powers as Commander in Chief, but conceded that these are 'not very clearly defined.' The admission that American sovereignty is being bargained away was made before the Senate Foreign Relations Committee. . . . The witnesses before the Foreign Relations Committee, headed by Senator Wiley (Republican, Wisconsin) were State Under Secretary Smith and Herman Phleger, legal adviser to the State Department."

184:1 *New York Times*, October 26, 1957. The statement was an eight-year-old echo: "The democracies must learn that the world is now too small for the rigid concepts of national sovereignty that developed in a time when the nations were self-sufficient and self-dependent for their own well-being and safety. None of them today can stand alone." Eisenhower, *Crusade In Europe*, page 523.

The totality of Eisenhower's willingness to surrender national sovereignty was observed by the *London Times* (September 23, 1960): Eisenhower "asked delegates (to the Fifteenth UN General Assembly) to contemplate a United Nations taking on almost limitless responsibilities, extending even to outer space. . . . They [the responsibilities] imply turning the United Nations into something that is at least an effective nucleus of world government."

Chapter Fifteen

188:1 See *New York Times*, September 5, 1950.

188:2 It was grimly ironical for Jackson to be heading up an outfit with the title of Radio *Free Europe*.

Julius Epstein writes: "What, for example, went on in the addled heads of officials who in April 1945 decided to drop leaflets urging Soviet nationals to surrender to Americans for 'speedy return to their Russian fatherland.' Speedy return, as any tyro in the business should have known, meant speedy liquidation by firing squads. Meanwhile other leaflets and broadcasts addressed to Russian enemies of the Kremlin promised that they would never be sent back; many of those who believed that promise

would soon pay for it with their freedom or their lives.

"Our Psychological Warfare Division, headed by General Robert A. McClure, with C. D. Jackson as his deputy, cannot slough off its share of responsibility for confusions and deceits of this character. The pattern, however, was set at much higher levels. It was a pattern such as Moscow itself might have prescribed. For its effects were (1) to turn the Soviet peoples, in particular the enemies of the regime, against the democracies; (2) to convince the Kremlin's internal foes that it was futile to count on the understanding and help of the West; and (3) to strengthen Stalin's hand as against the population in his difficult postwar period of readjustment." Julius Epstein, "How We Served As Partners In A Purge," *American Legion Magazine*, December 1954, pages 14-15; 43-45.

189:1 See Kurt Glaser, *Czecho-Slovakia* (Caldwell: Caxton, 1961), especially pages 219-226.

189:2 *Czechoslovakia Enslaved* (London: Gollancz, 1950), page 183. See, also, page 135 where the same sentiments are expressed.

189:3 *East and West* (London: Lincolns-Praeger, 1944), page 58.

189:4 See the numerous references to Peroutka in Glaser, *Op. cit.*

190:1 Jiri Brada, "Radio Free Europe," (Part 3 of 3), *Facts Forum News*, March 1956, page 46.

193:1 Jiri Brada, "Radio Free Europe." (Part 1 of 3), *Facts Forum News*, January 1956, pages 11-16.

193:2 *Ibid.*

194:1 In its report of July 18, 1956 the Senate Committee On Government Operations (Chairman, John L. McClellan, Democrat from Arkansas) revealed that Harold Stassen as Director of the Foreign Operations Administration was responsible for allowing the Soviets to obtain radio transmitters that could be used for "jamming." For a summary of Stassen's exploits in the FOA, see *The*

Dan Smoot Report, June 17, 1957.

194:2 "On May 31, 1959 the US Information Agency announced that 49 paintings and works of sculpture had been selected for showing at the American National Exhibition in Moscow . . . billed by the USIA as containing 'cultural, scientific, and technological exhibits designed to further Soviet understanding of life in America. . . .'

"Of the 67 artists whose works have been chosen for exhibition in Moscow, 34 — . . . have records of affiliation with Communist fronts and causes. Of these 34, there are 12 whose records appear to be relatively inconsequential because they involve connections with only one or two Communist fronts or causes, and include no affiliation for a period of ten years or more. This leaves 22 . . . with significant records of affiliation with the Communist movement in this country . . . [and] these 22 artists have a minimum of 465 connections with Communist fronts and causes." Representative Francis E. Walter, Chairman of HCUA, "The Moscow Art Exhibit," *Human Events,* June 24, 1959.

194:3 See Eugene W. Castle's two books, *Billions Blunders And Baloney* (New York: Devin-Adair, 1955), especially Chapter 7, and *The Great Giveaway* (Chicago: Regnery, 1957), pages 62-64; 74-81.

195:1 Said the *New York Times* (April 30, 1955): "The Communists and indeed the whole of the extreme left were exultant after Signor Gronchi's election."

195:2 May 13, 1955, as quoted in *Deadline Data.*

195:3 One of the few places where the significance of Gronchi's visit could be studied was in *National Review.* See William S. Schlamm, "Foreign Trends," December 14, 1955, page 17, and January 18, 1956, pages 20-21. For accounts of Gronchi's reception by Eisenhower, see *New York Times,* February 28 and 29, 1956.

196:1 "Sukarno organized a colossal anti-American rally in Jakarta [formerly Batavia] on November 8, 1944. The Indonesian weekly *Djawa Baros* published photos of Sukarno burning bigger-than-life pictures of Western leaders. A caption under the picture read: 'Roosevelt, Churchill condemned.' " William Schulz, "Peace Corps Goes To Indonesia," *Human Events,* November 10, 1962, page 866.

196:2 The Eisenhower Administration — for public consumption — went through the motions of proclaiming neutrality during the course of the anti-Communist rebellion against Sukarno. But the proclamation was completely phony: Anti-Communist rebels from Indonesia "tried [but failed] to buy surplus U.S. equipment now in Okinawa and on Guam . . . [and] the worst blow came in the Philippines. The U.S. had been trying to dispose of a collection of B-25 twin-engine bombers, war surplus now at Clark Field. The rebels in the North Celebes wanted to use these planes to convoy their trading vessels. But when a rebel intermediary tried to buy the planes, the U.S. took them off the market."

At the same time: "The U.S. has some 158 Indonesian officers and men training in the U.S. under a pre-civil-war program. But, so far, the U.S. sells no arms to rebels. Rebel leaders are bitter. Here in Singapore one of their top representatives said last week: 'The U.S. is leaning over backward to stay neutral and keep out of war. But when you deny us the right to buy arms it's the same as if both Washington and Moscow were helping the Communists win the war.' " *U.S. News & World Report,* March 28, 1958, page 69.

Even the usually cautious *U.S. News & World Report* (April 25, 1958, page 31) accepted the fact that Sukarno's Communist character was no longer in doubt: "Indonesia's President Sukarno is going overboard in his alignment with Communists of that country. From Sumatra comes this report: 'When Sukarno's Army captured Pakanbaru, scores of Reds who had been jailed by the rebels were immediately released. Communists there are terrorizing local leadership. Reds are playing a tight game. In Java, they tell people that they are out to save Indonesia from 'foreign imperialists,' while in Sumatra they promise to give better schools, more food and clothing.' "

But at the very same time hypocrisy was the keynote in our State Department: Lincoln White, chief of the news division in the State Department, expressed regret "that Indonesia turns to the Communist bloc to buy arms for possible use in killing Indonesians who openly oppose the growing influence of Communism in Indonesia." He hoped "for an early resolution of the internal differences between Indonesians." *U.S. News & World Report*, April 18, 1958, page 19.

196:3 This was true up to that time. Since then I believe the Moroccan Premier Ibrahim's visit, and perhaps those of a few Soviet officials, have been longer.

196:4 See Rodney Gilbert, "Our Dear Friend Sukarno," *American Opinion*, February 1959, pages 48-55.

196:5 The fawning continues in the present Administration: "As an example of how not to deal with those who make the world a cold place for opponents of Communism, take the Administration's red carpet treatment of Indonesia's visiting President Sukarno. Following a 21-gun salute, President Kennedy hailed his guest as 'a distinguished national leader, father of his country, and a leader in the world.' That description was so extravagant that even Mr. Sukarno protested: 'I am just a small mouthpiece of the Indonesian nation.' " *The Wall St. Journal*, April 27, 1961.

196:6 Said the distinguished American journalist Constantine Brown: "Actually, Sukarno is being paraded by international communism as Exhibit A to the nations which have not yet joined the Communist bloc. He is being shown as one who has broken with impunity international laws and agreements; has flouted the once mighty West in the South Pacific

and has told the United Nations indirectly to mind its own business." *Manchester* (N.H.) *Union Leader*, January 24, 1958.

197:1 John T. Flynn, "Behind The Headlines," Broadcast over the Mutual Broadcasting System, May 4, 1958.

"During his [Sukarno's] stay here, a fifty-thousand dollar documentary film of his visit was made by the United States Information Agency. Subsequently, this film was exhibited in movie theaters throughout Indonesia for an admission fee, although both the film and the copies were a gift from our government." Castle, *The Great Giveaway*, page 118.

197:2 See Bella V. Dodd, "Strange White House Visitor," *National Review*, June 6, 1956, page 9. See, also, an interview with Karel J. V. Nikijuluw, South Moluccan representative in the United States, *U.S. News & World Report*, January 11, 1957, pages 82-84.

Sukarno's place in the international Communist Hierarchy was recognized in 1960 when he was awarded the Lenin Peace Prize. The Eisenhower policy of supporting Sukarno continued under the most fraudulent of pretenses. On February 8, 1959 the Indonesian Foreign Ministry announced that the United States approved the sale to Indonesia of small arms and other light military equipment, enough to supply twenty new battalions. The explanation for this move was given in the *New York Times* (February 10, 1959): "The United States arms deal . . . results from a reassessment [in Washington] . . . of Indonesian neutralism. Officials [in Washington] explained . . . that the United States Government had found leading members of the Indonesian regime increasingly wary of communism and Soviet influence. . . . President Sukarno's 'guided democracy' appears to involve limiting Communist activities and increasing the role of the army."

On March 18, 1959 the United States agreed to lend $70,800,000 to Sukarno for economic development. On April 12,

1959 the Export-Import Bank extended a credit of $6,900,000 to Indonesia for the purchase of United States machinery and construction materials.

Within the next two months Sukarno was paying his respects to his Communist colleagues by visiting them in the Soviet Union, North Vietnam, and throughout Europe and Latin America. And while Sukarno was still in North Vietnam, the United States announced that its Development Loan Fund would lend $9,000,000 to Indonesia for development projects. And on June 10, 1960 the United States Export-Import Bank loaned $45,500,000 for the construction of a fertilizer plant and power station in Indonesia. And before the end of the year more than $80,000,000 would be poured out to Sukarno by the United States in the form of loans and grants.

197:3 Nehru's total collaboration with the Communists at Panmunjom has been fully confirmed by Rear Admiral A. E. Jarrell, USN, "How India's 'Neutrality' Helped The Communist Cause," *U.S. News & World Report*, June 29, 1956, pages 98-104. Jarrell was the Senior United Nations Member of the Military Armistice Commission in Korea.

197:4 Published in February-March 1957. This is the magazine which is *American Opinion* today. See, also, statements of the Society for the Defense of Freedom In Asia, "Nehru And Democracy," *National Review*, February 22, 1956, pages 21-22, and "Nehru's Road To Communism," *Op. cit.*, April 11, 1956, pages 19-20.

198:1 And right while these notes are being written, in November, 1962, our Government is rushing huge jet freighter loads of arms, ammunition, etc. to Nehru, to help him "fight" the Chinese Communists — the whole "fight" having undoubtedly been planned and stage-managed by the Kremlin bosses of both Mao and Nehru in part for this very purpose of supplying an excuse for us to arm Nehru as we did Tito.

199:1 Nehru made the most of this opportunity to serve as liaison between Chou En-lai and Eisenhower and to serve as a propagandist for the Communist Chinese. He could not have been more insulting toward Nationalist China, our ally: "Obviously, the Formosan Government, at the · most, is the Formosan Government. It is not China." See the full text of the transcript of a press conference held by Nehru on December 19, 1956, *U.S. News & World Report*, December 28, 1956, pages 57-63.

199:2 Some of Nehru's most widely publicized anti-American actions took place in the UN either by anti-American votes or by abstention from voting: (1) On October 21, 1952, when the Soviet Union asked the UN to hear charges that the United States used germ warfare in Korea, India abstained; (2) on March 26, 1953, when the Communists introduced a resolution in the UN charging the United States with spying behind the Iron Curtain, India abstained; (3) on March 27, 1953 India voted to demand a hearing on charges that the United States conducted germ warfare in Korea; (4) on December 3, 1953 India abstained when a United States resolution was introduced condemning Communist atrocities in Korea; and, (5) on December 10, 1954 India abstained from condemning the Communist Chinese for holding American and other war prisoners in violation of the Korean armistice terms.

200:1 Department of State, *Press Release*, Number 454, and Department of Agriculture, *Press Release*, Number 2554; both releases dated August 29, 1956.

200:2 May 19, 1956, page 1.

201:1 S.I.S.S., Hearings: "Subversive Influence In The Educational Process," September 24, 1952, (Part 1), pages 193-199.

201:2 S.I.S.S., Hearings: "Subversive Influence In The Educational Process," March 24, 1953, (Part 5), pages 635-637.

202:1 April 1, 1958, page 3.

203:1 As quoted by L. Brent Bozell,

"The U.S. Pushes 'National Communism,' " *National Review*, June 1, 1957, pages 516-517; 530.

203:2 *Ibid.*

204:1 *U.S. News & World Report*, January 18, 1957, pages 108-112.

204:2 See *The Cry Is Peace* (Chicago: Regnery, 1952).

204:3 *London Times*, March 17, 1958.

205:1 *New York Times*, May 23, 1957.

205:2 *New York Times*, May 20, 1957.

206:1 "Now this is a very curious circumstance, and one of sad significance — sad because the President's endorsement will enormously increase the book's circulation, but sadder still that he and others in high office could conceivably be influenced by the cheap cynicism of Mr. Hoffer's indiscriminate sniping at all belief, all strongly held principle, all moral doctrine." Frank S. Meyer, "Principles And Heresies: The President And 'The True Believer,' " *National Review*, May 2, 1956, page 15.

206:2 See Howard Rushmore, "Heard On The Party Line," *American Mercury*, April 1955, page 128. See, also, Marian M. Strack, "There Are No Absolutes," *National Republic*, May 1956, pages 21-22 *et seq.* Mrs. Strack reveals. that, at Freedom House, a film-version of "The Investigator" was "being continually shown gratis to all comers."

206:3 See *Annual Report*, 1953, HCUA, page 49. For Ship's testimony, see HCUA, Hearings: "Communist Infiltration Of Hollywood Motion-Picture Industry," (Part V), September 20-25, 1951, pages 1771-1775.

206:4 Jack Gould, "Radio In Review," December 31, 1954. The passage of time certainly has not dulled the *New York Times* talent for fiction. In a *New York Times News Service* dispatch, Russell Baker writes: "No one ever laughed out loud at Senator Joseph McCarthy while he stood at the pinnacle. A Canadian [undesirable alien Communist] broadcaster [Ship] made a record parodying McCarthy's hearing-room manner, but most [Gallup poll?] record shops sold it only under the counter and the buyer played it low with windows and doors shut against potential eavesdroppers." *Boston Herald*, December 13, 1962.

206:5 Jack Gould, "Radio In Review," *New York Times*, December 31, 1954.

207:1 *National Review*, May 17, 1958, page 459.

208:1 "At the start of the conference Press Secretary James C. Hagerty said quite firmly that there would be no pictures. He said that it had been the White House custom 'for years' not to photograph a foreign envoy when he presented his credentials. But under the apparently cordial circumstances that surrounded the conference, the long-standing custom was abruptly reversed." *United Press* dispatch, *Memphis Press Scimitar*, February 11, 1958. For a good summary of Menshikov's career, see "The Menshikov Behind The Smile," *U.S. News & World Report*, May 9, 1958, pages 54-58.

208:2 Syndicated column ("The Washington Merry-go-Round"), July 31, 1955.

208:3 *Inside Russia Today* (New York: Harper, 1957), page 79. "On July 12, 1956, Jacob Malik, Soviet Ambassador to the United States . . . said: 'Senator Knowland has announced that Ike is going to be a candidate. This is fine news. I'm for Eisenhower. The people of Europe know him. They like him and trust him. We can do business with President Eisenhower.' " *The Dan Smoot Report*, July 20, 1956, page 6.

209:1 *Los Angeles Times*, November 8, 1955.

209:2 The most recent account of this incident is to be found in William C. Bullitt, "A Talk With Voroshilov," *The Great Pretense*. (Prepared and released by the House Committee On Un-American Activities, May 19, 1956), pages 18-19.

210:1 *Los Angeles Times*, November 8, 1955.

210:2 *New York Times*, January 2,

1958.

210:3   *New York Times*, July 23, 1957.

211:1   *New York Times*, November 30, 1957.

211:2   The Eisenhower Administration had made a practice of tossing such bouquets to Tito. A New York businessman, who had considerable experience in Yugoslavia, wrote in an "open letter" to Members of Congress, Secretary Dulles, and President Eisenhower: "How have the President and Mr. Dulles given hope to the Poles and the other enslaved peoples and assured them of our interest in their liberty? By the summit conference at Geneva or Mr. Dulles' visit to slavemaster Tito at Brioni last year? By giving aid to Communist Tito, enabling him and his mob to hold the Yugoslavs in slavery? Or by their Ambassador [James D. Riddleberger] to Yugoslavia's joining a group of Tito's top aides in the drinking following a Tito-given hunting-party for diplomats, and embracing two of them as they sang, 'Tito We Swear Our Loyalty To You,' and other Communist songs, as reported under the item, 'Gay Diplomats,' page 3, Belgrade *Politika* for May 25, 1956." William H. Smyth, Letter released on June 28, 1956.

211:3   The flirtation continued, at least as late as 1960. "Anastas Mikoyan, No. 2 man in the Soviet Union, after visiting U.S., gave the following size-up . . . : *Eisenhower* — 'Sentimental' not hard. He kept making nostalgic references to Marshal Zhukov as a wartime comrade, when he knew Zhukov had been discredited." *U.S. News & World Report*, July 18, 1960.

212:1   News conference at the White House, March 26, 1958, as reported in *U.S. News & World Report*, April 4, 1958, page 103.

213:1   *U.S. News & World Report*, July 26, 1957, pages 86-87.

Said *National Review* in an editorial (August 3, 1957, page 125), under the heading of *The Breathless General And The Honest Marshall*: "Mr. Eisenhower, alas, does not mean to say that *he* unique-ly — owing to unique personal or intellectual shortcomings, or because he was faced with an adversary of unique powers, or because the circumstances militated against his success — is incapable of defending the West, in terms of idealism. Mr. Eisenhower doesn't hold *himself* responsible for the lost debate with Mr. Zhukov; he holds the West responsible. He does not mean that *he* had difficulty defending the West: he means the West is difficult to defend — as witness the fact that, with so able a spokesman as himself there to put forward its claims, it failed, up against the superior claims of Communism."

Chapter Sixteen

215:1   In this chapter, dealing with Associates And Appointments, there have been omitted altogether a few paragraphs dealing with individuals who, so far as I know, are no longer active or important on the political scene or in the total picture on which this searchlight is focused. And in this chapter, also, some slight changes in phrasing have been made, in the interest of fairness and restraint, from the expressions of opinion which were boldly stated in a confidential letter never intended nor offered for sale.

215:2   Menon's visit was made on the eve of the Summit conference of 1955. See *Human Events*, August 13, 1955, page 1.

216:1   J. B. Matthews, "The Years Of Betrayal," *American Mercury*, February 1954, pages 34-45.

When Belfrage was asked in the House Committee on Un-American Activities to tell whether he had served either Great Britain or the United States during the war, he declined to answer on grounds that an answer would tend to incriminate him. HCUA, Hearings: "Investigation of Communist Activities In The New York Area," (Part 2), May 5, 1953, pages 1285-1286.

In 1943 Belfrage, while working for British Intelligence in London, was turning British secrets over to Soviet agents

Golos and Elizabeth Bentley. Elizabeth Bentley, *Out Of Bondage* (New York: Devin-Adair, 1951), pages 201-202.

216:2 HCUA, Hearings: "Investigation Of Communist Activities In The New York Area," (Part 2), page 1280.

216:3 " . . . Established by the American Labor Party in 1947 as a 'progressive' weekly. . . . Although it denies having any affiliation with the Communist Party, it has manifested itself from the beginning as a virtual arm of Soviet Russia." HCUA, Report: "Trial By Treason," August 25, 1956, page 12.

216:4 S.I.S.S., Hearings: "Institute of Pacific Relations," (Parts 1 and 2); Chambers' testimony of August 16, 1951; Budenz' testimony of August 22, 1951; Barmine's testimony of July 31, 1951; Wittfogel's testimony of August 7, 1951; and, Massing's testimony of August 2, 1951. For more details of Barnes' background see Suzanne La Follette, "The Case Of Joseph Barnes," *The Freeman*, August 27, 1951, pages 742-744.

John Gunther, after visiting Eisenhower's headquarters in Paris, confirmed Barnes' role in writing *Crusade In Europe.* See *The Freeman*, March 10, 1952, page 356.

During the war years few pro-Communist propaganda moves were more successful than Wendell Willkie's round-the-world trip. As George N. Crocker describes it: "The flighty Wendell Willkie, after losing in his try for the Presidency in 1940, suddenly 'got religion' and became an ebullient emissary for Roosevelt, traveling to London, Moscow, and Chungking in an Army transport plane, emotionally overcome by his precipitate arrival in the upper regions of international fame. His much-publicized slogan 'One World,' served well to cover up the real state of affairs. . . . Whether other Republican leaders, such as Hoover and Taft, and dissident Democrats, such as former Secretary of War Harry H. Woodring, looked upon these antics of Wendell Willkie as those of an opportunistic hypocrite or an impressionable

dupe, we know not. They themselves had no hallucinations about 'a *grand coalition* of peoples, fighting a common war of liberation.' " *Roosevelt's Road To Russia* (Chicago: Regnery, 1959), pages 50-51. Accompanying Willkie on his infamous trip and helping him to write his account was none other than Joseph Barnes! Wendell L. Willkie, *One World* (New York: Simon and Schuster, 1943), page x.

217:1 According to John T. Flynn, the financial windfall realized by Eisenhower with his *Crusade In Europe* was "super-intended" by Davies. See "Our Phoney War On Communism," *American Mercury* (February 1954), pages 17-21.

217:2 For information on the Bilderbergers, see Smoot, *Invisible Government*, page v. In 1958 "Hauge was lured away from the White House (after serving as an economic adviser to Eisenhower) when ubiquitous Wall Streeter Sidney Weinberg . . . persuaded him to become chairman of the finance committee at Manufacturers Trust Co." *Time Magazine*, January 4, 1963, page 62. For Weinberg, see Smoot, *Op. cit.*, pages 81ff., and 95ff.

217:3 For an appraisal of Case's leftism, see Finis Farr, "Hopeless Case," *Human Events*, November 18, 1959.

217:4 "Not content with this, Davies proclaimed that Communism — which clearly denies God and religious faith — 'is protecting the Christian world of free men,' and urged all Christians 'by the faith you have found at your mother's knee, in the name of the faith you have found in temples of worship,' to embrace the Soviet Union." Budenz, *The Cry Is Peace*, pages 3 and 4.

218:1 Richard L. Stokes uncovered an authoritative account of Hopkins' relationship to the Kremlin: "Late in July, 1941 . . . Moscow learned that President Roosevelt was sending Harry L. Hopkins for Lend-Lease negotiations with Premier Stalin. The name was a surprise. Not many Red officials had ever heard of their future benefactor. A wireless, asking who Harry L. Hopkins was, went to

Ambassador Constantine Oumansky in Washington. His reply was limited to generalities that might have been copied from *Who's Who*. The envoy was admonished to get details about Hopkins' political temper and attitude towards the U.S.S.R.

"It was taken as a matter of course in Moscow . . . that Hopkins would bring heavy demands for concessions and guarantees . . . in return for Lend-Lease favors. . . . Hopkins arrived in Moscow on July 30. But a day or so earlier [Foreign Minister] Molotov had saluted his colleagues with one of his infrequent broad grins. . . . The Minister explained that he now had a full report on Harry L. Hopkins. It was based, Molotov declared, on intelligence supplied by 'a certain man at the very highest level of the Roosevelt administration.' The name was concealed. [Mr. Stokes' source] . . . gathered it was that of an American spy for Russia either in the State Department or in Mr. Roosevelt's entourage at the White House. The information was impeccable, whatever that agent's identity.

"With an assurance justified by the event, Molotov announced: 'Mr. Hopkins will demand no concessions whatever. His desire is to ask nothing and give everything. What he wants is to keep us in the fighting — and that is all. Mr. Hopkins is completely on our side and may be trusted absolutely.'" "A Tragic Tale Of Lend-Lease," *Human Events*, April 1, 1953.

Mr. Stokes' source was Colonel Igor Bogolepov, formerly Counsellor to the Soviet Foreign Office before escaping from Russia. Bogolepov testified in the Institute of Pacific Relations hearings before the McCarran Committee in 1952 when he gave extremely damaging evidence against Owen Lattimore, Joseph E. Davies, and other Americans. In this country at that time Bogolepov was working in a confidential capacity for a federal agency.

218:2 *New York Times*, February 1, 1946. General Wedemeyer thought of Hopkins and his *alter idem*, Roosevelt, as

something other than "loyal" Americans: "There sat Harry Hopkins, Churchill writes in *The Grand Alliance*, 'absolutely glowing with refined comprehension of the Cause.' This 'Cause,' as Hopkins told Churchill on behalf of Roosevelt, was to be 'the defeat, ruin and slaughter of Hitler, to the exclusion of all other purposes, loyalties or aims.' Thus did the President of the United States through the mouth of Harry Hopkins renounce adherence to the Constitution of the United States and repudiate his pledged word to the American people to keep them out of foreign wars for the sake of an aim he conceived to be higher, namely the 'slaughter' of Hitler." Albert C. Wedemeyer, *Wedemeyer Reports* (New York: Holt, 1958), page 9.

218:3 *The Leftist Background of Ralph J. Bunche* (New York: Alliance, 1954). See, also, Harold Lord Varney, "Who And What Is Ralph Bunche?," *American Mercury*, May 1956, pages 29-35; and, Manning Johnson, *Color, Communism, And Common Sense* (New York: Alliance, 1958), page 65. Bunche's role in the Bang-Jensen affair is described in Julius Epstein's "The Bang-Jensen Tragedy," *American Opinion*, May 1960, see, especially, Chapter III.

It is of interest to note that Henry Cabot Lodge, the 1960 Republican Vice-Presidential candidate, thought it would be a "wonderful idea" to have a man such as Ralph J. Bunche in the President's cabinet. *New York Times*, October 14, 1960.

218:4 Manly, *The UN Record*, page 144. Mr. Manly devotes six pages (139-144) of his penetrating study to Ralph Bunche. And from Manly's vantage point as the *Chicago Tribune's* correspondent at the UN for eight years, he has pulled together some interesting pieces of the Ralph Bunche story.

For example, in 1954, Bunche, who had served as Director of the UN's Trusteeship Division, was made Undersecretary-General. In Bunche's background—aside from his long-time proclivity for left-wing organizations—were his close connections with Alger Hiss. Bunche had rushed to Hiss' defense almost as soon as Hiss had been identified as a Communist by Whittaker Chambers. And when Bunche had first applied for a position in the UN, he had listed Hiss as a reference. But in 1954 the Eisenhower Administration came to Bunche's rescue so that there would be no difficulty surrounding his promotion on the UN staff.

Mr. Manly writes of a report that Max Rabb, then Eisenhower's trouble-shooter with minority groups, "was insistent that Bunche should be whitewashed to avoid any risk of offending Negro voters in the 1954 elections." The whitewash was applied by the Eisenhower Administration's special loyalty board for international organizations. This group was headed by Pierce Gerety, a political associate of John Lodge, brother of UN Ambassador Henry Cabot Lodge, who, when a United States Senator, had employed Max Rabb as his administrative assistant.

218:5 In 1954 the NCEC letterhead bore the names of Paul H. Appleby, George Backer, Stringfellow Barr, Laird Bell, George Biddle, Henry Seidel Canby, Evans Clark, George Hamilton Combs, Morris L. Cooke, Thomas H. Elliott, Tom Fizdale, Alan Green, Oscar Hammerstein II, Alvin H. Hansen, Mark deWolfe Howe, Gardner Jackson, Donald Jecks, Mrs. Albert D. Lasker, Susan Mary Lee, Isidore Lipschutz, Marshall MacDuffie, Robert R. Nathan, George Outland, Charles Rose, Maurice Rosenblatt, Robert W. Ruhl, Thibaut de St. Phalle, Sidney H. Scheurer, Arthur M. Schlesinger, Harry Louis Selden, Robert E. Sherwood, Marshall K. Skadden, Edward S. Skillin, Michael Straight, Nathan Straus, Telford Taylor, Gerhard Van Arkel, Walter Walker, and Sumner Welles. *Congressional Record*, August 11, 1954, page 13414.

Appearing on the 1952 NCEC letterhead were Frederick L. Allen, Thurman Arnold, Mark Ethridge, George M. Glassgold, Eduard C. Lindeman, Ruth Bryan Rohde, James Roosevelt, and Vincent E. Sutliff. In 1961 additional names on the Committee included George E. Agree,

Hannah Arendt, George R. Donahue, Archibald MacLeish, Duncan Phillips, Bishop James A. Pike, Francis B. Sayre Jr., and David E. Scoll.

Soliciting support for the Committee's "increasingly important work" in 1961 were United States Senators Clifford P. Case, Eugene J. McCarthy, John Sherman Cooper, Lee Metcalf, and Estes Kefauver. *Letter in our files* from these Senators to "Dear Friends," dated June 2, 1961.

Father Richard Ginder, in his column "Right or Wrong" (*Our Sunday Visitor*, December 16, 1958), pointed out that the NCEC "contributed a total of $73,372 to the censure of the late Senator McCarthy. This was disclosed in a report made under the requirements of the Corrupt Practices Act." And in its own 1961 promotional literature, under the heading "The NCEC Is Known For The Results It Gets," the NCEC quotes, without comment, the late Senator Joseph R. McCarthy: "The National Committee for an Effective Congress 'masterminded the censure movement.'"

218:6 See page 87, note 1.

219:1 The group included John Sparkman of Alabama, Richard Stengel and Paul Douglas of Illinois, Richard Neuberger and Wayne Morse of Oregon, Estes Kefauver of Tennessee, James Murray of Montana, Joseph O'Mahoney of Wyoming, John Carroll of Colorado, Frank Church of Idaho, R. M. Evans of Iowa, Claude Wickard of Indiana, William Marland of West Virginia, Earle Clements of Kentucky, and Millard Tydings of Maryland.

219:2 In one instance the National Committee For An Effective Congress went all out against the candidacies of Senators Herman Welker and Everett M. Dirksen through a subsidiary front called "A Clean Politics Appeal." See "The Committee That Lost Its Reason," *National Review*, March 23, 1957, pages 277-280.

219:3 See William F. Buckley Jr. and Brent Bozell, *McCarthy And His Enemies* (Chicago: Regnery, 1954), pages 97-

124; 346.

219:4 National Emergency Conference; National Emergency Conference for Democratic Rights; American-Russian Institute for Cultural Relations with the Soviet Union; and, American Law Students Association.

219:5 Even Jessup's wife got into the act. After Whittaker Chambers had identified Hiss as a Communist, Mrs. Jessup interceded with Henry Luce to have Chambers fired from his position on *Time Magazine's* editorial staff. See Whittaker Chambers, *Witness* (New York: Random House, 1952), page 616.

220:1 See testimony of Jessup before the Subcommittee of the Senate Committee on Foreign Relations, Hearings: "Nomination of Philip C. Jessup," September 27-October 18, 1951. Compare Jessup's testimony with those of Professor Kenneth Colegrove of Northwestern University in S.I.S.S., Hearings: "Institute of Pacific Relations," Part 3, September 25, 1951, especially pages 917-926; Brigadier General L. Joseph Fortier, September 20, 1951, pages 843-864; and, Harold Stassen, Part 4, October 1, 1951, pages 1035-1074, and October 5, 1951, pages 1111-1138.

220:2 Subcommittee of the Senate Committee on Foreign Relations, Hearings: "Nomination of Philip C. Jessup," September 27-October 18, 1951.

When the Senate adjourned in 1951 Truman went ahead and appointed Jessup anyway. Then on January 17, 1952, Soviet Foreign Minister Vishinsky, at a UN conference in Paris, said: "I learned the other day with some dismay that 37 Senators had asked the United States Government if it would dismiss Mr. Jessup from here because he was rather sympathetically inclined toward an un-American way of thought. . . . I must express my sympathy for Mr. Jessup." *New York Times*, January 18, 1952.

220:3 And of course Mr. Jessup is still equally alive today as a Judge on the International Court of Justice at The Hague. Jessup was nominated by the United States members of the Permanent Court of Arbitration: David W. Peck, former Justice of the Appellate Division of the New York Supreme Court; Bethuel M. Webster, former president of the American Bar Association, and a leading opponent of the Bricker Amendment; Harold A. Smith, a senior partner in the Chicago law firm of Winston, Strawn, Smith & Patterson; and, Herman Phleger, former legal adviser to Secretary of State Dean Acheson. This nominating committee was appointed by Eisenhower on the recommendation of Secretary of State Dulles. See "Letter Of Herman Phleger to the Editor," *Richmond News-Leader*, December 15, 1960.

221:1 Dr. Felix Wittmer summarized the character of Milton Eisenhower in an "open letter" to the President: "You have never denied your faith in Dr. Milton Eisenhower's political wisdom; you have sought his advice; you are seeking it today. But it was at the request of the Soviet dupe Henry Agard Wallace that Milton Eisenhower, in 1938, was charged with coordinating the land use programs of the Department of Agriculture. In the early war years, Milton Eisenhower was an Associate Director of Elmer Davis' left-wing OWI. Doesn't it make you suspicious at all, sir, that in 1945 the Production and Marketing Administration was set up on the special recommendation of brother Milton? This agency, which reshaped the New Deal Administration's program of agricultural control, was a socialistic apparatus. Clinton P. Anderson, champion of the Robin Hood ill-fare state, called Milton Eisenhower 'the best equipped man in the country to carry out the policies I have in mind for the producers of food and the consumer.' Brother Milton has been a stalwart of Paul Hoffman's Committee for Economic Development, in which the internationalist-minded businessmen of the eastern seaboard hobnob with the foremost New Deal planners. He has been on the International Committee of the socialistic National Planning Association. He has been in the front ranks of those educators who are spreading the disintegrating ideas of UNESCO in our schools." "Where Is Your Crusade, Mr. Eisenhower?," *Human Events*, August 19, 1953.

Contrast Doctor Wittmer's summary of Milton Eisenhower's qualifications for office-holding with the promise for house-cleaning in the Republican Platform of 1952: "We shall eliminate from the State Department and from every Federal office, all, wherever they may be found, who share responsibility for the needless predicaments and perils in which we find ourselves."

221:2 There can be little doubt that Milton is a highly vocal propagandist for Khrushchev. For example, the *Baltimore Sun* on February 23, 1960, quoted Milton as telling a meeting of Alumni of Johns Hopkins University that Khrushchev "has become a champion of peace" and "Khrushchev is very different from Stalin."

Human Events (March 3, 1960, page 2), in commenting upon these remarks, said that foreign policy observers "point out that Milton Eisenhower apparently overlooks the fact that it was Khrushchev who carried out the bloody purge in the Ukraine in 1938, a typical Stalin action. They also recall that it was Khrushchev, not Stalin, who sent troops to carry out the sanguinary suppression of the Hungarian freedom revolt in 1956. Further, it has been under the prodding of Khrushchev, not Stalin, that Red China has penetrated Burma, flattened the independence of Tibet, and taken over 46,000 square miles of territory of India. Finally — it is pointed out — it has been under Khrushchev, not Stalin, that the Soviet Union has taken the audacious step which Stalin never even attempted — the creation of a Soviet satellite on the doorstep of the US. It was under Khrushchev, not Stalin, that the Communists in Guatemala took over full power, armed with a shipment of weapons sent by Red satellite Czechoslovakia, before failing in the attempt to

set up an outright Communist regime there in 1954. Today, under Khrushchev, and in the wake of Camp David [private meeting with Dwight Eisenhower], the USSR has succeeded in establishing a Communist puppet regime in Cuba, just 90 miles off the coast of Florida."

222:1 *New Bedford* (Mass.) *Standard-Times*, May 29, 1954.

222:2 It was Chesly Manly, we believe, who first used the term "Hissites" to describe the prominent individuals who rallied to the defense of Alger Hiss' character. It was an imposing list — Ralph Bunche, Felix Frankfurter, Philip Jessup, Eleanor Roosevelt, and Adlai Stevenson, among others. But the most important Hissite in the Eisenhower Administration was John Foster Dulles, who knowingly, at least as early as 1946, covered up Hiss' connections with the Soviet underground. See Mr. Manly's, *The UN Record*, Chapter VII, and especially pages 146-148.

222:3 See, also, Bundy, *Collectivism In The Churches*, Chapter 12, "Mr. Dulles And Some Collectivistic Churchmen."

223:1 For what this association implies, see Felix Wittmer, "Freedom's Case Against Dean Acheson," *American Mercury*, April 1952, pages 3-17.

223:2 1952-1953 edition, which was on sale in September 1952.

223:3 The State Department, even by the time of Dulles' appointment, was clearly recognized as a haven for security risks and, above all others, this Department needed a Secretary in whom some confidence could be vested to do a real housecleaning.

The appointment certainly appeared strange and disillusioning to William F. Buckley Jr., who wrote: "The principal reason why the Senate and the people should have no confidence in [John F.] Dulles on matters relating to loyalty and security is his reversal, in February, of the Civil Service Loyalty Board's finding that a 'reasonable doubt' does indeed exist as to John Carter Vincent's loyalty.

Not only did Dulles overrule this highly cautious board, he also exonerated Vincent on the lesser, looser, laxer score by declaring that neither is there 'reasonable doubt' that Vincent is a security risk! Now, the evidence against Vincent, garnered from a study of his career, is very persuasive. At the very least, it argues that he is a security, if not a loyalty risk.

"But even apart from Vincent's activities and associations in China, there is the testimony of Louis Budenz, who asserts he knew Vincent to be a member of the Communist Party. Therefore, in exonerating Vincent under the present loyalty standard ('reasonable doubt' — Executive Order 10241, April, 1951) and the security standard ('reasonable doubt' — State Department Memorandum, June 8, 1948), Mr. Dulles in effect declared that there is no reasonable doubt but that Louis Budenz is a liar. And this in spite of the fact that on the basis of thousands of pages of secret testimony, corroborated wherever possible, the FBI gives Budenz the highest reliability rating. . . . Mr. Dulles dealt the federal security program . . . an Achesonian blow." "Two To Get Ready," *Human Events*, April 8, 1953.

223:4 See Bundy, *Collectivism In The Churches*, page 209.

223:5 Of course there are exceptions. One of the strongest indictments of Dulles' policies was made by Frank S. Meyer. Mr. Meyer called attention to Dulles' statement before the UN General Assembly (September 17, 1953): "We can understand the particular desire of the Russian people to have close neighbors who are friendly. We sympathize also with that desire. The United States does not want Russia encircled by hostile peoples."

Said Mr. Meyer: "Surely, if the Administration had the faintest sense of reality about the character of the struggle, the tightest possible encirclement of the Soviet Union by the most hostile of peoples would be one of our first aims. What is Secretary Dulles saying? That any friends we have in the periphery of the Soviet empire are to be sacrificed to the Russian desire for captive neighbors? How does this differ from the policy of Yalta, the sellout of Poland in 1945?" "Where Is Eisenhower Going?," *American Mercury*, March 1954, pages 123-126.

224:1 "Not even Franklin Delano Roosevelt and Harry S. Truman had dared to woo labor so openly." Victor Riesel, "Labor And Eisenhower," *American Mercury*, February 1953, pages 59-66. See, also, *Human Events*, September 30, 1953, page 1.

225:1 Nothing better explains the total inadequacy of Streibert to present a pro-American program than his own words. For example, see "The New 'Voice Of America,'" an interview with Streibert in *U.S. News & World Report*, March 26, 1954, pages 58-64. See, also, the numerous references to Streibert in Castle, *Billions Blunders And Baloney*.

225:2 *The Freeman*, November 30, 1953, page 153.

225:3 As these notes are being written, early in November, 1962, Mr. Streibert has just been appointed President of the Radio Free Europe Fund.

225:4 In the Kennedy Administration, Bowles served as Undersecretary of State for ten months, but since November 27, 1961 Bowles has held the imposing title of President Kennedy's "Special Representative and Adviser on African, Asian and Latin American Affairs."

225:5 When Bohlen finished his mission to Moscow "Khrushchev put his arm around U.S. Ambassador Charles E. Bohlen . . . [and] declared expansively: 'We do not understand why they are taking you away from us and sending you so far away. We understand you and you understand us. We hate to see you go.'" *Time Magazine*, as quoted by Frank Kirkpatrick, *The American Way*, Volume III, No. 4, 1957, page 10.

225:6 "Let us take Mr. Eisenhower at his repeated words of last summer that our retreat from victory was not a historical necessity, that bad judgment by flesh and blood American citizens was a strong factor in the expansion of Russia, and in the shrinking of the free world. Now, *who* were the Americans responsible for bad judgment? Certainly right at the top of the list are the men who authorized the Teheran, Yalta and Potsdam agreements. The principals at the diplomatic Waterloos are dead or dismissed. But some subordinate staff members are still around, and some of them, in the course of things, are graduating upwards. The question is, have time and experience matured their judgment? Not Mr. Bohlen's, by his own, admirably frank admission. He still thinks Yalta was a good thing, all things considered. So what have we got? An ambassador to Russia who is endorsed not only by the Republican President of the United States, but also by Mr. Arthur Schlesinger, Jr., author, as far as I know, of the legend of the Necessity of Yalta, who dubs Bohlen 'the best possible candidate for the job.' " William F. Buckley Jr., "Two To Get Ready," *Human Events,* April 8, 1953.

". . . Dulles insists on the appointment of Bohlen. What for? The issue of Bohlen need not enter into what lies in that controversial FBI file on that gentleman. It need concern not much more than what is in his own official biography in *Who's Who*: 'Accompanied Sec. of State to Moscow Conf., 1943; attended Teheran Conf., 1943; 1st Sec., Moscow, Nov. 1942-Jan. 1944; chief Dv. Eastern European Affairs, 1944; area adviser, U.S. Group Dumbarton Oaks Conversations on Internat. Orgn., Washington 1944; Asst. to Sec. of State for White House Liaison, 1944; accompanied Pres. Roosevelt to Crimea Conf., 1945 (Yalta).' In short, Mr. Bohlen was a big wheel in the machinery which produced the disastrous policy of appeasing our Soviet co-belligerent." *Human Events,* March 25, 1953, page 2.

226:1 James Burnham, "Was Bohlen A Blunder?," *The Freeman,* May 4, 1953, pages 551-554.

226:2 Richard L. Stokes describes Bohlen as a protégé and personal appointee of Harry Hopkins during World War II. "A Tragic Tale Of Lend-Lease," *Human Events,* April 1, 1953.

226:3 Mr. Bohlen is another one of the left-wingers from the Eisenhower hive who seems to have been indispensable to Mr. Kennedy's program. He is now Ambassador to France. When Bohlen was appointed, *United Press International* quoted an unnamed American diplomat describing Bohlen as one who would drive "as hard a bargain as any horse trader." *St. Louis Post-Dispatch,* August 16, 1962. The late Senator Styles Bridges saw Bohlen in a different light: "In most every diplomatic horsetrade at which Bohlen was present, the Russians got the fat mare and the U.S. ended up with the spavined nag. Bohlen is an experienced failure." Douglas Caddy, "Architect Of Appeasement," *U.S.A.,* September 25, 1959, pages 4-6.

For recent appraisals of Bohlen, see M. Stanton Evans et al., *The Fringe On Top* (New York: American Features, 1962), pages 152-159, and, M. Stanton Evans, "Trends," *National Review Bulletin,* September 4, 1962, page 6.

226:4 *New York Times,* January 23, 1954.

John Foster Dulles had anticipated Dean by at least four years: "If the communist government of China in fact proves its ability to govern China without serious domestic resistance, then it, too, should be admitted to the United Nations." *War Or Peace* (New York: Macmillan, 1950), page 190.

And by 1955 Dean was willing for the United States not only to accept Communist China as the "government of China in fact" but urged that the United States recognize and trade with Communist China. See Arthur F. Dean, "United States Foreign Policy And Formosa," *Foreign Affairs,* April 1955, pages 360-375.

227:1 And Mr. Dean, too, still carried on officially — and disastrously, from the Americanist point of view — under Kennedy, as head of the U.S. delegation to the nuclear disarmament negotiations at Geneva. Dean resigned from this post, effective December 31, 1962. For a recent appraisal of Dean, see Evans, *The Fringe On Top*, page 114-118.

227:2 For his work with the Office of Strategic Services during World War II, Dulles received the Medal of Merit. Part of the citation for this award said: "He assisted in the formation of various Maquis groups in France and supported the Italian partisan groups both financially and by pin-pointing airdrops for supplies." As quoted in Sanche de Gramont, *The Secret War* (New York: Putnam's, 1962), page 135. The Communist domination and objectives of the Maquis have been described in Sisley Huddleston, *France, The Tragic Years, 1939-47* (New York: Devin-Adair, 1955); of the Italian partisans, see Luigi Villari, *Italian Foreign Policy Under Mussolini* (New York: Devin-Adair, 1956), and *The Liberation Of Italy* (Appleton: C. C. Nelson, 1959); and, Veale, *War Crimes Discreetly Veiled*, especially Chapter III.

227:3 Eleanor Dulles retired from the State Department and government service in January 1962. Her final post was Berlin, where she had the title of Special Assistant to the State Department's Director of Intelligence and Research. Columnist Bill Henry in the *Los Angeles Times* (February 10, 1959) described her as "the source of all factual knowledge as to what the Soviet is up to in regard to West Berlin." But the real kiss-of-death for Eleanor Dulles' reputation came in a farewell telegram to her from Berlin's slippery mayor, Willy Brandt, who expressed his heartfelt thanks for "everything you have done for Berlin." *Washington Evening Star*, January 26, 1962.

227:4 From the same office came "Marshall McDuffie — former law partner of the Dulles brothers, one-time head of the UNRRA mission to the Ukraine, acquaintance of Moscow Trial impresario Andrei Vishinsky, friend of Nikita Khrushchev, unofficial ambassador extraordinary to Moscow — [who] again pops up in the news: this time as broker for an outfit called International Trade Fairs, Inc., that will stage a big agricultural fair in Moscow next summer, with 'at least $15,000,000' of U.S. goods on display." *National Review*, August 1, 1956, page 4.

228:1 In connection with the Dulles brothers it is worth remembering too that both Allen and John Foster Dulles, as still quite young men, were a part of the small "brain trust" of Colonel Edward Mandell House, in carrying out the plans of that sinister character at the Paris Peace Conference after World War I.

Allen Dulles certainly behaved in a highly suspicious manner with regard to Povl Bang-Jensen, the Danish diplomat who served as assistant secretary to the UN Committee on Hungary. Bang-Jensen incurred the wrath of Dag Hammarskjoeld when he refused to identify Hungarian witnesses who testified before the UN Committee on events surrounding the Hungarian revolt of 1956. Bang-Jensen sought in vain the cooperation of Allen Dulles when he tried to inform the CIA Director of Soviet infiltration of the UN Secretariat and American intelligence agencies. Bang-Jensen died November 24, 1959 — undoubtedly a murder victim. See S.I.S.S., Report: "The Bang-Jensen Case," September 24, 1961. Also see, De Witt Copp and Marshall Peck, *Betrayal At The UN* (New York: Devin-Adair, 1961).

228:2 *Christian Economics*, February 8, 1955, page 2.

229:1 *Human Events*, May 19, 1956, page 3.

230:1 On the television program, *Meet The Press*, August 26, 1956, as quoted in *National Review*, September 8, 1956, pages 5 and 6.

230:2 Stevenson as a "centrist" certainly had his share of left-wing support.

When Eleanor Roosevelt formed a "Stevenson For President Committee" in 1956, at least fifty-two members of the committee had been sponsors of Communist fronts. See J. B. Matthews, "Now They're For Stevenson," *National Review*, February 8, 1956, pages 20-21.

230:3 On the television program, *Meet The Press*, August 26, 1956, as quoted in *National Review*, September 8, 1956, pages 5 and 6.

For the Eisenhower-Larson beliefs, see Arthur Larson, *A Republican Looks At His Party* (New York: Harper, 1956).

230:4 Larson is now Director of the World Rule of Law Center at Duke University. But in May 1961 he took time out from his internationalist duties there to attend a week-long unofficial conference on Soviet-American relations in the town of Nizhnyaya Oreanda in the Crimea. See *New York Times*, May 13, 1961, and Dan Smoot, *The Invisible Government*, pages i-iii.

231:1 See Barron, *Inside The State Department*.

231:2 Hagerty's role against McCarthy did not go unnoticed. "C. D. Jackson and James Hagerty, propaganda advisers to President Eisenhower, were congratulated by British officials at Bermuda for masterminding the White House and State Department statements critical of the ideas of Senator Joseph McCarthy." *U.S. News & World Report*, December 11, 1953, page 12.

Hagerty recently caused a nation-wide furore in his present position as Vice President of the American Broadcasting Company. On November 11, 1962 an ABC television program ("The Political Obituary Of Richard M. Nixon," narrated by the ultra-liberal Howard K. Smith) featured Alger Hiss. Hiss took advantage of this opportunity to smear Nixon as Hiss has smeared just about every prominent individual who had anything to do with his conviction for perjury in 1950. It will be recalled that the perjury involved in the Hiss case concerned his lying when charged with

giving information to the Russians. Protests against the appearance of Hiss were dismissed by Hagerty on grounds that he, Hagerty, was defending "the principle of a free press."

Willard Edwards, the distinguished correspondent of the *Chicago Tribune*, said: "Even Hiss must have been startled at the invitation. Lucky Luciano, the late vice lord, might have been similarly surprised if invited to comment to a national audience on the political career of Thomas E. Dewey, the man who sent him to prison, after Dewey's defeat for the Presidency." "How Probers Tripped Up Alger Hiss," *Human Events*, December 8, 1962.

232:1 The nomination of Conant was approved in the Senate by a vote of four to two. Senator Leverett Saltonstall of Massachusetts, the Republican whip, engineered the confirmation on a Friday night at seven o'clock when he knew that most of the Senators had left Washington for the weekend. The major wire services failed to report that the vote had been four to two. And the only newspaper in the country which carried this news was the *Boston Post*. See John Kelson, "Inside Story of Conant 'Coup' Finally Told By Sen. Dworshak," *Boston Post*, March 22, 1953.

232:2 ". . . Mr. Bruce is labelled, in Europe, as America's most conspicuous diplomatic supporter of the 'third force concept' . . . that it is the Continent's fate to reorganize itself as a neutral region separating the U.S. from the Soviets." William S. Schlamm, "Foreign Trends," *National Review*, March 23, 1957, page 281.

232:3 See *Human Events*, February 9, 1957, page 4, and March 2, 1957, pages 2 and 3.

233:1 See HCUA, Hearings: "Investigation of Dr. Edward U. Condon," March 5-10, 1948; "Report (on Dr. Edward U. Condon) to the Full Committee of the Special Subcommittee on National Security," March 18, 1948; Hearings: "Testimony of Dr. Edward

U. Condon," September 5, 1952. One of Condon's colleagues at the Corning Glass Works, Weldon Bruce Dayton, a nuclear-cosmic ray scientist, was refused a passport by the State Department. See *Human Events*, February 18, 1956, pages 2 and 3. Another colleague of Condon's is Robert D. Murphy, vice president at Corning Glass. For more on Murphy see page 166, and notes 166:4 and 248:4.

234:1　See *Human Events*, June 2, 1956, pages 1 and 2; and, *National Review*, June 27, 1956, page 4.

235:1　See the review of Stewart's record in *Report of the Special Committee to Investigate Tax-Exempt Foundations and Comparable Organizations*, House of Representatives, 83rd Congress, 2nd Session, 1954, pages 375-381. Stewart was identified as a Communist by Louis Budenz. S.I.S.S., Hearings: "Institute of Pacific Relations," Part 2, August 22, 1951, pages 563-564.

235:2　For an excellent description of the extent to which the ILO was taken over by Communists and Socialists, see William L. McGrath, "Socialism By Treaty," *National Review*, May 9, 1956, pages 11-13.

236:1　There were early and harsh judgments of Warren's record on the bench: ". . . The record reveals Chief Justice Warren as a dogmatic ideologue . . . with Justices Douglas and Black. These three judicial horsemen of the Liberal apocalypse . . . are always on the side of the central government as against the states. Always . . . they favor the rights of unions as against the rights of individuals. Nearly always, as in the Slochower and Cole and Communist registration and Steve Nelson cases, or in their dissent from the Cutter Laboratories decision, they upheld privilege for Communists against claims of national security." Editorial, *National Review*, July 4, 1956, pages 5 and 6.

237:1　See *Human Events*, August 31, 1957, page 3, and September 7, 1957, page 1. See, also, Fulton Lewis Jr., *Exclusive*, August 28, 1957, pages 3 and 4.

237:2　McKinney is presently United States Ambassador to Switzerland.

238:1　Mr. Cain is now a resident of Miami and a bank executive. During the election campaign of 1962 he directed the efforts of Claude Pepper's opponent but along the way paused to do some whitewashing: ". . . I consider Mr. Pepper's loyalty to our country to be as positive as is my own." *Miami Herald*, November 25, 1962. See other characterizations of Pepper on page 74 and 74:1.

238:2　*Exclusive*, January 9, 1957, page 1.

239:1　See *Congressional Record*, 85th Congress, 1st Session, pages 3937-3946.

239:2　For a glimpse at Brennan's early pro-Communist activities as a Justice of the Supreme Court, see Rosalie Gordon, *Nine Men Against America* (New York: Devin-Adair, 1958), pages 107-109.

240:1　The utter dishonesty of this White House Conference was clearly indicated in L. Brent Bozell, "National Trends," *National Review*, December 21, 1955, page 13.

Dr. Adam S. Bennion, who was a major participant in the Conference, said: "The White House Conference was a stimulating experience. It was well set up and allowed full and free discussion on the part of some 1,800 people around 166 conference tables. Those in charge planned the gathering to be thoroughly democratic, *but once again a capable, well-organized* and directed minority showed how effective it can be against an unorganized and undirected miscellaneous group. . . .

" . . . The major addresses at the conference — before and after the table discussions — presumed some form of Federal Aid. *Objections and reservations had been siphoned off in the progressive discussions.*" (Italics added.) Address of Dr. Bennion to the Sixtieth Congress of American Industry, Hotel Waldorf-Astoria, New York, December 9, 1955.

240:2　While McElroy was showing such a determined penchant for intruding the Defense Department into political-economic-social areas, Admiral Hyman G. Rickover, told a Senate Armed Services Preparedness Committee: "The Sputnik has stirred up a lot of feeling, but I think — it looks to me as though there is still a lot of play-acting on the thing. I think people are going through the motions and nearly everybody comes up and says we should appropriate a couple of billion dollars more, and that will solve the problem. That will not solve our problem. I don't think it is all money and I don't think it is all organizational, either. The easiest thing to do in Washington when something goes wrong is to reorganize, and from what I have seen in many years all that usually gets reorganized are the telephone numbers." *U.S. News & World Report*, January 17, 1958, page 55.

240:3 *U.S. News & World Report* (April 18, 1958, page 29) stated flatly: "Neil McElroy, Secretary of Defense, is the real architect of President Eisenhower's plan to reorganize the Defense Department." A plan devised only a few months after McElroy succeeded Charles E. Wilson.

240:4 The "reorganization plan" was outlined in Eisenhower's State of the Union Message on Jan. 9, 1958 and spelled out in detail in a special message from Eisenhower to the Congress on April 3, 1958.

Representative Carl Vinson of Georgia, Chairman of the House Armed Services Committee, led the opposition to the measure. Said Mr. Vinson: "One point that puzzles me is the President's vigorous criticism of the chain of command to the unified commands. This chain of command, according to the President's message, is 'cumbersome and unreliable in time of peace and not usable in time of war.' And yet . . . what is being thus criticized in the President's message . . . is the very system which was established by the President in connection with the proposal and enactment of the President's Reorganization Plan No. 6 of 1953. . . . The actual result of the President's proposal is a supreme Prussian-type general staff." *U.S. News & World Report*,

April 25, 1958, pages 80-81, 123-124.

For an excellent summary and analysis of the reorganization plans, see L. Brent Bozell, *National Review*, April 26, 1958, page 392.

241:1 See *U.S. News & World Report*, April 18, 1958, page 8.

242:1 Much more recently, as a carry-over under the Kennedy Administration, Mr. Bunker has helped to deliver West New Guinea to Sukarno. See *American Opinion*, October 1962, page 67, and November 1962, pages 59-60. See, also, the *Reuters* dispatch, describing Dutch reaction to Bunker's meddling. *Quincy* (Mass.) *Patriot Ledger*, September 5, 1962. The Kennedy Administration in this instance concluded a policy long established by the Eisenhower Administration. On March 12, 1956 Secretary of State Dulles, paying a state visit to Indonesia, "made it clear to President Sukarno that the United States was giving no support to the Dutch on the [Netherlands New Guinea] issue . . . 'the general trend is in your favor' [Dulles told Sukarno]." *New York Times*, March 18, 1956.

243:1 Since 1957 Emmerson has served in France, Nigeria, and Southern Rhodesia during the Eisenhower Administration.

In February 1961 he was promoted to the rank of Minister and President Kennedy appointed him to be Minister to Tokyo in 1962. "Tetsuma Hashimoto, head of the influential Shiunso Society in Japan, has written Amb. Reischauer to protest appointment of John K. Emmerson as U.S. Minister in Tokyo. Hashimoto points out that Emmerson's most quoted statement while he served in Japan during Occupation was: 'There is no person I can ever trust in Japan. The only people I believe in are the Communists imprisoned during the Pacific War. Let them be set free and have Japan reconstructed with those Communists taking leadership.'" *National Review Bulletin*, August 7, 1962, page 3.

Fulton Lewis Jr. reports that since arriving in Japan, Emmerson has engaged in "a strange campaign to woo Japanese leftists" and "those being wooed are leaders of Sohyo, the Japanese labor federation. They hold membership cards in the Japanese Socialist party, an extremist group that is loudly anti-American" and "under Emmerson's program, some 40 leftists have come to the United States as guests of Uncle Sam, according to a State Department spokesman." *Los Angeles Herald-Examiner*, November 9, 1962.

For an earlier, but excellent, summary of Emmerson's activities, see Frank Kirkpatrick, *The American Way*, Volume III, No. 4, 1957, pages 3-9.

246:1 See Lane, *I Saw Poland Betrayed*.

246:2 The only exceptions then left were the tiny country of Greece and the city of Istanbul.

247:1 When Bohlen's tour of duty was completed at that post, *Human Events* (October 21, 1959, page 2) said that "Bohlen leaves [Manila] with U.S.-Philippine relations at their lowest ebb since independence was granted to those Pacific Islands."

247:2 After Thompson had been in Moscow six months, *U.S. News & World Report* (January 24, 1958, page 51) summarized the type of information and suggestions he was sending to Washington: "The Ambassador thinks he detects among Russia's leaders a new willingness to permit more freedom of thought in the satellite countries and among the Soviet's own scientists and intellectuals. He is looking for means by which the U.S. may foster this development, urges increased exchanges of intellectuals and scientists between the two countries."

247:3 Mr. Zellerbach has died since this paragraph was originally written. But he played too important a part in pro-leftist activities of the "double-crossing decade" for his name to be omitted here. The nature of these activities have been outlined in *The Dan Smoot Report*, January 28, 1957, pages 7 and 8; and, *The American Legion Firing Line*, February 1, 1957, pages 1 and 2.

247:4 For those curious as to the nature of the Fund while Mr. Zellerbach was

associated with it, see William Henry Chamberlin, "Anti-Anti-Communism: A Ford Investment," *National Review*, April 11, 1956, pages 16-18.

248:1 See *Congressional Record*, January 30, 1957, pages 1237-1244.

248:2 From the very beginning of the Eisenhower administration, Jackson's influence was considerable:

"(1) Last Spring [1953], when the ailing Taft was preparing a speech to be given in Cincinnati, he showed it to Ike before delivering it and got his approval. Taft's remark in the speech that we might have to 'go it alone' in the Far East hit the headlines. Jackson is believed to have been the man who got the President to make such comments so many observers concluded: Ike repudiates Taft.

"(2) Attorney General Brownell cleared his historic speech (attacking Truman on the [Harry Dexter] White case) with Ike before delivery. Jackson again — according to reliable sources — stepped in and influenced Ike to adopt the rather chilly and negative line which impaired but failed to spoil the Brownell case and eventual victory over Truman [in the White case]. These matters are known and discussed in GOP circles. There is naturally, therefore, speculation that Jackson also prompted Ike's expressed hope for 'no Communist issue in 1954.'" *Human Events*, December 2, 1953, pages 1 and 2 .

248:3 An *Editorial* entitled "Unseeing Eyes" in *National Review* (November 2, 1957, pages 389-390) called attention to many alarming features of Rabi's background, when he was appointed to Eisenhower's Science Advisory Committee:

(1) Rabi was 'especially enthusiastic' over [J. Robert] Oppenheimer's 'moral character.'

(2) Rabi was a leading opponent of the proposal to develop an H-bomb.

(3) Rabi (along with Oppenheimer, Jerrold Zacharias, and Charles Lauritsen) belonged to "the notorious ZORC cabal, exposed in 1953 by *Fortune* [*Magazine*]. ZORC tried to promote passive con-

tinental air defense and its distant radar warning lines at the expense of the Strategic Air Command and offensive striking power. . . . "

(4) Rabi "succeeded Oppenheimer as Chairman of the AEC General Advisory Committee. Before his defense of Oppenheimer and his involvement in ZORC he became known to a wide public when, in 1946, he, Philip Jessup . . . and others signed a letter to the *New York Times* calling on the United States to stop nuclear bomb production and to dump all U-235 into the ocean."

(5) "Less known to the public has been Rabi's service as a scientific consultant to the State Department. His conduct in that post led certain other agencies of the government, when setting up a highly confidential project, to include an entire special security procedure to cut off all lines of communication to Rabi."

Incidentally, Doctor Rabi was appointed by President Kennedy to be a member of the General Advisory Committee to the United States Arms Control and Disarmament Agency.

248:4 See page 166, and notes 166:4 and 233:1.

Mr. Murphy has evidently not ceased his meddling. In April, 1961 Murphy went on a confidential mission for President Kennedy to the Dominican Republic. Intermediaries between the President and Murphy were former Ambassador Joseph P. Kennedy, the President's father, and Igor Cassini, a society columnist for the Hearst newspapers.

Cassini and his brother, Oleg, a *couturier* for Jacqueline Kennedy, the President's wife, are directors of Martial, Inc., a public relations firm which handles foreign accounts, but the Dominican Republic was supposedly not one of these accounts. From all appearances, however, the Cassinis were anxious to land this client.

The Murphy mission was ostensibly made to convince the Dominican Republic's Government that it would be wise to adopt a "liberalization of its policies,"

which in the context of 1961 meant to go soft on Communists. The details of the mission, hazy for the most part, appeared in Tad Szulc's special dispatch, *New York Times,* July 22, 1962.

And the haze has not been lifted by either the recent profile of Igor Cassini in the *Saturday Evening Post* (Peter Maas, "Boswell Of The Jet Set," January 19, 1963, pages 28-33) or the confusion created by Cassini's recent indictment by the Justice Department. Igor Cassini has been charged, along with four associates in Martial, Inc., with failing to register as an agent for the Dominican Republic. See *Time Magazine,* February 15, 1963, page 43; and, *Newsweek,* February 18, 1963, page 23.

But the results of the mission to the Dominican Republic are explained by the *Richmond News Leader,* August 1, 1962: "Anyhow, Murphy went to the Dominican Republic; Igor introduced him to Generalissimo Trujillo. But strangely, nothing happened. Mr. Murphy stood by while the Generalissmo was assassinated on May 30, 1961. Suddenly U.S. warships appeared on the horizon while the proper left-wing politicians took over. Mr. Murphy and Mr. Cassini stayed around for a few weeks winding up loose ends, then finally went their separate ways."

249:1 Mr. McCone has proved to be another "indispensable man" to successive left-wing administrations, whether labeled Republican or Democrat. He has recently (in 1962) been appointed successor to Allen Dulles as head of the CIA.

249:2 Sherman Adams was "a Rasputin in the White House . . . [who] seemed intent upon destroying the Republican party. Given two more years as 'Assistant President,' his mission might have been accomplished. But fate intervened; Bernard Goldfine's vicuna coat was ripped off his back, leaving Adams exposed as a two-faced small-time chiseler." James L. Wick, "Enemy Columnists Hope To 'Help' GOP," *Human Events,* March 31, 1960.

249:3   See Lionel Lokos, *Who Promoted Peress?* (New York: Bookmailer, 1962).

249:4   The objective in such cases, of course, is to bring discouragement and despair to those who are trying to expose and stop the Communists, as well as to show that Communist sympathizers will be rewarded despite all opposition.

249:5   "By the time the Zwicker confirmation came to a vote, every member of the Senate, this correspondent is informed, had been honored by a personal call from either a high Pentagon official or a member of the White House Staff. The results: 70 ayes, 2 nays (McCarthy and Malone)." L. Brent Bozell, "National Trends," *National Review,* April 20, 1957, pages 371-372.

Chapter Seventeen

251:1   The significance of the word "treason" was not overlooked by Eisenhower when he was campaigning for the presidency in 1952, and, at the same time, reaching new heights of hypocrisy:

"I have come to Milwaukee tonight to talk with you about communism and freedom.

"These two plain words—we all know—bespeak two distinct worlds. They signify two titanic ideas, two ways of life, two totally irreconcilable beliefs in the nature and destiny of man.

"The one—freedom—knows man as a creature of God, blessed with a free and individual destiny, governed by eternal and natural laws.

"The second — communism — claims man to be an animal creature of the state, curses him for his stubborn instinct for independence, governs with a tyranny that makes its subjects wither away.

"These two ideas are opposed as danger is to safety, as sickness is to health, as weakness to strength, as darkness to light.

"Great truths can, at times, be startlingly simple. This one is of that kind. It is so simple a truth that it seems almost too obvious, almost stale.

"But let not our memories be too short. Only a few years have passed since many moved among us who argued cunningly against this plain truth. Their speech was persuasive, and their vocabulary clever. Remember? It went like this: 'After all, while we stand for political democracy, they stand for economic democracy. Fundamentally, there are but two slightly different roads to the same goal. We both believe in freedom.'

"We all must remember that sophisticated lie. We will never forget it. For it partly poisoned two whole decades of our national life. It insinuated itself into our schools, our public forums, some of our news channels, some of our labor unions, and—most terrifyingly—into our Government itself.

"What did this penetration into Government mean? It meant contamination in some degree of virtually every department, every agency, every bureau, every section of our Government. It meant a Government by men whose very brains were confused by the opiate of this deceit.

"These men were advisers in a foreign policy that—on one side of the world—weakly bowed before the triumph in China of Communists hailed as 'agrarian reformers.'

"On the other side of the world this policy condoned the surrender of whole nations to an implacable enemy whose appetite for conquest sharpened with every victory. This penetration meant a domestic policy whose tone was set by men who sneered and scoffed at warnings of the enemy infiltrating our most secret counsels.

"It meant—in its most ugly triumph—treason itself.

"These years have, indeed, been a harrowing time in our history. It has been a time of both honest illusion and dishonest betrayal—both terribly costly. It has been a time that should have taught us, with cold finality, the truth about freedom and communism.

"Most of us, young or old, wise or naive, have learned. An important few have not. They have learned very little—and they admit nothing.

"They are men about whom there is

nothing great except their vanity and their complacency. They are proud prisoners of their own mistakes.

"Who are these men?

"They are those who cheered the blithe dismissal of the Alger Hiss case as 'a red herring.' They are those who applauded two weeks ago when an Administration servant declared that Communists in our national life were 'not very important' and that we should not waste time chasing 'phantoms.' They are those who slapped their sides with laughter when the same man dismissed the quest for Communists in our government as a kind of silly game played in the Bureau of Wild Life and Fisheries.

"Do you think these fish stories, ghost stories and animal stories are really very amusing? Such comedy touches do little to relieve the tragic knowledge that we have been for years the gullible victims of Communism's espionage experts. These experts in treason have plundered us of secrets involving our highest diplomatic decisions, our atomic research. Tragically, we do not know how much more our security may have been jeopardized.

"This, I repeat, has been a calamity of immeasurable consequence. It is not irreparable: We are strong enough and wise enough to survive it. But for a disturbed people it is made easier to bear—not by making light of it, but by assuring the people it cannot be repeated. To minimize it is criminal folly.

"You can never cure malignant growth just by a hearty bedside manner!

"I must be blunt, for this is a serious matter. I speak not as a partisan or as a candidate but simply as an American Citizen—moved to honest anger by this persistent, gnawing threat of Communist treason in our national life. I know that millions of both parties today are moved to anger and to action.

"Neither these millions nor I can understand a politician who one week makes jokes about this menace, and another week—after public reaction has dampened his humor—promises to offer a serious solution.

"Now, my fellow Americans, we must do more than recognize a menace in order to defeat it. When a free country frankly faces this menace, what should it do—and what should it not do?

"As a people we must be wise enough to know this principle: Freedom must defend itself with courage, with care, with force and with fairness. Failing to remember this principle, freedom in destroying its mortal enemy, could destroy itself.

* * *

"Armed with a clear and uncompromising respect for freedom, how then shall we defend it?

"To begin with: All of us—citizens, jurists, officials—must remember that the Bill of Rights contains no grant of privilege for a group of people to join together to destroy the Bill of Rights. A group—like the Communist conspiracy—dedicated to the ultimate destruction of all civil liberties cannot be allowed to claim civil liberties as its privileged sanctuary from which to carry on subversion of the Government.

"At the same time we have the right to call a spade a spade. That means, in every proved case, the right to call a Red a Red. The time is past when we can hide our heads in the sands of stubborn ignorance or spend our days in the leisurely indulgence of abstract argument.

* * *

"Every official of government must bear clear responsibility for the loyalty and fitness of his own immediate subordinates. And every official of the Federal Government—on every level—must answer any question from appropriate sources touching upon his loyalty and devotion to the United States of America.

"If we add candor to our fidelity to freedom's principles, I sincerely believe our attack on the Communist threat will be well under way. I am confident that a new administration—but only a completely new one—can organize and press this attack successfully.

* * *

"But above all there is needed firm and determined leadership. The climate of our

Federal Government must be one that Communists and their sympathizers would find not only uncongenial but thoroughly hostile.

"I am confident that millions of Americans of both parties will, in this autumn of 1952, demand—with the fervor of an aroused people—the appointment of new guardians of our country's security.

"We have all had enough, I believe, of those whose thinking is still haunted by past illusions, those who are prisoners of their own fuzzy thinking and their own mistakes.

"We have all had enough, I believe, of those who have sneered at the warnings of men trying to drive Communists from high places—but who themselves have never had the sense or the stamina to take after the Communists themselves. . . ."

And Eisenhower was campaigning in 1952 on a Republican Platform which said:

"We charge that they [leaders of the Government of the United States under successive Democratic Administrations, and especially under this present Administration] have shielded traitors to the Nation in high places, and that they have created enemies abroad where we should have friends.

* * *

"By the Administration's appeasement of Communism at home and abroad it has permitted Communists and their fellow travelers to serve in many key agencies and to infiltrate our American life. When such infiltration became notorious through the revelations of Republicans in Congress, the Executive Department stubbornly refused to deal with it openly and vigorously. It raised the false cry of 'red herring' and took other measures to block and discredit investigations. It denied files and information to Congress. It set up boards of its own to keep information secret and to deal lightly with security risks and persons of doubtful loyalty. It only undertook prosecution of the most notorious Communists after public opinion forced action.

"The result of these policies is the need-less sacrifice of American lives, a crushing cost in dollars for defense, possession by Russia of the atomic bomb, the lowering of the Iron Curtain, and the present threats to world peace. Our people have been mired in fear and distrust, and employees of integrity in the Government service have been cruelly maligned by the Administration's tolerance of people of doubtful loyalty.

"There are no Communists in the *Republican Party*. We have always recognized Communism to be a world conspiracy against freedom and religion. We never compromised with Communism and we have fought to expose it and eliminate it in government and American life.

"A Republican President will appoint only persons of unquestioned loyalty. We will overhaul loyalty and security programs. In achieving these purposes a Republican President will cooperate with Congress. We pledge close coordination of our intelligence services for protecting our security. We pledge fair but vigorous enforcement of laws to safeguard our country from subversion and disloyalty. By such policies we will keep the country secure and restore the confidence of the American people in the integrity of our Government."

* * *

On March 9, 1961 Senator Everett Dirksen of Illinois placed in the *Congressional Record* (pages 3334-3342) twenty-four columns of small print purporting to be a list of "achievements during eight years of a Republican Administration." Mr. Dirksen described the account as an "authentic compilation" but nowhere is there the slightest reference to anything the Eisenhower Administration even attempted—much less achieved—in order to fulfill the promises made in the Milwaukee speech and 1952 Platform, with regard to ridding the government of subversives or those who shielded subversives in one way or another.

As a matter of fact any Republican, worthy of the name, who wishes to find out what happened to the Grand Old Party after 1952, would do well to compare the 1952 Platform and Senator Dirksen's interminable catalogue of "achievements."

252:1 *U.S. News & World Report,* December 18, 1953, pages 67-70.

"President Eisenhower's speech to the United Nations . . . was a fresh move in the direction of appeasement of Soviet Russia." Editorial in *The Freeman,* December 28, 1953, page 221.

252:2 See Fulton Lewis Jr., *Exclusive,* May 8, 1957, page 3.

252:3 "After the end of the war the [uranium] workings of St. Joachimsthal in Czechoslovakia and those in Eastern Germany, in the Erzgelrign in Saxony and the Marsfield copper-belt, were taken over for the Soviet atom-bomb project." Werner Keller, *East Minus West = Zero* (New York: Putnam's, 1962), page 303.

253:1 Pavel Winkler

253:2 David Shea Teeple, "Atoms For Peace—Or War?," *National Review,* January 12, 1957, pages 35-37.

253:3 *Ibid.*

254:1 For example, Doctors J. Robert Oppenheimer, Donald J. Hughes, and Leo Szilard. *Ibid.*

254:2 See William Henry Chamberlin, "Atomic Giveaway," *The Wall St. Journal,* May 14, 1957; and, Medford Evans, "They First Make Mad," *Human Events,* March 26, 1955.

255:1 See Medford Evans, "Have They Really Got It?: Fact And Myth About Soviet Atomic Strength," *Human Events,* June 1, 1957. For earlier appraisals, see Richard L. Stokes, "The U.S. Has No Secrets," pages 263-266; and, Medford Evans, "Are Soviet A-Bombs Russian?," pages 266-268, *The Freeman,* January 12, 1953. A recent and pertinent study is Keller, *East Minus West = Zero.*

255:2 On October 21, 1956 Gomulka formally assumed control of Poland. Two days later Eisenhower offered aid to Poland "if Poland wants it." Needless to say Poland not only wanted but received

$95,000,000 worth of aid on June 7, 1957, and they were back for more on October 31, 1957. As the *New York Times* (November 1, 1957) described it: "The Poles . . . want this time to get the balance of their shopping list filled." And most of the list was filled when a sales and credit agreement totalling $98,000,000, in addition to the June 7 aid, was negotiated in Washington.

256:1 Senator William F. Knowland, Republican of California, as quoted in *American Mercury,* September 1957, page 47.

256:2 The United States is still being visited by the sins of Eisenhower's aid to Communist Poland. For example: "On July 11, 1961—less than three months after the Bay of Pigs tragedy—Kennedy's Ambassador to communist Poland—Jacob D. Beam—ceremonially opened a new production line at the big Lenin steel works at Nowa Huta, Poland.

"The *New York Times News Service,* reporting this event, said: 'The new facility, the only continuous steel galvanizing line in the Soviet bloc, was built out of American machinery and financed with a $2,500,000 United States credit.' (*Dallas Morning News,* July 13, 1961.)

"This plant has produced part of the essential galvanized steel which went into the missile bases in Cuba; and we should have known the plant would do just that when we gave communist Poland the money to build the facility. Proof that Washington officialdom *knew* our money would be used to produce war goods for Cuba? On April 2, 1960, the *New York Times* carried a front-page article entitled 'Cubans and Poles Sign Trade Treaty.' Here are passages from the story: 'Cuba announced last night a far-reaching trade pact with Poland . . . . The list of products Poland will deliver includes sea-going ships and fishing vessels, planes, helicopters, complete industrial plants, steel foundries and lamination mills, sugar mills, chemical plants, power plants, industrial machinery plants, road-building equipment, textile machinery, tractors, Diesel and electrical motors and tools.' " *The Dan Smoot Report*, October 29, 1962, page 349.

257:1 See Eugene W. Castle, "Sputnik Speeds Up Spending," *Christian Economics*, March 4, 1958, page 4.

257:2 *Associated Press* dispatch, *Boston Traveler*, June 20, 1956.

258:1 See *Human Events*, May 27, 1957, page 2.

The extent of help to Tito apparently had no bounds: "The United States last week presented to Marshal Tito a U.S. Atomic Energy Commission 'atoms for peace' library. It consisted of 13,100 technical reports." *National Review*, June 15, 1957, page 558.

258:2 And under the Kennedy Administration, of course, as first exposed by Major Knickerbocker, we have been training, at our airfields in Texas, some of the Yugoslav Communist pilots who fly these planes.

World (the weekly news journal), June 19, 1962, reported that U.S. training for Yugoslav soldiers, sailors, and airmen had a cash value of five million dollars. And that American military hardware to Yugoslavia included 212 jet-fighters, 126 piston-engine fighters, 918 tanks, 33,800,000 rounds of ammunition, and 424,405 rockets. The same journal (April 10, 1962) reported that in the few months after December 1, 1961 export licenses were approved for the shipment to Yugoslavia of American commodities valued at more than $6,700,000. The commodities were mostly electronic equipment, iron, steel, and copper scrap, and various types of industrial machinery.

259:1 (Chicago: Regnery, 1957), page xiv.

259:2 See Page 263, note 2.

259:3 *United Press* dispatch in *Manchester* (N.H.) *Union Leader*, February 11, 1957.

260:1 See HCUA, Hearings and Appendix to Hearings: "Communist Political Subversion," (Parts 1 and 2), November 12-December 14, 1956.

260:2 See Robert C. Alexander, "A Study Of Our Immigration Laws," booklet published in May 1960 by The American Coalition Of Patriotic Societies, Washington, D. C. Mr. Alexander is a former Deputy Director of the Visa Office in the Department of State.

261:1 Press dispatch of July 23, 1953, as quoted by Attorney Robert B. Dresser in an *Open Letter* to Eisenhower, dated and released to the press on March 16, 1957.

261:2 *Manchester* (N.H.) *Union Leader*, February 11, 1957.

262:1 "Rarely was mention made of the fact that there were an estimated 600,000 Communists in Hungary at the start of the revolution *and that most of the refugees in the initial period were running from the patriots.*" Edna R. Fluegel, "The New Attack On Our Immigration Act." *American Mercury*, June 1957, pages 93-100.

262:2 Richard Arens on the *Manion Forum Network*, July 6, 1958. Mr. Arens, at the time, was staff director of the House Committee on Un-American Activities. "The well-informed late Senator Pat McCarran stated, on the Senate floor in 1951, that there were *then* five million *illegally* in our country." Edna F. Fluegel, "The New Attack On Our Immigration Act," *American Mercury*, June 1957, pages 93-100.

262:3 Fluegel, *Loc. cit.*

262:4 See Page 263, note 2.

263:1 See next footnote.

263:2 The speech, which was delivered to the Sixty-sixth Continental Congress of the Daughters of the American Revolution, is published and distributed by that organization's National Defense Committee. See, also, *American Mercury*, March 1958, pages 103-110, where Mr. Arens' speech is reprinted under the title: "The Communist Campaign Against Our Immigration System."

264:1 Holland Roberts, a candidate for the office of State Superintendent of Public Instruction. See *Tenth Report*

(1959), California Senate Fact-Finding Committee On Un-American Activities, pages 39-40.

264:2 (New York: Abelard-Schuman, 1956). The subtitle of Mr. Joyce's book is worth noting: *The Twilight Of National Sovereignty.*

264:3 For example, see *U.S. News & World Report*, January 18, 1957, pages 135-138.

265:1 The position now carries the title: Undersecretary for Political and Security Council Affairs. In this office at the present time is Eugeny Kiselev of the USSR. His predecessors were Arkady Sobelov, Constantine Zinchenko, Ilya Tchernychev, Dragin Protitch, Anatoly F. Dobrynin, and Georgy Arkadev—all from the USSR, with the exception of Protitch from Yugoslavia. See S.I.S.S., Report: "The Bang-Jensen Case," released on September 14, 1961, page 21.

265:2 As of this writing the thumbs belong to the Burmese Marxist U Thant, the ubiquitous Ralph Bunche, and Eugeny Kiselev of the USSR.

265:3 Stassen is now in oblivion, helped on his way by the Republican electorate of Pennsylvania who refused him nomination in that state's gubernatorial primary in 1958. Herter, who succeeded John Foster Dulles as Secretary of State, has been the subject of two studies in *American Opinion*: June 1959, pages 32-34 *et seq.*, and June 1960, pages 14-26. And on November 15, 1962 President Kennedy appointed Herter as his Special Representative for Trade Negotiations with nations of the European Common Market.

265:4 See Page 173, note 1.

265:5 For example, on March 15, 1956, in a speech before the Chicago Council on Foreign Relations, Herter said: ". . . We should offer to coordinate our [foreign] aid with whatever assistance the Soviet Union is willing to provide. If the Soviet proposes to build a steel mill, we should not feel bound to offer to build the same mill on more favorable conditions. We should, on the contrary, be willing to

work out both with the Soviet and with the recipient country a program to which both the Soviet and ourselves can each contribute." *Human Events*, December 15, 1956, pages 1 and 2.

Mr. Herter certainly was prophetic, since in 1962 the House Foreign Operations and Monetary Affairs Subcommittee learned that American foreign aid funds built a *Soviet* radio station and a *Soviet* multi-million dollar hospital in Cambodia while Herter was Undersecretary and Secretary of State. And officials of the foreign aid program admitted that, as of 1962, American aid *may* be building similar Soviet projects in eighteen other countries. *Human Events*, March 31, 1962, page 238. The Cambodian story has also been told in *World* (the weekly news journal), May 1, May 8, May 15, May 22, and June 19, 1962.

266:1 Joseph C. Harsch, November 6, 1956.

267:1 "A Letter To The South: On Segregation," *One Man's Opinion* (now *American Opinion*), September 1956, pages 28-37.

268:1 Since this was written the invasion of Mississippi by Federal Marshals and Federal troops has simply confirmed and emphasized everything said in the paragraphs noted. It has also shown further how the actions and purposes of the present Administration make it simply a continuation of the last one. The same evil forces are guiding and controlling both.

268:2 Wayne L. Hays, Democrat of Ohio.

269:1 Westbrook Pegler in the *New York Journal-American*, January 9, 1955.

The attitude of the White House had been reported earlier: "This week the Reece Committee opened its doors for public hearings but it is uncertain how much of a job it will be able to do. The Committee became unpopular at the White House from its birth—and already the funds expected for the investigation have been drastically cut . . . . Observers are pointing to the Reece Committee as just another example of an inexplicable and tragic hostility of the White House toward efforts of Congress to cope with the Communist menace." *Human Events*, May 12, 1954, pages 2-3.

269:2 "The fact that the United States, with its advanced scientific and material resources, was not able to launch the first earth satellite should be the subject of serious thought and investigation. In my opinion, it indicates the work of well-organized Soviet spy rings in the United States missile production system. These rings on the one hand are pumping out of the United States valuable scientific and other information and on the other hand are sabotaging and delaying the United States missile effort under all kinds of seemingly logical excuses." *Letter from Gouzenko to Eisenhower*, October 6, 1957, as quoted in *New York Times*, October 7, 1957.

Gouzenko had served as Code Clerk in the Soviet Embassy at Ottawa, Canada, and was instrumental in exposing the vast Soviet espionage network covering Canada and the United States, emanating from the Embassy. See, especially, Gouzenko's own book, *The Iron Curtain* (New York: Norton, 1948), and his testimony before the Senate Internal Security Subcommittee on January 4, 1954, published as Senate Document No. 5, 84th Congress, 1st Session, 1955.

Gouzenko's conclusions were confirmed later by Vladimir Shabinsky (a former colonel in the Soviet Army), "How I Found The Nazi Missile Secrets," *Look Magazine*, February 4, 1958, pages 20-21; and, Peter Van Slingerland, "How We Let The Missile Secrets Get Away," *Op. cit.*, pages 22-23.

269:3 As quoted in *American Mercury*, May 1958, page 53.

270:1 See Jules Dubois, "Problem In Panama," *American Mercury*, March 1954, pages 79-84.

270:2 The surrender of United States interests in Panama continues. For example, on September 17, 1960, the eve of Soviet Premier Khrushchev's arrival in the United States, Eisenhower took the voluntary and unilateral action of ordering the flag of Panama to be flown with the flag of the United States in the United States Canal Zone. On February 2, 1960 the House of Representatives had voted 381-12 against Panamanian demands for the display of the Panamanian flag in the Zone. The House felt it would be a "major departure from established policy" and "should not be accomplished through executive fiat." See *House Report* 2218, 86th Congress, August 31, 1960.

270:3 Fulton Lewis Jr. in *Exclusive*, March 27, 1957, page 1.

Representative Michael A. Feighan, Democrat of Ohio, cites another example of mendacity with regard to the Hungarian revolt:

"You will recall the revolution broke out on October 23, 1956, and that by October 28, the Hungarian patriots had rid their country of the Russian oppressors. A revolutionary regime took over and there was a political hiatus for five days.

"Then the State Department, allegedly concerned about the delicate feelings of the Communist dictator Tito, sent him the following cabled assurances of our national intentions in the late afternoon of Friday, November 2, 1956. 'The Government of the United States does not look with favor upon governments unfriendly to the Soviet Union on the borders of the Soviet Union.'

"It was no accident or misjudgment of consequences which led the imperial Russian Army to reinvade Hungary at 4 a.m. on the morning of November 4, 1956. The cabled message to Tito was the go ahead signal to the Russians because any American school boy knows that Tito is Moscow's Trojan Horse. It took less than 48 hours for him to relay this message of treason to his superiors in the Kremlin." *Congressional Record*, August 31, 1960, page 17407.

Eisenhower's callous treatment of the revolt in Hungary was especially significant on the very day he heard of the fighting there. In a statement to the press he said: "The United States deplores the intervention of Soviet military forces, which under the treaty of peace should have been withdrawn and the presence of which in Hungary as is now demonstrated is not to protect Hungary against armed aggression from without, but rather to continue an occupation of Hungary by the forces of an alien government for its own purposes. The heart of America goes out to the people of Hungary." *U.S. News & World Report*, November 2, 1956.

If there was anything the Hungarians did not need it was "heart"—their needs were arms. Yet, on the same day in a nation-wide radio and television address, Eisenhower interrupted his campaign oratory only long enough to say that the "people of Poland and of Hungary—indeed, of all Eastern Europe—are men and women whom America has never forgotten, nor ever will," and "it remains the firm purpose of America to strengthen the love of liberty everywhere, and to do all within our *peaceful* power to help its champions." *Op. cit.*, pages 98-100.

"In November, 1956, the halls of the United Nations rang with the speeches of United States delegate Henry Cabot Lodge, Jr., who offered the Hungarian patriots indignant oratory instead of the physical help for which they cried so desperately. Said Lodge, five hours after the Soviet attack on Budapest had begun, 'if ever there was a time when the action of the United Nations could literally be a matter of life and death for a whole nation, this is that time.' *Hungary died because the only nation capable of saving it, the United States, chose to let it die*—pretending that we could default on our own responsibility by calling upon an organization incapable of handling such a situation." (Italics added.) Frank J. Johnson, *No Substitute For Victory* (Chicago: Regnery, 1962), page 148.

271:1   January 1957, pages 5-6.

271:2   For a blow-by-blow account of the July 14 meeting, see Fulton Lewis Jr., *Exclusive*, July 23, 1958, pages 1 and 2.

272:1   *Boston Herald*, July 27, 1958.

The net effect of the intervention in Lebanon was to replace President Camille Chamoun with General Fouad Chehab, originally sponsored by Egypt's Nasser (See *New York Times*, September 24, 1958). But the real power was to be exerted by Chehab's Premier, Rashid Karami, who not only also held the portfolios of Minister of the Interior and Minister of Defense, but was the open and recognized leader of the Communists in Lebanon. On December 10, 1958 Karami would tell the world that the Eisenhower Doctrine had served its purpose and it was now "out of date . . . we no longer feel bound by . . . [its] terms." *Deadline Data*, December 10, 1958.

272:2   "From the rostrum of the United Nations we shall convince the colonial and semicolonial people to liberate themselves, and to spread the Communist theory all over the world. We recognize the United Nations as no authority over the Soviet Union, but the United Nations serves us to detect the capitalists and the warmongers in the Western World." Soviet General Bondarenko at the Frunze Military Academy in Moscow, as quoted by Slovakian Colonel Jan Bukar in his testimony before the House Committee on Un-American Activities, May 13, 1953, page 15.

272:3   For an excellent analysis of the United States policy with regard to the Suez crisis, see L. Brent Bozell, "Mr. Dulles Finds Himself," *National Review*, September 29, 1956, pages 8 and 21. Says Mr. Bozell: ". . . No one knew better than Mr. Dulles that the real aggressor at Suez was not Nasser, but the Kremlin; and that the real danger was not that Egypt would control the Canal, but that the U.S.'s mortal enemy, the Soviet Union, would."

273:1   Forty million dollars per year for Laos would, per capita, be the equivalent of well over a billion dollars per year for England, or over six billion dollars per year for India. For the four years, 1955-1958, International Cooperation Administration officials admitted that United States aid to Laos amounted to $166,000,-000, *excluding military aid*. See House Subcommittee On Government Operations, Hearings: "United States Aid Operations In Laos," March 11-June 1, 1959), pages 252-253.

Chairman Porter Hardy (Dem.-Va.) said: "Laos is the only country in the world where we support the entire military budget. Some *85 percent or more of our total aid* to Laos goes into support of a 25,000-man military force." *Ibid.*, page 2. (Italics added.)

By December 31, 1961, aid disbursements (excluding military aid) to Laos amounted to $388,000,000. See Lawrence Sullivan, Coordinator of Information, House of Representatives, as quoted in Fulton Lewis Jr., *The Top Of The News*, October 8-12, 1962, page 328.

And at the present time the aid to Laos continues at a rate of at least three million dollars a month. For recent developments in Laos, see Slobodan M. Draskovich, "Laos: For Whom The Bell Tolls," *American Opinion*, July-August 1962, pages 15-20.

274:1 *World Survey* (England), June-July 1956, page 4.

275:1 "What, then, does justice mean to him (Eisenhower), when he moves against France and England in defense of Moscow's puppet, Nasser, and stands by while Hungary is murdered? How does it square with devotion to justice to woo Tito and Gomulka, whose system of thought and government, in its fundamentals identical with that of the Soviet Union, is as alien to justice as ever was Stalin's?" Frank S. Meyer, "The Ethics Of Mr. Eisenhower's Rhetoric," *National Review*, February 9, 1957, page 137.

275:2 ". . . a Soviet-appeasing mood has markedly expanded in the Western leaders, very conspicuously in the American President, leader of the West's leaders." James Burnham, *National Review*, September 7, 1957, page 204.

275:3 See Page 63, note 1.

275:4 See Page 231.

275:5 See Page 128, note 1.

278:1 The reluctance on the part of so many individuals to dispel the aura which surrounded Eisenhower puzzled Frank Kirkpatrick:

"When we get to President Eisenhower, it is one of the most amazing paradoxes of our time that the same people, who believe Roosevelt and Truman protected the Reds, close their eyes and their minds to both the suggestion and the overwhelming evidence that the communists have been given as much or greater protection and encouragement by Eisenhower.

"This does not mean that there are more or even as many party members who have access to the White House—nor does it mean that open infiltration of the Federal Departments is continuing. The protection for and aid to the domestic communists is a far more subtle matter in the Eisenhower administration. There is nothing subtle, however, about the result:

"(a) The Communist Party, which had gone underground in the late forties, has come out of hiding and both bluntly and accurately pointed to Ike's fraternizing at Geneva as evidence that communism is not a conspiracy.

"(b) The active anti-communists in Congress have been given an example of what can and will happen to them if they attempt the housecleaning promised by the Republicans—McCarthy was condemned by White House orders.

"(c) The Communist Program, advanced in April of 1954, has been followed almost to the letter in American foreign policy, and in domestic affairs a perceptible current toward communist objectives can be observed." *The American Way*, Volume II, No. 8, 1956, page 28.

278:2 At this point in the original manuscript there was one paragraph in which I expressed my own personal belief as to the most likely explanation of the events and actions which this document had tried to bring into focus. In a confidential letter, neither published nor offered for sale, and restricted to friends who were expected to respect the confidence but offer me in exchange their own points of view, this seemed entirely permissible and proper. It does not seem so for an edition of the letter that is now to be published and given, probably, fairly wide distribution. So that paragraph, and two explanatory paragraphs, connected with it, have been omitted here. And the reader is left entirely free to draw his own conclusions.

279:1   When Truman, as candidate for the vice presidency, was asked if he welcomed the campaign support of Earl Browder, he said he welcomed the support of "anyone who will help keep the President [Roosevelt] in office." *New York Herald Tribune*, October 18, 1944.

281:1   "Fears May Be Liars," an address by Frank R. Barnett at the National Military-Industrial Conference in Chicago, Illinois, March 14, 1957.

281:2   *Ibid.*

282:1   *Ibid.*

282:2   See Matthew B. Ridgway, *Soldier* (New York: Harper, 1956).

282:3   For example, Lieutenant General James M. Gavin, head of the Army's research and development program, told a Senate Armed Services Preparedness Subcommittee: "We have seen our Army deteriorate steadily. We have seen the Soviet Army grow . . . . Then we come before a committee on the Hill and try to defend a budget we don't believe in. It·is an untenable position." General Gavin explained that when he arrived in Washington in 1954 the Army had 27 divisions and a 12.6-billion-dollar budget, but in 1958 there were only 15 divisions and an 8.6-billion-dollar budget. *U.S. News & World Report*, January 17, 1958, page 53.

282:4   *The Kiplinger Washington Letter*, April 20, 1957, page 4.

283:1   Evans, *The Secret War For The A-Bomb*. See, especially, Chapter 9. See, also, Doctor Evans' "Are Soviet A-Bombs

Russian?," *The Freeman*, January 12, 1953, pages 266-268.

285:1   C. L. Sulzberger, *New York Times*, May 30, 1956.

285:2   Dorothy Healey Connelly, Chairman of the Communist Party in Los Angeles- County, as quoted in Rosalie Gordon, *Nine Men Against America* (New York: Devin-Adair, 1958), page 143. For other joyful reactions by Communists to these decisions, see *The American Legion Firing Line*, February 15, 1958, pages 1-3.

285:3   FBI Director J. Edgar Hoover said in his 1958 Annual Report to the Attorney-General: "Sensing a more favorable atmosphere the Communist Party, USA, and its dupes and sympathizers gained further courage and became more vocal in their attacks upon law enforcement and other professions which are dedicated to preserving our freedoms." Quoted in *Human Events*, January 7, 1959, page 3. And that publication commented that "students of subversion note gravely a marked relationship between this 'more favorable atmosphere' for communism and the left-wing decisions of the Supreme Court" in 1958.

286:1   Especially the order issued by Eisenhower on May 17, 1954.

287:1   Lattimore has recently taken a position at Leeds College in England, but during the spring and summer of 1961 he performed yeoman service for the international Communist conspiracy by helping Outer Mongolia attain membership in the U.N.

M. Stanton Evans and his co-authors, Alan H. Ryskind and William Schulz, present a concise summary of the latest Lattimore escapade: "Lattimore popped up in Ulan Bator, with a United States passport, just as U.S.-Mongolian negotiations toward recognition were getting under way. 'I do not think it is an accident,' [Senator Thomas] Dodd [D-Conn.] said, 'that at the very moment when there was a big drive on to persuade the State Department to grant recognition to Outer Mongolia, Owen Lattimore should arrive there as a VIP visitor.' It is reasonable to conclude that Lattimore was in Mongolia, if not at the direction, at least with the connivance, of the Kennedy State Department. Fulton Lewis Jr. reported: 'Lattimore's visit is shrouded in secrecy. Travelling on two grants, Lattimore's ostensible purpose was to study Mongolian *progress*. State Department officials admit they knew of Lattimore's visit, but deny that he was dispatched on official business. They say that they will consult with the Baltimore professor upon his return.' " *The Fringe On Top*, pages 109-110.

287:2   For an account of this disgraceful exhibition, see "Alger Hiss At Princeton," *National Review*, May 16, 1956, pages 9-10; 22.

288:1   Alexander Orlov, a former NKVD agent, testified to the existence of thirty-eight espionage rings in the United States —with only two, in his knowledge, exposed as a result of the work done by Whittaker Chambers and Elizabeth Bentley. S.I.S.S., Hearings: "Scope Of Soviet Activity In The United States," (Part 51), February 14 and 15, 1957.

288:2   S.I.S.S., Hearings: "Scope Of Soviet Activity In The United States," (Part 27), June 14, 1956, page 1481.

288:3   *Exclusive*, August 14, 1957, page 3.

290:1   Speech in May, 1955 before the 16th Freedom Forum at Harding College, Searcy, Arkansas, as quoted in the *National Program Letter*, June 1955, page 1.

290:2   See J. Edgar Hoover, "Red Spy Masters In America," *Reader's Digest*, August 1952, pages 83-87; "Where Do We Stand Today With Communism In The United States?," *American Legion Magazine*, March 1954, pages 14-15, 58 *et. seq.*; "Reds Still Recruit Ready Help In The U.S.," *U.S. News & World Report*, March 8, 1957, pages 110-111; and, "The Communists Are After Our Minds," *American Magazine*, October 1954, pages 19, 85-88.

290:3   Of course there are moments when the patience and forbearance of

Americans are strained to the breaking point. For example, in August 1959 Khrushchev was invited to visit the United States. Vice President Nixon told the press that the invitation "was initiated by the President himself." Senator Thomas Dodd of Connecticut called the invitation "a national disgrace." Representative August Johansen of Michigan said: "The Khrushchev invitation reflects incredible confusion, illogic and contradictions." Constantine Brown, foreign affairs editor of the *Washington Star*, wrote: "This is the greatest disaster to our foreign policy in a generation." Newspapermen recalled that Secretary Dulles, on June 16, 1958, admitted that if Khrushchev managed to get a meeting with Eisenhower that the result for Khrushchev might be "the greatest triumph of his career." Richard Cardinal Cushing protested the visit "in behalf of millions of people in Russia and in countries held in bondage and slavery . . . who cannot speak for themselves." *Human Events*, August 12, 1959, pages 1 and 2.

Archbishop William O. Brady of St. Paul asked: "How stupid can we get?" George Resnick, New Hampshire Commander of the Jewish War Veterans, suggested: "The invitation to Khrushchev should also include an invitation to our Russian imprisoned GI's." *Op. cit.*, August 19, 1959, pages 2 and 3.

Eugene Lyons said, of the Khrushchev visit, that "it adds prestige to every Communist group in every country . . . [and] will be taken by Communists, their fellow-travelers, their victims, as a symbol of our weakness . . . ." *Op. cit.*, October 7, 1959, page 4.

Ironically it was Khrushchev, himself, who dispelled any and all illusions with regard to his trip: "When I was preparing for the trip to the United States at the invitation of President Eisenhower, some people in America said: Khrushchev will come to our country, he will see our wealth, our strength, and he will change his views. Perhaps they hoped that I would change my views and abandon communist ideas? But, of course, only foolish people could think that." Speech at Vladivostok, October 6, 1959, as quoted in A. Ajubei *et. al.*, *Face To Face With America* (Moscow: Foreign Languages Publishing House, 1960), page 114. This 616-page volume is a Soviet propaganda account of Khrushchev's visit to the United States and is profuse with illustrations of smiling Americans, both in and out of government.

In Peiping, after his visit to the United States, Khrushchev told Chou En-lai: "If enough people follow Eisenhower we will get what we want, over a great deal of opposition from some quarters. He is most discreet and does not bring up unpleasant subjects like some of the American warmongers." SPX Research Associates *Periodic*, Third Quarter, 1959, Annex "B."

291:1 *The Enemy At His Back* (New York: The Bookmailer, 1956).

295:1 The magazine, *American Opinion*, has continued to publish a revised annual scoreboard every year, as planned and promised. The rising level of the various percentages, as listed respectively against the various countries, is conservative but realistic—and terrifying. And the history of the five years of 1958 to 1963 has shown that every demonstrable error in these annual scoreboards has been on the side of *under appraisal* of the degree of Communist influence in various countries.

298:1 See S.I.S.S., *Annual Report*, 1956, pages 47-48; and, "Subversive Infiltration In The Telegraph Industry," (Parts 1 and 2), May 14, 1951-January 22, 1952.

298:2 HCUA, Hearings: "Investigation Of Communist Penetration Of Communications Facilities," (Part 1), July 17-August 9, 1957.

298:3 See testimony of Wilbur M. Brucker, General Counsel of the Department of Defense, S.I.S.S., Hearings: "Defense Facilities Protection Act," April 29-June 2, 1955, pages 5-24; also, see S.I.S.S., Hearings: "Scope Of Soviet Activity In The United States," (Part 44), November 21, 1956; and, HCUA, Hearings: "Communist Penetration Of Radio Facilities (Conelrad-Communications)," Part 1, August 23-24, 1960; Hearings and Report, Part 2, October 26, 27, and November 29, 1961.

299:1 We recommend the July-August 1962 issue of *American Opinion* for those who wish to see the latest scoreboard. And we are sorry to have to inform our readers that the score for the United States, as thus estimated in the summer of 1962, stands at 50-70%. But every one of the experts involved thinks that this is a *conservative* figure.

300:1 It is no surprise to us that Eisenhower looks at Khrushchev in a kindly light: "Now, I don't think that Mr. Khrushchev is himself a cruel man, but he's raised in the doctrine of force. . . . I'm sure he loves children. He's always talking about his own family. When he met my grandchildren here, he invited them right to Russia. He extracted from them a promise that they would come if he could influence their parents to let them come. Oh, he's very, very much of a family man that way. . . ." Dwight D. Eisenhower on *C B S Reports*, "Eisenhower On The Presidency," February 15, 1962. (Khrushchev has been described in much different fashion by the House Committee On Un-American Activities in its seven-part report, "Crimes Of Khrushchev," September 4, 1959-January 8, 1960.)

It is not without significance that these fawning remarks concerning Khrushchev were made by the same individual whom Khrushchev described as "completely lacking in will power" and as unfit to be leader of a great power. See *New York Times*, June 4, 1960.

And for the benefit of the Communists' world-wide propaganda warfare, Khrushchev's spokesman, Foreign Minister Andrei Gromyko, discarded Eisenhower in a speech before the Supreme Soviet. Gromyko accused the Eisenhower Administration of having caused *the* deterioration in US-Soviet relations. Then Gromyko, always the master of confusion, said: "It is no secret that definite hopes, particularly for the improvement of relations between the United States and the U.S.S.R., are pinned . . . on the coming to power of Mr. Kennedy. The Soviet Government would like Soviet-American relations to return . . . to the course along which they developed during the days of Franklin D. Roosevelt." *Deadline Data*, December 23, 1960.

But this was nothing new in the way of tactics used by the Communists to ridicule and downgrade the office of the American Presidency: "Nikita Khrushchev, to whom he [Eisenhower] tendered a civility St. Francis might have shrunk from showing to a rabid dog, responded with violence and disdain." Editorial, *National Review*, January 14, 1961, page 8.

Epilogue

xviii:1 See Nathaniel Weyl, *Red Star Over Cuba* (New York: Devin-Adair, 1960); Earl E. T. Smith, *The Fourth Floor* (New York: Random House, 1962); S.I.S.S., Hearings: "Communist Threat To The United States Through The Caribbean," (13 Parts); Hearings: "Cuban Aftermath — Red Seeds Blow South," March 16, 1961; Hearings: "State Department Security: The William Wieland Case," February 15, 1961 — April 12, 1962; "State Department Security: Testimony Of William Wieland," January 9, and February 8, 1961, and February 2, 1962; and, Report: "State Department Security — The Case Of William Wieland," released October 16, 1962.

xxi:1 Congressional investigations, combined with strong reactions from patriotic Americans, in and out of government, have caused some shifting of these individuals. And during the Kennedy Administration Rubottom was moved to the Naval War College at Newport, Rhode Island. Wieland was assigned to the Foreign Service Institute of the State Department. Bonsal was appointed as Ambassador to Morocco. Allen Dulles was retired, as was his Deputy, Bissell.

But Bissell fell into a bed of roses. He is now the $45,000-a-year President of the Institute of Defense Analysis: "Bissell's institute is now advising top Disarmament Agency officials to de-emphasize the need for 'on site' inspections in their present nuclear test ban and disarmament talks with the Soviet. Instead, the institute favors adopting 'verification' methods similar to those used by the U.S. in checking Russia's reported withdrawal of missiles and bombers from Cuba. This new disarmament approach is contained in a Bissell group study, prepared at Woods Hole, Mass., in consultation with Soviet and U.S. scientists." Columnists Robert S. Allen and Paul Scott, *Tallahassee Democrat*, January 25, 1963.

xxiii:1 The truth of the slowdown in the United States satellite program is not easy to come by, but some light has been shed on the situation in J. B. Medaris, *Countdown For Decision* (New York: G. P. Putnam's, 1961). General Medaris was head of the Army Ballistic Missiles Agency, from 1955 to 1958, and for the next two years, until his retirement, was head of the U.S. Army Ordnance Missile Command at Redstone Arsenal.

xxiv:1 *The Dan Smoot Report*, December 11, 1961, page 394.

xxiv:2 *U.S. News & World Report*, November 2, 1956, page 99.

xxiv:3 Telegram from Eisenhower to Indian Prime Minister Nehru, as quoted in *U.S. News & World Report*, January 3, 1958, page 86.

xxv:1 Suspension of nuclear testing was absolutely contrary to the best sources of advice: General Nathan Twining, Chairman of the Joint Chiefs of Staff, categorically endorsed nuclear weapons testing as vital to the safety of the United States and its allies. *U.S. News & World Report*, April 18, 1958, pages 66 and 67.

In testimony before the Senate Disarmament Committee, on April 16, 1958, Dr. Edward Teller, "father of the H-bomb," said: "If we stop nuclear tests, then we have made a further step in the direction of making the use of nuclear explosives very difficult and virtually impossible even in a limited way. This would leave the non-nuclear war machine of Russia free to take over the countries on the periphery of the Communist empire. And I am sure that, under those conditions, Russia would — or rather the Communists would — conquer the world, slice by thin slice, and we could not do anything about it." *U.S. News & World Report*, April 25, 1958, page 67.

Lewis L. Strauss, Chairman of the Atomic Energy Commission, could not even conceive of the unilateral cessation of nuclear testing, and as for cessation by a simple agreement with the Communists, he described this as "getting into a boxing ring with an opponent who agrees with you that he will have no horseshoes in his gloves but who will not agree to let the referee examine them." *U.S. News & World Report*, May 2, 1958, page 67.

xxvi:1 Mr. Kennedy's views were made known in an address to the UN General Assembly on September 25, 1961. The complete text of the address is in the *Congressional Record*, April 19, 1962, pages 6498-6501.

xxvi:2 For an excellent summary and analysis of these developments, see John Rousselot, "Disarmament," *American Opinion*, February 1963, pages 11-17.

xxxiii:1 An *Editorial* in *National Review* (June 18, 1960, page 381) described Khrushchev's tirade as made "in terms more vulgar, more wrenching, more debasing than any used throughout history between heads of states." And the accuracy of this description can be appreciated even from a reading of watered-down versions of Khrushchev's remarks. For example, see one translation printed in *U.S. News & World Report*, May 30, 1960, pages 90-91.

INDEX

Index

Index

K

Kadar government, 180, 181
Kansas, 69
Karamanlis, Constantin, 162
Karelian Isthmus, 292
Kashmir, 199
Katanga, xxvi
Katyn Forest Massacre, 28
Katz, Milton, 217
Kecskemeti, Paul, xxiv
Kefauver, Estes, 242
Kennedy Administration, xxi, xxv
Kennedy, John F., xxv, xxvi, xxvii, xxxi
Kentucky, 122
Kern, Erich, 37
Keynesian doctrine, 112
Khrushchev, Nikita, 55, 153, 157, 158, 200, 212, 300, xxv, xxvi, xxvii, xxviii, xxix xxxii, xxxiii, xxxiv
Kiev, 209
Kimmel, Husband, 13, 45
Kiplinger, 145, 200, 282
Knowland, William, 54, 114
Koniev, Marshall, 39
Koo, Wellington, 208
Korean War, 136
Korea, 3, 4, 136, 140, 183, 219
Kossuth, 192
Kotelawala, John, 4
Kremlin, 3, 4, 15, 17, 49, 50, 92, 105, 106, 119, 134, 143, 144, 147, 152, 154-156, 159-161, 163, 165, 166, 170, 172, 175, 178-180, 188, 194, 197, 200, 203, 204, 205, 208, 210, 213, 217, 218, 227, 245, 255-258, 267, 272, 274, 283, 284, 292, x, xviii, xix, xxi, xxix, xxx, xxxi, xxxii
Kridl, Manfred, 100, 101, 103
Kriendler, Max, 76, 78

L

Lamont, Corliss, 101
Lamphier, Thomas, 269
Lane, Arthur Bliss, 275, 276
Lange, Oscar, 256
Laos, 273
La Rochefoucauld, 10
Larson, Arthur, 230, 248
Laski, Harold, 77
Latin America, xxi, xxviii, xxxii, xxxiii
Lattimore, Owen, 116, 220, 221, 287
Latvia, 217, 292

Latvian Americans, 179
Lawrence, David, 269
Lawton, Kirke, 81, 86, 249
League Against Imperialism, 197
Lebanon, 242, 243, 271-273, xx
Leftwing Socialists (Italian), 195
Lehman, Herbert, 173, 187, 226, xxvi
Lenin, Nikolai, 47, 91, 191, 215, 291, 292, 299, 300
Lewis, Fulton, 180, 193, 219, 238, 288, xviii
Libya, 299
Life Magazine, 148
Life of John Birch, The, 79
Lindsey, Howard, 76
Lippmann, Walter, 50, 183
Lithauer, Adele, 201
Lithuania, 217, 292
Lithuanian Americans, 179
Little Red Schoolhouse, 201
Little Rock, Ark., 57, 267
Litvinov, Maxim, 16
Lodge, Henry Cabot, 67, 109, 242
Lodge, John Davis, 119
Loew, Arthur, 76
London, 17
London Economist, xxii
Los Alamos, N. M., 248
Los Angeles, Cal., xx
Louisiana, 69
Lovestone, Jay, 74, 227
Lowell, James Russell, 272
Lowman, Myers, 85
Lublin Gang, 37, 174, 187, 188, 211
Ludden, Raymond, 245
Lynd, Robert S., 245

M

Mabley, Jack, x
MacArthur, Douglas, 58, 189, 244
MacLeish, Archibald, xviii
Macmillan, Harold, 184
Madison Square Garden, 78
Magsaysay, Ramon, 4
Mahlanobis, P. C., 256
Maine, 122, 219, 298
Majer, Vaclav, 189
Malenkov, Georgi, 143, 154
Manchuria, 292
Manikov, 3, 179
Manila, 164, 204, 247
Mann, Thomas, 77

Index   cxci

The Politician

Index